DARD

Philosophical Perspectives, 3
Philosophy of Mind and Action Theory, 1989

Previously Published Volumes
Volume 1, Metaphysics—1987
Volume 2, Epistemology—1988

Forthcoming Volumes
Volume 4, Action Theory and Philosophy of Mind—Spring 1990
Volume 5, Philosophy of Religion—Fall 1991
Additional Titles to be announced.

Philosophical Perspectives, 3
Philosophy of Mind and Action Theory, 1989

Edited by
JAMES E. TOMBERLIN
California State University, Northridge

Ridgeview Publishing Company ● Atascadero, California

Paper Text: ISBN 0-917930-48-7
Cloth Text: ISBN 0-917930-88-6

The typesetting and illustrations were done by the CSUN Graphics Department (Randall Tucker, Manager). The typesetter was Robert Olsen.

Published in the United States of America
by Ridgeview Publishing Company
P. O. Box 686
Atascadero, California 93423

Printed in the United States of America

Philosophical Perspectives, 3
Philosophy of Mind and Action Theory, 1989

CONTENTS

vi / Contents

PREFACE

The nature of belief, meaning, and understanding, perceptual thoughts, reason and cause, narrow versus wide content, individualism and anti-individualism, mental causation, folk psychology, intentional action, personal identity and freedom of the will—these are some of the central issues addressed in twenty-two original essays in this the first of two volumes devoted to action theory and the philosophy of mind.

A new series of topical philosophy studies, *Philosophical Perspectives* aims to publish original essays by foremost thinkers in their fields, with each volume confined to a main area of philosophical research. The intention is to publish volumes annually.

Philosophical Perspectives could not have come to fruition without the precious encouragement it received from Administrative Officials at California State University, Northridge. I am particularly grateful to Dr. James W. Cleary, President of this institution, and Dr. Bob H. Suzuki, Vice President for Academic Affairs, who provided essential financial support through the Special Projects Fund of the California State University Foundation, Northridge. I also thank Dr. Jerome Richfield, Dean, School of Humanities, and Dr. Daniel Sedey, Chair, Department of Philosophy, for their consistent efforts in advancing this project. Pat Boles, Administrative Program Specialist, School of Humanitites, maintained logistical supervision and arranged for many valuable services. Dorothy Johnson, Betsy Leighton, and Susana Nugent contributed ever so many hours of invaluable clerical assistance and support.

April 1989   **JAMES E. TOMBERLIN**

Philosophical Perspectives, 3
Philosophy of Mind and Action Theory, 1989

REASONS AND CAUSES[1]

Fred Dretske
University of Wisconsin, Madison

I am a materialist who thinks that we sometimes do things because of what we believe and want. I pretty much have to accept the idea, then, that reasons are causes. If beliefs and desires are not causally relevant to behavior, I, for one, fail to see why it would be worth having them. We need beliefs and desires because our wanting this and believing that, besides being our reasons *for* doing what we do, are—sometimes at least— the reasons *why* we do it. If reasons aren't causes, one of the chief— indeed (for certain people) the *only*—motive for including them in one's inventory of the mind, vanishes. They are no longer capable of doing the job—actually getting us to *do* what they justify us in doing—that was their primary excuse for existing.

But if this is so, and I shall, following Donald Davidson, take it to be so, it is hard not to accept what seems like an immediate, but *not* so Davidsonian, corollary—namely, that the semantic aspect of reasons, the what-it-is we believe and desire, is the property that, in addition to rationalizing or justifying what we do, also figures essentially in the causal *explanation* of what we do. A causal explanation of an event is, I assume, more than a specification, under some description or other, of the event's cause. An explanation requires, in addition, and perhaps among other things, some indication of which of the properties of the cause, by being law-instantiating properties, underlie the cause's efficacy in producing that effect.[2] Meaningful sounds, if they occur at the right pitch and amplitude, can shatter glass, but the fact that these sounds have a meaning is surely irrelevant to their having this effect. The glass would shatter if the sounds meant something completely different or if they meant nothing at all. This fact doesn't imply that the sounds don't have a meaning, but it *does* imply that their having meaning doesn't help explain their effects on the glass. To know *why* the glass shattered, you have to know something about the amplitude and frequency of these sounds, properties of the sound that are relevantly involved in its effect on the glass. Events are causes, but facts explain, and facts, at least in the case of causal explanations, have to do with the properties of the cause that make it a cause. Meaningful sounds *are* causes, to be sure. So in this sense their existence must be recognized by acoustical engineers. For explanatory purposes, however, for purposes of understanding *why* they have the effects they do, there is no meaning in the science of acoustics.

If the causal efficacy of reasons is like this, then although materialists such as myself can comfort themselves with the idea that reasons, just like other well-accredited physical events and conditions, *are* causes (and can therefore produce behavior by contracting the muscles and stimulating the glands in living systems), there are, *for explanatory purposes*, no reasons in the science of behavior. It may still turn out that reasons, by helping to *rationalize* behavior, help to explain why we *should* do some of the things we do, but on this account of matters, reasons will never explain why we actually do what it is in our interest to do. There will be no reasons in the science of behavior.

Some philosophers find this result perfectly acceptable. It helps to explain, among other things, why behavioral biologists never bother about beliefs and desires, not to mention other content-bearing internal states (e.g., hopes, regrets, fears), in their quest to understand the activities of living systems—including humans. The idea is that they, as good (*hard*, as we like to say) scientists, are trying to explain behavior; and for purposes of explanation the semantic character of our inner states, supposing (for the moment) that some of these inner states have a semantic character, is irrelevant. To put the point in Jerry Fodor's terms, although the language of thought has both a syntax and a semantics, it is the syntax, the shape and form, not the semantics, of its representational elements that does all the explanatory work. It may be useful to couch generalizations in semantic terms, but that is a methodological expedient; semantics is merely a device for generalizing over causally relevant formal properties. The best we can hope for, those of us who look for some vindication of common-sense (i.e., belief-desire) psychology in the developments of cognitive science, is that some (most? all?) of the relevant semantic niceties, those we allude to in describing what a person intends, believes and wants, will be reflected in, or correlated with, the output-determining *shape* or *form* (i.e., the syntax) of the internal representations. Meaning itself is causally inert, powerless to initiate, modify, or influence behavior. The best we can hope for is that it supervenes on something, presumably electrical and chemical events in the nervous system, that packs a real behavioral punch.

I find this result quite unacceptable. It implies that *what* we believe, intend, and desire has no bearing on what we do. It implies that *what a person thinks* has as much relevance to what he does as *what a sound means* has to the amount of pressure it exerts on a glass. Given our ordinary way of thinking about these matters,[3] the belief that there is a beer in the refrigerator (together, of course, with a desire for a beer) causes Clyde to go to the refrigerator because of what this belief is a belief *about* and what this desire is a desire *for*. Beliefs and desires *are* causes, yes, but what explains their causal properties, why they cause Clyde to move from his comfortable spot on the sofa and head for the kitchen (rather than, say, the garage), is the fact that he believes the beer is there, in the kitchen, not in the garage, and the fact that he is thirsty enough, wants a beer enough, to make the necessary trip. If all he wanted was something to drink, he needn't have moved. There was (and he knew it) water within arm's reach. If the semantic properties of reasons, the what-it-is we believe and desire, is irrelevant to explaining their causal properties, what it is they make us do, then the fact that they are causes, taken by itself, is or should be very little solace indeed. For it leaves us without the resources for understanding the *explanatory* role of reasons, the why and wherefore of our doing something because of what we want and believe.

It is always easier to complain about broken thingamabobs, gadgets that don't work the way we want them to work, than it is to actually fix them. I expect to be told that the contraption I am tinkering with is already working about as well as can be expected. The brain is a marvelous instrument, to be sure, but it is, after all, merely a hunk of matter. You can't make it do *everything* the ghost it replaces is supposed to have done. Davidson, by showing that what justifies behavior can also cause behavior, did about all that could be done in this regard. There are, furthermore, compelling reasons to suppose that if reasons are thought of as internal states, internal *physical* states of course, having (essentially) a meaning or propositional content (the what-it-is we believe, intend, and desire), then this meaning or content *cannot* be construed as a causally relevant factor in the determination of action. It can't be the internal state's possession of *this* property that explains the state's causal influence on behavior.

Without trying to summarize these arguments, we can give their gist. It goes something like this: Even if the things that have meaning are in the head, the meanings themselves aren't in the head. Even if one doesn't subscribe to the kind of causal theory of meaning that motivated Putnam's well-known remark,[4] it is surely plausible to suppose that what something means, whether it be tracks in the snow, a blinking light on a CRT screen, or certain electrical activity in the cortex, is a matter determined, in part at least, by the *relations* that obtain between the elements that have this meaning (the stuff in the head, the tracks in the snow, the blinking light) and the sorts of conditions that comprise their meaning. Meaning certainly isn't an intrinsic property of meaningful things, something you could discover by looking *in* the head, by taking the measure of the tracks, or by studying the light under a magnifying glass. This kind of investigation would be as silly as trying to discover the meaning of words by an acoustical analysis of speech. But if this is so, then whatever it is in the head that causes the muscles to twitch and the glands to secrete, whatever it is, in other words, that is responsible for our behaving the way we do (or at least our moving the way we do when we behave),[5] is something that will have its causal role determined, not by its meaning— for that is a matter, in part at least, of how things on the inside stand to things on the outside—but by whatever intrinsic properties it (the stuff in the head) possesses, presumably the electrical and chemical properties that neurobiologists study, that are capable of making muscles contract and glands secrete. As Stich expresses it in formulating what he calls the principle of autonomy, the only psychological states that do any genuine work in the explanation of behavior are those that supervene on the current, internal physical state of organisms.[6] Psychological differences that do not manifest themselves as *biological* differences are irrelevant to the explanation of motor output. But meaning is not in the head nor does it supervene on the stuff that is in the head. Therefore, meaning, or something (in the head) having meaning, is irrelevant to the explanation of behavior.

The upshot of such arguments is that we may believe things and we may desire things. And our beliefs and desires may even cause us to behave in certain ways. But nothing about *what* we believe and desire, not even (it seems) the fact that we believe and desire something, is pertinent to understanding *why* we behave this way. If you want to know *why* we do things—why, for instance, Clyde is headed for the kitchen—ask a neurobiologist. He or she will tell you (or will some day) what it is about our internal states, states which (if things turn out right) are our reasons for acting the way we do, that explains why we act this way.

As I said, I find this conclusion unacceptable. I may be forced to accept it nonetheless. Whether I am or not depends, in part, on whether a plausible case can be made for the explanatory role of meaning. That is, can we maintain, not only that reasons are causes, but that their being reasons, their having the kind of semantic content or meaning that enables them to function so as to rationalize or justify behavior, is what underlies and determines their efficacy in the causal production of behavior? What we have to show is that what we think and know, what we desire and intend, the content of our psychological states and attitudes, unlike the meaning of glass-shattering sounds, *is* actually the property of our internal states that explains their distinctive causal efficacy, their effects on behavior.

Unfortunately, this project gets bogged down at the very beginning by the fact that there is no widely shared, or widely *enough* shared, theory of meaning to which one can appeal. How is one supposed to demonstrate the causal efficacy of something's having meaning if no one can agree about what meaning is? How does one show that what we believe makes a difference, a causal difference, to what we do if nobody can agree about what constitutes the objects of belief?

One way to finesse this difficulty, a strategy that I find tempting, is to turn the tables by choosing among otherwise plausible theories of meaning on the basis of how easy they make the job of exhibiting the explanatory role of meaning. Any theory of meaning that doesn't make a thing's having meaning into a causally relevant property of the thing (and hence the fact that it has this meaning into an explanatorily important fact about the thing) is a theory of meaning that can be rejected at the outset. It would be like having a theory of pain that made its occurrence something of which the sufferer could not be aware.

But this strategy is obviously too grand for a short paper, especially a short paper that is already half over. Let me, therefore, take a tactical detour by arguing that the kind of relational properties that might (plausibly?) underlie the assignment of meaning or propositional content to a physical state, relational properties that do *not* supervene on the intrinsic, non-relational properties of the state in question (and are, therefore, more or less plausible candidates for meaning-constitutive properties), are, nonetheless, properties that can shape, modify, and determine, and hence, to this extent at least, explain the causal role of the state or structure whose meaning they constitute. This still won't get me *exactly* where I want to go because I will not yet have shown that behavior (in contrast to a state's causing a certain pattern of bodily movements[7]) can be explained by the fact that a state has certain meaning-constitutive properties. Nevertheless, if I can get this far, I will, I hope, have come close enough to a really interesting thesis to make my near miss intriguing.

Suppose I give you a design problem. I want a system S that will do A when, but only when, conditions C obtain. Make me something that will behave this way.

This is a common enough problem in engineering circles. I want a device that will turn the furnace on whenever the room temperature gets too low. Or I want something that will open a valve whenever the pressure exceeds a certain level, make an irritating noise when passengers fail to buckle their seat belts, or restrict the flow of fuel when the engine runs too fast.

This kind of problem is also common enough in nature. Reflexes and other rigid, relatively unmodifiable, patterns of behavior—in fact, virtually all behavior we think of as innate or instinctive—is nature's solution to this same design problem. When the object being touched is hot, withdraw. Fast! When a certain silhouette, the kind a hawk makes, appears in the sky, freeze, run, or hide. When you encounter a cliff, stop or change direction.

We also encounter a similar problem in simple learning situations: How does one get the pupil to say "oak" (not "maple" or "pine") when shown the distinctive markings of an oak tree? How do you get the rat to press the bar when, and only when, the light is red? How do I figure out when to put the "i" before the "e" and when after? I will call any problem having this general structure The Design Problem.

In very general terms, the solution to The Design Problem is always the same—whether it is the deliberate invention of an engineer, the product of evolutionary development, or the outcome of individual learning. The system *S* must embody (and if it doesn't already embody, it must be supplied with) some kind of internal mechanism that is selectively sensitive to the presence or absence of condition *C*. It must be equipped with something that will indicate or register the presence of those conditions with which behavior is to be coordinated. There must be a temperature indicator in the thermostat, a hawk indicator in the chicken, a color indicator in the rat, and an oak tree indicator in the child. If there isn't, the design problem can never be solved. You can't build a system *S* to do *A* under conditions *C* unless there is something in *S* to indicate when *C* exists. The indicators don't have to be infallible, of course, but the more reliable the indicator the better the solution to The Design Problem. We don't want our chickens running for cover every time a sparrow flies by or our pupil shouting "oak tree" at every large bush, but a few mistakes, in the interests of economy and speed, can be tolerated in the design of the detector system as long as they don't endanger the system of which they are a part.

So the first requirement is that system *S* be equipped with an appropriate indicator, some internal mechanism whose various states register the presence or absence of condition *C*. Once this requirement is satisfied, all that remains to do in solving The Design Problem is to harness this indicator to effector mechanisms in such a way that it produces output *A* when (and only when) it positively registers the presence of condition *C*. The only thing left to do, in other words, is to make the indicator of *C* into a cause of *A*. This is exactly what engineers do with the thermostat—or, indeed, *any* device that is supposed to do something under a specified set of conditions. They make the internal indicator of temperature into an electrical switch for the furnace. They *give* the internal indicator a control function. They, by the way they design, wire, and install the device, make this internal indicator into a cause of furnace ignition, and they do so because this is the most direct way of solving The Design Problem, of making *S* do *A* when *C* exists.

This, too, is what nature does in its own non-purposeful way. It converts, by means of natural selection, sensory indicators into behavior switches. It does so (*when* it does so) either by equipping organisms with appropriate C-indicators (giving them sensory capabilities they did not formerly possess) or by deploying an already existent indicator in new, control-relevant ways (as a cause of A). Because of the benefits of doing A in conditions C, those occasional organisms will be favored whose heritable constitution, as chance would have it, is such that their internal C indicator causes A or some reasonable approximation thereof. Such behavior will, by hereditary means, become more widespread in succeeding generations. Eventually, members of this species will all do A instinctively in conditions C. Not much different, except for the kind of system and the manner in which the behavior is acquired, from engineering artifacts.

Furthermore, though it may sound odd to describe it this way, a similar process is taking place in the simple kind of learning situations already mentioned. We[8] begin with a pupil already endowed with the requisite internal indicators, already possessed of the kind of sensory powers needed to see oak trees and distinguish them (perceptually) from bushes, telephone poles and maple trees. That is, the pupil's eyesight is good enough so that, when seen in decent light and at close enough range, oak trees *look different* from the things in the relevant contrast set, the set of things he or she is learning to distinguish oak trees from. What discriminative learning of this sort amounts to is converting these internal sensory indicators into behavioral switches, converting the simple sensory process of *seeing* oak trees into the capacity to respond, in some distinctive way, *to* oak trees—a capacity that is fundamental to acquiring the kind of conceptual or cognitive skills associated with identification, classification, and recognition. What the engineer does by soldering wires in the right places, and nature does by selecting systems whose "wires" are already secured more or less permanently in the right places, we do, in simple learning situations of the kind now in question, by the timely (i.e., in conditions C) encouragement of right (i.e., A-like) responses. Somehow, appropriately timed rewards and punishments are enough to get some systems to re-wire themselves—enough, that is, for some systems to effect a conversion of their internal indicators (of C) into behavior switches. A little bit of magic that some biological systems are capable of performing.

So, in a variety of different ways, The Design Problem is solved by making an indicator of C into a switch for A. Deliberate design, biological evolution, and individual learning are all methods of achieving the same result.

Very interesting, you may say, but what does all this have to do with the role of meaning in the explanation of behavior?

Note, first, that for any system *S* for which The Design Problem has been solved, we have some internal state or condition in *S* that indicates, means (in Grice's natural sense of meaning), or represents (in, I think, *one* sense of this word) something about how things stand outside of *S*. This is, as everyone knows, a pretty anemic sort of meaning, not rich or intentionally robust enough to serve as the propositional content of a belief or a desire. Nevertheless, it does define a content, a *propositional* content, of sorts for *S*'s internal states—a content, I hasten to point out, that does not supervene on the intrinsic physical properties of the internal indicator or representation. You can't tell what an indicator indicates by looking at the indicator, what a representation represents by examining the representation itself. Try it with the blinking light on the CRT screen. What it indicates or represents is determined, not by the color or intensity of the light, not even by the little explanatory symbols printed for user convenience on the screen (or in the manual),[9] but by how the CRT is wired to the rest of the computer, the printer, the modem, and so forth—by the relations, primarily causal and informational, it bears to other parts of the system. To find out what it indicates or represents you must look to these relations, and these relations can change— hence changing what the instrument indicates or represents—without ever changing the representation itself. There is no reason I can't, by changing the relations between the monitor and the rest of a system, by (in other words) re-wiring things, convert the blinking light into a representation of something quite different. You will never know, just by looking at the screen itself or at the representation (the blinking light), that, after re-wiring, it *means* something completely different. There are possible worlds, sufficiently different from ours, in which smoke *doesn't* mean fire.

Note, second, that this propositional content of simple indicators, though it lacks, as I said, the robust intentionality of mature (what Grice calls non-natural) meaning, is not totally impoverished in this respect. It has something analogous to *aboutness*: The gas gauge in your car, because of the way it is hooked up, says or indicates something about your tank, that it is half full; it says nothing about my tank. The gauge doesn't say that this is what it is talking about, but, given the connections, this *is* what it is representing as half full. Furthermore, the sentential expression of this content exhibits a degree of intensionality (with an "s"): Your gauge doesn't indicate how much gas I have even if there happens to be an *extensional* equivalence between how much gas you have and how much gas I have—even if, as chance would have it, our tanks always have the same amount of gas in them.

So, for any system for which The Design Problem has been solved, we have a system occupying internal states having a content or meaning exhibiting some of the properties of fully intentional systems. The relations, primarily causal and informational, underlying this content are certainly not, not by themselves anyway, enough to constitute genuine meaning,[10] the kind of meaning we associate with *belief*, but because of their special properties, they do show promise of being *among* the relations out of which more robust content, richer intentional structures, might be manufactured. I hope I have said enough, at least, to make plausible the idea that these relations are candidates for genuine meaning-constitutive relations.

The question that remains, then, is whether a state's possessing the kind of meaning—or, if it is still too early in the game to speak about meaning, whether an internal state's standing in these indicator relations to external affairs—can help to determine the state's causal role in the operation of the system of which it is a part. Can a state or structure's meaning what it does, in this constricted sense of "meaning," explain its causing what it does? If so, we have a model, crude and oversimplified to be sure but a model nonetheless, of the explanatory role of what we believe. We will have a model, not only of beliefs producing output, but of how the output they produce is influenced, and hence partly explained, by *what* is believed.

Though I do not think artifacts, the sorts of things our engineers design and build, have beliefs and desires, I think they *do* things, and it is useful to think a moment about our explanations for their behavior, about *why* they do the things they do. This can, I believe, teach us something important about why living systems do some of the things they do. The comparison is especially revealing when the behavior in question, on the part of both the instrument and the animal, is an expression of the system's satisfactory solution to The Design Problem.

Instruments behave the way they do because that is the way they are designed and built. When things are working right, the movement of the temperature-sensitive strip in the thermostat causes the furnace to ignite. The device is wired to the furnace and supplied with electricity so that it will have this effect. *We*, the designers, manufacturers, and installers of this system, in the interest of solving a particular instance of The Design Problem, *give* this internal indicator its causal role. The reason we give it this causal role is that it is an indicator of the condition *to which* we want a coordinated response. So, in one sense, and leaving aside (for the moment) *our* involvement in the proceedings, this component causes what it does (thereby making the thermostat *do* what it does) because of what it, the component, indicates or means about external conditions. Or if, once again, it is premature to speak of meaning in this regard, the system behaves the way it does because of the special way its internal states are related to external conditions. This, I submit, comes suggestively close to a system doing something because its internal states stand in certain relations, in this case the indicator relation, to external affairs.

Though suggestive, this tendentious description of the thermostat ignores *our* involvement in the proceedings, the fact that *we* design and install these devices with particular intentions and purposes. The thermal sensor in this device does not cause furnace ignition because of what it means or indicates about temperature. It causes furnace ignition because of what we, its makers, *thought* it indicated about temperature and, thinking this, what we *wanted* to happen when this temperature varied. This *is*, to be sure, a case of an indicator's causing something, but what explains why it causes what it does is not the fact that it indicates, but the fact that *we believe* (or *know*) *that it indicates. This* situation cannot help us reach a philosophical understanding of the explanatory role of content or meaning because it *presupposes* the phenomenon of interest— presupposes, that is, that we, the makers of such instruments, make things happen because of what we believe and want. What we want is some account of whether—and if so, how—this is possible.

This result should come as no surprise. In talking about simple mechanical instruments we are, after all, looking for suggestive analogies, not thoughtful thermostats. What the behavior of a thermostat, not to mention a variety of other control devices, should teach us is that systems which have, in one way or another, solved The Design Problem (or systems *for* which this problem has been solved) are systems in which, in one way or another, either directly or indirectly, either (as in the case of artifacts) via a purposeful designer or (as in the case of living systems) via natural selection or learning, an internal element acquires a control function, a causal role in the determination of output, *because of the way it is related to external conditions*, because of what it (in virtue of these relations) indicates or means about the circumstances in which that behavior is produced. We need to find cases in which, unlike simple artifacts, this process occurs *without* the services of intentional intermediaries. In such cases meaning itself and not, as in the case of artifacts, some intermediate understander-of-meaning, influences, and thereby helps explain, the causal properties of the elements having that meaning.

I skip over the details of why evolutionary solutions of The Design Problem do not yield the desired account.[11] The basic reason is that natural selection produces systems whose internal states have their causal properties determined, not by the meaning-constitutive relations in which *these* states stand to external affairs, but by the relations in which the internal states of distant ancestors stood to external affairs. Natural selection produces systems that behave the way they do because of *earlier* solutions to The Design Problem, solutions that are now encoded in, and explained by, the genes of those organisms that now do A, instinctively, in conditions C.

It is only when we examine the changes occurring during the life history of individual organisms, internal changes that occur when an organism *learns* to do A in conditions C, that we find a plausible instance of an internal indicator (of C) acquiring its causal efficacy (in the production of A) because of what *it* means or indicates about external affairs. If The Design Problem is going to be solved, if behavior is going to be coordinated with the external conditions on which its effectiveness depends, as it must be if it is to be successful in the satisfaction of needs and desires, then, as we have seen, this behavior must be guided by internal indicators. No use biting if there is nothing in the mouth. No use running if nothing is chasing you. Hence we need internal indicators for prey in the mouth and predators behind us, indicators that exercise some control over the jaw and the legs. But in contrast to cases already discussed (artifacts and genetically determined behavior), discriminative learning *is* a process in which the internal determinants of behavior acquire their control over output, their power to produce an appropriate A, in virtue of their relationship to those conditions, C, in which (and only in which) that behavior is supposed to occur.

Learning is a process in which The Design Problem, the problem of how to produce A when condition C exists, is solved, not (as it is in the case of artifacts) by some purposeful agent designing a system to solve it, not (as in the case of evolution) by the natural selection of systems that have (by chance) already solved it, but by a process (roughly) of rewarding *A* when (and only when) it occurs in conditions *C*. That process, when it works, automatically makes the internal indicator of *C* into a cause of *A* and it does so, not because of the intrinsic, non-relational properties of this indicator, but because of its relational properties, because it is an indicator of *C*.

We may not understand, at the biological level, why or *how* rewarding behavior in certain conditions tends to make internal indicators into causes, but that it does, for *some* organisms, for *some* observable conditions, and for *some* behavior, is undeniable. What the Law of Effect tells us, at least for this simple kind of learning, is that some behavior, that which we think of as voluntary behavior, is produced, in part at least, by internal states which acquire their initial control over behavior because of their special relation to external conditions. If we take these special relations as being meaning-constitutive relations, this is, as far as I can see, another way of saying that not only is some behavior caused by internal states that have a meaning, but the fact that they have this meaning is what helps explain why they have this causal role, why they influence behavior the way they do. Unless I miss something, this comes intriguingly close to saying, not only that thoughts make a difference (that reasons are causes), but that what we think—what makes these reasons the reasons they are—makes a difference too.

Notes

1. An earlier version of this paper was prepared for, and read at, the North Carolina Colloquium in Philosophy in September 1986. Donald Davidson was my commentator and I thank him for his remarks. I wish also to thank the Center for Advanced Study in the Behavioral Sciences at Stanford University for the time and editorial assistance needed to prepare a final draft, and to the National Endowment for the Humanities #FC-20060-85 and the Andrew Mellon Foundation for financial assistance.
2. This point has been made by a variety of philosophers. Dagfinn Follesdal puts the point well in his "Causation and Explanation: a Problem in Davidson's View on Action and Mind," *Actions and Events: Perspectives on the Philosophy of Donald Davidson*, Ernest LePore and Brian McLaughlin (eds.); New York: Basil Blackwell Ltd. (1985). He also mentions (p. 312), and provides useful references for, a variety of other people, including Frederick Stoutland, Raimo Tuomela and Ted Honderich,

who have raised similar objections to Davidson's apparent conflation of causation and explanation in his classic paper, "Actions, Reasons and Causes." See, also, the excellent treatment in Sosa's "Mind-Body Interaction and Supervenient Causation," in *Midwest Studies in Philosophy*, vol. 9, ed. P. French et. al. (Minneapolis: University of Minnesota Press).

3. I do not hold sacred our ordinary ways of thinking about these matters. But I do think it is a reasonable place to begin. And it is, other things being equal, and assuming a manageable philosophical cost, a desirable place to end.

4. Even if, that is, one subscribes to some version of functionalism about belief content (e.g., conceptual role semantics), one will need what Ned Block colorfully calls a "long armed" notion of conceptual role, one that includes an element's functional relations to the external world (the sort we find in our ordinary descriptions of perception and action). See Block's discussion (pp. 635-39) of this point in "Advertisement for a Semantics for Psychology," *Midwest Studies in Philosophy*, X, French, Uehling, & Wettstein (eds.); Minneapolis, Minn.; University of Minnesota press (1986). See also, in the same volume, "Solipsistic Semantics" (pp. 595-614), Ernest Lepore and Barry Loewer's account of the inadequacies of a purely solipsistic semantics (one in which meaning supervenes on what is in the head).

5. There is a lot of important stuff buried in this parenthetical remark. My only excuse for keeping it buried is that it would take at least another twenty pages to uncover it in a responsible way. I *do* distinguish between behavior and the bodily movements that occur in the course of this behavior, and this distinction *is* critical to a *full* understanding of the role of reasons in the explanation of behavior. But I think, at least I hope, that the point I am making in this paper can be made without going into all this.

6. Stephen Stich, *From Folk psychology to Cognitive Science: The Case Against Belief*; Cambridge, Mass; The MIT Press, A Bradford Book (1983), pp. 164-65.

7. Actually, I think this is a bogus contrast. Behavior is the causing (by internal states) of bodily (and other external) change. But, once again, I don't want to raise and, for the limited objectives of this paper, I don't think I have to raise, this controversial issue.

8. Teachers aren't really necessary to this process. The relevant kind of learning can, and most often *does*, occur without the assistance of another person.

9. Printing "temperature" on a barometer, even if you mark off its face in degrees Fahrenheit, will not make a barometer into a thermometer.

10. In particular I have said nothing about the matter of *mis*representation, how a state could mean that P when P was not the case. As I am using the idea of indication (as Grice used the idea of natural meaning), it is not possible for something to indicate (or mean$_n$) that a state of affairs exists when it does not exist. This is, however, an important property of genuine meaning: Our beliefs can be false.

11. For the details see *Explaining Behavior: Reasons in a World of Causes* (Boston, Mass; The MIT Press. A Bradford Book. 1988).

References

Block, Ned (1986) "Advertisement for a Semantics for Psychology." In French, Uehling and Wettstein 1986.

Davidson, Donald (1963) "Actions, Reasons and Causes." Reprinted in Davidson (1980).

Davidson, Donald (1980) *Essays on Actions and Events*. Oxford University Press.

Dretske, Fred (1988) *Explaining Behavior: Reasons in a world of Causes*. Cambridge, Mass.: MIT Press. A Bradford Book.

Follesdal, Dagfinn (1985) "Causation and Explanation: A Problem In Davidson's View On Action and Mind." In *Actions and Events: Perspectives on the Philosophy of Donald Davidson*, Ernest Lepore and Brian McLaughlin, eds.; New York: Basil Blackwell.

French, Uehling, and Wettstein (1986). *Midwest Studies in philosophy* X; Minneapolis: University of Minnesota Press.

LePore, Ernest and Barry Loewer (1986). "Solipsistic Semantics." In French, Uehling & Wettstein (1986)

Sosa, Ernest (1984) "Mind-body Interaction and Supervenient Causation." In *Midwest Studies in Philosophy*, vol. 9, ed. P. French, Ted Uehling, and Howard Wettstein. Minneapolis: University of Minnesota Press.

Stich, Stephen (1983) *From Folk Psychology to Cognitive Science: The Case Against Belief*. Cambridge. Mass.: MIT Press. A Bradford Book.

Philosophical Perspectives, 3
Philosophy of Mind and Action Theory, 1989

REASONS EXPLANATION OF ACTION: AN INCOMPATIBILIST ACCOUNT

Carl Ginet
Cornell University

Incompatibilism is the thesis that any free action must be an undetermined event. By a *free* action I mean one such that until the time of its occurrence the agent had it in her power to perform some alternative action (or to be inactive) instead. By an *undetermined* event I mean one that was *not* nomically necessitated by the antecedent state of the world. (Hence, a determined event is one that *was* nomically necessitated by its antecedents.) By saying of an event that it was *nomically necessitated* by the antecedent state of the world, I mean that the antecedent state together with the laws of nature determined that that event, rather than some alternative, would occur.

I believe that a compelling argument for incompatibilism can be given but I will not undertake to give it here.[1] I want rather to rebut two arguments *against* incompatibilism that have been put forward from time to time. One of these, to which I will give by far the larger response, combines the consideration that a free action can be influenced by the agent's intentions, desires, and beliefs—can have an explanation in terms of reasons for which the agent did it—with the assumption that only a determined event can have such an explanation.[2] My response to this will be to counter the assumption by offering an adeterministic or *anomic* account of such explanations. The other argument does not assume that reasons explanations are deterministic (nor does it assume the contradictory) but simply claims that where we have an undetermined action we do not have an agent in control of (determining) what her action is to be: we do not have an action that the agent chooses, freely or otherwise.

I.

Let me first dispose of this latter argument. It is contained (though mingled with and not clearly distinguished from the other argument) in the following remarks of Frithjof Bergmann:

> Would indeterminacy, even if its existence could be demonstrated, really vouchsafe freedom, or would it not fulfill this expectation? ... Where or when would [the indeterminacy] have to occur to provide us with freedom? ... Imagine Raskolnikov walking up the steps to the old pawnbroker woman's room and assume that his mind still vacillates, that with every tread he climbs his thinking alternates from one side to the other. ...he mounts the staircase thinking "I shall kill her," "no, I shall not." This continues till he stands right before her door. Now let us hypothesize that his last thought just as he pushes the door open is "no, I shall not do it" and that the sought-for indeterminacy occurs right after these words crossed his mind. The thinking of this thought is the last link in a causal chain, but now there is a gap between this and the next event, which is his bringing the axe down on her head.
>
> What would this mean? Would the occurrence of a disjuncture in this place render Raskolnikov's act more free; would it provide him with a power or a control that he lacks otherwise? ... The implication, if anything, would be the reverse. If his last thought really is "no, I shall not do it" and this thought is somehow disconnected from the next event so that it has no causal influence on it and he then kills her, then one could only say that the indeterminacy has rendered his will ineffectual, that instead of giving him greater power or control the causal gap *decreased* it.
>
> ...one could envision two alternatives: either something other than his own last thought "influences" him so that he does commit the murder, or the last reversal was quite strictly not effected by anything whatever and occurred entirely "by chance." ...in either case it was not *he* that

made the decision, and *he* certainly did not exercise his freedom. We therefore can conclude that the occurrence of a causal gap in this particular location—between his last thought and his action—would not furnish him with freedom, but on the contrary would undermine the agent and make him a victim.[3]

Bergmann is suggesting that there is an absurdity in the thought that positing a break in the causal necessitation just before Raskolnikov's action helps to make it one that *he* chooses. In fact, he suggests, it would do just the opposite: it would go against its being the case that Raskolnikov determines whether or not he delivers the murdering blow. And if Raskolnikov does not determine that, then surely his delivering the blow is not his freely chosen action for which he can be held morally responsible.

Why exactly is the indeterminacy just before the action supposed to deprive the agent of control over his action? One reason, Bergmann seems to suggest, is that (as he thinks) if the action is undetermined then it is in no way influenced by his antecedent intentions or thoughts, and its being influenced by them is essential to its being controlled by the agent. But his words, particularly the last few sentences quoted, also invite the thought that the implication is more direct and does not depend on taking a deterministic view of how motives influence actions or on taking any particular view as to what agent control consists in: it is, one may think, just obvious that if an action is undetermined then the agent does not control (determine) it, has no say in whether or not it occurs.

We also find this latter idea in the argument that van Inwagen (1983) refers to as "the third strand of the *Mind* Argument" for compatibilism. The premiss of that argument, as van Inwagen phrases it (p. 144), is "the principle that no one has any choice about the occurrence of an undetermined event". I believe we adequately capture the idea here if we express it as follows:

(1) For any time t and any undetermined event occurring at t: it is not possible for it to have been in anyone's power to determine whether that event or some alternative (undetermined) event instead would occur at t.

From this premiss we can in two short steps derive a conclusion severely damaging to incompatibilism:

(2)   Therefore, for any time t and undetermined action occurring at t: it is not possible for it to have been in the agent's power to determine whether that action or some alternative (undetermined) action instead would occur at t.

(3)   Therefore, it is not possible for a free action to be undetermined.

It is impossible for the conclusion (3) and incompatibilism both to be true *if* it is also true that free action is at least possible (whether or not actual). The metaphysical possibility of free action is something that most incompatibilists assume, myself included, as of course do most compatibilists. That assumption conjoined with (3) does entail that incompatibilism is false. Since the argument is obviously valid, if free action is possible, either incompatibilism or the argument's premiss is wrong. A little reflection will show us that the latter is the problem.

Whatever plausibility this premiss has derives, I think, from ambiguity in sentences of the following form when they are about events that are actions.

(A)   It was in S's power to determine whether undetermined event E or some alternative undetermined event instead would occur at t.

When the event E is *not an action of S's* a natural reading of this sentence does make it express a plainly impossible proposition:

(A1) It was in S's power so to act that S's action (in concert with other circumstances at the time) would have nomically necessitated that E would occur at t and have been undetermined; and it was in S's power so to act that S's action would have nomically necessitated that some alternative instead of E would occur at t and have been undetermined.

Here each conjunct is impossible, for it implies that it was in S's power to make the case something that is impossible, namely, that an event at t would have been both determined and undetermined. On this inconsistent reading of (A) the premiss of the argument, (1) above, obviously holds.

But when the event E is an action of S's, another reading of (A) is possible, one that is perfectly consistent:

(A2) It was in S's power to act in a certain way at t without being nomically necessitated to do so; and it was in S's power to act in some alternative way at t without being nomically necessitated to do so.

Here each conjunct attributes to S the power to make the case something that in itself is perfectly possible, namely, S's performing an undetermined action. If an undetermined action is possible then there is no reason to say that an undetermined action cannot be in the agent's power to perform.

To determine an event is to act in such a way that one's action makes it the case that the event occurs. Let us grant (for the sake of this discussion) that if the event is *not* one's own action then this requires that the event be causally necessitated by one's action (in concert with other circumstances) and thus that it not be an undetermined event. But if the event *is* one's own action then one's determining it requires only that one perform it; and one's performing it, which is just the action's occurring, is compatible with the action's being undetermined, not causally necessitated by antecedents.

Suppose that S's raising her arm at t did occur as an undetermined action: S raised her arm at t without being nomically necessitated to do so. In that case, it was open to S, in S's power, up to t to raise her arm at t without being nomically necessitated to do so. There is no reason to doubt it. Nor is there any reason to be puzzled as to how this can be so. But van Inwagen (in uncomfortable company with some compatibilists) seems to find a mystery here. He says:

I must reject the following proposition:
If an agent's act was caused but not determined by his prior inner state, and if nothing besides that inner state was causally relevant to the agent's act, then that agent had no choice about whether that inner state was followed by that act.
I must admit that I find it puzzling that this proposition should be false...

Now I wish I knew *how it could be* that, for example, our thief had a choice about whether to repent [or instead rob the poor box], given that his repenting was caused, but not determined, by his prior inner states, and given that no other prior state "had anything to do with"—save negatively: in virtue of its non-interference with—his act. I have no theory of free action or choice that would explain how this could be.[4]

As I understand him, what puzzles van Inwagen is how an agent could have a choice about whether or not his action occurred, i.e., could determine that it occurred rather than something else instead, *if* the only antecedent things causally relevant to its occurrence, the agents motives for it (his "prior inner state"), left it undetermined, nomically unnecessitated. How, by what means, van Inwagen seems to want to ask, did the thief ensure that that action (rather than some alternative) occurred? The answer is: by no *means*, by nothing distinct from and productive of the action, but simply by performing the action itself. If an event is S's action then *S* (but, of course, no one else) can ensure its occurrence, determine *that* it occurs and thus *whether or not* it occurs, just by performing it.

So I attribute the puzzlement van Inwagen feels here to failure to distinguish the two very different readings sentences of form (A) can have when E is one of S's own actions. He wants to say that (A) can be true in such a case but he wonders *how* it can be. His feeling that (A) can be true is traceable to the (A2) interpretation, which gives a proposition whose possibility is clear and straightforward. His conflicting feeling that there is no way (A) can be true in such a case is traceable to the (A1) interpretation, which gives an inconsistent proposition.

II.

Let us turn now to the other argument against incompatibilism I mentioned earlier. This one crucially assumes that if an action is not a purely chance or random event, if it is influenced by or has an explanation in terms of the agent's reasons or motives for doing it, then it is *ipso facto* determined. A.J. Ayer (1946), for instance, says

> Either it is an accident that I choose to act as I do or it is not. If it is an accident, then it is merely a matter of chance that I did not choose otherwise; and if it is merely a matter of chance that I did not choose otherwise, it is surely irrational to hold me morally responsible for choosing as I

did. But if it is not an accident that I choose to do one thing rather than another, then presumably there is some causal explanation of my choice: and in that case we are led back to determinism.[5]

J.J.C. Smart (1968) argues that

the question of pure chance or determinism is irrelevant to the question of free will, though, so far from free will and determinism being incompatible with one another, a close approximation to determinism on the macro-level is required for free will.

Some philosophers would...say that in free choice we act from reasons, not from causes, and they would say that acting from reasons is neither caused nor a matter of pure chance. I find this unintelligible.

...the free choice is supposed to be not deterministic and not a matter of pure chance. It is supposed to be pure chance in the sense of "not being determined" but the suggestion is that it is also not merely random and is "acting from reasons". The previous paragraph [not quoted here; see note 16 for a description of its content] suggests, however, that acting from reasons is not merely random precisely because it is also acting from causes.[6]

We can formulate the argument these authors make as follows:

(1) Incompatibilism entails that an action cannot be both free and determined by an antecedent state of the world.
(2) If an action is not determined by an antecedent state of the world then it has no explanation in terms of its antecedents.
(3) But some free actions do have explanations in terms of their antecedents.
(4) Therefore, incompatibilism is wrong.

Premiss (1) is true by the definition of incompatibilism. Premiss (3) is obviously undeniable. We frequently give explanations of our own actions, and accept explanations of others' actions, like the following:

S opened the window in order to let the smoke out.

S wanted to get out of the country quickly and realized it would take days unless she gave the official a bribe, so she handed him all her rubles.

These are explanations of actions because they answer the question "Why did S do that?" The first explains why S opened the window. The second explains why S handed the official all her rubles. These examples illustrate a category of explanations that apply only to actions: they are explanations that give us the agent's reasons for acting as she did. For most of our actions, or most that we have occasion to reflect on, we believe that they have such reasons explanations. Very often some of the intentions, desires, or beliefs that we bring into such an explanation are antecedents of the action. It would be preposterous to suggest that free actions can never have such explanations, to deny premiss (3).

Some philosophers seem to think that premiss (3) would be acceptable even if it were stronger and said that an action *must* have an explanation in terms of its antecedents, or that this must be true of *responsible* actions or of ones that the agent *chooses*, ones that are truly the agent's actions. Bergmann, for example, seems to suggest this in the remarks quoted above (p. 2). But I can see no reason to accept these much stronger claims. When I cross my legs while listening to a lecture, that action (usually) has no explanation in terms of reasons for doing it that I had antecedently. I just spontaneously do it. A spontaneous action, not arising from any antecedent motive, can even be undertaken with a further intention that begins to exist just when the action does. For example, a bird catches a person's eye and, without having antecedently formed the intention to keep watching it, she moves her head when the bird moves, in order to keep her eyes on it.

But premiss (3) itself is obviously true. As I said, it would be absurd to suppose that a free action could not have an explanation in terms of the agent's antecedent reasons for doing it. It is premiss (2), that an action has no explanation in terms of its antecedents if it is not determined by them, that is the substantive and deniable premiss in the argument. Ayer clearly assumes that there are only two alternatives: either an action is determined or it is a purely chance event. He says, "if it is not an accident that I choose to do one thing rather than another, then presumably there is some causal explanation of my choice: and in that case we are led back to determinism." Smart finds unintelligible the suggestion that there is a third alternative, "that acting from reasons is neither caused [determined] nor a matter of pure chance."

To assume premiss (2) is to assume that *all* explanations of events must be law-governed or *nomic*. That is to assume that an explanation can be true only if laws of nature guarantee that the explaining factors plus other circumstances are accompanied by the explained event. Applied specifically to reasons explanations of actions, this means the following:

> (B) A reasons explanation can be true only if laws of nature guarantee that the agent's reasons for performing the action plus other circumstances are accompanied by the explained action.

This bold, bald assumption is false.

III.

Some philosophers have thought that the laws of nature that govern reasons explanations in the way required by assumption (B) are fairly obvious. J.S. Mill, for example, in his *Examination of Sir William Hamilton's Philosophy* says that "Necessitarians", of whom he counts himself one,

> affirm, as a truth of experience, that volitions do, in point of fact, follow determinate moral antecedents with the same uniformity, and (when we have sufficient knowledge of the circumstances) with the same certainty, as physical effects follow their physical causes. These moral antecedents are desires, aversions, habits, and dispositions, combined with outward circumstances suited to call those internal incentives into action. ... A volition is a moral effect, which follows the corresponding moral causes as certainly and invariably as physical effects follow their physical causes.[7]

One may object that, in point of fact, the same volition or action does not invariably follow the same set of "moral" antecedents and this is particularly clear in cases (which are common) where the moral antecedents include the agent's having two or more desires that conflict, so the agent can satisfy at most one of these desires. For example, on a Saturday afternoon I have a desire to spend the rest of the afternoon doing some philosophical work and also a desire to spend it watching a football game on television. Suppose this same set of conflicting motives recurs on several Saturday afternoons. Can't I choose to satisfy one of the motives on some of these occasions and the other on others of them, without there being any relevant difference in the antecedents on these several occasions? Mill says no.

> When we think of ourselves hypothetically as having acted otherwise than we did, we always suppose a difference in the antecedents: we picture ourselves as having known something that we did not know, or not known something that we did know; which is a difference in the external inducements; or as having desired something, or disliked something, more or less than we did; which is a difference in the internal inducements.[8]

It is already clear to Mill what the general law must be in such cases of conflict of motives: the chosen action will be the one that satisfies whichever of the conflicting motives is stronger than all the others: the strongest motive prevails.[9]

Thomas Reid (writing more than sixty years before Mill) makes the following remarks about this way of dealing with conflict-of-motives cases.

> When it is said, that of contrary motives the strongest always prevails, this can neither be affirmed nor denied with understanding, until we know distinctly what is meant by the strongest motive...when the motives are of different kinds, as money and fame, duty and worldly interest, health and strength, riches and honor, by what rule shall we judge which is the strongest motive? Either we measure the strength of motives, merely by their prevalence, or by some other standard distinct from their prevalence. If we measure their strength merely by their prevalence, and by the strongest motive mean only the motive that prevails, it will be true indeed that the strongest motive prevails; but the proposition will be identical, and mean no more than that the strongest motive is the strongest motive. From this surely no conclusion can be drawn... We are therefore

brought to this issue, that unless some measure of the strength of motives can be found distinct from their prevalence, it cannot be determined, whether the strongest motive always prevails or not. If such a measure can be found and applied, we may be able to judge of the truth of this maxim, but not otherwise.[10]

This suggests that one can secure confidence in Mill's law only by making it true by definition: "the strongest motive" *means* the motive that prevails. If this term is defined by some logically independent criterion, so that the proposed law will be a non-trivial proposition, then it is an open question whether the facts would give us reason for confidence in it. Reid presents Mill with a dilemma: either the strongest motive law is true by definition, in which case it is not the law of nature that was wanted, or some independent test of the strongest motive is to be found, in which case we do not know yet whether the proposed law holds.

Mill attempts to reply to this line of thought. He says there are two flaws in the argument that "I only know the strength of motives in relation to the will by the test of ultimate prevalence; so that this means no more than that the prevailing motive prevails."

First, those who say that the will follows the strongest motive, do not mean the motive which is strongest in relation to the will, or in other words, that the will follows what it does follow. They mean the motive which is strongest in relation to pain and pleasure; since a motive, being a desire or aversion, is proportional to the pleasantness, as conceived by us, of the thing desired, or the painfulness of the thing shunned. ... The second [flaw] is, that even supposing there were no test of the strength of motives but their effect on the will, the proposition that the will follows the strongest motive would not...be identical and unmeaning. We say, without absurdity, that if two weights are placed in opposite scales, the heavier will lift the other up; yet we mean nothing by the heavier, except the weight which will lift up the other. The proposition, nevertheless, is not unmeaning, for it signifies that in many or most cases there *is* a heavier, and that this is always the same one, not one or the other as it may happen, In like manner, even if the strongest motive meant only the motive which prevails,

> yet if there is a prevailing motive—if, all other antecedents being the same, the motive which prevails today will prevail tomorrow and every subsequent day—Sir W. Hamilton was acute enough to see that the free-will theory is not saved.[11]

This fails to wriggle out of the dilemma. Mill's proposed independent criterion of motive strength is the degree of pain and pleasure anticipated. On any ordinary understanding of this, the facts will not support the proposed law: people sometimes choose an alternative they believe will be more painful or less pleasant than another alternative they believe open to them, in order to keep a promise, for example. In his second point Mill seems to give the game away, apparently without quite realizing it. He says that, even if there were no other test of strongest motive but the one that prevails, this would make the strongest motive law no more absurd and unmeaning than "the heaviest weight always lifts the other up". To this Reid should reply: Exactly so. No more unmeaning *and no less tautologous*.

Mill goes on to claim that the proposition, "The heavier weight lifts the other up", "signifies that in many or most cases there is a heavier *and this is always the same one*, not one or the other as it may happen" (emphasis added). He implies that the corresponding proposition, "The strongest motive prevails", implies a corresponding thing, that the prevailing motive in recurrences of the same set of conflicting motives is always the same one. But, of course, neither tautology can have the implication claimed for it. It is a contingent proposition, and therefore compatible with "the heavier weight lifts the other up", that two objects should change over time with respect to which is the heavier of the two. Likewise it is contingent, and therefore compatible with the tautological interpretation of "the strongest motive prevails", that when the same set of conflicting motives recurs a different one prevails from the one that prevailed earlier. And, more important, this is not only a logical possibility but actually happens, often. Sometimes when my desire to work conflicts with my desire to watch football the first motive prevails, and sometimes the other prevails. Sometimes when my desire to get an early start on the day conflicts with my desire to sleep a bit more the first desire prevails, and sometimes the other does. If there are laws of nature that explain why the prevailing motive does prevail in such cases, that explain this in terms of antecedents of the action, it is far from obvious what the contents of those laws are and it seems unlikely that they deal entirely in terms of "moral" antecedents (i.e., the agent's antecedent reasons or motives), for it seems that we already know all the relevant facts about them: the agent had the conflicting motives and it seemed a tossup which to satisfy.

There is another sort of case, noted by Reid, where the strongest motive law cannot apply at all, even on its tautological interpretation, because there is no motive that distinguishes the chosen alternative from another one.[12] On my computer's keyboard there are two keys such that if I press either of them the result is that an asterisk appears on the screen. I know this about these keys and I want to produce an asterisk, so I have a motive or reason for pressing one of them. Now suppose further that I have no desire such that pressing one but not the other of these two keys satisfies it. I have no motive for pressing one of them that is not also equally a motive for pressing the other. I am utterly indifferent between these two equally good means to my end of putting an asterisk on the screen. So I arbitrarily choose to press one of them. Here we cannot say that my pressing one rather than the other signified the prevailing of one over another of two conflicting motives I had. There *were no* conflicting motives such that one motive favored the one key and the other motive favored the other key. Yet I did press the key I pressed for a reason, namely, in order to produce an asterisk. The answer to "Why did he press that key?" is "Because he wanted to produce an asterisk".

Of course, I did not have a reason for pressing that key *rather than the other*. There is no answer to "Why did he press that key rather than this other one?", at least no answer that is a reasons explanation. I chose to press that key for a certain reason, but it is not the case that I had a reason for *not* pressing this other one instead. A similar thing holds in a conflict-of-motives case where it seems to the agent a tossup which motive to satisfy. The answer to "Why did he get out of bed just then?" is "Because he wanted to get an early start on his day". But to the question "Why did he get out of bed rather than stay in it for a while longer?" there may be no answer, because there may be no answer to "Why did he choose to get an early start rather than to get more sleep?".

In this case it is plausible to suppose that, *if* there is a *nomic* explanation of why he got out of bed rather than remaining in it, his desire to get an early start will figure in it, since it was a reason for that action but not a reason for the alternative. Of course it cannot be the only relevant antecedent in a nomic explanation here and the available reasons explanation affords little clue as to what might be the other antecedents that would subsume the case under laws of nature. In the indifferent means case, however, we have no good reason to suppose that, if there is a nomic explanation of why I pressed that key rather than the other one, my motive for pressing that key will figure in it, since it was an equally good motive for the other alternative. It seems that here the available reasons explanation for my action gives little hint as to what any of the antecedents of this nomic explanation might be if there is one.

So, contrary to what Mill appears to suggest, our reasons explanations for our actions do not always show us, or even give us much of a clue to, what the laws are (if any) that govern the determination of our actions by their antecedents.

IV.

But to show that we do not know any causal laws governing our reasons explanations is not to show that no such laws obtain[13] or that their obtaining would be incompatible with the reasons explanations. Some philosophers have tried to make this latter claim of incompatibility,[14] but their arguments do not succeed, as Davidson (1963), among others, has shown.[15] But that issue is not relevant here, for assumption (B) makes a much stronger claim than that a reasons explanation of an action is *compatible* with the action's being nomically necessitated by its antecedents. Assumption (B) is that reasons explanations *require* such necessitation. That is something that Davidson (1963) does *not* argue for but simply assumes. Neither does Ayer or Smart argue for this requirement. Smart writes as if he has done so when he says, "The previous paragraph suggests...that acting from reasons is not merely random precisely because it is also acting from causes", but in the paragraph he refers to he argues only that reasons explanations *can* be nomic.[16] That is not the same thing. The possibility of nomic reasons explanations does not imply the impossibility of anomic reasons explanations.

There are arguments that might be given for assumption (B). It might be said, for instance, that in giving a reasons explanation we are giving *causes* of the action—we do frequently use the word "because" in giving reasons explanations—and where there are causes there must be nomic necessitation. But this last premiss amounts to just another way of stating assumption (B). A more worthy argument is this: in any explanation of an event in terms of its antecedents there must be some relation between explanans and explanandum in virtue of which the one explains the other. What else could this explanatory connection be if it is not that the explanans plus other antecedent circumstances nomically necessitates the explanandum?

That is a fair question. We can show that the right answer is *not* "There is nothing else it could be" by showing that for paradigm reasons explanations there are conditions that

> are obviously sufficient for their truth,
> obviously do not entail that there is any true law covering the case (any nomic explanation of the action),
> but do involve another sort of obviously explanatory connection between the explained action and its explanans.

Any condition satisfying these criteria I will call an *anomic* sufficient condition for a reasons explanation. It is not difficult to specify such conditions.

Consider first a very simple sort of reasons explanation, the sort expressed in a sentence of one of the following forms:[17]

> (1) a. S V-ed in order (thereby) to U.
>   b. By V-ing S intended to U.
>   c. S V-ed with the intention of (thereby) U-ing.

I take these different forms to give us different ways of saying the same thing.[18] Some instances of these forms:

> S rubbed her hands together in order to warm them up.
> By flipping the switch S intended to turn on the light.
> S opened the window with the intention of letting out the smoke.

A statement of any of the forms (1a-c) is an answer to the question, "Why did S V?"; it offers an explanation of S's V-ing. It says that S's reason for V-ing was that she believed and intended that by V-ing she would U. Actually, "believed and intended" is redundant. S's intending that by V-ing she would U implies that S believes that by V-ing she has enough chance of U-ing to make V-ing worth the effort, and that is all the belief that the explanation requires. So we can say that such an explanation says that S's reason (or at least one of S's reasons) for V-ing was her intention thereby to U.

The only thing *required* for the truth of a reasons explanation of this sort, besides the occurrence of the explained action, is that the action have been *accompanied* by an intention with the right sort of content. Specifically, given that S did V, it will suffice for the truth of "S V-ed in order to U" if the following condition obtains.

> (C1) Concurrently with her action of V-ing, S intended by *that* action to U (S intended *of* that action that by it she would U).

If from its inception S intended of her action of opening the window that by performing it she would let in fresh air (from its inception she had the intention that she could express with the sentence "I am undertaking this opening of the window in order to let in fresh air") then *ipso facto* it was her purpose in that action to let in fresh air, she did it in order to let in fresh air.

This is so even in the possible case where there is also true some independent explanation of the action, in terms other than the agent's reasons. Imagine that by direct electronic manipulation of neural events in S (through, say, electrodes planted in the part of S's brain that controls voluntary bodily exertion) someone else caused S voluntarily to open a window. Now the (C1) condition (where "V" is "open the window" and "U" is "let in fresh air") could also be true in such a case. The accompanying intention required by (C1) is at least conceptually compatible with the direct manipulation of S's voluntary exertions by another. Indeed, there appears to be nothing incoherent in the supposition that the controllers of the implanted electrodes might arrange to produce both S's voluntary exertion and the accompanying intention about it. If the (C1) condition were also true then it would be the case that S intended by her opening the window to let in fresh air. So it would be the case that S opened the window because of the other's manipulation of S's brain events *and* S opened the window in order to let in fresh air. There is no reason to think that the truth of either explanation must preclude the truth of the other.

Note that the content of the intention specified in (C1) refers *directly* to the action it is an intention about. That is, it does not refer to that particular action via a description of it but rather, as it were, demonstratively. The content of the intention is not the proposition,

"There is now exactly one action of V-ing by me and by it I shall U", but rather the proposition, "By *this* V-ing (of which I am now aware) I shall U".[19] It is owing to this direct reference that the intention is about, and thus explanatory of, *that particular* action. Such an intention, which is directly about a particular action, could not begin before the particular action does. In general, whether the propositional attitude be intending or believing or desiring or any other, for the proposition involved to contain direct or demonstrative reference to a particular requires that the particular have an appropriate sort of role in causing whatever constitutes the reference to it, a relation that is precluded if the reference comes before the particular begins to exist. (It is enough if the particular has begun to exist, even if it is an event: one can demonstratively refer to a particular event by demonstratively referring to a part of it.) This means that we have a factor, the agent's concurrently intending something of the action, that is sufficient to verify a reasons explanation of the action and that not only does not but could not be antecedent to the action. We have a sufficient condition that entails nothing about what happened before the action that is relevant to explaining it. We have a reasons explanation that is entirely in terms of a concurrent state or process and not at all in terms of any antecedent one.

Usually, some explanatory antecedent is in the background of this sort of reasons explanation, "S V-ed in order to U". Usually, the intention concurrent with S's V-ing is the outcome of an antecedent intention, or at least desire, to U in the very near future. Usually, maybe even always, when an agent opens a window in order to let in fresh air, or pushes on a door in order to open it, she has already formed the intention to perform such an action for such an end and the action is undertaken in order to carry out that antecedently formed intention, or at least she antecedently possessed a desire for that end and the action is undertaken in order to satisfy that antecedently existing desire. But, however common it may be, there is no necessity that it be so: one can quite spontaneously do such things with such intentions.

So we see that our sufficient condition for explanations of sort (1), in terms of a concurrent intention regarding the particular action, does not entail that the action has a nomic explanation in terms of its antecedents. We should also see that it does not entail that the action has a nomic explanation in terms of concurrent conditions.

Of course the following generalization is true of such cases: for any agent S and time t, if S intends of her V-ing at t that she thereby U then S Vs at t. But this is logically necessary and not a law of nature. It may be, of course, that when S has an intention directly about a current action of hers, intends of *this* V-ing that by it she U, there is a mental state of S that is necessary for her having this intention but is compatible with the non-occurrence of the action of V-ing, a mental state that needs to be supplemented only by the right relation to the action for the whole to be her intending something *of* that action. But it will not be plausible to suppose that it is a law of nature that whenever an agent has this sort of mental state—ingredient in intending something of a concurrent V-ing but compatible with there being no V-ing—she does concurrently V. Her belief of her concurrent action that it is a V-ing could be false. Even if that belief could not be false (as might plausibly be held for the case where V-ing is a mental act of volition), there is no case for saying that our sufficient condition entails a nomic connection. Either there is an ingredient of the agent's direct intention about her V-ing that is compatible with her not V-ing or there is no such ingredient. If the latter, then the intention does not give us the non-entailing condition necessary for a nomic explanation. If the former then, although this aspect *could* be part of a nomically necessitating factor, there is nothing in the condition itself that entails that it must be so. There is, we have noted, a causal connection between the action and the intention required for the latter to refer directly to the former. But even if this must involve a nomic connection—and it is by no means clear that it must—the causation goes in the wrong direction, opposite to that from explaining intention to explained action. (In general, when one's thought contains a direct reference to a particular, it is in virtue of the particular's producing something in the thought, not vice versa.)

If the explanatory connection between the explaining intention and the explained action is not nomic necessitation then what is it? Well, it stares one in the face. In reasons explanations of sort (1) the concurrent intention explains the action simply in virtue of being an intention of that action that by or in it the agent will do a certain thing, in virtue, that is, of being that sort of propositional attitude (an intention) whose content has that feature (its being that by or in that action a certain thing will be done). That is all there is to it. It is simple but for the purpose of explaining the action it is sufficient. Aside from the relation required for the direct reference, this is an *internal* relation between the explaining factor and the explained action. It follows from the direct reference plus *intrinsic* properties of the relata, namely, the property of one that it is an action of S's and the property of the other that it is an intention of S's with a certain sort of content, namely, that the item to which it directly refers be an action with such-and-such properties. The explanatory connection is made, not by laws of nature, but by the direct reference and the internal relation.

Are reasons explanations of sort (1) *causal* explanations? They are if all one means by "causal" is that the explanation can be expressed with a "because" linking the explanandum and the explanans. ("She opened the window because she intended thereby to let out the smoke.") If, on the other hand, one requires that a cause, properly so called, precede its effect, then these are not causal explanations. And it perhaps sounds odd to speak of a *concurrent* intention about an action as *causing* or *producing* or *resulting in* or *leading to* the action.

None of these expressions sounds odd, however, when speaking of a motive or reason the agent had prior to the action. One case where the explaining factor is antecedent to the action is the case where we explain the action as the carrying out of a decision the agent had made, an intention she had formed. One class of such explanations are expressible by sentences of the following form:

(2) a. S V-ed then in order to carry out her intention to V when F.
b. S V-ed then because she had intended to V when F and she believed it was then F.

Here (2b) simply spells out more fully what (2a) implies. Some examples of this sort of explanation:

S opened the window in order to carry out her intention to open the window when people started smoking.
S raised her hand in order to carry out her intention to raise it as soon as the Chair called for the votes in favor of the motion.

What is an anomic sufficient condition for the truth of such an explanation? The wording of (2a) suggests that it should include, besides the explained action and the antecedent intention, an intention concurrent with the action to the effect that the action be a carrying out of the prior intention. This will make it the case that S performed the action *in order to* carry out that prior intention, performed it, that is, with the intention of carrying out that prior intention. So we can say that an explanation of sort (2) is true if (C2) is true.

(C2) (a) Prior to this V-ing S had an intention to V when F, and (b) concurrently with this V-ing S remembered that prior intention and its content and intended of this V-ing that it carry out that prior intention (be a V-ing when F).

Note that S cannot have the concurrent intention specified in (C2b) without believing that F now obtains; so it guarantees the second conjunct of (2b).

It is obvious that this sufficient condition is anomic. That is, it is obviously compatible with the truth of (C2) in a particular case of S's V-ing that there should be another case (involving S or some other agent) that is exactly similar in everything antecedent to the action (including other circumstances as well as the agent's intention to V) but lacks the agent's V-ing. Thus (C2) could hold even if there were no nomic explanation of S's V-ing in terms of the prior intention plus other antecedent circumstances. What then makes the explanatory connection here, if it is not nomic connection? Well, in the concurrent intention required by (C2) S intends of her current action that it be of just the sort specified in the content of the required prior intention (to which the content of the concurrent intention must refer), namely, a V-ing when F. It is this internal and referential relation between the contents of the prior and the concurrent intention, together with the explanatory relation of the concurrent intention to the action, which we have already discussed, that makes the explanatory connection between the prior intention and the action. The connection has two links, from prior to concurrent intention and from concurrent intention to action.

Following the model of (C2) for explanations of sort (2), it is not difficult to work out anomic sufficient conditions for other forms of reasons explanations in terms of antecedent states of the agent. Consider, for example, the sort expressed by sentences of the following form:

(3) a. S V-ed in order to carry out her (antecedent) intention to U.

> b. S V-ed because she had intended to U and believed
> that by V-ing she would (might) U.

Here (3b) spells out more fully what is implied by (3a). Some examples
of instances of this form of explanation:

> S shouted in order to carry out her (antecedent) intention to
> frighten away any bears there might be in the vicinity.
> S uttered, "They're gone," because she had intended to let R
> know when they had gone and believed that by such an
> utterance she would do so.

The following is an anomic sufficient condition for the truth of explanations of sort (3).

> (C3) (a) Prior to V-ing S had the intention to U and (b)
> concurrently with V-ing S remembered that prior
> intention and intended that by this V-ing she would
> carry it out.

S's having the concurrent intention specified in (C3b) requires that
S believe that by this V-ing she would or might U, and thus it entails
the second conjunct of (3b).

Still another sort of reasons explanation in terms of antecedents
is expressible in sentences of the following form.

> (4) S V-ed because she had desired that p and believed that
> by V-ing she would (might) make it the case that p (or
> contribute to doing so).

Examples of this sort of explanation:

> S opened the window because she had a desire for fresher
> air in the room and believed that opening the window
> would let in fresher air.
> S voted for the motion because she wanted it to pass and
> believed that her vote would help it to do so.

The following gives an anomic sufficient condition for explanations
of this sort.

> (C4) (a) Prior to V-ing S had a desire that p and (b)
> concurrently with V-ing S remembered that prior
> desire and intended of this V-ing that it satisfy (or
> contribute to satisfying) that desire.

Our anomic sufficient conditions for explanations of actions in terms of antecedent reasons, (C2)-(C4), require S to remember the prior mental state (of intention or desire) while engaged in the action that that prior state explains. This will be a feature of any anomic sufficient condition for a reasons explanation of an action in terms of a prior state of the agent. If at the time the agent begins the action she has no memory at all of the prior desire or intention, then it can hardly be a factor motivating that action. Now it is not necessary in order for (C4), for example, to be an anomic sufficient condition for the truth of (4) that this memory connection be anomic as well. Even if it were true that there is remembering of the prior desire only if there is a nomic connection between the prior state (plus its circumstances) and some current state, it would not follow from this and (C4) that there must be a nomic connection between the prior desire (plus its circumstances) and the action for which, given the truth of (C4), it provides a reasons explanation. But it is interesting to note, incidentally, that it is possible to specify an anomic sufficient condition for remembering, for the connection between an earlier state of mind and a later one that makes the latter a memory of the former. S's seeming to remember a prior intention to do such-and-such will be a memory of a particular prior intention *if* S had such a prior intention and nothing independent of that prior intention has happened sufficient to produce S's seeming to remember such an intention. More generally, one's having had prior experience of a certain sort is the *default* explanation of one's later seeming to remember having had such experience, in the sense that it is the explanation *unless* this role is preempted by something else, independent of it, that was sufficient to cause the memory impression.[20]

Like those in terms of concurrent intentions, our anomic sufficient conditions for reasons explanations in terms of antecedent motives are compatible with the truth of independent explanations in terms other than the agent's reasons. Consider again our example of S's voluntarily opening a window *both* as a result of another's manipulation of events in S's brain *and* in order to let in fresh air. Add to it that S had earlier formed a desire for fresher air in the room and concurrently with her opening the window remembered that desire and intended of that action that it satisfy that desire, making true the appropriate instance of (C4). Then you have a case where S opened the window both because of the signals sent to the volitional part of her brain and in order to satisfy her antecedent desire. Again there is no reason to think that the truth of either explanation excludes the truth of the other.

A noteworthy fact about (C4), the anomic sufficient condition for an explanation of the form "S V-ed because she had desired that p and believed that by V-ing she would satisfy that desire", is that it suggests a way of distinguishing between (i) a desire that was a reason for which the agent acted as she did and (ii) a desire that was *not* a reason for which the agent acted as she did although it was a reason for so acting that the agent was aware of having at the time. A desire of the agent's fits description (i) if the agent acts with the intention that that action satisfy that desire; and a desire of the agent's fits description (ii) if, and only if, the agent has no such intention concurrent with the action despite being aware of the desire and of the fact that it is a reason for acting as she did (given her beliefs).

One may wonder, however, if and how there *could* be cases that fit description (ii). Our account does not answer this question, but only turns it into the question whether it could be that an agent at the time of acting believes that her action will satisfy a certain desire she has without intending of the action that it satisfy that desire. Suppose S urgently needs her glasses which she left in R's room where R is now sleeping. S has some desire to wake R, because she would then have R's company, but also some desire *not* to wake R, because she knows that R needs the sleep. S decides to enter R's room in order to get her reading glasses, knowing as she does so that her action will satisfy her desire to wake R. Could it nevertheless be true that S did not intend of her action that it wake R? Bratman (1987) offers an illuminating account of how this could be so.[21] It seems right to say that S did not intend to wake R if S was so disposed that, had it turned out that her entering the room did not wake R, S would not have felt that her plan had failed to be completely realized and she must then either wake R in some other way or decide to abandon part of her plan. And S's being thus *uncommitted* to waking R is quite compatible with S's expecting and desiring to wake R.

V.

The anomic sufficient conditions we have given for explanations of actions in terms of antecedent reasons allow the possibility that the very same antecedent state of the world could afford a reasons explanation for either of two or more different alternative actions. Suppose, for example, that there have been two different occasions when I have formed the intention to produce an asterisk on my computer screen and have known that either of two keys will do the job. If on one of those occasions I pressed one of those keys, my action can be explained by saying that I pressed that key in order to produce an asterisk; and if on the other occasion I pressed the other key, that action can be explained by saying that I pressed *that* key in order to produce an asterisk. The only differences we need to suppose in the two situations are in the action explained (my pressing the one key rather than the other) and its concurrent intention (which I could have expressed, "By this pressing of *this* key I intend to produce an asterisk"). We need suppose no differences at all in the relevant *antecedent* intention. On both occasions it was just an intention to produce an asterisk.

In that example the agent was indifferent between alternative means to an intended end. In another sort of example the agent chooses arbitrarily between incompatible desired ends. Suppose S desires the motion to pass and at the same time desires to avoid offending her friend who opposes the motion. Whether she votes for the motion or votes against it, the explanation can be that S did it in order to satisfy the relevant prior desire. Again, the only differences in the two alternative situations that we need to suppose, in order to make the alternative explanations hold in them, are differences in the actions and their concurrent accompaniments. We need suppose no difference in the antecedents.

Here we have a striking difference between the anomic explanatory connection we have found in explanations of actions in terms of antecedent reasons and the nomic explanatory connection in deterministic explanations of events. The nomic, deterministic connection, by its very nature, can go from a given antecedent state of the world to just one subsequent development. If the antecedent state of the world explains a subsequent development via general laws of nature then that same antecedent state could not likewise explain any alternative development. Given fixed laws of nature, a given antecedent situation has the potential to explain nomically and deterministically at most one subsequent alternative development. But the same antecedent state can explain in the anomic, reasons way any of several alternative possible subsequent actions. If the antecedent situation contains the agent's having desires for two or more incompatible ends or her being indifferent between alternative means to an intended end, then it has the potential to explain in the reasons way whichever of the alternative actions occurs. The one that occurs needs only to have the right sort of accompanying memory and intention.[22]

It is true, as we noted earlier, that when an agent chooses arbitrarily between incompatible ends or between alternative means to an intended end we do not have an explanation of why the agent acted as she did *rather than* in one of the other ways. Nevertheless, we do have an explanation of why the agent acted as she did: she so acted in order to carry out the intention or to satisfy the relevant desire. The truth of that explanation is not undermined by the agent's not having any reason for, there not being any explanation of, her not doing one of the other things instead.

But now one may wonder about cases where the antecedents explain an action in the reasons sort of way but do *not* have the potential to explain alternative actions equally well, where the antecedents give the agent's reason for acting as she did and also explain why she did not act in any alternative way instead. If such explanations must be nomic, must imply that sufficiently similar antecedents will (as a matter of the laws of nature) always lead to the same sort of action rather than to any alternative, then incompatibilism is still in serious trouble. For it would be absurd to say that any such reasons explanation of an action renders it unfree.

Incompatibilists need not worry. Such explanations need not be nomic either. Consider again reasons explanations of sort (3).

(3) S V-ed in order to carry out her intention to U.

Our anomic sufficient condition for such an explanation was (C3).

(C3) (a) Prior to V-ing S had the intention to U and (b) concurrently with V-ing S remembered her prior intention and its content and intended that by this V-ing she would carry it out.

What sort of enriched condition will be sufficient for the truth of a similar explanation of why S V-ed *and* did not do something else instead (either some other sort of action or being inactive)? A commonly occurring condition that accomplishes this is the following.

(C3*)(a) Just before V-ing the agent intended to U at once and preferred V-ing then to any alternative means to U-ing then that occurred to her that she thought she could then perform, and (b) concurrently with V-ing she remembered her prior intention and intended by this V-ing to carry it out and she continued to prefer V-ing to any alternative means of U-ing that occurred to her that she thought she could then perform.

It is obvious that (C3*) is sufficient for the truth of a reasons explanation of the sort under consideration, one of the form:

(3*) S V-ed then rather than doing something else or being inactive instead because she intended to U at once and she preferred V-ing to any other means of U-ing that occurred to her that she thought she could then perform.

It should be equally obvious that (C3*) does not entail that S's V-ing was nomically necessitated by its antecedents. There certainly is no plausibility in the proposition that the antecedents given in (C3*a) must always issue in S's V-ing. Often enough such antecedents are followed by S's doing something else instead, owing to some new alternative occurring to S at the last minute, or to S's changing her mind about what alternatives are open to her, or to S's suddenly abandoning (perhaps even forgetting) her intention to U at once, or to S's weakness of will (though S believed that V-ing was definitely the best means to U-ing and therefore intended to take that means, there was in some other means a temptation that she was in the end unable to resist). As with the antecedents that explain why S V-ed (those given in (C3a)), the antecedents that explain why not any other alternative instead (added in (C3*a)) do so completely only in conjunction with conditions concurrent with and not antecedent to the action explained (specified in (C3*b)). To suppose that there occurs another case where the antecedents are exactly the same but S does not V but is inactive or does something else instead is not to suppose anything incompatible with the truth of the explanation entailed by (C3*).

VI.

I hope to have made it clear that incompatibilism does not entail certain absurdities it has been alleged to entail. The thesis that a free action cannot be nomically determined by its antecedents does not entail that an agent cannot determine which free action she performs or that an agent cannot perform a free action for reasons. When one sees how easy it is to give anomic sufficient conditions for reasons explanations of actions, one may find it surprising that many philosophers should have subscribed to the assumption that such explanations must be nomic. (Even some incompatibilists have been guilty of this assumption; they have typically also been "hard" determinists, denying that we in fact have free will.[23]) Perhaps the error is less surprising if we see it as a case of over-generalizing a well-understood and highly respected paradigm, in this case the explanatory paradigm of the natural sciences where laws of nature are what make explanatory connections. Fascination with this paradigm can, it seems, blind one to the fact that the explanatory paradigm of our ordinary reasons explanations of action is quite different. There an internal and referential relation is sufficient to make the explanatory connection and has no need of a nomic connection. Neither does it rule out a nomic connection. Reasons explanations are not *in*deterministic, only *a*deterministic; but that is all that the defense of incompatibilism requires.

Notes

1. Versions of the argument that are substantially adequate though flawed in minor ways can be found, among other places, in Ginet (1966), van Inwagen (1975), Ginet (1980), Ginet (1983), and van Inwagen (1983).
2. The earliest appearance of this argument, or one closely akin to it, that I know of is in Hume's *Treatise*, Bk. II, Pt. III, Sec. 2.
3. Bergmann (1977), pp. 234-5. This is the central argument in an Appendix titled "Freedom and Determinism".
4. van Inwagen (1983), pp. 149-150.
5. Ayer (1959), p. 275.
6. Smart (1968), pp. 300-301.
7. Mill (1872), pp. 449-50.
8. Mill (1872), p. 451.
9. See Mill (1872), pp. 451-453.
10. Reid (1815), quoted from Dworkin ed. (1970), pp. 88-89.
11. Mill (1872), pp. 468-469.

12. See Dworkin ed. (1970), p. 87, excerpted from Reid (1815).
13. As Davidson (1963) points out.
14. For example, Melden (1961) and Malcolm (1968).
15. See Goldman (1969), which focusses on Malcolm (1968).
16. He argues (Smart, 1968, p. 300) that a computer programmed to select items from a set according to certain criteria can be said to have been "programmed to act in accordance with what we would call 'good reasons'."
17. In these forms "V-ed" is a variable ranging over past-tense singular forms of action verb phrases (for example, "opened the door"), "to U" ranges over infinitive forms ("to open the door"), and "V-ing" ranges over progressive forms minus their auxiliaries ("opening the door").
18. Certainly (1b) and (1c) are equivalent and each implies (1a), and in normal sorts of cases where (1a) is true (1b-c) will be true also. Bratman (1987), Ch. 8, describes unusual sorts of cases where it seems right to say that (1a) is true but (1b-c) are not, given the plausible assumption that, if one believes that ends E1 and E2 cannot both be achieved, one cannot (without being criticizably irrational) intend to achieve both, but one can both undertake action A1 in order to achieve (aiming at achieving) E1 and undertake action A2 in order to achieve E2.
19. Wilson (1980), Ch. V, calls attention to such directly referring intentions. He calls them "act-relational" intentions and contrasts them with "future action" intentions. To be exact, it is the statements attributing these two kinds of intentions, rather than the intentions themselves, that he calls "act-relational" and "future action". An act-relational statement attributes, as he puts it, an intention *with which* the agent acts, an intention the agent has *in* the action.
20. I have argued this point more fully in Ginet (1975), pp. 160-65.
21. See Bratman (1987), pp. 155-60. The example he discusses differs from mine in that the agent in his example believes that the expected but unintended effect (the "side" effect) will help to achieve the same end that his intended means is intended to achieve, whereas in my example S does not believe this but desires the expected side effect, waking R, for reasons independent of her intended end, getting her glasses. But this difference seems immaterial to Bratman's account of how the side effect can, though expected and even desired (or believed to promote desired ends), can still be unintended.
22. We have here a solution to another puzzle of van Inwagen's, concerning how an agent can have a choice about, can have it in her power to determine, which of competing antecedent motives will cause her action, be the reason for which she acts. He expresses this puzzle in a footnote appended to his remarks I quoted above (p. 6):

> Alvin Plantinga has suggested to me that the thief may have had a choice about whether to repent owing to his having had a choice about whether, on the one hand, DB [a certain complex of desire and belief in the thief] caused R [the thief's repenting], or, on the other, his desire for money and his

belief that the poor-box contained money (DB*) jointly caused the event *his robbing the poor-box* (R*). We should note that the two desire-belief pairs, DB and DB*, both actually obtained; according to the theory Plantinga has proposed, what the thief had a choice about was which of these two potential causes became the actual cause of an effect appropriate to it. This may for all I know be the correct account of the "inner state" of a deliberating agent who has a choice about how he is going to act. But if this account is correct, then there are two events *its coming to pass that DB causes R* and *its coming to pass that DB* causes R** such that, though one of them must happen, its causally undetermined which will happen; and it will have to be the case that the thief has a choice about which of them will happen. If this were so, I should find it very puzzling and I should be at a loss to give an account of it. (van Inwagen, 1983, p.239, n.34)

The proper account seems to me straightforward. The thief determines which of the antecedent motives he acts out of simply by acting in the way recommended by one of them while concurrently remembering the motive and intending his action to satisfy it. His doing so is obviously compatible with his action's being nomically undetermined by the antecedent state of the world.

23. For example: Holbach (1770), Chs. XI-XII; Ree (1885), Chs. I-II; Darrow (1922).

References

Ayer, A. J., 1946, "Freedom and Necessity", *Polemic* 5; reprinted in Ayer (1959).

Ayer, A. J., 1959, *Philosophical Essays*, Macmillan & Co., London.

Bergmann, Frithjof, 1977, *On Being Free*, University of Notre Dame Press, Notre Dame, IN.

Bratman, Michael, 1987, *Intentions, Plans, and Practical Reason*, Harvard University Press, Cambridge, MA.

Darrow, Clarence, 1922, *Crime, Its Cause and Treatment*, Crowell, New York.

Davidson, Donald, 1963, "Actions, Reasons, and Causes", *Journal of Philosophy* 60, pp. 685-700; reprinted in Davidson (1980).

Davidson, Donald, 1980, *Essays on Actions and Events*, Clarendon Press, Oxford.

Dworkin, Gerald ed., 1970, *Determinism, Free Will, and Moral Responsibility*, Prentice Hall, Englewood Cliffs, NJ.

Edwards, Paul and Pap, Arthur eds., 1973, *A Modern Introduction to Philosophy* Third Edition, Free Press, New York.

Ginet, Carl, 1966, "Might We Have No Choice?", in Lehrer ed. (1966).

Ginet, Carl, 1975, *Knowledge, Perception, and Memory*, D. Reidel, Dordrecht.

Ginet, Carl, 1980, "The Conditional Analysis of Freedom", in van Inwagen ed. (1980).

Ginet, Carl, 1983, "In Defense of Incompatibilism", *Philosophical Studies* 44, pp. 391-400.

Goldman, Alvin, 1969, "The Compatibility of Mechanism and Purpose", *Philosophical Review* 78, pp. 468-82.

Holbach, Paul Henri Thiry, baron d', 1770 (1808), *Systeme de la Nature (System of Nature* or *The Laws of the Moral and Physical World)*, London (Philadelphia).

Lehrer, Keith ed., 1966, *Freedom and Determinism*, Random House, New York.

Malcolm, Norman, 1968, "The Conceivability of Mechanism", *Philosophical Review* 77, pp. 45-72.

Melden, A.I., 1961, *Free Action*, Routledge & Kegan Paul, London.

Mill, John Stuart (Robson, J.M. ed.), 1872 (1979), *An Examination of Sir William Hamilton's Philosophy*, University of Toronto Press, Toronto.

Rée, Paul, 1885, *Die Illusion der Willens Freiheit*, Berlin; an English translation of the major parts of Chs. 1-2, by Stefan Bauer-Mengelberg, is published in Edwards and Pap eds. (1973) under the title, "Determinism and the Illusion of Moral Responsibility".

Reid, Thomas, 1815, *The Works of Thomas Reid*, Vols. III-IV, Samuel Etheridge, Jr., Charlestown, MA.

Smart, J. J. C., 1968, *Between Science and Philosophy*, Random House, New York.

van Inwagen, Peter, 1975, "The Incompatibility of Free Will and Determinism", *Philosophical Studies* 27, pp. 185-99.

van Inwagen, Peter ed., 1980, *Time and Cause: Essays Presented to Richard Taylor*, Reidel, Dordrecht.

van Inwagen, Peter, 1983, *An Essay on Free Will*, Clarendon Press, Oxford.

Wilson, George, 1980, *The Intentionality of Human Action*, North Holland, Amsterdam.

Philosophical Perspectives, 3
Philosophy of Mind and Action Theory, 1989

MENTAL QUAUSATION

Terence Horgan
Memphis State University

I.

Even if individual mental events and states are causally efficacious, are they efficacious *qua* mental? I.e., do the mental types (properties) tokened by mental events and states have the kind of relevance to individual causal transactions which allows these properties to figure in genuine causal explanations? This question has arisen with increasing frequency and urgency in recent philosophy of mind.

My project here has four stages. First, I shall argue that our common-sense belief in the efficacy of the mental presupposes a positive answer to the question just posed; thus a negative answer would constitute a version of epiphenomenalism hardly less offensive to common sense than is the version which denies that mental events have any effects at all. Second, I shall consider and reject several possible accounts of what it is for two events c and e, together with two properties F and G, to jointly instantiate the 4-place relation expressed by the locution 'c *qua* F causes e *qua* G'. (I call this relation *quausation*.) Third, I shall propose— albeit somewhat sketchily—a positive account of quausation. And fourth, I shall argue that this account, despite its sketchiness, makes very plausible an affirmative answer to the question of the causal efficacy of the mental *qua* mental.

I shall take for granted several theses which are widely held in contemporary philosophy, and whose popularity is largely due to Donald Davidson.[1] I'll assume (i) that causation is a relation between concrete, spatio-temporally located, events or states; (ii) that every token mental event or state is identical to some token physical event or state; (iii) that every action is caused by a reason of a certain sort, viz., a so-called "primary reason"; and (iv) that a token primary reason for performing an action of kind K is a complex state consisting of a token belief b and token desire d which jointly "rationalize" performing an action of kind K, in the sense that b is a belief that performing a K-action would (or probably would) bring about the object of the desire d. But although these assumptions will play a central role in my exposition, I doubt that they are essential either in generating the problem I shall address or as a component of my proposed solution; the subsequent discussion probably can be reformulated to avoid some or all of them.[2]

In addition, I shall speak freely of both properties and possible worlds; but I leave it open whether such talk can be paraphrased into more austerely nominalistic terms, or can otherwise be so construed as to eliminate any genuine ontological commitment to such entities. And I shall sometimes use the rubric 'event' in a broad sense, to include states, processes, and any other entities that can be causal relata.

2.

The problem of mental quausation can be motivated by considering the seminal account of rationalizing explanations of actions in Davidson (1963).[3] Davidson there points out that an agent who has a particular primary reason for performing an action of a certain kind, and who does perform an action of that kind, might not perform the action *because* of that reason. Something is needed, in order to turn the first 'and' into 'because' in sentences like

(1) He exercised and he wanted to reduce and thought exercise would do it.

Davidson's position, essentially, is that all we need to add is

(2) His exercising was caused, in an appropriate way, by his desire to reduce and his belief that exercise would do it.[4]

I.e., he maintains in effect that the truth of (1) and (2) is both necessary and sufficient for the truth of

> (3) He exercised because he wanted to reduce and thought exercise would do it.

But although the conjunction of (l) and (2) surely expresses a *necessary* condition for the truth of (3), it does not express a *sufficient* condition.[5] Sometimes the cause of a given effect has a certain property which is not appropriate to cite in a causal explanation of that effect. The following examples, from Fred Dretske and Ernest Sosa respectively, nicely illustrate the point:

> Meaningful sounds, if they occur at the right pitch and amplitude, can shatter glass, but the fact that these sounds have a meaning is irrelevant to their having this effect. The glass would shatter if the sounds meant something completely different, or if they meant nothing at all. This doesn't imply that the sounds don't have a meaning, but it *does* imply that their having meaning doesn't help explain their effects on the glass. To know *why* the glass shattered you have to know something about the amplitude and frequency of these sounds, properties of the sound that are relevantly involved in its effect on the glass. (Dretske, this volume.)

> A gun goes off, a shot is fired, and it kills someone. The loud noise is the shot... In a certain sense the victim is killed by the loud noise. But not by the loud noise as a loud noise, but only by the loud noise as a shot, or the like... The loudness of the shot has no causal relevance to the death of the victim. Had the gun been equipped with a silencer the shot would have killed the victim just the same. (Sosa, 1984, pp. 277-8.)

When one keeps such examples in mind, it becomes quite evident why the conjunction of (l) and (2) does not entail (3). Suppose that sentences (l) and (2) are true, but that the cause's being a primary reason for exercising has no more relevance to the causal transaction than does, in these examples, the meaning of the sounds *vis-a-vis* their causing the glass to shatter, or the loudness of the shot *vis-a-vis* its causing the victim's death.[6] Then sentence (3) is just false. This is so even though the primary-reason property of the cause-state does provide a *rationale* for the effect-event, i.e., shows that the effect-event had something to be said for it from the agent's point of view. Providing such a rationale does not, by itself, establish that the primary-reason property of the cause is any more relevant to the causal transaction than is the sounds' meaning in Dretske's example, or the shot's loudness in Sosa's.

Sosa remarks that although the victim's death is caused by the event which is a loud noise, it is not caused by that event "as a loud noise." As one might say, the death is not caused by that event *qua* loud noise. This use of 'qua'-constructions is quite natural, and also quite common, when questions of explanatory relevance are at issue. As I said at the outset, the neologism 'quausation' will here be used to refer to the 4-place relation between two events and two properties that is expressed by the locution "c *qua* F causes e *qua* G." I shall construe this locution in such a way that the truth of (4) is both necessary and sufficient for the truth of (3)—assuming, as I do, that reasons are indeed causes:

(4) His exercising, *qua* the property *being an exercising*, was caused by his desire to reduce and his belief that exercising would result in reducing, *qua* the respective properties *being a desire to reduce* and *being a belief that exercising would result in reducing*.[7]

Quausation, as I shall understand it, may be partially explicated as follows:

For any two events c and e and any two properties F and G, c *qua* F causes e *qua* G iff:

(i)   c causes e;
(ii) c instantiates F;
(iii) e instantiates G; and
(iv) the fact that c instantiates F is explanatorily relevant to the fact that e occurs and instantiates G.

Clause (iv) is the crucial one, and is itself in need of further explication. This clause, as I am employing it here, expresses (by stipulation) the additional condition required to make statements like (3) come out true, over and above what is asserted in statements like (1) and (2).[8] I shall use the phrase 'quausal relevance' for this particular kind of explanatory relevance. Providing an account of quausal relevance will be a central concern below.[9]

Now, suppose that statements like (4) are never (or virtually never) true when the cited properties of cause and effect are reason-types and act-types, respectively. More generally, suppose that such statements are never (or virtually never) true when the cited property of the cause is mental—regardless whether the cited property of the effect is mental, actional, or something else. Then the corresponding mentalistic 'because' statements, like (3), also are never (or virtually never) true. But this latter claim is surely an outrageous offense against our common-sense belief in the efficacy of the mental. We believe not merely that reasons *are* causes, but also that people act the way they do *because* they have reasons which rationalize their actions. More generally, we believe not merely that mental events and states *are* causes, but also that they have the effects they do *because* they instantiate the specific mental properties they do.[10] In short, common sense holds not merely that mental events and states are causally efficacious, but also that their mental properties are explanatorily relevant to the causal transactions in which those events figure as causes. Accordingly, any view which denies the latter claim surely qualifies as a kind of epiphenomenalism, a kind I shall call *quausal epiphenomenalism.*

If one claims, with Davidson, that token mental events and states are identical to token physical events and states, then one thereby fends off traditional epiphenomenalism—the view that mental events lack any effects at all. But unless and until it can be shown that the mental *qua mental* is efficacious, i.e., that mental properties are quausal, there remains the possibility that quausal epiphenomenalism is true anyway—token physicalism notwithstanding. The problem of quausal epiphenomenalism is therefore very real, and very pressing. Indeed, it can fairly be called the latest incarnation of the Mind-Body problem, in a form especially applicable to the "nonreductive materialism" so prevalent in recent philosophy of mind. Successfully fending off quausal epiphenomenalism will require doing two things: first, giving a plausible account of quausal relevance; and second, using this account to argue that the mental *qua* mental is causally efficacious.

3.

Suppose that an event c causes an event e, and that c and e instantiate two properties F and G respectively. What is required in order for F and G to be explanatorily relevant to the causal transaction between c and e? One suggestion, with an accompanying line of reasoning to support it, goes as follows:

> For two events to be causally related is for them to have descriptions which jointly instantiate what Davidson calls a "strict law"—a law which is as precise and exceptionless as possible, which contains no *ceteris paribus* clauses, and which contains no causal-dispositional notions which themselves need cashing out in terms of more fundamental scientific concepts and laws. So whenever we give a causal explanation of an event, the explanatorily relevant properties of the cause and the effect will be properties which are connected by a strict law.

This line of thought has a certain initial plausibility, especially if one accepts Davidson's conception of causation as subsumability under a strict law. But, whether or not Davidson is right about the nature of causation itself, the strict-law criterion of *quausal relevance* is really far too stringent to be credible.[11] For, there are all kinds of garden-variety causal explanations citing properties of the cause and effect which, although explanatorily relevant, almost certainly do not figure in strict laws. ("The bridge collapsed because a truck drove onto it which exceeded its weight bearing capacity." "The fire was caused by a short-circuit." Etc.) Causal explanation is a highly context relative, highly interest relative affair, and attention to numerous examples of this kind— both in science and in ordinary life—makes clear the implausibility of insisting that the only properties of a cause and effect that are relevant to causal explanation are ones which figure in a strict law.

Davidson himself, incidentally, has never advocated a strict-law criterion of explanatory relevance; on the contrary, he has long repudiated such a view. Toward the end of Davidson (1963), for example, the following passage occurs:

> Ignorance of valid causal laws does not inhibit valid causal explanation, or few causal explanations could be made. I am certain the window broke because it was struck by a rock—I saw it all happen; but I am not (is anyone?) in command of laws on the basis of which I can predict which blows will break which windows. A generalization like, 'Windows are

fragile, and fragile things tend to break when struck hard enough, other things being right', is not a predictive law in the rough—the predictive law, if we had it, would be quantitative and would use very different concepts. The generalization, like our generalizations about behavior, serves a very different function: it provides evidence for the existence of a causal law covering the case at hand.... [It] is an error to think no explanation has been given until a law has been produced. (Davidson, 1980, pp. 16-17.)

Davidson has consistently maintained this position about causal explanation. And, although various commentators seem to have thought otherwise, the position is not incompatible with his "anomalism," the doctrine that there are no strict psychophysical or psychological laws.[12]

Since the strict-law criterion of quausal relevance is too stringent, we need a more liberal one. Presumably, an appropriate criterion should be suitably flexible, allowing for the interest relativity and context relativity of explanation itself. One possibility, suggested by Davidson's remarks in the above-quoted passage, is this: two properties F and G, instantiated by a cause-event c and an effect-event e respectively, are explanatorily relevant to the causal transaction between c and e just in case F and G are connected by a generalization which, although it may not be a strict law itself, at least *provides evidence for* the existence of a strict causal law that subsumes c and e. But this suggestion is quite implausible. For, if F and G are only relevant to the causal transaction in this evidential way, then it seems just wrong to employ 'because' statements as we do in causal explanations. Consider statement (3) above, for instance. When we say of someone that he exercised *because* he wanted to reduce and believed exercising would do it, what is the force of this claim—over and above what is claimed by the conjunction of (1) and (2)? Surely *not* that the rational appropriateness of the action, *vis-a-vis* the reason, provides evidence for the existence of a strict causal law subsuming the two events! If that sort of epistemic role were the only way that the respective reasonal and actional properties were relevant to the causal transaction, then it seems the most these properties could do would be to provide evidence for the *existence* of a genuine causal explanation; they would not really be explanatorily relevant themselves. *Bona fide* quausal relevance is not merely epistemic, but metaphysical: relevant properties must somehow pertain directly to the causal transaction *itself*, and not merely to our knowledge that it *is* a causal transaction.

A slightly different suggestion about quausal relevance, with an accompanying line of reasoning to support it, is this:

> Causal explanation is a matter of subsuming the cause and the effect under some counterfactual-supporting generalization. However, such a generalization need not be a *strict law* in order to serve this purpose. Many of our causal explanations advert, explicitly or implicitly, to the kinds of generalizations which Davidson calls "heteronomic"—i.e., looser, vaguer, exception-ridden generalizations which often employ ineliminable *'ceteris paribus'* clauses and/or ineliminable causal-dispositional concepts. Mentalistic causal explanation is no exception. And there are certainly generalizations of *this* kind linking mental event-kinds and to action-kinds, even if Davidson is right in claiming that there are no strict psychological or psychophysical laws. Accordingly, if two logically and metaphysically independent properties F and G are respectively instantiated by the cause-event and the effect-event in a given causal transaction, then F and G will be explanatorily relevant to that transaction provided that they are *at least heteronomically connected*. Furthermore, the reason why properties connected by a merely heteronomic generalization are relevant to causal explanation is *not*, contra Davidson, that the generalization provides evidence for the existence of a strict law which "covers" the events c and e (even though the generalization may happen to serve this evidential role too). Rather, the reason is that the heteronomic generalization *itself* covers c and e. I.e., built into our concept of causation, as the key criterion for two events' being causally related, is that they are subsumed by a generalization which is at least heteronomic. Even if no two events could ever satisfy this criterion without also being subsumed by some strict law, the fact remains that strict-law subsumability is not itself *criterial* for being causally related, i.e., is not part of the very concept of causation itself.

But this line of reasoning is quite dubious, for at least three reasons. First, there are cases where two events, although subsumable under a robust, counterfactual-supporting, heteronomic generalization, simply are not causally related at all. Suppose, for instance, that a certain disease causes progressive liver failure in humans, and also causes an intense desire to eat worms. Then the following will be a perfectly respectable heteronomic generalization: '*Ceteris paribus*, anyone who eats worms will die of liver failure'. Yet *ex hypothesi*, eating worms doesn't cause liver failure at all; the disease does.

Second, there are examples of causal transactions in which the cause and the effect have properties which evidently are not connected by even a heteronomic generalization, but which seem explanatorily relevant anyway. Suppose, for instance, that Barry's noticing a flower shop causes him to remember that tomorrow is his wife's birthday.[13] The properties *being a noticing that there is a flower shop yonder*, and *being a remembering that tomorrow is one's wife's birthday*, certainly appear explanatorily relevant to the causal transaction; yet generalizations like

> *Ceteris paribus*, a (married) man who notices that there is a flower shop yonder will remember that the following day is his wife's birthday

seem just false.[14]

Third, even in cases where the proposed criterion yields the intuitively right verdict, one doesn't feel intuitively that the rightness rests on satisfaction of *this* putative criterion. Take, for instance, action/reason causal transactions. Nobody doubts that there are *ceteris paribus* generalizations linking reason-types to the act-types they rationalize. But intuitively, the existence of such generalizations just doesn't seem good enough to guarantee that actions are caused by reasons *qua* reasons. On the contrary, there persists the intuitive worry that unless reasonal and actional properties meet some further criterion, they are ultimately superfluous to these causal transactions—that the only properties of the cause and the effect with any *real* quausal relevance are properties cited in the homonomic laws of natural science.

What is wanted, therefore, is an account of quausal relevance which links up more directly with our pre-theoretic intuitions about this matter, and which yields the correct verdict in cases where the heteronomic generalization criterion yields the wrong one.

4.

I shall now sketch the broad outlines of a positive account of quausal relevance which evidently meets these desiderata. Articulating the proposed account in detail would be a project in itself, well beyond the scope of this paper. But I will try to say enough to make plausible the claim that the mental properties of mental events really are explanatorily relevant to the causal transactions in which these events figure as causes.

Consider again Dretske's example of meaningful sounds' causing a glass to shatter, and Sosa's example of a loud shot's causing a victim's death. What is it about the sounds' meaning, and the shot's loudness, which renders these properties irrelevant to the shattering and to the victim's death, respectively? It seems evident that *part* of what is required, in order for properties F and G of the respective cause-event c and effect-event e to be explanatorily relevant to the causal transaction between c and e, is that F's being instantiated is a *counterfactually necessary condition* for the occurrence of an event that falls under the event-type G. I.e., a counterfactual of the following form must be nonvacuously true:

> (N) If there had not occurred an event with property F, then there would not have occurred an event with property G.

Or rather, a counterfactual of form (N) must be nonvacuously true *unless* the causal transaction involves overdetermination, the presence of a preempted potential cause, or some such familiar kind of non-standard feature which makes problems for analyses of causation generally; in addition, the properties F and G must be logically and metaphysically independent of one another.[15] (These provisos will carry over to what I shall say below, even when I do not explicitly mention them.)

The operative instances of (N), for Dretske's and Sosa's examples respectively, are the following. (Assume that in the glass shattering case, the sounds meant 'shatter'.)

> (N1) If there had not occurred sounds which meant 'shatter', then the glass would not have shattered.
> (N2) If there had not occurred a loud shot, then the victim would not have been killed.

If (N1) and (N2) each fail to be nonvacuously true, then the sounds' meaning 'shatter' and the shot's loudness each would thereby fail to satisfy a necessary condition for quausal relevance. However, it is doubtful whether (N1) and (N2) really *do* fail to satisfy this condition. Given the right sort of background stories, they evidently both are non-vacuously true. This is the case, for instance, if we suppose that the glass-shattering sounds were sung by a soprano who was strongly determined either to sing 'shatter' high and loud or to sing nothing at all; and if we suppose that the person who fired the shot had no means at hand to muffle its sound. So the moral is this: although the non-vacuous truth of a statement of form (N) is evidently a *necessary* condition for the quausal relevance of properties F and G, it is not a *sufficient* condition.

What more is required? One suggestion is that (N) should be strengthened to this:

(N′) If c had not instantiated property F, then there would not have occurred an event with property G,

where c is the event which was the cause in the actual world (or the "counterpart" of that event).[16] But when one examines this suggestion carefully, it appears seriously problematic. Consider, for instance, Dretske's glass shattering example, with respect to the properties of the sounds which clearly *are* quausally relevant: pitch, amplitude, etc. Call these the sounds' *R-properties*. Then the operative instance of (N′), for the R-properties, is this:

(N1′) If c had not possessed the R-properties, then the glass would not have shattered.

But is this counterfactual nonvacuously true? Arguably not. For, it might be claimed, with considerable plausibility, that if sounds in another possible world lack the R-properties, then they cannot be identical with (or counterparts of) the sounds which actually occurred. After all, it is at least arguable that the R-properties are essential properties of the sound-events in question, so that they could not have been *those* sounds without possessing the R-properties.[17] These considerations suggest that it is a mistake to try to understand quausal relevance solely in terms of counterfactuals whose antecedents explicitly cite the event (or its counterpart) which was the actual cause-event itself. Better to seek an account which remains neutral about the highly vexed issue of the transworldly individuation of events—and which takes into consideration what would have happened, under various pertinently similar circumstances, if there had occurred (or had not occurred) an event which both (i) instantiated property F, and (ii) was *pertinently similar* to the actual cause-event c.[18]

What seems required for quausal relevance, then, is a wider pattern of counterfactual dependence of the occurrence and non-occurrence of events with property G upon the occurrence or non-occurrence of events with property F. In characterizing the requisite pattern it will be useful to employ the terminology of possible worlds. Suppose that an event c causes an event e. Associated with this causal transaction, I suggest, is a set P[c,e] of *pertinently similar worlds* (PSW's). Each PSW contains a situation pertinently similar to—although perhaps somewhat different from—the situation in which c caused e in the actual world W. Also, each PSW w contains exactly one event c* which is *pertinently similar* to the event c of the actual world W; and w might, or might not, contain an event e* which is pertinently similar to the event e of W. An event in w, in order to be pertinently similar to c (or e) of W, not only must resemble c (or e) of W in pertinent intrinsic respects; it also must occur in *circumstances* in w what are pertinently similar to the circumstances in W in which the causal transaction between c and e transpired. If you like, the transworld pertinent-similarity relation holds between c* (of a PSW w) and c (of W) only if (i) c* is a good *prima facie* candidate for being identical with (or the counterpart of) c; and (ii) c* is also a better such candidate than any other event in w. Likewise, *mutatis mutandis*, for pertinent similarity between an event e* (of w) and e (of W). But, for the reason given above, it is best to allow the transworld pertinent-similarity relation to be weaker than the transworld identity (or counterpart) relation.

Quausal relevance of the properties of a cause-event and effect-event, I suggest, depends upon what happens across the range of PSW's in the class P[c,e]. My proposal is this:

> If (i)   event c causes event e,
> (ii) c and e respectively instantiate properties F and G,
> (iii) F and G are logically and metaphysically independent, and
> (iv) the causal transaction between c and e does not involve preemption, overdetermination, or the like,[19]

then the fact that c and e instantiate F and G, respectively, is explanatorily relevant to the fact that c causes e iff[20] the following *Relevance Condition* is satisfied:

(R) For any world w in P[c,e], if c^* is the event in w that is pertinently similar to c of W, then

(i) if c^* instantiates F in w, then c^* causes (in w) an event e^* which both instantiates G (in w) and is pertinently similar to the W-event e; and

(ii) if c^* does not instantiate F in w, then c^* does not cause (in w) an event which is pertinently similar to the W-event e.[21,22]

Patterns of counterfactual dependence of the kind described by condition (R) are often sought empirically, by means of controlled experimentation. Mill's methods of causal inquiry can be construed as techniques for experimentally probing for just such patterns.[23] Mill's joint method of agreement and difference is especially germane. The primary form of *agreement*, among the various PSW's in which the c^*-event instantiates the property F, is that in each such world w, c^* of w causes an event e^* that is pertinently similar to the effect-event e of W. And the primary form of *difference* between the PSW's in which F is instantiated by the c^*-event and those in which F is not so instantiated is that in each world w of the latter kind, c^* does *not* cause such an event e^*.[24] This direct connection between Mill's methods and condition (R) is encouraging, because it suggests that (R) reflects well our pre-theoretic intuitions about what it is for the properties F and G to be explanatorily relevant to the causal transaction between the events c and e.

Fleshing out this skeletal account of quausal relevance would require saying something systematic about what determines the class of PSW's, relative to a given causal transaction, and about what standards govern the transworld pertinent-similarity relation. I shall not undertake this task here. Various questions would need addressing within a more complete account, such as these: (l) Does the class of PSW's, and/or the operative pertinent-similarity relation, depend in part upon our current scientific theories, and if so how and why? (2) Do context-relative parameters, such as features of the pragmatics of explanation, partially determine the appropriate class of PSW's, and/or the appropriate standards of transworld pertinent similarity between events?[25] (3) Is it always fully determinate which worlds are PSW's and which are not, or is the borderline sometimes vague and indeterminate? (4) Is the vagueness of transworld pertinent similarity always completely resolved by contextual parameters, relative to a particular explanatory situation and a particular causal transaction, or is there sometimes (or always) a residual degree of vagueness?[26]

Even in the absence of a more complete account of quausal relevance, however, one finds oneself with fairly strong pre-theoretic *intuitions* about possible worlds—and about certain events in those worlds—which seem clearly pertinent, or clearly not pertinent, to questions about the explanatory relevance of specific properties *vis-a-vis* specific causal transactions. Such intuitions, being data which any adequate theoretical account of quausal relevance would need to accommodate, have fairly strong *prima facie* credibility. Admittedly, any particular intuitive judgment about these matters is defeasible; in the end of the judgment might prove mistaken, if it gets over-ruled on weighty grounds by a developed theory of quausal relevance which accommodates lots of *other* relevant data. But meanwhile, the presumption of correctness should be accorded to one's strong intuitive judgments about which worlds count as PSW's and which do not, and about which events within the PSW's count as pertinently similar to the actual cause-event or effect-event.[27]

One important feature of the class of PSW's, for a given causal transaction, does require mention. Roughly put, it is this: the class does not include nearby worlds in which an event occurs which is pertinently similar to the actual cause-event c, which lacks the property F of c, but which instead has a property F* with these two features: (i) F* is of the same general type as F; and (ii) F* is a property which, if F itself is quausally relevant, would also be quausally relevant in essentially the same way that F is.[28] Refining this vague formulation, in an informative and non-circular way, is an important part of the task of fleshing out the account of quausal relevance I am sketching. I will not attempt to do so here, but will merely illustrate the point with an example. Consider again the quausally relevant properties in Dretske's glass shattering case—the ones I am calling *R-properties*, like the sounds' specific pitch and amplitude. Suppose that certain properties which are only slightly different from the R-properties— say, slightly different properties of pitch and amplitude—also have glass-shattering capacity; call these *R* properties*. It clearly won't do to include among the PSW's a possible world in which (i) the situation is pertinently similar to the actual situation; and (ii) there occur sounds, quite like the sounds in the actual causal transaction, which instantiate R* properties but not the R-properties.

I am ready now to draw out some morals from the account of quausal relevance here suggested. To begin with, the account explains quite naturally why, in Dretske's example, the content of the sounds is irrelevant to their causing the glass to shatter. For, among the PSW's are worlds in which pertinently similar sounds occur but either mean something different or mean nothing at all; and the glass's shattering or not shattering is not correlated, across the PSW's, with the presence or absence of sounds which mean 'shatter'.[29] As Dretske remarks, "The glass would shatter if the sounds meant something completely different, or if they meant nothing at all" (Dretske, this volume).[30]

Sosa's example of the shot's loudness fares similarly. Among the PSW's, relative to the shot's causing the victim's death, are worlds where although (i) there occurs a shot that is pertinently similar to the actual-world shot, nevertheless (ii) this shot is not loud—for instance, worlds in which a quieter gun is used, worlds where the actual gun is fitted with a silencer, and so forth. The loudness of the actual shot is irrelevant, *vis-a-vis* the causal transaction in question, because the presence or absence of a *loud* shot is not correlated, across the PSW's, with the victim's dying or not dying. As Sosa remarks, "Had the gun been equipped with a silencer the shot would have killed the victim just the same" (Sosa, 1984, p. 278).

5.

When one turns from examples like Dretske's and Sosa's to typical cases of mental causation, however, things look very different. Typically, when a mental event c causes another event e, the following principle of *Supervenient Relevance* holds for some salient mental property F of c and some salient property G of e that is logically and metaphysically independent of F:

> (S.R.) For any world w in P[c,e], if c* is the event in w that is pertinently similar to c of the actual world W, then (i) c* instantiates F in w, and (ii) c* causes (in w) an event e* that both instantiates G and is pertinently similar to c of W.

This principle asserts a form of dependence, or supervenience, of the properties F and G upon other properties of the various c*-events and e*-events in the various PSW's: viz., in every PSW w, (i) the event c* has the property F; and (ii) an e*-event occurs in w, caused by c*, which has the property G. Thus principle (S.R.) does indeed express the "supervenient relevance" of F and G.[31]

Consider, for example, a case where a mental event causes an action: Fred experiences a desire for a beer, and this desire causes him to walk to the refrigerator. The mental cause c has the property *being a desire for a beer*. Now, there are PSW's in which Fred experiences a desire for a beer in a situation that is modestly different from the actual situation—for instance, worlds in which Fred is located at a slightly different position in his house than his actual-world position at the time he experiences the desire for a beer. In these PSW's, Fred's desire causes a sequence of bodily motions that is somewhat different from his actual-world motions; however, the otherworldly sequence still qualifies as an action of walking to the refrigerator, and hence counts as pertinently similar to Fred's actual-world action.

But are there any PSW's in which an event occurs which both (i) is pertinently similar to the actual-world event of Fred's desiring a beer, and yet (ii) lacks the mental property *being a desire for a beer*? I submit that there are not. In making this claim, I do not mean to take issue with the widely accepted view that the content of people's propositional attitudes does not normally supervene on "what's in the head."[32] I am prepared to allow that there are possible worlds in which there occurs, in Fred's head or in the head of a Fred-*doppelganger*, an event c* which is physically just like the actual-world event that was his desire for a beer, which causes bodily motions that are physically just like the motions that constituted his actual-world action of walking to the refrigerator, but which does not instantiate the property *being a desire for a beer*. But although there may be such worlds, my claim is that they are far too different from the actual world to count as PSW's. Hence they are just not pertinent to the question whether the property *being a desire for a beer* is explanatorily relevant to the causal transaction here at issue.

Consider, after all, how much alteration of actuality it would take to get a possible world of the kind envisioned. One mode of alteration would be head-external: leave Fred's brain and body just as they were in the actual world, but place him (or a *doppelganger* of him) in a larger environment which differs enough from his actual-world environment that the physical event which would otherwise have been a desire for a beer no longer qualifies as a desire with this same content. (Maybe Fred's *doppelganger* desires schmeer, even though he calls it 'beer'; schmeer, of course, is made from XYZ rather than water.) Fine, but why on earth should what happens in such Twin Earthly environments be considered pertinent to questions about the quausal relevance of properties instantiated by cause-events in our own earthly environment? Possible worlds in which the agent's environment has Twin Earthly qualities seem far too gratuitously different from actuality to qualify as PSW's.[33] Anyone who would claim otherwise takes on a very heavy burden of proof.[34]

Another mode of alteration would be head-internal: leave intact the physical event in Fred's brain which was his desire for a beer, but alter the surrounding "neural wiring" so drastically that physical events like the one in question now figure so differently in the head-internal causal nexus that they no longer token the property *being a desire for a beer*. But such worlds, surely, are again too weird to count as PSW's. The actual-world neural wiring surrounding the event which was Fred's desire for a beer, being an important background condition within which that event caused Fred's action, surely remains intact within all the worlds which are PSW's, relative to the causal transaction in question.[35]

These remarks carry over, *mutatis mutandis*, not only to other instances of the mental causation of action, but also to cases where one mental event causes another. We routinely engage in (putative) mentalistic explanation; our very criteria for attributing propositional attitudes and other mental states presuppose the soundness of this practice; and (putatively) mental events interact with each other, with sensory events, and with behavior in content-appropriate ways that are systematic enough to render the practice of (putative) mentalistic causal explanation a useful and viable enterprise. These facts constrain the class of PSW's, relative to a given causal transaction in which a mental event is the cause, in the following way: content-determining features of the cause's environment take on the status of background conditions, and hence are held fixed across the PSW's.[36]

Consider again the case where Barry's noticing the flower shop causes him to remember that tomorrow is his wife's birthday. Now, there are certain psychological background conditions present, at the moment when Barry notices the flower shop, without which this event would not have caused him to remember that tomorrow is that all-important day. In any PSW in which there occurs an event c^* that is pertinently similar to the actual cause-event c, c^* takes place in the presence of such background conditions, and also instantiates the property *being a noticing that there is a flower shop yonder*; in each such PSW, c^* will cause Barry to remember that tomorrow is his wife's birthday. Furthermore, in each PSW in which Barry does not notice (in the pertinently similar situation) that there is a flower shop yonder, he does not remember the birthday (while in that situation). As in the earlier example, there simply is no PSW in which there occurs an event c^* that is pertinently similar to the actual cause-event c and yet fails to instantiate the mental property *being a noticing that there is a flower shop yonder*. For, any world in which there occurs an event that is physically like c, but lacks this mental property, is a world too distant from the actual world to qualify as a PSW. Again: weird worlds are not PSW's.[37]

It appears, therefore, that the mental properties of mental events are indeed explanatorily relevant in the causal transactions in which those events are causes.[38] Even though we humans evidently are physico-chemical systems all of whose behavior and inner goings-on are explainable, in principle, in terms of the laws of physics as applied to our microphysical parts, we are also creatures whose mental states, *qua* mental, are causally efficacious. It is nice to have philosophical justification for believing in mental quausation, since most of us—myself included—could no more believe otherwise than we could fly.[39]

Notes

1. See, for instance, Davidson (1963, 1967, 1970), reprinted in Davidson (1980). Although I shall cite Davidson's writings by their original date and source, all the page numbers I give for quoted passages will refer to Davidson (1980).

2. In fact, I regard the assumptions as expository fictions. Elsewhere (Horgan, 1978, 1981, 1982) I have argued for an event-free ontology, as part of a general program of minimalizing ontological commitments by resorting to non-standard logico-grammatical devices such as adverbial operators and non-truth-functional sentential connectives. See also Tye (1984a, 1984b, 1984c, forthcoming), Horgan and Tye (1988), and Horgan (forthcoming). For an argument against the token-token psychophysical identity theory, which complements the no-event ontology favored by Michael Tye and me, see Horgan and Tye (1985).

3. Quite a number of philosophers have objected to Davidson's action theory, and/or his overall philosophy of mind, similarly to the way I shall—although nobody has formulated the problem quite as I do. See, for instance, Stoutland (1976, 1980), Toumela (1977), Hess (1981), Honderich (1982, 1984), Hornsby (1982), Kim (1984), Skillen (1984), Sosa (1984), Follesdal (1985), and Johnston (1985). For related discussion, see LePore and Loewer (1987), and Dretske (this volume). In my view, the problem of mental quausation does not show that Davidson's views are fundamentally inconsistent, or that he is unavoidably committed to a form of epiphenomenalism; however, the problem does reveal a lacuna in his position, a gap which needs filling. As far as I can tell, the account of mental quausation I shall propose below is consistent with—and even complementary to—the central tenets of Davidson's philosophy of mind.

4. Why the qualifier 'in an appropriate way'? Because of the problem of "wayward causal chains," which was later illustrated in Davidson (1973a) with the following example:

> A climber might want to rid himself of the weight and danger of holding another man on a rope, and might know that by loosening his hold on the rope he could rid himself of the weight and danger. This belief and want might so unnerve him as to cause him to loosen his hold, and yet it might be the case that he never *chose* to loosen his hold, nor did he do it intentionally. (Davidson, 1980, p. 79.)

Characterizing the difference between appropriate and wayward causal chains, in Davidson's view, is beyond the conceptual resources of our common sense mentalistic psychology, and would require dropping to the level of detailed and accurate physical laws. I myself suspect that common sense can do better than Davidson thinks, by virtue of the way our notion of quausation operates; more on this below.

5. By this I mean that there is more to the meaning of (3) than is captured by the conjunction of (1) and (2); a further condition needs to be met, to be spelled out below. But for reasons to be explained, I would claim that this further condition cannot fail to be satisfied if (1) and (2) are true; in this *modal* sense of sufficiency, the conjunction of (1) and (2) is indeed sufficient for (3).

6. Let me stress that in making this hypothetical supposition, I do not mean to suggest that I think it is metaphysically *possible* for the supposition to be true. In fact I do not, for reasons to be explained below.

7. It is worth noting that the mentalistic and behavioral predicates in (3) express mental and actional properties of an agent, whereas those in (4) express corresponding mental and actional properties of concrete events and states. The two kinds of properties are systematically related, and both kinds can be (and have been) regarded as types which are tokened by concrete events and states. In Horgan (1984), section 2, I propose a theory which treats both kinds of properties as event types, which spells out the various systematic interconnections in some detail, and which defines two kinds of type/token relation.

8. One can, if one likes, view clause (iv) as expressing a relation between facts of a certain kind. I myself prefer, however, to construe the locution 'the fact that...is explanatorily relevant to the fact that...' as having the logico-grammatical status of a non-truth-functional sentential connective, and hence as not ontologically committed to facts. Elsewhere (Horgan, 1978, 1982) I have argued that singular causal statements should likewise be regimented using a non-truth-functional causal connective (rather than a predicate over events), and that the statements flanking this connective should contain no putatively event-denoting terms. (Typically these flanking statements can be obtained by simply "unnominalizing" the nominalized sentences that flanked the causal predicate in the original unregimented singular causal sentence.) Were I to approach quausation in the same spirit, I would dispense with the 4-place quausal predicate. Instead I would focus directly upon 'because'-statements like (3), which I would regiment this way:

> (3') *The fact that* he wanted to reduce and thought exercise would do it *causally explains why* he exercised,

with the italicized words viewed as expressing a non-truth-functional sentential connective. (Under such an approach, the apparent distinction between causation and quausation might dissolve; this would depend upon whether or not there turned out to be adequate theoretical motivation for positing two distinct connectives, one causal and the other quausal.) I have various reasons for not pursuing the no-event format in the present paper, including these: (1) it is philosophically tendentious; (2) the central ideas I want to stress here, being largely independent of issues concerning the ontology of causation, are most readily grasped within the commonly accepted picture of causation as a relation between events; and (3) reformulating these ideas under the no-event format presumably requires first working them out within the standard framework anyway.

9. Perhaps clause (iv) should be qualified with 'in the appropriate way', for the same reason that this phrase was inserted into (2). Or perhaps appropriateness can be cashed out as part of an account of quausal relevance. I leave this question open, although I am inclined to think that the latter will turn out to be the case under the approach to quausal relevance sketched below.

10. By 'we' I mean those of us who believe in mentality at all, which is just about everybody except "eliminative materialists" like Churchland (1981) and Stich (1983). For a critique of Churchland's and Stich's arguments, see Horgan and Woodward (1985); and for some positive arguments in favor of realism about propositional attitudes, see Graham and Horgan (1988). If the causal efficacy of the mental *qua* mental cannot be sustained, however, then realism loses its point; one might as well go eliminativist.

11. LePore and Loewer (1987) distinguish between two notions of causal relevance, and they invoke this distinction to defend Davidson's anomalous monism against the charge of epiphenomenalism. They write:

Consider the following locutions:
a) Properties F and G are relevant$_1$ to making it the case that
c causes e, and
b) c's possessing property F is causally relevant$_2$ to e's
possessing property G.
    We will say that (a) holds iff c has F and e has G, and there
is a strict law that entails Fs cause Gs. It is in this sense
that...c's having F and e's having G "make it the case" that c
causes e. Relevance$_2$...holds when c's being F brings it about
that e is G. We shall argue that those who charge [anomalous
monism] with epiphenomenalism are guilty of confusing
relevance$_1$ with relevance$_2$. (pp.634-635)

As I understand this passage, relevance$_1$ is meant to capture the idea
that the properties F and G are related to one another in a way that
is *criterial* for c's being a cause of e. I.e., it is supposed to be part of
our very concept of causation that two events cannot qualify as being
causally related unless they respectively instantiate properties F and G
that are related to one another in the relevance$_1$ way. (For Davidson,
this way is the existence of a strict law entailing that F's cause G's.)
Relevance$_2$, I take it, is meant to be what I am here calling quausal
relevance. (Although LePore and Loewer's wording of (b) suggests that
the only pertinent explanatory question is why e instantiates G, their
overall discussion suggests otherwise. It appears that they also regard
the question why e *occurred* as highly pertinent, and thus that their actual intent is better captured by clause (iv) in my above partial explication of quausation.) If this is a fair reformulation of their distinction, then
I agree with them about two crucial points: first, that if the properties
F and G are relevant$_2$ in the causal transaction between c and e, then
F and G are not epiphenomenal in the transaction; and second, that those
philosophers who charge Davidson with epiphenomenalism often just
conflate relevance$_2$ with relevance$_1$. (Of course someone might, without
conflating these notions at the outset, try to argue explicitly that
relevance$_2$ entails relevance$_1$. But under a Davidsonian strict-law conception of relevance$_1$, at least, I am quite dubious about the prospects
for any such argument.)
12. On anomalism, see Davidson (1970, 1973b, 1974). Even in Davidson (1963),
    one already finds this passage:

> [G]eneralizations connecting reasons and actions are not—and
> cannot be sharpened into—the kind of law on the basis of
> which accurate predictions can reliably be made.... [It] is easy
> to see why this is so. What emerges, in the *ex post facto*
> atmosphere of explanation and justification, as *the* reason was,
> to the agent at the time of action, one consideration among
> many, a reason.... The laws whose existence is required if
> reasons are causes of actions do not, we may be sure, deal in
> the concepts in which rationalizations must deal. (Davidson,
> 1980, pp. 15-17.)

13. The example is due to Barry Loewer.
14. One might try becoming so liberal about what counts as "*ceteris paribus*" that the generalization comes out true after all. But *prima facie*, this is quite implausible. And in any case, if one adopts this position then it will be very hard to avoid allowing all sorts of explanatorily superfluous properties to qualify as quausally relevant—like the meaning of the sounds, in Dretske's glass-shattering example.
15. By 'logically independent' (and 'metaphysically independent') I mean that it is logically (metaphysically) possible for F to be instantiated by an event e without G being instantiated either by e itself or by some event which is either a cause or an effect of e; and likewise for G, *vis-a-vis* F.
16. On counterparts, see Lewis (1968, 1971).
17. I am assuming that for counterfactuals of the form (N′), the antecedent holds at a world w iff the event c *occurs* in w but fails to instantiate property F in w. Loewer and LePore (1987) invoke counterfactuals which look similar to (N′), viz., ones with the form

$$(N^*) \quad \sim Fc \ > \ \sim Ge,$$

where c and e are (or are the counterparts of) the actual world's cause-event and effect-effect, respectively. They say that the non-vacuous truth of such a counterfactual is a necessary condition for the causal relevance of the cause-property F. However, they also read such counterfactuals differently than I do: they say that one way for the antecedent (or consequent) to hold, at a possible world, is for c (or e) *not to occur* in that world. But this difference between their reading and mine ultimately doesn't matter, for present purposes. If one reads (N′) and (N*) my way, then it is arguable that *neither* is such that its non-vacuous truth is a necessary condition for the quausal relevance of properties F and G—for the reasons just given. On the other hand, if one reads (N′) and (N*) their way, then although the non-vacuous truth of these counterfactuals evidently is a necessary condition for the quausal relevance of F and G, it is not a *sufficient* condition—for the same reason that the non-vacuous truth of (N) is not a sufficient condition.
18. Davidson (1987) argues, in effect, that counterfactuals like (N1′) are virtually never non-vacuously true, because an event in another possible world which differs in any interesting way from a corresponding actual-world event is bound to differ somehow with respect to causes and effects, and hence cannot be identical to that actual-world event. (He also took this line in his oral comments on Dretske, at the 1986 Chapel Hill Colloquium.) Now, one certainly might take issue with Davidson's trans-worldly application of his own famous identity criterion for events. Nevertheless, the possibility of such a hyper-essentialist position concerning trans-world event identity does underscore the desirability of an account of quausal relevance which does not presuppose that the only pertinent counterfactuals concern what would have happened had the cause-event *itself* been different in various respects from how it actually was.

19. Strictly speaking, one should distinguish between causal and *quausal* preemption or overdetermination. Quausal preemption involves not a preempted potential cause, but rather a preempted, potentially instantiated, quausally relevant property—i.e., a property F', not instantiated by the actual cause c, such that (1) if F had not been instantiated by c then F' would have been instantiated by an event pertinently similar to c; and (2) in every PSW w in which F' but not F is instantiated by the event c* (of w) that is pertinently similar to c, c* causes an event e* that is pertinently similar to e. Quausal overdetermination involves not the simultaneous occurrence of two events each of which separately causes the given effect, but rather the simultaneous instantiation, by the actual cause c, of two properties J and K, logically and metaphysically independent of one another, such that (1) if only one of the two properties J and K had been instantiated by an event pertinently similar to c, then that event would have caused an event pertinently similar to e; and (2) in any PSW w in which only one of the two properties J and K is instantiated by the event c* (of w) that is pertinently similar to c, c* causes an event e* that is pertinently similar to e. Condition (iv) in the antecedent of my proposed account of quausal relevance is probably best construed as excluding only quausal preemption, quausal overdetermination, or the like. I.e., the account actually seems applicable in cases of ordinary causal preemption or overdetermination, provided one is willing to describe causal overdetermination as involving two distinct causes.

20. Even if satisfaction of the following Relevance Condition should turn out to be only necessary for quausal relevance, rather than both necessary and sufficient, this still would go a long way toward refuting quausal epiphenomenalism. For, as shall be seen presently, although the proposed condition is not satisfied by examples of quausally superfluous properties like Dretske's and Sosa's, it evidently *is* satisfied by mental properties of cause-events in typical instances of mental causation. This fact shifts the burden of proof to those who would espouse quausal epiphenomenalism.

21. One might ask why clause (ii) of (R) is not worded this way:

> if c* does not instantiate F in w, then c* does not cause (in w) an event which both instantiates G and is pertinently similar to the W-event e.

The reason for eschewing this formulation is that (R) is supposed to express the explanatory relevance of the properties F and G to the causal transaction *itself*—and not merely the relevance of the fact that c instantiates F to the fact that e instantiates G. Some additional comments are in order here. Sometimes, in a singular causal statement, the effect is designated by a description which cites a quausally irrelevant property of that event—as in "The sounds caused Fred's favorite event," where Fred's favorite event happens to be the glass's shattering. More commonly, however, the description of the effect cites a property (perhaps a sortal property) which does seem pertinent to questions of quausal relevance—as in "The sounds caused the glass's shattering." Often in these latter cases, the property attributed to the effect figures as a contextual parameter which partially determines (1) which other-worldly events count as being pertinently similar to the actual effect e of W, and (2) which possible worlds count as PSW's relative to the given causal transaction. In the example just given, for instance, it is clear that an event e*, in a possible world w, can qualify as pertinently similar to the actual effect e even if e* (in w) differs quite substantially from e (in W) at the level of microphysical detail—provided that e* is indeed a glass shattering. And this fact, in turn, influences the extent to which a given possible world can differ from W while still qualifying as a PSW.

22. The letters 'F' and 'G' (and/or the letters 'c' and 'e') might best be construed as dummy expressions replaceable by specific property-designators (event-designators), rather than as variables ranging over properties (events). Under this construal (R) is a schema, rather than a formula with two event-variables and two property-variables. The schema interpretation would be called for if the class of PSW's, and/or the transworld pertinent-similarity relation among events, should turn out to depend in part upon how we designate the cause and effect, and/or their respective properties. Compare Lewis (1971), where it is argued that the trans-world counterpart relation is subject to this sort of description-relativity.

23. Sometimes, however, Mill's methods are used not to determine which properties of the cause are quausally relevant, but rather to determine which event is the cause. In such cases the appropriate pattern of counter-factual dependence will be somewhat different from the one I have described. In particular, the class of PSW's will include worlds in which there does not occur an event that is pertinently similar to the actual cause c; and the occurrence or non-occurrence of an event pertinently similar to c (of W) will be correlated, across the PSW's, with the occurrence or non-occurrence of an event pertinently similar to e (of W).

24. Mill's method of concomitant variation, and his method of residues, come into play with respect to patterns of counterfactual dependence among properties which admit of varying *degrees*, like the quantitative magnitudes so ubiquitous in physics. I shall not discuss such degree-related dependence patterns, because I am not immediately concerned with causal claims in which the cause and/or the effect are characterized in terms of the degree to which a given property is manifested.

25. Here I should remark that both the class of PSW's and the operative transworld pertinent-similarity relation among events can depend upon which specific properties F and G, instantiated by c and e respectively, are being scrutinized for quausal relevance; cf. notes 20, 27, and 34. Indeed, perhaps it would be better to explicitly relativize the class of PSW's, and the pertinent-similarity relation, to the properties F and G (and not merely to the given causal transaction). I have refrained from doing so largely in order to simplify exposition.

26. Various questions about causal explanation also would bear explora-
tion, in connection with a more fully developed account of quausal
relevance. Such an account could be expected to yield insights about
matters including: (i) the nature of causal explanation itself; (ii) the different types of causal explanation; (iii) the role(s) played by heteronomic
generalizations in various kinds of causal explanation; (iv) the role(s)
played by strict laws; and (v) the strengths and deficiencies of the classic
Hempel-Oppenheim "deductive-nomological" model of explanation. For
pertinent discussion see Woodward (1979, 1984, 1986). These papers by
Jim Woodward are one source of inspiration for the general approach
to quausal relevance I am here proposing.
27. Let me add some additional methodological remarks, in light of the fact
that the centerpiece of this paper is a biconditional in which 'iff' is flanked
on the right by the Relevance Condition (R). One potential use of bicon-
ditionals in addressing philosophical problems is the strategy of *hard
core conceptual analysis* (for short, HCCA). Here the idea is to find an
'iff' statement whose left side (the analysandum) expresses a concept
central to the issue at hand, and whose right side (the analysans) provides clear, precise, non-circular necessary and sufficient conditions for
the analysans. The proposed conceptual analysis should be free of
counterexamples; also, the terms employed in the analysans should be
"conceptually prior" to the term expressing the analysandum, and also
conceptually prior to other terms that are closely cognate to the
analysandum-term. The HCCA strategy for dealing with a philosophical
conundrum consists of proposing an analysis which supposedly has the
features just mentioned, and then arguing that this analysis—perhaps
together with additional relatively uncontroversial premises—entails the
desired solution to the problem. Another approach, however, is the
strategy of *soft core conceptual geography* (SCCG). Here the idea is to
propose a biconditional whose left side expresses a concept central to
the discussion, and whose right side reveals something illuminating about
the how this concept fits together with various other concepts. The right
side of the biconditional may well be somewhat vague, allowing for varying resolutions (or partial resolutions) of its vagueness depending on context, speakers' interests and purposes, and the like. The terms occurring on the right side need not be "conceptually prior" to the term on
the left; and notions closely cognate to the concept expressed on the
left may well re-appear in one's descriptions of how the vagueness of
the right-hand terms gets resolved in certain contexts of usage. Such
descriptions need not rest upon purely *a priori* considerations, but instead may appeal to certain empirical facts (for instance, facts about
the kinds of putative explanations that people actually employ) as having normative import concerning what counts as a contextually appropriate vagueness resolution. The SCCG strategy for addressing a
philosophical problem consists of proposing such a biconditional, and
then using it as part of an overall argument that the desired solution
to the problem comports best with the global conceptual geography of
the concept in question and various cognate concepts. I regard my ap-

proach in this paper as an instance of the SCCG strategy. (I doubt that the concept of quausal relevance, or indeed most other concepts either inside or outside of philosophy, have precise necessary and sufficient conditions of the kind sought in traditional "analytic" philosophy. But I think the SCCG strategy is philosophically useful in any case, whether or not old-style conceptual analysis is a viable enterprise.) The SCCG approach reveals itself, for instance, in notes 29, 36, and 37 below.

28. The intuitive rationale for this proviso is that we are asking whether or not the presence or absence of F would make a difference in the causal transaction. In addressing this question, it is not appropriate to consider worlds in which, although F itself is not instantiated, there is instantiated a property F* of the kind described.

29. Suppose the soprano's vocal apparatus is so constructed that she cannot shatter glass with her voice except by emitting sounds which happen to mean 'shatter'; suppose, in fact, that this is true of all humans. Would this mean that the property *means 'shatter'* turns out, wrongly, to count as quausally relevant under my account? No. For, sounds in another world w can qualify as being pertinently similar to the actual sounds, and w itself can qualify as a PSW relative to the given causal transaction, even if the sounds in w are produced quite differently— say, by a noise-emitting artifact. Gratuitous departures from actuality won't do, either with respect to the class of PSW's or with respect to the pertinent similarity relation among events. But in some unusual cases, a fairly substantial non-gratuitous departure will be appropriate, in order to reach a world w where an event c* occurs which, although it instantiates (in w) the same quausally relevant properties that were instantiated by c in W, does not instantiate F (in w).

30. As I interpret this counterfactual conditional, the phrase 'the sounds' nonrigidly designates the sounds that occur in the envisioned counterfactual situation; these need not be identical to (or counterparts of) the sounds that actually occurred. Such usage is familiar enough. If one says, for instance, "The Vietnam War would have continued into the early 1970's even if the President had been Humphrey," one does not mean that the war would have continued even if Nixon had been Humphrey. Cf. Kripke (1972).

31. Supervenience is, I recognize, a modal notion: here the operative modal claim is that there *could not* occur an event c* (or an event e*) which is pertinently similar to the actual world's cause (or effect) and yet lacks the property F (or G). It is important to remember, however, that the accessibility relation governing modal assertions is a context-relative parameter of discourse—a point well argued by Lewis (1979). When a question of quausal relevance is at issue, it is natural to use modal language in such a way that all and only the PSW's, relative to the causal transaction in question, count as accessible; after all, these are the worlds that pertain to questions of quausal relevance. So it is of no small importance that mental properties are supervenient, in the way here described, under the contextually appropriate accessibility relation.

32. See Putnam (1975), Stich (1978), and Burge (1979, 1982, 1986).

33. Again I stress that one must keep in mind the reference class of possible worlds (i.e., the contextually appropriate accessibility relation), when one asks about the pertinence of supervenience or nonsupervenience of mental properties to questions about quausal relevance. Relative to a broad enough class of worlds, it is true that mental properties don't supervene on what's in the head. But this class is much broader than the class of PSW's for a given causal transaction involving a mental cause. When one restricts one's attention to PSW's, one finds that mental properties of causes normally obey principle (S.R), and hence are quausally relevant.

34. Two additional observations should be added. First, I already pointed out that the class of PSW's should not include worlds where, although there does not occur an event with the property F, there does occur an event with a property F* which belongs to the same general type as F and would be no less quausally relevant than F itself. The property *being a desire for a schmeer* may well be such an F* property, in which case we have another reason to exclude such a Twin Earthly world from the class of PSW's. Second, if we ask what sorts of head-external alterations of actuality it would take to get a world where an event occurs that is physically just like Fred's actual-world desire but which is not a propositional attitude at all, then things start getting so weird that such a case is very hard even to describe.

35. Besides, if we were to include, among the PSW's, worlds in which Fred's neural wiring is altered, then presumably we also should do so when applying Mill's methods to determine which event in W caused Fred's action; cf. note 22. Thus, c's status as the *cause* would come into question.

36. This interdependence between actual explanatory practice and the operative class of PSW's presumably would be accommodated, in a more thoroughly developed version of the account of quausal relevance I have sketched here, by wedding the account to an appropriate theory of causal explanation—perhaps along the lines of Woodward (1979, 1984, 1986). It should be noted, too, that the interdependence cuts both ways. I.e., features of the situation in which the actual causal transaction took place will qualify as causal "background conditions," and hence will remain fixed across all PSW's, only if the class of worlds which thereby count as PSW's has the following attribute: there are properties F and G, instantiated by the actual cause-event and effect-event respectively, such that (i) G-events depend counterfactually upon F-events, relative to the given class of PSW's, in the way specified by the above Relevance Condition (R); and (ii) this pattern of counterfactual dependence is rich enough and varied enough to render useful, illuminating, and pragmatically appropriate the general practice of citing the properties F and G in explaining those G-events that are caused by F-events.

37. But suppose there is an all-female society of Amazons, each of whom can produce, and can perceptually distinguish, sounds with the properties of pitch and amplitude which, in Dretske's glass shattering example, were the quausally relevant ones (the R-properties). Suppose, also, that sounds instantiating the R-properties, and *only* such sounds, hap-

pen to mean 'shatter' in the Amazon language. When Amora, queen of the Amazons, first encounters something made of glass, she reacts by saying 'shatter' (in Amazon); and it promptly shatters. Would this mean that the property *means 'shatter' in Amazon* turns out, wrongly, to count as quausally relevant under my account? No. For, a situation in another possible world w can count as pertinently similar to the actual situation, and w itself can count as a PSW relative to the given causal transaction, even if the object in w which Amora orders to shatter is made of something other than glass (e.g., clay); and if this object in w does shatter upon Amora's command, then its shattering will count as an event pertinently similar to the actual world's effect-event. But of course the clay object does not shatter in such a counterfactual situation, and hence the property *means 'shatter' in Amazon* turns out not to be quausally relevant in the actual causal transaction after all. Here we see an application of the point I made in note 36. When the question of the quausal relevance of the sound's intentional property is at issue, the fact that the object was made of glass does not qualify as a background condition that remains fixed in all PSW's. Why not? Because if we do hold this fact fixed across all PSW's, then the resulting pattern of counterfactual dependence of shatterings upon sounds that mean 'shatter' (in Amazon) just is not rich enough and varied enough to be illuminating. Objects made of other substances don't shatter in such circumstances; glass doesn't shatter on command when the order is given in any language except Amazon; etc. Hence it is clearly just coincidental that the glass-shattering properties of the Amora's utterance happen to be precisely the properties which, under the linguistic conventions of the Amazon language, qualify this sound as a token of the Amazon word for 'shatter'.

38. Although my examples of mental causal transactions all have involved propositional attitudes, I think my discussion here also is applicable to the qualitative, or phenomenal, properties of mental events. There is a close connection between my present appeal to principle (S.R), as grounds for the quausal relevance of the mental, and my defense of the supervenience of qualia in Horgan (1987).

39. For helpful discussion, and/or useful comments on prior drafts, I thank Fred Dretske, Gary Gleb, Barry Loewer, John Tienson, Jim Woodward, and especially Brian McLaughlin. A version of this paper was presented at the University of Massachusetts at Amherst, where I benefited from the ensuing discussion; specific changes were prompted by comments from Fred Feldman, Michael Jubien, and Gareth Matthews.

References

Burge, T. (1979). "Individualism and the Mental." In P. French, T. Uehling, and H. Wettstein, eds., *Midwest Studies in Philosophy, Volume 4*. Minneapolis: University of Minnesota Press.

Burge, T. (1982). "Two Thought Experiments Revisited," *Notre Dame Journal of Formal Logic*, 23, 284-293.

Burge, T. (1986). "Individualism and Psychology," *Philosophical Review*, 95, 3-45.

Churchland, P. (1981). "Eliminative Materialism and Propositional Attitudes," *Journal of Philosophy*, 78, 67-90.

Davidson, D. (1963). "Actions, Reasons, and Causes," *Journal of Philosophy*, 60, 685-700.

Davidson, D. (1967). "Causal Relations," *Journal of Philosophy*, 64, 691-703.

Davidson, D. (1970). "Mental Events." In L. Foster and J. Swanson, eds., *Experience and Theory*. Amherst: University of Massachusetts Press. London: Duckworth.

Davidson, D. (1973a). "Freedom to Act." In T. Honderich, ed., *Essays on Freedom of Action*. London: Routledge and Kegan Paul.

Davidson, D. (1973b). "The Material Mind." In P. Suppes *et. al.*, *Logic, Methodology, and Philosophy of Science, Vol. 4*. Amsterdam: North Holland.

Davidson, D. (1974). "Psychology as Philosophy." In S. Brown, ed., *Philosophy of Psychology*. New York: Harper and Row.

Davidson, D. (1980). *Essays on Actions and Events*. Oxford: Oxford University Press.

Davidson, D. (1987). "Knowing One's Own Mind," *Proceedings and Addresses of the American Philosophical Association*, 60, 441-458.

Dretske, F. (This volume). "Reasons and Causes." Presented at the 1986 Chapel Hill Philosophy Colloquium.

Follesdal, D. (1985). "Causation and Explanation: A Problem in Davidson's View on Action and Mind." In LePore and McLaughlin (1985).

Hess, P. (1981). "Actions, Reasons, and Humean Causes," *Analysis*, 41, 77-81.

Graham, G. and Horgan, T. (1988). "How to be Realistic about Folk Psychology," *Philosophical Psychology*, 1, in press.

Honderich, T. (1982). "The Argument for Anomalous Monism," *Analysis*, 42, 59-64.

Honderich, T. (1984). "Smith and the Champion of Mauve," *Analysis*, 44, 86-89.

Horgan, T. (1978). "The Case Against Events," *Philosophical Review*, 87, 28-47.

Horgan, T. (1981). "Action Theory Without Actions," *Mind*, 90, 406-414.

Horgan, T. (1982). "Substitutivity and the Causal Connective," *Philosophical Studies*, 42, 47-52.

Horgan, T. (1984). "Functionalism and Token Physicalism," *Synthese*, 59, 321-338.

Horgan, T. (1987). "Supervenient Qualia," *Philosophical Review*, 96, 491-520.

Horgan, T. (forthcoming). "Attitudinatives," *Linguistics and Philosophy*.

Horgan, T. and Tye, M. (1985). "Against the Token Identity Theory." In LePore and McLaughlin (1985).

Horgan, T. and Tye, M. (1988). "Braving the Perils of an Uneventful World," *Grazer Philosophische Studien*, 30, in press.

Horgan, T. and Woodward, J. (1985). "Folk Psychology is Here to Stay," *Philosophical Review*, 94, 197-226.

Hornsby, J. (1982). Review of *Essays on Actions and Events*, by Donald Davidson, *Ratio*, 24, 87-93.

Johnston, M. (1985). "Why the Mind Matters." In LePore and McLaughlin (1985).

Kim, J. (1984). "Self-Understanding and Rationalizing Explanations," *Philosophia Naturalis*, 21, 309-320.

Kripke, S. (1972). "Naming and Necessity." In D. Davidson and G. Harman, eds., *Semantics of Natural Language*. Dordrecht: Reidel.

LePore, E. and Loewer, B. (1987). "Mind Matters," *Journal of Philosophy*, 84, 630-642.

LePore, E. and McLaughlin, B., eds. (1985). *Actions and Events: Perspectives on the Philosophy of Donald Davidson*. Oxford: Basil Blackwell.

Lewis, D. (1968). "Counterpart Theory and Quantified Modal Logic," *Journal of Philosophy*, 65, 113-126.

Lewis, D. (1971). "Counterparts of Persons and Their Bodies," *Journal of Philosophy*, 68, 203-211.

Lewis, D. (1979). "Scorekeeping in a Language Game," *Journal of Philosophical Logic*, 8, 339-359.

Putnam, H. (1975). "The Meaning of 'Meaning'." In K. Gunderson, ed., *Language, Mind, and Knowledge: Minnesota Studies in the Philosophy of Science, Vol. 7*. Minneapolis: University of Minnesota Press.

Skillen, A. (1984). "Mind and Matter: A Problem that Refuses Dissolution," *Mind*, 93, 514-526.

Sosa, E. (1984). "Mind-Body Interaction and Supervenient Causation." *Midwest Studies in Philosophy*, 9, 271-282.

Stich, S. (1978). "Autonomous Psychology and the Belief-Desire Thesis," *The Monist*, 61, 573-591.

Stich, S. (1983). *From Folk Psychology to Cognitive Science: The Case Against Belief*. Cambridge, MA: MIT Press, Bradford Books.

Stoutland, F. (1976). "The Causation of Behavior," *Acta Philosophica Fennica*, 28, 286-325.

Stoutland, F. (1980). "Oblique Causation and Reasons for Action," *Synthese*, 43, 351-367.

Toumela, R. (1977). *Human Action and its Explanation*. Dordrecht: Reidel.

Tye, M. (1984a). "The Adverbial Approach to Visual Experience," *Philosophical Review*, 93, 195-226.

Tye, M. (1984b). "The Debate about Mental Imagery," *Journal of Philosophy*, 81, 678-691.

Tye, M. (1984c). "Pain and the Adverbial Theory," *American Philosophical Quarterly*, 21, 319-328.

Tye, M. (forthcoming). *The Metaphysics of Mind*. Cambridge, UK: Cambridge University Press.

Woodward, J. (1979). "Scientific Explanation," *British Journal for the Philosophy of Science*, 30, 41-67.

Woodward, J. (1984). "A Theory of Singular Causal Explanation," *Erkenntnis*, 21, 231-262.

Woodward, J. (1986). "Are Singular Causal Explanations Implicit Covering-Law Explanations?" *Canadian Journal of Philosophy*, 16, 253-280.

Philosophical Perspectives, 3
Philosophy of Mind and Action Theory, 1989

MECHANISM, PURPOSE, AND EXPLANATORY EXCLUSION

Jaegwon Kim
Brown University

I want to reopen the question whether the same bit of behavior, say an action we perform such as climbing a ladder, can be given both a "mechanistic" explanation, in terms of physiological processes and laws, and a "purposive" explanation, in terms of "reasons" (e.g., goals and beliefs). In a paper published in 1968,[1] Norman Malcolm defended a negative answer. He argued that once an action has been explained by setting forth its physiological causal antecedents it is no longer open to us to explain it by citing the agent's reasons, that is, his beliefs, desires, intentions, and the like. Alvin Goldman immediately replied to Malcolm,[2] arguing that mechanistic and purposive explanations are indeed compatible, that we can in fact characterize a type of situation in which one and the same behavior can be seen to be explainable both physiologically and rationally.

I want to reopen this debate not only because there is more to be said on this issue but also, and more importantly, because the issue has significant implications for some problems of much current interest in the philosophy of mind. A proper appreciation of the broader methodological issues and options involved will, I believe, help us to get clearer about some matters of current controversy. As we shall see, the question of explanatory compatibility leads us to more general questions about the possibility of *multiple explanations of a single explanandum*, and the relationship between two distinct explanatory theories covering overlapping domains of phenomena. Ultimately, these issues will be seen to arise from some basic assumptions about the epistemology and the metaphysics of explanation, and, in particular, the question of "realism" about explanations.

What Malcolm calls a "purposive explanation" of an action is one that conforms to the familiar "belief-desire" pattern of action explanation. Such an explanation explains an action by specifying the "reason for which" the agent did what he did, that is, by indicating what he wanted to accomplish and what he took to be an optimal way of realizing his want. We shall refer to such explanations as "rationalizing explanations"; these explanations provide us with the agent's considerations, explicit or implicit, that rationalize the actions to be explained. We need not think of belief-desire explanations as the only kind of rationalizing explanations ("I hit him because he insulted my wife"); nor need we think of rationalizations as the only mode of action explanation in vernacular psychology. However, belief-desire explanations seem to have a central place in our common everyday understanding of what we, and our fellow humans, do, and one could rightly claim, I think, that they constitute the basic mode of understanding actions in intentional psychology. Moreover, the question whether or not such explanations can coexist with physiological explanations of behavior is certain to generalize to other modes of intentional explanations, and how we answer this question will have direct implications for the current debate concerning the relationship between vernacular ("folk") psychology and the systematic science of human behavior, whether the latter is taken to be a relatively high-level "cognitive science" or a lower-level "neuroscience".[3]

But this problem of the relationship between vernacular and systematic psychology can itself be further generalized: What is the relationship between two explanatory theories (especially, two successive theories) of the same phenomena? Can the same phenomena be correctly explained by two different theories? Can we accept two such theories, each purporting to provide independent explanations of the same data? Suppose we accept either the compatibility thesis, or the incompatibility thesis, regarding the two types of action explanation. Could either position be generalized? Is it *in general* the case that an event can be given more than one explanation—or more than one type of explanation? Or is it the case that *in general* no event (perhaps, nothing) can be given more than one explanation? Are there general conditions under which explanations *exclude* each other?

I shall now place my cards on the table. On the question of the compatibility of action explanations, I think Malcolm is fundamentally right, although, as we shall see, this does not necessarily show Goldman to be wrong. I shall argue that the criticisms that have been raised against Malcolm, while they point to some interesting possibilities and need to be reckoned with, do not refute what I take to be the heart of Malcolm's arguments, and that on the special auxiliary assumptions Malcolm appears to accept, rationalizing explanations and physiological explanations do exclude each other. My central considerations will not depend on any special features of reasons and causes, or of mind and matter, but involve instead some broad reflections on the nature of explanation and causation— in particular, kinds of situation in which explanations with mutually consistent explanantia can yet compete against each other. This will lead me to formulate what I shall call "the principle of explanatory exclusion", something that many will, I am afraid, consider absurdly strong and unacceptable. Roughly, this principle says this: No event can be given more than one *complete* and *independent* explanation. What "complete" and "independent" may mean in this context is obviously important, and my discussion will be sensitive to the need of making these notions clearer; I should say right now, though, that I shall not be offering general definitions of these notions, but depend rather on the discussion of specific cases to generate reasonably cohesive senses for these terms. Rather, my strategy will be this: I shall argue my case principally for *causal explanations*, advancing at the same time some general considerations that will, I hope, make the exclusion principle seem a plausible constraint on explanations in general.

1. Malcolm's Argument

Although the exact form of a physiological explanation of behavior, and also exactly how we view the structure of a rationalizing explanation, are ultimately unimportant (as they should be if our results are to be of general interest), it will be useful to have some fixed points of reference. For this purpose we may simply turn to Malcolm's own view of the matter. He takes a physiological explanation of behavior to have the familiar form of a Hempelian "covering-law" or "deductive-nomological" ("D-N") argument:

> (N) Whenever an organism of structure S is in neurophysiological state q it will emit movement m. Organism O of structure S was in neurophysiological state q.
> Therefore, O emitted m.

A rationalizing explanation for Malcolm has the following, again familiar, form:

> (R) Whenever an organism has goal G and believes that behavior B is required to bring about G, O will emit B.
> O had G and believed B was required for G.
> Therefore, O emitted B.

Whether (R), too, is a D-N argument (Malcolm argues it is not) will play no role in the discussion to follow, although we need to assume, with Malcolm, that (R) represents the goal-belief complex as a "cause" or "condition" of the occurrence of the behavior. This is important: as will become clear, the incompatibility between these explanations stands out in the starkest way when they are both construed as causal explanations—as attempts to provide causal conditions from which the action or behavior issued.[4]

Before presenting his incompatibility argument, Malcolm tries to exclude the possibility that a rationalizing explanation of the form (R) is "less basic than" and "dependent on"[5] physiological explanations. I think that Malcolm's attempt is unsuccessful, for various reasons.[6] But whether or not Malcolm is successful here is less interesting for our purposes than why he makes the attempt. Recall that the provisional formulation of the explanatory exclusion principle I gave earlier prohibits only more than one *complete* and *independent* explanation for a given phenomenon. Although Malcolm does not say why he takes up the question of explanatory dependence at this point, a rationale is not far to seek: if the rationalizing explanation is *dependent* on the physiological explanation in an appropriate sense (e.g., by being *reducible* to it), then in truth there is only one explanation here, and the question of explanatory compatibility does not arise. The two explanations could peacefully coexist, but the peace is purchased at a price: they are no longer independent explanations. The explanatory efficacy of one would have been shown to derive from the other, and ultimately the physiological explanation would have to be taken as telling a deeper and more inclusive story of how the behavior came about.

What then is "the exact logical relationship between neural and purposive explanations of behaviour",[7] as Malcolm puts it? He asks: "Can explanations of both types be true of the same bit of behaviour on one and the same occasion?".[8] This is the problem of explanatory compatibility. But you will have noticed that the two explanatory schemes, (N) and (R), do not, strictly speaking, have the same explanandum; their explanatory conclusions are different, one speaking of the "emission of (bodily movement) m" and the other of the "emission of (behavior) B". Given this apparent difference in the explananda, it might appear that the question of compatibility could not arise. Malcolm is aware of this "dual explanandum solution" (as we might call it), and responds as follows:[9]

> Take the example of the man climbing a ladder in order to retrieve his hat from the roof. This explanation relates his climbing to his intention. A neurophysiological explanation of his climbing would say nothing about his intention but would connect his movements on the ladder with chemical changes in body tissues or with the firing of neurons. Do the two accounts interfere with one another?
> I believe there *would* be a collision between the two accounts if they were offered as explanations of one and the same occurrence of a man's climbing a ladder.

Although exactly how this is a response to the dual explanandum problem is somewhat uncertain, Malcolm seems to think that there is some concrete event here, the man's movement up the ladder, represented by the two conclusions, which serves as the shared explanandum of the explanations. In our discussion we will assume this is the case (Goldman does not dispute this assumption); if we do not, the problem of explanatory incompatibility could be restated, though this would bring in complications.[10] We may simply note here that although the two explanandum *statements* are not equivalent or synonymous, there is an evident sense in which they "describe" one and the same event, the same concrete happening, and that we could consider the compatibility problem stated with respect to this event however described. For now it will not matter exactly what this shared explanandum is, as long as it exists.

Malcolm's argument for the claim that not both explanations can hold seems to make use of the following assumption:[11]

(I)   If event C is nomologically sufficient for the occurrence of event E, then no event wholly distinct from C is necessary for E.

Using this principle, Malcolm appears to argue as follows: Suppose there is a physiological explanation of a man's ladder climbing conforming to schema (N) above. This explanation shows a certain physiological event ("neurophysiological state q") to be nomologically sufficient for the behavior. If this physiological event is indeed *sufficient* for the climbing, the climbing should occur whether or not any *other* event (such as beliefs and desires) occurred. That is, no other event should be necessary for the occurrence of the climbing, and the physiological explanation in itself should be deemed complete and sufficient as an explanation of the behavior. Once we know the physiological condition is present, we can be wholly confident that the ladder climbing will occur; it isn't necessary to verify whether other events, such as beliefs and intentions, are also present.[12] That the climbing would have occurred whether or not the rationalizing belief and desire occurred surely demonstrates the causal and explanatory irrelevance of the belief and desire.[13] For an explanatory connection can hold only if a dependency relation of some sort is present; perhaps, the condition that explains why an event occurred must at least be necessary in the circumstances for the occurrence of the event. Notice, by the way, that, as thus formulated, this is a general argument entirely independent of the subject matters of the two explanations; it makes no use of the fact that one of the explanations deals in psychological states and the other in neurophysiology, or the fact that the explanandum concerns human action or behavior. This is clear from the fact that (I) is wholly general and topic-neutral.

The crucial principle (I) as stated is obviously implausible if we consider causal conditions obtaining at different times:[14] e.g., let C be nomologically sufficient for E, and E for C*, where C occurs before E, and E before C*. Then C* is nomologically necessary for E. But seemingly there is no incoherence here. Or suppose C is sufficient for C*, which occurs later, and C* in turn is necessary for E, where E is later than C*. Again, there is no evident incoherence. Following Goldman, therefore, one might revise the principle like this:

(II) If C is sufficient for a later event E, then no event occurring at the same time as C and wholly distinct from it is necessary for E.

And it is this weaker principle that Goldman tries to undermine in his discussion of Malcolm's incompatibility argument.[15]

Goldman's objection to (II) is this: Suppose that two events, C and C*, are "simultaneous nomic equivalents"[16] in the sense that as a matter of law, C occurs (to an object) at a time if and only if C* occurs at the same time. Then if C is sufficient for E, then C*, too, is sufficient for E. If if C is necessary for E then so is C*, and we may suppose C to be both necessary and sufficient for the subsequent event E. This means two distinct events, C and C*, are such that C is sufficient, and C* is necessary, for E.

There are various complex issues here involving the inter-relations among necessity, sufficiency, cause, explanation, and the like. But fortunately we can largely ignore them, for what is crucial to the issue of explanatory compatibility is just this claim: *if C and C* are simultaneous nomic equivalents, in the sense explained, then one constitutes an explanation for a given event if and only if the other does.* If this claim is correct, the existence of physiological correlates for beliefs and desires would guarantee the possibility of both a rationalizing and a physiological explanation of an action. If all mental events have nomic equivalents in physiological states and processes (we may call this "the psychophysical correlation thesis"), every rationalizing explanation would have a physiological counterpart with the same explanandum.

2. Nomic Equivalents and Dependent Explanations

The claim just mentioned, to the effect that if C and C* are simultaneous nomic equivalents, one is an explanation of a given event just in case the other is, holds on the Hempelian account of explanation. But this unrestricted claim is surely dubious: it could be that although the situation is as described, C* is only an "epiphenomenon" of C, and, although C* is nomologically sufficient (and perhaps also necessary) for E, it does not explain why E occurs.[17] Thus, C could be the underlying pathological state of some disease, C* a simultaneous symptom of this state, and E a later stage of the disease. A case like this, therefore, is not one in which there are two explanations for one explanandum; for epiphenomena do not explain.

But let us not dwell on this possibility (although, as will be seen, it foreshadows others to be considered below), assuming instead something like the Hempelian nomic sufficiency account as our working model of explanation (this is what both Malcolm and Goldman do). The explanatory compatibilist may be willing to concede the possibility of epiphenomena just mentioned; for all he needs to refute Malcolm's claim is just one case in which each of two simultaneous nomic equivalents constitutes an explanans for the same event; surely, he may reason, not every case in which we have simultaneous nomic equivalents is one in which one of them is an epiphenomenon of the other. In any case, on the Hempelian model, if C and C* are nomic equivalents, the two explanations making use of them are "nomically equivalent explanations" in a straightforward sense; also, under the nomic-subsumptive account of causal relations, C and C* may be called "nomically equivalent causes". For it would be a matter of law that one is an explanation of a given event if and only if the other is, and that C is a cause of a given event if and only if C* is also its cause. Thus, if beliefs and desires have nomological coextensions in physiological states, for every rationalizing explanation of an action there is a nomologically equivalent physiological explanation (which we could formulate if we had sufficient knowledge of psychophysiological correlating laws). The fact that these explanations are nomically equivalent in this sense should alert us to the possibility that here we do not have two *independent* explanations of the same action. As I said, as a matter of nomological necessity, one is an explanation of that action just in case the other is.

Thus, our interim conclusion appears to be this: In the sort of situation Goldman asks us to consider, either one of the two nomically equivalent states is an epiphenomenon of the other so that we do not have two explanations of the same event, or else we have two explanations that are not nomologically independent. But what is wrong with nomologically dependent or equivalent explanations in this sense? Aren't they sufficient to show the possibility of giving two distinct explanations of one and the same event? And if the psychophysical correlation thesis holds, aren't we assured of the general possibility of explaining behavior both rationally and physiologically?

And there seem to be instances of just this sort in other areas of science. For example, we might explain the behavior of some substance subjected to certain conditions by an appeal to its gross physical dispositional properties (ductility, conductivity, viscosity, etc.)

on the one hand, and on the other by formulating a more theoretical account by invoking the micro-structures that underlie these dispositions as their "nomic equivalents". Don't we in such cases have exactly the kind of example that fits Goldman's argument? Such examples seem legion: we often deepen and enrich our understanding of natural phenomena by moving away from their observable features and the rough "phenomenological laws" that govern them, to their underlying micro-structures, and by invoking more systematic "theoretical laws" appropriate to these states. (At least, that is the textbook account of progress in scientific theorizing.) Perhaps, rationalizing explanations are related to physiological explanations in just this way—that is, as macro- to underlying micro-explanations—via a pervasive system of correlation laws providing for each psychological state a physiological "simultaneous nomic equivalent".

Whether such correlation laws exist, especially for contentful intentional states ("propositional attitudes") such as belief, desire, and intention, is a controversial question on which much has been written in the past two decades. I think that a preponderance of philosophical evidence is now on the side of "psychophysical anomalism", the thesis that there are not, and cannot be, precise laws connecting intentional states with physiological states of the brain (or any physical states).[18] If we have no confidence in the existence of such correlating laws, whether the correlations are species-or structure-specific, or uniform across all organisms and structures, the solution in terms of "nomic equivalents" would only be an idle possibility. But I do not want to pursue this issue of psychophysical laws here; for the general question still remains whether the existence of nomologically equivalent states opens for us the possibility of having multiple explanations of a single event. That is, we want to know how things would stand if there were psychophysical correlations.

What I want to claim is this: the kind of situation Goldman describes, namely one in which two events C and C* are seen to be nomologically necessary and sufficient for each other, and in which each of them is thought to constitute an explanans for one and the same event E, is *an inherently unstable situation*. This is so especially when C and C* are each a member of a system of events (or concepts) such that the two systems to which they respectively belong show the kind of systematic nomological connections Goldman envisages for the psychological and the physiological. The instability of the situation generates a strong pressure to find an acceptable account of the relationship between C and C*, and, by extension, that between the two systems to which they belong; the instability is dissipated and a cognitive equilibrium restored when we come to see a more specific relationship between the two explanations. As we shall see, in cases of interest, the specific relationship replacing equivalence will be either identity or some asymmetric dependency relation.

Another way of putting my point would be this: a certain instability exists in a situation in which two distinct events are claimed to be nomologically *equivalent* causes or explanations of the same phenomenon; stability is restored when *equivalence is replaced by identity or some asymmetric relation of dependence*. That is, either two explanations (or causes) in effect collapse into one or, if there indeed are two distinct explanations (or causes) here, we must see one of them as dependent on, or derivative from, the other—or, what is the same, one of them as gaining explanatory or causal dominance over the other.

The tension in this situation that gives rise to the instability can be seen in various ways. First, if C and C* are each a sufficient cause of the event E, then why isn't E *overdetermined*? It is at best extremely odd to think that each and every bit of action we perform is overdetermined in virtue of having two distinct sufficient causes.[19] To be sure, this differs from the standard case of overdetermination in which the two overdetermining causes are not nomologically connected. But why does the supposed nomological relationship between C and C* void the claim that this is a case of causal overdetermination? Notice the trade-off here: the closer this is to a standard case of overdetermination, the less dependent are the two explanations in relation to each other, and, correlatively, the more one stresses the point that this is not a case of standard overdetermination because of the nomic equivalence between the explanations, the less plausible is one's claim that we have here two distinct and independent explanations.

Second, if C and C* are nomic equivalents, they co-occur as a matter of law—that is, it is nomologically impossible to have one of these occur without the other. Why then do they not form a *single jointly sufficient* cause of E rather than two individually sufficient causes? How do we know that each of C and C* is not just a partial cause of E? Why, that is, should we not regard C and C* as forming a *single complete* explanation of E rather than two separately sufficient explanations of it? How do we decide one way or the other?

When we reflect on the special case of psychophysical causation, where C, let's say, is a psychological event, C* is its physiological correlate, and E is some bodily movement associated with an action, it would be highly implausible to regard C as directly acting on the body to bring about E (e.g., my belief and desire telekinetically acting on the muscles in my arm and shoulder and making them contract, thereby causing my arm to go up); it would be more credible to think that if the belief-desire pair is to cause the movement of my arm, it must "work through" the physical causal chain starting from C*, some neural event in the brain, and culminating in a muscle contraction. If this is right, we cannot regard C and C* as constituting *independent* explanations of E. We must think of the causal efficacy of C in bringing about E as dependent on that of its physical correlate C*.[20]

I believe that these perplexities are removed only when we have an account of the relation between C and C*, the two supposed causes of a single action, and that, as I shall argue, an account that is adequate to this task will show that C and C* could not each constitute a *complete* and *independent* explanation of the action.

A case that nicely illustrates this is the identity solution: by saying that C and C* are in fact one and the same event, we can neatly resolve the situation. Malcolm is clearly aware of this (as is Goldman); for in the course of his incompatibility argument he explicitly rejects the psychophysical identity thesis.[21] On the identity view, there is here one cause of E, not two whose mutual relationship we need to give an account of. As for explanation, at least in an objective sense, there is one explanation here, and not two. The two explanations differ only in the linguistic apparatus used in referring to, or picking out, the conditions and events that do the explaining; they are only descriptive variants of one another. They perhaps give causal information about E in different ways, each appropriate in a particular explanatory context; but they both point to one objective causal connection, and are grounded in this single causal fact.[22]

What are other possible accounts of the relation between C and C*? The standard model of theory reduction has it that for a theory to be "reduced to" another, the primitive theoretical predicates of the target theory must be connected via "bridge laws" with predicates, presumably complex ones, of the base theory to which it is reduced, in such a fashion as to enable the derivation of the laws of the target theory from those of the reducer.[23] It is clear that if a bridge law of the biconditional form were available for each primitive predicate of the theory to be reduced, its reducibility is assured. For all we need to do is to rewrite the basic laws of the target theory in the vocabulary of the reducer by the use of the biconditional laws, and add these rewrites, as needed, to the axioms of the reducer. In any event, the point is that if each psychological event has a simultaneous physiological nomic equivalent, all the conditions necessary for the reduction of psychology to physiology, in the currently standard sense of reduction, are satisfied. Our intentional psychology, with all its rationalizations, would be ripe for reductive absorption into physiology and associated sciences, and rationalizing explanations would cease to be *independent* explanations of actions.[24] The relation between a rationalizing explanation and the physiological explanation to which it is reduced would indeed be like that between a macro-explanation of—to resort again to a stock example—some thermal phenomenon (the expansion of a gas upon being heated) and its underlying micro-explanation (in terms of the increasing kinetic energies of the gas molecules). Here we are not dealing with two independent stories about the phenomenon; the main difference between them is that one tells a more detailed, more revealing, and theoretically more fecund story than the other. The sort of tension that Malcolm tries to exploit when we have both a rationalizing and a physiological explanation of an action no longer exists. The reason is that the two explanations are no longer independent—one is reducible to the other.

The supposed existence of psychophysical nomic coextensions, therefore, does not show that rationalizing explanations and physiological explanations could coexist as independent explanations of actions; on the contrary, it would show that explanations of one type are reductively dependent on those of the other type. For it would place us precisely in a situation tailor-made for the physiological reduction of psychology, namely one in which rationalizing explanation will be deprived of its status as an independent mode of understanding actions, a situation that, as we saw, Malcolm wanted to exclude. If such reducibility should obtain, the claim that rationalizing explanation provides us with a distinctive mode of understanding human action would be undermined. What explanatory efficacy rationalizing explanation possesses would derive from that of the underlying physiological explanation—at least in this sense: we would be able to give a physiology-based explanation of why, and how, it is that reasons explain actions, and if we take a causal view of the situation, then precisely how, and by what mechanism, reasons cause actions.

3. Causal Explanations and Explanatory Exclusion

The general principle of explanatory exclusion states that two or more complete and independent explanations of the same event or phenomenon cannot coexist. The meanings of "complete" and "independent" are obviously crucial. I shall not be offering definitions of these terms; rather I shall focus on some specific cases falling under the intended distinctions, with the hope that, in the course of my discussion, reasonably determinate core meanings will emerge that will give the exclusion principle clear and substantial enough content. A thorough examination of explanatory exclusion will inevitably spill over into the long-standing debate over the nature of explanation, a topic on which nothing like a consensus now exists. The discussion to follow will inevitably rest on certain intuitive assumptions about how explanations, especially causal explanations, work; however, I hope that the discussion will succeed in showing that whatever model of explanation you accept, unless you take a wholly fictionalist or instrumentalist view of explanation, the principle of explanatory exclusion is a plausible general constraint.

It seems to me that the case for explanatory exclusion is most persuasively made for causal explanations of individual events. Suppose then that we have two such explanations of a single event:

Explanation A cites C as a cause of E
Explanation B cites C* as a cause of E.

What are we to think of such a situation? Various possibilities can be distinguished:

Case 1. We find that C = C*. That is, there is one cause here, not two. We saw how this works for the case of psychophysical causation under the mind-body identity theory.[25] This, when available, is the simplest and perhaps the most satisfying way of relieving the tension created by the existence of the two explanations. Such identities are often found in a reductive context where one of the explanations specifies the cause by a deeper, and more theoretical and systematic, description.

Case 2. C is distinct from C*, but is in some clear sense "reducible" to, or "supervenient" on, C*. This sort of situation will arise in a reductive context of the sort just considered provided that for whatever reason we stop short of *identifying* the reductively related events or states. Thus, the psychophysical case considered earlier would be an instance of this kind if we believed in the nomological reducibility of psychological states to physical states, without, however, wishing to identify psychological states with their physical correlates; or if we believed in the "supervenience" in an appropriate sense of the psychological upon the physical, without identifying a supervenient psychological state with its physical base. In such a situation it is possible to treat causal relations involving psychological events and states as themselves supervenient upon, or reducible to, more fundamental physical causal processes. I have discussed "supervenient causation" extensively elsewhere.[26] In any event we do not have in cases of this kind two *independent* causal explanations of the same event. The two explanations can coexist because one of them is dependent, reductively or by supervenience, on the other.

Case 3. Neither C nor C* is in itself a "sufficient cause" of E, though each is an indispensable component of a sufficient cause. As has often been observed, when we are called on to provide a cause or an explanation for an event we usually select a causal factor that, for various epistemological or pragmatic reasons, is believed to be the most appropriate to the situation. A stock example goes like this: we might explain why an automobile accident occurred by citing, say, the congested traffic, or the icy road, or the faulty brakes, or the driver's inexperience, etc., depending on the explanatory context, even though each of these conditions played an essential role in causing the accident. If C and C* are related in this way we do not have two *complete* explanations— in one sense of "complete explanation", namely one in which a complete explanation specifies a sufficient set of causal conditions for the explanandum. It is clear that two incomplete explanations, in this sense, of the same event can coexist. The explanatory exclusion principle only bans more than one complete and independent explanation of the same event.

Case 3a.[27] C is a proper part of C*. If so, C as an explanation of E is neither complete in itself nor independent of C*.

Case 4. C and C* are different links in the same causal chain leading, say, from C to C* and then to E. In this case again we do not have two *independent* causal explanations; the explanans of one, C*, is causally dependent on the explanans of the other, C.

Case 5. C and C* are distinct and each a sufficient cause of E. We may think of them as belonging to two distinct and independent causal chains. This then is a case of *causal overdetermination*: E would have occurred even if either C or C* had not occurred, or had not caused it; the other would have been sufficient to bring it about. Thus, a man is shot dead by two assassins whose bullets hit him at the same time; or a building catches fire because of a short circuit in the faulty wiring and a bolt of lightning that hits the building at the same instant. It isn't obvious in cases like these just how we should formulate an explanation of why or how the overdetermined event came about; however, it is not implausible to think that failing to mention either of the overdetermining causes gives a misleading and incomplete picture of what happened, and that both causes should figure in any *complete* explanation of the event. If this is right, the present case is not one in which two complete and independent explanations are possible for one event.

Thus I disagree with Hempel when he says that when we have a case of "explanatory overdetermination", in which we have two or more complete D-N arguments with the same explanandum statement (e.g., "The length of this metallic rod increased"), then either argument *singly* can be considered as "complete" (one of them might explain it by invoking the fact that the rod was heated, and another might explain it by citing the fact that it was subjected to longitudinal stress).[28] Given Hempel's overriding concern with the inferential-predictive dimension of explanation, his position on this issue is not surprising. For as a predictive inference either D-N argument is wholly complete and sufficient. However, when it is a causal explanation of the lengthening of the rod that we are looking for, when we want to know *why* the rod's length increased, the situation seems radically altered: our understanding of why the event occurred is at best incomplete, and perhaps flawed, if we were unaware of one or the other "explanation".

The sense of "completeness" of an explanation I have just invoked is different from that used in characterizing the case of "partial cause" (Case 3 above), although this does not preclude a broader sense covering both. However, exactly how we deal with cases of causal overdetermination is not crucial to my general claims about explanatory exclusion; for it is unlikely that those who want to allow for multiple explanations of a single event would be willing to restrict them to instances of causal overdetermination. The exclusion principle would retain substantial content even if cases of overdetermination were exempted. In any event, the important point to note is this: that we have a case of causal overdetermination on hand is one way in which a satisfactory account of the relation between C and C* can go, removing the perplexities generated by the claim that each is a cause of some single event.

These considerations suggest the following simple argument for explanatory exclusion for causal explanations: Suppose that C and C* are invoked as each giving a complete explanation of E. Consider the two questions: (1) Would E have occurred if C had not occurred? and (2) Would E have occurred if C* had not occurred? If the answer is a "yes" to both questions, this is a classic case of overdetermination, and, as was discussed in preceding paragraphs, we can treat this case as one in which either explanation taken alone is incomplete, or else exempt all overdeterminative cases from the requirement of explanatory exclusion. If the answer is a "no" to at least one of the questions, say the first, that must be because if C had not occurred, C* would not have either. And this means that C and C* are not independent, and hence that the two explanations are not independent explanations of E.

The foregoing discussion of the subcases is useful as a way of making clearer what could be meant by the "completeness" and "independence" of explanations. When we examine the particular possibilities that seem to permit two distinct explanations of one event, we seem to be able to find— and we seem compelled to look for—reason for saying that either they are not independent or at least one of them is not complete. Two explanations of one event create a certain epistemic tension, a tension that is dissipated only when we have an account of how they, or the two causes they indicate, are related to each other. Finding out which of the cases canvassed holds for the given case is what is needed to relieve the tension.

4. Remarks on the Epistemology and Metaphysics of Explanation

When we look for an explanation of an event, we are typically in a state of puzzlement, a kind of epistemic predicament.[29] A successful explanation will get us out of this state. If our discussion is not too far off target, what it shows is that too many explanations will put us right back into a similar epistemic predicament, which can be relieved only when we have an explanation of how the explanations are related to one another.

Perhaps there is the following account of why this is so. Some writers have emphasized the unifying or simplifying role of explanation and tried to connect this with understanding.[30] It makes sense to think that multiple explanations of a single explanandum are presumptively counterproductive in regard to the goal of simplification and unification. When two distinct explanations are produced to account for a single phenomenon, we seem to be headed in a direction exactly opposite to the maxim of explanatory simplification "Explain as much as you can with the fewest explanatory premises". Unity is achieved through the promotion of interconnections among items of knowledge, and simplicity is enhanced when these interconnections are seen or interpreted as dependency relations. For the main role of dependency relations in a system is that they help reduce the number of required independent assumptions or primitives. If simplicity and unity of theory is our aim when we seek explanations, multiple explanations of a single phenomenon are self-defeating—unless, that is, we are able to determine that their explanatory premises are related to one another in appropriate ways. It is clear that showing that the explanatory premises of one explanation are dependent on those of the other, in any of the senses of dependence distinguished in the preceding section in connection with causal explanations, is in effect an attempt to reduce the number of independent explanatory premises—that is, a move toward restoring the simplifying and unifying role of explanations.

These reflections, though sketchy and programmatic, provide us with a clue to a possible way of understanding the concept of dependence for explanations, a notion that we have made a rather liberal use of without a general explanation. One theme that runs through the various different cases of "dependent explanations" we have surveyed seems to be this: if an explanation is dependent on a second, the two explanations taken together are committed to no more independent assumptions about the world than is the second explanation taken alone. This dovetails nicely with the view that explanations enhance understanding through simplification and unification. Here we would be trading in the notion of "independent explanation" for that of "independent assumption"; but that, I think, may well be progress.

These are general considerations not restricted to causal explanations. However, explanatory exclusion seems most obvious, and almost trivial, for causal explanations of individual events, and the reason seems to be this: we think of these explanations as directly tied to the actual causal histories of the events being explained, and their "correctness" as explanations is determined by the accuracy with which they depict the causal connections as they exist. When two such explanations of one event are on hand, we need to know how they are situated in relation to each other on the causal map of the event; one thing that cannot be allowed to happen, if our explanations are to be coherent, is that they tell two different stories about the same region of the causal map.[31] Explanatory exclusion may seem obvious for causal explanations, but this is not to say it is trivial: the above considerations at least assume "causal realism", the belief that there is a determinate objective fact of the matter about the causal history of any given event.[32] We must also assume certain metaphysical principles about causation, e.g. the principle (II) cited in section 1 above.

I take it that *explaining* is an epistemological activity, and that an *explanation*, in the sense of the "product" or "theoretical content" of such an activity,[33] is something about which we can have various cognitive attitudes (e.g., accepting, doubting, having evidence for, etc.). To be in need of an explanation is to be in an epistemically incomplete and imperfect state, and to gain an explanation is to improve one's epistemic situation; it represents an epistemic gain. However, knowledge must involve the real world: to know that p requires the truth of p, and to have a causal explanation of an event requires that the event specified as its cause be, in reality, a cause of that event. Let us once again focus on causal explanations of individual events, and set aside other sorts of explanation (e.g., explanation of laws and regularities, of what a word means, of how to interpret a rule, of how a mathematical proof works, etc.) The kind of view I have just alluded to, namely that a causal explanation of E in terms of C is a "correct explanation" only if C is in reality a cause of E, can be called an "objectivist" or "realist" conception of explanation. And the view that explanations must be "real" or "objective" in this sense can be called *explanatory realism*.

More generally, a realist conception of explanation holds that such notions as "objective truth" or "correctness" or "accuracy" make sense for explanations, and do so in a more or less literal way, and that an explanation is correct or accurate *in virtue of* there obtaining "in the real world" a certain determinate relationship between the explanandum and what is adduced as an explanation of it. Further, it maintains that an explanation represents a real addition to knowledge only if it has this property of correctness or accuracy, and that an explanation is epistemically acceptable only if we have good reason to think that the explanatory relation it purports to portray in fact holds in this objective sense. In short, it holds that explanations are appropriately evaluated on the basis of such objective criteria as accuracy and truth. Saying all this is not to slight the epistemological dimension of explanation. On the contrary: just as knowledge that something is so is canceled if the thing is not so, an explanation of X in terms of Y is voided if either Y does not exist or an appropriate relationship between X and Y does not in reality obtain. And just as the claim to know that p is, and must be, withdrawn when there is reason to believe that p does not hold, an explanation of X in terms of Y must be withdrawn, on explanatory realism, if we have reason to think that the claimed relationship does not in fact obtain between X and Y. Such things as understanding, intellectual satisfaction, making things intelligible, dispelling puzzles and apparent inconsistencies, etc. are crucial; however, we do not believe these things are *properly earned* unless an explanation is correct in some objective sense. The case for explanatory realism is best made—at least, can be made most explicitly— with respect to causal explanations, for here the notion of an "objective correlate" of explanation has an acceptably clear sense, clear enough for explicit consideration.[34]

It is helpful to distinguish between two versions of the exclusion principle. Suppose, for some given event, you have an explanation and I have another, distinct explanation. It can be rational, from an epistemological point of view, for you to accept yours, and for me to accept mine. But can they both be "correct" or "true" explanations? The *metaphysical* principle of explanatory exclusion says this: they can both be correct explanations only if either at least one the two is incomplete or one is dependent on the other.[35] There is a corresponding *epistemological* exclusion principle: *No one may accept both explanations unless one has an appropriate account of how they are related to each other.* What counts as an "appropriate account" of the relationship, in case of causal explanations, is as illustrated in the preceding section: ideally we must know which of these cases holds, or at least be satisfied that one of these cases, though we may not know which, does.

I should add a few remarks about the individuation of explananda. Some believe that an explanandum is fixed only when a statement representing it is fixed, a view closely tied to the inferential view of explanation;[36] this is often allied with the view that it is not events as concrete occurrences but *aspects* of events (or why a given event has a certain property) that are the proper objects of explaining. Thus, we do not explain, say, the Japanese surrender to the Allied Forces or Harry's accident, but rather such things as, say, why the Japanese surrender came as late as it did or how Hirohito was able to override the objections of the powerful military leaders, or why Harry's car ran off the road in broad daylight. These disputes, however, seem largely immaterial to my present concerns: if it is aspects of events, rather than events *simpliciter*, that are explained, then explanatory exclusion would apply to these event aspects.[37] If concrete occurrences are explainable, at least in the sense of explaining *why they occurred*, then they, too, would be subject to explanatory exclusion. Matters here are somewhat complicated because there are different views about the proper construal of events in causal and explanatory contexts.[38] But trying to heed these complexities and subtleties would be a largely pointless exercise in philosophical precision for the purposes at hand.[39]

The metaphysical principle makes sense only if some form of explanatory realism is accepted—that is, only if it makes sense, literal sense, to speak of the "correctness", "accuracy", and "truth" of explanations. And the acceptance of the metaphysical principle will provide a ground for abiding by the epistemological rule of exclusion. I think, though, that the epistemological principle can hold even if explanatory realism is rejected. Even if we abandon the idea that there are objective explanatory relations in the world, we may still find something cognitively and unsettling and dissonant about having to face, or accept, two or more independent explanations of the same phenomenon. The explanatory premises of one explanation need not logically contradict those of another, and there may be sufficient evidential warrant for thinking each set to be true. However, accepting the two sets of premises as constituting explanations of the same event (or any one thing), each complete in itself and independent of the other, may induce a sort of incoherence into our belief system. This may be one instance of epistemic incoherence that is not a case of logical (deductive or inductive) inconsistency or incoherence. I earlier tried to explain why this might be so on the basis of the view that the primary epistemic role of explanation is simplification and unification of our belief system. In connection with the coherence theory of justification, "explanatory coherence" is often prominently mentioned—how explanatory relations generate mutually supportive coherence in a system of beliefs. If our speculations here have a point, it can be summarized thus: *too many explanations can be a source of incoherence rather than increased coherence.*

It is interesting to contrast this situation with *predictions* or *proofs*. As I noted briefly above, it seems that, unlike explanatory overdetermination, predictive overdetermination does not create any sort of epistemic tension, any need to look for an account of how two predictive arguments, both predicting the same phenomenon, are related. Predictive or inferential overdetermination is simply a matter of overabundance of evidence. I infer that Peggy is in, because I can hear her typing and also because her lights are on. We predict that this steel rod will get longer because we know it's being stretched, and also because we know it's being heated. There are no problems here.[40] It is when such inferences are invested with explanatory import that a need for an account of their mutual relationship arises. And this is so, it seems to me, because explanations make a claim about how things are connected in the world, a claim that is absent in mere proofs or inferences. If this is right, the fact of explanatory exclusion shows that explanations cannot be construed as mere proofs or arguments.[41]

As I said, explanatory realism seems to fit comfortably with explanatory exclusion, although it is not, I think, entailed by it. One interesting possibility is *not* to argue for explanatory exclusion on the basis of explanatory realism, but rather to go the opposite route, namely to give independent considerations favoring the epistemological version of explanatory exclusion and then advocate explanatory realism as the most natural account of it.

Before moving on to the final section I would like to deal with a possible objection: it might be said that there is no need to appeal to any special, and potentially controversial, epistemological or metaphysical views concerning explanation in order to justify something like the rule of explanatory exclusion, and that all we really need is Ockham's Razor, the familiar principle of simplicity, that enjoins us to get by with the fewest possible entities, hypotheses, theoretical principles, and, of course, explanations. In reply, I would first note that the general simplicity requirement is vague and its application requires a more precise interpretation of the situation to which it is to be applied. In particular, we need to determine exactly at what point the entities in question begin to be multiplied "beyond necessity". In fact, determining where the excess baggage starts is the difficult part; the rest is trivial. The exclusion principle does the difficult work: it says that for any event more than one complete explanation is excess baggage. More, the principle helps us answer the following question: If, as is usually thought, explanations represent epistemic gains, why aren't two explanations better than one? It is not at all obvious that considerations of parsimony alone should mandate us to reject all but one explanation. We can indeed think of explanatory exclusion as a special case falling under the general simplicity requirement: it is a specific rule concerning one important way in which simplicity is to be gained in explanatory matters, and it explains why this form of simplicity is to be desired. That is, the explanatory exclusion principle provides a rationale for the application of Ockham's Razor to multiple explanations of a single explanandum.

5. Applications

In this final section I want to describe two examples from recent philosophical discussions in which the explanatory exclusion principle seems to be employed in a tacit but crucial way. The examples I shall discuss are not intended to constitute an argument for the exclusion principle; rather, they are intended to show that the principle is often accepted or presupposed, if only implicitly. Alternatively, they can be thought of as "applications" of the explanatory exclusion principle. Evidence such as this shows that, even apart from general theoretical considerations, the principle does carry a degree of prima facie plausibility, and should not be rejected without good reason.

The account of theory reduction we earlier referred to, one that was formulated by Ernest Nagel, is a model of *conservative reduction*. For in a reduction of this kind the reduced theory survives the reduction, being conserved as a subtheory of the reducing theory.

Its concepts are conserved by being tied, via the "bridge laws", to the concepts of the reducing theory, and its laws are reincarnated as derived laws of the more fundamental theory. For a theory to be reduced in this way to another theory whose legitimacy is not in question is for it to be vindicated and legitimatized.

There is another account of reduction, due to John Kemeny and Paul Oppenheim,[42] that is thought to give us an analysis of *eliminative* or *replacement reduction*. A theory is reduced to another, on this model, just in case all the data explainable by the first theory are explainable by the second. In cases of interest, the second theory, that is, the reducer, will do a good deal better than the first, the reducee. There need be no direct conceptual or nomological connections between the theories themselves; their theoretical vocabularies may be wholly disjoint and there may be no "bridge laws" connecting them. Nor need there be a logical incompatibility or a negative inductive or evidential relationship between them. It is just that one theory, the reducer, does its job better than (or at least as well as) the reducee, relative to their shared domain.

It is clear that any case of Nagelian reduction can be construed as a case of Kemeny-Oppenheim reduction, so that it is not strictly correct to characterize all cases of the latter as replacement or eliminative reductions. But it is also clear that any case of Kemeny-Oppenheim reduction that is not also a case of Nagel reduction is one that involves, or ought to involve, the elimination of the weaker reduced theory by the richer theory that reduces it. Thus, the phlogiston theory of combustion was reduced in the sense of Kemeny and Oppenheim to the oxidation theory, and was replaced by it. The impetus theory of motion was reduced, and eliminated, in the same sense, by modern dynamic theory of motion. And so on. A general principle like the following seems to be at work here: *If a theory is confronted by another that explains more, the only way it can survive is for it to be conservatively reduced to the latter.*

The question I want to raise is why this holds, or ought to hold. Why should we replace, and abandon, a Kemeny-Oppenheim reduced theory in favor of its reducer? Notice that the reducing theory does not in general *logically exclude* the reduced theory; there need be no logical incompatibility between them. Further, the reduced theory need not have been falsified; in fact, as far as direct evidence goes there may be good reason to think it is true. So why not keep them both? Notice the consequences of abandoning the reduced theory: its characteristic theoretical entities, properties, events, and states are no longer to be recognized as "real". They share the fate of the discarded theory: phlogiston had to go when the phlogiston theory was thrown out.

The reason I raise these points is that they help to give structure to the current debate concerning the future of vernacular psychology, the rich and motley collection of truisms and platitudes about our motives, desires, beliefs, hopes, actions, etc. It is in terms of such truisms that we explain, and predict at least in a limited way, the behavior of our fellow humans and ourselves. It strikes many of us as inconceivable that we can entirely dispense with this framework of intentional psychology; it is not clear that our conception of ourselves as persons and agents could survive the loss of the vernacular psychological scheme.

However, many philosophers have raised doubts about the reality of vernacular psychology—and the reality of such states as belief, desire, and intention. The thought is that the rapidly developing and expanding "cognitive science" will likely supersede the vernacular so that at some point in the future the rational thing to conclude is that there are no such things as beliefs and desires, and there never were. But in what sense of "supersede"? How should vernacular psychology be related to cognitive science if it is to survive, and if the states it recognizes, such as beliefs and desires, are to continue to be recognized as real?

Those who argue for the potential, and likely, elimination of vernacular psychology, and intentional psychological states that constitute its core, often point to two considerations: first, compared with systematic cognitive science the vernacular suffers from explanatory failure, and second there is no prospect of reducing it to a systematic scientific theory. For example, Paul Churchland, a forceful proponent of this position, writes:[43]

> As examples of central and important mental phenomena that remain largely or wholly mysterious within the framework of FP [folk psychology], consider the nature and dynamics of mental illness, the faculty of creative imagination...the nature and psychological functions of sleep...the common ability to catch an outfield fly ball on the run...the internal construction of a 3-D visual image...the rich variety of perceptual illusions...the miracle of memory...the nature of the learning process itself...

There are phenomena, Churchland is saying, that are adequately explained within cognitive science but untouched by the vernacular. A further implicit assumption is that cognitive science can explain everything explained by vernacular psychology. The claim then is that the vernacular is Kemeny-Oppenheim reducible to systematic cognitive science.

Churchland is also skeptical about the conservative Nagel reducibility of vernacular psychology to cognitive science. He says: "A successful reduction cannot be ruled out, in my view, but FP's [folk psychology's] explanatory impotence and long stagnation inspire little faith that its categories will find themselves neatly reflected in the framework of neuroscience".[44] Here he is saying that a conservative reduction is unlikely because there is little reason to believe in the existence of the bridge laws connecting vernacular psychological states with neurophysiological states. Thus the structure of Churchland's argument exemplifies the pattern we discerned earlier: vernacular psychology must be eliminated because it is Kemeny-Oppenheim reducible to cognitive neuroscience without being conservatively reducible to it.[45]

Thus, we are faced with the following question: granted that neuroscience has a wider explanatory range than vernacular psychology, why can't the two coexist anyway, without vernacular psychology being nomologically reduced to neuroscience? Why should we discard the vernacular and conclude that there aren't, and never have been, such things as beliefs, hopes, regrets, and wishes?

The explanatory exclusion principle provides a simple explanation of why the two theories, even if they do not logically or evidentially exclude each other, compete against each other and why their peaceful coexistence is an illusion. For vernacular psychology and neuroscience each claim to provide explanations for the same domain of phenomena, and because of the failure of reduction in either direction, the purported explanations must be considered independent. Hence, by the exclusion principle, one of them has to go.[46]

I think similar considerations can account for an otherwise puzzling aspect of Thomas Kuhn's celebrated theory of scientific "paradigms".[47] According to Kuhn, successive paradigms addressing the same range of phenomena are "incommensurable" with each other. They make use of different concepts, different methodologies, different criteria for generating problems and evaluating proposed solutions. As is well known, Kuhn says in various places that different paradigms do not, perhaps cannot, even share the same problems; nor can they, strictly speaking, share the same data. But I am here assuming that Kuhn must allow a sense in which different successive paradigms can, and do, share an overlapping domain of subject matters. Otherwise much of his theory of paradigms makes little sense.

Now one might raise the following question about paradigms: If they are, as Kuhn says, mutually incommensurable, and hence cannot even contradict each other, why can't we accept them all? Why must we discard the old paradigm when we construct a new one? After all, no paradigm is ever literally falsified, according to Kuhn, and every paradigm serves useful explanatory and predictive purposes, making its unique scientific contributions. So why not accumulate paradigms? We could do this without fear of logical incoherence or inconsistency, for paradigms are mutually incommensurable and hence cannot contradict each other. We would have a "cumulative theory" of scientific progress through accumulation of paradigms instead of the usual cumulative theory of scientific knowledge which Kuhn rejects.

Again, an answer is forthcoming from the explanatory exclusion principle: Kuhn takes for granted the incompatibility of successive paradigms directed at the same phenomena because he tacitly accepts the explanatory exclusion principle, and we go along with him because we, too, do not question it. I take it that, for Kuhn, each paradigm purports to provide complete and independent explanations of the data within its domain—complete and independent relative to other competing paradigms. It follows from the explanatory exclusion principle: No more than one paradigm for a single domain.[48]

Notes

1. "The Conceivability of Mechanism", *Philosophical Review* 77 (1968): 45-72. Reprinted in Gary Watson (ed.), *Free Will* (Oxford: Oxford University Press, 1982). Page references to this article are to the reprinted version in Watson. For an earlier defense of a position similar to Malcolm's see Alasdair C. MacIntyre, "Determinism", *Mind* 66 (1957): 28-41.
2. "The Compatibility of Mechanism and Purpose", *Philosophical Review* 78 (1969): 468-82; also in his *A Theory of Human Action* (Englewood Cliffs, N.J.: Prentice-Hall, 1970), pp. 157-65. For another defense of the compatibility position and a critique of MacIntyre, see Daniel C. Dennett, "Mechanism and Responsibility", in Dennett, *Brainstorms*

(Montpelier, Vt.: Bradford Books, 1981). G. H. von Wright defends a "two explanandum solution" in *Explanation and Understanding* (Ithaca: Cornell University Press, 1971), pp. 118-31.

3. See, e.g., Paul Churchland, *Scientific Realism and the Plasticity of Mind* (Cambridge: Cambridge University Press, 1979); Stephen P. Stich, *From Folk Psychology to Cognitive Science* (Cambridge: The MIT Press, 1983); Terence Horgan and James Woodward, "Folk Psychology Is Here To Stay", *Philosophical Review* 94 (1985): 197-226.

4. This means that one way in which one might try to eliminate the incompatibility is to interpret rationalizing explanation as a fundamentally *noncausal* mode of understanding actions. I believe that this is an approach well worth exploring: a rationalizing explanation is to be viewed as a *normative assessment* of an action in the context of the agent's relevant intentional states. For some elaboration on this idea see my "Self-Understanding and Rationalizing Explanations", *Philosophia Naturalis* 21 (1984): 309-20.

5. Malcolm, "The Conceivability of Mechanism", p. 131.

6. For one, the notion of "dependence" used is too narrow and seems at best to characterize a special subcase; for another, his argument makes use of special assumptions needing justification and exploits what appears to be local features of the particular case on hand. For a discussion of Malcolm's argument see William L. Rowe, "Neurophysiological Laws and Purposive Principles", *Philosophical Review* 81 (1971): 502-508.

7. Malcolm, "The Conceivability of Mechanism", p. 132.

8. Ibid.

9. Ibid., p. 133.

10. I believe there is much to be said in favor of the "two explananda" approach in the case of action explanations (see my "Self-Understanding and Rationalizing Explanations"). I am being somewhat cavalier about this issue here because our two disputants do not raise it and my real focus is on the general question of explanatory compatibility. For an interesting recent instance of this dual explanandum approach see Fred Dretske's forthcoming book, *Explaining Behavior: Reasons in a World of Causes* (Cambridge: MIT Press).

11. As spelled out by Goldman (with minor changes of wording).

12. This assumes, as Malcolm is aware, that beliefs and desires are not identical with physiological events—namely, that the so-called identity thesis about the mental is false. If the identity holds, we do not have two *independent* explanations. More on this later.

13. Unless, perhaps, the behavior is overdetermined by the neurophysiological event and the belief-desire pair. This possibility is discussed below.

14. Goldman, *A Theory of Human Action*, pp. 160-61.

15. Malcolm would be ill advised to rest his argument on this revised principle (although the principle may be valid). For he would be powerless to show the incompatibility between a rationalizing explanation and a physiological explanation which makes use of physiological initial conditions occurring a little later or earlier than the belief and desire in-

voked in the rationalizing explanation. What is crucial is not that the two conditions for E occur at the same time; it's rather that they belong in distinct, independent causal chains (or chains of conditions).

16. So we are treating C and C*, and also E, as "event types" or "generic events". In fact, talk of "necessity" and "sufficiency" seems to make clear sense only for generic events. But our discussion can be taken to concern individual events if we take these latter to be instantiations of generic events. See for details on this conception of events my "Events as Property Exemplifications" in Myles Brand and Douglas Walton (eds.), *Action Theory* (Dordrecht: Reidel, 1976). However, no particular views concerning the nature of events are presupposed in the present discussion.

17. On epiphenomena see, e.g., David Lewis, "Causation", *Journal of Philosophy* 70 (1973): 556-67.

18. Perhaps the most influential argument for psychophysical anomalism is one defended by Donald Davidson in "Mental Events", reprinted in his *Essays on Actions and Events* (New York: Oxford University Press, 1980). See my "Psychophysical Laws" in Ernest LePore and Brian McLaughlin (eds.), *Actions and Events: Perspectives on the Philosophy of Donald Davidson* (Oxford: Basil Blackwell, 1985), for an exegesis and discussion of Davidson's argument and additional references.

19. Goldman is aware of this point but does not follow up its implications; in fact, he, like Malcolm, considers the possibility that beliefs and desires are neural states. See below for this "identity solution".

20. I believe this picture can be generalized; see my "Epiphenomenal and Supervenient Causation", *Midwest Studies in Philosophy* 9 (1984): 257-70.

21. Malcolm, "The Conceivability of Mechanism", p. 134.

22. An identity account in the present context would be a form of the so-called "type identity" theory (talk of "nomic equivalence" between C and C*, for example, implies that these represent "generic events" or event types, not concrete events); however, the point applies to the "token identity" theory as well. For example, Donald Davidson's causal theory of action is one example: reasons (e.g., beliefs and desires) are causes of action, but they are redescribable in physical (presumably, physiological) terms and hence *are* physical events; and it is under their physical descriptions that reasons and actions are subsumed under law. Thus, for Davidson, the duality of explanation vanishes (whether this is Davidson's intended result is another question, however).

23. See Ernest Nagel, *The Structure of Science* (New York: Harcourt, 1961).

24. So, on the present construal, both Malcolm and Goldman come out right about the two types of explanation. For we are construing Malcolm to be saying that rationalizing and mechanistic explanations are not compatible as *independent* explanations; and Goldman does *not* claim that the two types of explanations are independent in our sense. In "Mechanism and Responsibility" Daniel C. Dennett, too, addresses the compatibility issue; however, his focus is different. His main aim is to show that the behavior of finite mechanisms, "tropistic systems", can be explained from "the intentional stance". Even if Dennett's conclu-

sion is accepted, our problem remains: What is the relationship between "intentional-stance explanations" and "physical-stance explanations"? Are the two types of explanations compatible when given of the same bit of behavior?

25. The precise formulation here would be affected somewhat by whether one takes the "token identity" or the "type identity" theory, and what view of the nature of events is adopted. However, the general point should apply regardless of the positions taken on these matters.

26. In "Causality, Identity, and Supervenience in the Mind-Body Problem", *Midwest Studies in Philosophy* 4 (1979):31-49; and "Epiphenomenal and Supervenient Causation", *Midwest Studies in Philosophy* 9 (1984):257-70. See also Ernest Sosa, "Mind-Body Interaction and Supervenient Causation", *Midwest Studies in Philosophy* 9 (1984): 271-81. For a general discussion of supervenience see my "Concepts of Supervenience", *Philosophy and Phenomenological Research* 65 (1984): 153-76.

27. I owe this case to Karl Pfeifer.

28. Carl G. Hempel, *Aspects of Scientific Explanation* (New York: The Free Press, 1965), p. 419.

29. Sylvain Bromberger calls it a "p-predicament" or "b-predicament" in his "An Approach to Explanation" in R.J. Butler (ed.), *Analytic Philosophy*, 2nd series (Oxford: Basil Blackwell, 1965).

30. See, e.g., Michael Friedman, "Explanation and Scientific Understanding", *Journal of Philosophy* 71 (1974): 5-19; Philip Kitcher, "Explanation, Conjunction, and Unification", *Journal of Philosophy* 73 (1976): 207-12.

31. Cf. Peter Railton's notion of an "ideal explanatory text" in "Probability, Explanation, and Information", *Synthese* 48 (1981): 233-256; also, David Lewis, "Causal Explanation" in *Philosophical Papers II* (New York: Oxford University Press, 1986).

32. I discuss this and related topics in some detail in "Explanatory Realism, Causal Realism, and Explanatory Exclusion", forthcoming in *Midwest Studies in Philosophy* 12 (1988): 225-240.

33. For some of the basic terminological distinctions see Bromberger, "An Approach to Explanation"; and Peter Achinstein, *The Nature of Explanation* (New York and Oxford: Oxford University Press, 1983), esp. Introduction and ch. 1.

34. Some would want to *analyze* the very notion of causation in terms of explanation, but I believe that is a mistake. See, e.g., Michael Scriven, "Causation as Explanation", *Nous* 9 (1975): 3-16; Kim, "Causes as Explanations: A Critique", *Theory and Decision* 13 (1981): 293-309.

35. It might be possible for the two explanations to be each dependent on a third, without one of them being dependent on the other. It seems that in such a situation both explanations could stand.

36. See Hempel, *Aspects of Scientific Explanation*, pp. 421-22.

37. These seem similar to what Fred Dretske has called "event allomorphs" in "Referring to Events" in Peter A. French et al. (eds.), *Contemporary Perspectives in the Philosophy of Language* (Minneapolis: University of Minnesota Press, 1977).

38. For a discussion of these matters and further references see my "Causation, Nomic Subsumption, and the Concept of Event", *Journal of Philosophy* 70 (1973): 217-36.

39. Robert Cummins has made an interesting distinction between explanation "by subsumption" (under a causal law) and explanation "by analysis" (into component parts). See his *The Nature of Psychological Explanation* (Cambridge: The MIT Press, 1983), esp. chs. 1 and 2. Could one and the same explanandum be given explanations of these two types? According to Cummins, however, subsumptive explanation explains *changes* and analytical explanation explains *properties*, so that the explananda are different. It seems also possible to construe the two explanations as mutually complementary but each only a partial explanation of a single explanandum, under a coarse-grained individuation of explananda.

40. Nor when we see that the same mathematical propositions can be given two different proofs. Some philosophers think, however, that certain proofs are more "explanatory" than others, in the sense that they seem to give us an explanation of "what makes the theorem hold". However, one could argue, I think, that the same principle of exclusion must apply to multiple *explanatory proofs* of the same mathematical proposition.

41. These remarks tie in with the standard discussion of "realism" vs. "instrumentalism" about scientific theories—especially, the common view that an instrumentalist conception of scientific theories, though viable as an account of their predictive utility, deprives them of explanatory significance.

42. "On Reduction", *Philosophical Studies* 7 (1956): 6-19.

43. "Eliminative Materialism and the Propositional Attitudes", *Journal of Philosophy* 78 (1981): 67-90. The quotation is from p. 73.

44. Ibid, p. 75.

45. Churchland also intimates that laws of vernacular psychology have been falsified. This is a controversial point, and even if it is true, it would not force the *elimination* of vernacular psychology (at least, that of intentional psychology); all it would show is that the vernacular needs improvement. To argue for an outright elimination, some principle like explanatory exclusion seems essential; and if we have such a principle, we don't need the premise about the falsity of vernacular psychology.

46. The right way to save vernacular psychology, in my view, is to stop thinking of it as playing the same game that "cognitive science" is supposed to play—that is, stop thinking of it as a "theory" whose primary raison d'etre is to generate law-based causal explanations and predictions. We will do better to focus on its normative role in the evaluation of actions and the formation of intentions and decisions. If vernacular psychology competes against cognitive science in the prediction game, it cannot win, and the best thing it can hope for is reductive absorption into its more systematic (and better funded) rival.

47. *The Structure of Scientific Revolutions* (Chicago: University of Chicago Press, 1962).

48. My thanks to David Benfield, John Biro, Brian McLaughlin, Joseph Mendola, and Michael Resnik for helpful comments.

References

Achinstein, Peter *The Nature of Explanation* (New York and Oxford: Oxford University Press, 1983).

Bromberger, Sylvain "An Approach to Explanation" in R.J. Butler (ed.), *Analytic Philosophy*, 2nd series (Oxford: Basil Blackwell, 1965).

Churchland, Paul *Scientific Realism and the Plasticity of Mind* (Cambridge: Cambridge University Press, 1979).

Churchland, Paul "Eliminative Materialism and the Propositional Attitudes", *Journal of Philosophy* 78 (1981): 67-90.

Cummins, Robert C. *The Nature of Psychological Explanation* (Cambridge: The MIT Press, 1983).

Davidson, Donald "Mental Events", in Davidson, *Essays on Actions and Events* (New York: Oxford University Press, 1980).

Dennett, Daniel C. "Mechanism and Responsibility", in Dennett, *Brainstorms* (Montgomery, Vt.: Bradford Books, 1981).

Dretske, Fred "Referring to Events" in Peter A. French et al. (eds.), *Contemporary Perspectives in the Philosophy of Language* (Minneapolis: University of Minnesota Press, 1977).

Dretske, Fred *Explaining Behavior: Reasons in a World of Causes* (Cambridge: MIT Press, 1988).

Friedman, Michael "Explanation and Scientific Understanding", *Journal of Philosophy* 71 (1974): 5-19.

Goldman, Alvin I. "The Compatibility of Mechanism and Purpose", *Philosophical Review* 78 (1969): 468-82.

Goldman, Alvin I. *A Theory of Human Action* (Englewood Cliffs, N.J.: Prentice-Hall, 1970).

Hempel, Carl G. *Aspects of Scientific Explanation* (New York: The Free Press, 1965).

Horgan, Terence and James Woodward, "Folk Psychology Is Here To Stay", *Philosophical Review* 94 (1985): 197-226.

Kemeny, John and Paul Oppenheim, "On Reduction", *Philosophical Studies* 7 (1956): 6-19.

Kim, Jaegwon "Causation, Nomic Subsumption, and the Concept of Event", *Journal of Philosophy* 70 (1973): 217-36.

Kim, Jaegwon "Events as Property Exemplifications" in Myles Brand and Walton, Douglas (eds.), *Action Theory* (Dordrecht: Reidel, 1976).

Kim, Jaegwon "Causality, Identity, and Supervenience in the Mind-Body Problem", *Midwest Studies in Philosophy* 4 (1979):31-49.

Kim, Jaegwon "Causes as Explanations: A Critique", *Theory and Decision* 13 (1981): 293-309.

Kim, Jaegwon "Concepts of Supervenience", *Philosophy and Phenomenological Research* 65 (1984): 153-76.

Kim, Jaegwon "Epiphenomenal and Supervenient Causation", *Midwest Studies in Philosophy* 9 (1984):257-70.

Kim, Jaegwon "Self-Understanding and Rationalizing Explanations", *Philosophia Naturalis* 21 (1984): 309-20.

Kim, Jaegwon "Psychophysical Laws" in Ernest LePore and Brian McLaughlin (eds.), *Actions and Events: Perspectives on the Philosophy of Donald Davidson* (Oxford: Basil Blackwell, 1985).

Kim, Jaegwon "Explanatory Realism, Causal Realism, and Explanatory Exclusion", *Midwest Studies in Philosophy* 12 (1988): 225-240.

Kitcher, Philip "Explanation, Conjunction, and Unification", *Journal of Philosophy* 73 (1976): 207-12.

Kuhn, Thomas *The Structure of Scientific Revolutions* (Chicago: University of Chicago Press, 1962).

Lewis, David "Causation", *Journal of Philosophy* 70 (1973): 556-67.

Lewis, David "Causal Explanation" in *Philosophical Papers II* (New York: Oxford University Press, 1986).

MacIntyre, Alasdair C. "Determinism", *Mind* 66 (1957): 28-41.

Malcolm, Norman "The Conceivability of Mechanism", *Philosophical Review* 77 (1968): 45-72. Reprinted in Gary Watson (ed.), *Free Will* (Oxford: Oxford University Press, 1982).

Nagel, Ernest *The Structure of Science* (New York: Harcourt, 1961).

Railton, Peter "Probability, Explanation, and Information", *Synthese* 48 (1981): 233-256.

Rowe, William L. "Neurophysiological Laws and Purposive Principles", *Philosophical Review* 81 (1971): 502-508.

Scriven, Michael "Causation as Explanation", *Nous* 9 (1975): 3-16.

Sosa, Ernest "Mind-Body Interaction and Supervenient Causation", *Midwest Studies in Philosophy* 9 (1984): 271-81.

Stich, Stephen P. *From Folk Psychology to Cognitive Science* (Cambridge: The MIT Press, 1983).

von Wright, G. H. *Explanation and Understanding* (Ithaca: Cornell University Press, 1971).

Philosophical Perspectives, 3
Philosophy of Mind and Action Theory, 1989

TYPE EPIPHENOMENALISM, TYPE DUALISM, AND THE CAUSAL PRIORITY OF THE PHYSICAL

Brian P. McLaughlin
Rutgers University

1. Two Kinds of Epiphenomenalism

Sixty three years ago, C.D. Broad distinguished two kinds of epiphenomenalism. He said:

> Epiphenomenalism may be taken to assert one of two things. (1) That certain events which have physiological characteristics have *also* mental characteristics...And that an event which has mental characteristics never causes another event in virtue of its mental characteristics, but only in virtue of its physiological characteristics. Or (2) that no event has both mental and physiological characteristics; but that the complete cause of any event which has mental characteristics is an event or set of events which has physiological characteristics. And that no event which has mental characteristics is a cause-factor in the causation of any other event whatever, whether mental or physiological (1925, p. 472).

(The inserted numerals are mine.) The following distinction is inspired by Broad's (1) and (2) respectively:

> *Type Epiphenomenalism* (Type-E). (a) Events can be causes in virtue of falling under physical types, but (b) events cannot be causes in virtue of falling under mental types.
> *Token Epiphenomenalism* (Token-E). (i) Physical events can

cause mental events, but (ii) mental events cannot cause anything.

The 'cannot' here is that of at least causal impossibility; and 'event' is used in a broad sense that includes states as well as changes.

Both types of epiphenomenalism deny the mental a place in the causal order, though in different ways. Token-E implies that mental events cannot have causal efficacy: in no causally possible world does a mental event cause anything. Type-E implies that events cannot have causal efficacy *qua* mental: in no causally possible world does an event cause anything in virtue of falling under a mental type. Thus, while according to Token-E, mental events cannot be causes, according to Type-E, mental event types are not, so to speak, causal powers.

Conjunct (ii) of Token-E implies conjunct (b) of Type-E: if mental events cannot be causes, then events cannot be causes in virtue of falling under mental types. (The reason is obvious: if an event can cause something in virtue of falling under a mental type, then an event can be both a cause and a mental event.) The converse, however, may well not hold: (b) may well not imply (ii). It will not if a mental event can cause something in virtue of falling under a non-mental event type. For, then, mental events can be causes, even if they cannot be causes qua mental.

But suppose that mental events can participate in causal relations in virtue of falling under non-mental types. Then, one can coherently reject Token-E while embracing Type-E. Indeed, in the past twenty years or so, a variety of views of the mental have been proposed that deny Token-E but either assert or are silent about Type-E: for example, certain functionalist views of the mental, Donald Davidson's Anomalous Monism (Davidson, 1980e), Keith Cambell's "new" epiphenomenalism (Cambell, 1970, Ch. 6), and James Cornman's neutral monism (Cornman, 1981, pp. 234-242). These views arguably imply that mental events are causes in virtue of falling under physical event types; and they either leave open whether, or deny that, events can be causes in virtue of falling under mental types. The question of whether Type-E is true arises even for those who reject Token-E.

2. The Problematic

Recent debates about epiphenomenalism have been about Type-E, rather than about Token-E. Indeed, it is fair to say that in the last decade or so discussions of the so-called mind-body problem have focused on whether Type-E is true. And the issues involved are related to such hotly debated issues as the status of "folk psychology" and the possibility of an intentional science. So I shall focus in what follows on Type-E.

It is not my aim, however, to determine whether Type-E is true. My primary aim is far more limited: I want to consider whether certain claims that are alleged to imply Type-E in fact imply it. I shall first present the claims in question, and then cite a secondary aim.

The claims are these:

> *Physical Comprehensiveness.* It is causally necessary that when two events causally interact, they do so in virtue of falling under physical event types.
> *Type Dualism.* There are mental event types, and no mental event type is identical with a physical event type.

My primary concern is whether Physical Comprehensiveness and Type Dualism imply Type-E. Of course, Physical Comprehensiveness implies (a) of Type-E, the claim that events can participate in causal relations in virtue of falling under physical event types. So what is at issue is whether Physical Comprehensiveness and Type Dualism jointly imply (b), the claim that events cannot participate in causal relations in virtue of falling under mental types.

Let us say that an event type is *causal* iff in some causally possible world an event token participates in a causal relation in virtue of falling under it. And let us say that an event type is *epiphenomenal* iff it is not causal. According to Type-E, then, at least some physical event types are causal while all mental event types are epiphenomenal. The primary issue, then, boils down to this:

> (Q) Do Physical Comprehensiveness and Type Dualism exclude the existence of causal mental event types?

I shall argue in due course that the answer to (Q) is "no." One can hold Physical Comprehensiveness and Type Dualism without, thereby, being committed to Type-E. My primary aim is to show this.

Of course, if Physical Comprehensiveness and Type Dualism imply (ii) of Token-E, then they imply (b) of Type-E. Physical Comprehensiveness implies that it is causally necessary that every event that participates in a causal relation is a physical event. But Physical Comprehensiveness and Type Dualism do not, however, imply (ii) if a mental event can be identical with a physical event. I sympathize with the Davidsonian view that a concrete event can be both mental and physical. This issue has been much discussed, and I have nothing to add here to that discussion. I shall simply assume in what follows that mental events can be physical.

Even if Physical Comprehensiveness and Type Dualism do not imply (ii), however, the question remains whether they imply (b). Question (Q) has emerged in recent literature mainly, though not exclusively, in connection with Davidson's views about psychophysical causal interaction. Davidson (see, e.g., 1980a) has long been an opponent of Token-E,[1] but he has been silent about Type-E. Despite this silence, it has been fairly widely charged that his doctrines of the Anomalism of the Mental and the Principle of the Nomological Character of Causality (described below in section 4) commit him to it.[2] I shall leave open whether they do. But I shall, however, attempt to undermine a central premise in the leading argument that they do. This is my secondary aim.

So much, then, by way of setting out the problematic. Six sections remain. In section 3, I discuss Type-E. In 4, I discuss the Anomalism of the Mental and the Principle of the Nomological Character of Causality. In 5, I present the central argument that the doctrines imply that all mental event types are epiphenomenal. In 6, I digress and discuss some responses that have been made to the claim that Davidson is committed to Type-E.[3] In 7, I try to cast doubt on a central premise of the argument in question. Finally, in 8, I try to make a case that Physical Comprehensiveness and Type Dualism do not imply Type-E.

3. Type Epiphenomenalism

Type-E is, perhaps, a less familiar doctrine than Token-E; so let us consider Type-E in more detail.

To begin, it is fairly widely held that the relata of the causal relation are event tokens but that they participate in causal relations in virtue of falling under event types. The idea is that while event tokens participate in causal transactions, such transactions must be *grounded* or *backed* by appropriate type-type relations. There is no received view about what sorts of type-type relations count as appropriate for grounding singular causal transactions. But whatever view is correct, an event type is causal iff it participates in a causation grounding relationship. So, Type-E is true iff at least some physical event types enter into causation grounding relationships and no mental event type does.

We need not decide here what sorts of type-type relations are singular causation grounding. But, to help fix our ideas, let us consider a leading view. According to nomic subsumption views of causation, events causally interact in virtue of instantiating event types that are nomologically related. On this view, causation requires laws that are such that if events fall under them, the events, thereby, count as causally related.[4] Such laws are *causal* laws. An analysis of the notion of a *causal* law would specify the features in virtue of which a law is such that when events fall under it, they, thereby, count as causally related. Whether a noncircular analysis of the notion is possible need not concern us here. The point to note for present purposes is just this: given a nomic subsumption view of causation, if Type-E is true, then physical event types do and mental event types do not figure in the causal laws of this world.

Suppose, then, that a nomic subsumption view of causation is correct. Then, figuring as a partial or complete cause-factor in a causal law suffices being a causal event type. To elaborate, if an event type C figures in a causal law as a *complete* cause-factor for the realization of a type E, then it is a causal law that whenever C is realized, E is, and C, thereby, counts as a causal event type. Suppose that an event type C figures in a causal law as a *partial* cause-factor for the realization of an event type E. Then, there is a condition D such that (i) the realization of D logically requires the realization of C and (ii) the realization of D nomologically suffices for the realization of E. For example, suppose it is a causal law that whenever F and G are realized, then H is. Then, the joint realization of F and G (in the same circumstance) nomologically suffices for the realization of H. So, F figures in the law in question as a partial cause-factor for the realization of H, and thereby counts as a causal event type. Suppose that it is a causal law that whenever F is realized, then, ceteris paribus, H is. (Events count as falling under a ceteris paribus law, of course, only if the ceteris paribus condition is satisfied in the circumstances of their occurrence.) Then, F figures as a partial cause-factor in the ceteris paribus law for the realization of H. And F, thereby, counts as a causal event type.

Finally, suppose that *only* nomological relationships between types count as causation grounding. (As we shall see in section 7, this implies but is not implied by a nomic subsumption view of causation.) Then, Type-E is true iff there are physical causal laws and no mental event type is a partial or complete cause-factor in a causal law. So much, then, by way of presenting a leading view of causation grounding relations.

Following Broad, I used the locution 'in virtue of' in formulating Type-E. While widely used in philosophical literature, the locution admittedly calls for explication. So, I shall close this section with a partial explication of it.

What is it, for instance, for some x to A in virtue of B-ing? I suggest the following initial answer: x As in virtue of B-ing iff that x Bs makes it true that x As. But this just shifts the burden to explicating 'make it true that'. So let us consider the in virtue of relation in more detail.

To begin, let us note some of its modal properties. If x As in virtue of B-ing, then either x's B-ing suffices for x's A-ing or else x's B-ing is necessary for something, x's C-ing, that occurs on the occasion in question and that suffices for x's A-ing. X can A in virtue of B-ing, however, even if B-ing is not required for A-ing. For example, one can live in New Jersey in virtue of living in New Brunswick, even though living in New Brunswick is not required for living in New Jersey. Likewise, a macro-property P might be realized in virtue of the realization of a micro-property $m(P)$, even if P is "multiply realizable" at the micro-level in question, and so the realization of $m(P)$ is not required for P's realization.

The in virtue of relation cannot be understood in modal terms alone. If x As in virtue of B-ing, then there must be an *appropriate explanatory connection* between x's A-ing and x's B-ing. As Quine has correctly noted 'in virtue of' "is almost 'because of'" (1974, pp. 8-9).[5] Indeed, statements employing 'in virtue of' imply statements employing 'because'. If Tim lives in New Jersey in virtue of living in New Brunswick, then he counts as living in New Jersey because he lives in New Brunswick. If an object has a certain temperature T in virtue of having a certain mean-kinetic energy E, then it counts as having T because it has E. Similarly, if two events are causally related in virtue of falling under certain event types, then they count as causally related because they fall under the types in question. Thus we sometimes explain why something counts as A-ing by citing the fact that it Bs, or why a group of things count as A-ing by citing the fact that they *Bs*. I suggest that: *x As* in virtue of *B-ing* if *x* counts as *A-ing* because *x Bs*. The kind of explanatory connection involved can vary. In the micro-macro case, it is something like "material causation," while in the case of event types and singular (efficient) causal transactions, it is something like "formal causation." In any case, a full explication of the in virtue of relation is a topic for a theory of explanation and need not be pursued further here.[6]

So much, then, by way of explicating Type-E. Turn to the doctrines of Davidson that are alleged to imply it.

4. The Davidsonian Doctrines Alleged to Imply Type-E

They are:

> *The Anomalism of the Mental.* There are no strict
> psychological or psychophysical laws.[7]
> *The Principle of the Nomological Character of Causality.* If
> events are causally related, they fall under a strict law.

It is uncertain what Davidson intends the modal status of these doctrines to be. But, for the sake of argument, I shall follow Davidson's critics in taking the intended modal force of the doctrines to be that of logical (or analytical, or conceptual) necessity.

Both doctrines employ the notion of a strict law. How to understand the notion is a topic for Davidsonian scholarship. I have discussed it at length elsewhere (McLaughlin, 1985). But as will become clear, nothing will turn here on the details of what makes a law strict. Some remarks will, however, help to fix our ideas.

Davidson holds that laws are true, counterfactual supporting generalizations that are confirmable by their positive instances. He characterizes the notion of a strict law in terms of the notion of a closed comprehensive theory (1980e, p. 219, and pp. 223-224; and 1980f, p. 230). A theory *T* is *closed* iff events within the domain of *T* causally interact only with other events within the domain of *T*. A theory *T* is *comprehensive* only if whenever an event within its domain participates in a causal interaction, that interaction is subsumed by some law of *T*. Let us say that a set of terms is the *minimal vocabulary* of a closed comprehensive theory iff it is the vocabulary of such a theory and no proper subset of it is. The notion of a strict law can be understood, then, as follows: a law is a *strict* law iff it is couched solely in the minimal vocabulary of a closed comprehensive theory or it can be derived via bridge laws from laws couched solely in such a vocabulary (cf., McLaughlin, 1985, pp. 342-348).[8] One of the main ideas underlying The Principle of the Nomological Character of Causality (hereafter, 'The Principle of Causality') is that whenever two events are causally related, their causal interaction is subsumed by a law that is a non-redundant part of a comprehensive system of laws. According to Davidson, such a system will be couched in the minimal vocabulary of a closed comprehensive theory or in terms reducible to the terms of such a theory.

Davidson claims that physics *promises* to be closed and comprehensive (1980e, pp. 223-224). The idea is, I take it, that an ideally completed physics would be closed and comprehensive. (Hereafter, I shall drop the qualifier 'ideally completed'). If so, laws couched in its minimal vocabulary and laws derivable from such laws by means of bridge laws would be strict. Moreover, Davidson explicitly claims that *most of science* employs non-strict laws (1980c, p. 219). He holds that *only* the vocabulary of physics is the minimal vocabulary of a closed comprehensive theory; and he doubts that even the vocabulary of biology can be reduced via bridge laws to terms in such a vocabulary, though he acknowledges that he does not know how to show this (Davidson, 1980c, p. 241). (He maintains that he can show, however, that mental terms do not reduce via bridge laws to terms in such a vocabulary; but whether he can show that need not concern us here.[9]) Suppose that, indeed, only the vocabulary of physics is the minimal vocabulary of a closed comprehensive theory. Then, all strict laws are either laws of physics or derivable from such laws via bridge laws.

In any case, be all this as it may, it should be mentioned that The Principle of Causality and the claim that all strict laws are physical laws together imply that every event that participates in a causal relation with a physical event is a physical event. (Thus they imply that the physical is causally closed: physical events causally interact only with other physical events.) And the Anomalism of the Mental (hereafter, 'Anomalism') and this version of token physicalism constitute Davidson's doctrine of Anomalous Monism (see, McLaughlin, 1985). This is the doctrine that (a) every event that causally interacts with a physical event is a physical event and that (b) there are no strict psychological or psychophysical laws. So much, then, by way of presenting Davidson's views.

Of course, whether The Principle of Causality and Anomalism are true is a question beyond the scope of this paper. My concern here is not with their truth, but rather with whether they jointly imply Type-E.

5. The Central Argument

One finds in the critical literature on the Davidsonian views in question a family of arguments that Anomalism and The Principle of Causality imply Type-E. One argument in the family is this: Anomalism implies Type Dualism. The Principle of Causality implies Physical Comprehensiveness. Type Dualism and Physical Comprehensiveness imply Type-E. So, Anomalism and The Principle of Causality imply Type-E. I won't challenge the claims that The Principle of Causality implies Physical Comprehensiveness and that Anomalism implies Type Dualism. But it should be noted that Physical Comprehensiveness and Type Dualism seem far more widely held than Anomalism and The Principle of Causality. And if former doctrines do indeed imply Type-E, commitment to Type-E would be fairly widespread even among realists about the mental. Consider Fodor's popular account (1974, and 1979 "Introduction") of the relationship between the special sciences and physical theory. On this account, it is causally necessary that whenever events within the domain of a special science causally interact, they do so in virtue of falling under some physical causal law or other. Moreover, Fodor maintains that nomic properties of the special sciences are typically not identical with nomic properties of physical theory. If Physical Comprehensiveness and Type Dualism implied Type-E, then Fodor's account of the special sciences would imply that nomic properties of the special sciences are typically epiphenomenal. It would follow that the laws of the special sciences are typically non-causal.[10] (This shocking conclusion should tip one off that something is rotten in Denmark.)

In the final section of the paper, I shall, as I mentioned earlier, challenge the claim that Type Dualism and Physical Comprehensiveness imply Type-E. The point to note now is that even if they do *not* imply Type-E, Anomalism and The Principle of Causality still might. For even if strict laws must be physical laws, The Principle of Causality *logically* requires subsumption under a physical law, while Physical Comprehensiveness only causally requires subsumption under a physical law. In this section, I want to examine an argument in the family of arguments in question that is *specifically aimed* at proponents of Anomalism and The Principle of Causality. (Once we see why this argument fails, we will be in a position to see why Physical Comprehensiveness and Type Dualism do not imply Type-E.)

Before explicitly stating the argument in question, it is useful to turn first to some philosophers who charge Davidson with commitment to Type-E. I shall present a large sample of characteristic passages in which he is so charged. The reasons why I present a large sample will emerge in section 6, where I argue that the responses that have been made to Davidson's critics are inadequate; so please bear with me.

Ted Honderich (1982, p. 62) says that a "causally relevant property" is a property in virtue of which an event can enter into a causal relationship. He espouses a principle he calls "the Principle of the Nomological Character of Causally-Relevant Properties," which asserts that only *nomic* properties are causally relevant. According to Honderich, The Principle of Causality implies this principle; and this principle together with Anomalism excludes there being causally relevant mental properties. Citing a debt to Honderich, Frederick Stoutland says:

> Davidson's view amounts to the claim that events are causes only in virtue of their having certain properties—namely, properties which figure in causal laws—nomic properties. His view that all causal laws are physical means that only *physical* properties are nomic. A reason cannot, therefore, cause an action in virtue of its psychological properties, for those are non-nomic; there are no nomological ties between the psychological and the physical. But if a reason causes an action only in virtue of its physical properties, then the psychological as psychological has no causal efficacy... (1985, p. 53).

Essentially the same concerns lead Jaegwon Kim to say that given Anomalism and The Principle of Causality, an event's

> causal powers are wholly determined by the physical description or characteristic that holds for it; for it is under its physical description that it may be subsumed under a causal law. And Davidson explicitly denies any possibility of

a nomological connection between an event's mental description and its physical description that could bring the mental into the causal picture (1984b, p. 267).

He claims that Davidson: "fails to provide an account of psychophysical causation in which the mental *qua mental* has any real causal role to play" (1984b, p. 267). Kim initiates his discussion of Davidson's position by saying that it is "strikingly similar" to Broad's version (1) of epiphenomenalism (quoted at the outset of the paper[11]), according to which "an event which has mental characteristics never causes another event in virtue of its mental characteristics, but only in virtue of its physiological characteristics." I take it that Kim holds that for the mental qua mental to have "a real causal role to play," at least some mental properties would have to be properties in virtue of which events can be causes. And he holds that The Principle of Causality and Anomalism imply that no mental property can be such a property. Similarly, Ernest Sosa says:

> assuming the anomalism of the mental, though my extending my hand is, in a certain sense, caused by my sudden desire to quench my thirst, it is not caused by my desire qua desire but only by my desire qua *neurological* event of a certain sort (1984, p. 278).

According to Sosa (1984, p. 279), an event, c, qua possessor of some property P, causes an event e, qua possessor of some property Q, only if P and Q figure in a law of the sort that can ground causal relations. And he holds that given The Principle of Causality and Anomalism, no event can cause another qua possessor of a mental property. Finally, Mark Johnston remarks that:

> According to anomalous monism if there are mental properties or types none of them figure in laws. (In the formal mode, no mental predicate figures in any statement of law.) (1985, p. 423)

And he holds that, given The Principle of Causality and Anomalism, the *truth* of any singular causal statement can be "accounted for" only by laws that relate physical properties. He concludes from this that: "There is then a clear sense in which, according to anomalous monism, no mental properties are causally relevant" (1985, p. 424). This completes my sample survey.

(These authors speak of properties rather than event types. But nothing turns on this. Let us say that the property of being an event of a certain type is causal iff the event type is causal. And let us mean by a 'mental property', a property of falling under a mental event type. So, given our broad use of 'event type', the property of being a belief that water is wet, for example, counts as a mental property.)

The leading argument that emerges here is this: The Principle of Causality implies that only nomic properties are causal. Anomalism implies that no mental properties are nomic. So Anomalism and the Principle of Causality imply that no mental properties are causal, that is, that mental properties are epiphenomenal.

It should be noted first of all, however, that The Principle of Causality and Anomalism are claims about *strict* laws. As I have argued elsewhere (McLaughlin, 1985, pp. 342-348), understanding the distinction between strict and non-strict laws is essential to understanding The Principle of Causality and Anomalism. In every paper in which Davidson discusses Anomalism, and in all of his published replies to commentaries on those papers, he is careful to distinguish strict laws from non-strict laws (see, 1980c, pp. 240-241; 1980e, pp. 219; 1980f, pp. 230-231; 1980g, p. 250). While all strict laws are laws, not all laws are strict. However the notion of a strict law is to be understood, it is compatible with Anomalism that there are non-strict psychological and psychophysical laws. And if there are, then there are nomic mental properties. So The Principle of Causality and Anomalism do not themselves exclude the existence of nomic mental properties.

Indeed, Davidson explicitly claims that there are psychological laws (see, e.g., 1980g, p. 250). He says, however, that such laws: "unlike those of physics, cannot be sharpened without limit, cannot be turned into the strict laws of a science closed within its area of application" (1980g, p. 250). Moreover, he holds that there are psychophysical laws, but that they are either only "roughly true" or "insulated from counterexample by generous escape clauses" (1980e, p. 219). And he says that: "psychophysical generalizations must be treated as irreducibly statistical in character, in contrast to sciences where in principle exceptions can be take care of by refinements couched in a homogenous vocabulary" (1980c, p. 240).[12] If I understand him, Davidson holds that there are non-strict psychological and psychophysical laws. But whether or not he holds this, as I said, it is compatible with Anomalism and The Principle of Causality that there are such laws.

Davidson's critics, for the most part, ignore his distinction between strict and non-strict laws.[13] The leading reason is, I suspect, this: they hold that even if it is compatible with The Principle of Causality and Anomalism that some mental properties are nomic, it is incompatible with these doctrines that there are *causal* mental properties. For, they hold, I suspect, that The Principle of Causality commits Davidson to the view that non-strict laws, if there are such, cannot be *causal* laws. Recall that, by stipulation, a causal law is a law such that if events fall under it, they, thereby, count as causally related. The critics maintain that the Principle of Causality implies that only strict laws are causal laws in this sense. If so, the existence of non-strict psychological or psychophysical laws is indeed irrelevant to whether there are causal mental properties or types. For non-strict nomological relationships will, then, not be causation grounding. It is for this reason, I suspect, that the distinction between strict and non-strict laws is so often ignored.

Even if Anomalism does not exclude the existence of nomic mental properties, it excludes the existence of strictly nomic mental properties. And if only strict laws are causation grounding, then only strictly nomic properties are causal. The argument under consideration, then, can be recast so as to make explicit reference to strictly nomic properties. Pedantically, it can be recast as follows:

(I) (p1) The Principle of Causality implies that only strictly nomic properties are causal.

(p2) Anomalism implies that no mental property is a strictly nomic property.

(c) Thus, The Principle of Causality and Anomalism imply that no mental property is a causal property (i.e., that mental properties are epiphenomenal).

Premise (p2) is true. I shall argue in due course, however, that (p1) is false and so that (I) is unsound.

A point should be stressed here, however, to avert possible misunderstanding: nothing I say in arguing that (p1) is false will turn on the distinction between strict and non-strict laws. While understanding this distinction is essential to understanding Anomalism and The Principle of Causality, it is *not* essential to understanding why (p1) is false. Nothing will turn on my having recast the premises of the argument in terms of strictly nomic properties. For The Principle of

Causality does not even imply that only *nomic* properties are causal. Even if there are neither strictly nomic nor non-strictly nomic mental properties, that fact and The Principle of Causality would not exclude the existence of causal mental properties or types. For it is compatible with The Principle of Causality that events can participate in causal relations in virtue of instantiating non-nomic properties. Premise (p1) implies this: The Principle of Causality implies that only nomic properties are causal. And this weaker claim is also false. More about this in section 7.

6. Some Would-be Defenses of Davidson

Let us first consider some recent responses to the charge that Davidson is committed to Type-E. (This section can be skipped without losing the thread of my argument against (p1).)

Norman Melchert (1986, pp. 267-274) defends Davidson by claiming that Davidson denies there are mental properties. Presumably, Melchert holds that since Davidson denies this, he does not hold that mental properties are epiphenomenal. It should be added that it is far from certain whether, when push comes to shove, Davidson thinks there are *any* properties at all, mental or physical. But conjunct (b) of Type-E does not imply that there are mental properties. It implies that if there are mental properties, they are epiphenomenal. And that concerns some friends of properties.

Moreover, Davidson (e.g., 1980e, pp. 210-211) holds that events can satisfy mental descriptions or open sentences, that mental predicates can be true of events. Nothing of relevance in what follows essentially turns on whether they are true of events in virtue of the fact that the events' have the properties expressed by the predicates. As Davidson's critics recognize, their argument can be recast in the formal mode for those with scruples about countenancing properties. It can be recast this way: The Principle of Causality implies that events can participate in causal relations only in virtue of satisfying strictly nomic descriptions. Anomalism implies that no mental description is strictly nomic. So The Principle of Causality and Anomalism imply that no event can participate in a causal relation in virtue of satisfying a mental description.

Turn, then, to a different reply to Davidson's critics. Ernest LePore and Barry Loewer claim that the charge of epiphenomenalism leveled by Honderich, Stoutland, Kim, Sosa, and Johnston, among others,

> rests on a simple, but perhaps not obvious, confusion. The confusion is between two ways in which properties of an event c may be said to be causally relevant and irrelevant (1987, p. 634).

Abbreviating 'Anomalous Monism' as AM, and treating The Principle of Causality as a subthesis of Anomalous Monism, they say:

> The heart of our response to the claim that AM is committed to epiphenomenalism is this: AM entails that mental features are causally irrelevant$_1$, but does not entail that they are causally irrelevant$_2$ (1987, pp. 635-636).

They claim that properties F and G are causally relevant$_1$ to c's causing e just in case c's having F and e's having G *makes it the case* that c causes e (1987, pp. 634-635). The notion of causal relevance$_2$ is introduced as follows: "Relevance$_2$ is a relation among c, one of its properties F, e, and one of its properties G. It holds when c's being F brings it about that e is G" (1987, p. 635). They explicate this last notion by appeal to certain kinds of counterfactual dependency relationships. And they say: "AM is compatible with there being counterfactual dependencies between events in virtue of their mental properties" (1987, p. 641). They hold that Anomalism and The Principle of Causality are consistent with the claim that mental properties can be causally relevant$_2$. It is in this way, they maintain, that, on Davidson's view, "mind can matter."

The charge made by Honderich, Stoutland, Kim, Sosa, and Johnston does not, however, rest on a confusion between causal relevance$_1$ and causal relevance$_2$. These authors do not deny that mental properties can be causally relevant$_2$. Rather, as the earlier quotes reveal, they deny that mental properties can be causally relevant$_1$. Recall that properties F and G are causally relevant$_1$ to c's causing e iff c's having F and e's having G makes it the case that c causes e. The critics in question all essentially argue that Anomalism and The Principle of Causality imply that an event's having a mental property cannot *make it the case* that it causes another: it is in this way, they claim, that "mind cannot matter" on Davidson's view. If an event c causes an event e in virtue of c's having F and e's having G, then c's having F and e's having G makes it the case that c causes e. So if mental properties cannot be relevant$_1$ to any singular causal transaction, then they are not causal properties. Thus in conceding that on Davidson's view, mental properties are invariably irrelevant$_1$, LePore and Loewer, thereby, concede that mental properties are epiphenomenal in the sense at issue.

Let us see why LePore and Loewer maintain that Davidson is committed to the causal irrelevance$_1$ of mental properties. First, they hold that, given that he holds The Principle of Causality, he is committed to the following: c's having F and e's having G makes it the case that c causes e only if F and G figure in a strict law (1987, p. 631). So they hold that The Principle of Causality implies that relevant$_1$ properties must be strictly nomic. And they hold that Anomalism implies that mental properties cannot be strictly nomic. So, they hold that Anomalism and The Principle of Causality imply that mental properties cannot be relevant$_1$. As we saw, if a property cannot be relevant$_1$, then it is not a causal property. LePore and Loewer are thus committed to the view that Anomalism and The Principle of Causality imply Type-E for essentially the reasons stated in argument (I). If I am right that (p1) of (I) is false, then LePore and Loewer fail to show that Davidson is committed to the irrelevance$_1$ of mental properties.

Of course, it may well be that mental properties can be relevant$_2$. But, be this as it may, as LePore and Loewer acknowledge, relevance$_2$ does not suffice for relevance$_1$. They should be viewed as attempting to mitigate severity of the charge of Type-E rather than as attempting to refute it. Their main point seems to be that while Davidson cannot hold that mental properties can be properties in virtue of which events participate in causal relations, he can hold that mental properties can be causally relevant$_2$; and that that should satisfy realists about the mental. Whether LePore and Loewer succeed in mitigating the severity of the charge that Davidson is committed to Type-E is, however, not my concern here.[14] My concern is with whether the charge can be made to stick.

7. Premise (P1) Examined

Consider, once again, premise (p1): The Principle of Causality implies that only strictly nomic properties are causal. I am unaware of any argument for (p1) in the literature. So let us start by addressing the following question: Why might one think (p1) is true?

To begin, recall The Principle of Causality: if events are causally related, then they fall under a strict law. As I mentioned, Davidson's critics take the modal force of this claim to be that of logical (or analytical, or conceptual) necessity. (Hereafter, to avoid prolixity, I shall, for the most part, drop 'analytical' and 'conceptual'.) They understand the principle to be stating a logically necessary singular causation-making property: namely, the property of falling under a strict law. Thus, they understand The Principle of Causality to state that it is logically necessary that if events are causally related, they are so in virtue of falling under a strict law. Whether Davidson intends The Principle of Causality to be understood in this way is, I think, doubtful. (He nowhere, for instance, speaks of events being causally related *in virtue of* falling under strict laws.) But, for the sake of argument, let us understand The Principle of Causality in the way in question. If I understand proponents of (I), then, they take The Principle of Causality (so understood) to imply this:

> *Exclusion Principle.* Events are causally related *only* in virtue of falling under strict laws.

Of course, the Exclusion Principle implies that only strictly nomic properties are causal. So if The Principle of Causality implies the Exclusion Principle, it implies that too. On the other hand, if The Principle of Causality does not imply the Exclusion Principle, it leaves open whether properties other than strictly nomic properties can be causal. Premise (p1) is true, then, iff The Principle of Causality implies the Exclusion Principle. I shall now try to make a case that it does not.

By an '*A*-making property', let us mean a property in virtue of which something is *A*. Then, of course, if a logically necessary *A*-making property is ipso facto the only *A*-making property, then The Principle of Causality indeed implies the Exclusion Principle. However, as I shall argue shortly, it is not the case that a property is ipso facto the only *A*-making property if it is a logically necessary *A*-making property. Of course, showing this would not *demonstrate* that The Principle of Causality does not imply the Exclusion Principle. But I think that the assumption that a logically necessary *A*-making property is ipso facto the only *A*-making property lies behind the view that The Principle of Causality implies the Exclusion Principle. It is hard to see what other reason one might think that the former principle, *by itself*, implies the latter. So I shall try to undermine the claim that The Principle of Causality implies the Exclusion Principle by arguing that the assumption in question is false.

For starters, note that it is not the case that a necessary A-making property is ipso facto the only A-making property. If one lives in New Jersey, then one does so in virtue of living in some county of New Jersey. But it is not the case that one can live in New Jersey only in virtue of living in a county of New Jersey. For one can live in New Jersey in virtue of living in a city of New Jersey. To take an example involving metaphysical necessity, suppose that if something has a certain temperature T, then it has it in virtue of having a certain mean-kinetic energy E. This would not imply that something can have T only in virtue of having E. For this is compatible with something having T in virtue of having a property that is not identical with the property of having E. There may be some micro property $m(E)$ whose realization counts as the realization of E, but whose realization is not required for E's realization. For E may be multiply realizable at the level of $m(E)$. Yet something could have a certain temperature T in virtue of having $m(E)$. To take an example involving logical (or analytical, or conceptual) necessity, if one is a brother, then one is so in virtue of being is a male sibling. But one can be a brother in virtue of possessing a property that is not identical with the property of being a male sibling. For example, the property of being a male with a sister is not identical with the property in question, and one can be a brother in virtue of being a male with a sister. Thus, being a male sibling is not the only brother-making property, despite the fact that it is a logically necessary brother-making property. To belabor the point, on standard accounts of basic actions, if one acts, then one does so in virtue of performing some basic action or other. But there are non-basic actions, and one can of course act in virtue of performing one. We see, then, that even if B is a logically (or analytically, or conceptually) necessary A-making property, it does not follow that B is the only A-making property. I contend that The Principle of Causality leaves open whether falling under a strict law is the only singular causation making property. The Principle of Causality does not imply the Exclusion Principle. The former principle does not itself exclude the existence of causal properties that are not strictly nomic. A proponent of The Principle of Causality can consistently hold, for instance, that the fact that two events are subsumed by a certain non-strict law makes it the case that they are causally related; that is, a proponent can consistently hold this provided that events are subsumed by the non-strict law only if they are subsumed by some strict law or other.

Indeed, The Principle of Causality does not even exclude the existence of non-nomic causal properties. For it leaves open whether there are non-nomological causation grounding relations. The Principle of Causality does not imply that only strict laws are causation grounding, or even that only laws are causation grounding. What it implies, rather, is that whenever events are causally related in virtue of falling under a causation grounding relation, they are causally related in virtue of falling under some strict law or other. (It is easy to see why: if two events instantiate a causation grounding relationship, then they are causally related. And, given The Principle of Causality, if two events are causally related, they fall under some strict law or other.)

A general point should be noted. According to nomic subsumption views of causation, events are causally related iff they fall under a causal law. Such views do not, however, thereby, imply that only causal laws are causation grounding. It is compatible with such views that falling under a causal law is not the only causation-making property. Nomic subsumption views do not, for example, exclude the possibility that there are certain kinds of counterfactual dependency relationships that can ground singular causal transactions. But such views imply that if events participate in a causal transaction in virtue of participating in a counterfactual dependency relationship, then participating in that relationship requires falling under some causal law or other. Nomic subsumption views do not imply that all causal properties or event types are nomic. What they imply, rather, is that if an event participates in a causal relation in virtue of having a certain property, then the event participates in the relation in virtue of having some nomic property or other. And this leaves open whether an event can participate in a causal relation in virtue of having a non-nomic property.

To sum up my main point, then: The Principle of Causality does not by itself imply the Exclusion Principle. So, (p1) is false. And since it is, (I) is unsound.

Now what type-type relations ground singular causal relations is a question for the theory of causation. Davidson does not attempt to offer a complete answer to it. For, as we have seen, The Principle of Causality leaves open whether there are causation grounding relationships that are not strict laws. The only requirement that The Principle of Causality imposes on such type-type relations is that whenever they are instantiated by events, some strict law or other is instantiated by the events.

We need not decide here how Davidson might provide a complete account of causal properties. Nevertheless, it is instructive to ask how a proponent of Anomalism and The Principle of Causality might defend the claim that there are causal mental properties. One natural suggestion is that he or she might first claim that a property is a causal property in virtue of and only in virtue of figuring as a partial or complete cause factor in a causal law. Recall that Anomalism does not exclude there being mental properties that figure in non-strict laws. A proponent of The Principle of Causality and of Anomalism might then try to argue that Type-E is false on the grounds that some mental properties figure in non-strict causal laws.[15] For if a mental property figures in a non-strict causal law, it is a causal property. Moreover, as we saw, The Principle of Causality is compatible with the claim that there are non-nomic causal properties. So it is also open to a proponent of The Principle of Causality and of Anomalism to try to argue that there are non-nomic, but causal, mental properties.

Of course, if a proponent of The Principle of Causality and of Anomalism rejects the Exclusion Principle, and so maintains that there are indeed causation grounding type-type relations that are not strict laws, he or she must *argue* that when events instantiate such relations, they instantiate some strict law or other. An argument for The Principle of Causality would yield such an argument. For, given The Principle of Causality, if causation requires falling under a strict law, then falling under a causation grounding relationship requires falling under a strict law. But the point is that if there are causation grounding relationships that are not strict laws, an argument for The Principle of Causality must show that such relationships require the instantiation of some strict law or other in order to be instantiated. It would have to be argued that causation grounding relationships that are not strict laws (say, non-strict causal laws) are *non-basic* causation grounding relationships in that they require the instantiation of some distinct causation grounding relationship (a strict law) in order to be instantiated.

The point to underscore, however, is that Davidson's position on causation is more flexible than his critics acknowledge. As we saw, The Principle of Causality does not imply the Exclusion Principle.

In seeing this, we see that Davidson is relieved of a burden. For while he must defend The Principle of Causality, he need not defend the Exclusion Principle. And that is all to the good since the latter principle at least seems widely implausible: it would, for instance, count most of the nomic properties of the special sciences as epiphenomenal. To be sure, The Principle of Causality is also open to challenge. But a defense of this principle need not be burdened with a defense of the Exclusion Principle. And any plausible defense of The Principle of Causality would, I believe, allow for causation grounding relationships that are not strict laws. Any such defense would, then, proceed, in part, by showing why such relationships require the instantiation of a strict law to be instantiated. Whether and how this can be done must, however, be left open here.

Finally, it is worthwhile making the obvious point that even if (I) is unsound, The Principle of Causality and Anomalism might, in conjunction with certain (at least causally) necessary truths about causal properties, imply Type-E. For example, despite the fact that The Principle of Causality is compatible with the existence of non-strict causal laws and Anomalism is compatible with the existence of psychological and psychophysical laws, it *may* of course be the case that the doctrines in question in conjunction with certain necessary truths about causal properties imply that there are no psychological or psychophysical *causal* laws. But to show that this *is* indeed the case, it would have to be shown that the Exclusion Principle follows from the doctrines and the truths in question.[16] My main point is that The Principle of Causality does not itself imply the Exclusion Principle. From the fact that falling under a strict law is a logically necessary causation making property, it does not follow that it is the only causation making property. And by arguing that (I) is unsound, I hope to have hit the ball into the other court. As I mentioned at the outset, I leave open whether Davidson is committed to Type-E. But if he is, he is not so committed for the reasons given in (I). His position on causation has more flexibility than his critics acknowledge.[17]

8. Return to Question Q

My primary concern in this paper, recall, is to see whether the epiphenomenality of mental properties is implied by the following claims:

> *Physical Comprehensiveness.* It is causally necessary that when events are causally related, they are so in virtue of falling under physical event types.
>
> *Type Dualism:* There are mental event types, and no mental event type is identical with a physical event type.

Thus, recall our earlier question:

> (Q) Do Physical Comprehensiveness and Type Dualism exclude the existence of causal mental event types?

The answer to this question is "yes" iff Physical Comprehensiveness implies that only physical event types are causal. For suppose that it does. Then, given Type Dualism, no mental type is causal. Suppose Physical Comprehensiveness does not imply that only physical types are causal. Then, even granting Type Dualism, it remains an open question whether there are causal mental types. So the answer to (Q) turns on whether Physical Comprehensiveness implies that only physical types are causal.

It should be easy to see now that Physical Comprehensiveness does not imply this. As we saw earlier, a logically necessary A-making property is not ipso facto the only A-making property. It follows that a causally necessary A-making property is not ipso facto the only A-making property. Even if following under a causation grounding physical type-type relation is causally necessary for one event to cause another, it does not follow that only physical type-type relations are causation grounding. What follows, rather, is that causation grounding relationships are either physical or, by causal necessity, require for their realization the realization of some physical causation grounding relationship or other. But an event type can, by causal necessity, require for its realization the realization of a physical event type without itself being a physical event type. This is so even if, for instance, the event type must be realized *in virtue of* the realization of some physical type. For an event type may be multiply realizable by physical types and not be identical with any physical type. Physical Comprehensiveness is compatible with events participating in causal relations in virtue of falling under non-physical types. So Physical Comprehensiveness and Type Dualism do not exclude the existence of causal mental properties. The answer to (Q) is, in a word, "no." One can hold Physical Comprehensiveness and Type Dualism without, thereby, being committed to denying that mental events can be causes or that they can be so qua mental.

To be sure, a proponent of Physical Comprehensiveness and Type Dualism who rejects the claim that only physical properties are causal properties must *argue* that non-physical causation grounding relationships *causally* require the realization of some physical causation grounding relationship or other for their realization. But how this might be argued need not concern us here. I want to close, however, by suggesting that at least the following relationship holds between physical properties and any causal property:

> *Causal Priority of the Physical.* For any causally possible world *w*, and for any causally possible world *w'*, if all and only the same physical properties exist in each, then all and only the same causal properties exist in each.

(Of course, a property can exist in a world without being exemplified in that world.) Given this, what non-physical causal properties, if any, there are in a causally possible world is fixed by the physical properties of that world. But this leaves open whether there are non-physical causal properties. Thus, suppose that the nomic properties of some special science fail to be identical with physical properties. It would not follow that the nomic properties of the special science are epiphenomenal, even if the Causal Priority of the Physical and Physical Comprehensiveness hold. Even given the truth of the doctrines in question, the laws of the special science in question may be *causal* laws, laws *in virtue of* which events participate in causal relations.[18, 19]

Notes

1. See LePore and McLaughlin 1985 for a detailed discussion of Davidson's view that reasons are causes and that rationalization is a species of causal explanation.
2. The literature is vast, but see especially Stoutland (1976), (1985); Honderich (1982), (1983); Kim (1984); Sosa (1984); and Johnston (1985).
3. I discuss Melchert (1986) and LePore and Loewer (1987).
4. On some views of causal laws, falling under a causal law does not suffice for being causally related, other conditions must be satisfied. For example, the events must be appropriately spatio-temporally related in ways that need not be specified in a causal law. For a discussion of this issue, see Kim's discussion of the 'pairing problem' (Kim, 1973). For present purposes, we can ignore the issue.

5. Quine (1974, pp. 9-12) thinks 'because' and 'in virtue of' are intentional connectives of some sort, and, of course, he shies away from such connectives.

6. Frank Jackson (1977, chap. One) treats 'in virtue of' as expressing a two-placed relation. I favor treating it as a nonstandard sentential connective; but I shall continue here to put matters in the material rather than the formal mode. It should be noted, however, that the reader can choose his or her preferred way of treating 'because'—as a relation or as a non-standard connective—and treat 'in virtue of' likewise.

7. Davidson explicitly restricts his discussion of the psychological to the propositional attitudes (belief, desire, intention, and the like). And so what is at issue is whether he is committed to the view that proposi-tional attitude types are epiphenomenal. But I shall not mention this again, since it does not matter for the points I make below.

8. Two points are in order. First, I provided only a necessary condition for a theory's being comprehensive. Any statement of necessary and sufficient conditions for comprehensiveness must, I believe, invoke the notion of a *maximally explicit* law (see McLaughlin, 1985, pp. 342-348). But I do not attempt such a statement here since doing so would take me too far afield of my central concerns in this paper. Second, while Davidson takes laws to be true generalizations of a certain sort, I have been treating laws as singular relations between event types. But nothing will turn on this difference in what follows. As we shall see in section 6, the central issues here can be recast in the formal mode. Suffice it for now to note that if laws are understood to be singular relations bet-ween event types, then the above account of strict law can be recast as an account of what makes a statement expressing a law the expres-sion of a strict law.

9. I examine Davidson's *argument* for the claim that all strict laws are physical and point out some gaps in the argument in McLaughlin 1985, pp. 348-360; but it is not my concern here whether in fact all strict laws are physical.

10. Fodor (1987b) maintains that the special sciences employ causal laws, laws that can back or ground singular causal relations.

11. I owe the Broad quotation to Kim.

12. As I mentioned in footnote 7, Davidson restricts his discussion of the psychological to the propositional attitudes. So a point should be noted here so as to avert possible misunderstanding. I am not suggesting that Davidson takes the vocabulary of the propositional attitudes to be a promising one for a scientific psychology. Davidson gives reasons for doubting the prospects of a scientific propositional attitude psychology in 1980c. For present purposes, suffice it to note that a scientific psychology *may* have to be framed in other terms. In any case, this alone is no reason to doubt that there are non-strict laws that invoke proposi-tional attitudes. And Davidson does not, I think, doubt that there are.

13. One possible exception is Stoutland (1985, pp. 51-53), though he does not actually speak of strict and non-strict laws.

14. But I do not think that they succeed in this either. To see why, consider the following. First of all, they define relevance$_2$ (1987, p. 635) as follows: c's being F brings it about that e is G iff (1) c causes e, (2) c is F and e is G, (3) if c were not F, then e would not be G, and (4) c's being F and e's being G are logically and metaphysically independent. And they note that (1)-(4) would have to be supplemented to handle pre-emption and overdetermination. (Note by the way that any essential property of c will be causally relevant$_2$ to e's being G, provided (1) and (4) hold, and barring pre-emption and overdetermination.) Embracing a Lewis-Stalnaker view of counterfactuals, they hold that the sort of counterfactual cited in (3) is true iff in all the most similar worlds to the actual world it fails to be the case that c (or a counterpart of c) is F. And they correctly note that there are two ways that it may fail to be the case in a world that c (or a counterpart of c) is F. One way is if c (or a counterpart of c) occurs but is not F. Another way is if c fails to occur altogether (and no counterpart of c occurs). Given this and some quite plausible assumptions, however, mental properties can be relevant$_2$ if and only if mental events can be causes. The implication from left to right is, of course, trivial: given that relevance$_2$ requires that conditions (1) and (2) be satisfied, if mental properties can be relevant$_2$, mental events can be causes. On two plausible assumptions, we can establish the implication from right to left. The first assumption is that if a mental event m causes a physical event p, then barring overdetermination and pre-emption, if m had not occurred, p would not have occurred. The second is that it *can* happen that all the most similar worlds to ours in which it failed to be the case that c (or a counterpart of c) is M are worlds in which c fails to occur (and no counterpart of c occurs). Given these assumptions, mental properties can be relevant$_2$ if mental events can be causes. I won't pursue how LePore and Loewer might try to revise their definition to avoid this since, for one thing, I am uncertain what intuitive notion they are attempting to capture. For another, I am not concerned here with whether the severity of the charge of Type-E can be mitigated.

15. LePore and Loewer respond to Honderich at one point by claiming that Davidson can allow that there are non-strict causal laws (1987, pp. 637 638). However, Honderich and the other critics in question seem to hold that if a law is causal, then the properties it invokes can be causally relevant$_1$ to a singular causal transaction: for falling under a causal law makes it the case the events are causally related. LePore and Loewer do not think that Davidson can hold that there are non-strict causal laws in *this* sense. Rather, they hold that Davidson can hold that there are psychological and psychophysical ceteris paribus generalizations that are true, counterfactual supporting, and confirmable by their positive instances. But Davidson's critics need not deny this. LePore and Loewer's disagreement with Davidson's critics, on this point at least, is, I believe, merely verbal.

16. As I say below, it seems enormously plausible that causal properties must

supervene on physical properties. It is, of course, an open question whether psychophysical supervenience is compatible with Anomalism (see Kim 1984, Sosa 1984, and McLaughlin 1985). I think that these claims are compatible since I think that psychophysical supervenience does *not* imply the existence of *strict* psychophysical laws. But this issue is beyond the scope of this paper.

17. Moreover, as I said at the outset, I leave open here whether Type-E is true. A wide variety of arguments have been offered for Type-E. And I have not even mentioned here what I take to pose the most serious threat of Type-E. If content fails to supervene on what's in the head, the question of whether intentional mental properties are epiphenomenal naturally arises. Suffice it to say that I think this threat too can be answered, but I leave that for another occasion. (For attempts to respond to this threat see Fodor 1987a and Dretske 1988.)

18. Of course, one would like to see an explanation of why the Causal Priority of the Physical holds, but I leave that for another occasion.

19. In addition to the help that I have cited above, I wish to thank the following for helpful discussions and/or useful comments on prior drafts: Gerald Barnes, Jerry Fodor, Gary Gleb, Jaegwon Kim, Ernest LePore, Barry Loewer, Tim Maudlin, Bradford Petrie, and the late William L. Stanton. I owe special thanks to Terence Horgan.

References

Broad, C.D., 1925, *The Mind and Its Place in Nature*, London.
Cambell, Keith, 1970, *Body and Mind*, New York.
Cornman, James, 1981, "A Nonreductive Identity Theory about Mind and Body," in *Reason and Responsibility*, Belmont, California, Joel Feinberg ed. (1981).
Davidson, Donald, 1980, *Essays on Actions and Events*, New York, Oxford.
Davidson, Donald, 1980a, "Actions, Reasons, and Causes," reprinted in Davidson (1980).
Davidson, Donald, 1980b, "Causal Relations," reprinted in Davidson (1980).
Davidson, Donald, 1980c, "Comments and Replies," reprinted in Davidson (1980).
Davidson, Donald, 1980d, "Hempel on Explaining Action," reprinted in Davidson (1980).
Davidson, Donald, 1980e, "Mental Events," reprinted in Davidson (1980).
Davidson, Donald, 1980f, "Psychology as Philosophy," reprinted in Davidson (1980).
Davidson, Donald, 1980g, "The Material Mind," reprinted in Davidson (1980).
Dretske, Frederick, 1988, *Explaining Behavior*, Cambridge, Bradford.
Fodor, Jerry, 1974, "The Special Sciences (Or: The Disunity of Science as a Working Hypothesis)," *Synthese*, 28, 97-117.
Fodor, Jerry, 1975, *The Language of Thought*, Cambridge, MIT.
Fodor, Jerry, 1987a, *Psychosemantics*, Cambridge, MIT.

Fodor, Jerry, 1987b, "Making Mind Matter More," presented at the Eastern Division Meetings of the American Philosophy Association as a commentary on LePore and Loewer (1987).

Honderich, Ted, 1982, "The Argument for Anomalous Monism," *Analysis*, XLII, 59-64.

Honderich, Ted, 1983, "Anomalous Monism: A Reply to Smith," *Analysis*, XLIII.

Horgan, Terence, 1981, "Token Physicalism, Supervenience, and the Generality of Physics," *Synthese*, 49.

Jackson, Frank, 1977, *Perception: A Representative Theory*, Cambridge, Cambridge University Press.

Johnston, Mark, 1985, "Why Having a Mind Matters," LePore and McLaughlin (1985).

Kim, Jaegwon, 1973, "Causation, Nomic Subsumption, and the Concept of Event," *Journal of Philosophy,* LXX, 217-230.

Kim, Jaegwon, 1984a, "Concepts of Supervenience," *Philosophy and Phenomenological Research*, XLV, 153-176.

Kim, Jaegwon, 1984b, "Epiphenomenal and Supervenient Causation," *Midwest Studies in Philosophy*, 9, P. French, T. Uehling, Jr., and H. Wettstein, eds., Minneapolis, University of Minnesota Press (1984).

Kim, Jaegwon, 1987, "'Strong' and 'Global' Supervenience Revisited," *Philosophy and Phenomenological Research*, X:VIII, 315-326.

LePore, Ernest, Loewer, Barry, 1987, "Mind Matters," *Journal of Philosophy*, LXXXIV, 630-641.

LePore, Ernest, McLaughlin, Brian, 1985, *Actions and Events: Perspectives on the Philosophy of Donald Davidson*, Blackwell.

LePore, Ernest, McLaughlin, Brian, 1985, "Actions, Reasons, Causes, and Intentions," in LePore and McLaughlin (1985).

McLaughlin, Brian, 1985, "Anomalous Monism and the Irreducibility of the Mental," in LePore and McLaughlin (1985).

McLaughlin, Brian, 1983, "Event Supervenience and Supervenient Causation," *Spindel Conference, Southern Journal of Philosophy*, 22.

Melchert, Norman, 1986, "What's Wrong With Anomalous Monism," *Journal of Philosophy*, LXXX, 265-274.

Quine, W.V.O., 1974, *The Roots of Reference*, Illinois, Open Court.

Smith, Peter, 1984, "Anomalous Monism and Epiphenomenalism: A Reply to Honderich," *Analysis*, XLIV.

Sosa, Ernest, 1984, "Mind-Body Interaction and Supervenient Causation," *Midwest Studies in Philosophy*, IX, 276-281.

Stanton, William L., 1983, "Supervenience and Psychological Law in Anomalous Monism," *Pacific Philosophical Quarterly*, 64, 74-76.

Stoutland, Fred, 1976, "The Causation of Behavior," *Essays On Wittgenstein in Honor of G. H. von Wright, Atca Philosophica Fennica*.

Stoutland, Fred, 1985, "Davidson on Intentional Behavior," in LePore and McLaughlin (1985).

Philosophical Perspectives, 3
Philosophy of Mind and Action Theory, 1989

FUNCTIONAL EXPLANTIONS AND REASONS AS CAUSES

Geoffrey Sayre-McCord
University of North Carolina at Chapel Hill

That a conceptual connection, of sorts, holds between a person's reasons for acting and her actions, has served as grounds for embracing two dramatic theses:

1. Reasons (as they manifest themselves in beliefs and desires) do not cause actions. (*The Anti-Causal Thesis*)
2. The explanation of nature is fundamentally different from the explanation of action. (*The Explanatory Dualism Thesis*)

If we assume that a conceptual connection does hold between reasons and action, the arguments for both theses are strikingly simple. In defense of the first thesis, all that need be added is Hume's Principle: between cause and effect only a (logically) contingent relation holds. For given Hume's Principle, and the conceptual connection (which after all is not a contingent one), it follows that no causal connection holds. In defense of the second thesis, all that need be added is one assumption and one observation. The assumption is that the covering-law model of explanation is adequate to the natural sciences; the observation is that if a conceptual connection does hold, then covering-laws are not required to explain a person's action given the presence of the relevant beliefs and desires (because the presence of the latter entail the performance of the former). Together the assumption and the observation undermine the view that one model of explanation will fit both natural science and human psychology.

In the face of these arguments, three counter-arguments are initially attractive (and often given). Regrettably, each faces serious problems.

First, one might simply reject the shared assumption of a conceptual connection between reasons and action. Then Hume's principle would be irrelevant, and room would be left to insist that action explanations (explanations which invoke beliefs and desires) suppress a premise containing a relevant covering-law.[1] In that case, both the Anti-Causal Thesis and the Explanatory Dualism Thesis would lose their footing. The problem with this response is that (as I shall argue) there really is a conceptual connection between beliefs, desires, and actions.

Second, one might acknowledge the conceptual connection, and then maintain that this very connection renders action 'explanations' as unexplanatory as they are non-causal. In that case, the Anti-Causal Thesis would be allowed, but at the expense of our explaining what people do by appeal to their beliefs and desires. The problem with this response is that we can and do explain why a person acts by appeal to her beliefs and desires.

Third, one might argue that the Anti-Causal Thesis confuses relations among descriptions with relations among the things described. Only descriptions can bear logical relations to one another, the argument would run, while only the things described can bear causal relations. Hence there being a logical connection between descriptions of beliefs and desires, and descriptions of actions, is perfectly compatible with there being a contingent and so causal connection between the things described.[2] In that case, the Anti-Causal Thesis would be rejected. But the Explanatory Dualism Thesis would remain unshaken, since explanations operate at the level of descriptions. Moreover, this last response may even fail to meet the anti-causalist challenge. For if psychological descriptions (which bring to bear an agent's reasons for acting) are irrelevant to the causal explanation of why people behave as they do, it is hard to see how the fact that a person has any particular reason can legitimately count as causing her actions—even if what does cause the behavior can be described in psychological terms.[3]

Although each of these counter-arguments is problematic, a proper account of the conceptual connection which holds between beliefs and desires will, I think, provide the leverage needed to dislodge both the Anti-Causal Thesis and the Explanatory Dualism

Thesis. In what follows I attempt to develop such an account. Central to my arguments will be an emphasis on the fact that beliefs and desires are (at least nominally) defined in functional terms.[4] Against the anti-causalists I shall argue that even if a conceptual connection holds between a person's reasons for action, and the actions to which they give rise, there may nonetheless be a causal connection as well. As I have said, the anti-causalist's argument depends on Hume's Principle that cause and effect are not conceptually linked. Yet, I shall argue, the principle doesn't apply to functionally characterized entities, properties, or events—between them both a conceptual and a causal connection may hold. Against the Explanatory Dualists I shall argue that to the extent the covering-law model is inappropriate to action explanations, it is (for just the same reasons) inapplicable to many explanations offered in the natural sciences. In particular, the covering-law model is inadequate for all explanations which invoke functionally characterized entities, properties, or events and the covering-law model is no more adequate to functional explanations in natural science than in psychology. Hence the model's inadequacy for psychology reveals not some deep methodological divide between the sciences of nature and those of man, but a deep inadequacy in the model.

Action Explanations

A fairly standard picture of action explanations seems to underwrite the view that a conceptual connection holds between a person's reasons for acting and her actions. According to this picture, any action (in contrast to mere behavior) is susceptible of explanation in terms of beliefs and desires.[5] In fact, the (in principle) availability of such an explanation is a necessary condition for some behavior to count as an action. To explain a person's action we must fit it into the context of the agent's beliefs and desires. We do this by treating the action as the conclusion of a practical inference and providing a description of the belief and desire which formed the premises of the inference. Suppose, for example, that we want to explain Isolde's leaving her room surreptitiously. We could offer the following:

1. Isolde wanted (more than any other competing option) that she see her beloved alone.[6]

2. Isolde believed that the best way for her to see her beloved alone (all things considered) was for her leave surreptitiously.
3. So, Isolde left surreptitiously.

We might, of course, be mistaken; Isolde may not have left the room at all, or her leaving may not have been intentionally surreptitious, or her reasons for leaving surreptitiously may have been different than the ones we think. Thus, we might be wrong about whether Isolde performed an action, or about what the action was that she did perform, or about the reasons she had for performing it. Regardless, if we do offer an explanation of the action we take her to have performed, the explanation will fit the following schema:

1. *A* wanted (more than any other competing option) that *x*.
2. *A* believed that the best way to insure that *x* (all things considered) was for her to *y*.
3. So, *A* *y*-ed.

It is worth emphasizing that our action explanations use *descriptions* of beliefs and desires; our practical inferences, in contrast, rest on the *contents* of our beliefs and desires. Isolde may have left surreptitiously because she wanted to be alone with Tristan and believed that the best way to insure their being alone (all things considered) was for her to sneak away; yet if she did, her reasons for disappearing—the considerations that entered into her practical inference—made no reference to her wants and beliefs but only to (what she took to be) some feature of their being alone that she in fact found attractive and to what (she took to be) the best way to insure that they get to be alone. It is the *contents* of beliefs and desires (and not that she has the beliefs and desires) which serve as an agent's reasons for acting, while it is by being the content of *beliefs* and *desires* that these contents manage to serve as an agent's reasons. Recognizing this is central to an appreciation of the hazy sense in which beliefs and desires constitute an agent's reasons.[7]

In any case, when explaining a person's action, we attribute two things to the agent: a relevant occurrent want that is stronger than all competing wants and a belief as to the best way (all things considered) to satisfy the want.[8] The want involved will, in effect, be the motivational consequence of a constellation of background desires. As opposed to the complex of background desires, which may conflict, the relevant occurrent wants exist only undefeated, often as a compromise between various conflicting urges and inclinations, commitments and plans.[9] Although occurrent wants, so thought of, may coincide with long term desires, and the relevant beliefs may coincide with standing convictions, these background desires and beliefs are relevant to the explanation of particular actions only as they manifest themselves as occurrent wants and beliefs. Occurrent wants and beliefs are of interest, not because of the firmness with which they are held, but because of the impact they have on a person's behavior.

The relevant belief is, importantly, an *evaluative* belief about how *best* to insure the realization of some end. Often the evaluative nature of the belief is over-looked, probably because people assume all the work of evaluation is reflected in an agent's desires. Yet this evaluative component is central to explaining why a person chooses one way of securing a desired end rather than another equally effective way.[10] While the relevant evaluations will frequently reflect the agent's desires (the desired often seeming desirable), they won't always.[11] Some evaluative beliefs, for instance, concern which desires are best, and they do so often without having an eye to which desires best satisfy others.[12]

Moreover, the evaluative belief about how best to insure the realization of some end (the end being the content of a desire) will only be one among many of the evaluative beliefs held by the agent.[13] Thus, the simple picture of action provided by the explanation schema glosses over almost everything relevant to deliberation; it applies only to what emerges from the all too hectic clash among evaluative beliefs and between these beliefs and an agent's desires. The schema also leaves out of account all the interesting relations which hold between our experiences and our beliefs and desires. Even so, the schema pick-up on what is central to those folk-psychological explanations of particular actions that appeal to an agent's reasons for acting.

Action explanations, as the schema suggests, invoke an agent's belief concerning the best way *all things considered* to satisfy a relevant desire. The 'all things considered' rider, though crucial, is misleading in two ways.

In the first place, the truth of an action explanation does not depend on the agent *consciously considering* anything. What is important for action is an appropriate link to beliefs and desires, not an awareness either of the beliefs and desires, or of the link which ties them to behavior.[14] People do sometimes act without having deliberated at all, and people do sometimes act because of beliefs and desires of which they are unaware. Nonetheless, a belief will count as considered (in the relevant, albeit attenuated, sense) as long as it has affected what the agent believes to be the best course of action. As a result, a belief has been considered if it has played a role (not necessarily decisive) in determining what the agent takes to be the best way to insure the realization of her desired end under the circumstances. Clearly, some belief can affect another, and so be considered (in this somewhat artificial sense) without the person being aware of the influence.[15] Hence, the 'all things considered' clause should not be read 'all things consciously considered' but instead 'all considerations that will have an influence, having done so.'

In the second place, the belief invoked to explain action is not the belief the person would have had had all things (or even all relevant things or even all relevant things available to her) actually been considered. Instead, it is the belief the person actually had about what the best course of action was, given only what the person actually considered (consciously or not). This sort of belief is often worthy of ridicule; people can ignore the obvious, and they can give improper weights to their considerations. Even so, given the considerations, and the significance the agent assigned to them, people who have, in fact, performed an action, will have had a belief about the best course of action. It is this belief which is ultimately invoked in action explanations.[16]

Causalists and anti-causalists alike can agree with what has been said so far. Certainly some causalists, as well as some anti-causalists, will want to add, subtract, or otherwise amend various details, depending on their preferred accounts of practical syllogisms. Yet these differences in detail are not crucial to what follows. The important difference between causalists and anti-causalists comes out in the positive accounts each offers of the relationship between beliefs, wants, and action. The causalists, not surprisingly, offer an account which takes beliefs and wants to be the causes of action. Anti-causalists, in turn, hold that beliefs and desires do not cause actions, rather they simply provide a way of describing behavior and are merely a story we tell about others (and ourselves). According to the anti-causalists, there are neither properties, nor states, nor processes, nor events, nor things, of or within a person which can be identified as that person's desires and beliefs, and which can cause, or fail to cause, action. Instead, people behave in ways which, at least usually, lend themselves to interpretations as intentional. We explain a person's action, so say the anti-causalists, by fitting it into a coherent story which displays its reasonableness, not by enumerating its causes. Understanding some behavior as intentional—viewing it as an action performed for a reason—is a matter of seeing its point. Thus, G. H. von Wright:

> Behavior gets its intentional character from being seen by the agent himself or by an outside observer in a wider perspective, from being *set* in a context of aims and cognitions.[17]

In the same vein, although not directly in the service of the anti-causalist's position, Daniel Dennett argues that "being intentional is being the object of a certain stance."[18] And elsewhere he argues that "*all there is* to being a true believer is being a system whose behavior is reliably predicted via the intentional strategy...".[19] The availability of a coherent (and predictively valuable) story for a person's behavior is taken as the sole criterion for the ascription of wants and beliefs; people have whatever beliefs and desires we attribute to them in constructing a coherent biography. On this view, intentionality of behavior depends essentially on norms and practices; on the conventions, expectations, and interpretations of others.[20]

The anti-causalist account of the connection between beliefs, wants, and actions, faces two serious—and commonly recognized—problems. The first is that actual behavior dramatically underdetermines our ascriptions of beliefs and wants. We may construct different, and incompatible, coherent accounts of a person's behavior.[21] The anti-causalists can't plausibly maintain that people have whichever reasons go with the particular hypothesis *we* happen to adopt. *We may end up accepting the wrong hypothesis.* (Or at least so it seems.)

The second problem is that, so long as one is willing to ascribe unusual or peculiar wants and beliefs, any behavior, of any thing, can be put into a context of aims and cognitions. We can offer coherent accounts, laden with intentionality, of the strikingly sedate life which rocks lead. All we need do is say that rocks 'want' to make people happy, and that they 'believe' that the best way to make people happy is to remain passive and get pushed around by gravity, slingshots, etc..[22] If the sedate life of rocks seems insufficiently complex, imagine instead a hollow Tin Foil Man manipulated by magnets from a roof top. No matter how complex his behavior (and we can imagine it to be very complex indeed), his empty-headedness seems quite conclusive grounds for thinking he has no beliefs or desires. So the availability of a coherent biography cannot serve as the sole criterion for the possession of beliefs and desires since rocks and the Tin Foil Man lack both.[23]

We do not, then, satisfactorily explain an action simply by providing a description of a practical inference which has the appropriate conclusion. Not just any intelligible story will do. The wants and beliefs attributed to the agent must be ones the agent actually has. While we must fit the action into a context of reasons, the reasons must be the agent's.

Yet even if we get an action explanation that attributes the right desires and beliefs to the person (ones she actually has), we still might have the wrong explanation for her behavior. Isolde may want to be alone with Tristan, and she may believe that leaving surreptitiously is the best way (all things considered) to insure that they are alone *and* her leaving unnoticed might be unintentional on her part (for instance if she is swept away in the night). A person's wants and beliefs explain behavior only when they are responsible for it.

We may push the point further: not just any connection between an agent's reasons for acting, and her behavior, is acceptable. Suppose that Tristan, Isolde's love, knows that Isolde wants to be alone with him and that she believes they can be alone only if her departure goes undetected. Suppose also that, for this reason, he steals Isolde away while she is asleep. When this happens, Isolde's reasons *are* responsible for her exit going unnoticed (if only indirectly), but not in any way which allows her leaving to be an action she performed.[24]

To explain a person's action correctly, (1) we must attribute to the agent wants and beliefs she actually had, and (2) these wants and beliefs must be responsible for the agent's behavior in the appropriate (as yet unspecified) way. So far I have limited myself to saying merely that the psychological states invoked in the explanation must be 'responsible' for the behavior explained in some appropriate way. This leaves the formulation vague enough to be acceptable even to sophisticated anti-causalists; they might maintain that the responsibility involved is not *causal* responsibility.[25] Nonetheless, a common, although more contentious, requirement does seem attractive: (3) the beliefs and wants invoked in the explanations must be *causally* responsible for the behavior in some suitably direct way and their status as reasons—their content—must be relevant to their having the effects they do. Only if this third requirement is satisfied will reasons and actions find a comfortable place within the world.

The best sort of account, I think, would require that the people (or things) whose behavior is being explained, have some sort of internal representational system that serves to record and guide interaction with the world. On this view, only things with representational systems have beliefs and desires. This would allow us to rule out both rocks and the Tin Foil Man (they have no internal representational system) and would countenance ascribing beliefs and desires to people and animals (and perhaps to sufficiently sophisticated computers). Also, it would explain how there can be preferred coherent explanations; the bad explanations misrepresent the representational states of the agent. At the same time, to the extent the representational character of the system plays a role in the etiology and regulation of behavior, content would plausibly be explanatorily relevant. All this is compatible, of course, with a naturalized account of representation and content. If standard functionalism is true, for instance, a mental state gets its identity (and thus its content) from the complex of causal relations it bears to other mental states, to the world, and to behavior; and so, happily, the mental state's having the content it does will figure in the best explanation of why it has the causal effects it does.[26] However adequate this sort of account proves to be, neither it nor even a non-reductionistic semantic functionalism is available to anti-causalists. For if there are internal states which represent the world and have an appropriate impact on behavior, then there would be good reason to identify them as beliefs and desires which cause (or at least partially cause) actions. And that is something an anti-causalist, no matter how sophisticated, must resist.

In any case, the anti-causalist's positive account of the relation between reasons and actions is unacceptable. It makes beliefs too dependent on interpretation and too easy to have, for it leaves each of us with whatever beliefs others ascribe to us and it makes believers out of rocks (and empty-headed metal mannequins). Despite the problems facing the anti-causalist position, though, a causal account is doomed unless there is some acceptable way to undermine either

Hume's Principle or the Conceptual Connection Thesis. Fortunately, Hume's Principle simply will not bear the weight of the anticausalists' argument. And by rejecting the principle we can see our way clear to a reasonable, causal, account of the relationship between reasons and action.

Certainly one could counter the anti-causalists by attacking the Conceptual Connection Thesis rather than Hume's Principle. Yet several considerations point to there actually being a conceptual connection, of sorts, between a person's reasons for acting and her actions. So, after trying to spell out these considerations, I'll argue that, even granting a conceptual connection, there's room for a causal one as well.

The Conceptual Connection Thesis

Arguments concerning the Conceptual Connection Thesis are intimately tied to arguments concerning the role of covering laws in action explanations. On the one hand, according to those who hold that there is a conceptual connection, one may give a complete (i.e. non-enthymatic) explanation of an action simply by describing the premises of a practical inference—no covering-law need be invoked to link explanans to explanandum. The conceptual connection, they argue, renders covering-laws superfluous. On the other hand, according to those who deny that there is a conceptual connection, the force of action explanations is standardly taken to depend crucially upon suppressed premises containing covering-laws. The nature of explanation, they argue, renders covering-laws essential.

Defenders of the covering-law model of explanation argue that action explanations (when tenable) implicitly rely on premises like:

> Any person who is disposed to act rationally will, when she has occurrent want w and occurrent belief b, invariably (or: with high probability) do action a. And the person in question is, or was, disposed to act rationally at the appropriate time.[27]

An agent who had the appropriate wants and beliefs, but was irrational, they argue, would fail to perform the action her reasons justified. It is only on the assumption that a person is rational that we can explain her actions by appeal to her reasons. More generally, it is only by relying on an empirical law (to the effect that if a person has certain beliefs and desires, and is rational, she will act in a certain way) that we can explain the way she acts by appeal to her beliefs and desires. If such empirical premises are lurking in the background, then action explanations which only mention the beliefs and desires of the agent are really disguised covering-law explanations after all—or, failing a covering-law, simply not really explanations. And, if we discover the need for the suppressed premise, then (and this is undisputed) it is appropriate to think of action explanations as causal explanations.

Those who defend the conceptual connection thesis have offered three arguments for thinking that the having of relevant wants and beliefs guarantees the forming of an appropriate intention and, *ceterus paribus*, the performing of an appropriate action.[28]

The first of these turns, in effect, on the claim that the premises of an action explanation cannot be identified without making reference to the conclusion. Alan White puts the argument this way:

> It is characteristic of what serves as a cause that it is independent of its particular effect, in the sense that its description need not make any reference to such an effect... On the other hand, the desire that is alleged to be the cause of a particular deed is necessarily characterized either as a desire to do that deed or as a desire for something to which that deed is thought to be a means.[29]

This argument may be interpreted in either of two ways. Neither interpretation, though, raises any difficulties for the covering-law model of explanation. Taking the argument at face value, it runs into trouble immediately because we can accurately characterize a person's desires without making any reference to what they are desires for—say, as 'the desire Isolde had yesterday evening' or 'the desire she has that will get her into a great deal of trouble' or even 'the desire that is alleged to be the cause of a particular deed'. Instead, then, we might interpret the argument as resting on the more plausible claim that descriptions which differentiate one kind of desire from another ('individuating descriptions' we might call them) can only do so by making reference to their intentional objects; what makes a desire the desire it is is what it is a desire for.[30] Plausible as this claim is, it is perfectly compatible with there being no connection, logical or otherwise, between having a particular desire and actually performing the action desired. So it raises no problems for the covering-law model of explanation.

The second argument concentrates on the actions to be explained rather than on the beliefs and desires that do the explaining. A person may want to perform some action and never succeed (that's what raises problems for the first argument). But, the second argument points out, a person cannot have performed an action without having acted for reasons—even in cases where a person fails to do what she intends, her attempts count as actions (when they do) only because they were performed for a reason. What marks behavior as intentional is its having a point, and it has a point only if it is done for some reason. Moreover, what makes the particular action the action it was, are the reasons for which it was performed; it's one thing to leave surreptitiously to be alone with Tristan, quite another to sneak out to go to the disco. In either case, of course, Isolde will have left surreptitiously, yet we won't know what it was she was doing, in leaving surreptitiously, unless we know why she did it. And, to the extent she would have been doing the same thing, that is, leaving surreptitiously, there will be an explanation of her action that is the same for both cases (for instance, that she wanted (more than any competing option) that she not be followed and believed that the best way to insure that she not be followed was for her to leave surreptitiously). Even if we are dealing with a single action under different descriptions (e.g., 'leaving', 'leaving surreptitiously', 'leaving surreptitiously to avoid being followed', 'leaving surreptitiously to be alone with Tristan') each description will be true only if the ascription of reasons that goes with it is true.[31] This all suggests that there is a logical connection both between someone having performed an action and her having acted for reasons and between her having performed some particular action and her having acted for specific reasons.

The third, and most compelling, argument for thinking there is a conceptual connection turns on the observation that an agent's failure to perform the appropriate action (or at least her failure to form the appropriate intention) constitutes *conclusive* evidence that either the wrong belief or the wrong desire (or both) has been ascribed to the agent. If an agent fails to perform the appropriate action and has not misunderstood her circumstances, forgotten the time, or changed her plans, we take this to prove the person did not have the occurrent wants and beliefs we had supposed. We in effect treat having the beliefs and desires ascribed as a sufficient condition for the forming of the appropriate intention and, under standard conditions, for the performing of the appropriate action. This wouldn't be so if there were a covering-law, implicitly relied on, that might be false.

One might maintain, of course, that there is after all a covering-law underlying action explanations—one that asserts that a person's occurrent wants and beliefs will combine in the appropriate way to give rise to action—which is so firmly entrenched that we will acknowledge no counter-examples.[32] Yet when a supposed covering-law becomes as well entrenched as this is, it seems reasonable to think of it as fixing the conceptual framework within which talk of actions makes sense and not as a tacit assumption invoked within the framework.

If this is right, action explanations work without invoking covering-laws because the occurrent wants and beliefs they ascribe are defined, at least in part, as having certain characteristic effects on behavior; together they move people to action (the wants do the moving while the beliefs do the orchestrating). If something does not combine in the appropriate way with occurrent beliefs to give rise to action, then *it is not an occurrent want*. Similarly, if something does not combine appropriately with occurrent wants, then it is not an occurrent belief. The functional characterization of occurrent wants and beliefs rules out the possibility of a person

1. who wants (more than any competing option) that x,
2. believes that the best way to insure that x (all things considered) is for her to y,
3. and yet who doesn't y (or at least set herself to y).

(where the wants and beliefs ascribed are occurrent). The assumption that (1) and (2) apply is falsified by the fact that the person did not perform the action (or at least form the intention) which would have been appropriate (i.e. rational) given these wants and beliefs. Defining occurrent wants and beliefs in functional terms eliminates the need for an independent covering-law in action explanations. No additional covering-law is needed to link wants and beliefs to actions.

On this account, really two steps link a person's beliefs and desires to her action. The first is the conceptual link between beliefs, desires, and the forming of intentions. The second, which is submerged when explaining actions already performed, is between the having of intentions and the performing of actions: if one really intends to perform an action, and one has neither forgotten the time nor misunderstood the circumstances, then, unless one is physically prevented, one will perform the action intentionally.[33] Clearly, there are several limiting clauses on the link between intentions and action. When we are explaining past actions we may safely assume the clauses are satisfied; when we are predicting future actions these clauses are usually collapsed into an all-encompassing ceteris paribus clause.[34]

As defenders of the covering-law model have argued, action explanations do presuppose the rationality of the agent; a person's behavior cannot be explained by her reasons unless she is rational. Yet rationality enters the picture not as an extra premise in our explanations, but as precondition for the agent's having the wants and beliefs our explanations ascribe. If a purported want does not combine with beliefs in the appropriate (*rational*) way, it is (temporarily at least) ruled out of court as not being an occurrent want at all. Similarly, if a purported belief does not combine with desires in the appropriate (*rational*) way, it too is (temporarily at least) ruled out of court as not being an occurrent belief at all.[35] The rationality requirement thus plays a crucial role in limiting what can count as a legitimate explanation of action. At the same time, it rules out the possibility of there being a person who has the appropriate wants and beliefs yet who fails, because of irrationality, to perform the appropriate action; if a person suffers this sort of irrationality, she fails to have the appropriate wants and beliefs.

Central though it is to the conceptual connection thesis, this rationality requirement is extremely weak. It is compatible with the fact that people are often amazingly irrational and with there being several, multiply incompatible, standards of rational choice. The rationality requirement demands only that a person's occurrent wants and beliefs combine in certain characteristic ways so as to give rise to action. The requirement does not touch on the content of either the wants or the beliefs, nor does it require that occurrent and standing wants be compatible. A person may meet the weak rationality requirement and still hold beliefs which are absurd or unfounded, as well as desires which are insatiable, conflicting, or self-destructive. Such people are surely irrational in some sense, but not in the sense presupposed by action explanations. All that the weak rationality requirement demands is that occurrent wants (the ones which give rise to the behavior in question) combine with relevant beliefs (however idiotic) in an acceptable way, to bring about action. To this extent, though, even the weak rationality requirement imposes some constraint on the content of beliefs and desires; for to combine in an acceptable way these contents must be such that, from the agent's point of view, they can serve as reasons for action.

Many considerations will influence a person's occurrent belief concerning the best course of action; moral convictions, estimates of risk, and evaluation tactics may all enter in. Among the evaluation tactics available are those often recommended in decision theory; minimax, the principle of insufficient reason, etc.. Adoption of one or the other of these tactics will no doubt affect a person's belief concerning the best course of action. Nonetheless, these different tactics enter as criteria for rationality only when we are concerned with substantive rationality; they enter only when the *content* of belief is under scrutiny. A person may be rational in the weak sense (and so may have beliefs and desires) regardless of which tactic, if any, is employed. Indeed, because the having of beliefs and wants presupposes weak rationality, the evaluation of an agent's substantive rationality presupposes the agent's weak rationality.

Weak rationality is, as I have emphasized, compatible with having ridiculous beliefs and conflicting desires. Even so, the requirement of weak rationality does have some bite: it eliminates as irrelevant states of a person which could not affect behavior, and among even those states which do or could have an effect, it eliminates those which would not combine in appropriate ways to give rise to actions.

So far the defense of the weak rationality requirement has been negative and rests on accommodating two facts: people are irrational and multiple standards of substantive rationality exist. A positive argument for accepting both the rationality requirement and the Conceptual Connection Thesis rests on noting that together they explain the way we interact with other people.

When we first meet people we assume both weak and substantive rationality. That is, we assume that they have reasonable beliefs and desires (by our own lights) and that these work together, in the appropriate way, to affect their behavior.[36] Having ascribed particular wants and beliefs to a person, we take a failure to act in the appropriate way as conclusive evidence that our ascriptions are inaccurate. As we get to know the person, and her behavior fails to conform to our predictions, we adjust our ascriptions of belief and desire so as to better accord with her behavior. Usually we need adjust our assumption of strong rationality only slightly. We do this by ascribing peculiar fears, strange attachments, or false beliefs. Sometimes, however, we are forced to wild extremes. We may find ourselves (though rarely) describing someone as 'believing she is Napoleon' or as 'wanting to be a rock' where these are meant literally, and not metaphorically. In the few rare cases in which even ascriptions of radical beliefs and wants fail, we do not simply abandon the assumption of weak rationality, we quit ascribing wants and beliefs to the person altogether. Wanting, believing, and (weak) rationality stand or fall together.

One might argue against the rationality requirement (and so the Conceptual Connection Thesis it helps to support), even in the face of these observations, by claiming that we stop ascribing wants and beliefs once the supposition of weak rationality is abandoned *not* because there is some necessary connection between belief, desire, and (weak) rationality, but simply because there is no pragmatic point to doing so: knowing about such beliefs and wants would be of no predictive value. Yet this response is implausible. Mistakenly, it assumes that our sole motive for ascribing beliefs and wants is the desire to predict future behavior. Often we do ascribe beliefs and wants to a person as an explanation of her behavior, even when these ascriptions promise no predictive power whatsoever. We are often interested in why people have done as they have even when there is no chance they will ever do it again. Lack of predictive power alone is not sufficient reason to stop ascribing beliefs and wants to a person.[37] In contrast, lack of weak rationality alone does appear to be a sufficient reason for not ascribing beliefs and desires to a person.

Instead of exploring these issues I will argue that even if a conceptual connection exists, reasons may cause actions. That wants and beliefs are *nominally* defined in functional terms, I shall argue, allows for there being both a conceptual and a causal connection between a person's reasons for acting and her actions.

Beliefs, Desires, and Nominal Definitions

In the *Posterior Analytics*, Aristotle introduces the distinction between (what has come to be called) nominal and real definitions.[38] Nominal definitions afford us handles by which to pick out something of interest for further investigation. They set out those characteristics of the thing 'defined' which we take it to have.[39] Real definitions, on the other hand, tell us what characteristics the thing really has. Thus water is nominally defined as being, say, clear and colorless and liquid at room temperature, while its real definition is spelled-out in terms of hydrogen and oxygen; anything which is H_2O is water, regardless of whether it is clear, colorless, etc..

Nominal and real definitions can diverge quite dramatically. To take a standard example, jade was nominally defined in terms of its characteristic color and its hard smooth texture, etc.. With the nominal definition in hand, science set out to provide a real definition. As it turned out, the things collected together under the nominal definition of jade are really of two natural kinds, jadeite and nephrite. The nominal definition failed to pick out a single homogeneous natural kind, and so no single real definition of jade is available. When apparent unity disintegrates, when the nominal definitions span natural kinds, we must either choose one of the natural kinds as setting the real definition or rule that there is no real definition to correspond to the nominal definition.

Alternatively, in some cases a nominal definition may lead to a real definition which establishes fundamental similarities between seemingly different things; apparent diversity may cover a deeper unity. Dogs might have been nominally defined as four-legged mammals of a characteristic size and shape. Yet with a real (in this case, biological) definition in hand we have found that dogs span an incredible range, some looking more like rats (chihuahuas) and others more like horses (Great Danes). Depending on what characteristics figured in our nominal definition, it might even be that the vast majority of dogs fail to fit the definition.

In still other cases, things might be even messier. Imagine a group of explorers in South America who discover a new animal which flies, has a striped body, and which emits a series of high pitched beeps. The explorers take these characteristics as a nominal definition and they warn others who enter the cave to 'watch out for those flying striped beasties that beep.' We shall call them Fergons. Suppose that, following a fair bit of hullabaloo, the local government sends in a zoologist to capture and examine some of these Fergons. After bringing them out of the cave, and studying them for a little while, the zoologist makes some startling announcements: Fergons are not striped, they just have wrinkled bodies which, under the artificial cave lighting, look striped (their wrinkled skin casts thin shadows); Fergons do not actually fly, they simply climb up the walls until they fall; and when they do fall they don't emit a series of beeps, they let out one single beep, which echoes. The explorers' nominal definition of Fergons, it turns out, was completely wrong.

Suppose the zoologist were to make another startling announcement (after studying hundreds of Fergons): some are squirrels, while others are cats, and still others are large rats. All are wrinkled beasts which climb walls, fall, and let out a beep. Of course they look quite different from each other in normal light, but in the cave they all looked pretty much the same. Has the nominal definition of a Fergon actually succeeded in picking something out? Or, is there really no such thing as a Fergon? Regardless of how we answer, the example shows that a nominal definition of x's need not mention an attribute which all or even some x's actually have. What a nominal definition of x's does provide is a way of picking things out as x's. We use nominal definitions to get science off the ground. Once off, there is no reason science should not tell us that common sense misrepresents the world.

It is open to a causalist to hold that the occurrent wants and beliefs invoked in action explanations are, like Fergon (or jade, or dog), nominally defined. The definitions that support a conceptual connection, on this view, are nominal definitions set out in functional terms. Because a functional account of wants and beliefs (which supports a conceptual connection between reasons and action) can operate at the level of nominal definitions, a functionalist needn't (and shouldn't) claim that wants and beliefs (as they really are) are fully (or even accurately) characterized functionally. In particular, a functionalist needn't hold either that all things which perform the functions of beliefs and desires are such, or that wants and beliefs are merely dispositions to act. We are still largely in the dark about what things play the role of wants and beliefs.

Illustrative parallels abound in physical science. Consider explanations that invoke magnets.[40] We may explain the fact that some iron filings, i, moved towards a rock, r, by pointing out that r is a magnet (in this case a lodestone). The explanation is a causal one: r caused i to move towards r. The explanation has this form:

1. *r* is a magnet
2. *i* is a collection of iron filings
3. So, *i* moved towards *r*

Although the magnet *caused* the iron filings to move, there is still a conceptual connection (of the sort there is in action explanations) between the premises and the conclusion of the explanation. If the filings did not move towards the rock, then either it is not really a magnet or else the filings are not iron (or else a *ceteris paribus* clause was violated). No third suppressed premise asserts a covering-law connecting magnets with the movement of the iron filings. Rather, magnets have been nominally defined in functional terms. To be a magnet is to be something which has certain characteristic effects on the world under standard conditions. A third premise which contained a covering-law would simply spell out these characteristic effects, and would therefore be otiose. Prior to the development of electromagnetic theory, events were often *properly* explained by pointing out that they were caused by magnets. (A magnet, not a ghost, caused the iron filings to move.) That such explanations were true has been born out by the development of electromagnetic theory. That they were informative is clear, for people learn something important about an event when they learn it was caused by a magnet (even if they do not know electromagnetic theory).[41]

If (and I think because) we lack a real definition of occurrent wants and beliefs, we have no conclusive way to settle the question of whether all occurrent wants and beliefs actually interact in a way our nominal definitions demand. Until real definitions are developed, the functionally specified nominal definition must determine what is to count as an occurrent reason. And our nominal definitions require that reasons have characteristic, rational, effects on behavior. This functional characterization of occurrent reasons accounts for what conceptual connection there is between reasons and action. Whether the connection underwritten by the nominal definitions remains intact depends, in the end, on whether the real definitions provided by psychology preserve the functional character of the nominal definitions. Action explanations will be vindicated to the extent that a well articulated theory of motivation both retains and explains the characteristic effects of beliefs and desires.

Explanations which invoke things nominally defined (in functional terms or not) are promissory explanations. They tell us, roughly, how a real explanation should go, and of what sort of things it ought to take account. If action explanations rely on nominal definitions, then, they are in some sense incomplete; nevertheless they are neither unenlightening nor likely to be false (so far as they go).[42]

Once a well-articulated theory has been developed, though, pragmatic considerations determine whether we tacitly assume or explicitly invoke the theory when offering an explanation. In cases where no such theory is yet available (action explanations now, and magnetic explanations prior to electromagnetic theory) our explanations presuppose the (at least in principle) availability of an acceptable theory. The force of a nominal definition lies in the possibility of cashing it out in terms of a real definition. Even so, explanations which contain elements only nominally defined are saved from vacuity by the assumption that a real definition is, in principle, available. Importantly, while action explanations may presuppose such real definitions, there is no reason to assume in advance that the real definitions at which psychology eventually arrives will abandon the functional characterizations of wants and beliefs—our nominal definitions might well be good real definitions. And if they are, then the action explanations which rely on them will be as well-credentialed as any other scientific explanation.

Although functional explanations will succeed only if there are things which fulfill the function, they do not presuppose any particular kind of thing; functional explanations are insensitive to differences in material instantiations so long as functional equivalence is maintained. Thus two systems can be functionally isomorphic, and so have the same wants and beliefs (at least as they are nominally defined), even though they are composed of radically different substances. What is significant about functional explanations is that, when they work, they often capture regularities and systematic connections that are undescribable, and so inexplicable, if one shifts attention to the particular things that happen to play the various functional roles. As Dennett has argued, for instance, certain features of the stock market will completely escape someone, a Martian say, who concentrates solely on physical goings-on:

> Take a particular instance in which the Martians observe a
> stock broker deciding to place an order for 500 shares of
> General Motors. They predict the exact motions of his
> fingers as he dials the phone, and the exact vibrations of his

vocal cords as he intones his order. But if the Martians do not see that indefinitely many *different* patterns of finger motions and vocal cord vibrations—even the motions of indefinitely many different individuals—could have been substituted for the actual particulars without perturbing the subsequent operation of the market, then they have failed to see a real pattern in the world they are observing.[43]

Functional explanations and structural explanations (that appeal to macro-level structural features of things) share an important characteristic that distinguishes them from material explanations (that operate at the level of ultimate constituents); they are both neutral with regard to material instantiation. But for our purposes, there is an important difference between functional and structural explanations; only structural explanations conform to the covering-law model. Things have the structure they do in virtue of *the way they are* (in virtue of their structure). Their *behavior* is explained by invoking general, covering-laws that connect structure with behavior. Functional explanations, in contrast, do not fit the covering-law model. Things play their function in virtue of *what they do*, and not because of what they are. Thus their behavior may be explained without invoking covering-laws; covering-laws would be superfluous. A covering-law would only tell us the thing's characteristic effects; but we know this already if we know the thing's function. Since we picked it out in the first place, as being the sort of thing it is, because of the function it plays, we do know its function. If x is a 'wurzil' in virtue of its fulfilling a certain function f, then there is no need for a covering-law to explain the fact that a 'wurzil' did f: it wouldn't be a 'wurzil' if it didn't.[44]

Plainly, there is room for, and presumably call for, an explanation of how x goes about being a 'wurzil.' What is it about x that allows it to play the function it does? An answer to this sort of question will be in terms of some background theory and will, perhaps, although not necessarily, invoke covering-laws. Whether it does involve covering-laws depends on the nature of the background theory. If it too invokes things functionally defined, then covering-laws will again be superfluous.

Conclusion

Recognizing that beliefs and desires are (at least nominally) defined in functional terms both allows that, and explains why, the Conceptual Connection Thesis is right in holding that a conceptual connection, of sorts, links a person's reasons for acting to her action. Against the backdrop of these functional definitions, something can qualify as an occurrent want or belief only if it would have a certain characteristic effect on a person's behavior. The content of our nominal definition of occurrent reasons justifies our inference from the having of certain wants and beliefs (each functionally defined) to the performance of the action they explain.

Recognizing that beliefs and desires are (at least nominally) defined in functional terms also provides grounds for rejecting Hume's Principle. The conceptual connection which exists between reasons and actions parallels the one between magnets and their characteristic effects. In fact, the same sort of connection holds between anything defined in functional terms, and its characteristic effects. Yet this kind of conceptual connection, as the magnet example shows, is perfectly compatible with there also being a causal connection. Moreover, as the magnet example also shows, scientific explanations, like action explanations, will fail to fit the covering-law model whenever they invoke things defined in functional terms. So the truth of the Conceptual Connection Thesis does not support belief in some deep methodological divide between psychology and the rest of science, even though it does undermine the covering-law model's claim to hegemony. Consequently, both the Anti-Causal Thesis, and the Explanatory Dualism Thesis, are unfounded—even though the Conceptual Connection Thesis, upon which they stand, is at least defensible.

The covering-law model is inappropriate for action explanations when the wants and beliefs invoked are functionally individuated. Still, it would be a mistake to conclude that the model can have no place in the explanation of action. In the first place, covering laws (although, no doubt, not strict laws) might well figure crucially in explaining why people come to form the various beliefs and desires that they do. In the second place, covering laws may be appropriate in explaining how the things (or events) which are the wants and beliefs (or the having of wants and beliefs) perform the functions they do. The things (or events) which really are occurrent wants and beliefs (or wantings and believings), and their effects, are perhaps—though not necessarily—explicable in terms of covering-laws. Whether covering laws will play a role once real definitions are in hand will depend on whether the real definitions themselves are functional. However, since there is good reason for doubting that anything more than token-token identities could be discovered, there is good reason for skepticism concerning the possibility of establishing interesting or useful laws which connect beliefs and desires (as they really are) with physical descriptions of people or their behavior. Regardless, unless psychologists succeed at dramatically fleshing out theories of belief and motivation, action explanations are doomed to being imprecise, schematic, and disturbingly *ad hoc*.[45]

Notes

1. C.G. Hempel defends this view in "Reasons and Covering Laws in Historical Explanation," in *The Philosophy of History*, Patrick Gardiner (ed.), (Oxford: Oxford University Press, 1974), pp. 90-105.
2. This is the line taken by Donald Davidson in his seminal paper "Actions, Reasons, and Causes," in *Essays on Actions and Events*, (Princeton: Princeton University Press, 1980), pp. 3-19.
3. This general worry has been pressed by Fred Dretske in "Reasons and Causes," a paper delivered at the Chapel Hill Philosophy Colloquium and a version of which appears in this volume; Ernest Sosa in "Mind-body Interaction and Supervenient Causation," *Midwest Studies* IX, P. French, *et. al.* (eds.) (University of Minnesota Press: Minneapolis, 1984), pp. 271-282; Fredrick Stoutland in "Oblique Causation and Reasons for Action," *Synthese* (1980), pp. 351-367; and Louise Antony in "Anomalous Monism and the Problem of Explanatory Force," unpublished manuscript. Ernest Le Pore and Barry Loewer, in "Mind Matters," *Journal of Philosophy* (1987), pp. 630-642, rightly point out that the 'levels of description' move is at least compatible with assigning causal relevance, of a sort, to mental properties. Specifically, mental properties might well prove causally relevant in the sense that they might pass an important counterfactual test; mental properties might be such that if some event did not have them, then it would not have had the effects it did. In another context, I've argued that this sort of relevance is insufficient to establish the explanatory credentials of disputed properties. See my "Moral Theory and Explanatory Impotence," *Midwest Studies* XII, P. French, *et. al.* (eds.) (University of Minnesota Press: Minneapolis, 1988), pp. 433-457.
4. The functionalism I rely on, unlike standard versions, does not assume that every type of mental state (nor even every type of belief and desire) can be fully specified in functional terms. Moreover, I steer clear of assuming that the relevant functional states can be specified noninten-

tionally. More about this follows.

5. Throughout this paper I shall be using 'wants' and 'desires' interchangeably (despite the mockery such a practice makes of the subtleties of the English language).

6. Where some option competes with the one apparently preferred if and only if the agent believes they cannot both be taken.

7. For this reason I think it a mistake to represent practical inferences from the first person point of view as always making reference to the fact that the agent wants something. Sometimes a person's reasons for acting have nothing to do with her wanting anything. See E.J. Bond's *Reason and Value*, (Cambridge: Cambridge University Press, 1983), and Stephen Darwall's *Impartial Reason*, (Ithaca: Cornell University Press, 1983).

8. Although action explanations invoke both beliefs and desires (wants), we often offer just one in explaining an action: to add more would be to belabor the obvious. Nonetheless, a non-enthymatic explanation will ascribe to her both beliefs and wants.

9. Buridan's ass stands still not because he is desireless, but because each of his desires is defeated by another—no occurrent want emerges. Of course, this terminological regimentation solves no puzzles (least of all the one posed by Buridan). It simply allows us to use the distinction between occurrent wants, and background wants (or desires), to capture motivation's equivalent of the distinction in moral theory between actual obligations and prima facie obligations.

10. Paul Churchland offers an argument in defense of the evaluative component in "The Logical Character of Action-Explanations," *Philosophical Review* 79 (1970), pp. 214-236.

11. Sometimes the belief attributed might only be a belief that the course of action is as good as any other. When this happens no explanation is given for the agent taking the actual course instead of one of the other equally attractive ones.

12. See Kolnai's "Deliberation is of Ends" in *Ethics, Value, and Reality* (Indianapolis: Hackett Publishing Co., 1978), pp. 44-62.

13. In some cases, say when doing something for its own sake, performing the action is not a means to some further end, but rather the end itself. So it would be misleading to characterize the relevant belief as a belief concerning the best means to some end. Hence my reliance on the more unusual phrase 'the best way to insure the realization of some end.'

14. Unlike Alvin Goldman, I shy away from holding that occurrent wants (or beliefs) are usually, let alone always, present to consciousness. In the process, I allow that we might be surprisingly ignorant of what we occurrently want (or believe), of what we are doing, and even of the fact that we are doing anything (for instance, competing with a friend, or undermining someone's confidence). See Goldman's *A Theory of Human Action*, (Princeton: Princeton University Press, 1970), pp. 86-88, 99, but also pp. 121-125 where he expresses reservations about occurrent wants always being conscious.

15. Often the most pernicious beliefs one has are those that influence our judgments subconsciously.
16. This raises some interesting difficulties for those who treat beliefs as reasons, since the relative influence of beliefs is largely independent of their justificatory force. See A.R. Mele, "*Akrasia*, Reasons, and Causes," *Philosophical Studies* 44 (1983), pp. 345-368.
17. G.H. von Wright, *Explanation and Understanding*, (Ithaca: Cornell University Press, 1971), p. 115. See also William Dray, *Laws and Explanation in History*, (Oxford: Clarendon Press, 1957).
18. Daniel Dennett, "Conditions of Personhood," in *Brainstorms* (Bradford Books, Montgomery, 1978), p. 271.
19. "True Believers: The Intentional Strategy and Why It Works," in *Scientific Explanation*, A.F. Heath (ed.), (Oxford University Press: Oxford, 1981), p. 68. Similarly, Davidson has held that "The limit placed on the social sciences is set not by nature, but by us when we decide to view men as rational agents with goals and purposes, and as subject to moral evaluation." "Psychology as Philosophy," in *Essays on Actions and Events* (Princeton University Press: Princeton, 1980), p. 239.
20. See for example G.E.M. Anscombe, *Intention*, (Ithaca: Cornell University Press, 1976).
21. Imagine, for example, that a respected art critic and dealer praises some work of mediocre quality done by his son. At least three plausible explanations are available for his aesthetic lapse. (1) The critic really likes the work, and would like it regardless of who the artist was. Or (2) The critic really likes the work, but largely because his love for his son has blinded him to its faults. Or, (3) the critic realizes the work is only of mediocre quality, but he praises it anyway so that he will not have to support his son. (Adding the third possible explanation, I have taken this example from D.C. Dennett's "Brain Writing and Mind Reading" in *Brainstorms*, *op. cit.*, pp. 39-50.) All three hypotheses may provide perfectly coherent accounts of the art critic's actual behavior. Yet they ascribe fundamentally different motives and beliefs to the critic, that in turn support significantly different counterfactual conditionals.
22. That this explanation attributes passivity, rather than action, to rocks, isn't important. People often do remain passive intentionally, and that is all that rocks are supposedly doing.
23. The Tin Foil Man example is William Lycan's. See his *Consciousness*, (Bradford Books, MIT Press: Cambridge, 1987). John Haugeland, in "The Mother of Intention," *Nous* 16, (1982) pp. 613-619, offers a nice discussion of these difficulties. Not surprisingly, though these criticisms are often made, their force is not universally acknowledged. Dennett responds to them, in "True Believers: The Intentional Strategy and Why It Works," *op. cit.*, primarily by emphasizing that a system must be very complex before the intentional stance recommends itself. He does, however, acknowledge that at least in the case of human behavior there are perfectly objective facts describable only from the intentional stance (pp. 25-29).

24. Whether we can legitimately talk here of *her* leaving surreptitiously is dubious since she has not done anything. For a discussion of the problems surrounding 'wayward causation' see Roderick Chisholm's "The Descriptive Element in the Concept of Action," *Journal of Philosophy* 61 (1964), pp. 613-625; Donald Davidson's "Freedom to Act," in *Essays on Actions and Events, op. cit.*, pp. 63-81; Gilbert Harman's "Practical Reasoning," *Review of Metaphysics* 29 (1976), pp. 431-463; and Irving Thalberg's "Do Our Intentions Cause Our Intentional Actions?", *American Philosophical Quarterly* 21 (1984), pp. 249-260.

25. This position is defended, for instance, by Fredrick Stoutland in "The Causal Theory of Action," in *Essays on Explanation and Understanding*, Manninen and R. Tuomela (eds.) (D. Reidel: Dorbrecht, 1976), pp. 351-367 and in "Davidson on Intentional Behavior," in *Actions and Events*, Ernest Le Pore and Brian McLaughlin (eds.) (Basil Blackwell: London, 1986), pp. 44-59.

26. See for instance Wilfrid Sellars' "Mental Events," *Philosophical Studies* 39 (1981), pp. 325-345; William Lycan's *Consciousness, op. cit.* and his *Judgment and Justification* (Cambridge University Press, 1988); Jerry Fodor's *Psychosemantics* (Bradford Books, MIT Press: Cambridge, 1987); and Dennis Stampe's "Towards a Causal Theory of Linguistic Representation," in *Midwest Studies* II, P. French, *et. al.* (eds.) (University of Minnesota Press: Minneapolis, 1977), pp. 81-102. Here I simply pass over well-known problems facing standard (i.e. causal) functionalism—most notably those that center on drawing a plausible distinction between narrow and wide content. See Lynne Rudder Baker's *Saving Belief* (Princeton University Press: Princeton, 1987).

27. See for example C.G. Hempel "Reasons and Covering Laws in Historical Explanation," *op. cit.*. If some such premise is presupposed by action explanations, then the strict analogy between action explanations and practical syllogisms won't hold since the covering-law will either not enter into the practical syllogism at all or else it will figure simply as the content of one of the agent's beliefs. Even so, if the agent is rational the action explanation will overlap with a description of the practical syllogism in a way that would preserve the relevance of an agent's reasons for acting.

28. See von Wright, *op. cit.*, as well as A. I. Melden's *Free Action*, (London: Routledge & Kegan Paul Ltd., 1961), Charles Taylor's *The Explanation of Behavior*, (London: Routledge & Kegan Paul Ltd., 1964), Richard Taylor's *Action and Purpose*, (Englewood Cliffs: Prentice-Hall Inc., 1966), and Alan White's *The Philosophy of Mind* (Random House: New York, 1967).

29. Alan White's *The Philosophy of Mind, op. cit.*, pp. 147-148.; see also Melden's *Free Action, op. cit.*, p. 53.

30. That this is what White has in mind is suggested by his writing "...we distinguish desires—e.g., a desire for X and a desire for Y-in terms of their possible effects and their potential fulfillments." *op. cit.*, p. 148. There is an important difference, though, between saying desires are distinguished by their possible effects and saying they are distinguished

by their potential fulfillments. The second claim seems to be what's relied on by the argument now under consideration. The first claim, in contrast, supports a distinct argument (the third one I will consider) for thinking there is a conceptual connection.

31. Whether what we have here are several actions or a single action under various descriptions is a ticklish issue, but not one that affects this argument. For a discussion of the issue, see Goldman, *op. cit.*, and Jennifer Hornsby's *Actions* (Routledge & Kegan Paul: London, 1980).

32. This is the position defended by Paul Churchland in "The Logical Structure of Action-Explanations," *op. cit.*.

33. See, for example, von Wright, *op. cit.*, pp. 93-118; Fredrick Stoutland, "The Logical Connection Argument," *American Philosophical Quarterly Monograph* 4 (Basil Blackwell: London, 1970), pp. 117-129; and Paul Churchland, "The Logical Structure of Action-Explanations," *op. cit.*. Just how intentions fit into the picture is not clear. It's tempting to equate intentions with appropriate belief-desire complexes. However, such an account has trouble explaining how we carry out plans and it has difficulty accommodating the fact that we might do intentionally either (or indeed both) of two actions we believe incompatible. See Michael Bratman's "Two Faces of Intention," *Philosophical Review* 93 (1984), pp. 375-405.

34. The claim that failure to form the appropriate intention constitutes conclusive evidence for the absence of at least one of the premises faces an obvious challenge. Cases may arise in which, despite the presence of the appropriate beliefs and wants, and the absence of any external hinderances, no action is forthcoming. Defenders of the Conceptual Connection Thesis can, quite legitimately, claim that the person's failure is (perhaps literally) one of nerve. The failure to act may be chalked up as a malfunction of his intentional system. In effect, then, the failure might reasonably be traced to a violation of the *ceteris paribus* clause which hovers over the link between intention and action.

35. Unfortunately, a positive account of this weak rationality requirement is elusive. Roughly, though, it stipulates that a person's occurrent wants and beliefs must combine in a way susceptible to being set out in an intelligible practical inference. Lacking a logic of practical inference, saying this is relatively unenlightening—still, we all probably, perhaps even necessarily, share a sense of what is an acceptable practical inference. There is an intimate, but I think surprisingly complex, relationship between intelligible practical inferences and Bayesian decision theory. Most of the complexities arise from the fundamental difference between the evaluative belief relevant to action explanations and a belief that has as its content simply a probability estimate.

36. There is always some worry that a philosopher's report of 'what we do' is a reconstruction and distortion that reflects philosophical prejudice rather than good sociology, so I find some consolation in knowing that Sherlock Holmes did as I say we do. In the "Musgrave Ritual" Holmes describes his method as follows: "I put myself in the man's place, and having first gauged his intelligence, I try to imagine how I should myself

have proceeded under the same circumstances." See *The Memoirs of Sherlock Holmes*, (A & W Publishers, Inc.: New York, 1975), p. 117.

37. Perhaps, though, we would stop ascribing beliefs and desires altogether if they were never useful in predicting peoples' behavior.

38. Aristotle II 7-10. Rather than doing justice to Aristotle's text, I take the terminology and cast the distinction so as to make my point (though I do hope not to abuse Aristotle's distinction). See Robert Bolton's "Essentialism and Semantic Theory in Aristotle," in *Philosophical Review* 85 (1976), pp. 514-544.

39. So construed, nominal definitions are not truth claims, not stipulative definitions, and not analytic explications; they are pragmatic devices used to pick things out for further investigation. They work as explanatory place holders indicating the sort of thing that must be invoked to complete an explanation.

40. I borrow this example from Churchland, *op. cit.*. Goldman uses it too, *op. cit.*.

41. For a defense of the informativeness of such explanations, see Elliott Sober's "Dispositions and Subjunctive Conditionals, or Dormative Virtues Are No Laughing Matter," *Philosophical Review* 91 (1982), pp. 591-596. An unflappable allegiance to Hume's Principle has led some to deny that functional explanations are causal explanations. For instance, W. Seager distinguishes functional from causal explanations specifically (and only) because functional explanations do not satisfy Hume's Principle. Consequently, Seager is committed to holding (unintuitively) that magnets don't cause iron filings to move. See Seager's "Functionalism, Qualia and Causation," *Mind* 92 (1983), pp. 174-188.

42. Here, of course, eliminative materialists will take exception. See, for instance, Paul Churchland's "Eliminative Materialism and Propositional Attitudes," *Journal of Philosophy* 78 (1981), pp. 67-90; and Stephen Stich's *From Folk Psychology to Cognitive Science* (Bradford Books, MIT Press; Cambridge, 1985). For a defense of (what might affectionately be called) retentive materialism, see "Folk Psychology is Here to Stay," by Terence Horgan and James Woodward, *Philosophical Review* 94 (1985), pp. 197-226; Lynne Rudder Baker's *Saving Belief, op. cit.*; and Jerry Fodor's *Psychosemantics, op. cit.*.

43. Daniel Dennett, "True Believers: The Intentional Strategy and Why It Works," in *The Intentional Stance* (Bradford Books, MIT Press; Cambridge, 1988), pp. 25-26. For a similar argument, see Hilary Putnam's "Philosophy and Our Mental Life" in *Mind, Language, and Reality*, (Cambridge: Cambridge University Press, 1975), pp. 291-303.

44. See John Haugeland's "The Nature and Plausibility of Cognitivism," *Behavioral and Brain Sciences* 1 (1978), pp. 215-226; and Hilary Putnam's "Philosophy and Our Mental Life," *op. cit.*.

45. This paper has been greatly improved thanks to comments and criticisms made by Walter Edelberg, Carl Hempel, Douglas Long, William Lycan, Nicholas Rescher, Wilfrid Sellars and Takashi Yagisawa.

Philosophical Perspectives, 3
Philosophy of Mind and Action Theory, 1989

ON A CAUSAL THEORY OF CONTENT

Lynne Rudder Baker
Middlebury College

The project of explaining intentional phenomena in terms of nonintentional phenomena has become a central task in the philosophy of mind.[1] Since intentional phenomena like believing, desiring, intending have *content* essentially, the project is one of showing how semantic properties like content can be reconciled with nonsemantic properties like cause. As Jerry A. Fodor put it,

> The worry about representation is above all that the semantic (and/or the intentional) will prove permanently recalcitrant to integration in the natural order; for example that the semantic/intentional properties of things will fail to supervene upon their physical properties.[2]

What is wanted is "a *naturalized* theory of meaning; a theory that articulates, in nonsemantic and nonintentional terms, sufficient conditions for one bit of the world to be *about* (to express, represent, or be true of) another bit." (p. 98)

My aim here is to examine Fodor's own response to the worry about representation, and to show that his Causal Theory of Content is not up to the task of naturalizing intentionality. Since Fodor's recent work is the most developed and most promising attempt to give an explicit solution to the "naturalization" problem, if I am right about that attempt, then very little headway has been made toward naturalizing intentionality in the intended sense.

Psychosemantics

Fodor offers a Representational Theory of Mind, according to which "to believe that *P* is to bear a certain relation to a token of a symbol which means that *P*."(p. 135) The immediate and pressing question is this: what makes a token mean that *p*? What makes a given token a 'red'-thought or a 'water'-thought?[3] More generally, how is the nonlogical, primitive vocabulary of the language of thought (Mentalese) to be interpreted? The task of psychosemantics is to specify sufficient conditions, in nonsemantical and nonintentional terms, for a given mental token to represent *A*.

Fodor begins by formulating a crude (and obviously false) view that he proceeds to refine: A symbol expresses a property, and its tokens denote the property, "if it's nomologically necessary that *all* and *only* instances of the property cause tokenings of the symbol."(p. 100)

Both the "only" and "all" clauses are then qualified. The "only" clause is modified to accommodate misrepresentation, and a necessary condition for "wildness" underwrites the modification: Only A's cause non-wild 'A'-tokenings. The "all" clause is restricted in application to observation terms. What is claimed for the resulting theory, the Slightly Less Crude Causal Theory of Content, is that

> it does what metaphysical skeptics about intentionality doubt
> *can* be done: it provides a sufficient condition for one part
> of the world to be semantically related to another part
> (specifically, for a certain mental representation to express a
> certain property); it does so in nonintentional,
> nonsemantical, nonteleological, and in general, non-question-
> begging vocabulary; and it's reasonably plausible....(p. 98)

Although I am no metaphysical skeptic about intentionality, I do not believe that the Slightly Less Crude Causal Theory of Content accomplishes what is claimed for it. In particular, I think that the "only" clause fails, because the account of misrepresentation or wildness actually applies to nothing; and I think that the "all" clause fails, because no psychophysically optimal conditions can be antecedently specified that guarantee that red instantiations produce 'red'-tokenings. I shall argue for these claims in the next two sections.

Misrepresentation

The tenet of the Crude Causal Theory that only A's cause 'A'-tokens leads straight to what Fodor calls 'the disjunction problem:' Suppose that horses reliably cause tokens of a certain type, but that sometimes cows cause tokens of that type. Although what we would like to say on such occasions is that a cow is misrepresented as a horse, what the "only" clause of the crude theory forces us to say is something else, something that eliminates the possibility of error: since cows as well as horses are sufficient to produce tokens of the given type, we must interpret the type as expressing not the property *horse*, but rather the disjunctive property *horse or cow*.[4] Since this has the consequence that misrepresentation of a cow as a horse is impossible, the "only" clause of the Crude Causal Theory must be modified.

To distinguish error from genuinely disjunctive properties, Fodor draws upon the observation that falsehoods are ontologically dependent upon truths. An instance of a B can cause an 'A'-tokening only when there is independently a semantic relation between A's and 'A'-tokenings; and the fact that a B causes an 'A'-tokening depends on the fact that A's cause 'A'-tokenings, but the fact that A's cause 'A'-tokenings does not depend on the fact that B's cause 'A'-tokenings. For example, a cow-caused token is a misrepresentation of a horse only if the fact that a cow causes the token depends on the fact that horses cause tokens of that type, but the fact that horses cause tokens of that type does not depend on the fact that a cow ever causes tokens of that type.

Thus, the causal connection between B's and 'A'-tokenings is asymmetrically dependent on the causal connection between A's and 'A'-tokenings. This seems to yield a necessary condition for misrepresentation, or wildness: "B-caused 'A'-tokenings are wild only if they are asymmetrically dependent upon non-B-caused 'A'-tokenings."(p. 108) Since the wild B-caused token would not have been an 'A'-token without an independent relation between A's and tokens of that type, a case of error without asymmetric dependence on truth would be a counterexample to this account of misrepresentation.[5]

Let us consider this account in light of a particular case. Suppose that, although there are many ordinary cats around, a certain person, *S*, learns a particular Mentalese symbol solely from artifacts (say, Putnam's robot-cats) that impinge on sensory surfaces in exactly the same way as cats.[6] Now (for the first time) *S* sees a real cat, which happens to be chasing a robot-cat. How should Fodor interpret the cat-caused token? His theory should apply to such a case, for S is in a world with the same fundamental physical laws as our world, and in a world in which reference is possible; the only difference between the imagined world and the actual world is a slight difference in environment—just the kind of difference to which reference is supposed to be responsive.

There seem to be three possibilities for interpreting the cat-caused token. Either (i) it is a correct representation of a cat (and the robot-caused tokens are misrepresentations of cats); or (ii) it is a misrepresentation of a robot-cat (and the robot-caused tokens are correct representations of robot-cats); or (iii) it is a correct representation of the disjunctive property *cat-or-robot-cat*.

(i) Suppose that the cat-caused token is a correct representation of a cat and the robot-caused tokens are misrepresentations of cats. Although this construal may seem implausible, Fodor explicitly allows it when he assumes that one can "learn 'horse' entirely from noninstances."(p. 109) So, for the moment, put aside qualms about what, on a Causal Theory, would make 'horse' the correct interpretation of a mental symbol whose tokening has never been caused by a horse and suppose that S has learned 'cat' entirely from noninstances. In that case, if Fodor's account is correct, there must be asymmetric dependence of the content of robot-caused tokens on the content of S's single cat-caused token. But as the story was told, the requisite dependence is missing; if there is any asymmetric dependence, it goes the other way. S's present disposition to apply 'cat' to a real cat depends upon her corresponding current disposition to apply it to robot-cats.[7] So, Fodor can not take the cat-caused token to be a representation of a cat.[8]

(ii) On the other hand, suppose that we interpret the robot-caused tokens as 'robot-cat'-tokens, and then say that the lone cat-caused token is a misrepresentation of robot-cats as cats. Not only does this move fly in the face of Fodor's assumption that one can learn a mental symbol entirely from noninstances, but also it opens Fodor up to the criticism that he leveled against Dretske (p. 104): this move ignores relevant counterfactuals. Since encounters with real cats, which are plentiful, would have produced the same type of tokens that were in fact produced by robot-cats, there seems to be no asymmetry whatever between tokens caused by cats and tokens caused by robot-cats, and hence no misrepresentation at all, on Fodor's account. The correlation that was established is "(not a nomological dependence of 'A's on A's but) a nomological dependence of 'A's on (A v B)s."(p. 104) In the case at hand, the correlation is between tokens of a certain type and (cats or robot-cats). It is simply an accident that the actual causes of *S*'s early representations were all robot-cats; representations of the same type would have been caused by real cats. So, consideration of counterfactuals suggests that we can not take the cat-caused token to be a misrepresentation of a robot-cat.

(iii) The symmetry between the cat-caused token and the robot-caused tokens just rekindles the disjunction problem. If cats and robot-cats are both sufficient for the causation of tokens of a certain type and if "symbols express the properties whose instantiations reliably cause them," then what tokens of that type must express is not the property *cat* (or the property *robot-cat*) but rather the disjunctive property *cat-or-robot-cat*. In that case, both the cat-caused and the robot-caused tokens are veridical after all—even when *S*, on subsequently discovering the difference between cats and robot-cats, exclaims, "I mistook that robot for a cat!" Fodor's account seems to preclude saying that *S* made an error, describable as mistaking a robot for a cat. We would have to say that her mistake was to think that she had made a mistake, and try (perhaps without success) to find some way to make sense of her "second-order" mistake. Since the same story could be told about any other mental symbol (at least any other mental symbol for nonobservables), this leaves us with no general account of misrepresentation.

The only way I see to reply is to confine the account of error to observation terms. In that case, no interpretation of the story about cats and robot-cats would impugn Fodor's account of error, because the account of error would not be taken to apply to natural kind terms anyway. However, this reply does not save the account of error in terms of asymmetric dependence.

First, the fact that Fodor develops his account of error with respect to 'horse' suggests that he wants it to apply more broadly than merely to cases concerning observation terms. Unless Fodor can find a way to develop an account of error for terms like 'cat' or 'horse,' it would seem that errors about cats and horses would have to be accounted for in terms of errors about more observable shapes, colors and so on. But in the cat/robot-cat case, there are no errors concerning such observables. So, confining the account of error to observation terms would still just leave us with no account of error for horses or cows.

Moreover, confining the account of error to observation terms—even if Fodor turned out to be right about observation terms—would have the effect of making the account of error apply to nothing at all. For Fodor builds an account of error (one not based on asymmetrical dependence) into his account of the semantics of observation terms. Fodor invokes psychophysics, which specifies in nonsemantic and nonintentional terms circumstances—e.g., the lighting is such and such, the visual system intact, and so on—in which observation terms are tokened. If S is in psychophysically optimal circumstances and *red* is instantiated, then by psychophysical law, S can not avoid producing a 'red'-token. The only source of error for observation terms is less-than-optimal circumstances; as Fodor describes psychophysics and its application to observation terms, we need no further account of error in terms of asymmetric dependence for observation terms.

Therefore, Fodor's account of misrepresentation solves no problems: For nonobservation terms, it leaves the disjunction problem in place and fails to provide a necessary condition for error, and for observation terms, it is otiose. But without an account of misrepresentation or wildness that has appropriate application, the change from the unmodified "only" clause of the Crude Causal Theory to the modified "only" clause of the Slightly Less Crude Causal Theory of Content has no effect. In the absence of a successful account of wildness, "Only A's cause nonwild 'A'-tokenings," or "All non-A-caused 'A'-tokenings are wild" is no better than "Only A's cause 'A'-tokenings," and the account remains inadequate.

Let me close this discussion of misrepresentation with a conjecture. Not only is the particular account of error in terms of an asymmetrical dependence on truth inadequate, but I believe that no such account, under the constraints imposed by the project of naturalizing intentionality, can succeed. My doubts stem from my suspicion that any such account entails a kind of type/type identity, which I think false.

To see how there can be error, Fodor says, "we need a difference between A-caused 'A'-tokenings and B-caused 'A'-tokenings that can be expressed in terms of nonintentional and nonsemantic properties of causal relations."[9] But if 'A'-tokenings are taken to represent A's, the question arises: What nonsemantic, nonintentional conditions make 'an 'A'-token' even a candidate as a description of the token caused by B? I suspect that the answer to this question leads straight into the arms of type/type identity.

To see why, consider Fodor's own description of the problem of error: "I see a cow which, stupidly, I misidentify. I take it, say, to be a horse. So taking it causes me to effect the tokening of a symbol; viz., I say 'horse.'"(p. 107) What does the error consist in? Fodor's answer is that there is "independently a semantic relation between 'horse'-tokenings and horses," and on this occasion a cow caused a 'horse'-tokening.

What nonintentional, nonsemantic conditions determine that the token caused on this occasion by a cow is a 'horse'-token? Whatever makes the Mentalese token a 'horse'-token can in no way depend on the English word 'horse' since a main point of psychosemantics is to show how mental tokens can represent without presupposing a public language. So if Fodor reports his token by saying in English, 'There's a horse,' that report is not constitutive of the error. Such a report is a semantic feature of the case, irrelevant under the constraints of psychosemantics. Furthermore, the fact that on this occasion, the cow looked like a horse to Fodor is an intentional feature and also is irrelevant.

So, in virtue of what is this cow-caused token a 'horse'-token? The only answer that I can think of in terms of nonsemantic and nonintentional conditions is this: (1) the causal relation previously established between horses and 'horse'-tokens was in fact a causal relation between horses and mental tokens of a nonsemantic type T; and (2) mental tokens of nonsemantic type T are 'horse'-tokens in virtue of this causal relation; and finally (3) the cow on this occasion caused a token of nonsemantic type T.

But if (1)—(3) give an accurate account of why the cow-caused token is a 'horse'-token, then Fodor's description of error commits him to a kind of type/type identity of the semantic and the nonsemantic. (1)—(3) entail type/type identity, because they entail that all tokens of a single semantic type (at least within an individual) are of a single nonsemantic type; what makes a token a 'horse'-token is that it is of a particular nonsemantic type caused by horses. But to suppose that all tokens that represent horses are of a single nonsemantic type is wildly implausible.[10]

Thus, we are left with no satisfactory account of misrepresentation. The notion of asymmetrical dependence of misrepresentation on accurate representation turned out to solve no problems, and, if my conjecture is correct, any account conforming to the constraints of psychosemantics will be committed to an implausible type/type identity theory. Therefore, I think that no account of error in terms of nonintentional and nonsemantic conditions is likely to succeed.

Local Color

The "all" clause of the Slightly Less Crude Causal Theory of Content, even when restricted to terms like 'red,' is no less flawed than the "only" clause.

For a certain class of mental symbols—so-called observation terms—Fodor claims that psychophysics, coupled with a Causal Theory of Content, solves the naturalization problem by providing "a plausible sufficient condition for certain symbols to express certain properties: viz., that tokenings of those symbols are connected to instantiations of the properties by psychophysical law."(p. 113)

Even if this is correct, Fodor points out, there is no obvious way to extend the naturalized account to nonobservation terms generally. Yet we need to be able to extend it "on pain of having the metaphysical worry that—excepting psychophysical concepts—*we have no idea at all* what a naturalized semantics would be like for the nonlogical vocabulary of Mentalese."(p. 118) I shall say little about Fodor's approach to extending naturalization to nonobservation terms; for I think that the difficulties arise right at the beginning.

In this section, I shall be concerned with the claim that the Causal Theory of Content, together with psychophysics, approximates a "complete solution to the naturalization problem" for a mind whose nonlogical vocabulary consists exclusively of observation terms like 'red.' In the next section, I shall consider the prospects for any project that relies on a comprehensive, context-free distinction between observation and nonobservation terms.

What psychosemantics needs are nonintentionally and nonsemantically specifiable sufficient conditions under which instantiations of *red* produce tokens that denote RED (or, equivalently, as I am using these terms, 'red'-tokens).

> All that matters is that there are concepts (Mentalese terms) whose tokenings are determined by psychophysical law; and that these concepts are plausibly viewed as expressing the properties upon which their tokening is thus lawfully

contingent; and that the psychophysical conditions for the tokenings of these concepts can be expressed in nonintentional and nonsemantical vocabulary.(p. 113-14)

It is not required, Fodor emphasizes, "that we view psychophysics as enunciating sufficient conditions for the fixation of *belief*"; the purpose will be served "if psychophysics enunciates sufficient conditions for the fixation of *appearances*."(p. 114) What one believes depends in part on the way things appear and in part on one's cognitive background.

> [Psychophysics] can't guarantee that you'll *believe* 'red there,' only that 'red there' will occur to you. But a guaranteed correlation between instances of red and tokenings of 'red there' in the occurs-to-me box will do perfectly nicely for the purposes of semantic naturalization; all semantics wants is *some* sort of nomologically sufficient conditions for instances of *red* to cause psychologically active tokenings of 'red.'(p. 114)

The claim, then, is that psychophysics specifies conditions in which instantiations of *red* appear red, or alternatively, conditions in which instantiations of *red* produce a token of 'red there.'

There is, I believe, a fundamental incoherence in this view, which elsewhere I have tried to bring out by thought experiments about molecular duplicates and their production of 'red'-tokens.[11] Here, I want to come at it from a different perspective—one more epistemic than semantic.

The basic epistemic difficulty, one that almost exactly parallels the basic semantic difficulty, can be illustrated by an example. So, to begin, consider three events on three possible worlds, which differ in local environmental conditions to be described shortly. There are no differences in physical laws among the worlds, only environmental differences that scientific laws should be able to accommodate. Let *S* be a sincere and competent English-speaking Earthian.

> Event 1: On Earth, in conditions psychophysically optimal on Earth, specified in terms of "wavelengths, candlepowers, retinal irradiations, and the like" *S* is placed in an empty room, with solid red walls.
> Event 2: On Mars, in conditions psychophysically optimal on

Mars, specified in terms of "wavelengths, candlepowers, retinal irradiations, and the like," S is placed in an empty room with solid green walls.

Event 3: On Venus, in conditions psychophysically optimal on Venus, specified in terms of "wavelengths, candlepowers, retinal irradiations, and the like," S is placed in an empty room with solid red walls.

Suppose that on Mars, atmospheric conditions transform light waves of the lengths that green objects on Earth reflect into waves of the lengths that red objects on Earth reflect. For example, if a green object is transported to Mars without any change in the object (such as painting it red), light reflected by that object on Mars has the same retinal effect as light reflected by red objects on Earth. Physical measurements reveal that light at the surface of the object on Mars is of the same wavelengths as light reflected by green objects on Earth, but that light 1 centimeter away from the object on Mars is of the same wavelengths as light reflected by red objects on Earth. Otherwise, Mars and Earth are similar. So, when S is placed in the green room on Mars, her visual system is affected in the way that it was when she was placed in the red room on Earth.

On Venus, by contrast, atmospheric conditions transform light waves of the lengths that red objects on Earth reflect into waves of the lengths that green objects on Earth reflect. For example, if a red object is transported to Venus without any change in the object (such as painting it green), light reflected by that object on Venus has the same retinal effect as light reflected by green objects on Earth. Physical measurements reveal that light at the surface of the object on Venus is of the same wavelengths as light reflected by red objects on Earth, but that light 1 centimeter away from the object on Venus is of the same wavelengths as light reflected by green objects on Earth. Otherwise, Venus and Earth are similar. So, when S is placed in the red room on Venus, her visual system is affected in the way that it would be if she were placed in a green room on Earth.

Now, ask: Do the walls appear the same to S on Earth and on Mars? On Earth and on Venus? In each case, one answer denies the Causal Theory of Content, and the other answer detaches appearances from internal physical states. I shall defer comment on an objection about optimal conditions until later; it will be easier to defuse the objection in light of attempts to answer these questions.

First, compare Earth and Mars. Do the walls appear the same to S on both? Suppose that the answer is yes. Then we would have to say that different causes (red instantiations and green instantiations) in optimal circumstances can produce the same appearances. In that case, we have a disjunction problem. For the token produced should not be interpreted as a 'red'-token, but as a 'red or green'-token. Even worse, in various other worlds, atmospheric conditions could transform wavelengths for blue, green, magenta or even wavelengths for Middle C into wavelengths produced by red things on Earth. Thus, there would be no limit on the different property instantiations sufficient in optimal conditions for the production of a token of a given physical type. However, to say that the interpretation of the token is as a 'red or green or magenta...or Middle C'-token is simply to say that we have no interpretation at all. The reappearance of the disjunction problem thus disables the Less Crude Casual Theory on this alternative.

So, suppose that the walls do not appear the same to S on both Earth and Mars. In the example, S is in the same internal physical state on Earth and Mars; her sensory stimulation is the same on both. Therefore, on this alternative a single internal state can subserve two types of appearances. Not only is this a violation of mind/brain supervenience, but also, since there are endless combinations of cause and atmospheric conditions in different worlds that would have the same sensory effects, a single internal state can subserve any appearance, on this alternative. Thus, neither answer to the question of whether the walls appear the same to S on Earth and Mars seems satisfactory.

Do the walls appear the same to S on Earth and Venus? Suppose that the answer is yes. Then since S's sensory stimulation on Venus is what it would be if produced in optimal conditions by green things on Earth, this answer, like the negative answer above, has the effect of detaching appearances from internal physical state. For on this alternative, different internal states subserve the same type of appearance. Again, endless combinations of cause and atmospheric conditions in various possible worlds would produce a single type of internal state. On this alternative, then, any internal state can subserve a given appearance.

So, suppose that the walls do not appear the same to S on Earth and on Venus. But since S is in optimal conditions on both, and red is instantiated on both, the putative psychophysical law must be false if the walls do not appear the same to S on both. This alternative thus becomes a straightforward counterexample to the Causal Theory of Content. Thus, neither answer to the question of whether the walls appear the same to S on Earth and Venus seems satisfactory. There simply seem to be no coherent answers to the questions of whether or not the walls appear the same to S on Earth and on Mars, on the one hand, and on Earth and on Venus, on the other.

There may seem to be an easy reply in terms of optimal conditions: Since my discussion relies on a difference in atmospheric conditions on Earth, Mars and Venus, perhaps we should make reference to atmospheric conditions in the specification of optimal conditions. There are two ways to incorporate atmospheric conditions: (i) we may continue to take 'optimal conditions' nonrigidly to refer to whatever conditions are optimal in a given world, or (ii) we may take 'optimal conditions' rigidly to refer to the conditions optimal on Earth.

(i) If we continue to relativize optimal conditions to world, then adding reference to atmospheric conditions makes no difference to the result of the discussion of Events 1, 2 and 3; for even though on this alternative, there is no single set of optimal conditions across possible worlds, for each Event, S is in optimal conditions in the world in which he is located. That is, on the nonrigid construal, since S is in atmospheric conditions optimal in each world, the objection that optimal conditions must include atmospheric conditions is just irrelevant to my point.

(ii) So, consider the rigid construal. Suppose that the only psychophysically relevant conditions are those that are optimal on Earth. I think that this construal is unsatisfactory for two reasons. First, it would entail, implausibly, that psychophysically optimal conditions never obtain on Mars. In any case, we need not go to Mars to see the implausibility of taking conditions that never obtain to be optimal. Suppose that, as a result of pollution, Earth's atmosphere changed in such a way that objects that formerly reflected light of green wavelengths then reflected light of red wavelengths. Suppose that 50,000 years later, scientists took the prevailing conditions to be optimal and formulated (what they took to be) psychophysical laws that were as well-confirmed as psychophysical laws are today. But if optimal conditions are those that are now optimal on Earth, as the rigid construal supposes, then psychophysics on future Earth would be impossible; for optimal conditions on future Earth, on the rigid construal, would simply never obtain. To suppose that there can be no psychophysics in such environmentally-altered circumstances seems to me a kind of planetary and temporal chauvinism.[12]

Second, the rigid construal of 'optimal conditions' in effect gives up the Causal Theory by reducing it to the role of a reference fixer. Here is the reason: The Causal Theory of Content is supposed to be a general theory of 'aboutness,' a phenomenon not confined to Earth. So, even if we take optimal conditions rigidly to be those optimal on Earth (including atmosphere), we still must be able to make comparisons between Earth and Mars. On this construal, do the walls appear the same to S on Earth and on Mars? If not, then (again) appearances get detached from internal states. So assume that the walls on Earth and on Mars *do* appear the same to S. The reason would be this: S is in the same internal sensory state on Mars that she would be on Earth when her mental token on Earth is a 'red'-token. But if S has the same appearances on Earth and on Mars on this rigid construal of 'optimal conditions,' the theoretical work would be done by type-type identity: Without type-type identity, there would be no grounds for supposing that the green instantiation on Mars produced a red appearance. What makes an appearance a 'red'-appearance, on this alternative, is its physical type, not its causal history.

Compare: we can fix the referent of 'water' by properties like being wet, being drinkable, and so on. But what determines that a particular liquid is water are not these properties at all, but its being a sample of a certain chemical type, H_2O, as opposed to a sample of the equally wet and drinkable XYZ. Similarly, on the alternative under consideration, what determines that an appearance is red is its being of a certain physical type. For example, we say that the grey-caused token on Mars is a 'red'-token only because of physical similarities between it and 'red'-tokens on Earth. Invocation of causal histories of tokens of that physical type in optimal circumstances merely serves to pick out the relevant physical type. Since content here is determined by physical type, not causal history, this alternative just abandons the Causal Theory of Content.

Thus, the objection concerning optimal conditions does not affect my argument on the nonrigid construal, and leads away from a Causal Theory of Content on the rigid construal. From the point of view of the Book of Nature, the conditions that we select as optimal seem to have no special status anyway. Insofar as a psychophysical law is written in the Book of Nature, its antecedent is an infinitely long disjunction of causes and conditions, one disjunct of which is of particular interest to us and is singled out as specifying conditions that are optimal. There is the same lawlike connection between red walls, one kind of light, and production of tokens of a certain type, on the one hand, as there is between green walls, a different kind of light, and production of tokens of the same type, on the other. Nomologically speaking, these are on a par. Conditions are optimal relative to our interests; optimality is not given by nature.

Why is the Causal Theory of Content unable to deliver answers to questions about the way the walls appear to *S*? The reason, I think, is that the Causal Theory implicitly employs two criteria for identity of appearances:

(A1) Same environmental causes (in optimal circumstances) --> same appearances.

(A2) Same sensory effects (in optimal circumstances) --> same appearances.

(A1) and (A2) could peacefully co-exist if any two appearances that were counted as the same according to one were counted as the same according to the other. But in trying to answer the questions about how the walls in Events 1, 2, and 3 appeared to *S*, we have seen that (A1) and (A2) come apart. Since their implicit conjunction leads to incoherence, perhaps we should just abandon one of them.

To give up (A1) would be to give up the Causal Theory of Content. For if we gave up (A1) in favor of (A2), we should say that the walls on Earth and on Mars appeared the same, because they have the same sensory effects. But different color properties were instantiated (even in optimal conditions) on Earth and on Mars. Therefore, on this alternative, types of appearance are not even correlated with types of causes in optimal circumstances, and *red* instantiations/*green* instantiations do not determine different appearances (red appearances/green appearances).

However, to give up (A2) would also be unpromising from the point of view of the naturalization problem. If we gave up (A2) in favor of (A1), we should say that the walls on Earth and on Venus appeared the same to *S*. But consider *S*'s point of view. This second alternative requires us either to disregard *S*'s point of view altogether, or to take what a sincere and competent speaker says to be *no* evidence of the way things appear to her; in either case, it cuts thought totally off from public language.

To see this, suppose that we asked S to compare how the walls appeared to her on Earth and on Venus. She would reply that on Earth the room appeared red to her. Since on Venus, the red room impinged on S's senses in the same way as a green room would on Earth, she would say that on Venus, the walls appeared green to her. Even if informed of the different color property instantiations and the differences in atmosphere, when asked how the rooms in each case appeared, she would still respond that they looked different on Earth and on Venus—just as an expert on refraction would say that the stick in water still *looked* crooked. However, on the option of giving up (A2) and retaining (A1), it follows that 'red there' in Mentalese occurred to S on Venus, despite the fact that she is a competent English speaker who insists that 'green there' occurred to her.

It is important to see that the difficulty here has nothing to do with any assumptions about incorrigibility. S is not exactly making a mistake about the way that she is being appeared to. Rather, her thought-token receives incompatible interpretations: 'red there' in Mentalese and 'green there' in English. Perhaps, alternatively, we could say that she is thinking two incompatible thought-tokens at once. Either way, there is an incoherence between Mentalese and English; different properties are being represented simultaneously. Unless this incoherence can be overcome (and I do not see how it can be), on the Causal Theory of Content, we must disregard all the subject's testimony.[13]

A corollary of this (still assuming that we give up (A2) in favor of (A1)) is that we all lack verbal access to what occurs to us, to the ways that things appear to us; our reports and any thoughts that we can put into words are no evidence at all as to the actual character of the way that things appear. Such a view would make the relations between spoken language and thought a total mystery. How could language be the expression of thought, as Fodor says it is, if the theory of thinking forces us to say that things appear red to a sincere and competent speaker of English who says that they appear not red, but green?

And to hold on to the Causal Theory of Content at the cost of saying that, his denials notwithstanding, the walls appear red to S vitiates Fodor's entire discussion in which he replaces Mentalese with English as the language of thought. In his attempt to solve the disjunction problem, Fodor says that he sets it up, "as it happens, for a token of English rather than a token of Mentalese; but none of the following turns on that."(P107) But if we lack verbal access to our Mentalese tokens—if 'red there' can occur to us when we would swear that 'green there' occurs to us—a lot turns on the substitution of English tokens for Mentalese tokens. The shift from Mentalese to English is thus far from innocent.[14]

Let me note two further consequences of giving up (A2): (1) any internal perceptual state could subserve any appearance whatsoever. (See initial discussion of Events 1, 2, and 3.) This makes internal physical state almost irrelevant to 'red'-tokenings.[15] (2) It seems that no contentful state ever supervenes on the brain. If, as Fodor argues (p. 33-44), causal powers do supervene on the brain, we seem to have the further consequence that causal powers and content swing free of each other.[16]

Before making a final determination that the conjunction of (A1) and (A2) leads to incoherence, let us consider a re-description of the cases. If we take optimal conditions to be those in which things appear the way that they are, we could re-describe the Event on Mars (and similarly the Event on Venus) in one of three ways: (a) We could take the walls on Mars to be green and S to be in optimal conditions, and then conclude that S's appearance was green. But this interpretation violates mind/brain supervenience by detaching internal state from appearance, and disregards S's point of view altogether—in the same way that we saw when we considered giving up (A2) below.

(b) We could take the walls on Mars to be green and S's appearance to be red, and then conclude that the conditions are not optimal. However, this suggestion allows conditions that *never* obtain to be optimal. Such a result would be unsatisfactory for reasons given in discussing the rigid construal of 'optimal conditions.'

(c) We could take S to be in optimal conditions on Mars and S to have a red appearance, and then conclude that the walls on Mars are red. Since light measured at the surface of the walls on Mars reflected wavelengths of green, this suggestion would detach the color of the walls from their reflective properties. Perhaps, then, one would hold that colors of objects are determined by their reflective properties *together with* atmospheric conditions. But suppose that the Martian atmosphere is intermittently polluted in such a way that colors look different on some days than on others (as actually happens on Earth). In that case, the current suggestion, which takes atmosphere as a determinant of actual color of objects rather than as a condition that may or may not be optimal for viewing would force us to say that the actual colors of objects, not just how the objects look, change from day to day. I do not think that we understand color in this way, nor do I think that we would if Earth's atmosphere were like Mars' supposed atmosphere.[17]

It seems, then, that although the conjunction of (A1) and (A2) leads to incoherence, the Causal Theory of Content can not dispense with either one.[18] Since the problems are perfectly general, it would be wrong to suppose that since contexts often do affect brain states, the difficulties raised here may be confined to "funny cases," as Fodor suggests (p. 159, 10n); for they arise with respect to 'red' or any other so-called observation term.

For these reasons, I do not believe that the Causal Theory of Content, coupled with psychophysics, has begun to solve the naturalization problem for observation terms, as Fodor formulates it. Therefore, it seems that neither the modified "all" clause nor the modified "only" clause of the Slightly Less Crude Causal Theory of Content can deliver what is claimed for it.

Saving Appearances?

Is a comprehensive, context-free distinction between observation and nonobservation terms a viable basis for any semantic theory? I am doubtful. For it is not even clear that 'red' is an instance of a semantically special type of term, a class that is supposed to include other terms traditionally linked to sensory experience and to exclude terms like 'water' whose interpretations are less directly accessible to the senses. On the one hand, comparison of 'red' with observationally equivalent observation terms 'magenta' and 'Middle C' shows that what is to distinguish 'red' as an observation term does not hold in the case of the other terms. On the other hand, comparison of 'red' with a nonobservation term like 'water' reveals an important semantic symmetry. Thus, the claim that there is a special class of observation terms and "the idea that the semantics of observation terms is somehow at the core of the theory of meaning"(p. 114) are not borne out.

What is supposed to distinguish terms like 'red' as observation terms?

> [W]hat makes RED special—what makes it a 'psychophysical concept' within the meaning of the act—is that the difference between merely seeing something red and succeeding in seeing it *as* red vanishes when the observer's point of view is psychophysically optimal. You can't—or so I claim—see something red under psychophysically optimal viewing conditions and *not* see it as red.

The Venus case has already given reason to be skeptical of this: under psychophysically optimal viewing conditions on Venus, our subject saw red things, but did not see them *as* red. But I don't want to press this as a counterexample so much as to point out that there is no temptation to generalize Fodor's claim about 'red' to terms less familiar but equally accessible, observationally speaking—terms that should be on a par with 'red' from the point of view of psychophysical law. In exactly the same sense that sufficient conditions for a token's being a 'red'-token can be specified, sufficient conditions for a token's being a 'magenta'-token or a 'Middle C'-token can be specified.

To paraphrase Fodor: there are circumstances such that magenta instantiations control a certain kind of tokening whenever those circumstances obtain; and it's plausible that 'magenta' expresses the property *magenta* in virtue of the fact that magenta instantiations cause tokenings of that kind in those circumstances; and the circumstances are nonsemantically, nonteleologically, and nonintentionally specifiable.(p. 112) Nevertheless, one could be covered by the relevant psychophysical law, see something magenta in the relevant circumstances and still not see it as magenta. I suspect that infants with intact visual systems can see magenta without having the concept MAGENTA.

Similarly, for Middle C. Middle C ought to be susceptible to psychophysical law in the same sense as red is; but to hear a tone *as* Middle C, even if one has "perfect pitch," requires a good deal of auxiliary information beyond what is immediately available in the nonintentionally and nonsemantically described perceptual circumstances. At the least, the disappearance, under optimal circumstances, of a distinction between seeing and seeing-as does not seems to distinguish "psychophysical concepts" from others. Moreover, since there is no reason to think that the concept RED is any less embedded in a system of concepts than is the concept MAGENTA or the concept MIDDLE C, it is not even clear that the distinction between seeing and seeing-as vanishes in the case of RED.

On the other hand, the similarity between 'red' and 'water' is immediately apparent. Molecular duplicates on Earth and on Twin Earth have different concepts: one of WATER and the other of WATER2, by virtue of environmental differences. Molecular duplicates on Earth and on Mars have different concepts: one of RED and the other of GREEN, by virtue of environmental differences (on one reading). The molecular duplicates on Earth and Twin Earth have the same causal powers; the molecular duplicates on Earth and Mars have the same causal powers. 'Red'-tokens are no closer to being "self-interpreting" than are 'water'-tokens. So, there does not seem to be a semantically special class of observation terms anyway; on one side, 'red' does not seem relevantly different from the nonobservation term 'water', and on the other side, what is supposed to make observation terms special clearly does not apply to most so-called observation terms—if it applies to any at all.

If the naturalization problem, under the constraints set out by Fodor, is a problem at all, it thus seems unlikely to be solvable by appeal to a general, context-free distinction between observation terms and other terms. So, if the naturalization problem as it has been recently conceived is genuinely a problem, I believe that we remain at a loss for a solution.[19]

Notes

1. See, for example, Dretske (1981); Stalnaker (1984); Block (1986); and Fodor (1987). Hereafter, references to the latter will be given in the text as 'p.' followed by a page number.
2. Fodor (1984): p. 232.
3. Fodor's usage of a key term is inconsistent. Is "A'-tokening' a semantic characterization that identifies the token in terms of its semantic type (interpretation)? Do 'A'-tokens represent A's? Sometimes yes, sometimes no. On the one hand, when Fodor says that only A's cause (nonwild) 'A'-tokens, the "A'-tokens' is a semantic characterization of tokens as representing A's. And he clearly uses "horse'-tokening' in such a way that 'horse'-tokenings represent horses, and similarly for 'red'-tokenings. On the other hand Fodor sometimes assumes that it is an open questions as to what properties 'A'-tokenings represent; he wants to distinguish the case in which 'A' expresses the property of being A (and hence B-caused 'A'-tokens misrepresent) from the case in which 'A' expresses the property of being A or B (and hence B-caused 'A'-tokens are veridical).(p. 101-102) (I think that it would be less misleading to express the distinction as one between 'A'-tokens and 'A or B'-tokens and to take 'A'-tokens as always representing A's.)

4. Following Fodor, I shall italicize names of properties (the property *red*), put names of concepts in all capitals (the concept RED). "RED is the concept which denotes (or expresses) *red*; and 'red' is a term (either of English or Mentalese) that encodes that concept."(p. 160 5n) On Fodor's view, concepts are expressions of Mentalese. The content of a symbol, as I am using the terms, is what it expresses or denotes or represents.

5. Fodor speaks of the asymmetric dependence of misrepresentation on *truth*; perhaps 'the asymmetric dependence of misrepresentation on accurate representation' would be better.

6. Putnam (1975): 238.

7. Fodor replies to an objection about learning 'horse' from noninstances (cows, say), in a way that requires him to distinguish (as Dretske also must) between training period and mastery period. As Fodor points out in his criticism of Dretske, it is far from clear that there is a principled distinction between the two periods. In any case, the example of the robot case can not be avoided by Fodor's reply to the cited objection. See Fodor's discussion of current dispositions (p. 109).

8. Bernard Kobes pointed out that there is room for asymmetric dependence if we assume that, on the basis of his participation in linguistic and other community practices, *S* learned the concept CAT even though she had only been exposed to robot-cats. Although I think that this is plausible, I do not think that it is available to Fodor. Since on Fodor's view, the meaning of public language is dependent on the meaning of mental representations, invocation of interpreted public language at the ground level of his account of the semantics of mental representation would be viciously circular.

9. P. 106. If, in this context, 'A'-tokenings need not be misrepresentations at all.

10. See, for example, Baker (1987), (1987b).

11. Again see Baker (1987), (1987b).

12. Moreover, referring to Earth's atmosphere in the specification of sufficient conditions would not guarantee that we had truly sufficient conditions anyway. For we could imagine that the inhabitants of all three planets always (even when they are doing their science) wear certain kinds of glasses, but that the glasses have different properties on the different planets. On Earth, they have no effect; on Mars, they transform waves of lengths that green objects on Earth reflect to waves of lengths that red objects on Earth reflect; on Venus, they transform waves of lengths that red objects on Earth reflect to waves of lengths that green objects on Earth reflect. It is implausible to suppose that we could formulate a law that anticipates all the conditions in which same causes produce different effects.

13. Although similar to a kind of converse of Kripke's puzzle about belief, the issues raised here are different. At least as David Lewis sees it, if beliefs are not narrow, Kripke's puzzle vanishes; however, the difficulty raised here does not. Kripke (1979); Lewis (1981): p. 288.

14. It is thus incoherent to say that " 'red' is a term (*either in English or Mentalese*) that encodes [the concept RED]." (p. 160, 5n; my emphasis)

15. For a discussion of related issues, see Pereboom (forthcoming).
16. One source of difficulty is that for (almost?) any specifiable context, there is a larger context that can embed the specified context and alter its effects. So, even if we can specify conditions in which an X-instantiation reliably produces an X-appearance or an 'X'-token, appeal to the counterfactual-supporting properties of causal statements licenses consideration of a larger set of conditions (which encompass the original set) in which it is implausible or even incoherent to claim that an X-instantiation produces an X-appearance. Although my argument calls into question all forms of mind/brain supervenience, as long as minds are characterized by intentional states like belief, it does not apply to the kind of "weak supervenience" that John Haugeland (1982) has advocated.
17. Bernard Kobes suggested re-description of the cases along the lines of (c).
18. Since I think that variants of (A1) and (A2) both have great intuitive appeal, I think that the conflict presented here is evidence of a deep problem, one that I do not yet know how to resolve. My point here is only that the Causal Theory of Content, which tends to pull away from mind/brain supervenience, is no solution.
19. I read versions of this paper at the University of Massachusetts at Amherst and at Arizona State University, where I received incisive comments, especially from Gary Hardegree, Gareth B. Matthews, Bernard Kobes, Gregory Fitch and Theodore Guleserian. I also wish to thank Hilary Kornblith for helping to improve an earlier draft and to acknowledge the Middlebury College Faculty Research Fund for support of this work.

References

Baker, Lynne Rudder (1987), "Content by Courtesy," *Journal of Philosophy* 84: 197-213.

Baker, Lynne Rudder (1988), *Saving Belief* (Princeton: Princeton University Press).

Block, Ned (1986), "Advertisement for a Semantics for Psychology," in *Studies in the Philosophy of Mind* (Midwest Studies in Philosophy, Vol. X), Peter A. French, Theodore E. Uehling, Jr., Howard K. Wettstein, eds. (Minneapolis: University of Minnesota): 615-678.

Dretske, Fred I. (1981), *Knowledge and the Flow of Information* (Cambridge, Mass: MIT/Bradford).

Fodor, Jerry A. (1984), "Semantics Wisconsin Style," *Synthese* 59: 231-250.

Fodor, Jerry A. (1987), *Psychosemantics* (Cambridge, Mass: MIT/Bradford).

Haugeland, John (1982), "Weak Supervenience," *American Philosophical Quarterly* 19: 93-103.

Kripke, Saul A. (1979), "A Puzzle About Belief," in *Meaning and Use*, Avishai Margalit, ed. (Dordrecht/Holland: D. Reidel Publishing Co.): 239-283.

Lewis, David (1981), "What Puzzling Pierre Does Not Believe," *Australasian Journal of Philosophy* 59 (1981): 283-289.

Pereboom, Derk (forthcoming), "Why a Realist Cannot Be a Functionalist."

Putnam, Hilary (1975), "It Ain't Necessarily So" in *Mathematics, Matter and Method: Philosophical Papers, Vol. I* (Cambridge, Cambridge University): 237-249

Stalnaker, Robert C. (1984), *Inquiry* (Cambridge, Mass: MIT/Bradford).

Philosophical Perspectives, 3
Philosophy of Mind and Action Theory, 1989

NEO-FREGEAN THOUGHTS

Steven E. Boër
The Ohio State University

0. Introduction: Neo-Fregeanism and object-dependent thought

Following the Russellian tradition, let us use the term 'singular thoughts' for thoughts of the sort that an L-speaking person S would conventionally express in a context c by uttering a sentence of L having the logical form '$F(t_1,...,t_n)$', in which each of 't_1',...,'t_n' is either a purely designational (i.e., non-attributive) name in L for some object or a deictic demonstrative phrase referring in c to some object. In recent years the so-called British neo-Fregeans[1] have revived the Russellian idea that S's singular thoughts are, unlike "general", "descriptive" thoughts, so intimately about their objects (for Russell: the sense-data referred to by 't_1',...,'t_n') as to be impossible for S to entertain in the absence of those objects. On the one hand, this idea about the essentially "contextual", "not-purely-conceptual", "*de re*" character of such thoughts has been daringly extended to include singular thoughts about contingent, extra-mental objects other than oneself and the present moment. On the other hand, the idea has been reconciled with the Fregean picture of thinking as a dyadic relation between a person and a proposition (construed as a structured entity composed of modes of presentation and possessing an absolute truth-value) by discerning in singular thoughts tokens of allegedly "object-dependent" or "*de re*" *types* of mode of presentation. These *de re* types are essentially context-bound ways of thinking of objects which are available to (can be tokened by) a subject S for thinking about a particular object x only in contexts where x exists and bears a certain special contextual (e.g., perceptual) relation to S, that relation being constitutive of the type in question.

The result of these moves is the distinctive neo-Fregean position according to which: (I) all thinking involves having genuinely *propositional* attitudes; (II) there are two possible kinds of propositional contents, those which involve *de re* modes of presentation and those which do not; (III) purely designational names and deictic demonstrative phrases are conventionally associated with such *de re* types of mode of presentation, tokens of these *term-types* having as their senses in a given context tokens (if such are available in that context) of the associated type of mode of presentation; (IV) 'that'-clauses designate propositions containing the senses of their ingredient words. Two particular conclusions about object-dependent thoughts follow from (I)-(IV) viz.,

> (ODT-1)   Singular perceptual-demonstrative thoughts are a species of object-dependent thoughts.

and

> (ODT-2)   The beliefs and other attitudes ascribed to people in English by means of 'that'-clauses containing nonempty, designationally used proper names are a species of object-dependent thoughts.

Both conclusions are *prima facie* counterintuitive, a fact which poses a major obstacle to accepting the Neo-Fregean position.

The aim of this paper is to remove this obstacle in three steps: first, to rehearse some independent motivation for accepting (ODT-1) and (ODT-2); second, to show how a neo-Fregean might handle some related problems about empty terms; and third, to undermine two rival accounts of perceptual-demonstrative thoughts which reject (ODT-1).[2]

1. Motivation

1.1. An argument for (ODT-1)

Let us begin with a modified version of Gareth Evans' "Argument from Understanding".[3] For technical reasons having to do with indexicality and the employment of substitutional quantification, the argument will be presented as a schematic piece of *first-person* reasoning which the reader is invited to instantiate upon being addressed by any person S with a remark of the form 'That G is F' such that (a) 'that G' is employed by S in the familiar "perception-based" way and (b) the reader *understands* the remark in question. One then proceeds to reason as follows.

Since I do understand S's remark, and since both

(1) The hearer H cannot understand S's (referentially intended perception-based) remark 'That G is F' unless H possesses, and brings to bear upon the interpretation of S's remark, the perceptual information '$G_1,...,G_n$' about the (appearance of) the shared environment invoked by S's use of 'that G'.

and

(2) In order for H to bring to bear this perceptual information upon the interpretation of S's remark, H must use this information to *justify* H's belief that

(2a) If what S says is true, then $(\exists x)(G_1 x \, \&...\& \, G_n x \, \& \, Fx)$

independently of any justification that H might have for believing that $(\exists x)(G_1 x \, \&...\& \, G_n x \, \& \, Fx)$ or for believing that what S says is not true.,

I must have appropriate justification for *my* belief that (2a). This justification could only reside in my tacitly reasoning in a way relevantly like (i)-(vi) below (where 'c' is to be thought of as having been replaced by my specification of the current context of S's utterance and 't' by whatever singular term of my idiolect actually figures in my tacit reasoning):

(i) True(What S expressed in c by 'F(that G)') [Supposition]

(ii) True(What S expressed in c by 'F(that G)') $\longleftrightarrow$ $(\exists x)(x =$ What S referred to in c by 'that G' $\& \, Fx)$ [semantic premiss]

(iii) $(\exists x)(x =$ What S referred to in c by 'that G' $\& \, Fx)$ [from (i) and (ii)]

(iv) $G_1 t \, \&...\& \, G_n t$ [perceptual premiss]

(v) $t =$ What S referred to in c by 'that G' [pragmatic premiss]

(vi) $(\exists x)(G_1 x \, \&...\& \, G_n x \, \& \, Fx)$ [from (iii)-(v)]

Moreover, I accept the principle that

(P1) For any person H, if H is justified in a certain belief and H's justification is essentially based upon a certain argument, then every premiss H uses in that argument must express a proposition which H believes.

To which, *provided that all starred quantifiers below are construed substitutionally with respect to the singular terms of my idiolect*, I may harmlessly add the following plausible principles (where, of course, 't' is replaced by that singular term of my idiolect which actually figures in (v) above):

(P2) If my premiss (v) expresses a proposition p which I believe, then, I believe that t = What S referred to in c by 'that G'.[4]

(P3) If I believe that t = What S referred to in c by 'that G', then for some* x, I believe that x = What S referred to in c by 'that G'.

But if my justification for believing (2a) essentially consists in (i)-(vi), then it follows from (P1)-(P3) that, for some* x, the belief which I express by (v) must be a belief that x = what S referred to in c by 'that G'. I conclude that

(3) I cannot come justifiably to believe that (2a) unless, for some* x, I believe that S is referring to x.

From (1)-(3) it trivially follows that

(4) I cannot understand S's referential remark 'That G is F' unless, for some* x, I believe that S is referring to x.

Adopting some obvious abbreviations, reading '$==>$' and '$<==>$' respectively as strict implication and strict equivalence, and restricting the range of propositional variables to exclude higher-order propositions about the semantic properties of propositions (e.g., their truth-values, entailments, etc.), I obtain, as corollary to (4):

(5) $(p)\{p$ is true $==> \{[K_Ip <==> U_I(S$'s remark 'That G is F')] $==> [K_Ip ==> (\exists^*x)B_I(S$ is referring to $x)]\}\}$

I now assume for *reductio*:

(6) POSSIBLY$\{ \sim(\exists x)(S$ is referring to $x) \& (\exists q)[S$'s remark 'That G is F' says that q]$\}$.

I am entitled to claim that

(7) $\{(6) ==> (\exists p)[p$ is true & $[K_lp <==> U_l(S$'s remark 'That G is F')]]\}$,

as may be seen by simply letting p be the proposition that S's remark 'That G is F' says that q.[5] And so I may conclude from (6) and (7) that

(8) $(\exists p)[p$ is true & $[K_lp <==> U_l(S$'s referential remark 'That G is F')]].

And from (8), (5), and (6) it follows that

(9) $(\exists p)\{p$ is true & $[K_lp ==> (\exists^*x)B_l(S$ is referring to $x)]\}$ & $\sim(\exists x)(S$ is referring to $x)$,

which, given the entirely plausible suppressed premiss

(10) $[(\exists^*x)B_l(S$ is referring to $x)]$ & $\sim(\exists x)(S$ is referring to $x)]$ $==> (\exists p)[p$ is false & $B_l(p)]$,

implies

(11) $(\exists p_1)[p_1$ is true & $(K_lp_1 ==> (\exists p_2)(p_2$ is false & $B_lp2))]$.

Invoking what Evans rather grandly calls the "axiom of the seamlessness of truth", viz. (12):[6]

(12) $\sim(\exists y)(\exists p_1)[p_1$ is true & $(K_yp_1 ==> (\exists p_2)(p_2$ is false & $B_yp_2))]$,

I infer from the ensuing contradiction with (11) the falsity of (6), i.e.,

(13) $\sim$POSSIBLY$\{\sim(\exists x)(S$ is referring to $x)$ & $(\exists q)[S$'s remark 'That G is F' says that q]$\}$;

or, equivalently:

(14) Necessarily, if nothing is referred to in S's referentially intended remark 'That G is F', then S's remark expresses no thought.

Since I am applying the foregoing considerations to a remark which I understand, and since by (14) there would be nothing for me to understand if there were no referent, I conclude that S's utterance expresses a thought which is object-dependent. [End of Argument-Schema]

By repeatedly applying the argument schema to perceptual-demonstrative remarks which one understands, one can convince oneself that (ODT-1) holds in at least these cases. This fact would seem to support, as an inference to the best explanation, concluding that (ODT-1) holds in general.

1.2. An argument for (ODT-2) yielding (ODT-1) as a corollary

We now turn to a broader argument which delivers both (ODT-1) and (ODT-2). The argument depends in part upon the following popular thesis about proper names, the reasons for which are too familiar to require rehearsal here:

> A nonempty proper name is an obstinately[7] rigid designator—i.e., it denotes its actual-world referent with respect to *every* possible world, regardless of whether that object happens to exist there.

Before presenting the case for (ODT-2), some technical preliminaries are in order. Let us treat an *utterance-context* as an ordered n-tuple consisting of a world, an utterer, a time, a place and whatever other coordinates are deemed salient; since for present purposes only the world-coordinate W really matters, we can represent utterance-contexts in the abbreviated style '$<W,...>$'. Now a standard way to think, in the abstract, of an interpreted indicative language (or language-fragment) L is to take L as a function from some antecedently specified set of sentences (the sentences of L) such that, for each s in the set, $L(s)$ is a (possibly partial) function from utterance-contexts to propositions. (Textbooks in Linguistics commonly speak of languages as "devices for pairing meanings and sound sequences".)

Now let L_E be the indicative fragment of English and consider the following sentence of L_E:

(*) There is an object which, necessarily, is Neptune.

Since, either here or in some other world, this sentence might belong to various different languages, let us write '(*L)', for variable L, as a way of referring to (*) *qua* sentence of interpreted indicative language L. Now for the argument.[8]

Let W be any world in which Neptune does not exist and $L_1,...,$ L_n be the languages (if any) spoken by denizens of W (if any). Then the sentence (*L_E), as hypothetically uttered in context $<W,...>$, is true in W—i.e., $(L_E((*)))(<W,...>)$ is a proposition true in W—since presumably 'Neptune' is in L_E an obstinately rigid designator of Neptune (denoting that planet with respect to every possible world, whether or not Neptune happens to exist there). Now the open sentence

(**) There is an object which, necessarily, is x.

is either such that $L_i((**)) = L_E((**))$ or not. If not, then clearly L_i is distinct from L_E. If, on the other hand, $L_i((**)) = L_E((**))$, then— since *ex hypothesi* Neptune does not exist in W to be "fixed" by inhabitants of W as the referent of 'Neptune' in any language spoken in W— there are only three possibilities: either (a) 'Neptune' is an empty singular term of L_i, or (b) speakers of L_i in W have fixed the reference of 'Neptune' as some other object which does exist in W, or (c) 'Neptune' is something other than a name in L_i. If either (b) or (c), then clearly L_i is distinct from L_E. And if (a), then (*L_i), as hypothetically uttered in context $<W,...>$, must be either false or truth-valueless with respect to W. That is to say, if $L_i((**)) = L_E((**))$ and 'Neptune' is an empty singular term of L_i, then the value of $L_i((*))$ for the context $<W,...>$ is either a proposition false-in-W or else $L_i((*))$ is only a partial function, undefined for $<W,...>$. If $L_i = L_E$ then $(L_E((*)))(<W,...>) = (L_i((*)))(<W,...>)$, in which case (*$L_i$), as hypothetically uttered in $<W,...>$, is true at W if and only if (*L_E), as hypothetically uttered in $<W, ...>$, is true at W—an equivalence which we have just seen to fail. Therefore, in any case: L_i is distinct from L_E. We are, then, in a position to lay down our first premiss:

(1) Any world in which Neptune does not exist is a world none of whose denizens speak L_E.

Now it seems independently plausible to say, with David Lewis[9], that

(2) L_E is an actual language of a population P in W if and only if there prevails among members of P in W a convention of trust and truthfulness in L_E,

It follows that

(3) Any world in which Neptune does not exist is a world none of whose denizens observe a convention of trust and truthfulness in L_E.

But the existence of such a convention consists in the existence of a regularity R of attempted truth-telling and imputed truthfulness in L_E backed by certain complex overlapping propositional attitudes regarding R in W among members of P. Let us collectively call the attitudes definitive of attempted and imputed truthfulness in L_E, together with the supporting attitudes regarding R, "the L_E-attitudes." Then we may regard it as a definitional consequence of (3) that

(4) Any world in which the object Neptune does not exist is a world in which no population P exhibits a regularity R involving their having the L_E-attitudes.

Now assume for *reductio*:

(5) The availability to a population in a world of a regularity R involving their having the L_E-attitudes is independent of the existence of Neptune in that world.

But that is just to say that

(6) There is a possible world in which Neptune does not exist but in which some population exhibits a regularity R involving their having the L_E-attitudes.

Since this contradicts (4), we may conclude that

(7) The availability to a population in a world of a regularity R involving their having the L_E-attitudes depends upon the existence of Neptune in that world.

Now it appears that, in the envisaged circumstances, one could not *in general* ultimately blame the unavailability in question on anything but the unavailability, due to the non-existence of Neptune, of the beliefs and other attitudes ascribable to the putative L_E-speakers by means of sentences containing 'Neptune' in appropriate 'that'-clauses. If so, then we may conclude that

(8) The best explanation of the truth of (7) is that those L_E-attitudes reportable by use of the term 'Neptune' in appropriate 'that'-clauses are a species of object-dependent thoughts.

But what holds for 'Neptune' presumably holds for any other referential proper name, in which case it would follow that attitudes reported by the use of such terms in content-clauses are object-dependent one and all![10] (One might dispute the account of the actual language relation that we have borrowed from Lewis. Fine; nothing save pedagogic ease hinges on appealing to it rather than any of its competitors in the literature.[11] For *any* plausible account of the actual language relation will presumably involve the members of an allegedly English-speaking population P having or being disposed to have propositional attitudes like the belief that a member of P wouldn't utter 'Neptune is a planet' unless he or she meant that Neptune is a planet, or believed that Neptune is a planet, or unless it were true that Neptune is a planet, etc.) This completes the case for (ODT-2).

The derivation of (ODT-1) as a corollary proceeds as follows. Consider any referentially intended and perceptually based utterance U at a time t of the form '$G(\text{this } F)$' by an actual-world English-speaker S who succeeds thereby in referring to some perceived, contingently existing external object X and expressing some perceptual-demonstrative thought θ_U about X. Let W be a world as much as possible like the actual world except that S (or his counterpart S^*) has at t in W a phenomenologically indistinguishable set of *hallucinatory* experiences and issues a referentially intended and perceptually based counterpart utterance U^* in which the counterpart token of 'this F' is accordingly (and unwittingly) empty.

Suppose for *reductio* that U^* actually expresses the thought θ_U despite the contextual failure of S^*'s token of 'this F' to refer to anything in W. Then, in principle at least, nothing would prevent both S and S^* from exploiting their respective perceptual settings to introduce into their counterpart languages a new proper name 'N' by means of the deictic formula 'Let this F henceforth be named "N"'. Of course, the name thus introduced by S^* in W would, *ex hypothesi*, be empty; but so long as S^* is unaware of this fact the naming ceremony in W will be illocutionarily successful, albeit defective. And, again in connection with the same respective perceptual settings, S could proceed assertively to utter some monadic predication

(M) $Q(\text{this } F \text{ called '}N\text{'})$

and S^* could proceed assertively to utter some counterpart (M^*) thereof.

Now if, in the envisaged circumstances, S^*'s utterance U^* actually expressed a thought (viz., the thought θ_U), so presumably would S^*'s subsequent assertive utterance of (M^*). Given our *reductio* hypothesis, then, it follows that S^*'s utterance of (M^*) in W does express some thought. But if S^* in W thus *shares* S's actual thought θ_U, then S^* presumably must share the thought, θ_M, which S expresses by uttering (M).

However, for one who introduces a name 'N' via a perception-based demonstrative 'this F' there will be a constitutive connection between the thoughts he could express by tokens of '$Q(N)$' and the thoughts he could express, immediately following the name-introduction, by tokens of 'Q(this F called "N")'. This connection is mediated by the fact that, within the context of the introductory circumstances,

$N = $ this F called "N"

is axiomatic for the introducer. Consequently, if S^* shares S's thought θ_M, S^* must also share the thought expressed by S's tokens of '$Q(N)$'.

But, by the lately established (ODT-2), the thought expressed by S's tokens of '$Q(N)$' cannot be entertained by S^*: the thought thus available to S is not available to S^*. *Ergo*, it is false that U^* actually expresses the thought θ_U despite the contextual failure of S^*'s token of 'this F' to refer to anything in W. Thus we obtain (ODT-1) as a corollary of (ODT-2).

2. Extension of the Account to Problem-cases

2.1. Negative existentials and statements about fiction

Any proponent of object-dependent thoughts clearly has to face up to the fact that we ordinarily and without the slightest hesitation ascribe truth-values to at least some kinds of sentences which we *know* to contain empty terms. The most notable examples, of course, are negative existentials like 'Santa Claus does not exist' and statements *about* fiction like 'Sherlock Holmes was a better detective than Hercule Poirot'. In the following passage Evans gives a clear statement of an attractive general strategy for coping with such "conniving" uses of empty singular terms:

> The fundamental idea is to regard utterances containing empty terms used connivingly as moves in a linguistic game of *make-believe*. We make believe that there is an object of

such-and-such a kind, from which we have received, or are receiving, information, and we act within the scope of that pretence. ... And just as a deliberate initial pretence on the part of a story-teller or film-maker can provide people with the informational props which encourage them to continue the make-believe, so those props can be provided by shared illusions (current or remembered), or mistaken testimony, not originally the product of any artistic or imaginative process.[12]

Evans elaborates an account of games of make-believe, on which make-believe truths (created by the game) are a kind of fictional truth, differentiated by their foundation in actual fact (other than facts of stipulation or imagination that it be so) and such that one can *discover* P to make-believedly be the case (for short: discover that *P*).

After explaining the principles governing such games and show-ing how to provide for make-believe propositional attitudes, Evans completes his account of the "conniving" use of empty singular terms by showing how we can, in Gricean fashion, introduce make-believe linguistic actions. These, together with the pretense that certain non-existent things actually do exist and that things are as the "informa-tion" we share presents them as being, enables us to have *make-believe thoughts* about such objects and *make-believedly to refer* to them.

The technical details of Evans' theory need not detain us here: the crucial point for our purposes is that games of make-believe which transpire against a backdrop of shared information permit the *make-believe* occurrence of the kind of referential communication which is secured by the normal information-invoking use of singular terms. The "merely apparent" sufficient conditions for genuine referential communication—viz., possession of information derived in knowledge-preserving way from common source (story-teller, novel, misperceived object, etc.)—turn out, Evans says, to be sufficient and necessary conditions for *make-believe referential communication*, at least within the game of make-believe resting upon a shared in-formational backdrop! Such make-believe communication involves make-believe understanding, or *quasi- understanding* as Evans calls it, which requires having make-believe thoughts one can only have by suppressing the impact of disbelief and engaging in the operative pretense.[13] In particular, such cases involve the participants' having *thoughts about an object* which *we* can report only by *engaging* in the game ourselves—e.g. *demonstrative thoughts about that pink elephant*. Subsequently, games of make-believe can be *exploited* to enable us to make serious statements *about* the game and what is make-believedly the case within it, as according to Evans we do when we talk about works of fiction.

As regards the problem of singular negative existentials, Evans lays down two plausible constraints on any putative solution (the motivation for which need not distract us here): first, the analysis of such statements— i.e., their alleged logical form—must not be represented as metalinguistic[14]; and, second, the analysis must represent such sentences as containing 'exists' as a basic first-level predicate 'E( )' which is true of everything.[15] As before, his guiding idea is that

> ...A singular negative existential statement involves a make-believe reference, which must bring with it the possibility of make-believedly having or soliciting an answer to the question...'Which one is it..that you are saying does not really exist?' And giving an answer...inevitably draws one into the pretence.[16]

Accordingly, he proposes that the logical form of '*t* does not exist' is the same as that of '*t* doesn't *really* exist', namely:

> Not[Really(E(*t*))],

where the deep-structure sentential operator 'Really' is interpreted by the following rule:

> For any sentence *s*, an utterance of <Really(*s*)> is true (absolutely) iff (∃*p*)(*p* is true (absolutely) & *s* expresses *p* when *s* is uttered as a move in the relevant game of make-believe).[17]

What was said earlier about "understanding" statements about fiction applies here as well: if someone is to *understand* an utterance of <Really(*s*)>, he must quasi-understand *s* (i.e., it must be true that *he understands s**) and realize that the whole utterance is absolutely true iff, in quasi-understanding *s* (i.e., in *entertaining a thought as expressed by *s**), he is in fact entertaining a thought which is true.

2.2. Propositional attitude ascriptions

There is, however, one rather glaring gap in Evans' treatment of conniving uses. Although he explains[18] how we might treat utterances of sentences like 'Zeus was powerful'—made during a contemporary discussion of Greek Mythology—as involving a kind of pretense on our part which is *not* the continuation of any pretense on the ancient Greeks' part, he has very little to say about conniving uses in *opaque* contexts such as

(BZ) The ancient Greeks *believed* that Zeus was powerful.

Although these cases, like the former, do not involve the continuation of pretense, they are much more problematic in that, unlike the former, they *are* intuitively capable of literal truth or falsity. After making some half-hearted suggestions, Evans just leaves the matter dangling with the disquieting remark that such sentences 'are not to be taken as *literally true*'![19] However, a more palatable treatment is possible within the confines of the neo-Fregean position.

Let 'N' be schematic for names and/or demonstrative phrases of English, and let 'F' be schematic for verb phrases of English other than 'exists' and its cognates. Then since an instance of

N {does/does not} really exist.

can on Evans' view make a genuine statement, so too can an instance of

A believes that N really {does/doesn't} exist.

We could then maintain that when 'N' is connivingly used by an utterer u in connection with a game of pretense (e.g., "Greek mythology") to which A is *not* regarded as a party, then u's utterance of

A believes that $F(N)$.

should be paraphrased as (or regarded as truth-conditionally equivalent to)

A takes A-self's belief that N really exists to be about something such that $F(\text{it})$.

The paraphrase reports a belief whose object is not the non-existent referent of 'N' but rather A's own (regrettably false) *assumption* that

N really exists. This proposal allows for the problematic belief-attributions by a non-believer to be literally true or false, while still withholding literal truth-values in other cases of conniving use. In defense of this proposal, we can at least offer a palliative for any twinges of *ad hoc*-ery.

First of all, the paraphrase describes, not some bizarre, *sui generis* sort of belief, but rather a kind of belief which at least tacitly *accompanies* ordinary singular beliefs about real objects. One who, e.g., believes that Toad Suck, Arkansas is pretty at least tacitly takes his/her belief that there is such a city to be about a pretty place. (Notice the practical—though not stylistic—interchangeability of 'Is *it* a pretty place?' with 'Are you talking about a pretty place?' in response to 'There is such a place as Toad Suck, Arkansas'.) The idea is that, in the special case at hand, only the "accompanying" belief is available to be reported, since, strictly speaking, the ancient Greeks expressed no thoughts by uttering the relevant theological sentences of their language.

Secondly, (against the backdrop of what we condescendingly call "Greek Mythology") the paraphrase manages to capture the explanatory role of saying things like (BZ). Why, for example, did the ancient Greeks sincerely utter certain sentences, build certain temples, perform certain rites of propitiation, and so on? We need not suppose that their theological sentences expressed thoughts in order to explain why they were uttered. They were uttered because the ancient Greeks took themselves (mistakenly, as it turns out) to have singular thoughts about beings with such-and-such properties and believed those sentences to express such thoughts.[20] They built the temples and performed the propitiatory rites because, as *we* can say, they thought that Zeus really exists, took themselves thereby to be thinking of a powerful being, and believed such things as that powerful beings ought to be kept happy!

No doubt some will object that the paraphrase would attribute too much "conceptual sophistication" to the subject(s)—i.e., that we could still truly report the ancient Greeks' theological beliefs without having to assume that they were capable of meta-beliefs about their own (or others') beliefs. There is no knock-down rebuttal of this. But the capacity for such meta-beliefs does seem to be a necessary condition of being able to be party to genuine *conventions*. And the sorts of beliefs whose ascription is under review do seem to involve the subject's having a language, hence being party to such general conventions as are constitutive of having a language (as well as certain specific conventions, such as those regarding the use of the Greek counterpart of 'Zeus' as a name.) Children can believe that Santa Claus will bring them goodies; it is rather doubtful that the family dog is up to it.

3. Assessment of Two Rival Accounts of Singular Thoughts

3.1. Kent Bach's theory of "de re" thoughts

Kent Bach has recently proposed a treatment of singular beliefs (or "*de re* beliefs" in his terminology) on which they are indeed essentially relational but *not* essentially "of" their objects, i.e. not object-dependent in the sense which concerns the neo-Fregean.[21] Thus conceived, *de re* beliefs can supposedly be accommodated within the confines of Methodological Solipsism.[22] According to Bach, the inherent relationality of such beliefs lies in their indexical form: the *mode* of relation to their objects is part of their contents. The object (if any) of a *de re* belief (token) is determined not by its content but by its context. The relevant part of the content, the mode of presentation, merely determines what the appropriate contextual relation is. Thus, when individuated "psychologically" (by mode of presentation), *de re* beliefs are no more essentially about their objects than are descriptive beliefs. But when individuated "semantically" (by object and predicative content in a context), a *de re* belief is essentially about its object, but only in a trivial sense.

In specifying the content of *S*'s *de re* belief state, the operative *de re* relation R must be represented in the content of the belief via some mode of presentation M_R, so as to determine how its predicative content is applied to an object. Thus (DR) below, taken as a whole, supposedly represents the belief's total truth-condition, whereas 'M_R' and 'Gx' represent respectively the indexical and predicative contents of the belief-state):

(DR) $(\exists!x)(Rx(M_R S)\ \&\ Gx).$[23]

In the special case of perceptual-demonstrative belief, Bach says, R would be the kind of causal relation essential to perceiving an object; and the mode of presentation M_R would be a *percept* (= a *way* of being appeared to); M_R need not be descriptive, for the object is already singled out perceptually. Since Methodological Solipsism

demands that we characterize perceptual states in such a way that
a person could be in the *same* perceptual state regardless of whether
he is really perceiving a physical object or merely hallucinating, Bach
adopts Chisholm's "adverbial" method of perceptual content-
individuation, whereby perceptual state-types are individuated by
how the perceiver is appeared to. Accordingly, where m is a sense
modality, f_x is a way of being appeared to by physical object x, and
'$A_m f_x S$' abbreviates 'S is appeared$_m$ to f_x-ly', (PB) represents the
truth-condition of S's belief, of the object that appears$_m$ f to him, that
it is G (i.e., the belief he might express with 'this [f-appearing$_m$ thing]
is G'):

(PB) $(\exists!x)[CAUSESx(A_m f_x S) \& Gx]$.

Bach's major positive aim in his paper is to present a conception
of perceptual-demonstrative belief which '...reconciles with
[Methodological Solipsism] the claim that perceptual beliefs are
psychological states properly so-called'.[24] He offers little by way of
direct argument that we *ought* to think of singular beliefs in the way
presented, perhaps because he tacitly assumes that *only* a view compatible with Methodological Solipsism could be correct and that his
view is the only such view. Be that as it may, an independent argument for a position essentially like Bach's has been attempted by
Michael McKinsey,[25] so it behooves us to look at that argument
before turning to internal criticism of Bach's view.

McKinsey alleges that there is linguistic evidence that not all instances of

(1) S assumes that an F (or just one F) is G, and S wishes
that *it* is H.

can be read as

(2) S assumes that an F (or just one F) is G, and S wishes
that *the F which is G* is H.

on the ground that

(3) Nob assumes that just one fish got away at t, and he
wishes he had caught *it* at t.

is a plausible ascription which imputes no inconsistency to Nob,
whereas construing (3) in terms of (2) would yield

(4) Nob assumes that just one fish got away at t, and he
     wishes he had caught at t the fish that got away at t.,

which implausibly ascribes to Nob a self-contradictory wish! Since, McKinsey avers, there is no plausible construal of (3) in terms of ordinary "bound variable" anaphora either[26], the only alternative is to see the anaphoric pronoun 'it' in (3) as representing Nob's attempt at a mental act of demonstrative reference, the actual referent (if any) of which would be *fixed* by some definite description contextually recoverable from prior discourse—in this case: 'the fish that got away from Nob at t'. (3) must thus be distinguished from other instances of (1) and related constructions in which the anaphoric pronoun *could* be taken as simply going proxy for such a description. (The parallel with Kripke's remarks about "reference-fixing" versus "synonym-fixing" should be obvious.)

McKinsey tentatively concludes (in effect) that there are Bach-style *de re* thoughts (wishes, beliefs, etc.), some of which are ascribed by true sentences like (3). These thoughts are not object-dependent, since sentences like (3) can be true regardless of whether the assumption ascribed by their first conjunct is true or not. Nor are these thoughts propositional, since the ingredient anaphoric pronoun cannot be replaced by any non-anaphoric expression like a name or definite description without manifestly altering the sense of the whole sentence.

McKinsey's data, it must conceded, are certainly suggestive of a position like Bach's. But it is premature to concede defeat. For McKinsey rests his entire case on our intuitions about the alleged counterexample involving (3) and (4). On inspection, however, these intuitions are less damaging that McKinsey supposes.

The counterexample arises only if we take the description in (4) flaccidly, so that

(5) Nob wishes he had caught at t the fish that got away
     at t.

is heard as reporting a wish whose fulfillment-condition impossibly requires there to be a world w such that:

In w, one and only one fish, x, is such that x gets away from [is not caught by] Nob at t and Nob catches x at t.

However, there is no obstacle to taking the description rigidly and reading (5) as reporting a wish whose fulfillment-condition is the perfectly intelligible one that obtains in a world w when:

> In the actual world, α, just one fish gets away from Nob at t; and, in w, ($\exists x$)(x = The fish-which-got-away-from-Nob-at-t-in-α & x is caught-by-Nob-in-w-at-t)

Now it may be objected that this secures a determinate fulfillment-condition for Nob's wish only at the cost of building the truth of Nob's assumption (of just one actual escaping fish) into the content of his wish, thus somehow "distorting" (5)'s truth-condition. But, we may reply, surely (5), *as embedded in (4)*, can be heard as attributing to Nob a wish with precisely this fulfillment-condition despite the fact that the truth of Nob's assumption is not explicitly stated but only presupposed by the wording of (5). Indeed, it seems generally to be the case that the total fulfillment-condition of the wish we ascribe using a 'that'-clause in a given context must include the satisfaction of any presuppositions attaching to the words of that clause—hence that there will often be more contextually involved in the propositional content than immediately meets the eye or ear. If the context (especially the linguistic context) can determine the identity of the proxied description in (3), there is no apparent obstacle to its also determining the status of that description as rigid or flaccid, nor to its helping to determine the content of what, using that description, the utterer of (4) would (perhaps elliptically) be holding Nob to want.

Let us turn now to assessing Bach's own remarks. According to Bach, the *type* of a perceptual-demonstrative belief-state is given by the type of its total (and *ex hypothesi* non-propositional) content. Taking **M** as a sensory mode and **F** and **G** as concepts, let us represent that total content as a pair $<<\mathbf{M,F}>,\mathbf{G}>$ in which $<\mathbf{M,F}>$ types the "percept serving as mental indexical" by its sensory mode **M** and presentational content **F**, and **G** types the predicative content. Now it appears from Bach's account that, in addition to the traditional dyadic belief-relation B between persons and propositions, there is also supposed to be a triadic belief-relation B^* among persons, (event-)tokens of perceptual content-type $<\mathbf{M,F}>$, and predicative contents **G**. This new, "narrow" primitive relation B^*, unlike the "wide" primitive relation of *de re* belief invoked by others, does *not* involve the object, if any, contextually determined by the $<\mathbf{M,F}>$-token. Consequently,

S bears B^* to a $<\mathbf{M,F}>$-token and a $\mathbf{G}$-token respectively [in symbols: '$B^*(S,<\mathbf{M,F}>,\mathbf{G})$']

cannot be translated by means of familiar, object-involving locutions such as 'believes-of' or 'believes-to-be'. On the contrary, '$B^*(S,<\mathbf{M,F}>,\mathbf{G})$' has no ordinary English counterpart: no verb-phrase of ordinary English expresses the alleged relation B^*. Rather, it is the familiar locution

S believes x to be $\mathbf{G}$

and its kin which are to be explained in terms of the hybrid newcomer

$(\exists\mathbf{M})(\exists\mathbf{F})(B^*(S,<\mathbf{M,F}>,\mathbf{G})$ & x is the unique cause of S's having that experience of type $<\mathbf{M,F}>$),

which conveniently factors into a "narrow" component (=the first conjunct) and a "wide", object-involving component (=the second conjunct). It will do no good to attempt to gloss '$B^*(S,<\mathbf{M,F}>,\mathbf{G})$' with anything like

S mentally predicates [or better: attempts mentally to predicate] $\mathbf{G}$ via (a token of) the perceptual mode of presentation $<\mathbf{M,F}>$,

for our grip on the notion of "mental predication" rests on an analogy with predication in overt speech acts. But, by the lights of traditional speech act theory, predication, unlike (speaker-)reference, is not a separate speech act but only an abstraction from a whole illocutionary act.[27] On Bach's view, however, there would, in the case of *de re* belief, be no inner analogue of the "whole" illocutionary act to support an analogous abstraction of "mental predication." This is one way in which the traditional problem of the "unity of thought" arises for Bach.

We are left, then, with the problem of how to understand this alien theoretical predicate 'B^*' in an appropriately narrow way, i.e. Bach faces the task of explaining to us what obtains when $B^*(S,<\mathbf{M,F}>,\mathbf{G})$ for some $S,\mathbf{M,F}$, and $\mathbf{G}$ *without* making reference to external objects contextually determined by the $<\mathbf{M,F}>$-token. The only way of doing this which comes to mind would be to attempt a purely *functional* definition, in which B^* is characterized by (i) the input-conditions under which (given such-and-such conditions) an organism S comes to be so related to the appropriate entities, (ii) the relations between such B^*-states of S and S's other (narrowly specifiable) psychological states, and (iii) the relations of S's B^*-states and other (narrowly specifiable) psychological states to S's (narrowly specifiable) behavior. What are the relevant principles? As we have seen, they cannot be folk platitudes involving 'believes-of', 'believes-to-be', etc. Perhaps the relevant principles would be the "narrow counterparts" of these folk platitudes in some fancy, yet-to-be-formulated psychological theory.

But this cannot be right. Ordinary *de re* attributions notoriously do not share the behavior-explanatory power which standardly accrues to *de dicto* attributions. So the relevant principles would either be the "narrow counterparts" of folk platitudes about *de dicto* belief or else would be principles peculiar to the yet-to-be-formulated psychological theory which embeds 'B^*'. In the latter case, we have no idea what these proprietary principles might be; and, in the former case, although we know lots of folk platitudes about *de dicto* belief and other attitudes, we are left in the dark about how to extract narrow, non-propositional counterparts featuring 'B^*'. Indeed, we have been given no reason to suppose that *any* well-defined, purely internal state of S is ascribed by the likes of '$B^*(S, <\mathbf{M,F}>,\mathbf{G})$'!

Bach's account of the truth-conditions of *de re* beliefs is equally puzzling. His detailed remarks about (DR) and (PB) are often equivocal as between (i) the view that empty *de re* beliefs, unlike their nonempty counterparts, have *no* determinate truth-conditions[28] and (ii) the view that empty *de re* beliefs have the very *same* truth-conditions as their non-empty counterparts.[29] Two internal considerations make it likely that (ii) is the intended view. First of all, if only a *de re* belief which actually is *de* some *res* O enjoys a truth-condition, surely its truth-condition should intuitively pertain to facts about O in particular! In other words: what is intuitively necessary and sufficient for the *truth* of S's belief, of an object O that visually appears f-ly to him, that it is a G, is that O alone causes S to be appeared to f-ly and O is a G—not the mere circumstance, alluded to in (PB), that *something or other* is such that it alone causes the appearing and is a G. The very way in which (DR) and (PB) are formulated thus supports reading them as expressing (ii). Secondly, since the "contents" of *de re* beliefs are, according to Bach, not fully propositional, truth can only be predicated of the *de re* belief-state-token (relative to the context of its occurrence): it is the belief-occurring-in-a-context, not "what is believed", whose truth-conditions are presumably at issue. But, since the existence of the *de re* belief-state-token is allegedly independent of the existence of any appropriately related *res*, it is once more natural to read (DR) and (PB) as schematically providing the condition which *any de re* belief-state-token occurring in a context c must satisfy if it is to be true-in-c.

Let us tentatively assume, then, that (ii) is Bach's view. Then the following problem arises. If S, while the victim of a wholesale hallucination, were to utter

(6) That pink elephant is wearing a tutu!,

he would thereby count as expressing what Bach would regard as an empty *de re* perceptual thought θ_1, whose content we might represent in the form

$<<M_{visual}, \text{pink elephant}>, \text{wears a tutu}>.$

By the natural principle that the truth-value of one's indicative utterance in a given context c is the same as that of the thought that utterance would conventionally count as expressing in c, the truth-value of S's utterance of (6) would be that of θ_1 in the context. According to (PB), the thought θ_1 would be *false* in the envisaged context, owing to the absence of an appropriate uniquely related object; so the utterance of (6) would be false too. Now suppose, on the other hand, that S, still hallucinating, had instead uttered

(7) That pink elephant is *not* wearing a tutu,

thereby counting as expressing what Bach would regard as an empty *de re* perceptual thought θ_2, whose content we might represent as

$<<M_{visual}, \text{pink elephant}>, \text{doesn't wear a tutu}>.$

By parity of reasoning, the absence of an appropriate uniquely related object would render both θ_2 and (7) false. So far, so good. But what if S, still hallucinating, had uttered

(8) Either that pink elephant is wearing a tutu or that pink elephant is *not* wearing a tutu,

instead of (6) or (7)? Being an instance of a tautology, (8) is presumably true in S's (or anyone's) mouth. Yet, again by parity of reasoning, both disjuncts of (8) are false in S's mouth, so (8) is *not* true in S's mouth, which, by the light of classical logic, is absurd!

Short of abandoning classical logic—the need for doing which would scarcely count in favor of Bach's theory—only one way of avoiding this paradox comes to mind, and that is to insist upon a distinction between the "external negation"

(EN) It is not the case that: That F is such that it is a G. (In symbols: '$\sim(\text{that } F)_z G_z$')

and the "internal negation"

(IN) That F is such that it is not a G. (In symbols: '$(\text{that } F)_z \sim G_z$')

as possible logical forms for (7), maintaining that (7) is false under the circumstances only when read along the lines of (IN), but true when read along the lines of (EN). It is difficult to find any such distinction in surface syntax, but if a bit *ad hoc*-ness at the level of logical form is the only price to be paid for this "solution", then Bach gets off the hook for a nominal fee.

Alas, the price of pursuing this escape-route turns out to be prohibitive. First of all, it severs the truth-conditions of sentences of the form 'That **F** is **G**' from any plausible account of what the utterer of such a sentence *asserts*.[30] For, intuitively, the utterer of "That **F** is **G**" does not assert anything about the *existence* of a referent for his token of "that **F**", or anything else that would prepare us for adoption of the truth-condition-schemata

$\text{True}_c('(\text{that } F)_z G_z')$ iff $(\exists x)[\text{Den}_c('\text{that } F',x) \ \& \ x \text{ is } G]$,
$\text{True}_c('\sim(\text{that } F)_z G_z')$ iff $\sim(\exists x)[\text{Den}_c('\text{that } F',x) \ \& \ x \text{ is } G]$,

and

$\text{True}_c('(\text{that } F)_z \sim G_z')$ iff $(\exists x)[\text{Den}_c('\text{that } F',x) \ \& \ \sim(x \text{ is } G)]$

that, in aid of semantically implementing the "internal/external negation" ploy, would be foisted upon demonstrative utterances in virtue of the (DR)-style truth-conditions of the *de re* thoughts they are alleged to express.

Worse still, another paradox looms. For, on Bach's view, if S is in a perceptual situation in which he unwittingly hallucinates the presence of an F which is G, his utterance of '$(\text{that } F)_z G_z$' would express a false *de re* thought, in consequence of which his utterance of '$(\text{that } F)_z \sim G_z$' would likewise express a false *de re* thought. But what about the "objectless" thought, θ, which would be expressed by S's utterance of '$\sim(\text{that } F)_z G_z$' in that situation? Since '$(\text{that } F)_z G_z$'

is held to express a thought, albeit a *de re* one, surely there *is* such a thought as θ, in which case θ must be a *true* thought. But then θ cannot be a *de re* thought, since Bach's view makes all objectless *de re* thoughts false. But—and here's the rub!—*θ cannot be a de dicto thought either*, unless Bach is willing to countenance the bizarre situation in which there can be a (true) *de dicto* thought that it is not the case that *p* without there being any such thing as the *de dicto* thought that *p*. So if the *de re/de dicto* distinction for thoughts is exhaustive, Bach faces a flat contradiction. Positing a third category seems wildly *ad hoc* and of dubious intelligibility anyway, while denying the existence of θ altogether seems equally unmotivated unless—like the neo-Fregeans but unlike Bach—one is prepared to deny the existence of any thought (of any sort) expressed by an empty occurrence of '(that $F)_z G_z$'.

In light of all this, it seems that Bach should abandon view (ii) in favor of view (i), which denies truth-conditions to empty *de re* beliefs, adopting instead of (DR) and (PB) a conditional formulation like

(CF) (x){CAUSES$(c,x,S$'s being appeared to $<\mathbf{M,F}>$-ly) $\rightarrow$
[TRUE$_c$(the state S is in when $B^*(S, < <\mathbf{M,F}>,\mathbf{G}>))$
$\leftarrow \rightarrow G(x)$]},

which would mesh neatly with the intuitively attractive truth-conditional schemata

(x){Den$_c$('that F',x) $\rightarrow$ [True$_c$('G(that F)') $\leftarrow \rightarrow x$ is G]}

and

(x){Den$_c$('that F',x) $\rightarrow$ [True$_c$('-G(that F)') $\leftarrow \rightarrow x$ is not G]},

('TRUE' being the counterpart for *de re* belief-states of 'True' for sentences) on which the truth-conditions of empty demonstrative utterances are simply left undefined. But, though formally workable as an account of sentential truth-conditions, this approach is much less attractive as an account of the truth-conditions of *de re* thoughts.

On the one hand, it does not fit all that well with our folk notions about such truth-conditions. There is some linguistic evidence that folk psychology inclines towards treating so-called *de re* beliefs as a species of *de dicto* beliefs. It equates '*S* believes *N* to be *F*' with '*S* believes of *N that it is F*', and (at least sometimes) allows both to be expressed as '*S* believes *that N is F*', with '*N*' occurring transparently—as, e.g., 'you' does in an utterance of

The police believe that *you* are still in New York.

to "Mad Dog" Mulligan by his moll in response to the newspaper headline

POLICE BELIEVE "MAD DOG" MULLIGAN STILL IN NEW YORK!

Folk psychology further identifies the truth-conditions of *de dicto* beliefs with those of their *dicta*, i.e., with the truth-conditions of "what is believed". Thus, where the absence of an object makes it impossible to issue a true report in any of these forms, where "what is believed" cannot be specified in the 'that'-clause format, the intuitive verdict seems to weigh in favor of saying that truth-conditions are absent simply because the subject has no such belief at all, as opposed to saying that the subject has an ineffable belief with no truth-condition. To put the same point another way, the inference from

There is nothing which *S* believes to be the case.

and

There is no object (or objects) and no property (or relation) such that *S* believes the former to have (or stand in) in the latter.

to

S has no beliefs at all.

seems pretheoretically valid, yet Bach's theory invalidates it where objectless *de re* beliefs are concerned.

On the other hand, prospects look dim for Bach's being able to ride roughshod over these folk intuitions in the mighty name of Real Science. For to pass off our gappy friend 'TRUE' (or any other contender) as the "correct", scientifically anointed truth-predicate for *de re* belief-states, Bach must *justify* his choice of 'TRUE' on suitable grounds. And one condition which he himself places on such justification is that it must be consistent with purely *solipsistic* antecedent characterizations of beliefs, desires, experiences, "contents", etc. It seems, however, that any such justification would have to rest ultimately on the obvious and crucial connection between perceptual input and the formation of *observational de re* beliefs, for it is here that a thing's having a property and its being believed to have that property are most intimately connected. But the requirement of Methodological Solipsism prevents this characterization from taking the natural form

> For any object x and observational property G: If it were the case that Gx, and x alone caused S's having an experience of type $<\mathbf{M,F}>$, then (under such-and-such "normal" internal and external conditions) it would be the case that $(B^*(S,<\mathbf{M,F}>,\mathbf{G})$,

forcing it instead to take something like the form

> For any observational properties F and G: If S were to have an experience (in mode $\mathbf{M}$) *as of* an F's being G, then (under such-and-such solipsistically specifiable conditions) it would be the case that $B^*(S,<\mathbf{M,F}>,\mathbf{G})$

(where $\mathbf{M,F}$, and $\mathbf{G}$ are likewise solipsistically specified). Only the former, however, relates S's B^*-state to the situations in which 'TRUE' is supposed to apply to B^*-states; the latter so divorces the characterization of B^*-states from the anything like the folk account of the truth-grounds of *de re* beliefs as to make it totally mysterious how anything like (CF) could ever be justified by such a narrow account. Matters only become worse when we consider that the allowable presentational content $\mathbf{F}$ and predicative content $\mathbf{G}$ will be so narrowly phenomenal as to make problematic any solipsistic account of *de re* beliefs which are not purely observational in content, as indeed most of our singular beliefs are not.

Rather than attempt repairs to Bach's account, which would surely begin with rejection of the stultifying burden of Methodological Solipsism, let us look instead at a rather different rival view of singular thoughts which is not thus handicapped at the outset.

3.2. Harold Noonan's theory of demonstrative thoughts

Harold Noonan[31] has recently directed a number of criticisms against the neo-Fregean view in the course of proposing his own account of perceptual-demonstrative thoughts, an account not resting upon acceptance of Methodological Solipsism. He begins by targeting two claims made by Christopher Peacocke in support of the claim that object-dependent thoughts are not psychologically redundant, viz.:

(IT) No set of attitudes gives a satisfactory psychological explanation of a person's (transparently described) acting *on* a given object unless the content of those attitudes includes a *demonstrative* mode of presentation of that object[32]

and

...[(IT)], if true, can contribute to an argument that the fact that a demonstrative type [of mode of presentation] is indexed with one object rather than another [i.e., the fact that one object rather than another is thought of in this demonstrative way] can feature in a propositional attitude explanation of why the thinker acts on one object rather than the other.[33]

First, Noonan proposes and argues for the following thesis (R), which entails the falsity of *either* (IT) *or* the claim that demonstrative thoughts are object-dependent:

(R) When an action is directed upon a concrete, contingent object other than its agent—in the sense that it is intentional under a description containing a term which denotes the object—then an adequate psychological explanation of it is available under a (possibly distinct) description containing a term denoting the object; *and in this explanation the only psychological states of the agent referred to are ones whose existence is independent of the object's existence.*

(R) bifurcates explanations of successful action into two parts: a "purely psychological" part, involving only object-independent attitudes of the agent; and a not-purely-psychological description of those features of the environment which underwrite the success of the action.

The argument for (R) proceeds as follows. Suppose, for *reductio*, that there were a counterexample to (R). Any such counterexample would involve an action which had no explanation (under an appropriate description) that did not involve object-dependent attitudes. But in an appropriately similar situation where the agent is *hallucinating* and there is no object, the agent will perform the *same* bodily motions. But the neo-Fregean cannot explain why. No "new" psychological states are involved, and some of the previous ones (i.e., the "object-dependent" ones) are *missing*! So the action would be *inexplicable* in the hallucination case— which is absurd. Therefore, (R) is true after all, and so either (IT) is false or else demonstrative thoughts are not object-dependent.

The key to resisting this argument lies in Peacocke's distinction between action *on* the object (e.g., *S*'s kicking Fido) and action *at* the location where the object happens to be (e.g, *S*'s kicking whatever happens to be at that location), the former being the notion which figures in (IT). In the hallucinatory cases, there is no action *on* an object to be explained, but only action *at* the location where the object appears to be. Suppose that, in reaching out for the hallucinatory object, *S* happens to lay hands on a similar (but *un*perceived) real object, *O*. *Ex hypothesi*, *S* would not be in a position to have demonstrative thoughts about either the hallucinated object or about *O*. *S* would, of course, undoubtedly have attitudes towards thoughts of the sort

(L) The thing *now* located at such-and-such a bearing and distance from *me* is *F*.

These attitudes would explain why *S* acted (reached) *at that place* (where *O* happened to be) but would *not* explain why *S* acted *on* *O*. In short, the neo-Fregean can explain why the hallucinating subject performs the same bodily motions even though the relevant demonstrative thoughts are not available to him, provided he holds that thoughts of the sort (L) are standardly involved whether or not the relevant demonstrative thoughts are available. And this proviso seems harmlessly true.

Noonan grants the intuition that the agent's action in the hallucinatory case (involving only action at the place occupied by some unperceived object) is not explicable in quite the same way as in the veridical case (involving action on a perceived object) but argues against Peacocke's assumption that the *only* explanation of this intuitive asymmetry is that the agent lacks certain demonstrative thoughts in the former case which he possesses in the latter. The real difference on which the asymmetry intuition is based is, Noonan alleges, that in the hallucinatory case the agent has only *accidentally true belief*, whereas in the veridical-perception case the subject has *knowledge*. Since knowledge generally provides a better explanation of successful action than does merely accidentally true belief, the intuited asymmetry is just a felt difference in the relative adequacy of the corresponding explanations. But since the same thing can be both believed and known, Noonan concludes that nothing in the nature of the case as described prevents us from saying that the subject *does* have the relevant demonstrative thoughts in the hallucinatory case too, though he does not know them to be true.

This criticism rests upon a questionable diagnosis of the asymmetry intuition. The chief difference anent explicability between the two cases could equally well be accounted for as follows. In the veridical case the correct explanation of, say, agent S's grabbing object O would advert to certain of S's attitudes $K_1,...,K_n$ based upon S's current experience *of* O, involving the operation of a perceptual information-link through which O feeds information to S and, so to speak, guides S and enables S to track O. By contrast, in the hallucinatory case—where there is no such information-link, the thing (if any) which is "victim" of the action playing no role in guiding the subject to it—the correct explanation of S's grabbing *it* would advert to certain of S's attitudes $B_1,...,B_k$ based upon S's experience *as of* O.

Nothing so far implies (as Noonan's putting the difference in terms of knowledge versus accidentally true belief would) that the K_i's and B_i's can coincide in content, whereas already there is reason for suspicion that they can't. For although it is surely correct that the agent has attitudes towards thoughts of the sort

There is an object of kind F in location l,

and that he knows such thoughts to be true in the one case, whereas they are for him merely accidentally true objects of belief in the other, it is far from obvious that the same holds for the crucial *demonstrative* thoughts in question. In the hallucinatory case, what sense can we make of the alleged demonstrative thought expressed by 'That object is F' being *true* at all, "accidentally" or otherwise? What *fact*, pray tell, is the *truth-maker* of this alleged thought? The only candidate available would be the fact, if it is a fact, that the ultimate victim of his action (the unperceived object, x) is indeed F. But there are two obvious reasons why this won't do.

First of all, x's actually being F is not a general feature of such cases: even though the agent may have an hallucinatory experience as of a red rubber ball before him, all the relevant features of his reaching, grasping, throwing, or whatever could be the same even if x were a green plastic ovoid. Secondly, even if x *does* happen to be F, our pretheoretic intuition is that this fact about *x* is utterly *irrelevant* to the truth-value of any supposedly "demonstrative thought about the object" generated by the hallucination—irrelevant precisely because there is no intuitively appropriate sort of *connection* between *x* and the agent's thoughts. In fact, these are just the intuitions standardly cited on behalf of Direct Reference theories: the case at hand is an analogue of Donnellan's famous case of Thales and the hermit.[34]

A connected intuitive difficulty is that it seems impossible to *specify* in any direct way *what* the hallucinating agent is supposed demonstratively to believe. If we say, 'He believes that *that object* is *F*', we undertake an obligation to answer the question 'What object?'. But, as we have seen, the answer cannot be 'The unperceived object, *x*'; and, on pain of admitting a bizarre ontology of hallucinatory objects, dream-objects, and the like, there is no other answer to be given.[35] (One could of course try an indirect specification of the form

S has a visual experience as of a *G*, and *S* believes that *it* is *F*.

But our discussion of the McKinsey argument should warn us off taking this as ascribing any "empty demonstrative belief" to *S*.)

Noonan actually tries to show how demonstrative modes of presentation *can* be object-*in*dependent by claiming that a demonstrative mode of presentation of an object can be regarded as resting upon a *disposition* which can be possessed regardless of whether the object exists. He writes, e.g., that

> Whether I actually see an array of pills or merely hallucinate one,...I am capable of thinking the very same thoughts, since when my perception is veridical and I concentrate on one of the pills and think some demonstrative thought about it, my thought has the *content* it has because of what I am disposed to do—which would be the same if I were hallucinating or not—and it is a thought *about* that particular pill I am attending to because it is that pill on which, in fact, my dispositions are uniquely targeted.[36]

Noonan's idea is that the right sort of dispositional connection with an object might be the ground of a demonstrative thought about it even though one has no information-link with the object. That there is a suitable object where the subject's dispositions are targeted may be sheer coincidence, and whether such a coincidence obtains supposedly makes no difference to the availability of demonstrative thoughts. So the relevant dispositions of the subject are not founded upon (i.e., intrinsically relational with respect to) any particular object. Instead, we are told,

> ...if one's demonstrative thought seems to one to be a thought about a stationary object, they will be dispositions concerning a certain place, to direct actions to whatever object of a certain type is located there, and to evaluate one's thought in light of information received from it. ... If one's demonstrative thought seems to one to be a thought about a moving object there will be no *one* place which will be the target of one's dispositions over time, rather a sequence of places; but one's dispositions-at-a-moment will remain the same as in the former case.[37]

We are then presumably in a position to explain actions in hallucination cases, for

> ...a demonstrative thought..., when it has an object, will be as much a thought about a place (or a connected series of places) as about an object, and can be a thought about a place even when it is not a thought about an object.[38]

Now Noonan is *not* suggesting that we *conflate* (a) thoughts containing a demonstrative mode of presentation of an object with (b) thoughts which merely contain an egocentric mode of presentation of a place at which there happens to be an object. But he owes us an account of the difference between them. His answer is that the real distinction between (a) and (b) is that

> ...one cannot have a demonstrative thought without one's having information—its seeming to one—that one's thought has an object, while one can have an egocentric thought about a place even though one has no information that there is an object at that place.[39]

It is important to remember that Noonan does not attempt to *reduce* demonstrative identification of spatially located things to the identification of locations in egocentric space—i.e. to replace 'this *F*' with 'the *F* there now' or the like. He thus avoids the powerful arguments

Evans[40] mounts against any such reduction. But there is another way of seeing what is wrong with Noonan's proposal.

Demonstrative modes of presentation are clearly associated with distinctive patterns of evidential sensitivity: in the case of thoughts employing perceptual demonstrative modes of presentation, the subject's judgment of such thoughts must be sensitive in obvious ways to evidence concerning those properties of the demonstratively identified object which are responsible in the causally appropriate ways for the subject's experience. While these patterns of evidential sensitivity are far too complex to permit of direct description, they can, as Peacocke[41] has pointed out, be specified indirectly by exploiting the idea that one person can exhibit the same pattern of evidential sensitivity as another person with a richer conceptual repertoire without having to share in that richer repertoire.

Peacocke calls this pattern the *constitutive role* of the mode of presentation in question and lays down the following necessary and sufficient condition for a description 'The object which is C' to specify the constitutive role of a type of mode of presentation, D:

> (a) any family of perceptions, beliefs and memories which would cause someone to judge a thought of the form '$[D_x]$ is F' would also cause someone with the requisite concepts to judge 'the object which is C is F,' and (b) any family of perceptions, beliefs and memories [not requiring possession of concepts beyond those required by D and forming the subject's total informational state at the time] which would cause someone with the requisite concepts to judge 'the object which is C is F would also cause him to judge '$[D_x]$ is F.'[42]

Against this background, Peacocke proposes that (where 'F' is an appropriate sortal) the constitutive role of a visual demonstrative mode of presentation [that F] is specified by the (attributive) description

> (C1) the F responsible, in the way required for perception, for the experience as of an F in *that* region of my visual field.

Here the italicized 'that' obviously cannot, on pain of circularity, correspond to a demonstrative mode of presentation of the same type as [that F]: rather, it (and all similarly occurring demonstratives in constitutive role specifications) corresponds to that way of thinking

of a particular current token conscious state which one enjoys simply in virtue of *being* in that state. (I.e., there is no need to think of
the state in any other way than that given by what it is intrinsically
like to be in that state.)

By contrast, Noonan's account of demonstrative thoughts seems
to amount to the rival proposal that the constitutive role of a visual
demonstrative mode of presentation, [that *F*], is given by something
like the (attributive) description

(C$_2$) the *F* occupying the place on which are targeted those
of my dispositions that arise from the experience as of
an *F* in *that* region of my visual field.

Assuming that Peacocke's definition of constitutive role specification
is a reasonable one, and noting that (C$_1$) appears to satisfy it with
respect to [that *F*], the question then is whether (C$_2$) could *also*
plausibly be taken to give the constitutive role of [that *F*]. If (C$_1$)
specifies the constitutive role of [that *F*], then (C$_2$) is capable of doing so only if it is *a priori* equivalent to (C$_1$). But (C$_2$) is not *a priori*
equivalent to (C$_1$), for there are epistemically possible circumstances
in which corresponding instances are not satisfied by the same thing.

Consider, e.g., a subject *S* with the sudden experience as of seeing
a flashing firefly in an otherwise completely dark room, prompting
some remark like 'That firefly is pretty'. A feature of such experiences
is that one often cannot immediately tell how far away the object
is, in consequence of which the firefly responsible, in the way required for perception, for *S*'s experience as of a firefly in such-and-
such region of his visual field may *not* be the firefly occupying the
place on which are targeted those of *S*'s dispositions that arise from
the experience as of a firefly in that region of his visual field. For
the darkness-induced disorientation may bring it about that *S*'s
dispositions arising from his experience are, at least initially, targeted
on a certain place within arm's reach, whereas the firefly causing
his experience is, at the moment, much farther away—its unusual
size and brightness compensating for the distance. Description (C$_2$)
might not net anything, or it might net a non-flashing firefly accidentally within arm's reach, but it would not be coextensive with (C$_1$).

A view like Noonan's not only distorts the constitutive role of
(visual) demonstrative modes of presentation but also offers a false
picture of the use of demonstratives in communication. On such a
view, there is of course no obstacle to subjects S_1 and S_2 sharing the

same perceptual-demonstrative belief when one or both fails to be appropriately related to any object, so long as S_1 and S_2 share the right sort of experiences and experience-induced dispositional connections with one and the same place. Nor does this view appear to offer any impediment in principle to each party knowing (or at least truly believing) that the other shares that perceptual-demonstrative belief. But if all this is so, then *communication* ought to be straightforwardly possible between S_1 and S_2 in such cases. For *if*, as he presumably can, S_1 says to S_2 something which expresses S_1's perceptual-demonstrative belief, and S_1 brings it about via the normal Gricean mechanisms both that S_2 comes to share this belief of S_1's and that each party knows (or at least truly believes) that his belief is thus shared, then surely S_1 has communicated with S_2!

But imagine now a situation in which S_1 and S_2 are talking to one another by telephone while looking out the windows of their adjacent motel rooms at the same courtyard, in the center of which there appears to be a small brown rabbit, standing immobile. Suppose further that, although in fact the courtyard is empty, both S_1 and S_2 are (allowing for slight perspectival differences, etc.) having similar visual experiences, in virtue of which they enjoy similar dispositions, regarding such-and-such a place in the center of the courtyard, to direct their actions toward whatever "rabbit-ish" object is located there. Finally, imagine an extended conversation between S_1 and S_2 "about that rabbit" in which there are many uses of 'that rabbit' and related demonstrative phrases putatively referring to a jointly seen rabbit in the courtyard before them.

On Noonan's model, it seems that S_1 and S_2 could be genuinely communicating with one another via their utterances containing 'that rabbit'. There is, however, a strong intuition to the effect that the lack of any common causal ground of the right sort—specifically, the lack of grounding in a common *object*—makes the alleged "communication" completely spurious in cases of the sort described. (Notice that the case above is stipulated to be one in which the parties suffer a common hallucination: it is *not* a case in which they merely *mistake* some common object—e.g. a rock in the center of the courtyard—for a small brown rabbit.) It is instructive to compare the "joint hallucination" case with a different scenario in which "failure to communicate" is also the verdict of common sense: viz., the familiar situation of a conversation in in which someone unwittingly dials a wrong number and proceeds to talk with the party at the other end (each mistaking the other for an acquaintance) until some- one finally says something that "gives away" the mistake. Here there is likely to be massive failure of communication not through lack of objects but through lack of *common* objects: the references of the parties' respective tokens of given name- and demonstrative phrase- types will (unbeknownst to them) be completely different. If, as this kind of case suggests, a necessary condition of information-based communication is the existence of common referents, it should come as no surprise that the "joint hallucination" case is not intuitively an instance of genuine communication!

4. Conclusion

The Neo-Fregean theses (ODT-1) and (ODT-2) have been seen to be supported by independently plausible arguments and to form part of a theoretical perspective which is not only well able to handle obvious problem cases but is also free from the defects that evident- ly beset prominent rivals which reject (ODT-1) and (ODT-2). Now that the idea of object-dependent thoughts and ways of thinking has been detoxified, the path is clear for an appreciation of its advantages.[43]

Notes

1. Most notably: Gareth Evans, John McDowell, Christopher Peacocke and Martin Davies.
2. In another paper, Boër [2], I rebut a host of specific objections to the material from Evans [6] presented below in sections 1.1 and 2.1-2.2.
3. Evans [6], Sec. 9.4.
4. It is our stipulation that all this reasoning is taking place

    (a) in the first person,
    (b) with respect to a singular perceptual-demonstrative remark which one understands, and
    (c) *in* the very perceptual context which forms the background for interpreting the remark

    that makes this principle true by enabling the reasoner simply to *reuse* the same (possibly context-dependent) term that figured in his or her ancillary reasoning (i)-(vi).
5. In terms of our earlier restriction on propositional variables, the pro- position that S's remark expresses such-and-such a proposition q is not excluded, since "being expressed by S's remark", like "being grasped by S", is not a *semantic* property of q.

6. Our earlier restriction on the range of the propositional variables is crucial here, otherwise (12) would be false when, e.g., p_1 = the true proposition that H has some false belief, and p_2 = the content of that false belief.

7. This expression is borrowed from Salmon [19], p. 34.

8. The argument for (ODT-2) was inspired by one found in Davies [4].

9. Lewis [7].

10. This is not compromised by the concession (in Section 2.2 below) of a sense in which an utterance of 'The ancient Greeks believed that Zeus is powerful' can be true absolutely, despite the non-existence of Zeus; for that concession, it will be seen, pertains only to the special circumstance of a "conniving" use by the utterer in connection with a subject not taken to be party to the game.

11. See, e.g., Peacocke [15], Loar [8] and Davies [4], Ch. I.

12. Evans [6], p. 353.

13. Quasi-understanding must *not* be equated with merely pretending to understand. Pretending to understand is, presumably, merely pretending to do those things in which real understanding consists. In contrast, as Evans stresses, quasi-understanding involves really *doing* some of the things constitutive of genuine understanding (e.g., bringing to bear shared information derived in typically knowledge-preserving ways from a common "source")—only in the absence of a real object and within the scope of a certain pretense (e.g., that there is an object from which the information appropriately derives).

14. Cf. Evans [6], p. 344. (It is not totally clear what Evans means by 'analysis' here: I have taken him to mean *proposed logical form*, yet his rejection (in the same breath) of Donnellan's suggestion, which is only a proposed truth-condition, suggests that he either meant *truth-conditions* or was confused about what Donnellan was proposing.)

15. Evans [6], p. 351.

16. Evans [6], p. 369.

17. Evans [6], pp. 369-70.

18. Evans writes:

> The pretence may exist only in [speaker and audience's] serious exploitation of it. The speaker and hearer who seem to see a little green man but doubt their eyes may find themselves expressing a serious disagreement about the nature of the illusion by uttering such sentences as "He's a hunchback" and "No! He's carrying something" ([5], p. 365).

This, Evans suggests ([5], p. 365, fn 37), is how we probably treat discourse about the Greek Gods (where the original story-tellers were not engaged in pretense).

19. Evans [6], p. 366n.

20. Cf. McDowell [9].

21. Bach [1].

22. By 'Methodological Solipsism', Bach means *Conceptual* Methodological Solipsism, which is not purely syntactic/computational but allows talk

of *conceptual content* of inner representations, provided of course that these "meaning" properties can be solipsistically specified.

23. Bach reads (DR) as 'S represents as being G the unique object that bears R (the relation determined by M_R) to the belief state (token) that S is in.'

24. Bach [1], p. 123

25. McKinsey [13].

26. This claim, however, is disputed in Pendlebury [18].

27. Cf. Searle [20].

28. Bach [1], p. 136 above.

29. Bach [1], p. 137 below.

30. This point is made in Davies [3].

31. Noonan [14].

32. (IT) is introduced and argued for in Peacocke [16].

33. Peacocke [17], p. 184.

34. Donnellan [5].

35. At this point there is a strong temptation to suppose that the relevant experiences in the two cases *must* be factored into something like

>   (i) "the appearance that an F is before me" (the appearance whose sensational and representational content is supposedly the same in both cases and whose representational content ("that an F is before me") provides the "common something" that supposedly is known in one case but just luckily believed in the other)

plus

>   (ii) a causal story about the genesis of the experience (which story will differ in the two cases).

But this is tendentious and potentially question-begging. The supposition is tendentious because it is open to us to say, with McDowell (in [10]), that the appearance that an F is before one can be either (in non-veridical cases) a *mere* appearance or (in veridical cases) *the fact that an F is before one* manifesting itself to one—an occurrence which enhances one's epistemic status. Such a disjunctive conception allows that what is given to experience in the two cases may be the same in so far as it is an appearance that an F is before one. Moreover, the supposition is potentially question-begging insofar as it incorporates at the level of perception the very sort of representationalism which the neo-Fregean opposes at the level of thought.

36. Noonan [14], p. 82.

37. Noonan [14], p. 88.

38. Noonan [14], p. 88.

39. Noonan [14], p. 89.

40. Evans [6], pp. 171-74.

41. Peacocke [17], Chapter 5.

42. Peacocke [17], p. 112. (Greek letters in the original have been replaced with italicized Roman letters.) A word about Peacocke's notation: where

D is a singular term type, $[D]$ is the *type* of mode of presentation conventionally associated with D; and, where x is an object, $[D_x]$ is the *token* of $[D]$ with respect to x, i.e., $[D_x]$ is the particular mode of presentation which "presents" x in that way. Since $[D]$ is object-dependent, it determines a token $[D_x]$ in a context only if x exists in that context; and a thinker S must be related to x in the $[D]$-constitutive way in order to employ $[D_x]$ in thinking (i.e., for there to be propositions containing $[D_x]$ towards which S can bear various attitudes). By 'thought of the form "$[D_x]$ is F"' Peacocke means an attitude towards the proposition appropriately composed of $[D_x]$, the sense of 'is', and the sense of 'F'.
43. On which, see McDowell [11] and [12].

References

1. Bach, K. (1982). "*De re* Belief and Methodological Solipsism," in A. Woodfield, *Thought and Object*. Oxford, Clarendon Press.
2. Boer, S. (forthcoming). "Object-Dependent Thoughts," *Philosophical Studies*.
3. Davies, M. (1982). "Individuation and the Semantics of Demonstratives," *Journal of Philosophical Logic* 11: 287-310.
4. Davies, M. (1981). *Meaning, Quantification, Necessity*. London, Routledge and Kegan Paul.
5. Donnellan, K. (1970). "Proper Names and Identifying Descriptions," *Synthese* 21: 335-58.
6. Evans, G. (1982). *The Varieties of Reference*. Oxford, Clarendon Press.
7. Lewis, D. (1983). "Languages and Language," in his *Philosophical Papers*, Vol. 1. New York, Oxford University Press.
8. Loar, B. (1976). "Two Theories of Meaning," in Evans, G. and J. McDowell, eds. *Truth and Meaning*. Oxford, Clarendon Press.
9. McDowell, J. (1977). "On the Sense and Reference of a Proper Name," *Mind* 86: 159-85.
10. McDowell, J. (1982). "Criteria, Defeasibility and Knowledge," *Proceedings of the British Academy* 68: 455-79.
11. McDowell, J. (1982). "Truth-Value Gaps," in L. Cohen *et. al.*, eds. *Logic, Methodology, and Philosophy of Science*, Vol. 6. Amsterdam, North-Holland.
12. McDowell, J. (1984). "*De Re* Senses," in C. Wright, ed. *Frege: Tradition and Influence*. Oxford, Blackwell.
13. McKinsey, M. (1986). "Mental Anaphora," *Synthese* 66: 159-75.
14. Noonan, H. (1986). "Russellian Thoughts and Methodological Solipsism," in J. Butterfield, ed. *Language, Mind and Logic*. Cambridge, England; Cambridge University Press.
15. Peacocke, C. (1976). "Truth Definitions and the Actual Language Relation," in Evans, G. and J. McDowell, eds. *Truth and Meaning*. Oxford, Clarendon Press.
16. Peacocke, C. (1981). "Demonstrative Belief and Psychological Explanation," *Synthese* 49: 187-217.

17. Peacocke, C. (1983). *Sense and Content*. Oxford, Clarendon Press.
18. Pendlebury, M. (1982). "Hob, Nob, and Hecate: The Problem of Quanti-fying Out," *Australasian Journal of Philosophy* 60: 346-54.
19. Salmon, N. (1981). *Reference and Essence*. Princeton, Princeton University Press.
20. Searle, J. (1969). *Speech Acts*. Cambridge, England; Cambridge University Press.

Philosophical Perspectives, 3
Philosophy of Mind and Action Theory, 1989

FOLK PSYCHOLOGY AND THE
EXPLANATION OF HUMAN BEHAVIOR*

Paul M. Churchland
University of California, San Diego

Folk psychology, insist some, is just like folk mechanics, folk thermodynamics, folk meteorology, folk chemistry, and folk biology. It is a framework of concepts, roughly adequate to the demands of everyday life, with which the humble adept comprehends, explains, predicts, and manipulates a certain domain of phenomena. It is, in short, a folk *theory*. As with any theory, it may be evaluated for its virtues or vices in all of the dimensions listed. And as with any theory, it may be rejected in its entirety if it fails the measure of such evaluation. Call this the *theoretical view* of our self understanding.

Folk psychology, insist others, is radically unlike the examples cited. It does not consist of laws. It does not support causal explanations. It does not evolve over time. Its central purpose is normative rather than descriptive. And thus it is not the sort of framework that might be shown to be radically defective by sheerly empirical findings. Its assimilation to theories is just a mistake. It has nothing to fear, therefore, from advances in cognitive theory or the neurosciences. Call this the *anti-theoretical view* of our self understanding.

Somebody here is deeply mistaken. The first burden of this paper is to argue that it is the anti-theoretical view that harbors most, though not all, of those mistakes. In the thirty years since the theoretical view was introduced (see esp. Sellars 1956, Feyerabend 1963, Rorty 1965, Churchland 1970, 1979, 1981), a variety of objections have been levelled against it. The more interesting of those will be addressed shortly. My current view is that these objections motivate no changes whatever in the theoretical view.

The second and more important burden of this paper, however, is to outline and repair a serious failing in the traditional expressions of the theoretical view, my own expressions included. The failing, as I see it, lies in representing one's commonsense understanding of human nature as consisting of *an internally stored set of general sentences*, and in representing one's predictive and explanatory activities as being a matter of *deductive inference* from those sentences plus occasional premises about the case at hand.

This certainly sounds like a major concession to the anti-theoretical view, but in fact it is not. For what motivates this reappraisal of the character of our self understanding is the gathering conviction that little or *none* of human understanding consists of stored sentences, not even the prototypically *scientific* understanding embodied in a practicing physicist, chemist, or astronomer. The familiar conception of knowledge as a set of 'propositional attitudes' is itself a central aspect of the framework of folk psychology, according to the reappraisal at hand, and it is an aspect that needs badly to be replaced. Our self understanding, I continue to maintain, is no different in character from our understanding of any other empirical domain. It is speculative, systematic, corrigible, and in principle replaceable. It is just not so specifically *linguistic* as we have chronically assumed.

The speculative and replaceable character of folk psychology is now somewhat easier to defend than it was in the 60's and 70's, because recent advances in connectionist AI and computational neuroscience have provided us with a fertile new framework with which to understand the perception, cognition, and behavior of intelligent creatures. Whether it will eventually prove adequate to the task of replacing folk psychology remains to be seen, but the mere possibility of systematic alternative conceptions of cognitive activity and intelligent behavior should no longer be a matter of dispute. Alternatives are already abuilding. Later in the paper I shall outline the main features of this novel framework and explore its significance for the issues here at stake. For now, let me acquiesce in the folk-psychological conception of knowledge as a system of beliefs or similar propositional attitudes, and try to meet the objections to the theoretical view already outstanding.

I. Objections to the Theoretical View

As illustrated in Churchland 1970, 1979, and 1984, a thorough perusal of the explanatory factors that typically appear in our commonsense explanations of our internal states and our overt behavior sustains the quick 'reconstruction' of a large number of universally quantified conditional statements, conditionals with the conjunction of the relevant explanatory factors as the antecedent and the relevant explanandum as the consequent. It is these universal statements that are supposed to constitute the 'laws' of folk psychology.

A perennial objection is that these generalizations do not have the character of genuine causal/explanatory laws: rather, they have some other, less empirical, status (e.g., that of normative principles, or rules of language, or analytic truths). Without confronting each of the many alternatives in turn, I think we can make serious difficulties for any objection of this sort.

Note first that the concepts of folk psychology divide into two broad classes. On the one hand there are those fully intentional concepts expressing the various propositional attitudes, such as belief and desire. And on the other hand there are those nonintentional or quasi-intentional concepts expressing all of the other mental states such as grief, fear, pain, hunger, and the full range of emotions and bodily sensations. Where states of the latter kind are concerned, I think it is hardly a matter for dispute that the common homilies in which they figure are causal/explanatory laws. Consider the following.

A person who suffers severe bodily damage will feel pain.
A person who suffers a sudden sharp pain will wince.
A person denied food for any length will feel hunger.
A hungry person's mouth will water at the smell of food.
A person who feels overall warmth will tend to relax.
A person who tastes a lemon will have a puckering sensation.
A person who is angry will tend to be impatient.

Clearly these humble generalizations, and thousands more like them, are causal/explanatory in character. They will and regularly do support simple explanations, sustain subjunctive and counterfactual conditionals, and underwrite predictions in the standard fashion. Moreover, concepts of this simple sort carry perhaps the major part of the folk psychological burden. The comparatively complex explanations involving the propositional attitudes are of central importance, but they are surrounded by a quotidian whirl of simple explanations like these, all quite evidently of a causal/explanatory cast.

It won't do then, to insist that the generalizations of folk psychology are on the whole nonempirical or noncausal in character. The bulk of them, and I mean thousands upon thousands of them, are transparently causal or nomological. The best one can hope to argue is that there is a central core of folk-psychological concepts whose explanatory role is somehow *discontinuous* with that of their fellows. The propositional attitudes, especially belief and desire, are the perennial candidates for such a nonempirical role, for explanations in their terms typically display the explanandum event as 'rational'. What shall we say of explanations in terms of beliefs and desires?

We should tell essentially the same causal/explanatory story, and for the following reason. Whatever else humans do with the concepts for the propositional attitudes, they do use them successfully to predict the future behavior of others. This means that, on the basis of presumed information about the current cognitive states of the relevant individuals, one can non-accidentally predict at least some of their future behavior some of the time. But any principle that allows us to do this—that is, to predict one empirical state or event on the basis of another, logically distinct, empirical state or event—*has* to be empirical in character. And I assume it is clear that the event of my ducking my head is logically distinct both from the event of my perceiving an incoming snowball, and from the states of my desiring to avoid a collision and my belief that ducking is the best way to achieve this.

Indeed, one can do more than merely predict: one can control and manipulate the behavior of others by controlling the information available to them. Here one is bringing about certain behaviors by steering the cognitive states of the subject—by relating opportunities, dangers, or obligations relevant to that subject. How this is possible without an understanding of the objective empirical regularities that connect the internal states and the overt behaviors of normal people is something that the anti-theoretical position needs to explain.

The confused temptation to find something special about the case of intentional action derives primarily from the fact that the central element in a full-blooded action explanation is a configuration of propositional attitudes in the light of which the explanandum behavior can be seen as sensible or rational, at least from the agent's narrow point of view. In this rational-in-the-light-of relation we seem to have some sort of super-causal *logical* relation between the explanans and the explanandum, which is an invitation to see a distinct and novel type of explanation at work.

Yet while the premise is true—there is indeed a logical relation between the explanandum and certain elements in the explanans—the conclusion does not begin to follow. Students of the subject are still regularly misled on this point, for they fail to appreciate that a circumstance of this general sort is *typical* of theoretical explanations. Far from being a sign of the nonempirical and hence nontheoretical character of the generalizations and explanations at issue, it is one of the surest signs available that we are here dealing with a high-grade theoretical framework. Let me explain.

The electric current I in a wire or any conductor is causally determined by two factors: it tends to increase with the electromotive force or voltage V that moves the electrons down the wire, and it tends to be reduced according to the resistance R the wire offers against their motion. Briefly, $I = V/R$. Less cryptically and more revealingly,

$(x)(V)(R)[(x$ *is subject to a voltage of* $(V))$ & $(x$ *offers a resistance of* $(R)) \supset (\exists I)((x$ *has a current of* $(I))$ & $(I = V/R))]$

The first point to notice here is that the crucial predicates—*has a resistance of (R), is subject to a voltage of (V)*, and *has a current of (I)*—are what might be called 'numerical attitudes': they are predicate-forming functors that take singular terms for numbers in the variable position. A complete predicate is formed only when a specific numeral appears in the relevant position. The second point to notice is that this electrodynamical law exploits a relation holding on the domain of numbers in order to express an important empirical regularity. The current I is the *quotient* of the voltage V and the resistance R, whose values will be cited in explanation of the current. And the third point to notice is that this law and the explanations it sustains are typical of laws and explanations throughout science. Most of our scientific predicates express 'numerical attitudes' of the sort displayed, and most of our laws exploit and display relations that hold primarily on the abstract domain of numbers. Nor are they limited to numbers. Other laws exploit the abstract relations holding on the abstract domain of vectors, or on the domain of sets, or groups, or matrices. But none of this means they are nonempirical, or noncausal, or nonnomic.

Action explanations, and intentional explanations in general, follow the same pattern. The only difference is that here the domain of abstract objects being exploited is the domain of propositions, and the relations displayed are logical relations. And like the numerical and vectorial attitudes typical of theories, the expressions for the propositional attitudes are predicate-forming functors. *Believes that P*, for example, forms a complete predicate only when a specific sentence appears in the variable position *P*. The principles that comprehend these predicates have the same abstract and highly sophisticated structure displayed by our most typical theories. They just exploit the relations holding on a different domain of abstract objects in order to express the important empirical regularities comprehending the states and activities of cognitive creatures. That makes folk psychology a very interesting theory, perhaps, but it is hardly a sign of its being *non*theoretical. Quite the reverse is true. (This matter is discussed at greater length in Churchland 1979, sec. 14, and 1981, pp. 82-4.)

In summary, the simpler parts of folk psychology are transparently causal or nomic in character, and the more complex parts have the same sophisticated logical structure typical of our most powerful theories.

But we are not yet done with objections. A recurrent complaint is that in many cases the reconstructed conditionals that purport to be sample 'laws' of folk psychology are either strictly speaking false, or they border on the trivial by reason of being qualified by various *ceteris paribus* clauses. A first reply is to point out that my position does not claim that the laws of folk psychology are either true or complete. I agree that they are a motley lot. My hope is to see them replaced entirely, and their ontology of states with them. But this reply is not wholly responsive, for the point of the objection is that it is implausible to claim the status of an entrenched theoretical framework for a bunch of 'laws' that are as vague, as loose, and as festooned with *ceteris paribus* clauses as are the examples typically given.

I will make no attempt here to defend the ultimate integrity of the laws of folk psychology, for I have little confidence in them myself. But this is not what is required to meet the objection. What needs pointing out is that the 'laws' of folk theories are *in general* sloppy, vague, and festooned with qualifications and *ceteris paribus* clauses.

What the objectors need to do, in order to remove the relevant system of generalizations from the class of empirical theories, is to show that folk psychology is significantly *worse* in all of these respects than are the principles of folk mechanics, or folk thermodynamics, or folk biology, and so forth. In this they are sure to be disappointed, for these other folk theories are even worse than folk psychology (see McCloskey 1983). In all, folk psychology may be a fairly ramshackle theory, but a theory it remains. Nor is it a point against this that folk psychology has changed little or none since ancient times. The same is true of other theories near and dear to us. The folk physics of the 20th Century, I regret to say, is essentially the same as the folk physics of the ancient Greeks (McCloskey 1983). Our conceptual inertia on such matters may be enormous, but a theory remains a theory, however many centuries it may possess us.

A quite different objection directs our attention to the great many things beyond explanation and prediction for which we use the vocabulary and concepts of folk psychology. Their primary function, runs the objection, is not the function served by explanatory theories, but rather the myriad social functions that constitute human culture and commerce. We use the resources of folk psychology to promise, to entreat, to congratulate, to tease, to joke, to intimate, to threaten, and so on. (See Wilkes 1981, 1984).

The list of functions is clearly both long and genuine. But most of these functions surely come under the heading of control or manipulation, which is just as typical and central a function of theories as is either explanation or prediction, but which is not mentioned in the list of theoretical functions supplied by the objectors. Though the image may be popular, the idle musings of an impotent stargazer provide a poor example of what theories are and what theories do. More typically, theories are the conceptual vehicles with which we literally come to grips with the world. The fact that folk psychology serves a wealth of practical purposes is no evidence of its being nontheoretical. Quite the reverse.

Manipulation aside, we should not underestimate the importance for social commerce of the explanations and predictions that folk psychology makes possible. If one cannot predict or anticipate the behavior of one's fellows at all, then one can engage in no useful commerce with them whatever. And finding the right explanations for their past behavior is often the key to finding the appropriate premises from which to anticipate their future behavior. The objection's attempt to paint the functions of folk psychology in an exclusively non-theoretical light is simply a distortion born of tunnel vision.

In any case, it is irrelevant. For there is no inconsistency in saying that a theoretical framework should also serve a great many nontheoretical purposes. To use an example I have used before (1986), the theory of *witches, demonic possession, exorcism,* and *trial by ordeal,* was also used for a variety of social purposes beyond strict explanation and prediction. For example, its vocabulary was used to warn, to censure, to abjure, to accuse, to badger, to sentence, and so forth. But none of this meant that demons and witches were anything other than theoretical entities, and none of this saved the ontology of demon theory from elimination when its empirical failings became acute and different conceptions of human pathology arose to replace it. Beliefs, desires, and the rest of the folk psychological ontology all are in the same position. Their integrity, to the extent that they have any, derives from the explanatory, predictive, and manipulative prowess they display.

It is on the topic of explanation and prediction that a further objection finds fault with the theoretical view. Precisely what, begins the objection, is the observable behavior that the ontology of folk psychology is postulated to explain? Is it bodily behavior as *kinematically* described? In some cases perhaps, but not in general, certainly, because many quite different kinematical sequences could count as the same intentional action, and it is generally the *action* that is properly the object of folk psychological explanations of behavior. In general, the descriptions of human behavior that figure in folk-psychological explanations and predictions are descriptions that *already* imply perception, intelligence, and personhood on the part of the agent. Thus it must be wrong to see the relation between one's psychological states and one's behavior on the model of theoretical states postulated to explain the behavior of some conceptually independent domain of phenomena (Haldane, 1988).

The premise of this objection is fairly clearly true: a large class of behavior descriptions are not conceptually independent of the concepts of folk psychology. But this affords no grounds for denying theoretical status to the ontology of folk psychology. The assumption that it does reflects a naive view of the relation between theories and the domains they explain and predict. The naive assumption is that the concepts used to describe the domain-to-be-explained must always be conceptually independent of the theory used to explain the phenomena within that domain. That assumption is known to be false, and we need look no farther than the Special Theory of Relativity (STR) for a living counterexample.

The introduction of STR brought with it a systematic reconfiguration of all of the basic observational concepts of mechanics: spatial length, temporal duration, velocity, mass, momentum, etc. These are all one-place predicates within classical mechanics, but they are all replaced by two-place predicates within STR. Each ostensible 'property' has turned out to be a *relation*, and each has a definite value only relative to a chosen reference frame. If STR is true, and since the early years of this century it has seemed to be, then one cannot legitimately describe the observational facts of mechanics save in terms that are drawn from STR itself.

Modern chemistry provides a second example. It is a rare chemist who does not use the taxonomy of the periodic table and the combinatorial lexicon of chemical compounds to describe both the observable facts and their theoretical underpinnings alike. For starters, one can just smell hydrogen sulphide, taste sodium chloride, feel any base, and identify copper, aluminum, iron, and gold by sight.

These cases are not unusual. Our theoretical convictions typically reshape the way we describe the facts-to-be-explained. Sometimes it happens immediately, as with STR, but more often it happens after long familiarity with the successful theory, as is displayed in the idioms casually employed in any working laboratory. The premise of the objection is true. But it is no point at all against the theoretical view. Given the great age of folk psychology, such conceptual invasion of the explanandum domain is only to be expected.

A different critique of the theoretical view proposes an alternative account of our understanding of human behavior. According to this view, one's capacity for anticipating and understanding the behavior of others resides not in a system of nomically-embedded concepts, but rather in the fact that one is a normal person oneself, and can draw on one's own reactions, to real or to imagined circumstances, in order to gain insight into the internal states and the overt behavior of others. The key idea is that of empathy. One uses oneself as a simulation (usually imagined) of the situation of another, and then extrapolates the results of that simulation to the person in question (cf. Gordon 1986; Goldman, forthcoming).

My first response to this line is simply to agree that an enormous amount of one's appreciation of the internal states and overt behavior of other humans derives from one's ability to examine and to extrapolate from the facts of one's own case. All of this is quite consistent with the theoretical view, and there is no reason that one should attempt to deny it. One learns from every example of humanity one encounters, and one encounters oneself on a systematic basis. What we must resist is the suggestion that extrapolating from the particulars of one's own case is the fundamental ground of one's understanding of others, a ground that renders possession of a nomic framework unnecessary. Problems for this stronger position begin to appear immediately.

For one thing, if *all* of one's understanding of others is closed under extrapolation from one's own case, then the modest contents of one's own case must form an absolute limit on what one can expect or explain in the inner life and external behavior of others. But in fact we are not so limited. People who are congenitally deaf, or blind, know quite well that normal people have perceptual capacities beyond what they themselves possess, and they know in some detail what those capacities entail in the way of knowledge and behavior. Moreover, people who have never felt profound grief, say, or love, or rejection, can nonetheless provide appropriate predictions and explanations of the behavior of people so afflicted. And so on. In general, one's immediately available understanding of human psychology and behavior goes substantially beyond what one has experienced in one's own case, either in real life or in pointed simulations. First-person experience or simulation is plainly not *necessary* for understanding the behavior of others.

Nor is it *sufficient*. The problem is that simulations, even if they motivate predictions about others, do not by themselves provide any explanatory understanding of the behavior of others. To see this, consider the following analogy. Suppose I were to possess a marvelous miniature of the physical universe, a miniature I could manipulate in order to simulate real situations and thus predict and retrodict the behavior of the real universe. Even if my miniature unfailingly provided accurate simulations of the outcomes of real physical processes, I would still be no further ahead on the business of *explaining* the behavior of the real world. In fact, I would then have two universes, both in need of explanation.

The lesson is the same for first-person and third-person situations. A simulation itself, even a successful one, provides no explanation. What explanatory understanding requires is an appreciation of the *general patterns* that comprehend the individual events in both cases. And that brings us back to the idea of a moderately general *theory*.

We should have come to that idea directly, since the empathetic account of our understanding of others depends crucially on one's having an initial understanding of oneself. To extrapolate one's own cognitive, affective, and behavioral intricacies to others requires that one be able to conceptualize and spontaneously to recognize those intricacies in oneself. But one's ability to do this is left an unaddressed mystery by the empathetic account. Self-understanding is not seen as a problem; it is other-understanding that is held up as the problem.

But the former is no less problematic than the latter. If one is to be able to apprehend even the *first*-person intricacies at issue, then one must possess a conceptual framework that draws all of the necessary distinctions, a framework that organizes the relevant categories into the appropriate structure, a framework whose taxonomy reflects at least the more obvious of the rough nomic regularities holding across its elements, even in the first-person case. Such a framework is already a theory.

The fact is, the categories into which any important domain gets divided by a learning creature emerge jointly with an appreciation of the rough nomic regularities that connect them. A nascent taxonomy that supports the expression of no useful regularities is a taxonomy that is soon replaced by a more insightful one. The divination of useful regularities is the single most dominant force shaping the taxonomies developed by any learning creature in any domain. And it is an essential force, even in perceptual domains, since our observational taxonomies are always radically underdetermined by our untrained perceptual mechanisms. To suppose that one's conception of one's *own* mental life is innocent of a network of systematic expectations is just naive. But such a network is already a theory, even before one addresses the question of others.

This is the cash value, I think, of P.F. Strawson's insightful claim, now thirty years old, that to be in a position to pose any question about other minds, and to be in a position to try to construct arguments from analogy with one's own case, is already to possess at least the rudiments of what is sought after, namely, a general conception of mental phenomena, of their general connections with each other and with behavior (Strawson, 1958). What Strawson missed was the further insight that such a framework is nothing other than an empirical theory, one justified not by the quasi-logical character of its principles, as he attempted unsuccessfully to show, but by its impersonal success in explaining and predicting human behavior at large. There is no special justificational story to be told here. Folk psychology is justified by what standardly justifies *any* conceptual framework: namely, its explanatory, predictive, and manipulative success.

This concludes my survey of the outstanding objections to the theoretical view outlined in the opening paragraph of the present paper. But in defending this view there is a major difference between my strategy in earlier writings and that of the present paper. In my 1970 paper, for example, the question was framed as follows: "Are action explanations *deductive-nomological* explanations?" I would now prefer to frame the question thus: "Are action explanations of the same general type as the explanations typically found in the sciences?" I continue to think that the answer to this second question is pretty clearly yes. The reasons are as covered above. But I am no longer confident that the D-N model itself is an adequate account of explanation in the sciences or anywhere else.

The difficulties with the D-N model are detailed elsewhere in the literature, so I shall not pause to summarize them here. My diagnosis of its failings, however, locates the basic problem in its attempt to represent knowledge and understanding by sets of sentences or propositional attitudes. In this, the framers of the D-N model were resting on the basic assumptions of folk psychology. Let me close this paper by briefly exploring how we might conceive of knowledge, and of explanatory understanding, in a systematically different way. This is an important undertaking relative to the concerns of this paper, for there is an objection to the theoretical view, as traditionally expressed, that seems to me to have some real bite. It is as follows.

If one's capacity for understanding and predicting the behavior of others derives from one's internal storage of thousands of laws or nomic generalizations, how is it that one is so poor at enunciating the laws on which one's explanatory and predictive prowess depends? It seems to take a trained philosopher to reconstruct them! How is it that children are so skilled at understanding and anticipating the behavior of humans in advance of ever acquiring the complex linguistic skills necessary to express them? How is it that social hunters such as wolves and lions can comprehend and anticipate each other's behavior in great detail, when they presumably store no internal sentences at all?

We must resist the temptation to see in these questions a renewed motivation for counting folk psychology as special, for the very same problems arise with respect to any other folk theory you might care to mention—folk physics, folk biology, whatever. It even arises for theories in the highly developed sciences, since, as Kuhn has pointed out, very little of a scientist's understanding of a theory consists in his ability to state a list of laws. It consists rather in the ability to apply the conceptual resources of the theory to new cases, and thus to anticipate and perhaps manipulate the behavior of the relevant empirical domain. This means that our problem here concerns the character of knowledge and understanding in general. Let us finally address that problem.

II. An Alternative Form of Knowledge Representation

One alternative to the notion of a universal generalization about *F* is the notion of a *prototype* of *F*, a central or typical example of *F* which all other examples of *F* resemble, more or less closely, in certain relevant respects. Prototypes have certain obvious advantages over universal generalizations. Just as a picture can be worth a thousand words, so a single complex prototype can embody the same breadth of information concerning the organization of co-occurrent features that would be contained in a long list of complex generalizations. Further, prototypes allow us a welcome degree of looseness that is precluded by the strict logic of a universal quantifier: not *all* *F*s need be *G*s, but the standard or normal ones are, and the non-standard ones must be related by a relevant similarity relation to those that properly are *G*. Various theorists have independently found motive to introduce such a notion in a number of cognitive fields: they have been called *paradigms* and *exemplars* in the philosophy of science (Kuhn 1962), *stereotypes* in semantics (Putnam 1970, 1975), *frames* (Minsky 1981) and *scripts* (Schank 1977) in AI research, and finally *prototypes* in psychology (Rosch 1981) and linguistics (Lakoff 1987).

Their advantages aside, prototypes also have certain familiar problems. The first problem is how to determine just what clutch of elements or properties should constitute a given prototype, and the second problem is how to determine the metric of similarity along which 'closeness' to the central prototype is to be measured. Though they pose a problem for notions at all levels, these problems are especially keen in the case of the so-called basic or simple properties, because common sense is there unable even to articulate any 'deeper' constituting elements (for example, what elements 'make up' a purple color, a sour taste, a floral smell, or the phoneme ā?). A final problem concerning prototypes is a familiar one: how might prototypes be effectively represented in a real cognitive creature?

This last question brings me to a possible answer, and to a path that leads to further answers. The relevant research concerns the operations of artificial neural networks, networks that mimic some of the more obvious organizational features of the brain. It concerns how they learn to recognize certain types of complex stimuli, and how they represent what they have learned. Upon repeated presentation of various real examples of the several features to be learned (*F, G, H*, etc.), and under the steady pressure of a learning algorithm that makes small adjustments in the network's synaptic connections, the network slowly but spontaneously generates a set of internal representations, one for each of the several features it is required to recognize. Collectively, those representations take the form of a set or system of similarity spaces, and the central point or volume of such a space constitutes the network's representation of a *prototypical F, G,* or *H*. After learning is completed, the system responds to any *F*-like stimulus with an internal pattern of neuronal activity that is *close to* the prototypical pattern in the relevant similarity space.

The network consists of an initial 'sensory' layer of neurons, which is massively connected to a second layer of neurons. The sizes or 'weights' of the many connections determine how the neurons at the second layer collectively respond to activity across the input layer. The neurons at the second layer are connected in turn to a third layer (and perhaps a fourth, etc., but we will here limit the discussion to three-layer networks). During learning, what the system is searching for is a configuration of weights that will turn the neurons at the second layer into a set of *complex feature detectors*. We then want the neurons at the third or 'output' layer to respond in turn to the second layer, given any *F*-like stimuli at the input layer, with a characteristic pattern of activity. All of this is achieved by presenting the network with diverse examples of *F*s, and slowly adjusting its connection weights in the light of its initially chaotic responses.

Such networks can indeed learn to recognize a wide variety of surprisingly subtle features: phonemes from voiced speech, the shapes of objects from grey-scale photos, the correct pronunciation of printed English text, the presence of metallic mines from sonar returns, and

grammatical categories in novel sentences. Given a successfully trained network, if we examine the behavior of the neurons at the second or intermediate layer during the process of recognition, we
discover that each neuron has come to represent, by its level of activity, some distinct aspect or dimension of the input stimulus. Taken
together, their joint activity constitutes a multi-dimensional analysis
of the stimuli at the input layer. The trained network has succeeded
in finding a set of dimensions, an abstract *space*, such that all more-
or-less typical *F*s produce a characteristic profile of neuronal activity across those particular dimensions, while deviant or degraded
*F*s produce profiles that are variously *close* to that central prototype.
The job of the third and final layer is then the relatively simple one
of distinguishing that profile-region from other regions in the larger
space of possible activation patterns. In this way do artificial neural
networks generate and exploit prototypes. It is now more than a suggestion that real neural networks do the same thing. (For a summary
of these results and how they bear on the question of theoretical
knowledge, see Churchland 1989a. For a parade case of successful
learning, see Rosenberg and Sejnowski 1987. For the *locus classicus*
concerning the general technique, see Rumelhart *et al* 1986.)

Notice that this picture contains answers to all three of the problems about prototypes noted earlier. What dimensions go into a prototype of *F*? Those that allow the system to respond to diverse examples
of *F* in a distinctive and uniform way, a way that reduces the error
messages from the learning algorithm to a minimum. How is similarity to a prototype measured? By geometrical proximity in the relevant parameter space. How are prototypes represented in real
cognitive creatures? By canonical activity patterns across an appropriate population of neurons.

Note also that the objective features recognized by the network
can also have a temporal component: a network can just as well be
trained to recognize typical *sequences* and *processes* as to recognize
atemporal patterns. Which brings me to my final suggestion. A normal human's understanding of the springs of human action may reside
not in a set of stored generalizations about the hidden elements of
mind and how they conspire to produce behavior, but rather in one
or more prototypes of the deliberative or purposeful process. To
understand or explain someone's behavior may be less a matter of
deduction from implicit laws, and more a matter of recognitional subsumption of the case at issue under a relevant prototype. (For a more

detailed treatment of this view of explanation—the *prototype activation model*—see Churchland 1989b.)

Such prototypes are no doubt at least modestly complex, and presumably they depict typical configurations of desires, beliefs, preferences, and so forth, roughly the same configurations that I have earlier attempted to express in the form of universally quantified sentences. Beyond this, I am able to say little about them, at least on this occasion. But I hope I have succeeded in making intelligible to you a novel approach to the problem of explanatory understanding in humans. This is an approach that is grounded at last in what we know about the brain. And it is an approach that ascribes to us neither reams of universally quantified premises, nor deductive activity on a heroic scale. Explanatory understanding turns out to be not quite what we thought it was, because cognition in general gets characterized in a new way. And yet explanatory understanding remains the same *sort* of process in the case of human behavior as in the case of natural phenomena generally. And the question of the *adequacy* of our commonsense understanding remains as live as ever.

Notes

Acknowledgement: This essay is a substantially expanded version of a short paper presented at the British Joint Session Meetings in 1988, and published in the *Proceedings of the Aristotelian Society*, supplementary volume LXII (1988). My thanks to the editors for permission to use that material here.

References

Churchland, P. M. (1970), "The Logical Character of Action Explanations", *Philosophical Review*, 79, no. 2.

Churchland, P. M. (1979), *Scientific Realism and the Plasticity of Mind*, (Cambridge: Cambridge University Press).

Churchland, P. M. (1981), "Eliminative Materialism and the Propositional Attitudes", *Journal of Philosophy*, LXXVIII, no. 2.

Churchland, P. M. (1984), *Matter and Consciousness* (Cambridge: The MIT Press).

Churchland, P. M. (1986), "On the Continuity of Science and Philosophy", *Mind and Language*, 1, no. 1.

Churchland, P. M. (1989a), "On the Nature of Theories: A Neurocomputational Perspective", in Savage, W., ed., *Scientific Theories: Minnesota Studies in the Philosophy of Science*, Vol. XIV (Minneapolis: University of Minnesota Press).

Churchland, P. M. (1989b), "On the Nature of Explanation: A PDP Approach", *A Neurocomputational Perspective* (Cambridge, Mass., The MIT Press).

Feyerabend, P. K. (1963), "Materialism and the Mind-Body Problem", *Review of Metaphysics*, 17.

Goldman, A. (forthcoming, 1989).

Gordon, R. (1986), "Folk Psychology as Simulation", *Mind & Language* 1, no 2.

Haldane, J. (1988), "Understanding Folk", *Proceedings of the Aristotelian Society*, Supplementary Vol. LXII.

Kuhn, T. S. (1962), *The Structure of Scientific Revolutions* (Chicago: University of Chicago Press).

Lakoff, G. (1987), *Women, Fire and Dangerous Things* (Chicago: University of Chicago Press).

McKloskey, M. (1983), "Intuitive Physics", *Scientific American*, 248, no. 4: pp. 122-30.

Minsky, M. (1981), "A Framework for Representing Knowledge", in Haugeland, J., ed., *Mind Design* (Cambridge: The MIT Press).

Putnam, H. (1970), "Is Semantics Possible?", in Kiefer, H. & Munitz, M. eds., *Languages, Belief, and Metaphysics* (Albany: State University of New York Press). Reprinted in Putnam, H., *Mind, Language and Reality* (Cambridge: Cambridge University Press).

Putnam, H. (1975), "The Meaning of 'meaning'", in Gunderson, K., *Language, Mind and Knowledge: Minnesota Studies in the Philosophy of Science*, Vol. VII. Reprinted in Putnam H., *Mind, Language and Reality* (Cambridge: Cambridge University Press).

Rorty, R. (1965), "Mind-Body Identity, Privacy, and Categories", *Review of Metaphysics*, 1.

Rosch, E. (1981), "Prototype Classification and Logical Classification: The Two Systems", in Scholnick, E., ed., *New Trends in Cognitive Representation: Challenges to Piaget's Theory* (New Jersey: Lawrence Erlbaum).

Rosenberg, C. R., and Sejnowski, T. J. (1987), "Parallel Networks That Learn To Pronounce English Text", *Complex Systems*, 1.

Rumelhart, D. E., Hinton, G. E., and Williams, R. J., (1986), "Learning Internal Representations by Error Propagation", in Rumelhart, D. E., and McClelland, J. L., eds., *Parallel Distributed Processing: Explorations in the Microstructure of Cognition* (Cambridge: MIT Press, 1986).

Schank, R., and Abelson, R. (1977), *Scripts, Plans, Goals, and Understanding* (New Jersey: John Wiley and Sons).

Sellars, W. (1956), "Empiricism and the Philosophy of Mind", in Feigl, H. & Scriven, M., eds., *Minnesota Studies in the Philosophy of Science*, Vol. I (Minneapolis, University of Minnesota Press). Reprinted in Sellars, W., *Science, Perception and Reality* (London: Routledge and Keegan Paul, 1963).

Strawson, P. F. (1958), "Persons", *Minnesota Studies in the Philosophy of Science*, Vol. II, eds. Feigl, H., Scriven, M., and Maxwell, G. (Minneapolis: University of Minnesota Press).

Wilkes, K. (1981) "Functionalism, Psychology, and the Philosophy of Mind", *Philosophical Topics*, 12, no. 1.

Wilkes, K. (1984), "Pragmatics in Science and Theory in Common Sense", *Inquiry*, 27, no. 4.

Philosophical Perspectives, 3
Philosophy of Mind and Action Theory, 1989

ILLOGICAL BELIEF*

Nathan Salmon
University of California, Santa Barbara

I

My purpose here is to present a defense against some criticisms that have been leveled against various doctrines and theses I advanced in *Frege's Puzzle*,[1] and to draw out some philosophically interesting applications and consequences of some of the central ideas utilized in my defense. The two principal objections I shall consider—one of which is offered by Saul Kripke and the other by Stephen Schiffer—as I reconstruct them, tacitly presuppose or assume one or both of a pair of closely related and largely uncontroversial principles concerning belief and deductive reasoning. The first is a normative principle, which I shall call *the belief justification principle*. It may be stated thus:

Suppose x is a normal, fully rational agent who consciously and rationally believes a certain proposition p. Suppose also that x is consciously interested in the further question of whether q is also the case, where q is another proposition. Suppose further that q is in fact a trivial deductive consequence of p. Suppose finally that x fully realizes that q is a deductive consequence of p and is fully able to deduce q from p. Under these circumstances, x would be rationally justified in coming to believe q on the basis of his or her belief of p (and its deductive relationship to q), or alternatively, if x withholds belief from q (by disbelieving or by suspending judgement) for independent reasons, x would be rationally justified in accordingly relinquishing his or her belief of p.

The second principle is similar to this, except that it is descriptive rather than prescriptive. I shall call it *the belief closure principle*:

Make the same initial-condition suppositions concerning x *vis a vis* the propositions p and q as given in the belief justification principle. Under these circumstances, if x consciously considers the question of whether q is the case and has adequate time for reflection on the matter, x will in fact come to believe q in addition to p on the basis of his or her belief of p (and its deductive relationship to q), unless x instead withholds belief from q (either by disbelieving or by suspending judgement) for independent reasons, and accordingly relinquishes his or her belief of p.

The belief justification principle, since it is normative rather than predictive, may seem somehow more certain and on sounder footing than the belief closure principle, but both principles are quite compelling. I shall claim that there are situations that present straightforward counter-examples to both principles simultaneously. Specifically, I claim that these principles fail in precisely the sort of circumstances to which my objectors tacitly apply the principles.

First, a preliminary exposition of the project undertaken in *Frege's Puzzle* is in order. The central thesis is that ordinary proper names, demonstratives, other single-word indexicals or pronouns (such as 'he'), and other simple (noncompound) singular terms are, in a given possible context of use, Russellian "genuine names in the strict logical sense."[2] Put more fully, I maintain the following anti-Fregean doctrine: that the contribution made by an ordinary proper name or other simple singular term, to securing the information content of, or the proposition expressed by, declarative sentences (with respect to a given possible context of use) in which the term occurs (outside of the scope of nonextensional operators, such as quotation marks) is just the referent of the term, or the bearer of the name (with respect to that context of use). In the terminology of *Frege's Puzzle*, I maintain that the *information value* of an ordinary proper name is just its referent.

Some other theses that I maintain in *Frege's Puzzle* are also critical to the present discussion. One such thesis (which Frege and Russell both more or less accepted) is that the proposition that is the information content of a declarative sentence (with respect to a given context) is structured in a certain way, and that its structure and constituents mirror, and are in some way readable from, the structure and constituents of the sentence containing that proposition.[3] By and large, a simple (noncompound) expression contributes a single entity, taken as a simple (noncomplex) unit, to the information content of a sentence in which the expression occurs, whereas the contribution of a compound expression (such as a phrase or sentential clause) is a complex entity composed of the contributions of the simple components.[4] Hence, the contents of beliefs formulatable using ordinary proper names, demonstratives, or other simple singular terms, are on my view so-called *singular propositions* (David Kaplan), i.e., structured propositions directly about some individual, which occurs directly as a constituent of the proposition. This thesis (together with certain relatively uncontroversial assumptions) yields the consequence that *de re* belief (or *belief of*) is simply a special case of *de dicto* belief (*belief that*). To believe *of* an individual x, *de re*, that it (he, she) is F is to believe *de dicto* the singular proposition about (containing) x that it (he, she) is F, a proposition that can be expressed using an ordinary proper name for x. Similarly for the other propositional attitudes.

There is an important class of exceptions to the general rule that a compound expression contributes to the information content of a sentence in which it occurs a complex entity composed of the contributions of the simple components. These are compound predicates formed by abstraction from an open sentence. For example, from the "open" sentence 'I love her and she loves me'—with pronouns 'her' and 'she' functioning as "freely" as the free variables occurring in such open sentences of the formal vernacular as '$F(a, x)$ & $F(x, a)$'—we may form (by "abstraction") the compound predicate 'is someone such that I love her and she loves me'. Formally, using Alonzo Church's 'λ'-abstraction operator, we might write this '$(\lambda x)[F(a, x)$ & $F(x, a)]$'. Such an abstracted compound predicate should be seen as contributing something like an attribute or a Russellian *propositional function*, taken as a unit, to the information content of sentences in which it occurs, rather than as contributing a complex made up of the typical contributions of the compound's components.

In addition to this, I propose the sketch of an analysis of the binary relation of belief between believers and propositions (sometimes Russellian singular propositions). I take the belief relation to be, in effect, the existential generalization of a ternary relation, *BEL*, among believers, propositions, and some third type of entity. To believe a proposition *p* is to adopt an appropriate favorable attitude toward *p* when taking *p* in some relevant *way*. It is to agree to *p*, or to assent mentally to *p*, or to approve of *p*, or some such thing, when taking *p* a certain way. This is the *BEL* relation. I do not say a great deal about what the third relata for the *BEL* relation are. They are perhaps something like *proposition guises*, or *modes* of acquaintance or familiarity with propositions, or *ways* in which a believer may take a given proposition. The important thing is that, by definition, they are such that if a fully rational believer adopts conflicting attitudes (such as belief and disbelief, or belief and suspension of judgement) toward propositions *p* and *q*, then the believer must take *p* and *q* in different ways, by means of different guises, in harboring the conflicting attitudes toward them—even if *p* and *q* are in fact the same proposition. More generally, if a fully rational agent construes objects *x* and *y* as distinct (or even merely withholds construing them as one and the very same—as might be evidenced, for example, by the agent's adopting conflicting beliefs or attitudes concerning *x* and *y*), then for some appropriate notion of a way of taking an object, the agent takes *x* and *y* in different ways, even if in fact $x = y$.[5] Of course, to use a distinction of Kripke's, this formulation is far too vague to constitute a fully developed *theory* of proposition guises and their role in belief formation, but it does provide a *picture* of belief that differs significantly from the sort of picture of propositional attitudes advanced by Frege or Russell, and enough can be said concerning the *BEL* relation to allow for at least the sketch of a solution to certain philosophical problems, puzzles, and paradoxes—including those in the same family as Frege's notorious 'Hesperus'-'Phosphorus' puzzle.[6]

In particular, the *BEL* relation satisfies the following three conditions:

(*i*) *A* believes *p* if and only if there is some *x* such that *A* is familiar with *p* by means of *x* and *BEL*(*A*, *p*, *x*);[7]

(*ii*) *A* may believe *p* by standing in *BEL* to *p* and some *x* by means of which *A* is familiar with *p* without standing in *BEL* to *p* and all *x* by means of which *A* is familiar with *p*;

(*iii*) In one sense of 'withhold belief', *A* withholds belief concerning *p* (either by disbelieving or by suspending judgement) if and only if there is some *x* by means of which *A* is familiar with *p* and not-*BEL*(*A*, *p*, *x*).

These conditions generate a philosophically important distinction between withholding belief and failure to believe (i.e., not believing). In particular, one may both withhold belief from and believe the very same proposition simultaneously. (Neither withholding belief nor failure to believe is to be identified with the related notions of disbelief and suspension of judgement—which are two different ways of withholding belief, in my sense, and which may occur simultaneously with belief of the very same proposition in a single believer.)

It happens in most cases (though not all) that when a believer believes some particular proposition *p*, the relevant third relatum for the *BEL* relation is a function of the believer and some particular *sentence* of the believer's language. There is, for example, the binary function *f* that assigns to any believer *A* and sentence *S* of *A*'s language, the *way A* takes the proposition contained in *S* (in *A*'s language with respect to *A*'s context at some particular time *t*) were it presented to *A* (at *t*) through the very sentence *S*, if there is exactly one such way of taking the proposition in question. (In some cases, there are too many such ways of taking the proposition in question.)

This account may be applied to the comic-book legend of Superman and his woman-friend Lois Lane. According to this saga, Lois Lane is acquainted with Superman in both of his guises—as a mild-mannered reporter and dullard named 'Clark Kent' and as the superheroic defender of truth, justice, and the American way, named 'Superman'—but she is unaware that these are one and the very same person. Whereas she finds our hero somewhat uninteresting when she encounters him in his mild-mannered reporter guise, her heartbeat quickens with excitement whenever she encounters him, or even merely thinks of him, in his superhero guise. Consider now the sentence

(0) Lois Lane believes that Clark Kent is Superman.

Is this true or false? According to my account, it is true! For Lois Lane agrees to the proposition that Clark Kent is Superman when taking it in a certain way—for example, if one points to Superman in one of his guises and says 'He is him', or when the proposition is presented to her by such sentences as 'Clark Kent is Clark Kent' and 'Superman is Superman'. That is,

> BEL[Lois Lane, that Clark Kent is Superman, f(Lois Lane, 'Superman is Superman')].

Lois Lane also withholds belief concerning whether Superman is Superman. In fact, according to my account, she believes that Superman is not Superman! For she agrees to the proposition that Superman is not Superman when taking it in the way it is presented to her by the sentence 'Clark Kent is not Superman'. That is,

> BEL[Lois Lane, that Superman is not Superman, f(Lois Lane, 'Clark Kent is not Superman')],

and hence, since Lois Lane is fully rational, it is not the case that

> BEL[Lois Lane, that Superman is Superman, f(Lois Lane, 'Clark Kent is Superman')].

II

It is evident that these consequences of my account do not conform with the way we actually speak. Instead it is customary when discussing the Superman legend to deny sentence (0) and to say such things as

> (1) Lois Lane does not realize that Clark Kent is Superman.

According to my account, sentence (1) is literally false in the context of the Superman legend. In fact, (1)'s literal truth-conditions are, according to the view I advocate, conditions that are plainly unfulfilled (in the context of the Superman legend). Why, then, do we say such things as (1)? Some explanation of our speech patterns in these sorts of cases is called for. The explanation I offer in *Frege's Puzzle* is somewhat complex, consisting of three main parts. The first part of the explanation for the common disposition to utter or to assent to (1) is that speakers may have a tendency to confuse the content of (1) with that of

> (1′) Lois Lane does not realize that 'Clark Kent is Superman' is true (in English).

Since sentence (1') is obviously true, this confusion naturally leads to a similarly favorable disposition toward (1). This part of the explanation cannot be the whole story, however, since even speakers who know enough about semantics to know that the fact that Clark Kent is Superman is logically independent of the fact that the sentence 'Clark Kent is Superman' is true (in English, according to the legend), and who are careful to distinguish the content of (1) from that of (1'), are nevertheless favorably disposed toward (1) itself—because of the fact that Lois Lane bursts into uncontrollable laughter whenever the mere suggestion 'Clark Kent could turn out to be Superman' is put to her.

The second part of my explanation for (1)'s appearance of truth is that (1) itself is the product of a plausible but mistaken inference from the fact that Lois Lane sincerely dissents (or at least does not sincerely assent) when queried 'Is Clark Kent Superman?', while fully understanding the question and grasping its content, or (as Keith Donnellan has pointed out) even from her expressions of preference for the man of steel over the mild-mannered reporter. More accurately, ordinary speakers (and even most nonordinary speakers) are disposed to regard the fact that Lois Lane does not agree to the proposition that Clark Kent is Superman, when taking it in a certain way (the way it might be presented to her by the very sentence 'Clark Kent is Superman'), as sufficient to warrant the denial of sentence (0) and the assertion of sentence (1). In the special sense explained in the preceding section, Lois Lane withholds belief from the proposition that Clark Kent is Superman, actively failing to agree with it whenever it is put to her in so many words, and this fact misleads ordinary speakers, including Lois Lane herself, into concluding that Lois harbors no favorable attitude of agreement whatsoever toward the proposition in question, and hence does not believe it.

The third part of the explanation is that, where someone under discussion has conflicting attitudes toward a single proposition that he or she takes to be two independent propositions (i.e. in the troublesome 'Hesperus'-'Phosphorus', 'Superman'-'Clark Kent' type cases), there is an established practice of using belief attributions to convey not only the proposition agreed to (which is specified by the belief attribution) but also the way the subject of the attribution takes the proposition in agreeing to it (which is no part of the semantic content of the belief attribution). Specifically, there is an established practice of using such a sentence as (0), which contains the

uninteresting proposition that Lois Lane believes the singular proposition about Superman that he is him, to convey furthermore that
Lois Lane agrees to this proposition *when she takes it in the way
it is presented to her by the very sentence 'Clark Kent is Superman'*
(assuming she understands this sentence). That is, there is an established practice of using (0) to convey the thought that

> *BEL*[Lois Lane, that Clark Kent is Superman, *f*(Lois Lane,
> 'Clark Kent is Superman')].

III

The last part of the explanation just sketched may be clarified by
considering an objection raised by Schiffer.[8] Schiffer sees my theory
as attempting to explain ordinary speakers' dispositions to utter or
to assent to (1) by postulating that in such cases a particular
mechanism, of a sort described by H. P. Grice,[9] comes into play. The
mechanism works in the following way: A speaker deliberately utters a particular sentence where there is mutual recognition by the
speaker and his or her audience that the speaker believes the
sentence to be false. The speaker and the audience mutually
recognize that the speaker is not opting out of Grice's conversational
Cooperative Principle (according to which one should make one's
conversational contribution such as is required, at the stage at which
it occurs, by the accepted purpose or direction of the conversation),
and hence that the speaker is subject to the usual Gricean conversational maxims. Yet the speaker and audience also recognize that there
is a *prima facie* apparent violation of the first conversational *maxim
of Quality*: "Do not say what you believe to be false." The audience
infers, in accordance with the speakers intentions, that the speaker
is using the sentence not to commit himself or herself to its literal
content (which is taken to be false) but instead to convey, or to "implicate," some saliently related proposition, which is easily gleaned
from the context of the conversation. In the case of sentence (1), on
this account, the speaker employs this mechanism to implicate that
Lois Lane does not agree to the proposition that Clark Kent is Superman when she takes it in the way it is presented to her by the very
sentence 'Clark Kent is Superman'. Schiffer's criticism is that this account flies in the face of the obvious fact that ordinary speakers do
not believe (1) to be false, but believe it true.

This criticism is indeed decisive against the explanation described above for our propensity to say such things as (1). But this is not the explanation I proposed in *Frege's Puzzle*. Oddly, the very example of sentence (1) comes from a particular passage in *Frege's Puzzle* that explicitly precludes Schiffer's interpretation:

> Now, there is no denying that, given the proper circumstances, we say things like 'Lois Lane does not realize...that Clark Kent is Superman'... When we make these utterances, we typically do not intend to be speaking elliptically or figuratively; we take ourselves to be speaking literally and truthfully. (p. 81)

My pragmatic account of the appearance of truth in the case of such sentences as (1) is meant not only as an explanation of the widespread disposition to utter or to assent to (1), but equally as an explanation of the widespread intuition that (1) is literally true, and equally as an explanation of the widespread belief of the content of (1). What is needed, and what I attempt to provide (or at least a sketch thereof), is not merely an explanation of the disposition of ordinary speakers to utter or assent to (1) given the relevant facts concerning Lois Lane's ignorance of Superman's secret identity, but an explanation why ordinary speakers who understand (1) perfectly well, fully grasping its content, sincerely utter it while taking themselves to speaking literally and truthfully, without being exactly similarly disposed toward such synonymous sentences as

Lois Lane does not realize that Superman is Superman

when they also understand these sentences perfectly well and the common content of these sentences is something these speakers believe.[10] The particular Gricean mechanism that Schiffer describes is no doubt part of the correct explanation in *some* cases of how ordinary speakers may use certain sentences to convey what these sentences do not literally mean. But the particular mechanism in question cannot yield a coherent account of why ordinary speakers believe that a given sentence is true. How would the alleged explanation go? "Here's why ordinary speakers believe that sentence *S* is true: They realize that it's false. This mutual recognition of its falsity enables them to use *S* to convey something true. Their use of *S* to convey something true leads them to conclude that *S is* true." This alleged explanation is incoherent; it purports to explain ordinary speakers' belief that a given sentence is true by means of their belief that it is false. Clearly, no attempt to explain the widespread view that (1) is literally true can proceed from the initial hypothesis that ordinary speakers typically believe that (1) is literally false!

Schiffer's criticism concerns only the third part of the explanation sketched in the preceding section: the hypothesis that there is an established practice of using such a sentence as (0) to convey that Lois Lane agrees to the proposition that Clark Kent is Superman when taking it in the way it is presented to her by the very sentence 'Clark Kent is Superman'. I do not claim that this practice came about by means of a special Gricean mechanism requiring the mutual recognition by the speaker and his or her audience that sentence (0) is literally true. Quite the contrary, I suppose that many ordinary speakers, and most philosophers, would take the proposition that they use the sentence to convey to be the very content of the sentence. That is why they would deem the sentence literally false. Schiffer describes a particular mechanism that allows speakers to use a sentence to convey ("implicate") what it does not literally mean by means of a mutual recognition that what is conveyed cannot be what the sentence literally means. I had in mind an alternative mechanism that allows speakers to use a sentence to convey something stronger than what it literally means, thereby creating a mutual misimpression that what is conveyed is precisely what the sentence literally means. There is nothing in the general Gricean strategy (as opposed to the particular strategy involving Grice's first conversational maxim of Quality) that requires ordinary speakers to recognize or believe that the sentence used is literally false. Grice (*op. cit.*) describes several mechanisms that involve speakers' using a sentence mutually believed to be true to convey ("implicate") something further that the sentence does not literally mean, and Schiffer himself cites such a mechanism in the course of presenting his objection. Surely there can be such a mechanism that, when employed, sometimes has the unintended and unnoticed consequence that speakers' mistake what is conveyed ("implicated") for the literal content. Consider, for example, the conjunction 'Jane became pregnant and she got married', which normally carries the implicature that Jane became pregnant before getting married. Utterers of this sentence, in order to employ it with its customary implicature, need not be aware that the sentence is literally true even if Jane became pregnant only after getting married. Some utterers may well become misled by the sentence's customary implicature into believing that the sentence literally means precisely what it normally conveys—so that, if they believe that Mary became pregnant only after getting married, they would reject the true but misleading conjunction as literally false. A similar situation may obtain in connection with certain English indicative conditionals ("If you work hard, you will be rewarded") and universal generalizations ("All white male cats with blue eyes are deaf"), which carry an implicature of some salient connection between antecedent and consequent that is more than merely truth-functional "constant conjunction." (The implicated connection need not be the temporal relation of earlier-later, as in the conjunction case.) It is this general sort of situation, or something very similar, that I impute to propositional-attitude attributions.[11]

Frege's Puzzle makes the suggestion that, in a certain type of case, a simple belief attribution ⌜c believes that S⌝ may be routinely used to convey the further information (not semantically encoded) that (assuming he or she understands his or her sentence for S) x agrees to the proposition p when taking it in the way it is presented to x by the very sentence S, where x is the referent of c and p is the content of the nonindexical sentence S.[12] The book does not include the much stronger claim that the manner in which such a belief attribution is routinely used to convey this further information must exhibit all of the features that characterize Gricean implicature—let alone does it include the highly specific claim that the phenomenon in question is an instance of Gricean particularized conversational implicature.

I have not thoroughly explored the relation of Grice's many rich and fruitful ideas to the sort of project undertaken in *Frege's Puzzle*; obviously, there is a great deal more to be investigated. It should be clear, however, that there is nothing in Grice's general apparatus that makes the sort of explanation I have in mind in connection with propositional-attitude attributions altogether impossible. Quite the contrary, some of the central ideas of the Gricean program are obviously directly applicable.

IV

In *Frege's Puzzle* I explicitly applied the various doctrines and theses sketched in Section I above to Kripke's vexing puzzle about belief.[13] Kripke considers a certain Frenchman, Pierre, who at some time t_1, speaks only French and, on the basis of deceptive travel brochures published by the London Chamber of Commerce and the like, comes to assent to the French sentence 'Londres est jolie' (as a sentence of French), which literally means in French that London is pretty. At some later time t_2, Pierre moves to London and learns the English language by direct assimilation (not by translation in an ESL course). Seeing only especially unappealing parts of the city, and not recognizing that this city called 'London' is the very same city that he and his fellow French speakers call 'Londres', Pierre comes to assent to the sentence 'London is not pretty' (as a sentence of English), while maintaining his former attitude toward the French sentence 'Londres est jolie'. Kripke presses the following question: Does Pierre believe at t_2 that London is pretty? The puzzle arises from Kripke's forceful demonstration that both the assertion that Pierre does believe this, and the denial that he does, appear deeply unsatisfactory (for different reasons). Likewise, both the assertion that Pierre believes at t_2 that London is *not* pretty and the denial that he does appear deeply unsatisfactory.

What does my account say about Pierre's doxastic disposition at t_2 *vis a vis* the propositions that London is pretty and that London is not pretty? I maintain that he believes them both. For he understands the French sentence 'Londres est jolie' when he assents to it, fully grasping its content. That content is the proposition that London is pretty. Since he agrees to this proposition when he takes it in the way it is presented to him by the French sentence, he believes it. Exactly the same thing obtains with regard to the negation of this proposition and the English sentence 'London is not pretty'. Hence he believes this proposition too. In fact, Pierre presumably also assents to the conjunctive sentence 'Londres is pretty but London is not', as a sentence of Frenglish, i.e. French-cum-English (French-English "word-salad"). And he understands this sentence in Frenglish. Hence he even believes the conjunctive proposition that London is pretty and London is not pretty. If he is sufficiently reflective, he will even know that he believes that London is pretty and London is not pretty. For given adequate time to reflect on the matter he can, with sufficient linguistic competence and ample epistemic justification, assent to the sentence 'You, Pierre, believe that *Londres* is pretty but London is not', taken as addressed to him as a sentence of Frenglish. The tri-part explanation sketched in Section

II above may easily be extended to account for our propensity to say such things (in Frenglish) as 'Pierre does not realize that London is *Londres*' despite their falsity.

Kripke objects to the sort of account I offer of Pierre's situation with some trenchant remarks. I quote at length:

> But there seem to be insuperable difficulties with [the position that Pierre believes both that London is pretty and that London is not pretty]... We may suppose that Pierre, in spite of the unfortunate situation in which he now finds himself, is a leading philosopher and logician. He would *never* let contradictory beliefs pass. And surely anyone, leading logician or no, is in principle in a position to notice and correct contradictory beliefs if he has them. Precisely for this reason, we regard individuals who contradict themselves as subject to greater censure than those who merely have false beliefs. But it is clear that Pierre, as long as he is unaware that the cities he calls 'London' and '*Londres*' are one and the same, is in no position to see, by logic alone, that at least one of his beliefs must be false. He lacks information, not logical acumen. He cannot be convicted of inconsistency: to do so is incorrect.
>
> We can shed more light on this if we change the case. Suppose that, in France, Pierre, instead of affirming "*Londres est jolie*," had affirmed, more cautiously, "*Si New York est jolie, Londres est jolie aussi*," so that [according to this account] he believed that *if* New York is pretty, so is London. Later Pierre moves to London, learns English as before, and says (in English) "London is not pretty." So he now [allegedly] believes, further, that London is *not* pretty. Now from the two premises, both of which appear to be among his beliefs, (a) if New York is pretty, London is, and (b) London is not pretty, Pierre should be able to deduce by *modus tollens* that New York is not pretty. But no matter how great Pierre's logical acumen may be, *he cannot in fact make any such deduction, as long as he supposes that* '*Londres*' *and* '*London*' *may name two different cities.* If he *did* draw such a conclusion, he would be guilty of a fallacy.
>
> Intuitively, he may well suspect that New York is pretty, and just this suspicion may lead him to suppose that

'*Londres*' and 'London' probably name distinct cities. Yet if we follow our normal practice of reporting the beliefs of French and English speakers, *Pierre has available to him (among his beliefs) both the premises of a modus tollens argument that New York is not pretty.* ... (pp. 257-258)

... Pierre is in no position to draw ordinary logical consequences from the conjoint set of what, when we consider him separately as a speaker of English and as a speaker of French, we would call his beliefs. He cannot infer a contradiction from his separate [alleged] beliefs that London is pretty and that London is not pretty. Nor, in the modified situation above, would Pierre make a normal *modus tollens* inference from his [alleged] beliefs that London is not pretty and that London is pretty if New York is. ... Indeed, if he *did* draw what would appear to be the normal conclusion in this case..., Pierre would in fact be guilty of a logical fallacy. (p. 262)

... The situation of the puzzle seems to lead to a breakdown of our normal practices of attributing belief... [The view that Pierre believes both that London is pretty and that London is not pretty] definitely get[s] it *wrong*. [That view] yields the result that Pierre holds inconsistent beliefs, that logic alone should teach him that one of his beliefs is false. Intuitively, this is plainly incorrect. ... [It is] *obviously wrong*...[a] patent falsehood... (pp. 266-267)

... when we enter into the area exemplified by...Pierre, we enter into an area where our normal practices of interpretation and attribution of belief are subjected to the greatest possible strain, perhaps to the point of breakdown. So is the notion of the *content* of someone's assertion, the *proposition* it expresses.

... Pierre's [case] lies in an area where our normal apparatus for the ascription of belief is placed under the greatest strain and may even break down. (pp. 269-270)

These passages indicate (or at least strongly suggest) that Kripke rejects as "plainly incorrect" the view, which I maintain, that Pierre believes at t_2 both that London is pretty and that London is not pretty.[14]

V

Schiffer raises a second objection to the theory advanced in *Frege's Puzzle*—one that is evidently similar in certain respects to Kripke's, but focuses more on the *de re* mode than on the *de dicto*. Schiffer's second criticism concerns such nesting (or second-level) propositional-attitude attributions as

(2) Floyd believes that Lois Lane does not realize that Clark Kent is Superman.

Schiffer tells a little story according to which Floyd is an ordinary speaker who is fully aware that the mild-mannered reporter is none other than the man of steel himself, and who is also aware of Lois Lane's ignorance of this fact. Schiffer argues that, whereas sentence (2) is straightforwardly true in the context of this little story—since Floyd believes that sentence (1) is true (and knows that if (1) is true, then Lois Lane does not realize that Clark Kent is Superman)—I am committed by my adherence to my central thesis (which Schiffer calls 'the 'Fido'-Fido theory of belief') to the falsity of (2), and further by my account of the dispositions of ordinary speakers to utter or to assent to (1), to the erroneous claim that Floyd does not believe that sentence (1) is true, and instead believes it to be false.

We have seen in Section III above that, contrary to Schiffer's interpretation, the explanation I offer for Floyd's propensity to utter (1) does not involve the obviously false claim that Floyd believes (1) to be false. How is it that I am committed to the claim that Floyd does not believe that Lois Lane does not realize that Clark Kent is Superman, and hence to the falsity of (2)? Schiffer argues that I am thus committed by invoking a certain principle that concerns *de re* belief, and which he has elsewhere called 'Frege's Constraint'.[15] Actually, the principle Schiffer explicitly cites is inadequate for his purposes, and should be replaced by a pair of principles which together entail the cited principle. The first might be called 'Frege's Thesis' and may be stated (using Schiffer's theoretical apparatus and terminology) as follows:

If x believes y to be F, then there is an object m that is a mode of presentation of y and x believes y under m to be F.

The second principle, which I shall call 'Schiffer's Constraint', is the following (again stated using Schiffer's theoretical apparatus and terminology):

> If a fully rational person x believes a thing y under a mode
> of presentation m to be F and also disbelieves y under a
> mode of presentation m' to be F, then $m \neq m'$ and x
> construes m and m' as (modes of) presenting distinct
> individuals.

Together these two principles pose a serious obstacle to my taking the position, which seems undeniably correct, that sentence (2) is true. For Floyd, whom we may suppose to be fully rational, no doubt believes that Lois Lane realizes that Superman is Superman. Yet given that Floyd is aware of Superman's secret identity, there do not seem to be the two modes of presentation required by Frege's Thesis and Schiffer's Constraint in order for Floyd to believe furthermore that Lois Lane does not realize that Clark Kent is Superman.

VI

Let us consider first Kripke's argument against the view that Pierre believes at t_2 both that London is pretty and that it is not. I briefly addressed Kripke's objection in *Frege's Puzzle*. I shall elaborate here on certain aspects of my reply.[16]

Kripke's primary critical argument might be stated in full thus:

> *P1*: Pierre sees, by logic alone, that the propositions (beliefs)
> that London is pretty and that London is not pretty are
> contradictory.
> *P2*: If Pierre has the beliefs that London is pretty and that
> London is not pretty, then he is in principle in a
> position to notice that he has these beliefs.

Therefore,

> *C1*: If Pierre has the beliefs that London is pretty and that
> London is not pretty, then he is in principle in a
> position to see both that he has these beliefs and that
> they are contradictory.
> *P3*: But Pierre, as long as he is unaware that the cities he
> calls 'London' and '*Londres*' are one and the same, is in
> no position to see that the propositions (beliefs) that
> London is pretty and that London is not pretty are
> simultaneously beliefs of his and contradictory, and

hence is in no position to see that at least one of his beliefs must be false.

Therefore,

> C2: As long as Pierre is unaware that the cities he calls 'London' and '*Londres*' are one and the same, it is incorrect to say that he has the beliefs that London is pretty and that London is not pretty.

An exactly similar argument may be stated, as Kripke proposes, replacing the belief that London is pretty with the more cautious belief that London is pretty if New York is, and replacing the logical attribute of contradictoriness with that of entailing that New York is not pretty. Furthermore, in this case we may replace the epistemic state of being in a position to see that at least one of the first pair of beliefs must be false with the disposition of being such that one would be logically justified in inferring that New York is not pretty from the second, more cautious pair of beliefs.

Both the displayed argument and the one obtained by making the suggested substitutions are extremely compelling. But they are fallacious. I do not mean by this that they proceed from false premises. I mean that they are invalid: the premises are all true, but one of the critical inferences is fallacious. Which one?

The fallacy involved may be seen more clearly if we first consider the following simpler and more direct argument:

> If Pierre has the beliefs that London is pretty if New York is and that London is not pretty, then (assuming that he consciously considers the further question of whether New York is pretty, that he fully realizes that the proposition that New York is not pretty is a trivial and immediate deductive consequence of the propositions that London is pretty if New York is and that London is not pretty, that he has no independent reasons for withholding belief from the proposition that New York is not pretty, and that he has adequate time for reflection on the matter) he will come to believe that New York is not pretty on the basis of these beliefs, and he would be logically justified in doing so. But Pierre, as long as he is unaware that the cities he calls 'London' and '*Londres*' are one and the same, will not come to believe that New York is not pretty on the basis of his

beliefs that London is pretty if New York is and that London is not pretty, and he would not be logically justified in doing so. Therefore, as long as Pierre is unaware that the cities he calls 'London' and '*Londres*' are one and the same, it is incorrect to say that he has the beliefs that London is pretty if New York is and that London is not pretty.

This argument is evidently at least very much like one of Kripke's, and it is valid. I have formulated it in such a way as to make obvious its reliance, in its first premise, on the belief closure and justification principles. (Let p be the conjunctive proposition that whereas London is pretty if New York is, London is not pretty, and let q be the entailed proposition that New York is not pretty.) I maintain that Pierre's inability to infer that New York is not pretty presents a bona fide counter-example to these principles, so that the first premise of this argument is false. The theses advanced in *Frege's Puzzle* show how Pierre's case may be seen as presenting a counter-example. Pierre fully understands the English sentence 'London is not pretty' and also the Frenglish sentence '*Londres* is pretty if New York is', grasping their content. In particular, he understands the Frenglish sentence to mean precisely what it does mean (in Frenglish): that London is pretty if New York is. (He does not misunderstand it to mean, for example, that *Rome* is pretty if New York is. If any French speaker who has never been to London can nevertheless understand French sentences containing the French name '*Londres*', Pierre understands the particular sentence '*Si* New York *est jolie, Londres est jolie aussi*' as well as its Frenglish translations.) When these sentences are put to him, he unhesitatingly assents; he agrees to the propositions that are their contents when he takes these propositions in the way they are presented to him by these very sentences. Hence he believes these propositions.

Pierre also fully understands the English sentence 'London is pretty if New York is', grasping its content. He is fully aware that the proposition so expressed, taken together with the proposition expressed by 'London is not pretty', collectively entail that New York is not pretty. Unfortunately for Pierre, he does not take this conditional proposition the same way when it is presented to him by the different sentences. He mistakes the proposition for two, logically independent propositions—just as he mistakes London itself for two separate cities. This is evidenced by the fact that he harbors conflicting doxastic attitudes toward the proposition. He believes it, since he agrees to it taking it one way (the way it is presented to him by the Frenglish sentence, or by its French translation), but he also withholds belief from it, in the sense specified in Section I above, since he does not agree to it taking it the other way (the way it is presented to him by the English sentence). It is this confusion of Pierre's—his lack of recognition of the same proposition when it is presented to him differently—that prevents Pierre from making the logical connection between his two beliefs and drawing the *modus tollens* inference. He fails to recognize that his belief that London is not pretty is the negation of the consequent of his belief that London is pretty if New York is.

It is precisely Pierre's sort of situation, in which there is propositional recognition failure, that gives rise to counter-examples to the belief closure and justification principles. The principles can, of course, be weakened to rescue them from vulnerability to this sort of counter-example. One way to do this is to adjoin a further initial-condition supposition: that x recognizes that q is a deductive consequence of his or her belief of p. That is, we must be given not only that x recognizes both that he or she believes p and that p entails q, but furthermore that x also recognizes that p is both a belief of his or hers and entailing of q. Since he is a logician, Pierre knows that the compound proposition that *whereas London is pretty if New York is, London is not pretty* entails that New York is not pretty, and he also knows (taking this proposition in a different way) that this proposition is something he believes, but since he fails to recognize this proposition when taking it differently, he does not recognize that this proposition is *simultaneously* something that entails that New York is not pretty and something he believes.[17]

One might be tempted to defend these disputed instances of the belief closure and justification principles by arguing that if a normal, fully rational agent x knows both that a particular proposition p is something he or she believes and furthermore that p deductively entails another proposition q, then x can easily infer that p is simultaneously both something he or she believes and something that deductively entails q. Since the former conditions are already included as initial-condition suppositions in the belief closure and justification principles, the new initial-condition supposition would be entirely superfluous.

This purported defense of the belief closure and justification principles does not succeed. Notice how it is supposed to go. We might begin by noting that the argument form $\ulcorner a$ is F and a is G; therefore a is both F and $G\urcorner$ is valid, since it is simply a special application of the 'λ'-transformation rule of *abstraction*, which permits the inference from a formula ϕ_a to $\ulcorner(\lambda_x)[\phi x](a)\urcorner$, i.e. to $\ulcorner a$ is an individual such that $\phi_{it}\urcorner$ (where ϕ_a is the result of uniformly substituting free occurrences of a for free occurrences of 'x' in ϕ_x–or for "free" occurrences of the pronoun 'it' in ϕ_{it}). In particular, then, there is a valid argument from 'x believes p, and p deductively entails q' to 'p is something that x believes and that deductively entails q'. We then invoke the belief closure and justification principles to argue that if x believes the conjunctive proposition that he or she believes p and p deductively entails q, then (assuming the rest of the initial conditions obtain) x will infer that p is something that he or she believes and that deductively entails q, and x would be justified in doing so. This would be a *meta-application* of the belief closure and justification principles, an application to beliefs concerning inference and belief formation. But this meta-application of these principles is part of a purported justification of these very principles! The problem with this defense of the two principles is that, like the misguided attempt to defend induction-by-enumeration by citing inductive evidence of its utility, it presupposes precisely the very principles it is aimed at defending, and hence suffers from a vicious circularity. If we let x be Pierre, p be the conjunctive proposition that whereas London is pretty if New York is, London is not pretty, and q be the proposition that New York is not pretty, then the resulting instances of the belief closure and justification principles are precisely special instances whose truth is explicitly denied by the sort of account I advocate.

More generally, the theory advanced in *Frege's Puzzle* distinguishes sharply between a complex sentence ϕ_a and the logically equivalent sentence $\ulcorner(\lambda_x)[\phi x](a)\urcorner$ (or $\ulcorner a$ is such that $\phi_{it}\urcorner$) as regards their proposition content. I have argued elsewhere for this distinction in some detail in connection with sentences ϕ_a that involve multiple occurrences of the name a.[18] Thus, for example, Pierre no doubt believes (putting it in Frenglish) that *Londres* is prettier than London, and (according to my view) he thereby believes the proposition (putting it in proper English) that London is prettier than London, but he does not thereby believe the unbelievable proposition that London exceeds itself in pulchritude (that London is something that is prettier than itself). Likewise, Pierre believes the conjunctive proposition that London is pretty and London is not pretty, but he surely does not believe that London has the unusual property of being both pretty and not pretty.

The fallacy in Kripke's argument, as reconstructed above, occurs in the inference from the subsidiary conclusion *C1* and the additional premise *P3* to the final conclusion *C2*. More specifically, the argument would apparently involve an implicit and invalid intervening inference from *C1* to the following:

C1' : If Pierre has the beliefs that London is pretty and that London is not pretty, then he is in principle in a position to see that these propositions (beliefs) are simultaneously beliefs of his and contradictory, and hence in a position to see that at least one of his beliefs must be false.

This intervening subsidiary conclusion *C1'* together with premise *P3* validly yield the desired conclusion *C2*. The implicit inference from *C1* to *C1'* is, in effect, a meta-application of one of the disputed instances of the belief closure and justification principles. Pierre is indeed in a position to know that he believes that London is pretty and that London is not pretty. Being a logician, he certainly knows that the propositions that London is pretty and that London is not pretty are logically incompatible. But he believes these facts about these propositions only when taking one of them in different ways, believing it to be two logically independent propositions, failing to recognize it as a single proposition. He is in no position to see or infer that these two propositions are simultaneously believed by him and contradictory.

There is a serious residual problem with the account given so far of Pierre's situation. There is an extremely compelling reason to deny that Pierre believes that London is pretty: when the sentence 'London is pretty' is put to him (after t_2), he sincerely dissents from it in good faith, while fully understanding the sentence and grasping its content. The theoretical apparatus of *Frege's Puzzle* makes it possible to dispel at least some of the force of this sort of consideration. Using that apparatus, where '*f*' refers to the function that assigns to a speaker and a sentence of the speaker's idiolect the corresponding third relatum of the *BEL* relation (e.g., the way the speaker would take the content of the sentence were it presented to the speaker at t_2 by that very sentence), we may say that at t_2

   BEL[Pierre, that London is pretty, *f*(Pierre, '*Londres* is pretty')],

or in Frenglish,

   BEL[Pierre, that *Londres* is pretty, *f*(Pierre, '*Londres* is pretty')],

whereas we must deny that at t_2

   BEL[Pierre, that London is pretty, *f*(Pierre, 'London is pretty')].

Pierre believes the proposition that *Londres* is pretty, taking it as presented by those very words, but he also withholds belief from (in fact disbelieves) the proposition that London is pretty, taking it as presented by those very words. Pierre's doxastic disposition towards the proposition depends entirely on how the proposition is presented to him. The reason offered for denying that Pierre believes that London is pretty is a decisive reason for affirming that he disbelieves that London is pretty (and therefore that he withholds belief), but it is highly misleading evidence regarding the separate and independent question of whether he believes that London is pretty.[19]

VII

I turn now to Schiffer's criticism that I am committed to the falsity of the true sentence (2). I fully agree with Schiffer that sentence (2) is straightforwardly true in his little story involving Floyd, as long as Floyd understands sentence (1) when uttering it or assenting to it. In fact, far from being committed to the claim that (2) is false, the theory advanced in *Frege's Puzzle* is in fact committed to the precisely the opposite claim that (2) is true! This virtually follows directly from the first condition on the *BEL* relation given in Section I above, according to which it is sufficient for the truth of (2) that Floyd should agree to the content of (1) when taking this proposition the way it is presented to him by the very sentence (1).[20] On my view, then, Floyd does believe that Lois Lane does not realize that Clark Kent is Superman. In addition, I also maintain (as Schiffer correctly points out) that Floyd believes that Lois Lane does realize that Clark Kent is Superman—since Floyd believes the proposition that Lois Lane realizes that Superman is Superman, and on my view this just is the proposition that Lois Lane realizes that Clark Kent is Superman. Thus, I maintain that Floyd both believes and disbelieves that Lois Lane realizes that Clark Kent is Superman.

Schiffer has uncovered a very interesting philosophical problem here. Before presenting my solution, I want to emphasize the generality of the problem. The general problem is not one that is peculiar to my own theory of propositional-attitude attributions (contrary to the impression created by Schiffer's presentation of his criticism), but is equally a problem for the orthodox, Fregean theory, and indeed for virtually any theory of propositional-attitude attributions.

Consider an analogous situation involving straightforward (strict) synonyms. Suppose that Sasha learns the words 'ketchup' and 'catsup' not by being taught that they are perfect synonyms, but by actually consuming the condiment and reading the labels on the bottles. Suppose further that, in Sasha's idiosyncratic experience, people typically have the condiment called 'catsup' with their eggs and hash browns at breakfast, whereas they routinely have the condiment called 'ketchup' with their hamburgers at lunch. This naturally leads Sasha to conclude, erroneously, that ketchup and catsup are different condiments, condiments that happen to share a similar taste, color, consistency, and name. He sincerely utters the sentence 'Ketchup is a sandwich condiment; but no one in his right mind would eat a sandwich condiment with eggs at breakfast, so catsup is not a sandwich condiment'. Now, Tyler Burge, who has a considerable knowledge of formal semantics and who is well aware (unlike Sasha) that 'ketchup' and 'catsup' are exact synonyms, would claim that Sasha believes that ketchup is a sandwich condiment but that Sasha does not believe that catsup is, describing his view in exactly so many words.[21] Clearly, Burge believes that Sasha believes that ketchup is a sandwich condiment. (See note 23 below.) When queried, "Does Sasha believe that catsup is a sandwich condiment?", however, Burge sincerely responds "No," while fully understanding the question and grasping its content. Given Burge's mastery of English, there would seem to be every reason to say, therefore, that he also believes that Sasha does not believe that catsup is a sandwich condiment. Yet by an argument exactly analogous to Schiffer's, we are apparently barred, by Frege's Thesis and Schiffer's Constraint, from acknowledging this. For we have granted that Burge believes ketchup to be something Sasha believes is a sandwich condiment. If, while remaining fully rational, Burge also believed catsup (i.e. ketchup) *not* to be something Sasha believes is a sandwich condiment, there would be a violation of the conjunction of Frege's Thesis with Schiffer's Constraint. There are no relevant modes of presenting ketchup that Burge construes as (modes of) presenting different stuff, as are required by Frege's Thesis together with Schiffer's Constraint. The conjunction of Frege's Thesis with Schiffer's Constraint thus apparently prohibits us from acknowledging that Burge does indeed disbelieve what he sincerely claims to disbelieve— that Sasha believes that catsup is a sandwich condiment.

Some philosophers will conclude that, despite his insistence to the contrary, Burge really does not disbelieve that Sasha believes that catsup is a sandwich condiment, and when he protests that he does, he is operating under a misunderstanding of the phrase 'believes that'. What Burge really disbelieves, they claim, is something linguistic, for example that Sasha believes that the sentence 'Catsup is a sandwich condiment' is true in English, or that Sasha satisfies the sentential matrix 'x believes that catsup is a sandwich condiment' in English (i.e. that the open sentence 'x believes that catsup is a sandwich condiment' is true in English when Sasha is assigned as value for the free variable 'x').[22] Yet this seems plainly wrong—and therein lies the problem. Burge correctly understands the sentence 'Sasha believes that catsup is a sandwich condiment'. He understands it to mean (in English) that Sasha believes that catsup, i.e. ketchup, is a sandwich condiment. He knows enough formal semantics to know that the sentence does not mean instead that Sasha believes that the sentence 'Catsup is a sandwich condiment' is true in English, nor that Sasha satisfies the sentential matrix 'x believes that catsup is a sandwich condiment' in English. Burge sincerely dissents from this sentence (as a sentence of English) because of his philosophical views concerning belief (which assimilate the proposition so expressed with the false proposition that Sasha accepts, or would accept, the sentence 'Catsup is a sandwich condiment', understood in a certain way). Burge's sincere dissent surely indicates a belief on his part (even if it is confused) that Sasha does not believe that catsup is a sandwich condiment— in addition to his correct belief that Sasha does believe that ketchup is a sandwich condiment, and in addition to his (erroneous) linguistic belief that Sasha fails to satisfy the sentential matrix 'x believes that catsup is a sandwich condiment' in English. The problem is that this apparently conflicts with Frege's Thesis in conjunction with Schiffer's Constraint.

This time the objection is not an objection to my theory of belief attributions in particular. If Schiffer's second criticism of my theory of belief attributions is sound, any reasonable theory of belief attributions, even a Fregean theory, would be required to deny that Burge believes that Sasha does not believe that catsup is a sandwich condiment.[23] Yet surely we are not barred by the demands of reasonableness (and consistency) from acknowledging that Burge does indeed disbelieve what he claims to disbelieve. Since it proves too much, there must be something wrong with Schiffer's argument. What?[24]

It is perhaps natural to point an accusing finger at Schiffer's Constraint. Since this principle (in conjunction with Frege's Thesis) apparently bars us—Fregeans, Russellians, and other theorists alike—from acknowledging what is patently true about Burge's beliefs, it would appear that it must be incorrect.

I was careful in *Frege's Puzzle* to avoid particular commitments concerning the nature of what I call 'proposition guises' or 'ways of taking propositions' or 'means by which one is familiar with a proposition'. However, I am prepared to grant, for present purposes, that *something* along the lines of Frege's Thesis and Schiffer's Constraint is indeed correct.[25] Does this, together with the doctrines and theses I advocate in *Frege's Puzzle*, lead to a commitment to the falsity of (2), as Schiffer argues? If so, then my position is strictly *inconsistent* since I also maintain that (2) is true.

Contra Schiffer, my granting that something along the lines of Frege's Thesis and Schiffer's Constraint is correct does not commit me to the falsity of sentence (2). For illustration, first instantiate the 'x' to Floyd, the 'y' to the fact (or proposition) that Clark Kent is Superman, and the 'F' to the property of *being realized by Lois Lane*. On my theory, the fact (or proposition) that Clark Kent is Superman is just the fact that Superman is Superman. The relevant instances of the two principles entail that, since Floyd both believes and disbelieves this fact to be realized by Lois Lane, if he is fully rational he must grasp this fact by means of two distinct modes of presentation of it, he must take this fact in two different ways. I am happy to say that Floyd does. In fact, my theory more or less requires that he does. Unless Floyd himself believes with me what Schiffer calls 'the 'Fido'-Fido theory of meaning', he may rationally proclaim 'The fact that Superman is Superman is trivial and something that Lois Lane realizes, whereas the fact that Clark Kent is Superman is neither;

hence they are distinct facts'. As the discussion in Section I made clear, whatever else my notion of a *way of taking* an object is, it is such that if Floyd believes that a proposition p is distinct from a proposition q, then Floyd takes these propositions in different ways (even if $p = q$). If Floyd is sufficiently philosophical, he may mistake the singular proposition about Superman that he is him, when it is presented to him by the sentence 'Clark Kent is Superman', for some general proposition to the effect that the mild-mannered reporter having such-and-such drab physical appearance is the superhero who wears blue tights, a big 'S' on his chest, and a red cape, etc. Or instead he may mistake the proposition, so presented, for the singular proposition *taken in a certain way*, or what comes to the same thing, the singular proposition together with a certain way of taking it. This is how he takes the singular proposition when it is so presented. The fact that he knows this proposition to be true does not have the consequence that he sees it as the very same thing, in the very same way, as the corresponding thing (general proposition or singular-proposition-taken-in-a-certain-way) that he associates with 'Superman is Superman'.

Consider Frege in place of Floyd. On my view, Frege mistook the singular proposition about the planet Venus that it is it to be two different propositions ("thoughts"). He took this proposition in one way when it was presented to him by the sentence '*Der Morgenstern ist derselbe wie der Morgenstern*' (the German version of 'Morningstar is the same as Morningstar') and in another way when it was presented to him by the sentence '*Der Morgenstern ist derselbe wie der Abendstern*' ('Morningstar is the same as Eveningstar')—despite the fact that he was well aware that the names '*Morgenstern*' and '*Abenstern*' refer to ("mean") the same planet. That he took this proposition in two different ways is established by the fact that he took it to be two different propositions. Floyd is in a similar state with respect to the singular proposition about Superman that he is him—even if Floyd has not formed a specific view about the nature of propositions in general or about the nature of this proposition in particular, as long as he takes this proposition to be two different propositions. Anyone who does not consciously subscribe to the sort of theory advanced in *Frege's Puzzle* is likely to have different perspectives on a given singular proposition of the form x *is* x when it is presented in various ways, seeing it as a different entity each time.[26]

Let us return to Frege's Thesis and Schiffer's Constraint. Suppose instead that the '*y*' is instantiated this time to Superman (or to Clark Kent) and the '*F*' to the property of *being an individual x such that Lois Lane realizes that x is Superman*, or *being someone that Lois Lane realizes is Superman*. Surely Floyd believes Superman to have this property. (We ask Floyd, "You know that man who calls himself 'Superman'. Does Lois Lane realize that he is Superman?" If Floyd understands the question, he should answer "Yes.") If at the same time Floyd disbelieves Superman to have this property, yet he remains fully rational, the conjunction of Frege's Thesis with Schiffer's Constraint will have been violated. As Schiffer points out, it will not do in this case to defend my theory by claiming that there are relevant modes of presentation *m* and *m'* of Superman that Floyd grasps but construes as (modes of) presenting different individuals, for there are no such modes of presentation in Schiffer's little story.

Does Floyd disbelieve Superman to be such that Lois realizes that he is Superman? Put another way, does Floyd believe Clark Kent to be someone that Lois Lane does not realize is Superman? I suspect that Schiffer assumed that if I were to concede that Floyd believes Lois Lane does not realize that Clark Kent is Superman, it would simply follow—according to my own theory—that Floyd believes Clark Kent to be someone that Lois Lane does not realize is Superman. That is, Schiffer's second criticism apparently involves an inference from

(2) Floyd believes that Lois Lane does not realize that Clark Kent is Superman

to

(3) Floyd believes that Clark Kent is someone that Lois does not realize is Superman.

On my theory, it virtually follows from (3) that Floyd believes Clark Kent not to be someone that Lois Lane realizes is Superman. The conjunction of Frege's Thesis with Schiffer's Constraint would thus bar me from acknowledging the truth of (2).

It is an essential part of the theory I advanced in *Frege's Puzzle*, however, that (3) does *not* follow from (2). The theory advanced in *Frege's Puzzle* distinguishes sharply between the proposition that Lois Lane does not realize that Clark Kent is such-and-such and the proposition that Clark Kent is someone that Lois Lane does not realize is such-and-such. These propositions differ in structure. Roughly put, Clark Kent is the subject of the latter proposition, but not of the former. According to my account, Floyd believes that Lois Lane does not realize that Clark Kent is Superman but, at least very likely, he does not also believe of Superman that he is someone Lois Lane does not realize is Superman.

In fact, it is precisely in the implicit inference from (2) to (3) that Schiffer might be invoking the belief closure principle (and perhaps the belief justification principle as well). Here again, the relevant logical entailment is an instance of the inference rule of abstraction. And here again, we seem to have an example of someone believing a proposition while being in no position to infer a simple deductive consequence from the proposition. Worse, if Schiffer's apparent implicit inference from (2) to (3) is indeed based on an application of the belief closure principle, as it seems to be, it is a fallacious application. For one of the initial-condition provisos of the belief closure principle is that the agent is aware of the deductive relationship between his or her current belief and its deductive consequence. But it seems likely in Schiffer's little story that Floyd does not believe that the proposition that Clark Kent is someone that Lois Lane does not realize is such-and-such is a valid deductive consequence of the proposition that Lois Lane does not realize that Clark Kent is such-and-such.[27] Given his favorable attitude toward sentence (1), it is evident that Floyd believes that Lois Lane does not realize that Clark Kent is Superman, but he is in no position to infer that Clark Kent is someone that Lois Lane does not realize is Superman, and he would not be logically justified in doing so. For we may suppose that Floyd also believes that Superman is someone that Lois Lane realizes is Superman. On my view, this is just to say that Floyd believes the singular proposition about Superman, i.e. Clark Kent, that *he* is someone that Lois Lane realizes is Superman. Floyd is not about to relinquish this belief of his. He would indeed be less than fully rational, in the sense used in Schiffer's Constraint, if at the same time he also formed the belief of Superman (i.e. Clark Kent) that he is someone that Lois Lane does not realize is Superman.

Floyd would be less than fully rational, that is, *unless* he has gained a *new* mode of familiarity with Superman, an additional mode of presentation, by encountering Superman on another occasion and failing to recognize him, *or* he somehow mistakes the logically incompatible properties of being someone Lois Lane realizes is Superman and of being someone Lois Lane does not realize is Superman—which are properties that such individuals as you, me, and Superman either have or lack in an absolute *de re* way—for properties of *individuals-under-guises* (or equivalently, for binary relations between individuals and ways of conceiving them).[28] Either of these predicaments might rescue Floyd from irrationality even when he both believes and disbelieves Superman to be someone Lois Lane realizes is Superman. For present purposes, we may assume that Floyd has acquired neither a new mode of presentation nor this philosophically sophisticated confusion.

Suppose we queried Floyd, "You know that man who calls himself 'Superman' and 'Clark Kent'. Does Lois Lane realize that he is Superman, or does she fail to realize that he is Superman?" If he understands the question, he should answer "She *does* realize that he is Superman." If he were sufficiently philosophical, he might describe his pertinent beliefs by adding, "Lois does not realize that *Clark Kent* is Superman. But if you're asking about the man himself (and not about the man-under-one-of-his-guises), she thinks he is two men. She *doubts* that he is Superman, but she also realizes that he is Superman. It all depends on the guise under which he is presented to her." Floyd cannot fully rationally add to this stock of beliefs a further belief that he would express by 'That man, Clark Kent, is someone Lois does *not* realize is Superman'. If he added this belief to his present stock, without relinquishing any of his current beliefs, he would believe of Superman that he simultaneously is and also is not someone Lois Lane realizes is Superman, that he both is and is not such that Lois Lane realizes that he is Superman. That would indeed be less than fully rational, in the sense used in Schiffer's Constraint (unless Floyd is under the sort of confusion mentioned in the preceding paragraph). To use a piece of terminology recently introduced by Schiffer, Floyd, in both believing and disbelieving that Lois Lane realizes that Clark Kent is Superman, exhibits *the belief/disbelief phenomenon with respect to* the phrase 'that Clark Kent is Superman' (which he does not construe as standing for the same thing as the phrase 'that Superman is Superman').[29] However, since on my view Floyd (unless he is under the sort of confusion mentioned above) does not disbelieve Clark Kent to be someone that Lois realizes is Superman, he does not exhibit the belief/disbelief phenomenon with respect to the name 'Clark Kent' (which he rightly construes as standing for the same individual as the name 'Superman'). Hence, my theory does not conflict here with the conjunction of Frege's Thesis and Schiffer's Constraint.[30]

VIII

Although the general philosophical problem uncovered by Schiffer does not refute my theory of propositional-attitude attributions (or Frege's), it does pose a very serious difficulty for—in fact, a refutation of—a proposal originally made by W. V. Quine in 1956 in his classic "Quantifiers and Propositional Attitudes,"[31] and more recently endorsed (and improved upon) by David Kaplan.[32] The proposal is one for translating (or in Quine's case, replacing) constructions involving quantification into intentional or content-sensitive operators by a certain type of construction—which Kaplan calls 'syntactically *de re*'—that avoids such quantifying in. In particular, a syntactically *de dicto* open sentence

c believes that ϕ_x,

where 'x' is the only free variable of the open sentence ϕ_x, and has only one free occurrence therein (positioned inside the scope of the content-sensitive syntactically *de dicto* operator 'c believes that'), is to be replaced by

c believes the property of being an object y such that ϕ_y of x

(Quine), or equivalently, to be translated into the syntactically *de re*

x is believed by c to be an object y such that ϕ_y

(Kaplan). The proposed substitutes artfully leave the free variable 'x' outside the scope of 'believe'.[33] Accordingly, on this proposal, the syntactically *de dicto* open sentence

(2′) Floyd believes that Lois Lane does not realize that x is Superman

is rewritten as

Floyd believes the property of being an object y such that Lois Lane does not realize the property of being Superman of y, of x

(Quine), or as

x is believed by Floyd to be an object y such that y is not realized by Lois Lane to be Superman

(Kaplan), or more colloquially as

(3′′) Floyd believes x to be someone that Lois Lane does not realize to be Superman.

Now, in Schiffer's little story, (2′) is true when Superman is assigned as value for the variable 'x', i.e. Superman satisfies (2′). Yet Schiffer's argument demonstrates that (3′′) is false when Superman is assigned as value for 'x', i.e. Superman does not satisfy (3′′). If (3′′) were true of Superman, Floyd would be less than fully rational, in the sense used in Schiffer's Constraint (unless he is under the confusion mentioned in the preceding section concerning the nature of the property of being someone Lois Lane realizes is Superman), since he would then both believe and disbelieve Superman to be someone Lois realizes is Superman, while lacking the required "modes of presentation" construed as (modes of) presenting distinct individuals. The proposed translation of (2′) into (3′′) thus fails, and for precisely the same reason as Schiffer's implicit inference from (2) to (3).[34]

Notes

*Part of the present paper was presented to the Pacific Division of the American Philosophical Association on March 26, 1987. It has benefitted from discussion with Stephen Schiffer and with Scott Soames. Thanks go also to Keith Donnellan and the participants in his seminar at UCLA during Spring 1987 for their insightful comments on *Frege's Puzzle*, and to the participants in my seminar at UCSB during Fall 1986 for forcing me to elaborate on my response to Kripke's objection to my position regarding his puzzle about belief.
1. Cambridge, Mass.: Bradford Books/MIT Press, 1986.
2. See Russell's "Knowledge by Acquaintance and Knowledge by Description," Chapter X of Russell's *Mysticism and Logic and Other Essays* (London: Longmans, Green and Company, 1911): 209-232, also in N. Salmon and S. Soames, eds., *Propositions and Attitudes* (Oxford University Press, Readings in Philosophy, 1988); and Russell's "The Philosophy of Logical Atomism," in his *Logic and Knowledge*, R. C. Marsh, ed. (London: George Allen and Unwin, 1956), pp. 177-281; also in his *The Philosophy of Logical Atomism*, D. Pears, ed. (La Sall: Open Court, 1985), pp. 35-155.
3. This separates the theory of *Frege's Puzzle* together with the theories of Frege, Russell, and their followers, from contemporary theories that assimilate the information contents of declarative sentences with such

things as sets of possible worlds, or sets of situations, or functions from possible worlds to truth-values, etc.

Both Frege and Russell would regard declarative sentences as typically reflecting only *part of* the structure of their content, since they would insist that many (perhaps even most) grammatically simple (noncompound) expressions occurring in a sentence may (especially if introduced into the language by abbreviation or by some other type of explicit "definition") contribute complex proposition-constituents that would have been more perspicuously contributed by compound expressions. In short, Frege and Russell regard the prospect of expressions that are grammatically simple yet semantically compound (at the level of content) as not only possible but ubiquitous. Furthermore, according to Russell's Theory of Descriptions, definite and indefinite descriptions ('the author of *Waverley*', 'an author', etc.), behave grammatically but not semantically (at the level of content) as a self-contained unit, so that a sentence containing such an expression is at best only a rough guide to the structure of the content. Russell extends this idea further to ordinary proper names and most uses of pronouns and demonstratives. This makes the structure of nearly any sentence only a very rough guide to the structure of the sentence's content. The theory advanced in *Frege's Puzzle* sticks much more closely to the grammatical structure of the sentence. (But see the following paragraph in the text concerning abstracted predicates.)

4. There are well-known exceptions to the general rule—hence the phrase 'by and large'. Certain nonextensional operators, such as quotation marks, create contexts in which compound expressions contribute themselves as units to the information content of sentences in which the expression occurs. Less widely recognized is the fact that even ordinary temporal operators (e.g. 'on April 1, 1986' + past tense) create contexts in which some compound expressions (most notably, open and closed sentences) contribute complexes other than their customary contribution to information content. See my "Tense and Singular Propositions," in J. Almog, J. Perry, and H. Wettstein, eds., *Themes from Kaplan* (Oxford University Press, forthcoming). The following paragraph in the text cites another largely overlooked class of exceptions.

5. An appropriate notion of a way of taking an object is such that if an agent encounters a single object several times and each time construes it as a different object from the objects in the previous encounters, or even as a different object *for all he or she knows*, then each time he or she takes the object in a new and different way. This is required in order to accommodate the fact that an agent in such circumstances may (perhaps *inevitably will*) adopt several conflicting attitudes toward what is in fact a single object. One cannot require, however, that these ways of taking objects are rich enough by themselves to determine the object so taken, without the assistance of extra-mental, contextual factors. Presumably, twin agents who are molecule-for-molecule duplicates, and whose brains are in exactly the same configuration down to the finest detail, may encounter different (though duplicate) objects, taking them

in the very same way. Likewise, a single agent might be artificially induced through brain manipulations into taking different objects the same way.

6. The *BEL* relation is applied to additional puzzles in my "Reflexivity," *Notre Dame Journal of Formal Logic*, 27, 3 (July 1986), pp. 401-429; also in N. Salmon and S. Soames, eds., *Propositions and Attitudes*.

7. I do not claim that a sentence of the form ⌜A believes p⌝ is exactly synonymous with the existential formula on the right-hand side of 'if and only if' in condition (*i*). I do claim that condition (*i*) is a (metaphysically) necessary, conceptually *a priori* truth. (See two paragraphs back in the text concerning the contents of predicates. It may be helpful to think of the English verb 'believe' as a *name* for the binary relation described by the right-hand side of (*i*), i.e., for the existential generalization on the third argument-place of the *BEL* relation.) My claim in *Frege's Puzzle* (p. 111) that belief may be so "analyzed" is meant to entail that condition (*i*) is a necessary *a priori* truth, not that the two sides of the biconditional are synonymous. (My own view is that something along these lines is all that can be plausibly claimed for such purported philosophical "analyses" as have been offered for ⌜A knows p⌝, ⌜A perceives B⌝, ⌜A (nonnaturally) means p in uttering S⌝, etc.)

8. "The 'Fido'-Fido Theory of Belief," in James Tomberlin, ed., *Philosophical Perspectives 1: Metaphysics* (Atascadero: Ridgeview, 1987), pp. 455-480. Schiffer's article includes a rejoinder, in an appended postscript, to many of the arguments of the present article. I think it is useful, however, to include in the present article my own statements of the arguments and replies that Schiffer is rejoining in his postscript. It is left to the reader to evaluate the relative merits of my replies to Schiffer's objections and Schiffer's rejoinder to my replies.

9. "Logic and Conversation," in P. Cole and J. L. Morgan, eds., *Syntax and Semantics*, volume 3 (New York: Academic Press, 1975), pp. 41-55; also in D. Davidson and G. Harman, eds., *The Logic of Grammar* (Encino: Dickenson, 1975), pp. 64-75; also in A. P. Martinich, ed., *The Philosophy of Language* (Oxford University Press, 1985), pp. 159-170.

10. Contrary to a proposal Schiffer makes in his postscript, the observation that the content of (1) is something ordinary speakers believe, *per se*, does not yield an adequate explanation here. For ordinary speakers are not similarly disposed toward 'Lois Lane does not realize that Superman is Superman' although they fully grasp its content, which (on my view) is the same as that of (1).

11. It is doubtful whether the conjunction and conditional cases, and the sort of situation I have in mind in connection with propositional-attitude attributions, qualify as cases of what Grice calls *particularized conversational implicature* (by far the most widely discussed notion of Gricean implicature); in a number of important respects, these cases better fit one or the other of Grice's two contrasting notions of *generalized conversational implicature* and *conventional* (nonconversational) *implicature*. Surely a great many speakers may be

confused by the conventional or generalized conversational implicature of a sentence into thinking that the sentence literally says (in part) what it in fact only implicates. Grice's notion of particularized conversational implicature apparently precludes the possibility of this sort of confusion. (See the third essential feature of particularized conversational implicature cited *op. cit.* on p. 169 of Martinich.) In some cases, it may also be possible to cancel explicitly the conventional or generalized conversational implicature of a sentence. I am not suggesting that the case of propositional-attitude attributions is exactly analogous to the conjunction and conditional cases. (The issues here are quite delicate.)

12. It might be thought that if ordinary speakers take a belief attribution $\ulcorner c$ believes that $S \urcorner$ to express the assertion that x agrees to the proposition p when taking it in the way it is presented to x by the very sentence S, and they use the attribution to convey (or "implicate") precisely this proposition, then this proposition cannot help but *be* (part of) the content of the attribution. The fact that the attribution does not literally mean what it is used to convey is attested to by the validity of the inference from the conjunction 'Floyd claims that Superman is mild-mannered, and Lois believes anything Floyd says concerning Superman' to 'Lois believes that Superman is mild-mannered'. The inference would be invalid if its conclusion literally meant that Lois agrees that Superman is mild-mannered when she takes this proposition in the way it is presented to her by the very sentence 'Superman is mild-mannered'. The premise gives information concerning only what propositions Lois believes, not how she takes them in believing them. (Grice also insists, *op. cit.* p. 69 of Martinich, that the supposition that an erstwhile implicature of a particular construction has become included in the construction's conventional meaning "would require special justification.")

13. "A Puzzle about Belief," in A. Margalit, ed. *Meaning and Use* (Dordrecht: D. Reidel, 1979), pp. 239-275; also in N. Salmon and S. Soames, eds., *Propositions and Attitudes*. Kripke's puzzle is addressed in appendix A of *Frege's Puzzle*, pp. 129-132.

14. I believe that a careful reading of "A Puzzle about Belief" reveals that Kripke probably ultimately rejects his schematic *disquotation principle* (pp. 248-249). The schema might be rewritten in the form of a single general principle (instead of as a schema), as follows: *If a speaker, on reflection, sincerely assents to a particular sentence S that he fully understands (as a sentence of his language), then he believes the content of S (in his language with respect to his context).* By contrast with Kripke's original principle schema, in this variation the sentence S may contain indexical or pronominal devices, and need not be a sentence of English. Either version, if correct, would entail that, since Pierre is a normal English speaker who fully understands, and on reflection sincerely assents to, the English sentence 'London is not pretty', he believes that London is not pretty, and since Pierre is also a normal Frenglish speaker who fully understands, and on reflection sincerely assents to, '*Londres* is pretty', he also believes that London is pretty. It is this disquotation

principle that is "subjected to the greatest possible strain, perhaps to the point of breakdown." In contrast to Kripke's skepticism, I endorse the disquotation principle and its consequences. In fact, the principle is virtually entailed by the first condition on the *BEL* relation given in Section I above.

15. "The Basis of Reference," *Erkenntnis* 13 (July 1978), pp. 171-206, at p. 180.

16. I treat logical attributes (such as the relation of deductive entailment and the property of contradictoriness) here as attributes of propositions, setting aside for the present purpose my contention that these attributes are primarily and in the first instance attributes of sentences in a language, and that whereas it is not incorrect, it can be quite misleading to treat them also as attributes of propositions.

17. Suppose x does not have the belief that p entails q, because (for example) x does not have the concept of logical entailment, but that x believes p and can nevertheless reason perfectly well, etc. Surely in some such cases we should expect that x would still come to believe q on the basis of his or her belief of p, and that x would be justified in doing so. One reformulation of the belief justification principle that seems both invulnerable to the sort of counterexample at issue in Pierre's case and more to the point makes explicit reference to the third relata of the *BEL* relation:

> Suppose x is a normal, fully rational agent who fully understands a particular sentence S (as a sentence of x's language) and that $BEL[x, p, f(x, S)]$, where p is the content of S (in x's context). Suppose also that x is consciously interested in the further question of whether q is also the case, taking q the way he or she does when it is presented to x by the particular sentence S' (of x's language). Suppose further that x also fully understands S' (as a sentence of x's language). Suppose finally that S' is uncontroversially a trivial deductive consequence of S (in x's language) by logical form alone (without the help of additional analytical meaning postulates for x's language). Under these circumstances, x would be rationally justified in coming to stand in *BEL* to q and $f(x, S')$ on the basis of his or her standing in *BEL* to p and $f(x, S)$ (and the deductive relationship between S and S'), or alternatively, if for independent reasons x does not stand in *BEL* to q and $f(x, S')$, x would be rationally justified in accordingly ceasing to stand in *BEL* to p and $f(x, S)$,

where f is the function that assigns to an individual speaker and a sentence of his or her idiolect, the corresponding third relatum of the *BEL* relation (e.g., the way the speaker takes the proposition that is the content of the sentence when it is presented to him or her by that very sentence). Cf. note 14 above. I am assuming here that 'London is *Londres*' is not a logically valid sentence of Frenglish (Pierre's language), despite the fact that it is an analytic sentence of Frenglish. Cf. *Frege's*

Puzzle, pp. 133-135.

An analogous principle may be given in place of the belief closure principle. These more cautious principles must be weakened even further to accommodate cases in which the function f is not defined, as in Kripke's 'Paderewski' case, *op. cit.*, pp. 265-266.

18. "Reflexivity," *loc. cit.*

19. A reply exactly similar to this can be offered to Steven Wagner's central criticism (in "California Semantics Meets the Great Fact," *Notre Dame Journal of Formal Logic*, 27, 3, July 1986, pp. 430-455) of the theory advanced in *Frege's Puzzle*. Wagner objects (at pp. 435-436) that the theory is incorrect to characterize someone who knows that 'Samuel Clemens' refers (in English) to Samuel Clemens as thereby knowing that 'Samuel Clemens' refers (in English) to Mark Twain, since any rational agent who knows the latter, and the trivial fact that 'Mark Twain' refers (in English) to Mark Twain, is *ipso facto* in a position to infer that 'Mark Twain' and 'Samuel Clemens' are co-referential, and that therefore 'Mark Twain is Samuel Clemens', and all of its Leibniz's-Law consequences, are true. (Wagner, at pp. 445-446, acknowledges the effectiveness of the sort of reply I am offering here, but finds it excessively reminiscent of the Fregean account of propositional-attitude attributions. There is considerable tension, however, between this reaction and some of his remarks on pp. 431-432. Cf. also note 5 above and *Frege's Puzzle*, pp. 2-7, 66-70, and especially pp. 119-126.)

On a related point, I argued in *Frege's Puzzle* (pp. 133-138) that the sentence 'Hesperus, if it exists, is Phosphorus' expresses a truth (in English) that is knowable (by anyone sufficiently *en rapport* with the planet Venus) *a priori*, by logic alone. One may also know, by principles of (English) semantics alone, that *if Hesperus, if it exists, is Phosphorus, then the sentence 'Hesperus, if it exists, is Phosphorus' is true (in English)*. But knowing these things does not *ipso facto* place one in a position to infer (and thereby to know by logic and semantics alone) that 'Hesperus, if it exists, is Phosphorus' is true (in English). The inability to draw this *modus ponens* inference (justifiably) is an instance of essentially the same phenomenon as Pierre's inability to draw the *modus tollens* inference.

20. In *Frege's Puzzle* I explicitly endorse (at pp. 129-130) Kripke's schematic disquotation principle. (Indeed, as pointed out in note 14 above, the principle is virtually entailed by the first condition on the *BEL* relation.) This disquotation principle (in turn) virtually entails the truth of (2) (in Schiffer's story), assuming Floyd fully understands (1) in assenting to it. Cf. also note 17 above.

21. See his "Belief and Synonymy," *Journal of Philosophy*, LXXV (March 1978), pp. 119-138.

22. Cf. the discussion of Mates's famous problem concerning nested propositional-attitude attributions in Alonzo Church, "Intensional Isomorphism and Identity of Belief," in N. Salmon and S. Soames, eds., *Propositions and Attitudes*. Whereas I disagree with Church concerning Burge's beliefs, I fully endorse his argument that the sentences 'Burge disbelieves

that Sasha believes catsup is a sandwich condiment' and 'Burge disbelieves that Sasha believes ketchup is a sandwich condiment' cannot differ in truth value in English if 'ketchup' and 'catsup' are English synonyms.

23. There is one potential difference between this case and that of sentence (2): Burge's belief that Sasha believes that ketchup is a sandwich condiment is very likely based, to some extent, on Sasha's readiness to assent to the sentence 'Ketchup is a sandwich condiment'. But whereas it is clear that Lois Lane fully understands the sentence 'Superman is Superman', and grasps its content, it is arguable that Sasha does not fully understand the sentence 'Ketchup is a sandwich condiment', since he takes it to be compatible with 'Catsup is not a sandwich condiment'. See the final footnote of Saul Kripke's "A Puzzle About Belief," concerning a "deep conceptual confusion" that arises from "misapplication of the disquotational principle" to speakers in situations like Sasha's. Kripke's view is that "although the issues are delicate, there is a case for" rejecting the claim that Burge believes that Sasha believes that ketchup is a sandwich condiment, on the grounds that Burge apparently misapplies the disquotation principle to Sasha's assent to 'Ketchup is a sandwich condiment', thereby betraying a misunderstanding of the term 'believe'. (Kripke adds that he does not believe that his brief discussion of this sort of situation ends the matter.)

Against this, the following should be noted. First, it is by no means obvious that Sasha fails to understand the term 'ketchup'; he has learned the term in much the same way as nearly everyone else who has learned it: by means of a sort of ostensive definition. If Sasha misunderstands the term 'ketchup', why does Lois Lane not similarly misunderstand the name 'Superman'? Second, even if Sasha's understanding of the term 'ketchup' is somehow defective, this does not make any difference to Burge's beliefs concerning Sasha's beliefs. Burge's philosophical views concerning belief allow that Sasha's grasp of the term 'ketchup', imperfect though it may be, is sufficient to enable him to form a belief that ketchup is a sandwich condiment. (See Burge's "Individualism and the Mental," in P. French, T. Uehling, and H. Wettstein, eds., *Midwest Studies in Philosophy IV: Studies in Metaphysics*, Minneapolis: University of Minnesota Press, 1979, pp. 73-121.) Even if Burge's philosophical views are incorrect, they are views concerning belief. It would be implausible to claim that Burge's views in this connection *must* indicate a misunderstanding of the term 'believe' (as used in standard English), as opposed to advocacy of a somewhat controversial theory concerning (genuine) belief. Last but not least, even if Sasha's understanding of the term 'ketchup' is somehow defective, the claim that Sasha therefore fails to believe that ketchup is a sandwich condiment is fundamentally implausible. Suppose Sasha points to a bottle labeled 'KETCHUP', and sincerely declares, "This stuff here is a sandwich condiment." Does he nevertheless fail to believe that ketchup is a sandwich condiment, simply because he does not realize that 'ketchup' and 'catsup' are synonyms?

24. The example of Sasha demonstrates that the difficulty involved is more general than it appears, arising not only on my own theory of propositional-attitude attributions but equally on a very wide range of such theories, including various Fregean theories. This feature is not peculiar to Schiffer's criticism. Although I cannot argue the case here, a great many criticisms that have been levelled against the sort of account I advocate—perhaps most—are based on some difficulty or other that is more general in nature than it first appears, and that equally arises on virtually any theory of propositional-attitude attributions in connection with the example of Sasha's understanding of the synonyms 'ketchup' and 'catsup'. The argument given here involving the terms 'ketchup' and 'catsup' is related to Kripke's "proof" of substitutivity using two Hebrew words for Germany, and to his argument involving 'furze' and 'gorse', in the conclusion section of "A Puzzle About Belief." All of these arguments are closely related to Church's famous arguments from translation. (See especially "Intentional Isomorphism and Identity of Belief.") I hope to elaborate on this matter in later work.

25. For several reasons, I do not accept the letter of Schiffer's Constraint as here formulated, though I do accept its spirit. I believe that Schiffer shares some of my misgivings over the principle, as here formulated. He mentions potential problems arising from the 'F' in the statement of the principle, and the need for "modes of presentation" for properties. A related difficulty is noted below. In addition, I do not accept the Fregean notion of a purely conceptual *mode of presentation* of an entity as an adequate substitute for my notion of a *way of taking* the entity in question. See note 5 above.

26. In *Frege's Puzzle* I wrote: "The means by which one is acquainted with a singular proposition includes as a part the means by which one is familiar with the individual constituent(s) of the proposition" (p. 108). Contrary to the interpretation advanced in Schiffer's postscript, I never suggested that the way an agent takes a structured complex object, such as a proposition, is made up *without remainder* of the ways the agent takes the separate constituents of the complex (with these ways-of-taking-objects structured in a similar way). The principal criticism of Schiffer's postscript challenges my contention that Floyd takes the singular proposition (or fact) about Superman that he is him in two different ways. It is difficult to understand, however, why Schiffer—who himself advanced (something along the lines of) Schiffer's Constraint in criticizing the theory of *Frege's Puzzle*—insists, as part of the same criticism, that the fact that a fully rational agent believes that whereas p is trivial, q is not, does not yield an adequate reason to conclude that this agent takes p and q in different ways (by means of different "modes of presentation").

27. Furthermore, it is highly controversial whether the former is a valid deductive consequence of the latter, and indeed, Floyd's views entail a negative answer to this controversial question. This renders the alternative belief justification principle cited in note 17 above also inapplicable.

28. The possibility of such confusion demonstrates a further difficulty with Schiffer's Constraint, as it is formulated here (see note 25), and that the principle should be stated more carefully—perhaps by adding a proviso concerning x's lack of confusion in regard to the nonrelativity, and the consequent logical incompatibility, of the property of being F and that of not being F, and in regard to the sort of entities that are candidates for having either.

29. Cf. Schiffer's "The Real Trouble with Propositions," in R. J. Bogdan, ed., *Belief* (Oxford University Press, 1986), pp. 83-117, at p. 107n.

30. Likewise, Burge believes ketchup, i.e. catsup, to be something that Sasha believes is a sandwich condiment, and he also believes ketchup to be something that Sasha disbelieves is a sandwich condiment. Furthermore, he disbelieves that Sasha believes that catsup is a sandwich condiment, but he does not disbelieve catsup to be something that Sasha believes is a sandwich condiment (I assume he is not under the sort of confusion mentioned in the preceding paragraph of the text)—otherwise he would not be fully rational in the relevant sense. Frege's Thesis and Schiffer's Constraint do not force us to deny that Burge disbelieves that Sasha believes that catsup is a sandwich condiment.

31. In Quine's *The Ways of Paradox* (New York: Randam House, 1966), pp. 183-194.

32. "Opacity," appendix B, in E. Hahn and P. A. Schilpp, eds., *The Philosophy of W. V. Quine* (La Salle: Open Court, 1986), pp. 229-294, at pp. 268-272.

33. The open sentence ϕ_y is the result of uniformly substituting free occurrences of the variable 'y' for free occurrences of the variable 'x' throughout ϕ_x. If 'x' has a free occurrence in ϕ_x inside the scope of a variable-binding operator on 'y', it will be necessary to use a different variable in place of 'y'. Kaplan's improvement on Quine's proposal introduces a somewhat more complicated translation, involving a procedure Kaplan calls *articulation*, in case ϕ_x contains more than one free occurrence of 'x' (as in 'x indulges x'). Such multiple-occurrence syntactically *de dicto* constructions will not concern us here.

34. No doubt, Superman himself agrees with Floyd concerning Lois Lane's ignorance of his secret identity, i.e. he believes with Floyd that Lois Lane does not realize that Clark Kent is Superman. But he also agrees with Floyd that Lois Lane realizes that he himself is Superman (since she realizes that Superman is Superman), and thus he believes himself to be someone Lois Lane realizes is Superman. Hence, being fully rational, he does not also believe himself to be someone that Lois Lane does not realize is Superman (although he believes himself to be someone that Lois Lane doubts is Superman). This refutes any attempt to analyze the so-called *de se* construction $\ulcorner a$ believes that $\phi_{\text{he-himself}}\urcorner$ by means of something along the lines of $\ulcorner a$ self-ascribes the property of being someone y such that $\phi_y\urcorner$. Such attempts are made by David Lewis, "Attitudes *De Dicto* and *De Se*," *The Philosophical Review*, 88 (1979), pp. 513-543, and Roderick Chisholm, *The First Person* (Minneapolis: University of Minnesota Press, 1981), at pp. 34-37 and *passim*.

References

J. Almog, "Form and Content," *Nous*, 19, 4 (December 1985): 603-616.

T. Burge, "Belief and Synonymy," *Journal of Philosophy*, LXXV (March 1978), pp. 119-138.

T. Burge, "Individualism and the Mental," in P. French, T. Uehling, and H. Wettstein, eds., *Midwest Studies in Philosophy IV: Studies in Metaphysics* (Minneapolis: University Of Minnesota Press, 1979): 73-122.

J. Barwise and J. Perry, "Shifting Situations and Shaken Attitudes," *Linguistics and Philosophy*, 8 (1985): 105-161.

A. J. Chien, "Demonstratives and Belief States," *Philosophical Studies*, 47 (1985): 271-289.

R. M. Chisholm, *The First Person* (Minneapolis: University of Minnesota Press, 1981).

A. Church, "Intensional Isomorphism and Identity of Belief," *Philosophical Studies* (1954):65-73; also in N. Salmon and S. Soames, 1988.

A. Church, "A Remark Concerning Quine's Paradox About Modality," in N. Salmon and S. Soames, 1988.

M. J. Cresswell, *Structured Meanings: The Semantics of Propositional Attitudes* (Cambridge, Mass.: Bradford Books/The MIT Press, 1985).

K. Donnellan, "Proper Names and Identifying Descriptions," in D. Davidson and G. Harman, eds., *Semantics of Natural Language* (Dordrecht: D. Reidel, 1972): 356-379.

K. Donnellan, "Speaking of Nothing," *The Philosophical Review*, 83 (January 1974): 3-31; also in Schwartz, 1977, pp. 216-244.

G. Evans, "Pronouns, Quantifiers and Relative Clauses (I)," in M. Platts, ed. *Reference, Truth and Reality* (London: Routledge and Kegan Paul, 1980): 255-317.

G. Frege, "*Über Sinn und Bedeutung*," *Zeitschrift für Philosophie und Philosophische Kritik*, 100 (1893): 25-50; in English in Frege, 1984, pp. 157-177; also in *Translations from the Philosophical Writings of Gottlob Frege*, translated by P. Geach and M. Black (Oxford: Basil Blackwell, 1952), pp. 56-78.

G. Frege, "*Der Gedanke*," in English in Frege, 1984, pp. 351-372; also in Frege, 1977, pp. 1-30; also in N. Salmon and S. Soames, 1988.

G. Frege, *Logical Investigations* (New Haven: Yale University Press, 1977).

G. Frege, *Collected Papers on Mathematics, Logic, and Philosophy*, B. McGuinness, ed. translated by M. Black, V. H. Dudman, P. Geach, H. Kaal, E.-H. W. Kluge, B. McGuinness, and R. H. Stoothoff (Oxford: Basil Blackwell, 1984).

G. Frege, *Philosophical and Mathematical Correspondence*, G. Gabriel, H. Hermes, F. Kambartel, C. Thiel, and A. Veraart, eds., abridged by B. McGuinness, translated by H. Kaal (University of Chicago Press, 1980); excerpts in N. Salmon and S. Soames, 1988.

P. French, T. Uehling, and H. Wettstein, eds., *Contemporary Perspectives in the Philosophy of Language* (Minneapolis: University of Minnesota Press, 1979).

P. T. Geach, *Reference and Generality* (Ithaca: Cornell University Press, 1962).

P. T. Geach, "Logical Procedures and the Identity of Expressions," in Geach, *Logic Matters* (University of California Press, 1972): 108-115.

H. P. Grice, "Logic and Conversation," in P. Cole and J. L. Morgan, eds., *Syntax and Semantics*, volume 3 (New York: Academic Press, 1975): 41-55; also in D. Davidson and G. Harman, eds., *The Logic of Grammar* (Encino: Dickenson, 1975), pp. 64-75; also in A. P. Martinich, ed., *The Philosophy of Language* (Oxford University Press, 1985), pp. 159-170.

L. R. Horn, "Metalinguistic Negation and Pragmatic Ambiguity," *Language*, 61, 1 (1985): 121-174.

D. Kaplan, "On the Logic of Demonstratives," in French, et al. 1979, pp. 401-412; also in N. Salmon and S. Soames, 1988.

D. Kaplan, "Demonstratives," in J. Almog, J. Perry, and H. Wettstein, eds., *Themes from Kaplan* (Oxford University Press, forthcoming).

D. Kaplan, "Opacity," in L. E. Hahn and P. A. Schilpp, eds., *The Philosophy of W. V. Quine* (La Salle, Ill.: Open Court, 1986): 229-288.

S. Kripke, "Identity and Necessity," in M. Munitz, ed. *Identity and Individuation* (New York: New York University Press, 1971): 135-164; also in Schwartz, 1977, pp. 66-101.

S. Kripke, *Naming and Necessity* (Harvard University Press and Basil Blackwell, 1972, 1980); also in D. Davidson and G. Harman, eds., *Semantics of Natural Language* (Dordrecht: D. Reidel, 1972), pp. 253-355, 763-769.

S. Kripke, "A Puzzle about Belief," in A. Margalit, ed. *Meaning and Use* (Dordrecht: D. Reidel, 1979): 239-275; also in N. Salmon and S. Soames, 1988.

D. Lewis, "Attitudes *De Dicto* and *De Se*," *The Philosophical Review*, 88 (1979): 513-543.

D. Lewis, "What Puzzling Pierre Does Not Believe," *Australasian Journal of Philosophy*, 59, 3 (1981): 283-289.

L. Linsky, *Oblique Contexts* (Chicago: University of Chicago Press, 1983).

B. Loar, "Names in Thought," *Philosophical Studies*, 51 (1987): 169-185.

R. B. Marcus, "A Proposed Solution to a Puzzle About Belief," in P. French, T. Uehling, and H. Wettstein, eds., *Midwest Studies in Philosophy VI: The Foundations of Analytic Philosophy* (Minneapolis: University of Minnesota Press, 1981): 501-510.

R. B. Marcus, "Rationality and Believing the Impossible," *Journal of Philosophy*, 80, 6 (June 1983): 321-338.

T. McKay, "On Proper Names in Belief Ascriptions," *Philosophical Studies*, 39 (1981): 287-303.

J. Perry, "Frege on Demonstratives," *The Philosophical Review*, 86 (1977): 474-497.

J. Perry, "The Problem of the Essential Indexical," *Nous*, 13 (1979): 3-21; also in N. Salmon and S. Soames, 1988.

J. Perry, "Belief and Acceptance," in P. French, T. Uehling, and H. Wettstein, eds., *Midwest Studies in Philosophy V: Studies in Epistemology* (Minneapolis: University of Minnesota Press, 1980): 533-542.

J. Perry, "A Problem About Continued Belief," *Pacific Philosophical Quarterly*, 61 (1980): 317-332. H. Putnam, "Synonymy, and the Analysis of Belief Sentences," *Analysis*, 14, 5 (April 1954): 114-122; also in N. Salmon and S. Soames, 1988.

H. Putnam, "Meaning and Reference," *The Journal of Philosophy*, 70, (November 8, 1973): 699-711; also in Schwartz, 1977, pp. 119-132.

H. Putnam, "The Meaning of 'Meaning'," in K. Gunderson, ed. *Minnesota Studies in the Philosophy of Science VII: Language, Mind, and Knowledge* (Minneapolis: University of Minnesota Press, 1975); also in Putnam's *Philosophical Papers II: Mind, Language, and Reality* (Cambridge University Press, 1975), pp. 215-271.

W. V. O. Quine, "Reference and Modality," in Quine, *From a Logical Point of View* (New York: Harper and Row, 1953): 139-159.

W. V. O. Quine, "Quantifiers and Propositional Attitudes," *Journal of Philosophy*, 53, 5 (March 1, 1956): 177-187; also in Quine's *The Ways of Paradox* (New York: Random House, 1966), pp. 183-194.

M. Richard, "Direct Reference and Ascriptions of Belief," *Journal of Philosophical Logic*, 12 (1983): 425-452; also in N. Salmon and S. Soames, 1988.

M. Richard, "Attitude Ascriptions, Semantic Theory, and Pragmatic Evidence," *Proceedings of the Aristotelian Society*, 1, 87 (1986/1987): 243-262.

B. Russell, "On Denoting," *Mind*, 14 (October 1905): 479-493; also in Russell, 1956, pp. 41-56.

B. Russell, "Knowledge by Acquaintance and Knowledge by Description," Chapter X of Russell's *Mysticism and Logic and Other Essays* (London: Longmans, Green and Company, 1911): 209-232; also in N. Salmon and S. Soames, 1988.

B. Russell, "The Philosophy of Logical Atomism," in Russell, 1956, pp. 177-281.

B. Russell, *Logic and Knowledge*, R. C. Marsh, ed. (London: George Allen and Unwin, 1956).

N. Salmon, *Reference and Essence* (Princeton University Press and Basil Blackwell, 1981).

N. Salmon, *Frege's Puzzle* (Cambridge, Mass.: Bradford Books/The MIT Press, 1986).

N. Salmon, "Reflexivity," *Notre Dame Journal of Formal Logic*, 27, 3 (July 1986): 401-429; also in N. Salmon and S. Soames, 1988.

N. Salmon and S. Soames, eds., *Propositions and Attitudes* (Oxford University Press, Readings in Philosophy, 1988).

S. Schiffer, "Naming and Knowing," in P. French, T. Uehling, and H. Wettstein, eds., 1979, pp. 61-74.

S. Schiffer, "The Basis of Reference," *Erkenntnis*, 13 (1978): 171-206.

S. Schiffer, "Indexicals and the Theory of Reference," *Synthese*, 49 (1981): 43-100.

S. Schiffer, "The Real Trouble with Propositions," in R. J. Bogdan, *Belief: Form, Content, and Function* (Oxford University Press, 1986): 83-118.

S. Schiffer, "The 'Fido'-Fido Theory of Belief," in J. Tomberlin, ed. *Philosophical Perspectives 1: Metaphysics* (Atascadero: Ridgeview, 1987): 455-480.

S. Schwartz, *Naming, Necessity, and Natural Kinds* (Cornell University

Press, 1977).

S. Soames, "Lost Innocence," *Linguistics and Philosophy*, 8 (1985): 59-71.

S. Soames, "Direct Reference, Propositional Attitudes and Semantic Content," in N. Salmon and S. Soames, 1988.

S. Wagner, "California Semantics Meets the Great Fact," *Notre Dame Journal of Formal Logic*, 27, 3 (July 1986): 430-455.

D. Wiggins, "Identity, Necessity and Physicalism," in S. Korner, ed. *Philosophy of Logic* (University of California Press, 1976): 96-132, 159-182.

D. Wiggins, "Frege's Problem of the Morning Star and the Evening Star," in M. Schirn, ed. *Studies on Frege II: Logic and the Philosophy of Language* (Stuttgart: Bad Canstatt, 1976): 221-255.

Philosophical Perspectives, 3
Philosophy of Mind and Action Theory, 1989

ON WHAT'S IN THE HEAD

Robert Stalnaker
Cornell University

"Cut the pie any way you like, 'meanings' just ain't in the head!"[1] So Hilary Putnam taught us some years ago. He made the point with some compelling examples all fitting a now familiar pattern: first we are asked to imagine a counterfactual person exactly like some actual person with respect to all purely internal psychological and physical properties, but situated in a counterfactual environment which differs from ours in some subtle way. For example, where we have aluminum, they have a metal that resembles aluminum superficially, but that has a different chemical structure. We are then invited to note that despite the intrinsic similarities of the two doppelganger, their utterances have different semantic properties. When the earthling says "Aluminum is used in the construction of airplanes," she say something that differs in content from what her twin says when she utters the same sounds. Since what is in the heads of the two is the same, while what they mean when they use certain words is different, the meanings of those words must depend on something other than what is in those heads. Tyler Burge developed this kind of example in more detail and extended the point in several ways.[2] First he argued that it is not just meaning and other semantical properties, but also intentional psychological properties that are shown to depend on external conditions: beliefs, desires, hopes and fears ain't in the head either. Second, he argued that social conditions—facts about the linguistic practices of members of the agent's community—were among the external conditions on which intentional mental states depend. Third, he emphasized that the dependence on external conditions was a pervasive phenomenon, one not restricted to some narrow range of concepts and expressions. It applies not just to de re attitudes or to attitudes expressed with proper names, indexical expressions and natural kind terms, but to de dicto attitudes and to all kinds of concepts and expressions. Burge called the thesis he was attacking—the thesis that intentional mental states are intrinsic properties of the individuals who are in those states—*individualism*.

In retrospect, it seems that we should not have been surprised by the conclusions of Putnam and Burge. Isn't it obvious that semantic properties, and intentional properties generally, are *relational* properties: properties defined in terms of relations between a speaker or agent and what he or she talks or thinks about. And isn't it obvious that relations depend, in all but degenerate cases, on more than the intrinsic properties of one of the things related. This, it seems, is not just a consequence of some new and controversial theory of reference, but should follow from any account of representation that holds that we can talk and think, not just about our own inner states, but also about things and properties outside of ourselves. But the conclusions were surprising, and they remain controversial. One reason is that the anti-individualistic thesis seems to have some paradoxical consequences. If what we mean or think is not in the head, it would seem that we cannot know, or at least cannot be authoritative about, what we mean or think.[3] Another reason is that this thesis seems to be incompatible with the explanatory role that intentional mental states are thought to play. We explain why people behave the way they do in terms of what they believe and want. In fact, it is often assumed that belief and desire states are to be defined in terms of the behavior they dispose the agents in those states to engage in. But how can such states be causally relevant if they are relational states— states that depend on things outside of the agent?

One response to the anti-individualist thesis is to grant it, but to deny its significance. If our ordinary concepts of belief, desire, and meaning are relational concepts that individuate mental states in a non-individualistic way, this only shows that our ordinary concepts are inappropriate for the purpose of the explanation of behavior. But, this response suggests, the revisions needed to render intentional concepts individualistic are not very radical. What such a revision must do is to factor out the "organismic contribution" to an intentional mental state— that component of the state that is dependent or supervenient on the internal states of the agent.

The revisionist response makes a negative and a positive claim. The negative claim is that no systematic explanatory theory of behavior will be tenable unless it is individualistic. The positive claim is that although ordinary intentional psychological concepts are not individualistic as they stand, they can be revised in a way that renders them individualistic while preserving the basic structure of intentional explanation. Jerry Fodor has defended both claims; Daniel Dennett has proposed ways to defend the positive thesis, and Stephen Stich and P. M. and P. S. Churchland have defended the negative thesis while rejecting the positive claim. In this paper, I want to explore both parts of the revisionist doctrine, beginning with the positive side.

After trying to get clear about what is required in general to define an individualistic analogue of a relational concept, I will look at two proposals for defining narrow content—a kind of content that is intended to render intentional states purely internal. Then I will turn to the negative side of the case, discussing a number of formulations of the negative thesis and a number of arguments in its defense. I will be arguing, first, that it is harder than some have assumed to define narrow content, and second that ordinary wide content is less mysterious than some have assumed.

A number of quite different issues are involved in the revisionist doctrine: some are relatively abstract questions concerning concept formation, methodology, and the distinction between intrinsic and relational properties; others are more specific questions concerning the nature of intentional concepts and the psychological mechanisms that underlie their application. To help separate these different issues from each other, I will begin by exploring an analogy: I will look at a very simple causal-relational concept—a concept that should be relatively transparent and uncontroversial—and consider what is involved in the attempt to define a narrow or purely intrinsic version of it. Then I will look back at the intentional concepts themselves and at the proposals for carving out narrow content.

Consider the concept of a *footprint*. This is a causal-relational concept: something is a footprint in virtue of the way it was caused. One might make the point that a footprint is not intrinsic to the sand or mud in which it is located by telling a Twin-Earth story: imagine a beach on Twin-Earth which is, at a certain moment on July 4, 1985, exactly like Jones Beach in every intrinsic detail. The difference is that the counterpart on Twin-Earth of a certain footprint on Jones Beach was caused, not by a foot, but by the way the waves happened to fall some hours earlier. So something on Twin-Earth that is intrinsically indistinguishable from a footprint is not a footprint. A philosopher with a gift for coining slogans might sum up the lesson of this thought experiment this way: *Cut the pie any way you like, footprints just ain't in the sand!*

The revisionist replies that this may be true of our ordinary folk concept of a footprint, but explanatory science is interested only in states that *are* intrinsic to the sand. So let us define a new concept that individuates the relevant state of the sand in a way that is independent of its causal history and environment: let us say that a *narrow footprint* is a foot-shaped indentation, whatever its cause. Can't we, in this way, isolate that component of the state of containing a footprint that is intrinsic to the medium that is in that state? The anti-individualist will note that the new concept is still a relational one. Footprints in the new sense no longer depend on the *particular* cause of the indentation, but they still depend on general facts that are extrinsic to the sand. An elaboration of the Twin-Earth story makes the point: suppose that on Twin-Earth feet have a different normal shape. If this is true, the indentation in the sand there will not only fail to be an ordinary footprint because of its different causal history, it will also fail to be a *narrow* footprint because normal footprints are differently shaped there, and so the indentation on the beach is not even shaped like a foot.

This pattern of conceptual revision—replacing a dependence on a specific causal interaction with dependence on a general regularity in the environment—is exemplified in less artificial cases. It seems reasonable to say that in defining dispositional properties, for example, we begin with a kind of causal interaction (a substance dissolves, or an object is observed). We then use suitably hedged counterfactuals to get at a stable property of one of the things involved in the interaction—a property that the thing has independently of the fact that the interaction took place. A sugar cube is soluble if it would dissolve if put in water (under normal conditions). An object is observable if it would be observed if a normal observer were suitably placed. Some such dispositional properties (such as solubility in water) may be purely intrinsic, but others will not be. Whether something is observable may depend on the capacities of normal observers, perhaps also on the lighting conditions that in fact obtain, or at least on the lighting conditions that normally obtain. The concept of belief may be this kind of narrowed version of the concept of knowledge, replacing a dependence on more specific causal relations between the fact known and a state of the knower with more general patterns of causal relations between facts and internal states.

One might further narrow our revised concept of footprint by taking the phrase "foot-shaped indentation" in a reference-fixing way. That is, by a narrow footprint we mean an indentation that is shaped the way feet are *actually* shaped. So whatever shape feet have on Twin-Earth, the counterpart on Twin-Earth of the footprint on Jones Beach is still a narrow footprint. Now, it seems, we have succeeded in isolating a purely internal state of the sand.

The pattern of concept formation now looks like this: we begin with a concept that classifies states of a thing in terms of a relational property—specifically, in terms of the way those states are caused. We then focus on the intrinsic properties of the states the concept picks out, classifying them in a new way: as states that share those intrinsic properties. This pattern too seems to be exemplified in less artificial cases. Consider, for example, the concepts of *mass* and *weight*. Weight is the quantity that is closer to the surface—more directly observed and measured. But it is a relational concept: what you weigh depends on the gravitational field you are in. Mass is the quantity that a body has, independently of its gravitational field, that explains why it weighs what it does in different gravitational fields. Even at an initial stage of inquiry when we may not know very much about the relevant intrinsic properties, we can still use this strategy of concept formation to point at the properties, whatever they are, that play a certain role in the explanation of a thing's behavior.[4]

Our definition of narrow footprint may make use of a sound strategy of concept formation, but the success of this kind of definition will always depend on a substantive presupposition: that the things picked out by the relational property are similar to each other in an appropriate way. The substantive presupposition will never be plausible unless one idealizes a bit: there are deformed feet, and distorting conditions that may give rise to footprints of an unusual shape. These will certainly be footprints, but if our definition of narrow footprint is to succeed, they, and other indentations shaped like them, must be excluded. By foot-shaped indentations we mean indentations that have the *normal* or *characteristic* shape that feet make under *normal* conditions. This kind of qualification is a familiar part of characterizations of dispositional properties: a thing is soluble in water if it would dissolve if put in water *under normal conditions*. The point of the qualification is to insure that what is defined is a stable property that we can generalize about. It might be that a thing would not dissolve if put in water in a particular situation because of anomalous environmental conditions even though the thing is intrinsically similar to soluble things. But we don't want to say that the thing loses its solubility under the abnormal external conditions. The qualification allows us to say that the thing remains soluble even though, in this case, it would not dissolve if put in water.

Even given such qualifications, a definition of this kind may fail. If the concept of footprint we begin with is the concept of a print made by a human bare foot, then the concept of a narrow footprint is perhaps well defined, since there is a relatively well defined shape that prints have, in normal cases, when they are made by such feet. But suppose we start with a more general notion: by "footprint" we mean a print made by a foot of some animal or other. This concept includes prints made by cloven hooves, webbed feet, and the paws of dogs as well as human feet, and it is not clear that these footprints have any one characteristic shape at all. If they do not, then our concept will collapse when we try to abstract away from the causal origin of the indentations we want to pick out. Or at best we will be left with a wildly disjunctive concept that will be of no interest.[5]

The moral of the story is that the narrowing of causal-relational concepts exemplifies a legitimate pattern of concept formation, but not a pattern that will in all cases yield a well-defined purely internal property. First, the pattern may succeed in eliminating a dependence of a property on specific interactions with other things, while leaving a dependence on general facts about the environment. Second, whether the pattern succeeds at all will depend on substantive presuppositions about the intrinsic similarities of things that share the causal-relational property. To evaluate the positive part of the revisionist thesis we need to see just what the presuppositions are in the case of intentional mental concepts, and to consider whether we have good reason to accept them.

The defense of the positive part of the revisionist thesis requires more than just the definition of narrow analogues for particular belief properties such as the property of believing that aluminum is used in the construction of airplanes; what is needed is a narrow analogue of belief in general. Like ordinary belief, narrow belief must be expressed as a relation between the believer and some kind of *content*. This is essential since the project is to explain mental states as internal states *while preserving the structure of intentional explanations*. The strategy is to change the notion of content in a way that makes belief states purely internal. But however content is explained, how is it possible for belief to be both a relation between a person and a content and also a purely internal state? To answer this we need to distinguish two ways in which a concept can be relational. Consider again the quantities weight and mass: a Twin-Earth thought experiment will show that weight is a relational property. William weighs three hundred pounds, but his twin on the less massive Twin-Earth weighs less. Mass, in contrast, is intrinsic; Twin-William is equally massive. But both weight and mass are relational in another sense: they are both *semantically* relational concepts. There is a relation—weight (or mass) in pounds—that William bears to the number three hundred and that Wilma bears to one hundred and two. Both weight and mass are concepts expressed by using a relational *predicate* together with a number to pick out a property. It is the fact that the family of properties—weight or mass properties—has a certain structure that makes it possible for them to be expressed in this way. But this is compatible with the properties being intrinsic in the sense that whether a thing has one of them is not contingent on anything external to the thing. The revisionist project requires a concept of belief that is semantically relational, but that expresses belief properties that are ontologically intrinsic; it proposes to accomplish this by changing or restricting the contents that are used to pick out the properties. Belief is to be narrowed by narrowing content.

So how is narrow content to be explained? The first answer I will consider is Jerry Fodor's.[6] Let me sketch, first Fodor's diagnosis of the problem—his explanation of the fact that content, in the ordinary wide sense, is not in the head—and then say how he proposes to revise the notion of content to get it back into the head where it belongs. The problem, Fodor says, derives from the following constraint on the identity conditions for content: beliefs that are true under different conditions have different contents. It is because the Earthling's thought or statement, "Aluminum is used in the construction of airplanes" could be true in possible circumstances in which her twin's corresponding statement or thought is false that we are required to conclude that the two have different content. Narrow contents cannot differ in this way, but if narrow content is not constrained by truth conditions, how can it be a notion of content at all? The solution, Fodor proposes, is not to give up the connection between content and truth conditions, but rather to relativize this connection to context. Narrow content will be something that determines the truth conditions of a belief or utterance as a function of the external environment of the believer or speaker. The model for this account of narrow content is David Kaplan's account of the semantics for demonstratives and indexicals. Kaplan makes a distinction between *meaning* (or what he calls *character*) and *content*, and this distinction provides the model for Fodor's distinction between narrow and wide content. According to Kaplan's account, when Daniels and O'Leary both say "I am bald," they say something with the same *character*, but with different *content*. Daniels's statement says that Daniels is bald, whereas O'Leary's says that O'Leary is. Character is explained as a function from context to content. The pronoun "I" has a constant character: it always refers to the speaker. But because different speakers use that pronoun, the same sentences containing it may be used to say different things. In general, the character of a sentence of the form "I am F" will be a function taking a context in which x is the speaker into the proposition that is true if and only if x has the property expressed by "F." Narrow content, on Fodor's account of it, is a generalization of character in Kaplan's sense, where the context includes any fact external to the believer that is relevant to the determination of wide content.[7]

Fodor suggests that once we are clear about the general nature of narrow content, "it's quite easy to see how the required principles of individuation should be formulated."[8] Here is his explanation of the "extensional identity criterion" for narrow content:

> There is presumably something about the relation between Twin-Earth and Twin-me in virtue of which his 'water'-thoughts are about XYZ even though my water-thoughts are not. Call this condition that's satisfied by [Twin-Me, Twin-Earth] condition C... . Similarly, there must be something about the relation between me and Earth in virtue of which my water-thoughts are about H_2O even though my Twin's 'water'-thoughts are not. Call this condition that is satisfied by [me, Earth] condition C' ... . Short of a miracle, it must be true that if an organism shares the neurophysiological

constitution of my Twin *and satisfies C*, it follows that its thoughts and my Twin's thoughts share their truth conditions.... . But now we have an extensional identity criterion for mental contents: two thought contents are identical only if they effect the same mapping of thoughts and contexts onto truth conditions.[9]

This argument tells us what kind of thing narrow content should be: a mapping from context into truth conditions; and it shows that *if* we succeeded in specifying such a mapping, it would have the right properties: it would be *narrow* (intrinsic) and it would be like *content* in the crucial way: it would determine the semantic or intentional properties of the thought (relative to context). But the argument tells us less than it seems about how such mappings are to be specified, and it obscures the fact that it is a substantive hypothesis that the internal states of believers contain thoughts that determine such mappings.

It is surely right that if the context (C or C') includes all information external to the believer that may be relevant to the determination of truth conditions, then context, together with the internal states of the believer, will determine truth conditions. That is only to say that truth conditions are determined by the conditions that are relevant to determining them. But pointing this out does not tell us what function from context to content narrow content is supposed to be, or explain how it is that the relevant function is determined by what is in the believer's head. If the abstract procedure outlined in the argument could, by itself, show how to narrow content, then it could be used to define a narrow analogue of any relational property.

Consider this parody of Fodor's characterization of the criterion for narrow content: Take the property of being exactly three miles from a burning barn. Suppose I have this property, even though my counterpart who is located at exactly the same place in a certain counterfactual situation does not. He, let us suppose, is instead exactly three miles from a snow-covered chicken coop. Now there is presumably something about the relation between my counterpart and his world in virtue of which he is three miles from a snow-covered chicken coop even though I am not. Call this condition C. Similarly, there is something about the relation between me and my world in virtue of which I am three miles from a burning barn, even though my counterpart is not. Call it C'. Whatever these conditions are, we *do* know this: short of a miracle, it must be true that anyone in the location that both I and my counterpart are in in our respective worlds would be three miles from a snow-covered chicken coop if condition C obtained, and three miles from a burning barn if instead C′ obtained. But this does not help us identify a specific function that takes condition C′ into the property of being three miles from a snow-covered chicken coop and also takes C into the property of being three miles from a burning barn—a function that is supposed to represent the contribution that an individual's location makes to the relational property. There are many such functions, and no reason to identify any of them with the contribution that my intrinsic location makes to the specific relational property. My counterpart cannot reasonably say, "I did my part toward being three miles from a burning barn by going to a place where, if conditions C′ had obtained instead of C, I would have been three miles from a burning barn." *Every* location is such that for some external conditions, if those conditions obtain, then anything in that location is three miles from a burning barn.

The exclusive focus on Twin-Earth situations makes it look easier than it is to factor out the contribution that the external environment makes to the possession of some relational property. In a Twin-Earth story, we are asked to consider a possible situation in which an individual shares *every* intrinsic property with its actual counterpart. So if the actual individual has the relational property in question, we can be sure that its Twin-Earth counterpart will have whatever property is supposed to be the purely intrinsic component of that relational property. But the story does not help us to identify the relevant intrinsic property. If we were to consider, not *Twin*-Earths, but, say, *Cousin*-Earth stories in which an individual resembles its counterpart in some but not all internal ways, it would be clearer that this strategy for defining intrinsic properties in terms of relations may leave many questions unanswered. Suppose, for example, that Cousin-Earth contains both H_2O and XYZ. In this world the two substances are easily distinguished. Their superficial properties are somewhat different from the superficial properties that H_2O has on Earth, and that XYZ has on Twin-Earth, and also somewhat different from each other. But both substances are somewhat like water in fact is. Suppose also that Cousin-English has different (non-scientific) words for the two substances, neither one of which is spelled or pronounced like "water," but that otherwise Cousin-English is a lot like English. Now suppose my counterpart on Cousin-Earth believes that salt is soluble in water, but does not believe that salt is soluble in the other stuff. Does his belief have the same narrow content as my belief that salt is soluble in water (and so the same narrow content as my Twin's belief that salt is soluble in the other stuff)? Fodor's abstract account, by itself, gives no guidance about how to answer this question.[10]

There are several disanalogies between Kaplan's notion of character and Fodor's proposed account of narrow content—disanalogies that suggest that Fodor's project is much more ambitious, and much more speculative. First, Kaplan's notion of context is not designed to include everything external to the individual, and the character of an utterance is not something determined by the purely internal properties of the speaker. As a result, characters are not required to have the counterfactual power that narrow contents must have. That the pronoun "I" has the character it has is a fact about a social practice—the practice of speaking English. The functions from context to content that Kaplan calls characters are not intended to tell us what speakers would be saying if they were speaking some other language. Kaplan's notion need not tell us this since the aim of his theory is not to isolate the purely internal component of what determines the content of speech acts, but simply to explain how some languages in fact work. The practice of speech is more efficient if speakers can exploit information about the environment—information available to all the participants in a conversation—in communicating. So languages make this possible by including rules that make what is said a function of that kind of information. That a language contains such rules (rather than, say, just lots of unsystematic ambiguity) is a substantive hypothesis, though in this case an obviously correct one. That our minds contain much more general systematic procedures for determining content as a function of context in a more general sense is a much more ambitious and speculative hypothesis.

Second, because Kaplan's theory is a theory of speech rather than a theory of thought we can identify, more or less independently of theory, the objects that the theory is interpreting: the objects that *have* character and content. A speech act can be described in terms of its content (O'Leary said that salt is soluble in water), but it also may be described in more neutral ways (O'Leary uttered the sentence, or the sounds, "Salt is soluble in water") But in the case of thought it is much less clear what it is that has a particular content, or narrow content. As with a speech act, we can describe a particular belief in terms of its content (O'Leary believes that salt is soluble in water), but in this case there is no easily identifiable mental state, describable independently of its content, that constitutes that person's having that belief. Of course a psychological theory might turn up such a mental state or object. It might be that what it is to believe that salt is soluble in water is to be storing in a certain location a mental sentence that says that salt is soluble in water. If this were true, then we could identify the thing that has the content independently of the content that it has. But it also might be that states of belief are more holistic. Suppose a total belief state were a complex cluster of dispositions to behave in various ways under various conditions. One might be able to use particular belief contents such as the belief that salt is soluble in water to describe such a state without it being possible to match up those contents with particular dispositions in the cluster. On this kind of account, the question "what makes it true (given the facts about the external context) that O'Leary believes that salt is soluble in water?" will be answered by describing how O'Leary is disposed to behave under various conditions. But the same behavioral dispositions that constitute O'Leary's total belief state will also make it true that he believes various other nonequivalent propositions. Compare: the question "what makes it true (given the facts about the external context) that O'Leary is three miles from a burning barn?" will be answered by describing O'Leary's location. But this same location will also make it true that O'Leary has various other nonequivalent relational properties (being more than two thousand miles from Los Angeles, being closer to Istanbul than to New Delhi, etc.). Even if we could find a narrow, purely internal characterization of the belief state as a whole, it wouldn't follow that we could find narrow analogues of the (relational) facts about the belief state that are expressed by ordinary attributions of belief.[11]

Fodor's abstract account of narrow content is motivated by a particular picture of belief and other mental states, a picture that he has made explicit and vigorously defended. Beliefs are internal sentences stored in the mind. The particular contents of those sentences depend on the believer's environment, but the sentences themselves can be identified as sentences, and as *beliefs*, independently of the particular environmental conditions that determine their interpretation. The sentences are beliefs in virtue of their internal functional role—the way they are affected by sensory inputs, interact with other internal states, and determine behavioral outputs. Their semantic properties will depend in part on what is going on outside—beyond the periphery—but the way they depend on what is going on outside is determined by the purely internal state. This is a very attractive picture, but it is not inevitable; it has strong, highly speculative, empirical presuppositions. Fodor's abstract account of narrow content as a function from context (in a very broad sense) to truth-conditional content may seem plausible given this picture, but it does not contribute much to defending the picture, or to explaining how it is to be developed. It does not, by itself, tell us how to identify narrow contents, and it does not give us reason to believe that internal states determine functions of this kind that will do any explanatory work. No general a priori argument will show that this is the way that things must be.

Is there a way to define narrow content that does not depend on the language of thought picture? Daniel Dennett, after criticizing the sententialist approach, makes some suggestions about how we might isolate what he calls the "organismic contribution" to the content of belief in a way that is neutral as to how that contribution is represented in the believer.[12] He calls his approach "*notional attitude psychology*," and contrasts it both with *propositional attitude psychology*, which describes attitudes in terms of the ordinary wide conception of content, and *sentential attitude psychology*, which takes the contents of attitudes to be syntactic objects—sentences of an inner language. The contents of notional attitudes are explained in terms of a kind of possible world, which Dennett calls a "notional world." "A notional world should be viewed as a sort of *fictional* world devised by a theorist, a third-party observer, in order to characterize the narrow-psychological states of a subject."[13] Notional worlds are supposed to be defined so that, "although my *Doppelganger* and I live in different real worlds—Twin-Earth and Earth— we have the *same* notional world."[14] The set of notional worlds that define the narrow contents of a person's beliefs is something like the worlds that *are* the way that the person takes the real world to be.

Notional worlds, it seems, are just the possible worlds that have been used to characterize ordinary wide contents in *propositional* attitude psychology. Possible worlds—at least all but one of them—are also fictional worlds in the sense that they are not actual. So how are notional attitudes different from propositional attitudes, characterized in this way? What difference explains why the contents of notional attitudes are narrow, while the contents of propositional attitudes are wide? The difference will not be found in the nature of the worlds themselves, or in the nature of the contents, which in both cases are just sets of worlds. So far as I can see, narrow contents, on Dennett's account, are just propositions. The difference between notional and propositional content is to be found in the different answers that the two theories give to the question, "in virtue of what facts do a believer's beliefs have the (notional or propositional) contents that they have?" According to propositional attitude psychology, the contents of an organism's attitudes are picked out as a function of relations between the organism and its actual environment. Just what relations do the job is a difficult and controversial question, but the Twin-Earth thought experiments show that the content of a belief, as ordinarily conceived, is not a function of purely internal properties of the believer. The task of narrow, notional attitude psychology is to explain how purely internal properties of an organism can be used to pick out a set of possible worlds—a perhaps different set that will characterize the organism's attitudes in a way that is different from the way it is characterized by an ordinary propositional attitude attribution. The idea is roughly this: O'Leary believes (correctly) that there is water in the basement. The proposition he believes is true in the actual world, but false in the counterfactual world where there is no water, but only XYZ in the basement. There is, however, a different proposition that does not distinguish the actual world from this counterfactual world—a proposition that we might roughly describe as the proposition that there is some water-like stuff in the basement. The first proposition is the wide content of O'Leary's belief; the aim of Dennett's project is to define narrow content so that the second of these propositions is the narrow content.

One can contrast Fodor's strategy with Dennett's in the following very abstract way: Fodor proposes to revise and narrow the folk concept of belief by changing the *kind* of thing that is the content of belief. Narrow contents are not propositions; they are functions from context to propositions. But for Dennett, in contrast, narrow contents are the same kind of thing as wide contents: both are propositions—functions from possible worlds (= notional worlds) into truth values. What is changed in the move to narrow content is the relation between a believer and a proposition in virtue of which that proposition correctly describes the believer's beliefs. To accomplish that change, Dennett needs to tell us just how the purely internal properties of individuals determine the narrow propositional content of their beliefs.

Here is Dennett's strategy for answering this question: suppose we know about an organism everything there is to know about its capacities and dispositions, but nothing about how it got that way: nothing about its historical properties, or about the environment that it came from. The problem is to say how to go from this limited information about the organism to a characterization of its notional world. "Our task," Dennett says, "is like the problem posed when we are shown some novel or antique gadget, and asked: what is it for?" We can't know, Dennett supposes, what it was actually designed for, but we could try to figure out, from its internal properties, what functions it is ideally suited to perform. "*We try to imagine a setting* in which...it would *excellently* perform some imaginably useful function."[15] In the same way, to find an organism's notional world—the world according to it—we try to imagine "the environment (or a class of environments) for which the organism as currently constituted is best fitted."[16] Propositions true in those possible environments will be the narrow contents of the organism's beliefs.

On the face of it, this doesn't look like what we want at all. Possible worlds picked out in this way look more like worlds in which the organisms needs or wants are satisfied than like worlds in which its beliefs are true. The antelope, for example, is aware of lions in its environment, and equipped to detect and escape from them. But it is not clear that it is better fitted for a lion-filled environment than for one that is lion-free. The antelope would have some useless defense mechanisms in certain lion-free environments, but it might still do a better job of "surviving and flourishing and reproducing its kind"[17] in such an environment. But, Dennett says, we are not supposed to understand "ideal environments" in a straightforward way: "By 'ideal environment' I do not mean the best of all possible worlds for this organism... . It might be a downright nasty world, but at least the organism is prepared to cope with its nastiness."[18] So ideal environments, in the intended sense, are environments for which the organism is prepared to cope. This is better: we do try to cope with the world as we believe it to be, and so worlds that are that way are presumably among the ones that our behavior is best fitted to cope with. But something essential still seems to be left out. Many features of organisms that help them cope with their environments seem intuitively to have nothing to do with their beliefs, and the fact that we have some feature that *would* help us cope with some counterfactual environment is surely not sufficient to say that such a counterfactual possibility is compatible with the world as we take it to be.

Consider the porcupine whose quills protect it from predators. It is best fitted, in Dennett's sense, for an environment containing animals that would attack and eat it if it weren't for the quills, and this will be true even if the porcupine's *only* defense mechanism is this passive one that does not require the porcupine to perceive or respond in any way to the presence of such predators. If the porcupine goes through life oblivious to the potential predators that its quills protect it against, it would surely be unreasonable to populate its notional world—the world according to it—with them.

The dangers that the porcupine's quills protect it from are real ones. The problem gets even worse if one considers, as Dennett's procedure requires, merely possible dangers that some actual feature we have might help to guard against. For example, consider a possible world containing fierce and powerful beasts that would love to eat human beings if it weren't for the fact that these beasts are repelled by the distinctive smell that humans in fact give off. We humans, as we actually are, are ideally fitted to cope with such predators, but I don't think worlds containing them can be used to characterize our beliefs.

It seems to me right that states of belief are states that help the believer to cope with an environment, and that the contents of those states are essentially connected with the kind of environment they help the believer to cope with. But to be a belief state, a feature of an organism must contribute in a particular way to the fitness of the organism to cope with its environment. At the very least, a belief state must involve the reception of information from the environment, and a role for this information in the determination of the behavior of the organism. While Dennett's general account of his procedure for identifying narrow content is not restricted to this kind of case, the examples he uses focus on it, and we can consider how his strategy fares if we apply it only to states of an organism that help it cope by receiving and storing information in a form that makes it available to help determine the organism's behavior.

Understood in this way, Dennett's procedure is a variation of one kind of naturalistic account of wide content that has been proposed.

According to this kind of account, a representational system is a system that is capable of being in a range of alternative internal states that tend to be causally dependent on the environment in a systematic way. Suppose that an organism is capable of being in internal states, $S_1, S_2, ..., S_n$, and that which of these states it is in normally depends on which of a corresponding range of alternative states the environment is in. Normally, for each i, the organism is in state S_i if (and because) the environment is in state E_i. Whenever a structure of causal dependencies of this kind obtains, it is appropriate to say that the organism *represents* the environment as being in state E_i in virtue of the fact that it is in state S_i, and that the organism's states contain *information* about the environment. Suppose further that the states of the organism are, or determine, behavioral dispositions, and that for each i, the behavior that state S_i disposes the organism to engage in is behavior that would be appropriate (given its needs or wants) in environment E_i. Then those representational states will be of the right general kind to be belief states.

This account of representation is like Dennett's account of narrow content in that it identifies content with a set of possible states of the environment. This account, like Dennett's, treats the descriptions of the relevant environments as the theorist's way of classifying internal states: the descriptions are not attributed to the organism. And like Dennett's, it does not distinguish information from misinformation. If the organism is in state S_i, then it represents the world as being in state E_i, whatever state the environment is actually in. But the notion of content that results from the causal account of representation will be a notion of *wide* content since the structure of causal relations in virtue of which the internal states are representational states will depend not just on the internal structure of the organism, but on general features of the environment. If the environment were radically different in certain ways, then the same states of the organism might tend to be sensitive to different features of the environment, or might not be sensitive to the environment at all. Content ascriptions, on this kind of account, are descriptions of internal states, but they describe them in terms of the organism's capacity to distinguish between a limited range of alternative possibilities, a range of possibilities that is constrained by certain facts about the organism's actual environment.

But even if our ordinary concept of content depends on facts about the actual environment in this way, might we apply this sort of procedure without relying on such facts? If we knew enough about the purely internal dispositional properties of a believer, might we be able to determine, from this information alone, a set of possible environments meeting this condition: if the believer were in such an environment it would tend to behave in ways that are appropriate (that tend to satisfy its needs better than alternative actions available in that environment), and it would do so *because* it is in such an environment? Dennett claims that if the believers were sophisticated enough we could, and that the resulting notion of content would be just the notion of narrow content we want.

> Highly adaptive organisms like ourselves...have internal structure and dispositional traits so rich in information about the environment in which they grew up that we could in principle say: this organism is best fitted to an environment in which there is a city called Boston, in which the organism spent its youth, in the company of organisms named...and so forth. We would not be able to distinguish Boston from Twin-Earth Boston, of course, but except for such virtually indistinguishable variations on a theme, our exercise in notional world formation would end in a unique solution.[19]

I see no basis for this optimism. I suspect that the attempt to recover information about a virtual environment without making any assumptions at all about the actual environment is just too unconstrained to work. Imagine a purely internal description of the movements that I am disposed to make under various internal conditions, as I walk down the streets of Boston going places to satisfy my wants and needs, a description that makes no reference to what is going on either specifically or in general beyond my skin. How could anything about *Boston*, or about Boston-like cities, be recovered from such a description? With a little imagination, one should be able to tell all kinds of wild fairy tales about environments in which the movements I am disposed to make are appropriate, but that are not anything like the way the world seems to me. The world beyond myself *could* be wired up so that the actions whose actual appropriateness depends on facts about Boston instead depended for their appropriateness on some totally different set of facts, say facts about the social organization of termite colonies. If the organism's internal structure and dispositional traits are rich and complex, then we will have to tell a long fairy tale. The world described by such a tale will perhaps have to share an abstract structure of some kind with the worlds that define the ordinary wide content of the organism's beliefs, but I don't see why they would have to share any content.

In normal everyday ascriptions of content we usually ignore not only fairy tale possibilities, but all possibilities except those that differ from the actual world only in very limited ways. When I say that O'Leary believes there is water in his basement, I may be saying only that O'Leary's conception of the world distinguishes the possibility that there is water in the basement from the possibility that his basement is dry. What this means, on the causal-informational account of representation, is that O'Leary is in a state that he would normally be in only if there were water in his basement. Further, that state is one that would normally cause O'Leary to behave in ways that would better serve his needs and wants if there were water in his basement than if the basement were dry: it disposes him to get out the mop, or call the plumber. But does O'Leary really believe that the liquid on his basement floor is *water*? Well, he certainly knows, or assumes, that it is not gasoline or olive oil. If it were any of a range of familiar alternative liquids, O'Leary's states and behavior would normally be different. But what about the possibility that it is a substance just like water in its superficial properties, but different from water in its underlying chemical structure? Does O'Leary's internal state contain information that distinguishes the actual situation from this one? Is there anything about him that would dispose him to behave differently (under normal conditions) if that situation were actual? In the usual context, that possibility is not relevant. When we claim that O'Leary thinks there is water in the basement, we are not claiming that he has ruled out the possibility that the stuff down there is really not water, but XYZ. We can, however, raise the question, and in this way change the range of relevant alternatives. The question will then shift, focussing on O'Leary's knowledge and beliefs about the chemical composition of water. If O'Leary is innocent of even the most elementary knowledge of chemistry, then nothing in his mind or behavioral dispositions will distinguish Earth from Twin-Earth, but that won't make it wrong to say, in a normal context in which Twin-Earth possibilities are ignored, that O'Leary believes that the stuff on his basement floor is water. That ascription of content distinguishes, in the right way, the relevant alternative possibilities that are compatible with O'Leary's conception of the world from the relevant possibilities that are not.

The revisionist may argue that it is this context-dependence of ordinary wide content ascriptions that makes them inappropriate for the purposes of theoretical explanation in cognitive science. Dennett's project might be seen as an attempt to eliminate the context-dependence by defining content relative to an absolutely neutral context that is free of all presuppositions about the external environment. But on the causal-informational account of representation, informational content is *essentially* relative to a range of alternative possibilities that are determined by general facts about the causal structure of the world in which the organism functions. It is internal states of the representor, on this kind of account, that contain information (or misinformation), but the system of causal relationships in virtue of which those internal states contain information cannot itself be something internal to the representor. The theorist, in describing the internal states of a representor in terms of informational content, has some choice in the range of alternatives relative to which content is defined. It may even be that for any possibility we can describe, there is a context in which we can ask whether the representor's beliefs distinguish that possibility from certain others. But this does not imply that there is an absolutely neutral context, a context free of all presuppositions about the environment, relative to which content ascriptions make sense.

In his attempt to characterize narrow content, Dennett has tied one hand behind his back. He proposes to extract a kind of content from facts about the believer while ignoring certain information that is available and that is used to determine ordinary wide content—information about the believer's historical properties and relation to the actual environment. I have argued that no reasonable notion of content will result from this procedure; one might also question the point of the exercise. Why bother? Why shouldn't an explanatory theory make use of historical and environmental information in defining content? To answer this we need to look at the other half of the revisionist's project: the arguments for the negative thesis.

The negative side of the revisionist doctrine has been formulated in various ways and given various labels: *methodological solipsism*,[20] *individualism*,[21] *the principle of autonomy*.[22] These different theses are sometimes distinguished from each other, but the general idea of all of them is that the states and properties that are described and expressed in an explanatory psychological theory should be intrinsic states and properties of the organism whose behavior is being explained. A number of similar arguments for this thesis have been advanced; they go roughly like this: an explanatory theory of human behavior, or of the behavior of anything else for that matter, should concern itself only with properties that are relevant to the causal powers of the thing whose behavior is being explained. Things that are intrinsically indistinguishable are indistinguishable with respect to causal powers, and so should not be distinguished by an explanatory theory. The Putnam-Burge thought experiments help to bring this point out: it is clear that people on Earth and their doppelganger on Twin-Earth will behave in exactly the same ways when put into the same environments. No tenable theory will explain their behavior in different ways, and so no tenable theory needs concepts that distinguish them.[23]

Before turning to this argument, we need to look more closely at the theses it is intended to support. First, here is Fodor's formulation of what he calls *individualism*: "Methodological individualism is the doctrine that psychological states are individuated *with respect to their causal powers*."[24] This doctrine is, Fodor says, a special case of a completely general methodological principle that all scientific taxonomies should conform to, a principle that can be defended on a priori metaphysical grounds. He emphasizes that individualism, in his sense, does not by itself rule out the individuation of mental states by relational properties.

> Relational properties can count taxonomically whenever they affect causal powers. Thus, 'being a planet' is a relational property par excellence, but it's one that individualism permits to operate in astronomical taxonomy. For whether you are a planet affects your trajectory and your trajectory determines what you can bump into; so whether you're a planet affects your causal powers.[25]

There is a shift in this characterization of individualism from a stronger to a weaker claim: it is one thing to individuate by causal powers, another to individuate by what *affects* causal powers. The fact that a planet is a planet is a fact about the configuration of its environment. This configuration plays a role in causing the planet to have the causal powers it has, for example its velocity. But the environmental facts do not *constitute* causal powers. Does individualism really require only that mental states be individuated by what causally affects causal powers? If so, then individualism in

Fodor's sense is a much weaker doctrine than the individualism that Burge has argued against. On this interpretation, individuation by ordinary wide content will be compatible with Fodor's individualism since, for example, the fact that it is *water* in O'Leary's basement— or at least the fact that there is water in his environment generally— surely plays a role in putting him into the internal state that disposes him to behave as he does. Of course as the Twin-Earth story shows, there are alternative causal histories that could have put O'Leary into the same internal state, but an analogous claim will be true for the planets. Imagine a Twin-Earth that is not a planet but is in a field of forces exactly like the one the Earth is in.

The defense of the negative thesis by Fodor and others trades on a conflation of the weaker and the stronger thesis. If the thesis is to have any bite—if it is to be a thesis that rules out the individuation of psychological states by ordinary wide content—it must be the stronger thesis. But the arguments and examples used to support individualism often count only against the weaker thesis. Fodor, for example, illustrates his version of individualism and defends its plausibility with an example of a causally irrelevant relational property: call a particle an h-particle if a certain coin is heads up, and a t-particle if the coin is tails up. No plausible theory, Fodor argues, will use this distinction to explain the behavior of particles. No one will disagree with this; it should be clear and uncontroversial that facts that are causally irrelevant to the internal states of a particle or an organism should play no role in characterizing its theoretically important physical or psychological states. But it does not follow from this that such states must be purely internal.

The same shift between a weaker and a stronger version of the negative thesis is evident in other discussions. Consider, for example Stephen Stich's principle of autonomy: "The basic idea of the principle is that the states and processes that ought to be of concern to the psychologist are those that supervene on the current, internal, physical states of the organism." This is clearly the strong thesis, restricting the psychologist to purely internal states. But causal language creeps into Stich's subsequent discussion of the principle: historical and environmental facts, he says, will be irrelevant to psychological theory except when they "make a difference" to the organism's internal state; such facts "will be psychologically relevant only when they *influence* an organism's current, internal, physical state." The facts about distant causal histories of a term that determine its reference are said to be psychologically irrelevant because they need not "leave their trace" on the current internal state of the subject using the term.[26]

Stich argues for his principle of autonomy with what he calls the *replacement argument*: "Suppose that someone were to succeed in building an exact physical replica of me—a living human body whose current internal physical states at a given moment were identical to mine at that moment.... . The replica, being an exact physical copy, would behave just as I would in all circumstances.... . But now, the argument continues, since psychology is the science which aspires to explain behavior, any states or processes or properties which are not shared by Stich and his identically behaving replica must surely be irrelevant to psychology."[27] Stich illustrates his point with an example of an industrial robot. Suppose we describe the robot by saying that it is successfully performing its millionth weld. This is, in Stich's terminology, a nonautonomous behavioral description. An exact physical replica behaving in a way that is, in a reasonable sense, exactly the same, might not satisfy it. The description is a "conceptual hybrid" of an autonomous description— "successfully performing a weld"[28]—and a purely historical description— "having performed 999,999 other welds". "If we are seeking a set of generalizations to explain robot behavior, it would be perverse to expect them to explain the latter fact or the hybrid into which it enters."[29]

The argument and the example seem compelling, I think, only if we assume that the historical property is causally irrelevant to the current state of the robot. But if we keep in mind that those first 999,999 welds must surely have taken their toll, then it may not seem so perverse to look for generalizations that explain the fact that the robot satisfies the hybrid description. Suppose that, because of metal fatigue, robots of this kind almost always break down soon after about nine hundred thousand welds. If the robot failed to break down, we might ask for an explanation: how was this particular robot able to perform its millionth weld? We might call robots "old" after their nine hundred thousandth weld, and generalize about the behavior of old robots. We certainly generalize about the behavior of human beings on the basis of historical properties such as age and experience.

If we replace our robots with new ones after 900,000 welds, they won't break down as often, but, Stich might point out, this is because real replacements won't be the exact replicas required by the replacement argument. If the new robots were really physically exactly like the ones they replace, then of course they would be similarly unreliable. If an eighty year old woman were physically exactly like a seven year old child, then she would behave like a seven year old child, falsifying biological and psychological generalizations about eighty year old women. But this counterfactual possibility does not, by itself, threaten the truth, or even the explanatory power, of such generalizations.

There may be a sense in which certain nonautonomous properties are causally irrelevant. Consider a simple causal chain: A causes B, which in turn causes C. Suppose that B is sufficient, in the circumstances, for C: that is, B would have caused C even if it had been caused by something other than A. So this causal chain contrasts with a more complex one where A is doing some additional work, perhaps not only causing B but also causing other things that enable B to cause C. To rule out this contrasting case, we might say that A is causally irrelevant to the fact that B causes C. But in another sense, A is causally relevant to this fact, since without A, B would not have happened, and so would not have caused C. Suppose we have a pair of alternative causal chains: alternative inputs A_1 or A_2 will cause a device to be in one of two alternative internal states, B_1 or B_2, which in turn will cause the device to produce outputs C_1 or C_2. If we ask why the internal state B_1 produces output C_1, it is not relevant to mention A_1. But if we ask why the device produces output C_1, it would be correct and informative to say, because it is in the B-state caused by A_1. It is one thing to explain why a particular internal state has the causal powers it has; it is another to explain why something is in an internal state that has those causal powers.

Does the internal state of the device contain *information* about how it came to be in that state? If there are alternative causes of B_1, then the fact that the device is in state B_1 does not distinguish them: the device does not 'know' that A_1 causes B_1, as contrasted with a counterfactual possibility in which A_2 causes B_1. But since it is A_1 that in fact causes the device to be in state B_1, and since the device would not have been in that state if A_1 hadn't happened, it 'knows', in virtue of being in state B_1, that A_1 happened.

In light of these distinctions, consider the following argument in defense of methodological solipsism from a paper by P. M. and P. S. Churchland:

> A neuron cannot know the distant causal ancestry...of its input... . An activated neuron causes a creature to withdraw into its shell not because such activation represents the presence of a predator—though it may indeed represent this—but because that neuron is connected to the withdrawal muscles, and because its activation is of the kind that causes them to contract. *The 'semantic' content of the state, if any, is causally irrelevant.*[30]

One cannot explain why the neuron's being activated causes the creature to withdraw by citing the fact that the activation represents the presence of a predator. But this does not prevent us from explaining why the creature withdraws by citing the presence of a predator, or by citing the fact that the creature is in a state that represents the presence of a predator. The semantic content is causally relevant to the behavior of the creature since if the creature had not been in a state with that semantic content, it would not have withdrawn into its shell. Can a neuron know the distant causal ancestry of its input? It cannot distinguish the situation in which its activation is caused by the presence of a predator from the situation in which it is caused by something else. But if in fact the neuron was activated by the presence of a predator, and would not have been activated if a predator had not been present, then it 'knows', in virtue of being activated, that a predator is present.

The critic of wide content might respond to these general considerations as follows: even if a theory *can* generalize about properties and states that are individuated by their causes, wouldn't it better, methodologically, to try to find a theory that individuates them more narrowly? Won't generalizations in terms of the internal properties be deeper and more accurate? Generalizations about the causal powers or behavioral dispositions of old robots, creatures that are representing the presence of a predator, or footprints will inevitably have exceptions; to the extent that they are true, they must hold in virtue of internal properties of those things, and we won't understand why the generalizations hold until we are clear about the relevant internal properties.

It is right that *one* explanatory task is the task of characterizing the mechanisms that underlie certain causal regularities. We want to know how the creature represents the presence of a predator, and how that representation causes it to withdraw into its shell. But there are at least three reasons why we may still want to generalize about causal and historical properties. First, we need to refer to such properties, and to generalizations about them, in order to pose the explanatory questions about the mechanisms. The creature has certain capacities: it can recognize predators and protect itself from them. The reason we are interested in the neurophysiological processes in the creature is that they explain how it is able to do such things. Second, we may not know enough to be able to generalize in terms of internal properties. Suppose our device is a black box and that all we know about the states B_1 and B_2 is that they are the states caused (or normally caused) by A_1 and A_2, respectively. Often we know something about the mechanisms that explain why a device has certain capacities or incapacities, but not enough to describe them in purely autonomous terms. We may have to wait for the completion of science before we are able to describe things in purely internal terms, if there are such terms. As Fodor said in another context, and in defense of the opposite conclusion, "No doubt it's all right to have a research strategy that says 'wait a while', but who wants to wait *forever*?"[31] Third, there may be generalizations that can be stated only in terms of non-individualistic states and properties. Different mechanisms explain how different creatures recognize predators, but we may still be able to generalize about the recognition of predators. Suppose there are lots of black boxes that take inputs A_1 and A_2 into outputs C_1 and C_2, but that they do it in different ways. It is, of course, the idea of functionalism that it is possible and useful to generalize about causal roles independently of the specific mechanisms by which those causal roles are realized. Functional theories are theories that characterize the internal states of individuals in nonautonomous terms in order to generalize at a certain level of abstraction. It is not a mysterious coincidence that such generalizations hold. There may be general causal pressures, such as evolutionary pressures, that tend to favor situations in which A causes C but that leave open the question of the means or intervening process by which this is accomplished. In such a case there may be two different questions about why A causes C. If the question is about the mechanism, one cites B. If it is about the general pattern, then one cites the general pressures. Why do chameleons change color to match their background? Because this provides camouflage and in this way helps them survive, or because certain chemical processes take place in the chameleon's skin.

Any psychological theory, folk or scientific, that understands mental states in terms of intentional states is a theory that sees a person or other organism as a receiver and user of information. The real lesson of Twin-Earth is that the fact that we are receivers and users of information is a fact, not just about us, but about the way we relate to our environments. In different environments, the internal states that in fact carry certain information would carry different information, or would not carry information at all. Ironically, the Twin-Earth stories that make this point so vividly also serve to obscure its significance in at least two ways: they make the dependence of intentional states on the environment seem, first, easier to avoid, and second, more mysterious, than it is. In the special case of Twin-Earth, it is easy to match up O'Leary's beliefs with corresponding beliefs of his twin, and to identify the narrow content with what these corresponding beliefs have in common. It is less easy to say, in general, how to factor out the purely internal component of a belief. I have argued that it is a highly speculative substantive hypothesis that there is any narrow notion of content that can be used to individuate intentional states autonomously. The special case of Twin-Earth also makes the dependence of intentional states on environment seem stranger than it is. Since the internal states of O'Leary's twin are exactly the same as O'Leary's, there is a sense in which the environmental differences between the two worlds make no difference to the internal states of the two twins, and so one is tempted to conclude that the environmental facts on which intentional states depend are therefore causally irrelevant. But the fact that a state might have had different causes does not show that the causes it does have are causally irrelevant.

Is O'Leary's belief that there is water in his basement an internal state of O'Leary? Is it in his head? Of course it is, in the same way that the mosquito bite on his nose is on his nose, and the footprint in the sand is in the sand. We can appeal to that belief to explain the fact that he is looking for the mop, just as we can appeal to the mosquito bite to explain why he is scratching his nose. We commonly individuate states and properties in terms of the way things interact with their environments, and use them to explain why things behave as they do. It is not easy to see how we could get along without doing this, or why we should try.[32]

Notes

1. Hilary Putnam, "The Meaning of 'Meaning'", in Keith Gunderson (ed.), *Language, Mind and Knowledge* (Minneapolis, University of Minnesota Press), 1975, 144.
2. Tyler Burge, "Individualism and the Mental," in P. French *et al*, eds., *Midwest Studies in Philosophy, 4, Studies in Epistemology* (Minneapolis, University of Minnesota Press), 1979.
3. It is not clear that this is right. What does follow is that the intrinsic state of the head is not authoritative: that is, it does not follow from the head's being in the intrinsic state it is in that it has certain beliefs. But unless we assume the kind of individualism that is being denied, this does not imply that *we* are not authoritative.
4. There is a rough but useful analogy between this strategy of concept formation and a popular account of the way natural kind terms acquire their content. According to that account, one kind of property—a cluster of superficial properties—determines a set of things—say a set of animals— and then this extension is used to determine a different type of property-structural or explanatory or essential properties. The relevant properties of this type are the ones shared by the things in the extension.
5. One might argue that concepts, such as the general concept of footprint, that collapse when we try to abstract away from causal origins are just the concepts that are of no interest to science. But this need not be true. It is conceivable, for example, that there be ecological generalizations about the role of footprints in the behavior of certain kinds of predators and their prey even if there were no interesting generalizations about the shapes of the relevant footprints. If there can be functional theories at all, then there can be theories that generalize about causal roles in abstraction from the intrinsic properties of the states that realize those roles.
6. Jerry A. Fodor, *Psychosemantics: The Problem of Meaning in the Philosophy of Mind* (Cambridge, MA: Bradford Books, The MIT Press, 1987), ch. 2.
7. An explanation of narrow content based on this analogy was developed in some detail in Stephen White, "Partial Character and the Language of Thought," *Pacific Philosophical Quarterly*, *63* (1982), 347-365.
8. Fodor, *Psychosemantics*, 30.
9. *Ibid.*, 48.
10. The point of my Cousin-Earth story is not just that narrow content may in some cases be indeterminate. That, I would argue and many would agree, is true of wide content as well. The point is that once we go beyond the Twin-Earth scenario, it becomes clear that we have been told nothing at all about how to identify narrow content. That there is such a thing to be identified is a substantive hypothesis.
11. The point is that it doesn't follow that one could find *interesting* purely internal analogues of the relational properties of belief states that are expressed by ordinary attributions of belief—internal properties that

might be expected to play a role in an explanatory theory of behavior. One could always, by brute force, define some sort of internal property. Consider the location analogy: there is a set of absolute locations that are (in fact, at a certain moment) three miles from a burning barn. The property of being in one of those locations is (assuming, as we have been for purposes of the analogy, absolute space) independent of the external environment, and it is distinct from the property of being in one of the locations in the set that is in fact at least two thousand miles from Los Angeles. But such properties will have no interest; at other times or in counterfactual situations where barns are burning at different places, there will be no point in distinguishing the locations where, at this time and in this situation, a barn is burning three miles away.

12. Daniel C. Dennett, "Beyond Belief," in Andrew Woodfield(ed.), *Thought and Object: Essays on Intentionality* (Oxford: Clarendon Press, 1982), 1-95.
13. *Ibid.*, 38.
14. *Ibid.*
15. *Ibid.*, 41.
16. *Ibid.*, 42.
17. *Ibid.*, 41.
18. *Ibid.*, 42.
19. *Ibid.*, 43.
20. This term is first used for this doctrine by Hilary Putnam in "The Meaning of 'Meaning'"(see note #1). Jerry Fodor defends the doctrine in "Methodological Solipsism as a Research Strategy in Cognitive Science," in *RePresentations* (Cambridge, MA: Bradford Books, The MIT Press, 1981).
21. This is Burge's term. Fodor distinguishes methodological solipsism from individualism in chapter 2 of *Psychosemantics*, though I think it is not clear that Fodor and Burge are using the term in the same sense.
22. This is Stephen Stich's term. Stich distinguishes the principle of autonomy from methodological solipsism. See Stich, *From Folk Psychology to Cognitive Science* (Cambridge, MA: Bradford Books, The MIT Press), 1983.
23. Fodor's chapter 2 of *Psychosemantics* contains a clear development of this argument. See also Stich's replacement argument in Stich, 165ff.
24. Fodor, *Psychosemantics*, 42. Fodor's emphasis.
25. *Ibid.*, 43.
26. Stich, 164-165.
27. *Ibid.*, 167.
28. Paul Teller has pointed out that "successfully performing a weld" is not really an autonomous description, since its application depends on a social and technological context. With a little imagination, one could tell a twin earth story in which what twin robot was doing did not count as performing a weld.
29. Stich, 168.
30. Patricia S. Churchland and Paul M. Churchland, "Stalking the Wild Epistemic Engine," *Nous, 17* (1983), 5-18. Emphasis mine.

31. Fodor, "Methodological Solipsism..." *RePresentations*, 248.
32. Many people provided me with helpful comments on an earlier version of this paper. I want to thank Kathleen Akins, Ned Block, Richard Boyd, Dan Dennett, Hartry Field, Sydney Shoemaker, Paul Teller, J. D. Trout, and Paul Weirich.

Philosophical Perspectives, 3
Philosophy of Mind and Action Theory, 1989

TURNING THE TABLES ON FREGE
OR
HOW IS IT THAT "HESPERUS IS
HESPERUS" IS TRIVIAL?

Howard Wettstein
University of Notre Dame

I. Introduction: The Charge of Cognitive Insensitivity

The following challenge, offered me by a friend some years ago, still represents the sense of at least a large sector of the philosophical community. This, as I will argue, is not as it should be.

> For some twenty years now philosophers have been carping about the inadequacies of the semantical approaches of Frege and Russell. It must be admitted that many counterexamples to the views of Frege and Russell have been offered, some of considerable intuitive merit. It is nothing less than scandalous, though, that the anti-Fregeans have never given due weight to the sorts of considerations that were absolutely central for Frege and Russell, considerations about "the cognitive significance of language." Indeed these questions, like the puzzle about informative identities with which Frege begins "On Sense and Reference," are barely mentioned by many leading anti-Fregeans.

Philosophers may have quite a number of things in mind when they speak of the cognitive significance of language. I'll focus, in this paper, upon two central facets of cognitive significance, two central ways in which the approach I favor—that of the anti-Fregeans[1]—has been thought to be cognitively insensitive.

1. The anti-Fregean orientation seems to violate an intuition that runs very deep in traditional thinking, "the intentionality intuition," as I'll call it. The idea is that in order to be thinking or speaking about something, one must have a substantial *cognitive fix* on the thing in question, that something in one's thought must correctly distinguish the relevant item from everything else in the universe.

One might motivate a cognitive fix requirement in several different ways. Russell's motivation was explicitly epistemic. One cannot think or speak about a thing, Russell maintained, *without knowing which thing is in question*. Frege's motivation was less explicit, but it seems plausible that an important strand in Frege's thinking was a very different intuition, one which Russell emphatically did not share, that conceptually unmediated reference is impossible, maybe even incoherent. Reference to a thing, on this view, essentially involves entertaining a concept. It may be useful here to compare Frege's semantical view with the view of the perceptual dualist: One cannot, according to the latter, immediately perceive physical objects. Perception of a thing, for the dualist, *just is* the apprehension of a sense-datum that, in some sense, represents the thing. So too for Frege, reference to an object cannot be unmediated, but rather consists in the apprehension of a sense that is satisfied by the object.[2]

Frege and Russell differ not only about the motivation for the intentionality intuition; they differ also about what exactly is required of the speaker or thinker. Russell demands, and this seems closely connected with the fact that his motivation was epistemic (and his epistemology Cartesian), that the speaker or thinker stand in an extremely strong epistemic relation to the referent, namely, that of direct acquaintance. Reference requires that the referent need be, as it were, smack up against one's mind. Otherwise, held Russell, the thinker or speaker would not really know which thing was in question, even if he possessed a concept that uniquely applied to it. Frege, motivated not so much (perhaps not at all) by epistemic considerations, but likely by what we might call his "referential dualism," maintains more modestly that one need merely (**merely?**) possess a uniquely denoting concept.

However one motivates the requirement, and whatever the details of the requirement, some such requirement might well appear obviously in order. We anti-Fregeans, on the other hand, often proceed as if we don't have to spend a moment worrying about this problem. Indeed, many of our examples seem simply to presuppose the incorrectness of any such requirement. Think, for example, about our claim that one who possesses a name, say, 'Cicero', may refer to its bearer even if one's beliefs about the relevant individual are very far off the mark; indeed, even if one has very little "in the head" on this topic.

Fregean sympathizers have often focused their attention on other alleged cognitive failings of the anti-Fregean approach, but the intentionality intuition, I submit, is a deep source of the sense so many have had that no matter how good the criticisms we anti-Fregeans have made of the traditional approach, our view remains deeply incoherent.

2. An arguably more famous, and certainly more specific "cognitive insensitivity" problem is posed by Frege's well-known discussion of non-trivial identity sentences like 'Hesperus is Phosphorus'. It's a commonplace that neither the Millian idea that, as Ruth Marcus put it, a name is a tag, or the Donnellan-Kripke way of reviving Mill, yields any simple, straightforward way of understanding the informativeness of 'Hesperus is Phosphorus,' or the obvious difference in informativeness of 'Hesperus is Hesperus' and 'Hesperus is Phosphorus'. Frege's view, on the other hand, yields a straightforward explanation.[3] On Frege's view, each name contributes its own distinctive sense to the thought content expressed, and so 'Hesperus is Phosphorus' can express a non-trivial content. The Millian approach, eschewing as it does anything like modes of presentation, or connoted properties, seems to give us no intellectual apparatus out of which we might fashion an explanation.

My aim in this paper is to reveal as baseless the contention that, as Alvin Plantinga once put it, the anti-Fregean approach founders on the rocks of cognitive significance.[4] Others in the anti-Fregean camp have presented putative solutions to puzzles about cognitive significance. What I have in mind, though, is not another solution, rather a dissolution. (If the reader, to paraphrase Santayana, is tempted to smile, I can assure him that I smile with him.) That the phenomena to which Frege draws our attention seem so puzzling is a tribute to the grip of the traditional way of thinking about language represented by the work of Frege and Russell, or so I will argue. Attention to what is perhaps the deepest lesson of the anti-Fregean revolution will suggest a very different way of sorting what is puzzling from what seems perfectly natural.

II. Conservative vs. Reform Anti-Fregeanism

I want to distinguish two ways of developing the anti-Fregean approach, one relatively conservative, and one more radical. The conservative theorist, whose views I describe in more detail below, wishes to avoid what he sees as the obvious pitfalls of Fregean orthodoxy. His hope, though, is to capture, in a less objectionable form than did Frege and Russell, the motivating spirit of the tradition, embodied in the idea that the connection between words and things is intellectually mediated, a matter of the way the referent is presented to the mind.

The more radical approach that I will advocate wants nothing of the spirit of Fregean orthodoxy. The conservative, as he himself emphasizes, has admittedly moved a substantial distance from orthodox Fregeanism. Some of the conservative's moves, moreover, and especially some of his examples, contain the seeds of genuine intellectual revolution. What the conservative fails to discern, excited as he is about his distance from Frege and Russell, is the extent to which he remains tied to traditional patterns of thought. The conservative's Fregean side, his emphasis on the way the referent is presented to the mind, obscures the natural approach to questions concerning the connection between words and things, as well as to questions about the cognitive significance of language.

The Problem of the Missing Cognitive Fix: The Conservative Response

There are many ways to develop a conservative strategy, and one finds what I have called the fundamental Fregean idea cropping up again and again throughout the anti-Fregean literature. I'll focus here on its presence in the work of Kaplan, where it is quite explicit, and in Kripke, where it is more surprising, in light of Kripke's sometimes explicit rejection of intellectually mediated reference.

Let's begin with what might well seem a natural place for an anti-Fregean with conservative leanings to begin, with indexical expressions, the first-person pronoun for example. Why might indexicals, as opposed to proper names, make for a natural conservative starting point? The answer is provided, in effect, by Kaplan in "Demonstratives," which might serve as a conservative handbook.[5] Kaplan argues that while proper names are, as Mill taught, "purely denotative"—they lack descriptive meanings— indexicals, like 'I', typically have descriptive meanings. Indeed, continues Kaplan, they have "easily stateable descriptive meanings." Descriptive meanings are, of course, grist for a Fregean's mill. Such meanings, maintains Kaplan, are known to the competent speaker, and provide the speaker with a kind of mode of presentation, a cognitive fix on the referent.[6]

Frege's orthodox notion of "sense," and his attendant conception of cognitive fix (not to speak of Russell's "direct acquaintance" approach to the appropriate sort of cognitive fix) were, according to Kaplan, too crude, too naive. We often do not carry around with us anything like purely qualitative individuating characterizations of the things about which we wish to speak. Indeed, we may lack such conceptions even of ourselves. Our concepts, and even our self-concepts, moreover, need not be accurate. I have a friend whose self-concept fits god better than it fits himself. Still, he speaks of himself when he uses 'I'. His ability to so refer to himself, despite his transcendent ego, reflects the fact, according to Kaplan, that associated with 'I', *by linguistic convention*, is a mode of presentation, although not a Fregean one. The crucial difference between Fregean and Kaplanian modes of presentation is this. Senses determine references "absolutely," while Kaplan's "characters" do so in a *context-relative* way; a character determines an object as reference only relative to a context of utterance. The character associated with 'I' is for Kaplan, (roughly) "the speaker of the context."

Kaplan's approach to indexical reference is thus compatible, at least in spirit, with the dictates of the intentionality intuition. The reference of an indexical is certainly not independent of the speaker's cognitive fix on the referent. Kaplan's conception, however, is of a context-relative cognitive fix, one that by contrast with Frege's conception, has been brought down to earth.

I've formulated Kaplan's approach so as to emphasize its continuities with Frege. There are, of course, substantial and impressive discontinuities that have been emphasized by Kaplan and others.[7] One important qualification that deserves explicit mention is that Kaplan never suggests, as some have, that indexicality is ubiquitous, and that Kaplan's treatment of indexicals can serve as a paradigm for the treatment of say, proper names and natural kind terms. Kaplan emphasizes, on the contrary, that names, entirely devoid of descriptive meaning, seem to require a very different sort of treatment.[8]

Nevertheless, the Fregean flavor of Kaplan's approach is striking. Kaplan's theoretical repertoire includes "ways of apprehending," conventionally associated with expressions, that provide a cognitive fix (relative to a context) and thereby determine the reference. Thus Kaplan, with Frege—and this is the point of great importance—gives great weight, with respect to the determination of reference, to the way the referent is represented to the mind.[9] Not only Kaplan, but many others as well, have either embraced, or have at least been tempted by, the conservative strategy. The feeling that reference must be intellectually grounded goes very deep. And the possibilities for attenuating the Fregean picture are extensive. One can, as we saw, try bringing the senses down to earth by making them context-relative. Another popular variation, tempting for one not quite ready to see proper names as entirely without descriptive content, is to assign to that content a semantically more humble role than did Frege, that of merely "fixing the reference" of a name, rather than that of providing a synonym for the latter.

Let's distinguish two ways in which the notion of "reference fixing by description" has been used, by Kripke as well as by others. First, one hears it said that names are sometimes, typically, or even always *introduced* by reference fixing definite descriptions. This, it should be noted, is a thesis about how names get going, so to speak, and not an account of how they later function. One who advances such a thesis need not maintain that later users of the name, or even later uses by the person who introduced the name, utilize a description to fix the reference. A second, and stronger, reference-fixing-by-description thesis consists in the claim that users of a name, even if they don't use the name synonymously with a description, must be fixing the reference of the name by some description.

This distinction is important for our purposes. It is the second and stronger reference fixing thesis in which I am here primarily interested, and which I see as most clearly exemplifying the conservative strategy.[10,11] Taking the reference of each use of a name to be determined by descriptions available to the speaker retains the intellectual character of the name-referent tie, and thus avoids the specter of semantic action at an epistemic distance.[12,13]

Kripke has, from time to time, explicitly disavowed this conservative position. He roundly asserts, in "Identity and Necessity,"[14]

> ...I...think, contrary to most recent theorists, that the reference of names is rarely or almost never fixed by description. And by this I do not just mean what Searle says: 'It's not a single description, but rather a cluster...'. I mean that properties in this sense are not used *at all*.[15]

Some, though, have taken Kripke to be, in my vocabulary, a conservative theorist, to be advancing the very view that Kripke denies in the passage just quoted. Indeed, Kripke himself sometimes seems much less definite on the matter. Lecture 3 of *Naming and Necessity* seems to place great emphasis on reference fixing by description. Consider the following passage.

Usually, when a proper name is passed from link to link, the way the reference of the name is fixed is of little importance to us. It matters not at all that different speakers may fix the reference of a name in different ways, provided that they give it the same referent.

The Fregean tone of this passage should not escape us. Frege, you remember, emphasizes that in natural language at least, different speakers will typically attach different senses to a name, but this will not matter much as long as reference is preserved.

Kripke, moreover, in his later "A Puzzle About Belief," in which he again rejects the reference-fixing-by-description approach to the semantics of names, suggests that it would not have been out of the question to read *Naming and Necessity* as suggesting the disputed view.

[In *Naming and Necessity*] I presupposed a sharp contrast between epistemic and metaphysical possibility: Before appropriate empirical discoveries were made, men might well have failed to know that Hesperus was Phosphorus, or even to believe it, even though they of course knew and believed that Hesperus was Hesperus. *Does not this support a Fregean position that 'Hesperus' and 'Phosphorus' have different "modes of presentation" that determine their references?* [Italics added.]... So it appears that even though, according to my view, proper names would be *modally rigid*—would have the same reference when we use them to speak of counterfactual situations as they do when used to describe the actual world—they would have a kind of Fregean "sense" according to how that rigid reference is fixed.[16,17]

A Radical Rejoinder

The radical sees philosophical backsliding in anti-Fregean attempts to satisfy the spirit of the intentionality intuition.[18] Doesn't the conservative strategy miss what the striking anti-Fregean counterexamples so strongly suggest? Recall the Donnellan-Kripke examples concerning proper names, examples in which a speaker, competent with a name, nevertheless has beliefs about the name's referent that are badly mistaken or extremely meager, for example, that Cicero was "some famous guy I think I heard about at school." What drives reference, such examples teach us, is simply not the mind's grip on the referent. The point, to particularize it to Frege, wasn't that we need to find more kosher senses—to bring senses down to earth. The point was that we can do without anything like senses, that the intentionality intuition is simply mistaken. The radical thus takes seriously the rhetoric about an anti-Fregean *revolution*, and proposes the following motto (every revolution needs one):

SEMANTIC CONTACT WITH THINGS DOES NOT DEPEND UPON SUBSTANTIVE EPISTEMIC OR CONCEPTUAL CONTACT WITH THEM[19]

The following remarks of Kripke, in *Naming and Necessity*, may help provide a feel for the contrast between the conservative, Frege-inspired, outlook, and the more radical one.

The picture which leads to the cluster-of-descriptions theory is something like this: One is isolated in a room [Descartes's study, we might add]; the entire community of other speakers, everything else, could disappear; and one determines the reference for himself by saying—"By 'Godel' I shall mean the man, whoever he is, who proved the incompleteness of arithmetic." Now you can do this if you want to. There's nothing really preventing it...

But that's not what most of us do. Someone, let's say a baby, is born; his parents call him by a certain name. They talk about him to their friends. Other people meet him. Through various sorts of talk the name is spread from link to link as if by a chain. A speaker who is on the far end of this chain, who has heard about, say Richard Feynman, in the market place or elsewhere [Question: where does Kripke shop?] may be referring to Richard Feynman even though he can't remember from whom he first heard of Feynman or

from whom he ever heard of Feynman... He doesn't know
what a Feynman diagram is... Not only that: he'd have
trouble distinguishing between Gell-Mann and Feynman. So
he doesn't have to know these things, but, instead, a chain
of communication going back to Feynman himself has been
established by virtue of his membership in a community
which passed the name on from link to link, not by a
ceremony that he makes in private in his study: "By
'Feynman' I shall mean the man who did such and such."

My point here is not to endorse the particulars of Kripke's sketch,
the idea that reference is determined by means of "chains of communication." I am increasingly skeptical about the adequacy of the
Donnellan-Kripke sketch.[20] My point is rather that however the
details go, it is the community's practice of using this name as a name
for *that* man that allows particular speakers to use the name to refer
to him. What drives reference is thus the institutionalized practice
of the linguistic community, and not the way the individual is
represented to the mind of the speaker (even where this is relativized to a context). The word-referent tie, as I put it above, is not an
intellectual tie. I thus want to take very seriously the platitude that
names are social instruments for making their bearers subjects of
discourse.[21]

What of indexicals? Indexicals, I said above, might seem to supply
a natural habitat for the Kaplan's brand of conservativism. Although
a full discussion is not possible here, I do want to argue that Kaplan's
approach to indexicals is far from trivial; indeed I believe it to be
implausible.

Kaplan's idea is that competence with an indexical involves knowing the rule that specifies the features of the context that determine
the referent of the indexical, and that this rule, in turn, captures the
speaker's cognitive perspective on the referent. Competence with
indexicals, though, seems more a matter of getting the hang of them,
of *knowing how* to use them, than it does of intellectually grasping
some rule that determines reference. Semantic theorists, not to speak
of ordinary mortals, seem to have quite a time discerning the sorts
of contextual features relevant to the determination of references
of demonstratives like 'that'. Imagine confronting an ordinary, competent speaker with an array of candidate rules, for example, that
the reference of a demonstrative is determined by a certain sort of

causal chain, or rather by the referential intentions of the speaker, or rather by the cues available to the competent and attentive auditor. Such a speaker, I submit, would not know where to begin. It is implausible, then, to suppose, as Kaplan does, that the semantic rules that govern our practices with indexicals are intellectually available to the competent speaker, and capture the speaker's cognitive perspective on the referent.[22]

One might find oneself sympathetic to the radical's reading of the original Donnellan-Kripke counterexamples, and to the considerations briefly mentioned that militate against Kaplan's approach to indexicals, but well feel that more needs to be said. The feeling may well linger that some deep incoherence attaches to the idea of epistemically unmediated reference. How indeed, to paraphrase Russell, can one speak of something without knowing what it is of which one speaks? Perhaps, then, the radical, in emphasizing the apparent lesson of the Donnellan-Kripke examples, has merely underscored what seems so perplexing about his view.

Second, even putting to one side the problem of the missing cognitive fix, is there any hope for dealing with the more specific problems of cognitive significance, Frege's famous puzzle for example, without recourse to something like modes of presentation? I turn now to Frege's puzzle, the discussion of which will afford us another chance to say the more that needs to be said.

Frege's Puzzle

Frege's discussion of cognitive significance, at the beginning of "On Sense and Reference," calls attention to cognitive data of undeniable importance, to what I'll call "Frege's data." I'll discuss Frege's data in the context of ordinary subject-predicate sentences, rather than, as Frege himself does, in the context of identity sentences, so as to avoid any special problems having to do with identity.[23] Consider, then, 'Hesperus appears in the morning' and 'Phosphorus appears in the morning. Or, for an example that involves indexicals, 'I am on fire' and 'He is on fire' (where unbeknownst to me, he and I are one). Here are Frege's data:

1. One can understand both sentences, but assent to only one.
2. One might find one of these old hat, but the other highly informative.
3. One's non-verbal behavior may change depending upon which of these he accepts.

Frege moves quickly from these uncontrovertible pieces of data to something much more controversial, to a theoretically infused way of describing the data, albeit one that looks harmless enough. Indeed, it sometimes hasn't been noticed that there is any movement here at all. Frege maintains that these sentences *express different propositions*, that they *have different thought contents*.

That Frege's description of his own data is far from inevitable is perhaps obvious enough once stated. Propositions, indeed the very category of propositional content, as acceptable as it is nowadays, was much less so just a few years ago. We can, though, reinforce this point—that Frege, in formulating his famous puzzle, imposes theory on the data—by reference to a view that takes propositions seriously, but that takes issue with Frege's contention that the respective pairs of sentences express different propositions.

Consider, then, Kaplan's view according to which both 'I am on fire' and 'He is on fire' express the same Russell-Kaplan "singular proposition," a proposition that contains me (in the flesh) as the subject constituent, and the property of being on fire as the predicate constituent. Kaplan, having posited a single proposition as the "content" of the two sentences, needs, of course, to address the obvious cognitive difference between the sentences. He needs to address, that is, Frege's data (1., 2., and 3. above), and indeed he proceeds to do so. We may like his subsequent explanation of Frege's data, or we may not.[24] What is clear, however, is that the cognitive data don't force us to conclude that the propositional contents are, as Frege supposed, distinct.

The distinction I am drawing between the uncontroversial cognitive data to be explained, and the data-as-described-in-terms-of-Fregean-categories, seems to me important. If this distinction is not observed it will indeed appear that the "cognitive data" refute the anti-Fregean approach. To observe the distinction is not yet to exonerate the anti-Fregean from the charge of cognitive insensitivity. What the anti-Fregean needs, though, is an explanation of Frege's data, and not an explanation of how the respective propositional contents can differ. The challenge, then, is this. 'Hesperus' and 'Phosphorus', for example, are equivalent along the dimension of reference, but may be strikingly inequivalent for a speaker along the cognitive dimension. How, given a Millian view of names, are we to account for this difference in cognitive role?[25]

The Conservative Approach To Differences In Cognitive Role

The conservative, we have seen, is not prepared to reject outright the traditional idea that reference depends upon what's in the head. The power of this Fregean intuition, however, pales before that of a related, perhaps even deeper, Fregean impulse, the idea that the *cognitive significance* of an expression is a matter of how the referent is presented to the mind.

Imagine that we could induce the conservative to reconsider his attempt to recover something intellectually available to the speaker that determines the reference (or does so in a context, etc.). We might attempt to move him by appealing, as I did above, to the Donnellan-Kripke counterexamples, and to the idea, suggested by these examples, that the correct interpretation of speech is, in the final analysis, in the public domain, a matter of the conventions of the linguistic community, and not, so to speak, in the jurisdiction of the individual speaker, not a matter of what's in his head.

Such an appeal, even if successful, would leave intact the more powerful Fregean impulse mentioned above—that cognitive significance is surely a matter of how the referent is presented to the mind. Even if reference is not a matter of what's in the head, how could the *cognitive significance* of an expression not be a matter of the individual's conceptual associations? Surely Frege was right about this much at least, or so thinks the conservative: 'Hesperus is Phosphorus' can be informative to a speaker only if he is thinking of the referent in different ways, one of which is associated for him with 'Hesperus' and one with 'Phosphorus'. Perhaps we can depart from the traditional account in more radical ways than we have envisaged, the conservative might (or might not) allow. Surely, though, we should not depart from what goes deepest in the tradition.

The challenge for the conservative, and it is not a trivial one, is to provide a non-Fregean account of these "ways of thinking," these modes of presentation. The conservative, despite his rejection of Fregean senses, still enjoys considerable latitude here, for his idea that cognitive differences are to be cashed out in terms of mode-of-presentational, or representational, differences does not commit him to any particular story about the relevant representational differences. One might look, for example, to the linguistic meanings of the relevant terms for the representational differences, as did Kaplan for the case of indexicals. This, however, seems implausible for the general case, since, as Kaplan noted, proper names lack descriptive meaning. Indeed, Kaplan's approach seems implausible even for indexicals when one considers examples like informative utterances of 'That is the same thing as that', where one cannot appeal to differences in the linguistic meanings of the indexicals.[26]

One might try a different conservative tack, and, focusing upon proper names, look to descriptions that merely fix the reference for an account of the relevant cognitive perspectives. Or, disabused of the notion that descriptions have even this much semantic relevance, one might simply give up the idea that anything of semantic import will be of help in explicating the relevant cognitive perspectives. The idea now would be to still insist that if two names differ cognitively, the speaker must be thinking of the thing(s) in different ways. These different "ways of thinking" will no longer be tied to how the names achieve reference. One might think, that is, that the key to cognitive significance are indeed associated properties, without thinking that these properties have anything to do with the determination of reference.

The Conservative's Problem

A central theme of the anti-Fregean literature is underscored in the following passage from Kripke's "A Puzzle About Belief," a passage in which Kripke presents what he refers to as "the clearest objection [to the Frege-Russell description theory]..."

...individuals who "define 'Cicero'" by such phrases as "the Cataline denouncer," "the author of *De Fato*," etc., are relatively rare... Common men who clearly use 'Cicero' as a name for Cicero may be able to give no better answer to "Who was Cicero?" than "a famous Roman orator," and they probably would say the same (if anything) for 'Tully'... Similarly, many people who have heard of both Feynman and Gell-Mann would identify each as "a leading contemporary theoretical physicist." Such people do not assign "senses" of the usual type [that uniquely identify the referent] to the names...(even though they use the names with a determinate reference). But to the extent that the *indefinite* descriptions attached or associated can be called "senses," the "senses" assigned to 'Cicero' and 'Tully', or to 'Feynman' and 'Gell-Mann', are *identical*. (p. 246)

Kripke's remarks here resonate with Putnam's early admission that although he was certainly competent with 'elm' and 'beech'—he, like the rest of us, was in a position to use these terms to refer to the respective kinds of trees—he was entirely ignorant about what distinguishes elms from beeches.

This common anti-Fregean theme—that two terms can share their (often meager) associated information without being co-referential—is by now not only common; it's a virtual commonplace. What is less appreciated is that this commonplace presents a dramatic obstacle to the conservative strategy. Examples like Putnam's "elm-beech" and Kripke's "Gell-Mann-Feynman," indicate not only that *reference is not a matter of what's in the head*. They indicate just as clearly that (to take only a bit of dramatic license) *cognitive significance is not a matter of what's in the head*. The names 'Gell-Mann' and 'Feynman', after all, are far from cognitively on a par, despite the lack of any difference in associated properties. Indeed, Kripke's just quoted remarks continue thus:

> Yet clearly speakers of this type [who associate the same indefinite information with both names] can ask, "Were Cicero and Tully one Roman orator, or two different ones?" or "Are Feynman and Gell-Mann two different physicists, or one?" without knowing the answer by inspecting senses alone. Some such speaker might even conjecture, or be under the vague false impression, that, as he would say, "Cicero was bald but Tully was not." (p. 246)

The conservative, wishing as he does to explain cognitive differences in terms of differences in associated properties, thus again seems to miss the point of the striking anti-Fregean examples. Nevertheless, it is not difficult to see what is driving the conservative, for the Fregean intuition that cognitive differences somehow *must* reflect representational differences runs very deep. If someone associates exactly the same properties with 'Cicero' as with 'Tully', then, wonders the conservative, how is it that he doesn't automatically take them to be a single person. Similarly, if one associates the same properties with 'elm' as with 'beech', then how can it be that one doesn't take them to be a single kind?

Dissolution of the Puzzle

To say that reference requires a substantive cognitive fix—a thesis common to traditionalists and conservatives—is to say, in effect, that reference requires a kind of mental apprehension of the referent. Think impressionistically for a moment of reference as involving a kind of intellectual gazing at the things of which we speak or think. This perspective immediately generates a puzzle from what I have been calling "Frege's data": How, a cognitive fix advocate will have to ask himself, can one be using two co-referring names—that is, be gazing at the same thing twice—without knowing that the same thing is in question?

One can, given such a mental apprehension conception, proceed in several directions. Russell's view was that if one is indeed gazing at the same thing (and it's genuine, unmediated gazing—that is, direct acquaintance), then one cannot wonder about whether there are two things. One would know that there is only one thing in question. If two terms, 'a' and 'b', are really functioning as logically proper names of the same thing, then 'a = b' cannot be informative. Conversely, if one can wonder whether, as it were, a is b, then one cannot really be gazing, and the terms must be functioning not as logically proper names, but as disguised descriptions.

Alternatively, Frege maintained that the relevant intellectual gazing is always mediated by the apprehension of a sense that uniquely individuates the referent. If the senses associated with the co-referring 'a' and 'b' are different, then one may be gazing at the same thing (under different aspects, we might say) and still not know that the referent is one and the same.

Notice the driving role of the mental apprehension picture in generating the sense of perplexity. Frege's data themselves—the idea that two names can, unbeknownst to the competent speaker, co-refer—don't seem all that dramatic. Is it, after all, so obvious, that we should know of any two co-referring names that they co-refer? But put Frege's data together with the mental apprehension picture and sparks fly. What may prevent appreciation of this point is the feeling that some sort of mental apprehension conception is inevitable, that it's radical denial is incoherent. I'll try, then, to further loosen the grip of the mental apprehension picture, with an eye towards throwing off its shackles. Whether or not I succeed, what I am really after is the sense that the mental apprehension conception is what propels the puzzle. Were we to radically deny the former and adopt an epistemically innocent way of thinking about reference, as I have suggested that we should, Frege's data would present no special problem.

The alleged difficulty with the radical's epistemically innocent conception of reference is that it makes reference entirely mysterious. What, or so the Fregean wants to ask, other than the mind's grip on a referent, could possibly secure reference? Where the Fregean sees a mystery, however, I see a fundamental and unproblematic feature of our name using practices, indeed a feature that has enormous social utility.[27]

Imagine our plight if we could only make those things subjects of discourse about which we had individuating knowledge (or even individuating belief). If that were the case, if our practices were so restrictive, then people like me could not refer to people like Herod by name. Given how little I believe about Herod, I wouldn't be able to ask, for example, who Herod was. Nor could I speculate that he lived in the first century. (To paraphrase Kripke, the idea that names like 'Cicero' must mean, for the competent speaker, something like "the Cataline denouncer," is a tribute to the excessive classical learning of some philosophers.) I can do these things now—refer to Herod by name, for example—just because our practices with names don't require anything like what the traditional picture presumes.

Names are thus not to be thought of as externalizations of inner gazings, mediated or not, but as social instruments, as tags that allow us to make into subjects of discourse those things with which the tags are conventionally associated. And it is crucial to the utility of these linguistic devices that they function even in the face of a referent's epistemic remoteness. Far from there being an epistemic requirement of any sort traditionally supposed, names allow speakers to bridge great cognitive gulfs. The mere possession of a name for an item, that is, *provides* a crucial kind of contact with it. One can now, as noted, ask questions, make assertions, and so on, that are *about* that very item. Names, from an epistemic point of view, ask very little of us, but generously provide for our needs.

So much for my attempt to loosen the grip of the traditional picture, to encourage a kind of gestalt switch in our thinking. I argued above that Frege's puzzle, so called, is generated not by Frege's data alone, but only in conjunction with the mental apprehension conception of reference. Is it so obvious, I asked, that there is something deeply puzzling about the very idea that a speaker can be competent with two co-referring names, and not know that they co-refer? The radical change in perspective I've been encouraging makes even more dramatic the dissolution of the puzzle. If one can refer to something without anything like a substantive cognitive fix on the referent, if the use of a name can be virtually blind epistemically, then why should it be the slightest bit surprising that a speaker might be competent with two co-referring names, but have no inkling that they co-refer?

A student who associates with 'Cicero' only that he was "a Roman orator," or "a famous Roman," subsequently hears about "Tully," another "famous Roman." He now stands in possession of two social instruments for making things subjects of discourse. *We* know that there is only one thing in question, but how in the world should he know this? Suppose he assumes that there are two people in question. Or suppose that he begins to wonder whether "Cicero is Tully." Why should anyone suppose that his wonder presents some special puzzle? Does the intelligibility of his wonder really require his associating *different* properties with the names? Why should it? Why can't he be thinking of both Cicero and Tully as "a Roman orator?"

To one in the grip of the mental apprehension picture, it will seem that the obvious and only way to explain what I've been calling "Frege's data," that co-referring names can be cognitively inequivalent, is in terms of a difference in cognitive perspectives, a difference in associated properties. Rejecting that picture, we can now see that there is no presumption whatever that co-reference should somehow be apparent to the competent name user, or that the possibility of its not being apparent is crucially dependent upon there being two different ways the referent is presented to the mind. That cognitive differences presuppose representational differences is a dogma, a product of the very conception that anti-Fregeans, at their best moments, have been at pains to reject.

Indeed, if there is any presumption to speak of here, it is in quite the opposite direction, that co-reference, except under unusual circumstances, will not be apparent. In general, then, "$a = b$" identities that are truths will nevertheless not be trivial, and this is no surprise. What is more surprising perhaps—and here we turn the tables on Frege—is that "$a = a$" identities are not, in general, trivial. One can, of course, simply repeat a name, intending to refer to the

same person, thus—barring seriously mind-bending circumstances—
guaranteeing that the same reference is in question. I can, for example, provide my class with an example of a triviality: "Susan (pointing to a student) is, of course, Susan." But the mere presence of the
same name, indeed the same name of the same party, surely does
not make the identity trivial. One can pick up Susan's name on two
occasions, and not know that the same Susan is in question.

Nor does the same name, along with the same identifying information, guarantee that the same individual is in question. Imagine
yourself hearing about "a famous Roman orator" named "Cicero"
in circumstances that lead you to believe that "another Cicero" is
in question, that is a Cicero other than the one about whom we've
all heard. You later forget just where you learned about this "other
Cicero," and just what it was that induced the belief that another
Cicero was in question. It may well be that you have no discriminating
information about the "two Ciceros," yet you don't therefore assume
that a single person was in question.

My conclusion, then, is that anti-Fregeans need not feel embarrass-
ed by allusions to Frege's puzzle or the problem of the missing
cognitive fix. We need neither to supply some missing epistemological
link to bridge the cognitive gulf between speakers and the references
of names that they use, nor to supply intellectual apparatus out of
which to fashion a solution to Frege's puzzle.

To say this is not to argue that the anti-Fregean has the upper hand
in the larger debate. This depends upon much larger questions—
methodological as well as substantive, questions in the philosophy
of mind, as well as in the philosophy of language—only some of which
I've touched upon here, and then all too briefly. It is not insignifi-
cant, though, that what was supposed to be *the* point of severe
pressure for the anti-Fregean, his inability to face squarely the questions that Frege and Russell took to be central, turns out to be
amenable to natural treatment.[28]

Notes

1. It has become customary to refer to those of us who oppose the traditional approach as anti-Fregeans—and this is a custom I follow here—
   but our opposition is to many of the main lines of Russell's approach
   as well. Anti-Fregeans, more specifically, oppose Russell's descriptivist
   view of names, as well as his idea that direct reference is possible only
   with respect to objects of direct epistemic acquaintance.

2. It might be supposed that what motivated Frege to introduce modes of presentation were not general considerations of the sort mentioned in the text, but were rather his concerns about informative identity sentences. This seems wrong. In his early *Begriffsschrift*, Frege's intellectual apparatus includes something very much like his later "modes of presentation," but the function of these is not to solve the famous identity puzzle. Indeed even with something like modes of presentation, Frege, in the *Begriffsschrift*, still feels the need for a metalinguistic account of identity to solve the otherwise apparently insoluble puzzles about how true identity sentences can have informative contents. So modes of presentation, it would seem, serve some more primitive need than the solution of the famous puzzle. For more on this point of Frege interpretation see Chapter 1, "Two Fundamental Problems: Frege's Classical Approach" of my forthcoming book, and also Richard Mendelsohn's seminal paper, "Frege's *Begriffsschrift* Theory of Identity," in the *Journal of the History of Philosophy* 22 (July 1982): 279-299.

3. But see note 27 below for the question of how straightforward Frege's solution really is.

4. There are, as noted, other aspects of what has been called "cognitive significance" that I do not touch upon here. At most, then, I show that the intentionality intuition and Frege's famous puzzle present no problem for the anti-Fregean. These two putative problem areas, however, are at the heart of the Fregean assault from cognitive significance. It is sometimes supposed, on the contrary, that at the heart of the Fregean approach, and at the heart of the Fregean attack on the allegedly cognitively insensitive anti-Fregean approach, is Frege's treatment of belief sentences, or, more generally, his treatment of "propositional attitude" ascriptions. It is also alleged that Frege's approach yields a natural account of the semantics of belief sentences, while the anti-Fregean is stymied here as well. I think that both of these points are mistaken, but I cannot pursue it here. I do so in the "Afterword" to "Has Semantics Rested On A Mistake?," *The Journal of Philosophy* 86 (April 1986): 185-209), and I will amplify on those remarks elsewhere. See note 25 below.

5. Kaplan's long-unpublished monograph appears in *Themes From Kaplan*, ed. J. Almog, J. Perry, and H. Wettstein, Oxford University Press, 1989. I owe to Joseph Almog the idea that what Kaplan calls the pure indexicals supply to the conservative a more easy target than the connotationless proper names.

6. See especially "Demonstratives," Section VII (part ii), Section XIV, and Section XVII.

7. Kaplan's "characters," while they determine the reference, are intellectually available to the competent speaker, and are crucial to the explanation of cognitive significance (in these respects they are like Fregean senses), do not, unlike Fregean senses, enter into the propositions expressed and, as already noted, they specify their referents only relative to a context.

8. It is interesting to note that Kaplan's emphasis on the lack of any sort of descriptive meaning for proper names does not induce him, in his later work, to reject an approach to names that is, in my vocabulary, fundamentally conservative. I have in mind here Kaplan's recent unpublished lectures, "Word and Belief," the doctrine of which is subtle and complicated, to which I cannot begin to do justice here. Kaplan's conservativism, then, is no mere reaction to facts about indexicals, but is a symptom of a Fregean tendency in his thought. I suggest below that Kaplan's conservative approach to indexicals is far from inevitable in any case.

9. Indeed, Kaplan's treatment of indexicals is, in one respect, more Fregean in spirit than Frege's own approach to indexicals. On Kaplan's view, each indexical is associated, *by the conventions of language*, with a (quasi-)sense. For Frege, of course, this was not so, and this was a defect in natural languages.

10. But see note 17 below for some discussion of the more innocuous, but not entirely innocent, thesis that reference fixing by description furnishes a paradigm of name *introduction*.

11. Kaplan, in the case of indexicals, attenuates Frege in two directions. He relativizes the descriptive contents to contexts, in the sense explained above, and assigns to the descriptive concepts the role of mere reference fixers. Like the second and stronger reference fixing thesis discussed in the text, the Kaplanian descriptive concepts are available to the users of the indexical and fix the reference for each use.

12. Other popular Frege-inspired variations less clearly avoid violating the intentionality intuition. Kripke, in *Naming and Necessity*, critically discusses a socialized description theory of names, an attempt to defeat anti-Fregean criticisms by socializing Frege's approach. One might, in this spirit, try to retrieve the sense of a name not from the individual speaker, but somehow from the linguistic community, perhaps in terms of commonly held beliefs about the referent. Notice that such an approach, to the extent it de-emphasizes the role of individual cognition, stands in tension with the intentionality intuition. Descriptional or not, such an approach faces the specter of semantic action at an epistemic distance. Also see note 18 below.

13. Notice that the moment one assigns to the descriptive concepts the role of reference fixers, as opposed to being full-blown senses and therefore propositional constituents, one produces an attenuated description theory that, as is evident from Kripke's discussion in the first lecture of *Naming and Necessity*, is immune to the modal argument championed by Kripke, Kaplan, and others. If one sees the modal arguments as at the core of the anti-Fregean approach, as I do not, one might conclude that intellectually mediated reference is not what the anti-Fregean revolution is about.

14. P. 157.

15. Kripke does not here mean that reference fixing descriptions are never used to introduce names. Indeed, he suggests that this may even be the standard case of name introduction, as I discuss in note 17 below.

16. Saul Kripke, "A Puzzle About Belief," in A. Margalit, ed., *Meaning and Use*, pp.239-283. The quotation is from pp. 243ff.

17. The Fregean intuition that the tie between words and things must—at some level—be descriptional seems not far from the surface in Kripke's discussion of the *introduction* of names (see *"Naming and Necessity*, p. 96, n. 42.). Kripke seems tempted by the idea that the paradigm of name-introduction is an occasion in which a name is introduced by means of a reference-fixing description, and that baptism by ostension might be subsumed under the description paradigm. "...the primary applicability of the description theory," Kripke writes, "is to cases of initial baptism."

Introduction of a name, of course, is quite a different matter than the subsequent use of a name. So even if one adopts a description theory of name-introduction, nothing follows about the subsequent use of the name. But why suppose that description of the bearer is essential even for name introduction? Why can't one baptize a child by pointing to it, where this doesn't involve anything like a description? Alternatively, consider a case in which someone simply starts using a name as a name for an individual without any formal name-introducing ceremony. If asked to whom he was referring, such a speaker might say all sorts of things (some of which, we might add, could be incorrect, not affecting his reference). Doesn't it seem artificial to insist that such a speaker must be fixing his reference by description?

Kripke, in informal discussions at Notre Dame during the academic year 1985-86, stood firm on the description theory of name introduction. Indeed, when faced with prima facie counter-examples to this description theory, Kripke suggested (albeit in a very tentative fashion) that "perhaps we need a cluster theory here." My own sense, which derives in part from Kripke's work, is that the suggestion that we need a cluster theory to save a descriptional picture is something about which we should be very suspicious, to put it mildly.

18. The examples of conservativism discussed so far have a Fregean—as opposed to a Russellian—flavor. These examples turn on the replacement of full-blown Fregean senses by context-relative concepts, or concepts that merely fix the reference. Still another sort of conservative strategy takes its cue from Russell's epistemic orientation. One might take ordinary proper names to be "directly referential," where Russell took only "genuine proper names" to be so. One could no longer require epistemic acquaintance of the name user, but one could still impose non-trivial epistemic constraints. One might suggest that some sort of causal connection with the referent is a necessary condition for referring to it by name, where the causal condition is somehow construed as providing a sort of epistemic connection. One thinks here of the work of Keith Donnellan, especially of his paper "The Contingent *A Priori* and Rigid Designators," in *Contemporary Perspectives in the Philosophy of Language*, eds. P. French, T. Uehling, and H. Wettstein (University of Minnesota Press, 1978).

19. The point of adding the word 'substantive' here is to allow me to avoid the issue of whether *any* sort of knowledge or belief about the referent

is required. If someone overhears a conversation between mathematicians, for example, in which the name 'Joan' is used as a name of a theorem, need the speaker know at least that it's the name of a theorem, as opposed to being the name of a woman, in order to use it, thereby referring to the theorem. If he says, "I bet Joan is tall," has he asserted something (false), or do we rather treat his utterance as radically defective. This is the sort of issue I wish to sidestep here.

20. Kaplan, in "Demonstratives," and more recently Joseph Almog in "Semantical Anthropology," in P. French, T. Uehling, and H. Wettstein, eds., *Midwest Studies in Philosophy*, vol. IX (University of Minnesota Press, 1984), pp.479-490, suggest that although historical chains need to be brought into the total picture of our practice with names, the chains are not to be brought into the semantics, *per se*. That is, contrary to the suggestion of Donnellan's and Kripke's original remarks, the historical chains do not, strictly speaking, determine reference. Kripke himself recently suggested a similar view in conversation.

21. As we saw in note 12 above, one might try to accommodate the social character of our practices with names within a fundamentally intellectualist picture of the name-referent tie. Such an approach would be more socially sensitive than Frege's, but it would still over-intellectualize language, at least from the point of view taken here. The crucial question is whether reference is to be tied to the community's *beliefs*, or rather to its *practices*. Couldn't it be, for example, that our current beliefs about a historical individual have become all fouled up, but that the continuity of usage secures reference nevertheless? Our beliefs about *him* are, in such a case, mistaken, but there remains an individual about whom we are talking, and about whom we are mistaken.

22. Nor does even the first-person pronoun present an easy target for Kaplan's approach. Competent speakers, it is true, no doubt possess a good *rough idea* of what contextual features determine the reference of 'I', something like, "being the speaker." This is not to say, however, that they can discern the sort of fine-print theoretical characterization which for Kaplan constitutes the character rule. Consider Kaplan's candidate rule: the reference of the first person pronoun is the agent of the context. Notice that "agent of the context" is a technical term for Kaplan. For technical reasons having to do with contexts in which no one is speaking, Kaplan doesn't understand 'the agent' to mean the same as 'the speaker'. The typical competent speaker, I submit, will not find Kaplan's "agent" idea the obvious one. See also pp. 202-203 of "Has Semantics Rested On A Mistake," for further discussion.

23. Focusing the discussion on the identity case may, in addition, induce a solution that fails to apply to the general case. Frege's meta-linguistic *Begriffsschrift* account is a case in point.

24. Kaplan's conservative-style explanation distinguishes the sentences cognitively in virtue of their different "characters" or linguistic meanings. 'I' and 'he', on Kaplan's view, present the referent under different aspects, and thus the sentences differ cognitively while expressing the same singular proposition. Kaplan's explanation applies, in any case,

only to cases that involve indexicals. What to do with proper names remains an open question.

25. The question just posed in the text concerns the cognitive roles of singular terms as these occur in simple, unembedded sentences. This, I want to emphasize, is not a question about the difficult-to-understand occurrences of singular terms when these are embedded in epistemic, e.g. belief, contexts. The latter problem is unaddressed in the present paper, as I explain in footnote 4 above. The latter problem is sometimes, I think misleadingly, referred to as "Frege's puzzle," although it is not the problem Frege takes up at the beginning of "On Sense and Reference," nor is it the problem that Kaplan discusses as "Frege's puzzle" in "Demonstratives." No doubt the two problems are related, but their relation is, I believe, quite complicated.

26. See "Has Semantics Rested On A Mistake?," pp. 195-196, for more along these lines.

27. One philosopher's mystery is another's fundamental tool for clarification. (Perhaps this is some sort of consequence of the customary *modus ponens-modus tollens* quip.) It's interesting, in this connection, that the Fregean's fundamental piece of intellectual apparatus, senses, are just what seem mysterious to the anti-Fregean. "What are these senses," we want to ask, "and how, in the world, can anything have such a non-conventional satisfaction relation to a referent?"

28. Versions of this paper were given at UCLA, The City University of New York, and Rutgers University, and I am grateful to participants in those discussions for helpful comments. I am especially grateful to Joseph Almog, Tom Blackburn, Jon Kvanvig, Genoveva Marti, Chris Menzel, Gilbert Plumer, and Bernard Reginster.

Philosophical Perspectives, 3
Philosophy of Mind and Action Theory, 1989

THE REVERSE FREGE PUZZLE

Takashi Yagisawa
California State University, Northridge

Introduction

Gottlob Frege's article "On Sense and Reference" has duly exerted enormous influence in philosophy of language and philosophy of mind. We speak of Fregean theories and Fregean arguments in discussing meaning, reference, attitudinal states, mental representations, and other related topics. The crux of Frege's contribution lies in the notion of *Sinn*, which he introduced in order to solve a certain puzzle. The puzzle in question, which we shall call 'Frege's puzzle,'[1] motivates the postulation of a particular understanding of *Sinn*, namely as mode of presentation. The mode of presentation associated with a term is understood to be something like the conceptual content of the term. Frege's puzzle may be formulated in various forms.[2] Since the gist of it is widely known among philosophers, I shall only disuss one simple version involving identity. Let 'a' and 'b' be two terms with the same reference or extension. Then the sentences 'a = a' and 'a = b' do not have the same cognitive value (*Erkenntniswerte*); the first is trivial and uninformative, whereas the second is nontrivial and informative. What is responsible for the difference? It is not reference or extension, for the two terms are coreferential or coextensional. Frege's solution to this puzzle is to postulate modes of presentation. The two terms in question have different modes of presentation associated with them. ('The morning star' and 'the evening star' are well-known examples. They are said to have some such modes of presentation as "the last visible heavenly body before sunrise" and "the first visible heavenly body after sunset," respectively.) The cognitive values of the two identity statements differ as a result. Frege's solution has been challenged by Kripke, Donnellan, Putnam, and others. I shall focus on Putnam's challenge, for it is the most misunderstood. His article "The Meaning of 'Meaning'"[3] has been widely read and almost equally widely persuasive. Its slogan is supposed by many to be that meanings are not "in the head." Whatever its precise meaning may be, this perceived slogan has led many philosophers to a further slogan in philosophy of mind, namely, that attitudinal contents are not "in the head." I diagree with this way of interpreting Putnam's argument, the so-called Twin-Earth argument, on two counts; I believe that it distorts the stated objective of Putnam's article and that it is prejudiced in favor of a particular pretheoretical intuition. I shall argue that Putnam's Twin-Earth argument generates a new puzzle complementary to Frege's puzzle. This new puzzle, which I shall call 'the Reverse Frege Puzzle,' forces a revision of the Fregean theory of *Sinn*. I shall conclude with a sketch of some consequences for attitudinal content ascriptions.

The Twin-Earth Argument

Twin Earth is just like Earth except that the words 'elm' and 'beech' are switched. In Twin Earth English 'elm' is true of beech trees and 'beech' is true of elm trees. $Oscar_1$ is an earthling, who knows that elms and beeches are different but does not know how they are different; to him elms and beeches are indistinguishable.[4] $Oscar_2$ is his Doppelgaenger on Twin Earth. Elms and beeches are indistinguishable to $Oscar_2$ exactly the same way as they are to $Oscar_1$. Indeed, the world appears to $Oscar_2$ exactly the same way as it does to $Oscar_1$.

Now, $Oscar_1$ sincerely utters the sentence 'Elms are deciduous.' Correspondingly, $Oscar_2$ utters the same sentence type 'Elms are deciduous' with equal sincerity. Do the two Oscars say the same thing? Do their beliefs so expressed have the same content? If the answer to the first question is in the affirmative (or negative), then given the sincerity of their utterances, the answer to the second question should also be in the affirmative (or negative). Tyler Burge gives the negative answers to both questions, maintaining that $Oscar_1$'s utterance of 'elm' means *elm* and Oscar$_2$'s utterance of 'elm' means *beech*.[5] He goes on to propose that attitudinal contents are not "in the head" but somehow socio-environmental.[6] Many philosophers seem to agree.[7] However, Putnam originally asked a different question: Is the extension of one Oscar's token of 'elm' the same as the extension of the other Oscar's token of 'elm'? Putnam answered this question in the negative. He then argued that this result shows that either the Doppelgaengers' corresponding utterances of 'elm' do not have the same meaning, i.e., meanings are not "in the head," or else meaning does not determine extension. Furthermore he proposed a theory of meaning which respects the above negative answer. A wide-spread misconstrual of the Twin-Earth argument compels me to spend some space for clarification of the Twin-Earth argument before discussing the generation of the Reverse Frege Puzzle and its solution.

It is a mistake to construe the original Twin-Earth argument along the following line:

(1) The two Oscars' utterances of 'elm' do not mean the same.

Therefore,

(2) Meanings are not "in the head" (for "the heads" of the two Oscars are exactly alike).

This popular but distorted construal unduly limits the scope of the argument and therefore weakens it. The original Twin-Earth argument is really a constructive dilemma:

(3) Either the two Oscars' utterances of 'elm' mean the same, or they do not.
(4) If they do, meaning does not determine extension (for the extensions of the two Oscars' utterances of 'elm' are different).
(5) If they do not, meanings are not "in the head" (for "the heads" of the two Oscars are exactly alike).

Therefore,

(6) Either meaning does not determine extension or meanings are not "in the head."[8]

The popularity of the popular version of the argument clearly stems from the widely shared opinion that the second disjunct of (3), which is also the premise (1) of the popular version, is true. This opinion is supposed to come directly from a pretheoretical intuition. Thus, those who happen to have a contrary intuition would find the popular version to be short-circuiting Putnam's original argument. Putnam himself apparently lacked a firm intuition that (1) is true; otherwise, why would he have stated the conclusion disjunctively? In any case, theoretical respectability of the intuition that (1) is false is important to the proper appreciation of the generality of the Twin-Earth argument.

Before claiming theoretical respectability for the intuition that (1) is false, I want to point out briefly how bizzare the popular view is. Burge's view typifies it. Burge maintains the following two propositions simultaneously:

(7) $Oscar_1$ does not fully understand the English term 'elm.'

(8) In sincerely uttering the sentence 'Elms are deciduous,' $Oscar_1$ expresses his belief that elms are deciduous.

To understand term t in language L, where t means M in L, is to do two things:

(i) to grasp what t means in L, i.e., given that what t means in L is M, to grasp M;

and

(ii) to associate M with t (as its meaning).

It is given that 'elm' means *elm* in English. Therefore, if (7) is true, so is (9):

(9) Either (i) $Oscar_1$ does not grasp *elm*, or (ii) $Oscar_1$ does not associate *elm* with 'elm.'

From (9i) it follows that

(10) $Oscar_1$ does not know that 'elm' means *elm*.

From (9ii) it follows that $Oscar_1$ either does not associate any meaning with 'elm' or associates a wrong meaning (a meaning other than *elm*) with 'elm.' But if so, then (10). Therefore, (10) follows from (7). Assuming an appropriate compositionality principle (which is not the target of Burge's attack), we can infer (11) from (10):

(11) Oscar₁ does not know that 'Elms are deciduous' means *that elms are deciduous.*

Now suppose that Oscar₁ acquired the belief he expresses in uttering 'Elms are deciduous' simply by reading a token t of that sentence in an encyclopedia. Thus, given (11), it follows that

(12) Oscar₁ does not know that t means *that elms are deciduous.*

But then, it is not clear at all how it is possible for Oscar₁ to acquire the belief that elms are deciduous simply by reading a sentence the meaning of which he does not know to be *that elms are deciduous.* Indeed, it seems impossible that Oscar₁ or anyone can acquire a belief the content of which is correctly specified by an English sentence by means of verbal communication in terms of that sentence, if he does not know the meaning of that sentence in English. Therefore, it seems that if Burge is right in maintaining (7) and (8), Oscar₁ acquired his belief that elms are deciduous by means quite independent of verbal communication in terms of the English sentence 'Elms are deciduous' (or its cognates). I find such belief acquisition by someone like Oscar₁ mysterious.

The Cartesian Intuition

The view that the Oscars' utterances of 'elm' do not have as diverse meanings as *elm* and *beech* but rather have the same meaning is more prevalent than the proponents of the popular version of the Twin-Earth argument would like us to believe. This view, which we may call 'the semantic parity thesis,' is most naturally supported by the intuition that the two Oscars have the same conception of what they call 'elm.' Let us call this intuition of the conceptual parity 'the Cartesian intuition' without any serious historical inuendos. The Cartesian intuition is fairly widely held and therefore provides a plausible starting point for a theory. But of course, a widely held intuition does not always promise a theoretical success. Insurmountable or excessively costly theoretical difficulties could force one to abandon an initially prevalent intuition. My goal in this section therefore is to flesh out the Cartesian intuition with theoretical consistency. If I am successful, then I will have shown that a respectable theoretical construction is possible on the basis of the Cartesian intuition. My reason for securing the respectability of the Cartesian intuition is twofold: first, taking the Cartesian intuition seriously is the most natural way to motivate the Reverse Frege Puzzle; second, the theoretical scaffolding which bolsters the Cartesian intuition provides us with the best theoretical foothold for the discussion, and ultimately a solution, of the Puzzle.

First of all, we should note explicitly that the meaning of a linguistic expression—type or token—is relative to a language. Failure to note this obvious fact could unfairly dispose one against the semantic parity thesis, hence against the Cartesian intuition. For example, *ex hypothesi* $Oscar_1$ and $Oscar_2$ are competent speakers of Earth English and Twin Earth English, respectively. In uttering 'Elms are deciduous,' $Oscar_1$ is speaking Earth English, and $Oscar_2$ Twin Earth English. $Oscar_1$'s 'elm' means *elm* in Earth English, and $Oscar_2$'s 'elm' means *beech* in Twin Earth English. Does this undermine the semantic parity thesis, hence also the Cartesian intuition? No. It is easily possible to understand the semantic parity thesis as consistent with this, by remembering the language-relativity of the meaning of an expression. *Any* token of 'elm,' including $Oscar_2$'s, means *elm* in Earth English, and *any* token of 'elm,' including $Oscar_1$'s, means *beech* in Twin Earth English.[9] The semantic parity thesis should then be understood as involving an implicit reference to the Oscars' idiolects as follows:

$Oscar_1$'s utterance of 'elm' means the same in his idiolect as $Oscar_2$'s utterance of 'elm' means in *his* idiolect.

What is in question in effect is the identity of the semantics of the two Oscars' idiolects. Failure to appreciate this fact could lead one to a hasty dismissal of the semantic parity thesis. For instance, the following objection to the semantic parity thesis exemplifies such failure:

"The Oscars are abducted while asleep and transported to a third planet. Upon waking up in the same room, they look out of the window to find a familiar-looking tree. They simultaneously shout, "That's an elm." The tree is a beech. It is clear that what $Oscar_2$ says is true and what $Oscar_1$ says is false. Therefore, they do not mean the same by 'elm.'"[10]

What is clear is that $Oscar_2$'s utterance is true *in Twin Earth English* and $Oscar_1$'s utterance is false *in Earth English*. Since $Oscar_2$ is a speaker of Twin Earth English and $Oscar_1$ a speaker of Earth

English, we tend automatically to assume these particular relativizations of semantic evaluation. This is perfectly consistent with the semantic parity thesis. The meanings of the Oscars' utterances in either English dialect are not in question. What is in question is *what the Oscars mean*, i.e., what their utterances mean *in their respective idiolects*.[11]

Noting the language relativity of semantic evaluation helps dismiss objections such as the above. However, there is a different line of objection. One version goes as follows:

"In Earth English 'elm' means *elm*. But Oscar$_1$ is a competent speaker of Earth English, *and not Twin Earth English*. So he must mean *elm* in uttering 'elm,' that is, 'elm' must mean *elm* in his idiolect. Likewise, 'elm' must mean *beech* in Oscar$_2$'s idiolect. *Elm* and *beech* are different meanings. Therefore, 'elm' does not mean the same in the two Oscars' idiolects."

This version is relatively easy to answer. That Oscar$_{1/2}$ is a competent speaker of Earth English/Twin Earth English does not entail that the semantics of his idiolect is identical with the semantics of Earth English/Twin Earth English. Generally, being a competent speaker of a certain English dialect does not entail having the idiolect the semantics of which is the same as the semantics of that English dialect. Otherwise, there would be little philosophical point in distinguishing an idiolect from a social language like English.[12]

However, another version of the objection may be formulated as a challenge:

"Show me how it is possible for a speaker whose idiolect does not have the same semantics as a certain social language, to be a competent speaker of that language." Or better, "Show me how it is possible that there be two speakers with the same idiolect and two different social languages such that one speaker is a competent speaker of one language and not the other, while the other speaker is a competent speaker of the other language and not the one. In particluar, show me how it is possible for Oscar$_1$ to be a competent speaker of Earth English and not Twin Earth English, and Oscar$_2$ a competent speaker of Twin Earth English and not Earth English."

At one, relatively superficial, level this challenge is not hard to meet. Take phonology. In order to be a competent speaker of British

English, it is not necessary to be able to duplicate the pronunciations of the Queen; a construction worker in London and a shop keeper in Liverpool may not enunciate like the Queen and yet be competent speakers of British English. This obvious fact points to an equally obvious fact that British Enlgish, a dialect of English, consists of many sub-dialects: Cockney English, Lancashire English, Oxbridge English, Scottish English, etc. One may qualify as a competent speaker of British English by speaking any one of them. Furthermore, the sub-dialects themselves consist of sub-sub-dialects: e.g., one may be a competent speaker of Scottish English by speaking Glasgow English rather than, say, Edinburough English or the Highlander English. And we have not hit the rock bottom level yet. Glasgow English further divides into various sub-sub-sub-dialects, each of which divides into still smaller dialects, until we reach idiolects. Every actual idolect has a different phonology from every other; everybody has different vocal folds, oral cavity, tongue, and other parts of the voice-producing mechanism from everybody else. Various individual speakers' various pronunciations are grouped together at a certain level of generality, to be called 'Glasgow accent,' 'Scottish accent,' or 'British accent.' If this is true of phonology, why can it not be true of semantics?

This reply answers, or at least defuses, one half of the challenge: "How is it possible for $Oscar_{1/2}$ to be a competent speaker of Earth English/Twin Earth English?" But it leaves the second half untouched: "How is it possible for $Oscar_{1/2}$ not to be a competent speaker of Twin Earth English/Earth English at the same time?" My answer to this in a nutshell is, "By not being a speaker of Twin Earth English/Earth English at all." The point of the challenge is that if $Oscar_2$ qualifies as a competent speaker of Twin Earth English and $Oscar_1$ has the same idiolect as $Oscar_2$, then it appears impossible for $Oscar_1$ not to be a competent speaker of Twin Earth English. I claim that $Oscar_1$ *is competent* in Twin Earth English. Thus if, and only if, he *spoke* that dialect, he would be a *competent speaker* of it. But he does not speak the dialect. So he is not a competent speaker of it. Since, while it is easy to accept that $Oscar_1$ is not a speaker of Twin Earth English, some may undoubtedly find it hard to accept that $Oscar_1$ is competent in Twin Earth English, let me elaborate a little. If he were suddenly to find himself on Twin Earth, $Oscar_1$ would pass muster as a perfectly competent speaker of Twin Earth English, as competent a speaker as $Oscar_2$; it would be impossible to tell them apart. Of course, $Oscar_1$ does not in fact pass muster as a competent speaker of Twin Earth English, for he is not in fact on Twin Earth or in contact with anyone who speaks Twin Earth English. But that only disqulifies him as a *speaker* of Twin Earth English. Linguistic competence may be compared to the ability to swim in this regard. It is possible to have the ability to swim without actually swimming or coming into contact with those who actually swim. The fact that $Oscar_1$ would pass muster if he were on Twin Earth is sufficient for his competence in Twin Earth English, no less than the fact that one would float and propel oneself if one were placed in a pool of water is sufficient for one's ability to swim in water. Remote isolation from Twin Earth is no more hindrance to $Oscar_1$'s comptence in Twin Earth English than it is a hindrance to his ability to swim in XYZ (H_2O's Doppelgaenger stuff on Twin Earth). If you are a Chomskian, I may also point out that $Oscar_1$ has internalized whatever grammatical knowledge in the Chomskian sense $Oscar_2$ has internalized; so if linguistic competence is determined by the internalized grammatical knowledge, as Chomsky thinks it is, then $Oscar_1$ has exactly the same linguistic competence as $Oscar_2$.

I said that the challenge was not hard to meet at one level. I have met it at that level. However, it *is* hard to meet at a deeper level: "What is a necessary and sufficient condition for a speaker to be competent in a language? And what is a necessary and sufficient condition for a speaker to be a speaker of a language?" I do not know the answer to either question. I can only say that linguistic competence is an entirely "internal" matter so that the two Oscars are exactly alike in their linguistic competence, whereas being a speaker involves "external" matters of communicational interaction with other speakers in rather intricate manners. I should also add that it is a mistake to assume that linguistic competence and speakerhood admit no degrees. A satisfactory theory should accommodate the possibility of someone being more or less competent, or more or less of a speaker, than someone else.

The Reverse Frege Puzzle

Twin Earth is set up so that 'elm' and 'beech' are switched in Twin Earth English and yet $Oscar_2$ is a true Doppelgaenger of $Oscar_1$, that is, despite the word switch, the two Oscars face the world in exactly the same way. In particular, $Oscar_1$ faces what he calls 'elm' in the same way as $Oscar_2$ faces what *he* calls 'elm,' and $Oscar_1$ faces what he calls 'beech' in the same way as $Oscar_2$ faces what *he* calls 'beech.' This is so because of the built-in assumption that $Oscar_1$ faces what he calls 'elm' in the same way as he faces what he calls 'beech' (plus the assumption that $Oscar_2$ is $Oscar_1$'s Doppelgaenger on Twin Earth). It is this underlying assumption that is the crux of Putnam's argument; the postulations of Twin Earth and $Oscar_2$ are embellishments to promote the picturesqueness of the argument. Since, according to the Cartesian intuition, the assumption in effect postulates conceptual parity for $Oscar_1$ between what he calls 'elm' and what he calls 'beech,' it can be put in the following Fregean terms: $Oscar_1$ associates the same *mode of presentation* with 'elm' and 'beech.' This gives rise to the Reverse Frege Puzzle.

Frege's solution to his original puzzle is based on the idea that different modes of presentation give rise to different cognitive values. And this naturally leads to the Fregean thesis that mode of presentation determines cognitive value. So no discrepancy in cognitive value is to be expected between two sentences which are identical except for different terms with the same mode of presentation. But the expectation is dashed by sentences like (13) and (14):

(13) Elms are elms.
(14) Elms are beeches.

Since 'elm' and 'beech' carry the same mode of presentation for $Oscar_1$, (13) and (14) should have the same cognitive value for him in his idiolect. But they do not. (13) is trivial and uninformative, whereas (14) is nontrivial and informative.

Two possible paths are open to solve this Reverse Frege Puzzle. One is to deny the Fregean thesis that mode of presentation determines cognitive value. The other is to note that either one of the following two compositionality principles is necessary for the generation of the puzzle and block it by denying both:

(A) The mode of presentation associated with a sentence is determined by the modes of presentation associated with its constituent parts and its syntactic structure.

(B) The cognitive value of a sentence is determined by the cognitive values of its constituent parts and its syntactic structure.

There are two ways in which the identity of the mode of presentation associated with 'elm' and 'beech' can result in the identity of the cognitive value of (13) and (14). One is via compositionality of mode of presentation: Since the two terms have the same mode of presentation, so do the two sentences; therefore, given that mode of presentation determines cognitive value, the two sentences have the same cognitive value. The other is via compositionality of cognitive value: Since the two terms have the same mode of presentation, they have the same cognitive value, given that mode of presentation determines cognitive value; therefore, the two sentences have the same cognitive value. By denying (A), one blocks the first way. By denying (B), one blocks the second way. In either case one blocks not only the generation of the Reverse Frege Puzzle but also Frege's original solution to his puzzle: in the absence of compositionality, attributing different modes of presentation to 'a' and 'b' would not explain the difference in cognitive value between 'a = a' and 'a = b.' I do not wish to allow myself to be as non-Fregean as possible in order to solve—or dissolve—the Reverse Frege Puzzle. I do not wish to destroy Frege's original solution to his puzzle in solving the Reverse Frege Puzzle. It is my goal to try to preserve as much Fregeanism as possible and solve the Reverse Frege Puzzle at the same time. I believe that this is a good methodological attitude; for the Reverse Frege Puzzle at least *prima facie* poses an immediate threat to the central notion in Frege's philosophy, viz., mode of presentation, and in particular, its relation to cognitive value, and the Reverse Frege Puzzle provides us with an opportunity to gain insight into the way in which mode of presentation is related to cognitive value. So, rather than throwing away the opportunity by denying Frege his original solution to his puzzle, why not seize the opportunity and try to escape the Reverse Frege Puzzle by refining the relation between mode of presentation and cognitive value without blaming the Puzzle on such a global principle as compositionality? Even if you are not much of a Fregean, I think that it is a better way to *understand* Fregeanism. This, of course, is not to say that I consider (A) and (B) obvious enough to be above all dispute. My position simply is that there is a more focused—and therefore more interesting and informative—solution to the Reverse Frege Puzzle than a sweeping solution by denying (A) and (B).

I shall now turn to that solution. It consists in rejecting the Fregean thesis that mode of presentation determines cognitive value without rejecting Frege's original solution to his puzzle. Frege's original solution to his puzzle was to say that different modes of presentation result in different cognitive values. My solution to the Reverse Frege Puzzle is to say that the same mode of presentation does not always result in the same cognitive value, i.e., that mode of presentation does not determine cognitive value.[13]

How does my rejection of the Fregean thesis solve the Puzzle? To begin with, note that the Reverse Frege Puzzle is a puzzle concerning the compossibility of the following two facts:

(15) In $Oscar_1$'s idiolect 'elm' and 'beech' are associated with the same mode of presentation.

(16) In $Oscar_1$'s idiolect (13) and (14) do not have the same cognitive value.

How is it possible to uphold (15) and (16) simultaneously? Why do (13) and (14) not have the same cognitive value for $Oscar_1$?

It is instructive to review Frege's notion of *Sinn*. Frege's puzzle motivates the postulation of *Sinn* as mode of presentation. It is the thesis that different modes of presentation result in different cognitve values that solves Frege's puzzle. But how is that thesis supported? It seems to have no independent support; instead, it is maintained as one half of a stronger thesis, i.e., the thesis that mode of presentation determines cognitive value. The stronger thesis is supported by the well-known Fregean thesis that *Sinn* determines *Beteutung*. In the context of our discussion, that thesis reads that mode of presentation determines extension. How is *this* thesis supported? The mode of presentation associated with a term as its conceptual content lays out the satisfaction condition for the term, that is, the condition for the membership in the extension of the term; necessarily, all and only objects that satisfy the condition are in the extension. This means that, assuming appropriate compositionality principles, mode of presentation lays out truth condition. The cognitive value of a sentence appears to be a matter of what truth condition is so layed out for the sentence. Thus, for Frege, mode of presentation plays the dual role of determining extension and cognitive value by performing a single job of laying out satisfaction condition. According to this picture, the truth condition for a sentence determines its cognitive value. (13) and (14) have different cognitive values for $Oscar_1$. So, they must have different truth conditions in his idiolect. This line of reasoning is in harmony with our initial reaction that the difference in cognitive value for Oscar$_1$ between (13) and (14) somehow arises from the fact that in his idiolect (13) has as trivial a truth condition as 'Everything is what it is,' while (14) has a non-trivial truth condition, a condition Oscar$_1$ happens to believe not to obtain. So, the task now is to uphold (15) and (17) simultaneously:

(17) In Oscar$_1$'s idiolect (13) and (14) do not have the same truth condition.

The only possible source of the difference in truth condition between (13) and (14), of course, is some difference between 'elm' and 'beech' that has an impact on the determination of the truth conditions of the two sentences. Following the Fregean picture in the preceding paragraph, we say that the difference is a difference in satisfaction condition; (13) and (14) have different truth conditions in Oscar$_1$'s idiolect because 'elm' and 'beech' have different satisfaction conditions in his idiolect. (13) is true if and only if the extension of 'elm' is a subset of the extension of 'elm,' whereas (14) is true if and only if the extension of 'elm' is a subset of the extension of 'beech.' Thus the task amounts to upholding (15) and (18):

(18) In Oscar$_1$'s idiolect 'elm' and 'beech' do not have the same satisfaction condition.

To uphold (15) and (18) together is to reject the Fregean thesis that mode of presentation determines satisfaction condition. In Oscar$_1$'s idiolect any object that is good enough for an application of 'elm' is also good enough for an application of 'beech,' and vice versa. For Oscar$_1$, what he calls 'elm' and what he calls 'beech' are conceptually indistinguishable, and yet they are distinct. How can we define satisfaction for the two terms in such a way that this is so?[14]

It might be suggested that we define satisfaction for 'elm' and 'beech' simultaneously, for the two terms operate *in tandem* in Oscar$_1$'s idiolect. From the universe of discourse U, one subset S is assigned to both 'elm' and 'beech.' S may be the extension for 'deciduous tree,' or 'tree,' or 'plant,' or some other more or less inclusive term. This captures the indistinguishability between 'elm' and 'beech.' Then the definitions go as follows:

Necessarily, for any member m of U, m *satisfies 'x is an elm'* if and only if m is a member of S and m does not satisfy 'x is a beech';

Necessarily, for any member m of U, m satisfies 'x is a beech' if and only if m is a member of S and m does not satisfy 'x is an elm.'[15]

Evidently, the above do not well define satisfaction for 'x is an elm' or for 'x is a beech'; an obvious circularity prevents the determination of whether any given object satisfies one predicate rather than the other. But this is not a defect, for it is precisely what is expected. The idea is that the complete satisfaction conditions for the two terms cannot be given separately. Note by the way that, given the usual recursive definitions for truth functional compounds, the satisfaction conditions for some compound predicates are well-defined: e.g., m satisfies the predicate 'x is an elm or a beech' if and only if m is a member of S; m satisfies the predicate 'x is an elm and a beech' if and only if m satisfies 'x is an elm' and m satisfies 'x is a beech,' which is the case if and only if m is a member of S and m does not satisfy 'x is a beech' and m satisfies 'x is a beech'—so nothing satisfies 'x is an elm and a beech.'

In case some should regard undesirable the fact that the above definitions mention S, let us note that they prejudge nothing concerning analytic relations between 'elm' or 'beech' and any particular inclusive term such as 'deciduous tree,' 'tree,' or 'plant.' As far as the definitions go, S could be any subset of U, even U itself.

Are the above definitions acceptable? The answer is "No." Their unacceptability stems from two defects. First, Oscar$_1$'s concept of what he calls 'elm' is in no way metalinguistic. His concept of what he calls 'elm' and his concept of what he calls 'beech' may operate *in tandem* indeed, but not in the matalinguistic manner manifest in the above satisfaction definitions. Frege refused a similarly metalinguistic solution to his puzzle for good reasons, and we should not hark back to it, either.[16] Second, they embody an elementary confusion between difference of satisfaction condition and difference of extension. To say that 'elm' and 'beech' have different satisfaction conditions is not the same as saying that they have different extensions; the first is weaker. Satisfaction of 'elm' is *different from* satisfaction of 'beech,' but the former does not *preclude* the latter. Nothing in the semantics of his idiolect justifies the presumption that no object could be what he calls 'elm' and what he calls 'beech' at the same time. Oscar$_1$'s conceptions do not exclude the possibility of one and the same object being what he calls 'elm' and what he calls 'beech';

for all he means, what he calls 'elm' and what he calls 'beech' may be one and the same kind of tree, or two disjoint kinds of tree, or two partially overlapping kinds of tree. The above definitions of satisfaction are too restrictive for this more general situation.

The lesson to be learned here is that it is wrong-headed to try to solve the Reverse Frege Puzzle by upholding (15) and (18). There seems to be little hope of fleshing out (18).[17] A more promising line seems to be to stick with the idea that if the satisfaction condition for a term in Oscar$_1$'s idiolect is determinate at all, it is fully determined by the mode of presentation Oscar$_1$ associates with the term.[18] Since I deny that the mode of presentation Oscar$_1$ associates with 'elm' fully determines the satisfacton condition for 'elm' in his idiolect, I deny that the satisfaction condition for 'elm' in his idiolect is determinate. This may be interpreted in two ways: that the term has an indeterminate satisfaction condition, or that the term has no satisfaction condition. However, if it has no satisfaction condition, (13) has no truth condition. Then (13) cannot be true. But it is. Therefore, the term should have an indeterminate satisfaction condition.

It seems to me to be impossible to reach an acceptable satisfaction condition which is biconditional; the conceptual indeterminateness in question is too profound to allow any biconditionsl definition. Instead one can only manage something like the following:

Necessarily, for any member m of U, m satisfies 'x is an elm' only if m is a member of S;
Necessarily, for any member m of U, m satisfies 'x is a beech' only if m is a member of S;
where S is an appropriate subset of U.

The two predicates are given an identical necessary condition, and no sufficient condition. Oscar$_1$ associates the same mode of presentation with 'elm' and 'beech,' but the mode of presentation is not articulate/detailed/complete enough to provide a necessary and sufficient condition for either term. It only gives a necessary condition. Since the condition is exactly the same for both terms, it does not account for the difference in cognitive value between (13) and (14).

The main question remains: What *does* account for the difference in cognitive value bewteen (13) and (14)? One answer which is unsatisfactory is simply to say that the obvious syntactic difference between (13) and (14) accounts for the difference in cognitive value.

Evidently the syntactic difference, or the lexical difference to be more specific, between (13) and (14) has to have something to do with the difference in cognitive value; for elimination of the former difference would result in one identical sentence and therefore elimination of the latter difference. But pointing out the former difference solves nothing; it is merely to register part of the Puzzle.

Cognitive value is a semantic notion. We therefore need to cash the former difference in semantic terms so as to account for the latter difference. To do so, let us note that even though 'elm' and 'beech' do in fact have the same satisfaction condition in Oscar$_1$'s idiolect, since the condition is incomplete, it is possible to be tightened toward completion. Some tightenings are inconsistent with the original incomplete condition, and therefore uninteresting. Among the consistent tightenings, some add more necessary conditions, others add sufficient conditions to make them necessary and sufficient conditions, and still others do both. No tightening alters a condition which is already necessary and sufficient; that is, any (indeed, the) tightening of a necessary and sufficient condition is that necessary and sufficient condition itself. Obviously, 'elm' and 'beech' need not be assigned the same tightening at the same time; 'elm' might receive one consistent tightening, while 'beech' receives another. It is false that for any consistent tightening T1 of the original satisfaction condition for 'elm' and for any consistent tightening T2 of the original satisfaction condition for 'beech,' if an object satisfies 'elm' according to T1, then it satisfies 'beech' according to T2. This is elementary, and Oscar$_1$ is quite aware of it. Indeed, it seems to capture the semantic difference between the two terms in his idiolect despite their parity with respect to mode of presentation and actual satisfaction condition. Thus, the Reverse Frege Puzzle is solved as follows:

Necessarily, (13) is true in Oscar$_1$'s idiolect if and only if for any x in U, if x satisfies 'elm,' then x satisfies 'elm.' Necessarily, (14) is true in Oscar$_1$'s idiolect if and only if for any x in U, if x satisfies 'elm,' then x satisfies 'beech.' For any consistent tightening T1 of the (actual) satisfaction condition for 'elm' and for any consistent tightening T2 of the (actual) satisfaction condition for 'beech' in his idiolect, necessarily, for any x in U, if x satisfies 'elm' according to T1, then x satisfies 'elm' according to T1. But it is not the case that for any T1 and for any T2, necessarily, for any x in U, if x satisfies 'elm' according to T1, then x satisfies 'beech'according to T2. Therefore it is not the case that for any T1 and for any T2, necessarily, (13) is true according to T1 and T2 if and only if (14) is true according to T1 and T2. *If two sentences could diverge in truth condition on some consistent tightenings of their (incomplete) truth conditions, then they have different cognitive values.* (13) and (14) could so diverge in Oscar$_1$'s idiolect. Therefore, (13) and (14) have different cognitive values in Oscar$_1$'s idiolect.

To repeat, the idea behind this solution is that the cognitive value of a sentence is determined by the truth conditions according to all consistent tightenings of its (actual) truth condition, rather than by its (actual) truth condition. It is a generalization of the idea behind Frege's solution to his puzzle, namely, the idea that mode of presentation determines cognitive value. If the mode of presentation associated with a sentence determines a necessary and sufficient (i.e., complete) truth condition, then since the consistent tightening of such a truth condition is the original truth condition itself, *it* determines the cognitive value of the sentence; so, the mode of presentation determines the cognitive value in such a case. If two sentences have different modes of presentation which determine incomplete but different truth conditions, then obviously some of their consistent tightenings are different, so the sentences have different cognitive values; therefore again, the mode of presentation determines the cognitive value. It is only when two sentences have the same mode of presentation which determines the same incomplete truth condition that the mode of presentation fails to determine the cognitive value. Frege's puzzle is solvable without considering the last kind of case, but the Reverse Frege Puzzle forces us to face it.

What does this say about *Sinn*? According to Frege, *Sinn* determines cognitive value. I have rejected the intermediate thesis that mode of presentation determines cognitive value; I have done so not by rejecting that mode of presentation determines truth condition but by rejecting that truth condition determines cognitive value. Do I accept that *Sinn* determines cognitive value? To do so with consistency, I would need to maintain that there is some other ingredient or aspect of *Sinn* than mode of presentation that, perhaps in conjunction with mode of presentation, determines cognitive value. Otherwise, I would have to reject the Fregean principle that *Sinn* determines cognitive value. Note that such a rejection could be made without the rejection of another Fregean principle that *Sinn* determines *Beteutung*. In any case I do reject the idea that the cognitive value of a term is always determinable by looking at the semantics of the term in isolation. The difference in cognitive value between 'elm' and 'beech' in Oscar$_1$'s idiolect does not arise in the following form:

The cognitive value of 'elm' is V1, the cognitive value of 'beech' is V2, and V1 is not identical with V2.

The two terms do not have different cognitive values independently of each other. Rather, we should say that {'elm,' 'beech'} is a pair of terms which are not on a par in cognitive value. Little more can be said, apart from the divergence in the tightenings of their satisfaction conditions as sketched above. They differ in cognitive value from each other *in tandem*.[19] Thus I reject that an aspect or ingredient of *Sinn* which attaches to a term in isolation determines cognitive value.

Ascriptions of Attitudinal Contents

The Cartesian intuition and the above solution to the Reverse Frege Puzzle yield a new perspective on ascriptions of attitudinal contents. Suppose that Oscar$_1$ sincerely assents to (13) and also to

(19) No elms are beeches.

Is that good evidence for concluding that he believes that elms are elms and that no elms are beeches? No. His sincere assent to a sentence is good evidence for his having a belief with a certain specific content only if the content matches what he understands the sentence to be saying. What he understands a sentence to be saying is a matter of what the sentence means in his idiolect, provided that the sentence is a sentence in his idiolect. But the Cartesian intuition supports the view that in his idiolect (13) does not mean *that elms are elms*, nor does (19) mean *that no elms are beeches*; for 'elm' does not mean *elm* in his idiolect, and 'beech' does not mean *beech*. What *do* they mean, then? English happens to lack necessary expressions to express their meanings by customary 'that'-clauses. No English words precisely capture the indefiniteness of 'elm' and 'beech' in his idiolect. This means that the precise contents of Oscar$_1$'s beliefs in question are not expressible in English.[20] This may be surprising at first glance. After all, Oscar$_1$'s conceptual situation with respect to 'elm' and 'beech' is not an extraordinary example of an exotic kind.

Each one of us is in more or less the same situation with respect to many, perhaps even most, terms in our linguistic repertoire. So, the precise contents of many, or most, of our beliefs and other attitudes are not expressible in English. In many, or most, cases our ascriptions of particular attitudinal contents in English are therefore false. And this may appear surprising to some. For we are quite successful in explaining and predicting fellow humans' behavior by means of content ascriptions in English of their attitudinal states. If the ascriptions are false, how can we be so successful? The rhetorical force of this question derives from the uncritical assumption that predictive or explanatory success is impossible without hitting the bull's eye of truth. But ascribing the precisely correct contents to the subject's attitudes is not the only way to be successful in explaining and predicting his behavior within common-sense psychology.

Suppose that a certain entity, call it 'the Agent,' exhibits a regular behavioral pattern which is dependent on its total internal states. Suppose also that we want to explain and predict its behavior. One of us, Bill, constructs a theory which says the following:

> If the Agent is in total internal state S1, it tends to exhibit behavior B1;
> If the Agent is in total internal state S2, it tends to exhibit behavior B2;
> .....
> If the Agent is in total internal state Sn, it tends to exhibit behavior Bn.

Another one of us, Phil, constructs a different theory which says:

> If the Agent is in total internal state S1*, it tends to exhibit behavior B1;
> If the Agent is in total internal state S2*, it tends to exhibit behavior B2;
> .....
> If the Agent is in total internal state Sn*, it tends to exhibit behavior Bn.

Assume that Phil's theory is incompatible with Bill's. Yet if the two theories are equally consistent with the rest of our world view, neither theory is superior to the other in point of explanatory and predictive success with respect to the Agent's behavior B1, B2, ..., Bn. But it is perfectly possible that one of the theories is true and the other false. Therefore, explanatory and predictive success need not be supported by truth. The crucial point here is that success is a pragmatic notion, whereas truth is not. Bill's theory is as successful as Phil's theory for B1 through Bn but might not be for the remainder of the Agent's behavioral repertoire. If we should have a chance to compare the two theories with respect to the Agent's behavior Bn+17 through Bn+89, Phil's theory might come out on top of Bill's. Note that the relevant additional behavior, Bn+17 through Bn+89, need not be *actually* exhibited, as long as it is *possible* for the Agent to exhibit them. The narrower the scope of the *explananda*, the wider the variation among those theories which are equally successful in explaining them. The scope of the *explananda* of common-sense psychology is usually limited to more or less mundane types of behavior in everyday life.

Describing Oscar$_1$'s attitudes in English by using English words 'elm' and 'beech' is something like a useful approximation for the purpose of explaining and predicting his behavior. Its utility derives from two facts: (i) Oscar$_1$'s behavior is a result of his psychological mechanism involving attitudinal states whose contents play important roles in generating his behavior[21] and can be precisely expressed in his idiolect; (ii) 'elm' and 'beech' in English are linked to 'elm' and 'beech' in his idiolect in an important way. The important way in question has something to do with pragmatics. Let us artificially stipulate two English words which correctly express the concepts expressed by 'elm' and 'beech' in Oscar$_1$'s idiolect: 'schmelm' and 'schmeech,' respectively. Then it is possible to capture Oscar$_1$'s attitudinal contents precisely in English by using 'schmelm' and 'schmeech.' Suppose that the content of Oscar$_1$'s particular attitude on a particular occasion is precisely captured in English by the phrase 'a belief that schmelms are F.' Correct explanations of his behavior should be couched in terms of the belief ascription 'Oscar$_1$ believes that schmelms are F,' among other attitudinal ascriptions. But we ordinarily do not employ words like 'schmelm.' Instead we would employ ordinary English words and say 'Oscar$_1$ believes that elms are F,' and be fairly successful. Why? Why should we be successful if our ascriptions are not true? Of course, 'Oscar$_1$ believes that elms are F' *is* true in Oscar$_1$'s idiolect. But not every ascriber's idiolect shares the relevant portions of semantics with Oscar$_1$'s idiolect. So, the above question is fully answerable only if we can show a certain link between the ascriber's use of the terms in English and Oscar$_1$'s use of the terms in his idiolect. The two terms have the same incomplete satisfaction condition in his idiolect, so Oscar$_1$ cannot rely on the satisfaction condition alone to apply the terms correctly and yet sincerely dissent from 'Elms are beeches.' How does he use them, then? I believe something like the following is the case. Oscar$_1$ intends his usage of 'elm' and 'beech' to be in harmony with other English speakers' usage, especially the experts' usage. (This is how I salvage Putnam's insight on the division of labor.) He intends extensional coincidence; he intends that he apply 'elm' ('beech') to all and only objects to which the experts apply 'elm' ('beech'). So, whenever he believes of a particular object that the experts call it 'an elm' ('a beech'), he is prepared to apply 'elm' ('beech') to the object in his idiolect, that is, he takes the object to be a schmelm (a schmeech); and vice versa. Thus, the role played by his belief about a particular object that it is a schmelm (schmeech) in his psychological mechanism for behavior generation can be said to be mirrored by the role of his belief about the object that the experts call it 'an elm' ('a beech'). The experts' usage determines the English usage, as Putnam points out. So, employment of terms 'elm' and 'beech' in English does capture enough to explain and predict Oscar$_1$'s behavior successfully.

The Disquotational Principle

The most handy way of belief ascription is by metalinguistic means. The so-called disquotational principle is widely held to be a reliable principle to follow. There is no doubt that the disquotational principle is such an intergral part of our daily practice of belief ascription that a human society without it would be radically different; cf. belief ascriptions to nonhuman animals, whose languages (if they have any) we do not know. However, I do not believe that the principle, as it is commonly formulated, is reliable in the sense of producing with some reasonable frequency belief ascriptions which are *true* in the language of the ascription. Ubiquitous and insistent applications of the principle in our daily practice of belief ascription again show that what is at stake in our practice is something other than the truth of the ascriptions. Since Kripke offers a discussion of the disquotational principle which is more sensitive than most others, I would like to elaborate briefly by discussing his treatment. Kripke states the disquotational principle as follows:

> If a normal English speaker, on reflection, sincerely assents
> to 'p', then he believes that p, where 'p' is to be replaced,
> inside and outside all quotational marks, by any appropriate
> standard English sentence.[22]

This obviously covers speakers of English only. It is obvious that in
every other (rich enough) language we can formulate the disquotational principle for that language. For mediation between different
languages, we may invoke the following *principle of translation*:

> If a sentence of one language expresses a truth in that
> language, then any translation of it into any other language
> also expresses a truth in that other language.[23]

Kripke then says,

> As Quine has pointed out, to regard others as speaking the
> same language as I is in a sense tacitly to assume a
> *homophonic* translation of their language into my own. So
> when I infer from Peter's sincere assent to or affirmation of
> "God exists" that he believes that God exists, it is arguable
> that, strictly speaking, I combine the disquotational principle
> (for Peter's idiolect) with the principle of (homophonic)
> translation (of Peter's idiolect into mine).[24]

I think Kripke is on the right track here. His immediate disclaimer,
however, is unfortunate:

> But for most purposes, we can formulate the disquotational
> principle for a single language, English, tacitly supposed to
> be the common language of English speakers. Only when
> the possibility of individual differences of dialect is relevant
> need we view the matter more elaborately.[25]

I say that the possibility of individual differences of *idiolect* is almost
always relevant. An obvious criterion for goodness of translation,
homophonic or heterophonic, is the above principle of translation.
But it is not the only one, as Kripke himself notes:

> Some of our ordinary practice of translation may violate (the
> principle of translation); this happens when the translator's
> aim is not to preserve the content of the sentence...[26]

I say that our ordinary practice of belief ascription typically involves a practice of homophonic translation the aim of which is "not to preserve the content of the sentence." You assent to the sentence 'Elms are pretty.' I apply the disquotational principle for your idiolect and infer that the sentence 'I believe that elms are pretty' is true in your idiolect. I then make a homophonic translation of that sentence into my idiolect and assert in my idiolect, "You believe that elms are pretty."[27] Suppose that you are botanically as ignorant as the Oscars, whereas I am a botanist and my 'elm'-concept and 'beech'-concept are appropriately clear and distinct. Then the sentence 'Elms are pretty' does not have the same content in our idiolects, and my translation of 'I believe that elms are pretty' in your idiolect into 'You believe that elms are pretty' in my idiolect does not conform to the principle of translation. But this does not mean that my translation is a failure. On the contrary, it serves well in my attempt at explaining and predicting your everyday behavior.

The disquotational principle as formulated above by Kripke is not true. What is true is the following language-non-specific version:

> If a person, on reflection, sincerely assents to sentence S of language L, with the correct understanding of the meaning of S in L, then he believes that P, where 'P' is to be replaced by the correct English translation of S in L.

Whatever plausibility Kripke's version may have is derivative of the plausibility of this version. And this version is immune to the complications and difficulties Kripke's version faces. But that is not to say that we should use this version instead of Kripke's. This version compromises practical usefulness for the sake of truth as much as Kripke's version compromises truth for the sake of practical usefulness. While it is usually easy to verify that a given person is a normal English speaker and that he is sincerely making an assent on reflection, it is usually not easy to verify that a given person (i) correctly understands the meaning of a sentence in an appropriate language, *and* (ii) correctly translate that sentence into English. When it is easy to translate the sentence into English correctly—say, the sentence is in English to begin with—it is usually the case that either the person in question does not correctly understand the meaning of the sentence, or else it is not easy to verify that he does—say, you have to ask a lot of awkward conceptual questions. If L is the person's idiolect, then it is usually not easy to translate the sentence into English correctly—say, you have to invent awkward words like 'schmelm' and 'schmeech.'[28]

Notes

1. We are following Nathan Salmon in adopting this appelation; cf. his *Frege's Puzzle* (Cambridge, Mass., The MIT Press/Bradford Books, 1986).
2. See Nathan Salmon, *op. cit.*.
3. In his *Mind, Language and Reality: Philosophical Papers, Volume 2* (Cambridge, Cambridge University Press, 1975), pp. 215-271.
4. The indistinguishability in question should be distinguished from perceptual indistinguishability. One can make a perceptual discrimination of relevant objects by relying only on completely extraneous cues. A man and a pig may appear exactly the same to one under some perceptual conditions even if one knows perfectly well how a man differs from a pig. To put it slightly tendentiously, the indistinguishability in question is tantamount to indistinguishability in one's conceptual network; nothing more, nothing less.
5. I shall use italics to refer to meanings. I do not thereby intend to reify meanings as entities. This is a practice purely for the sake of linguistic convenience without ontological underpinnings. I also use italics for a more conventional purpose of emphasis. Which use is intended should always be clear from the context.
6. See his "Individualism and the Mental," in French, P., Euhling, T., and Wettstein, H. (eds.), *Studies in Epistemology*, (Minneapolis, University of Minnesota Press, 1979), pp. 73-121, and "Other Bodies," in Woodfield, A. (ed.), *Thought and Object* (Oxford, Clarendon Press, 1982), pp. 97-120.
7. To cite but one recent example, Stephen Schiffer says matter-of-factly, "Twin Earth is simply a fanciful way of making a plain point: in order to have beliefs with contents ascribable with sentences containing 'cat,' one must have had some sort of contact, direct or indirect, with cats, ..." *Remnants of Meaning* (Cambridge, Mass, The MIT Press/Bradford Books, 1987), p. 36.
8. Putnam explicitly states his conclusion as a disjunction. See *op. cit.*, p. 219.
9. It might be said that a token expression carries a particular meaning essentially, for its actual context of utterance fixes the host language, which determines its semantic assignment once and for all. But surely, one and the same token expression could possibly occur in different contexts with different host languages. Also, semantic evaluations outside the host language are not philosophically problematic; an utterance of a sound sequence [hans li:pt] by a monolingual German speaker can be subject to evaluation according to English (phonology, syntax, and) semantics.
10. This objection is a modified version of the one communicated to me by Geoffrey Sayre-McCord.
11. Thus I disagree with William G. Lycan, who says, "Conceptual roles, then, are commonly not shared by speakers of the same language. What do the speakers share? Reference and truth-conditions"; *Logical Form in Natural Language*, (Cambridge, Mass., The MIT Press/Bradford Books,

1984), p. 243. The truth conditions assigned to a sentence by the idiolects of two English speakers could be different.

12. An idiolect can be shared by two or more speakers, as is the case with the Oscars according to the semantic parity thesis. So, an idiolect is not a private language. If I called English or any of its dialects 'public language,' I would create an impression by contrast that idiolects are private languages. Thus, I chose the adjective 'social,' intending to let it carry as few irrelevant philosophical nuances as possible.

13. Nathan Salmon draws a similar conclusion on p. 74 of *Frege's Puzzle*: "...we should conclude that the information value of 'elm' or 'beech' is not the conceptual content." His discussion on pp. 63-76 is highly sensitive and informative, and bears close relevance to mine. I should perhaps add, however, that I am not as certain as he is that proper names and single-word natural kind terms should receive the same treatment. See the end of my next note. I also disagree that belief should be construed in terms of a three-place BEL relation.

14. Expressions may have different cognitive values in different contexts of utterance. David Kaplan's prolonged utterance of 'That is that' which begins at dawn with a pointing finger at the morning star and ends at dusk (not on the same day) with a pointing finger at the evening star is informative. In *A Puzzle About Demonstrative Belief*, (Ithaca, NY, Cornell University Press, 1988), Chapter II, David F. Austin has purified this kind of case in his two-tubes setup, in which one looks into two independently manipulated tubes, the right tube with the right eye and the left tube with the left eye, and sees the same shade of red through both tubes. One says, "That is that," using the first 'that' to refer to the red patch seen through the right tube and the second 'that' to refer to the red patch seen through the left tube. In both Kaplan's and Austin's examples, the two occurrences of 'that' have different cognitive values, but that does not threaten Frege's solution to Frege's puzzle the way the Reverse Frege Puzzle does. For the first and second occurrences of 'that' do not have the same mode of presentation associated with them. Similarly, the sentence 'That is red,' where the demonstrative pronoun is uttered by Austin's observer to refer to the red patch seen through the right tube, has a different mode of presentation associated with it— hence a different cognitive value—from the sentence 'That is red,' where the demonstrative is uttered to refer to the red patch seen through the left tube. In any case, indexicals and their context sensitivity are not relevant to the Reverse Frege Puzzle. Proper names, on the other hand, might very well complicate the discussion of the Reverse Frege Puzzle. I stay away from proper names for that reason; general terms give us the purest form of the Puzzle without extraneous, albeit potentially interesting, wrinkles.

15. I am assuming that 'elm' and 'beech' are conceptually indistinguishable only from each other and not from any other term, e.g., 'birch,' 'maple,' 'pine,' 'spruce,' etc.. This assumption is inessential but simplifies discussion for obvious reasons.

16. For a brief but informative discussion of a metalinguistic solution, see Salmon, *op. cit.*, pp. 71-72.

17. According to Putnam's picture of linguistic division of labor, the satisfaction condition is determined by the mode of presentation (or if you insist on a neutral non-Fregean term, concept) associated with the term by appropriate *experts*. The mode of presentation associated with the term in the experts' idiolects determines the satisfaction condition for the term in their idiolects, and that satisfaction condition permeates, so to speak, throughout the linguistic community and becomes the satisfaction condition for the term in laypeople's idiolects as well. So satisfaction condition *is* determined by something that is "in the head" after all; only that the head has to be the head of an expert. I disagree with this. The satisfaction condition for a term in English may be determined by the experts' mode of presentation. But I do not believe that the satisfaction condition for the term in Oscar$_1$'s idiolect is so determined.

18. Some philosophers, like Stephen White in "Partial Character and the Language of Thought," *Pacific Philosophical Quarterly 63*, 1982, pp. 347-365, and Jerry A. Fodor in *Psychosemantics*, (Cambridge, Mass., The MIT Press/ Bradford Books, 1987), pp. 47-50, would disagree. According to them, the satisfation condition is not determined by what is common to the two Oscars. What is common to the two Oscars is a function from contexts to satisfaction conditions. That function maps the context in which Oscar$_1$ is embedded on Earth to the satisfaction condition, "For any x, x satisfies 'elm' iff x is an elm," and maps the context in which Oscar$_2$ is embedded on Twin Earth to the satisfaction condition, "For any x, x satisfies 'elm' iff x is a beech." This ingenious idea enables those philosophers to respect Putnam's claim that the extension of 'elm' in Oscar$_1$'s mouth is the set of elms and the extension of 'elm' in Oscar$_2$'s mouth is the set of beeches, and at the same time maintain that there is something common to the two Oscars' "narrow" psychological states which deserve our attention. However, for one thing, I do not believe that Putnam's claim about the extensions of 'elm' in the two Oscars' mouths is worth respecting. More importantly, I do not believe that the idea works. If it works for Oscar$_1$'s 'elm' and Oscar$_2$'s 'elm,' then it should also work for Oscar$_1$'s 'elm' and his 'beech'; for the only relevant kind of difference between Oscar$_2$'s 'elm' and Oscar$_1$'s 'beech' is an "external," socio-environmental kind, and those philosophers want to capture an interesting "internal" notion. But the context for the evaluation of Oscar$_1$'s 'elm' is the same as the context for the evaluation of Oscar$_1$'s 'beech' when he utters, say, 'Elms aren't beeches.' So, since the function and the context remain constant, the determined satisfaction conditions are the same. Therefore it follows that in Oscar$_1$'s idiolect for any x, x satisfies 'elm' iff x satisfies 'beech.' But in Oscar$_1$'s idiolect it is *not* the case that for any x, x satisfies 'elm' iff x satisfies 'beech.' A contradiction.

19. It is not the case that lexically different terms with the same *Sinn* always differ in cognitive value. For most English speakers, 'female fox' and

'vixen' have the same *Sinn* and the same cognitive value. This point refutes an obvious kind of metalinguistic solution to the Puzzle.

20. This of course does not mean that they are not expressible in some augmented English which contains artificially added vocabulary of an appropriate kind. Also, it is a mistake to think that the sentence "Oscar₁ believes that what satisfies 'elm' in his idiolect is what satisfies 'elm' in his idiolect" correctly expresses in English the content of the belief manifested in his assent to (13). Oscar₁'s belief in question is not metalinguistic; nor does it involve a semantic notion such as satisfaction.

21. This is obviously not the place to discuss the foes of the belief-desire psychology such as Stephen P. Stich (the syntactic theory of the mind) and Paul M. and Patricia S. Churchland (eliminative materialism). I am simply assuming the belief-desire psychology (not necessarily a version as primitive as folk psychology) as providing the background for discussion.

22. "A Puzzle About Belief", in *Meaning and Use*, Margalit, A. (ed.), (Dortrecht, Reidel, 1979), pp. 248-249.

23. *Ibid.*, p.250.

24. *Ibid.*, p.251. Kripke's emphasis.

25. *Ibid.*, p.251.

26. *Ibid.*, p.250.

27. Complete homophonicity is compromised by the obvious adjustment required for translating the indexical 'I' in the obvious manner.

28. Different drafts ancestral to the present paper were presented at East Carolina University, the Triangle Circle Discussion Group on Philosophy of Language and Mind, the University of North Carolina at Chapel Hill, and California State University, Northridge. I thank those who participated in the discussions on those occasions. I also thank James E. Tomberlin and Nathan U. Salmon for helpful comments.

Philosophical Perspectives, 3
Philosophy of Mind and Action Theory, 1989

FISSION AND THE FACTS

Mark Johnston
Princeton University

1.

How far is Common Sense, a thing only partly invented, only partly a useful fiction, committed to anything that is philosophically problematic? The answer one gives to that question must significantly determine one's conception of the point and scope of philosophy, one's view of how far philosophy legitimately can have revisionary aspirations, one's sense of how satisfying a description of our practices can be if that description indeed leaves everything as it is, if it aims only to dissolve or diffuse conflicts among the justifications we give for those practices, if, as a matter of principle, it never finds a place for the diagnosis of vitiating error.

The Revisionist makes his task easier by attributing to Common Sense proto-philosophical theories about features of our ordinary practices, theories which may then be shown to be internally incoherent, inconsistent with other things we take for granted or simply too primitive to take seriously. Thus philosophical pictures sometimes seem to be foisted on Common Sense. Our ordinary understanding of the passage of time is sometimes supposed to embody the picture of reality growing at one end and perhaps diminishing at the other at the same unspecifiable rate. Our ordinary conception of free will is sometimes supposed to involve a picture of free will as a kind of causation itself uncaused and yet somehow properly associated with particular human beings, where human beings are themselves depicted as morasses of causal determination. Our ordinary notion of being guided by a rule that determines a potentially infinite series of applications is sometimes supposed to depend upon picturing ourselves as being under the mysterious influence of a Platonic something which actually incorporates and organizes the infinite series of cases.

Only when we descend to the details can we see how far these attributions *merely* foist and how far they tease out the implicit commitments of Common Sense. Here I am concerned with the details of the Common Sense View, if there is such a view, of the facts of personal identity and difference. However, before we examine the metaphysical model of the facts of personal identity attributed to Common Sense by Revisionists and Non-Revisionists alike, and exhibit in detail what is mistaken in it, it is as well to notice that the Revisionist who goes by way of attributing a proto-philosophical theory or model to Common Sense faces a general dilemma.

Consider some proto-philosophical theory which such a Revisionist associates with some concept in ordinary use. Does that theory guide the actual use of the concept, i.e. determine its application in ordinary cases, or not? If it does, then to the extent that the Revisionist maintains the theory is shot through with falsity, to that extent he becomes an Eliminativist, depriving us of anything to have had a false view about. If it does not, the Revisionist's claim about the falsity of the theory is a claim about a more or less uninteresting epiphenomenon of ordinary practice, a bit of amateurish philosophizing on the part of Common Sense. The false theory would then be a curiosity, since ordinary practice does not rely on it any more than an aeronautical engineer who happens to be a logicist about mathematics relies on his logicism in his mathematical calculations. The Revisionist thus inherits the onus of explaining in particular cases how he finds a stable middle ground between adopting Eliminativism and simply remarking upon a theoretical epiphenomenon.[1]

In the particular case of personal identity the master of the Revisionist gambit is Derek Parfit.[2] He makes a case for the claim that we have a false view of our natures as persons, indeed that we think of ourselves as separately existing entities distinct from our brains and bodies, entities like Cartesian egos. So far from seeing the separately existing entity view as a theoretical epiphenomenon, Parfit argues that if we accept that this view is false then we should alter our practice in a certain way. Presently we use the concept of personal identity to guide our future-oriented concerns so that we care in a special and non-derivative way about *ourselves* as opposed to people merely continuous with us in rich and manifold respects. According to Parfit we should abandon or at least significantly weaken this non-derivative concern for ourselves once we see that we are not separately existing entities.[3]

In first setting out his Revisionist argument Parfit relied heavily on the case of fission, which is my central example here.[4] About it, I argue that even if Common Sense had a view of personal identity at odds with the right thing to say in the fission case, this view would be at most a theoretical epiphenomenon. It does not in general guide our use of the concept of personal identity in ordinary cases. At worst, this view would be an overgeneralization from consequences in ordinary cases of our independent employment of the concept. Fission is a case outside the ordinary and it is a case in which there are no determinate facts of personal identity. Although this latter claim may surprise, it occasions no deep revision.

2.

In discussions of personal identity consequent upon Parfit's "Later Selves and Moral Principles" *the Simple View* was mostly taken to be the view that personal identity was never and could not be an indeterminate matter nor a conventional matter nor a matter of degree.[5] While Richard Swinburne defended the Simple View in his paper "Personal Identity", Parfit attacked it, urging a parallel with the identity of nations and artefacts.[6] As emerges in his later debate with Sydney Shoemaker, Swinburne had in mind a particular metaphysical model which explained and organized the tenets of the Simple View.[7] Swinburne takes us to be indivisible immaterial souls, for whose persistence bodily and psychological continuity is mere evidence. Although the evidence can come in degrees and leave us epistemically in the dark, according to Swinburne, there is always an all or nothing fact of the matter as to personal identity and difference. Moreover, since according to Swinburne the relevant facts concern the persistence of indivisible immaterial souls they are therefore facts which conventions cannot create or project but only respect or fall foul of. Surprisingly, although this metaphysical view standing behind the Simple View is rejected by Parfit, he agrees with Swinburne in finding it to be an implicit commitment of Common

Sense. Parfit writes that when it comes to personal identity, we are adherents of the "Further Fact-View" and that this view can only be correct if we are "separately existing" (and indivisible) entities distinct from our brains and bodies.[8]

Perhaps it is natural and explanatory to associate with the Simple View the metaphysical model of persons as indivisible soul pellets. However, *if* Common Sense is implicitly committed to the metaphysical model then it is an idle commitment, a wheel that turns while nothing in our ordinary practice turns with it. As I have argued elsewhere, we cannot reasonably reconstruct our ordinary practice of identifying and re-identifying ourselves and each other in the easy and offhand ways in which we do as a practice which tracks indivisible soul pellets. Nor are our future-directed and retrospective self-regarding concerns as tentative as they ought to be if we took ourselves to be soul pellets; for then we should find ourselves difficult to trace behind the stage of mental and bodily states and events.[9]

What of the Simple View itself, is it embodied in our practice and is it true?

It should be emphasized that it is not sufficient to settle these questions to observe that our ordinary notion of personal identity is the notion of absolute identity restricted to persons, and that absolute identity, the simplest relation which holds "between" a thing and itself, never holds indeterminately between a thing and itself, never holds as a matter of mere convention and never holds less than completely. This observation can be allowed, while the question of the Simple View is still left open. For our concept of a person can be a source of indeterminacy, conventionality and partiality. Even if we insist that kinds specify determinate, non-conventional and non-partial conditions of persistence for their members, our concept of a person, alternatively our use of the terms "person" and "is the same person as", may be regarded as being associated with several competing kinds specifying different conditions. So the answer "Yes" to a question of personal identity may be neither determinately true nor determinately false because the answer would be "Yes" for instances of some of these kinds but not for instances of others. The answer "Yes" may be true due to adoption of a convention which has the effect that only the kinds for which this answer correct are to be considered. The answer "Yes" may be mostly true because the answer would be "Yes" relative to most of the competing kinds.

Hence the question about the Simple View is not a question about the truth of a metaphysical picture so much as a question as to whether our use of the terms "person" and "is the same person as" in our thought and talk associates a single kind with those terms. *Even if there were soul pellets this question about the philosophical reconstruction of our practice would still be left open.* There would still be a question as to what kind of thing *we* are, a question which might not have a fully determinate answer. Understanding this, which is to understand better what sort of question the question about the Simple View is, already makes it implausible that Common Sense has answered that question for itself and guides its use of the terms "person" and "personal identity" by means of its preferred answer. Yet this is just what opponents and advocates of the Simple View, Parfit and Swinburne most prominent among them, have assumed.

Having indicated in a preliminary way how harmless to our ordinary practice (as opposed to philosophical theories about it) it would be to allow that personal identity could sometimes be an indeterminate matter, let us now turn to the case of fission and see why we should allow this.

3.

The first thing to emphasize about fission is that it can be made to seem paradoxical. Here is the paradox of fission, presented for persons but easily generalizable to any continuant with at least two distinct subparts each such that its persistence, perhaps in conjunction with auxiliary parts drawn from elsewhere, could be sufficient for the persistence of the continuant in question.

(1) People can and do survive hemispherectomy (having one hemisphere removed). This surgical procedure is sometimes offered as the only means of saving the life of a patient with a massive and malignant tumor in one of his hemispheres. Patients who undergo these operations are mentally impaired, but what is surprising is that the impairment is not as radical as one might have thought. This is because the capacities to subserve some mental functions are duplicated in both hemispheres. Hemispheric specialization, i.e., the non-duplication across hemispheres of capacities to subserve the various mental functions, is far from complete in human beings. It is even less marked in the lower animals. There is evidence that

hemispheric specialization can be severely limited in individual humans by congenital defects which cut down the amount of cross-hemispheric communication.[10] Theoretically, in such a patient, there could be almost complete duplication of the various capacities to subserve his mental functioning, so that either hemisphere is able to take over most of his mental functioning. We may suppose that our subject Brown is such a patient.

(2) If Brown's brain were transplanted into the debrained body of his mental and physical twin Robinson, forming a composite Brownson, then Brown would survive as Brownson. This is Sydney Shoemaker's case set up so that there is no problem as to how the dispositions of Brown's brain mesh with those of Robinson's debrained body.[11] The claim that Brown survives as Brownson is the standard intuition about the case.

(3) Brown could survive having his brain transplanted into a receptive and brainless body and then survive hemispherectomy (left or right). This is just a consequence of (2) and (1) taken together. Suppose Brown survives as Brownson and Brownson survives hemispherectomy. Then Brown survives having his brain transplanted and having a hemisphere removed.

(4) Brown could survive if all but his left (or right) hemisphere were destroyed so long as the remaining hemisphere was kept alive and functioning and transplanted into Robinson's receptive but brainless body. Here we are to imagine the outcome described in case (3) but produced by a different method. We still end up with Brown's left (or right) hemisphere functioning in Robinson's old body. In case (3) we counted this as Brown surviving. Why not here? It might be urged that there is more sudden physical discontinuity involved in this second method of producing the outcome. Brown's body and one of his hemispheres are discarded at once rather than in two steps. But I do not think that someone who has granted our first three claims can plausibly maintain that the physical discontinuity involved in destroying half of Brown's brain and his brainless body is sufficient to prevent Brown's survival. By granting (1) through (3) one seems to be committed to the view that what is important for Brown's survival is the persistence of enough of Brown's brain to secure significant mental continuity. And cases (3) and (4) seem just alike so far as that goes. At least this is so, if, as we supposed, Brown lacks any significant hemispheric specialization, so that the remaining hemisphere can take over most of his mental functioning.

(5) (The Fission Case) Paradoxically, Brown can survive twice over. We get this result by playing through case (4) twice over, generating in the same situation a recipient of Brown's left hemisphere and a recipient of Brown's right hemisphere. But now Parfit's question "How can a double success constitute a failure?", originally urged by Parfit as a question about what it is rational for Brown to want in caring about survival, is at least as appropriately urged as a question about Brown's survival itself. A related question is: How can personal identity fail to be an intrinsic matter? That is, how can it be that in a given possible situation—the Fission Case—the operation of a process, which secures the survival of a person in another possible situation, fails to secure the survival of that person because of the co-occurrence in the given situation of a process which secures the survival of that person in some third possible situation? If it cannot be so, Brown survives twice over in the fission case, i.e. survives as two *seemingly* distinct people.

The paradox just exhibited has not been satisfactorily dealt with, even in elaborate and subtle discussions of identity over time. For example, two of David Wiggins's non-dispensable principles governing the persistence of individuals are[12]

(α) If F is a substance concept for a, then coincidence under F (i.e. being the same F as) must be determinate enough to exclude this situation: a is traced under F and counts as coinciding with b under F, a is traced under F and counts as coinciding with c under F, while nevertheless b does not coincide under F with c.

(β) What makes for the identity of a and b should be independent of objects distinct from a and b.

Since he intends this latter principle to have the effect of our claim that personal identity is an intrinsic matter, fission clearly places Wiggins's account of persistence in great jeopardy. Barring the view that Brown exists after the operation spatially separated from himself in the manner of a universal, we appear to have an argument that given (β), Brown, the recipient in the fission case of the left hemisphere, and the recipient in the fission case of the right hemisphere, satisfy the conditions deemed impossible by (α). Wiggins's brief remark on a related matter—his "fifty-one percent" solution—involves denying that a continuant can survive loss of half of the matter crucial to its survival.[13] In the present context, to avoid getting to (4), Wiggins would have to claim that no patient can survive left, or indifferently right, hemispherectomy.

Consider first the corresponding general claim about continuants, effectively the claim that there is no continuant with at least two distinct subparts each such that its persistence, perhaps in conjunction with auxiliary parts drawn from elsewhere, could be sufficient for the persistence of the continuant. Even if this "non-division principle" *were* true, we would not have a way out of the paradox unless we were prepared to maintain that it was not an empirical truth but a conceptual one. By a conceptual truth, I mean something derivable from a description of our use of terms for continuants and continuant identity rather than an empirical discovery about the things which these terms pick out. As we shall see, it will be implausible to maintain that (β), the claim that continuant identity is an intrinsic matter, is an empirical discovery. Rather, the way to defend it is by exhibiting a certain pattern in our use of terms for continuants and continuant identity, a pattern which we would adhere to under the impact of any (or almost any[14]) empirical discovery about continuants. Given that (β) is true as a matter of conceptual necessity then, if it is conceptually possible that there be a continuant with at least two distinct subparts each such that its persistence could be sufficient for the persistence of the continuant then it is conceptually possible that the continuant be wholly present in two non-overlapping places. But isn't this just what we would have antecedently thought to be conceptually impossible, i.e., a continuant, that is to say a persisting *particular*, exhibiting the prerogatives of a universal? That, briefly, is the general form of the paradox of fission. Prior to investigating alternative ways out, it is premature to take the paradox as a proof that the non-division principle, i.e. the principle that no continuant has at least two subparts of the problematic sort, is conceptually necessary. Indeed, so far from the non-division principle being conceptually necessary, reflection on worms, tunnels, nations, restorable artefacts and the like makes it seem simply false.

Mutatis mutandis for people and the claim that they do not survive left or indifferently right hemispherectomy. It is not enough to put this forward as an empirical claim. As a claim of conceptual necessity it looks difficult to defend. Since it is not the sort of obvious conceptual necessity which springs immediately from a description of our use of the terms "person" and "hemisphere" it looks as though the claim of conceptual necessity could only be defended by using the paradox as a proof. Prior to investigating alternative ways out this will be premature. Indeed, as in the general case, there seem to be good reasons not to take the paradox as such a proof. For it seems conceptually possible that we be confronted with someone whose hemispheres are such that either one could take over most of the psychological functioning of his whole brain. About him it will be plausible to say that he could survive left or indifferently right hemispherectomy.

This excursus into a developed form of Wiggins's suggestion about fission allows us to make a general point about the status of the paradox of fission. No solution is to be got by denying the empirical claims embedded in (1)-(5). Suppose for example that the midbrain turns out not to be divisible in the way required for the argument. "Phew! Thanks to empirical good fortune, natural extensions of our ordinary use of the terms 'person' and 'same person' do not lead to inconsistency." That this is not a satisfying solution to the paradox is made evident once we consider what it allows and implies. It is certainly a conceptual possibility that empirical fortune turned out to be bad, and if it had turned out badly then natural extensions of our ordinary use of the terms 'person' and 'same person' would be paradoxical. And now we simply have the obligation to offer a different solution to the paradox as it arises under the unfortunate possibility. Unless, that is, we are prepared to say that our concept of a person is so fragile, so dependent upon the graces of empirical fortune, as to be unworkable in such a possible situation.[15] The paradox of fission is harder than those who have dismissed it on empirical grounds have thought.

Derek Parfit presented something very like this paradox in his paper "Personal Identity", but curiously, so far as I can see, he does not really respond to it in a way that recognizes its full force.[16] The paradox is not dealt with by the main strategy of that brilliant and influential paper, namely, changing the subject, ceasing to talk seriously about personal identity, and instead talking about what matters to us in survival—the particular bodily and psychological connections which are the normal concomitants of survival. First, in caring about survival we typically want a package deal—identity plus the normal concomitants—so talking about what matters ought not really succeed in changing the subject. Secondly, changing the subject cannot be a response to the paradox unless one takes the paradox to show that the concept of personal identity is both inconsistent *and* unworkable in the sense that there is no consistent reconstruction of the concept possible and so no point in sticking to the old subject. Given our earlier observation that personal identity is just the relation of absolute identity restricted to persons, and given that the concept of absolute identity is evidently consistent and workable, this amounts to the view that the concept of a person is inconsistent and unworkable, a radical Eliminativism whose characteristic claim expressed in the material mode is that there are no people.

4.

Since the real force of the paradox of fission has been missed, we ought to make explicit the auxiliary assumptions employed in the paradox argument. There are five major assumptions which I wish to highlight. Each of the major views abut the fission case can be associated with the denial of one or more of these assumptions. The first assumption is

(A) The process which secures Brown's survival during the period when his body has been destroyed and his left (alternatively right) hemisphere is about to be transplanted has only to do with the persistence and functioning of the hemisphere. It does not involve the persistence of an indivisible immaterial soul or indivisible substantial form or entelechy which could be the companion of the left hemisphere or alternatively the right hemisphere but not both.

This is what Swinburne denies. According to Swinburne, Brown and his kindmates are indivisible immaterial souls. Brown the soul could accompany his left hemisphere or his right hemisphere but not both. That is why fission cannot really be a double success.

Despite Swinburne's recent attempt to argue in a relatively a priori fashion that we are essentially souls, it is hard to believe that (A) does not describe a conceptual possibility.[17] As Sir Peter Strawson maintained in his essay "Persons", any non-devious construal of our applications of mental and physical predicates to a person will have both sorts of predicates applying to a single subject of predication.[18] And as emphasized above, we cannot reasonably reconstruct our ordinary practice of identifying and reidentifying ourselves and each other as a practice which traces soul pellets not constituted by but only accidentally associated with human bodies.[19] Of course, the hylomorphism gestured at in (A) could have turned out to be true, and we need not fall in with the dogmatic materialism of the day and decisively deny that persons have indivisible non-physical aspects. All we need for the paradox is that whichever way this turns out, it is an empirical matter, so that (A) describes a conceptual possibility, something not ruled out by our present use of the terms "is the same person as", "hemisphere", etc. To be explicit, we need only

(A*) It is conceptually possible that distinct processes which in other possible situations secure the survival of an individual co-occur and when they co-occur they are intrinsically exactly as they were in the respective possible situations.

We need only this weak assumption about what is possible in the broadest sense, i.e. what is not conceptually incoherent, because the other assumptions involved are plausibly taken to be conceptual necessities, together partly constitutive of our concept of a persisting (human) person; which is to say that these claims are not in empirical jeopardy in any situation where we have settled it that we are considering persisting (human) persons. The principles are

(B) The identity through time of persons is an intrinsic matter.

(C) A person never survives spatially separated from himself in the fashion of a universal.

(D) Since persons are solid and not interpenetrable, no two people can be in exactly the same place at the same time.

(E) At no time is a person constituted by two independently functioning human bodies.

Principles (D) and (E) can be set aside for the moment, for they become relevant only when we consider a philosophical view of persisting individuals naturally associated with counterpart theory, a view discussed in section 5.

(B) is meant to capture the intent of Wiggins's (β), a principle which he calls "the only a and b rule". Wiggins intended this principle to rule out any theory, such as Robert Nozick's Closest Continuer

Schema, which makes the survival of a person turn on the absence of equally good continuers of that person.[20] Nozick's Schema would block our original argument at the step from (4) to (5). Although Brown could survive as the recipient of his left hemisphere or as the recipient of his right hemisphere he could not survive as both. Why? Well, if both recipients were equally good continuers of Brown then there would be no *closest* continuer of Brown so that neither would be Brown, and if one was the better continuer of Brown he would be Brown. So, at least, according to the Closest Continuer Schema which has it that the closest of the close enough continuers of a given individual (as measured by the standards of closeness appropriate to the kind of individual in question) is that individual.

If principle (B) is to rule out the Closest Continuer Theorist's account of the fission case, it must be expanded and explained, since it is easy to misformulate the idea behind it. Wiggins's (β) and Parfit's more recent formulation—"Whether a future person will be me must depend only on the intrinsic features of the relation between us. It cannot depend upon what happens to other people."[21]—do not actually rule out the Closest Continuer Theorist's claims about the fission case. Applying the theory to the fission case, we get the result that neither of the fission products is identical with Brown. We cannot say that according to the Closest Continuer Theorist one of these fission products *would have been* identical with Brown. For that would violate the necessity of identity: if neither of the fission products *is* identical with Brown, neither *can* be. If we hold to the necessity of identity and the Closest Continuer Schema then the comparison which Wiggins's (β) and Parfit's formulation invite us to make between the fission case and the two cases in which the one or the other hemisphere is transplanted while the rest of Brown is destroyed is not available. Neither fission product will turn up in these cases. We do not have a person turning up in a pair of cases, in one case identical with a given person and in the other not identical with this person because of the existence of an equally good competitor.

We can obscure this by using non-rigid designators and forgetting that we are. So we might say that the Closest Continuer Theory implies that in the fission case, the recipient of Brown's left hemisphere is not Brown while in the case in which Brown's right hemisphere is destroyed the recipient of Brown's left hemisphere *is* Brown. However, if either (β) or Parfit's formulation is to get a grip here an argument is needed that "the recipient of Brown's left hemisphere" picks out the same person in the two situations under consideration. The Closest Continuer Theorist has an argument that it does not.[22] How then should we formulate a plausible version of the idea that personal identity is an intrinsic matter, a version that is incompatible with the Closest Continuer Theorist's treatment of fission? The idea that personal identity is an intrinsic matter is the idea that the facts of personal identity do not float completely free of other facts. They are secured by or constituted by complex processes in a non-accidental way. To give expression to this idea of non-accidental connection we can resort to the idiom of possible worlds:

(B*) If in one possible world w a process p secures the survival of a person x then in any world w' in which p occurs and is intrinsically exactly as it is in w, in that world w' p secures the survival of x.

As it stands (B*) is a quite weak principle.[23] The process which secures the survival of a given person could be as inclusive as the world process or it could simply be the persistence of the person understood as a separately existing soul-pellet distinct from any brain or body. In conjunction with intuitive conceptions of the extent and nature of the processes which secure people's survival (B*) generates an interesting supervenience claim. Roughly, intuitive conceptions of the nature of the total process which secures a given person's survival will locate that process wholly within the space-time envelope or four dimensional total position swept out by that person's body over his lifetime. After all it is that on which we concentrate when trying to determine where and when the person survived. We do not look elsewhere and elsewhen. Intuitive conceptions will also allow that such processes, made up as they might be of many bodily and mental subprocesses, can be individuated without first settling the question of whether they have secured some person's survival. Given these intuitive conditions, we may suppose that the two diverging processes in the fission case are just the processes which in each of the other two worlds secured the existence of Brown. Moreover, these processes need not be intrinsically different as between the fission case where they occur together and the two simpler cases where each occurs alone. Since by hypothesis each process on its own secures the existence of Brown, (B*) tells us that in the fission case Brown is identical with each of the fission products. So, by the transitivity of identity, after the double transplant Brown is bilocated, exiting spatially separated from himself in the manner of a universal. This contradicts (C).

Notice that we need not employ the specific intuitive assumptions to generate this contradiction. (A*), and (B*) understood as a conceptual necessity, imply that it is conceptually possible that a person survives twice over spatially separated from himself in the manner of a universal. The general statement of the paradox is clear: about any kind of individual we need only assume the analogues of (A*), (B*) and (C) to generate a contradiction. As with (A*) and (B*), theorists have considered denying (C). Robert Nozick considers this only to reject it, and Andre Gallois has advocated it in discussion.[24]

Many will think that denying (C) is simply incoherent since it will lead us to say such things as that Brown weighs both 150 pounds and 151 pounds at the same time. But this is analogous to problems we have already solved. In order to make sense of the same individual having incompatible properties in the various worlds it inhabits we understand having a property as a function from worlds to sets of individuals, intuitively, the individuals that have the property in the argument worlds. In order to make sense of the same individual having incompatible properties at the various times it inhabits we understand having a property as a function from worlds and times to sets of individuals, intuitively, the individuals that have the property in the argument worlds at the argument times. In order to make sense of the strange, unprecedented circumstance of the same individual having incompatible properties at the various places it inhabits we understand having a property as a function from worlds, times and places to sets of individuals, intuitively, the individuals that have the property in the argument worlds, at the argument times and at the argument places. Topological, temporal and modal qualifications specify *modes* of having properties: *having* is having-in-w-at-t-at-p where 'w', 't', 'p' are variables for worlds, times and places respectively. By thus relativizing the relations of having holding between individuals and properties we can allow that individuals can have incompatible properties at the different worlds, times and places at which they exist.[25]

5.

The paradox is not completely tight. For there is a way of thinking about modality—counterpart theory—which allows one to hold (A*) and (B*) appropriately construed, and avoid violating (C). For our purposes the important idea in counterpart theory is that the otherworldly thing(s) which represent the possibilities for a given individual existing in a given world is (are) merely its counterpart(s) in the other world—the thing(s) in the world most resembling the given individual in important respects.[26] So the counterpart-theoretic version of (B*) will say that if the survival of x in w is secured by a process p then in any world w' where a counterpart of p occurs that process will secure the survival of a counterpart in w' of x. Appealing to (A*) and (B*) and taking w_1 to be the world in which only the left hemisphere of Brown survives and is transplanted, w_2 to be the world in which only the right hemisphere of Brown survives and is transplanted and w_3 to be the fission world we have

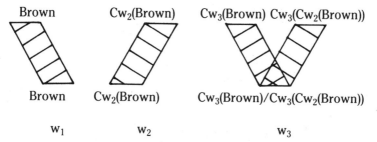

Brown Cw_2(Brown) Cw_3(Brown) Cw_3(Cw_2(Brown))

Brown Cw_2(Brown) Cw_3(Brown)/Cw_3(Cw_2(Brown))

w_1 w_2 w_3

where 'Cw_i(Brown)' denotes the counterpart in w_i of Brown.

Since we are not dealing with a theory of modality which licenses any such cross-world identities as Brown = Cw_2(Brown) = Cw_3(Brown) = Cw_3(Cw_2(Brown)) we are not forced to identify the two post-fission products in w_3 and thereby accept that Brown can survive spatially separated from himself in the fashion of a universal. But saying that Cw_3(Brown) and Cw_3(Cw_2(Brown)) are distinct implies that in w_3 there were two people all along; *before the fission these people were in exactly the same place.*

This co-occupancy problem can be made worse if we think of people as three-dimensional entities extended in space but not in time. Consider the cohabited envelope of space-time in w_3. If persons are three-dimensional entities then it is hard to see how the *subsequent* fission could have affected how many people were associated with this envelope of space-time. If there are two three-dimensional people associated with this envelope of space-time, and that is not the causal or logical consequence of what subsequently happens, then there would have been two people associated with this envelope of space-time even if the fission had not taken place, the brain and body in question being obliterated. But then we have an argument from (A*), (C), the counterpart theoretic variant of (B*) and the view that people are three-dimensional entities, entities with spatial but not temporal parts, to a quite dubious possibility—the possibility that two people exactly coincide throughout their entire lifetimes.

If we have adopted counterpart theory in response to the paradox generated by (A*), (B*) and (C) then we do better to take the view that people are four-dimensional entities, i.e. sums of temporal parts such that each part is psychologically and perhaps physically continuous with each other part, sums that are maximal in this respect. Then we can explain why in w_3 there are two distinct people in the same place before the fission while there would not have been two distinct people co-occupying that region if the fission had not taken place, the body in question being obliterated. The case of fission is a case of partial stage-sharing by two distinct maximal sums of psychologically and physically continuous temporal parts. By the definition of when a sum of temporal parts is a person, any such maximal sum is a person. But when we envisage a world which is like the fission world up to a time just before the fission, at which time the body in question is completely destroyed, we have only one such maximal sum and so only one person. On the temporal part view, partial stage-sharing is possible for two or more people but complete stage-sharing by two or more people makes no sense since we would then have just a single maximal sum of psychologically and physically continuous temporal parts and so just one person.

In effect, we have here an argument from (A*),(C), the counterpart-theoretic variant of (B*) and the impossibility of complete co-occupancy of two or more people, to David Lewis's treatment of the fission case.[27] Fission is a case where there are two people all along. Before the fission they shared stages, after the fission not. (Counting by person-stages, one became two). Of course this solution, exploiting as it does the idea of partial co-occupancy, conflicts with (D). But as we are beginning to see, every way out of the paradox of fission conflicts with one of (A)-(E).

Readers of Lewis's "Survival and Identity" might think that the argument Lewis gives there for his treatment of the fission case (which is independent of the present argument) combines with the present argument to show that denying (D) is not just one way out among others but has a special privilege. At the beginning of "Survival and Identity" Lewis asks "What is it that matters in survival?" and says that there are two plausible yet apparently competing answers.[28] First, identity is what matters. Contemplating some upcoming event one wants oneself to be around after the event. Secondly, one wants it to be the case that one's mental life should flow on, that one's present experiences, thoughts, beliefs, desires and traits of character should have appropriate future successors. According to this second answer what one wants is mental continuity and connectedness. Lewis says that these answers appear to conflict: identity is an all or nothing relation and it is transitive; the relation of mental continuity and connectedness can hold to various degrees and, as the fission case itself illustrates, it is not transitive. Lewis suggests that the conflict appears only because we make an unequal and inept comparison. The comparison can be seen to be unequal and inept if we take the view that persons are maximal sums of mentally continuous and connected temporal parts. Personal identity is a relation between continuant persons. Mental continuity and connectedness is a relation among the temporal parts or person-stages which make up continuant persons. On the temporal part view, wanting to be identical with some person around after some vicissitude amounts to wanting it to be the case that one's present stage is mentally continuous and connected with some stage after the vicissitude.

Hence the two answers do not really conflict. They complement each other, the one properly expressed in the language of the four-dimensional sums that are people, the other in the language of the shorter-lived parts that compose them. Indeed, Lewis's way of making apparent conflict disappear results in defining "person" and "personal identity" so that we never have personal identity without the holding of the particular mental relations which matter to us and we never have the holding of the particular mental relations without personal identity. In the fission case the particular mental relations hold twice over and in different directions, viz. between the pre-fission stages of the original patient and the post-fission stages of the recipient of the left hemisphere, and between the pre-fission stages of the original patient and the post-fission stages of the recipient of the right hemisphere. Since the post-fission stages of the recipient of the left-hemisphere and the post-fission stages of the recipient of the right hemisphere are not mentally continuous and connected they are not together stages of a single continuant person. The way out consistent with Lewis's definition of a person is to count the unconnected and discontinuous stages as stages of two distinct people, people sharing stages before but not after the fission. "The original patient", taken as a designator of a person is a rotten or multiply denoting description—each of the two persons is a good candidate to be its denotation.

I do not think we should accept Lewis's ingenious methodology and the argument it generates. For I do not see that the two answers from which Lewis starts are even apparently conflicting, any more than the answer "Romulus" and the answer "Remus" are apparently conflicting answers to the question "Name the legendary founders of Rome." The question "What matters in survival, i.e. what do we reasonably care about in caring about survival?" is properly answered by saying that what matters to us is personal identity *plus* its normal mental concomitants.In caring about survival we want a package deal. We want to exist in the future and be sufficiently connected to our present self to be able to carry out appropriate successors of the projects which presently give momentum to our lives. We regard each part of the package as considerably less worth caring about on its own. Thus there is the ordinary idea of pointless survival. One might for example be rationally indifferent as between a quiet death in one's sleep tonight and the onset in that sleep of ten years of uninterrupted deep unconsciousness terminating in death. The ten years of unconsciousness, though a form of survival or personal identity, offers nothing of what we value survival for, and this because of the absence of the typical mental concomitants of survival. There is no experience of our own activity, no community with others, no pursuit of the valuable and the diverting, no appropriate successors of the projects which give meaning to a life. There is personal identity but not the other part of the package. It is the whole package which we want in caring about survival, as is further shown by the fact that we would care significantly less about more or less mentally continuous successors just because we believed them not to be identical with us (cf. *The Invasion of the Body Snatchers*).

Of course Lewis's substantive philosophical thesis is that personal identity and the mental concomitants can never come apart. But since this is a substantive philosophical thesis and not clearly part of Common Sense it is not appropriate to use it to rule out the suggestion that Common Sense wants personal identity *plus* its mental concomitants, where these are understood as distinct but related parts of a package deal. If that is right, we cannot motivate the conflict from which Lewis starts in order to defend the substantive philosophical thesis.

That the substantive philosophical thesis and its consequences are not clearly part of Common Sense emerges in Lewis's discussion of Methuselah.[29] Methuselah lives 969 years. There is no mental connectedness between Methuselah when 300 and Methuselah when 900. Consider Methuselah on his 300th birthday. He foresees mental connectedness wearing out between himself then and himself 600 years on. The later person he is thinking of offers him little or nothing of the typical mental accompaniments of survival. This consideration, grounded in the gradual wearing out of mental connectedness, is enough for Lewis to take it that Methuselah when 300 and Methuselah when 900 are not (stages of) the same person. Here, defining personal identity in terms of mental continuity and connectedness seems to lead us wrong. For we have no reason to suppose that there is anything incoherent in the idea that Methuselah is a single long-lived person whose mental life varied a great deal between his 300th and 900th birthdays.

Since I wish to allow Lewis's stage-sharing account of the fission case as one acceptable account among many,[30] I not only need to deny that it has the privileged status which Lewis's argument for it seemed to provide, I also need to deny Parfit's charge that it radically misrepresents the ordinary concern to survive.[31] Parfit's charge arises in a case of fission in which one of the fission products survives some later event e while the other does not. In such a case, according to Lewis, we have two stage-sharing continuants, persons C_1 and C_2. C_2 survives e and C_1 does not. Consider a shared stage S at a time t_0 before the fission but after it is known that fission will occur. Lewis writes "The thought to be found in S is a desire for survival of the most commonsensical and unphilosophical kind possible. Since S is a shared stage, this desire is a shared desire. Certainly C_2 has the survival he desired, and likewise has what we think matters: mental continuity and connectedness (the R-relation) between S and much later stages... But how about C_1?"[32] Lewis claims that in such a case, despite the fact that C_1 does not survive e, C_1 will also get what he wanted at t_0. For the most commonsensical desire for survival available to S is not the "strong" desire—"Let both of us survive e."—but the "weak" desire "Let one of us survive e." The argument Lewis gives for this is that if we say that S had the strong desire then not only did C_1 miss out on what he wanted at t_0 but so also did C_2. Yet, Lewis maintains, C_2 clearly does get "what commonsensically matters in survival." C_2 does survive e.[33]

As just stated, this consideration can look insufficient. For it seems that there is a precisely parallel consideration in favor of the opposite conclusion: C_1 does not survive e, so C_1 clearly did not get what he commonsensically desired at t_0, so S, the stage of C_1 at t_0, had the strong desire, so C_2 did not get what he commonsensically desired at t_0, despite the fact that C_2 survives e.

Suppose this symmetry could be broken in favor of Lewis's way of going. We could still object on behalf of Parfit that Lewis misrepresents the commonsensical desire to survive. On the intuitive view of the matter there ought to be a single sense in which C_2 got what he commonsensically wanted at t_0 with respect to e and C_1 did not. But on the hypothesis of stage-sharing, and given Lewis's distinction between the strong and weak desires, either *both* got what they commonsensically wanted at t_0 or *neither* got it. So the hypothesis of stage-sharing prevents us from reconstructing the intuitive view of the matter.

This objection, and the worry about how to reconstruct the commonsense desire to survive e had by S in the circumstance in which S is ignorant of the upcoming fission, can be met by a reply that differs from Lewis's, a reply that does not make anything of the distinction between strong and weak desires.

Stage S, like all person-stages, is a bundle of events, states and processes within a particular spatio-temporal region. We are supposing that one of the mental events associated with S is the occurrent thought "Let me survive e", a thought which is the expression of a desire had at t_0 by both C_1 and C_2. As recent studies of the propositional attitudes have emphasized, we can mean by "desire" a desire event or state, understood as an item wholly included within the mental life of the individual in question, or we can mean the propositional attitude, a relation between an individual and a propositional content, a relation whose holding may depend both upon what is going on within the mental life of the individual in question and upon the extra-mental context in which the individual is located. The curious feature of S is that as far as associating a content with "its" occurrent thought "Let me survive e" goes, S is located in two competing and separable contexts. S is a stage of C_1, a person who does not survive e. But S is also a stage of C_2, a person who does survive e. In the first of these contexts, the thought "Let me survive e" is properly construed as having the content that C_1 survives e. In the second of these contexts the thought "Let me survive e" is properly construed as having the content that C_2 survives e. The second of these desired contents corresponds to the way things turn out. The first does not. So we should say that the desire to survive e, *considered as a desire of C_2*, i.e. assigned a content via the context that includes C_2, is satisfied, while the desire to survive e, considered as a desire of C_1, is not satisfied. And this is just the intuitive thing to say.

Compare a situation in which a supporter of Nixon and an infiltrator from the Nixon opposition together simultaneously raise a certain sign which has written on it "I will never abandon Nixon." Intuitively the token "I will never abandon Nixon" has two contents associated with it, depending on whether it is considered as a token used by the supporter or as a token used by the infiltrator. We may suppose that the supporter "uttered" (in the broad sense in which one utters cheques, etc.) a truth by means of the token and that the infiltrator uttered a falsehood by means of the token. So also, by means of the token "Let me survive e" C_2 gave expression to a desire that was subsequently satisfied while C_1 gave expression to a desire that was not subsequently satisfied. Thus we reconstruct, on the hypothesis of stage sharing, the intuitive view that C_2 got what he wanted while C_1 did not.

So far, we have met Parfit's objection to the stage-sharing account, and replaced Lewis's argument for this account with an argument from (A*), the counterpart theoretic version of (B*), (C) and the impossibility of complete co-occupancy. A final adjustment or addition to the stage-sharing view comes from (C), the counterpart theoretic version of (B*) and an intuition generated from a variant of the fission case.

Suppose that there is a process known as "brain cleaning", a process by which little bloodclots on the brain's surfaces are cleaned away. In order to get at the clots on the inside surfaces of the hemispheres the corpus callosum and other connective tissue has to be severed, and the hemisphere taken out of the patient and separately cleaned. They are then replaced in the patient, the connective tissue is sown up, and the patient leaves the hospital with a cleaned brain. This way of describing the case embodies the natural intuition that in such cases the patient survives brain cleaning. Barring intermittent existence, the patient survived during the operation, not bilocated in the manner of a universal but in a scattered state. If, during such a brain cleaning, the original debrained body was badly damaged and the cleaned hemispheres were transplanted into a duplicate debrained body our intuition would be the same. As in Shoemaker's case of Brown and Brownson this would be a case of body-transplanting and not brain-transplanting. The original patient would survive as the composite made up of his cleaned brain and the duplicate body. Barring intermittent existence, at one point during the whole operation the original patient is reduced to the condition of a mere scattered brain. That is to say at one point he survives as two separated hemispheres.

Now I do not pretend that this intuition is any more than a judgment about the case, but it is I think the judgment which we are on the whole inclined to make. And here, as opposed to many other bizarre cases, I do not think that we are *over*generalizing from our ordinary practice of re-identifying people, i.e. generalizing in a way that is best traced to the influence of distorting factors.[34] If we then have reason to respect the judgment, (B*), even in its counterpart theoretic form, requires that we read it over into the fission case. For consider: in the brain cleaning case in which the original debrained body is destroyed there is a 'Y'-shaped process ending at a time of which we are inclined to say that the original patient is then surviving in a scattered state. Suppose that the original patient in question is none other than Brown, and then observe that there is no obstacle to supposing that this very 'Y'-shaped process occurs in the fission case, and in a fashion which is no different from the way it was in the brain-cleaning cum transplanting case. But then the counterpart theoretic version of (B*) implies that there is a *third* person in the fission case, one who survives in a scattered state after fission, one who is made up first of the two separated hemispheres taken together and then perhaps of the recipient of the left hemisphere and the recipient of the right hemisphere taken together. This is reminiscent of a view about fission which Wiggins gestured at when he used the analogy of the Pope's crown—a single crown made up of distinct crowns.[35] And, of course, as with each of the responses to the paradox, we have a conflict with at least one of our principles. This time it is with (E): after the fission our third person will be constituted by two independently functioning human bodies.

6.

Principle (B*) may be beginning to look like the villain of the paradoxical piece so that friends of the Closest Continuer Theory, committed as they are to denying (B*), may be congratulating themselves. This would be premature self-congratulation, for we need to examine what would be involved in (B*)'s failure.

One way in which (B*) could fail is if *Extreme Haecceitism* about persons is true, i.e., if the facts of personal identity can float free of any other layer of facts, whether they be facts about the total world process, facts about the persistence of brains, bodies or minds or facts about processes of intermediate extent.[36] If such Extreme Haecceitism is true then the Closest Continuer Theorist, who characteristically takes some such a layer of facts to determine or settle the facts of closest continuation and hence settle the facts of personal identity, is in an embarrassing situation. He must admit that there is no necessary, analytic or conventional connection between any such layer of facts and the facts of personal identity. So there must be many worlds, indistinguishable from ours, in which the Closest Continuer Theory is mistaken, worlds in which although the underlying facts determine facts of closest continuation by the relevant parameters, these facts of closest continuation are no guide to the facts of personal identity; there being no regular association between the two kinds of facts. In claiming that this is not true of our world, the Closest Continuer Theorist can only then be understood as putting forward an hypothesis for which he can specify no evidence at all.

He might try to defend the Closest Continuer Theory by resort to a strategy reminiscent of Strawson on induction.[37] He might insist that it is simply part of what we mean by "reasonable" that it is reasonable to regard the closest continuer of a given person as that person. However the situation is not clearly parallel to the case of induction. The Closest Continuer Theorist who denies (B) on the grounds that Extreme Haecceitism is true is offering just one among several alternative accounts of our practice, accounts which agree over the non-puzzling cases which dominate in everyday life but accounts which deviate in the fission case by denying (C), (D) or (E). These accounts can be made to give the same answers as the Closest Continuer Theory in the ordinary range of cases, since it can be allowed that only in a special case like that of fission does the particular principle denied, be it (C) or (D) or (E), find a counterexample. In the presence of such competing theories, the Closest Continuer Theorist's claim that it is part of what we mean by "reasonable" that it is reasonable, even in the fission case, to regard the closest continuer of a given individual as that individual will not be very plausible.

Let us consider a more plausible account which the Closest Continuer Theorist has of how it is that (B*) is false. This account has it that there is a non-accidental connection between facts about certain underlying processes which make for close continuation and facts of personal identity, a connection of the general sort which (B*) expresses. However just because we will not tolerate a description of a situation as one in which a person survives twice over (in whatever sense) (B*) must be modified so as not to have this consequence in the fission case. The paradox of fission simply demonstrates this. While (B*) holds up in the ordinary range of cases, in which we have at most one excellent continuer of any given individual, it fails in any case in which there is a branching process which provides two or more excellent continuers. (Mutatis mutandis for fusion.)

This sort of account does have some plausibility. But evidently it does not especially distinguish the solution to the paradox offered by the Closest Continuer Theorist. The account has its analogue for each of the responses to the paradox which we have canvassed. Thus to take what will seem to some to be the most extreme example, the defender of the view that in the fission case Brown survives spatially separated from himself in the manner of a universal will say that (C) is true when restricted to ordinary cases, cases in which only non-branching patterns of continuation occur.

The non-partisan description of the situation seems to be this: the restrictions of (B*), (C), (D) and (E) to ordinary cases are very plausibly taken to be true. Our judgments of personal identity in the ordinary cases conform to the patterns which these principles predict. But when the principles are unrestricted and applied jointly to the fission case and its ilk they produce paradox. On the strength of our ordinary practice of re-identifying people and the fact that relative

to this ordinary practice (B) through (E) hold up, we do not have sufficient reason to subscribe to unrestricted versions of these principles.
To justify doing that we would have to show that their holding in
our ordinary practice does not depend on contingent features of the
cases we ordinarily consider. However the fission case suggests just
the opposite. By abstracting from the contingent feature of non-
branching continuity the fission case shows that we cannot subscribe
to the unrestricted versions of *all* of these principles. There is no consistent way of extending to the fission case *just* the principles which
hold up in everyday cases. So there is no determinate sense to be
made of the idea of what we *would* say about the fission case even
if we were fully lucid about our ordinary practice of re-identifying
people. We can make sense of what we *could* say, of there being
a number of legitimate consistent extensions of our ordinary practice, each one restricting some principle which holds up in that ordinary practice.

Absent some fact of the matter independent of our practice and
counterfactual extensions of it, a fact which makes it the case that
(B*) or (C) or (D) or (E) is *the* principle that is false when left
unrestricted, we should regard the fission case as a case of indeterminacy, a case in which there is no fact of the matter about personal
identity. Each of the restricted and consistent extensions of our practice to the fission case are associated with concepts of personal identity which are good competitors to be associated with our use of the
expression "is the same person as". Since the question of survival
in the fission case is answered differently by each of the competitors
there is no fact of the matter about how or whether one survives
fission. Personal identity is here an indeterminate matter.

Of course I do not rule out the possibility that a good pragmatic
case is made for *adopting* one or another of the competing concepts
of personal identity which gives a determinate answer in the fission
case. Perhaps adopting a particular one of these concepts makes practical matters go more smoothly. Then the question is the broadly
pragmatic question about how to extend our practice to serve our
interests. The answer to the question is not determined by the practice itself.

How stands the Simple View with its claims that personal identity
is never an indeterminate matter, never a matter of convention and
never a partial matter? These too are generalizations which hold up
in our ordinary practice. We naturally can be led to generalize beyond

our ordinary practice, perhaps even by employing a metaphysical picture of ourselves as indivisible soul pellets to explain and justify the generalization. But, as was suggested above, we are not in our ordinary practice tracing such soul pellets; the generalization and the metaphysical model backing it are not guiding our practice but are more or less epiphenomenal with respect to it. So even if we held the Simple View, and now need to revise or abandon it, this prompts no deep revision in our ordinary practice of identifying and re-identifying ourselves and each other. Nor I think does it call for deep revisions in the way in which we care about personal identity. More likely than not if we held the Simple View it was largely epiphenomenal to our actual practical concerns.

By way of an analogy with Revisionists who hope to make much of the failure of the Simple View I am reminded of John Mackie on colour.[38] Mackie held that we think of color as a feature of the surfaces of objects which can exactly resemble the intrinsic qualities of our color experience. Given Mackie's view a Revisionist might conclude that since science finds no such feature on the surfaces of objects but only complex patterns of molecular bonding nothing in the world corresponds to our conception of colour. So the world is colourless. The Revisionist strategy falls foul of an account of colour which defines what it is for objects to have particular colours in terms of our actual and counterfactual sensory responses under appropriate conditions. Such an internalist account of the facts of colour can allow that we might have a false picture of what it is for an object to be coloured. The false picture is largely epiphenomenal to our sensory responses and our practice of classifying objects in respect of colour as a result of these sensory responses. The Revisionist about colour will find it very hard going against such a combination of views. Here I intend to suggest the analogous combination of views about personal identity.[39]

Notes

1. Clearly the worry here expressed applies to that fashionable eliminativism about the psychological attitudes which stems from regarding "folk psychology" as a term-defining theory which has the singular vice of being largely false. A typical response is to accept the picture of folk psychology as a term-defining theory, not concede that it is *largely* false and conclude that there are legitimate restrictions of the theory— i.e. large enough sub parts of it—within which the constituent proposi-

tional attitude terms have extensions. But then the clear implication is that there are legitimate restrictions of the theory within which the terms have no extensions. So it's hard to see how the theorist who takes this line will be able non-artificially to claim that it is determinately true that people have beliefs. Better to take a different tack and examine the possibility that folk psychology is not a term-defining theory at all but a collection of rules of thumb which have accumulated as a result of a successful practice not itself guided by theory, *viz.* the practice of understanding each other as believers and desirers. We can regard ourselves as knowing how to do this without needing to assume we know a lot of propositional truths.

2. See "Personal Identity", *Philosophical Review* 80 (1971); "Later Selves and Moral Principles" in A. Montefiore (ed.), *Philosophy and Personal Relations* (McGill, Montreal, 1973); "Lewis, Perry and What Matters" in A.O. Rorty (ed.), *The Identities of Persons* (Berkeley: University of California Press, 1976); *Reasons and Persons* (especially Part III) (Oxford University Press, 1984).

3. See *Reasons and Persons, ibid.*, pp. 199-302.

4. See "Personal Identity", *op. cit.*, section 1.

5. The contrast between Simple and Complex views introduced in "Later Selves and Moral Principles", *op. cit.*, is replaced by the contrast between Reductionist and Non-Reductionist Views of personal identity in *Reasons and Persons, op. cit.* In the later work the Non-Reductionist View is associated with the Further Fact View which in its turn is assimilated to the view that we are separately existing entities, entities whose persistence through time is not an indeterminate matter.

6. "Personal Identity", *Proceedings of the Aristotelian Society* 74, 1973-4.

7. S. Shoemaker and R. Swinburne, *Personal Identity (Great Debates in Philosophy)* (Basil Blackwell Ltd., 1984).

8. *Reasons and Persons, op. cit.*, pp. 209-217.

9. See "Human Beings", *The Journal of Philosophy*, 84, 1987.

10. For a discussion of these matters see Charles E. Marks, *Commissurotomy, Consciousness and Unity of Mind* (M.I.T., Bradford Books, 1981).

11. See *Self-Knowledge and Self-Identity* (Cornell University Press, 1963), pp. 23-4.

12. *Substance and Sameness* (Oxford University Press, 1980), pp. 71, 91, 96, 105.

13. *Ibid.*, p. 97. Actually, Wiggins makes this claim specifically about artefacts.

14. I give the qualification only to suggest that even those who believe that the a priori/empirical distinction should be replaced by the idea of claims being more or less insulated from empirical refutation can make something of the point I express by means of the contrast between the empirical and the conceptually necessary. Perhaps a way of putting the point in their terms would be this: (β) is more immune to refutation than the claims about the independence of hemispheric functioning. So the problem of fission has to do with a central part of the web of belief which we would hold to pretty much however things went in more peripheral areas.

15. By 'unworkable' I here mean 'not such that some close approximation to it gives an acceptable answer in the case under consideration'. As will emerge, my own view about the fission case is that there are several ways of making the concept of personal identity "work" in that case and no need to choose between them.

16. *Op. cit.*, Section 1.

17. For a discussion of Swinburne's arguments see my review of S. Shoemaker and R. Swinburne, *op. cit.*, forthcoming in *The Philosophical Review*, 1987.

18. *Individuals* (Methuen, London, 1959), CH3.

19. See "Human Beings", *op. cit.*

20. Wiggins, *op. cit.*, pp. 95, 105. Robert Nozick's view is put forward in *Philosophical Explanations* (Harvard, Belknap Press, 1981), Chapter 1, "Personal Identity Through Time".

21. *Reasons and Persons*, p. 267.

22. This point has also been noted by Sydney Shoemaker *op. cit.* and H. Noonan "The Closest Continuer Theory of Identity", *Inquiry*, 1986. Shoemaker (wrongly to my mind) takes the difficulty to show that there is no substance to the idea that personal identity is an intrinsic matter.

23. But in fact it is still too strong, though the difficulty I have in mind is not germane to the main argument of the paper. Suppose that x has subparts y and z such that the survival of y or z could secure x's survival. Suppose that the process which secures x's survival in the actual world includes as proper sub-processes a process which secures y's survival and a process which secures z's survival. Then on the assumption that for each of these subprocesses there is some world in which they occur and are therein intrinsically as they actually are and therein secure the survival of x, (B*) gives a very strange result. In the actual world x is multiply located within himself; first in the improper subpart which makes up the whole of him, next in the proper subpart which is y and finally in the proper subpart which is z. This is intolerable—even though we might regard a wooden cube as surviving if its edges were ever so slightly shaved down we do not regard the unshaved cube as already consisting of the subpart which is it minus the anticipated shavings. In identifying the extent of the cube we look for the most inclusive cube-shaped bit of wood. Mutatis mutandis in the case of persons. So we should modify the consequent of (B*) so that it reads "in any world w' in which p occurs and is intrinsically as it is in w and *is not a part of some more inclusive process which secures the survival of a person*, in that world w' p secures the survival of x". I thank Mark Hinchliff for raising this nice problem.

24. *Philosophical Explanations*, *op. cit.*, p. 114.

25. For a defense of this way of understanding temporal and modal qualifications see my "Is There a Problem About Persistence?" in *Proceedings of the Aristotelian Society, Supplementary Volume*, 1987.

26. For counterpart theory see David Lewis "Counterpart Theory and Quantified Modal Logic", *Journal of Philosophy* 65, 1968, reprinted in his *Philosophical Papers, Volume 1* (Oxford University Press, 1983).

27. See "Survival and Identity" in A.O. Rorty (ed.), *op. cit.*, reprinted in *Philosophical Papers, Volume 1*.
28. *Ibid.*, pp. 55-56.
29. *Ibid.*, pp. 65-67.
30. Two caveats: first, one can allow the stage-sharing story without thinking that the unity relation among stages is to be given in terms of psychological continuity and connectedness. Bodily continuity may be more basic. But in any case one could take persisting people as unproblematic and just have the unity relation be the relation which holds between stages when and only where they are stages of (the history of) a single person. As this talk of histories suggests, I am not really happy with thinking of persons as temporally extended, but that is for reasons having nothing to do with fission.
31. See "Lewis, Perry and What Matters", *op. cit.*, and Lewis's "Postscript to Survival and Identity" in his *Philosophical Papers, Volume 1, op. cit.*
32. *Ibid.*, p. 73.
33. *Ibid.*, p. 74-75.
34. For a discussion of these matters see "Human Beings", *op. cit.*
35. D. Wiggins, *Spatio-temporal Continuity and Identity* (Basil Blackwell Ltd., 1967), p. 40.
36. For discussions of Haecceitism in its various forms see David Kaplan, "How to Russell a Frege-Church", *Journal of Philosophy* 72, 1975; Robert Adams, "Primitive Thisness and Primitive Identity", *Journal of Philosophy* 76, 1979; and David Lewis, *On the Plurality of Worlds* (Basil Blackwell Ltd., 1986), pp. 220-248.
37. See P. F. Stawson *Introduction to Logical Theory* (Methuen, London, 1952), Chapter 9.
38. See J. L. Mackie *Hume's Moral Theory* (Routledge Kegan Paul, 198), pp. 32, 60-1, 73-4.
39. I wish to thank Mark Hinchliff, David Lewis, Crispin Wright and Michael Smith for useful discussions on these matters.

Philosophical Perspectives, 3
Philosophy of Mind and Action Theory, 1989

WHEN IS THE WILL FREE?

Peter van Inwagen
Syracuse University

There is, it seems to me, something that might be called an "orthodox" or "classical" tradition in the history of thinking about the problem of free will and determinism. This tradition, as I see it, descends from Hobbes through Locke and Hume and Mill to the present day. I say "it seems to me" and "as I see it" because I am no historian and I freely grant that what appears to my untutored mind to be "the classical tradition" in the debate about free will and determinism may be an artifact of certain historians—or even of the editors of certain anthologies. (And, of course, in identifying this tradition as "classical," I exhibit the Anglo-Saxon bias that my education was designed to inculcate: Bergson, Heidegger, and Sartre are not going to appear in *my* list of the members of anything called "the classical tradition.")

However this may be, I speak as a member of this tradition, and I want to begin by describing its presuppositions—*my* presuppositions.

According to "the classical tradition," the history of the problem of free will and determinism is, primarily, the story of a debate between two schools of philosophers, the "compatibilists" and the "incompatibilists"; that is between those who hold that free will is compatible with determinism and those who hold that free will is incompatible with determinism. Now I am going to have almost nothing to say about determinism in this paper. In fact, I am not going to talk about the problem of free will and determinism—or not directly about it. I begin with a brief characterization of the history of this problem because, while the paper is not about the problem of free will and determinism, it presupposes the correctness of a certain way of looking at that problem. I do not propose to defend that way of looking at the problem—the way adherence to which defines membership in what I am pleased to call "the classical tradition"—, but I do want to make it clear what that way of looking at the problem is, and that it is my way. Since I shall have almost nothing to say about determinism, I shall not attempt to give any very careful explanation of this important idea. I will say only this. Determinism is the thesis that the past and the laws of nature together *determine* a unique future, that only one future is consistent with the past and the laws of nature. I am, however, going to have a great deal to say about free will and I will lay out in some detail the concept that the classical or orthodox tradition associates with the words 'free will'.

The term 'free will' is a philosophical term of art. (It is true that this term occurs in ordinary English, but its occurrence is pretty much restricted to the phrase 'of his own free will'—which means, more or less, 'uncoerced'. If someone uses the words 'free will' and does not use them within this phrase, he is almost certainly a participant in a philosophical discussion.) The first thing to realize about the use of the words 'free will' by philosophers belonging to the classical tradition is that, *now* at least, these words are a mere label for a certain feature, or alleged feature, of human beings and other rational agents, a label whose sense is not determined by the meanings of the individual words 'free' and 'will'. In particular, the ascription of "free will" to an agent by a current representative of the classical tradition does not imply that the agent has a "faculty" called 'the will'. It was not always so. Once upon a time, to say that X "had free will" was to imply that X had something called a 'will' and that this will was not only unimpeded by external circumstances (in which case the agent X *himself* was called 'free'), but that X's internal constitution left him "free" to "will" in various alternative ways. (The title of this paper is a relic of those times.) A tradition, however, is a changing thing, and the classical tradition has abandoned these implications of the words "free will." When a *current* representative of the classical tradition says of, e.g., Mrs. Thatcher, that she "has free will," he means that she is at least sometimes in the following situation: She is contemplating incompatible courses of action A and B (lecturing the Queen and holding her tongue, say), and she *can* pursue the course of action A and *can also* pursue the course of action B.

Now the word 'can' is one of the trickiest of all the little philosophically interesting Anglo-Saxon words. It is not only ambiguous; it is ambiguous in a rather complicated way. Accordingly, representatives of the classical tradition, when they are explaining the sense of their term of art 'free will', generally prefer to use some other words, in addition to 'can', to get their point across, rather as if they were trying to convey what someone looked like by displaying a photograph *and* a painted portrait *and* a pen-and-ink caricature. They say not only 'can do A and can also do B', but 'is able to do A and is also able to do B', and 'has it within his power to do A and has it within his power to do B', and 'has a choice about whether to do A or to do B'. They may also use language that is not ordinary English at all, but which seems somehow useful in conveying the sense they intend. They may, for example, talk of a sheaf of alternative possible futures that confront the agent, and say that he has free will just in the case that more than one of these futures is "open" to him or "accessible" to him.

Compatibilists, then, say that "free will" in this sense can exist in a deterministic world, and incompatibilists say that it cannot. The classical tradition sees the problem of free will and determinism as centered round the debate between the compatibilists and the incompatibilists. But what is at stake in this debate? Why should anyone care whether we have free will (in this special sense)? The answer is this: We care about morality, or many of us do, and, according to the classical tradition, there is an intimate connection between "free will" and morality. The connection is complicated, and various representatives of the classical tradition would describe it differently. But the following statement would, I think, be accepted by everyone within the classical tradition. Most within the traditional would want to say more; some *much* more. But this "highest common factor" by itself explains why many people care about whether we have free will.

> Some states of affairs are bad. They ought not to exist. And among these bad states of affairs are some that *are the fault of* certain human beings. These human beings are *to be blamed* for those states of affairs. The Nazis, for example, are to be blamed for the death camps: the existence of those camps is *their fault*. The Kennedy and Johnson and Nixon administrations are to be blamed for the U.S. involvement and actions in Vietnam. They (and perhaps others, but they

at least) can be *held to account* for that involvement and many of its consequences. On a more homely and personal level, our profession is to blame for the fact that many young men and women are being graduated from universities who cannot compose an English sentence or tell you who Galileo was. And, doubtless, each reader of this paper knows of bad states of affairs that are his fault and his alone. But if there were no free will—if no one were able to act otherwise—then no state of affairs would be anyone's fault. No one would ever be morally accountable for anything. The actions of some people might indeed be among the causes of various bad states of affairs, but those things they caused would never be their fault. For example, suppose a father has raped his nine-year-old daughter and, as a result, she has suffered immediate physical pain and terror and has experienced life-long psychological and emotional disorders. Unless the father had at least some measure of free will, the pain and terror and the rest are not his fault. He cannot be blamed for them. They are not something for which he can be held to account.

I have not argued for this position. I am only reminding you of what the classical tradition says about the relationship between being able to do otherwise than one does and moral accountability. It is because, rightly or wrongly, the members of the classical tradition believe in this relationship that they think it is an important question whether we have free will. Almost all of the members of the classical tradition have in fact believed in free will, although there are exceptions. Baron d'Holbach believed that determinism was true and that free will was incompatible with determinism and that there was thus no free will. C.D. Broad believed that free will was incompatible with both determinism and indeterminism, and was thus impossible. But d'Holbach and Broad were exceptions. Almost all of the members of the classical tradition believe in free will. What they differ about is what free will *is*—that is, about what it is to be able to do otherwise. Most incompatibilists, at least among trained philosophers, believe in free will. All compatibilists I am aware of believe in free will; there's not much point in being a compatibilist and not believing in free will.

Before going further, I want to point out what seems to me to be a blunder made by some writers on the problem of free will and determinism. Some writers speak of an "incompatibilist sense of 'can do otherwise'" and a "compatibilist sense of 'can do otherwise'." But when English-speaking compatibilists and incompatibilists argue about whether people could act otherwise in a deterministic world, they are using the words 'could act otherwise' in exactly the same sense. Otherwise they wouldn't be disagreeing about anything, would they? Each of them, being a speaker of English, knows what 'could have', 'was able to', and so on, mean when they are used in everyday life, and each means to be, and is, using these words in that everyday sense. Their case may be compared with the case of the dualist and the materialist in the philosophy of mind. Each uses phrases like 'feels pain' and 'is thinking about Vienna' in the same *sense*—the sense provided by the English language—though the two of them have radically opposed opinions as to the nature of the events and processes to which these terms apply. Similarly with the compatibilist and the incompatibilist: the two of them use phrases like 'could have acted otherwise' in just the same sense—the sense provided by the English language—and disagree about whether that one sense expresses something that could obtain in a deterministic world. Now it may be that a particular compatibilist or incompatibilist has a mistaken *theory* about what 'could act otherwise' means. But, in such a case, that philosopher does not *himself* mean by 'could act otherwise' what his mistaken theory says these words mean. For example, suppose that a certain compatibilist has published an essay the burden of which is that '*x* could act otherwise' means '*x* would act otherwise if he chose to'. And suppose that this is wrong: suppose that this is not a correct account of the meaning of the English phrase 'could act otherwise'. Then that compatibilist is not only wrong about what others mean by 'could act otherwise'; he is also wrong about what *he* means by these words. (Compare this case: if I mistakenly think that 'knowledge' means 'justified true belief', it does not follow that that is what I mean by 'knowledge'.) If philosophers always used words to mean what their theories said those words meant, no philosopher would ever revise a definition because of a counter-example. But this occasionally happens. Now if all anyone means by talk of an "incompatibilist sense" or a "compatibilist sense" of the central terms in the free-will debate is that philosophers have sometimes proposed theories about the meanings of these terms, theories that support compatibilism (or, it may be, incompatibilism),

I have no objection. But then we must remember that it remains an open question whether compatibilists use these terms in a "compatibilist sense" and whether incompatibilists use these terms in an "incompatibilist sense."

Finally, it is this single sense of 'can do otherwise', the sense provided by ordinary English, that compatibilists and incompatibilists contend is so intimately connected with the possibility of moral accountability. This is the classical tradition.

Let me now turn to my title. My question is, just how often is it that we are able to do otherwise? A belief in one's free will is the belief that one can sometimes do otherwise. But then it is consistent to say of X that he has free will despite the fact that he can almost never do otherwise. The central thesis of this paper is that while it is open to the compatibilist to say that human beings are very often—hundreds of times every day—able to do otherwise, the incompatibilist must hold that being able to do otherwise is a comparatively rare condition, even a *very* rare condition.

It is almost self-evident that compatiblism entails that being able to do otherwise is as common as pins. Or, at any rate, it is evident that typical versions of compatibilism entail this. Typical versions of compatibilism entail that being able to do otherwise is some sort of conditional causal power. For example, one primitive version of compatibilism—a version pretty generally agreed to be unsatisfactory— holds that for one to have been able to act differently is for one to have been such that one would have acted differently if one had chosen to act differently. (More generally, for one to be able to do A is for one to be such that one would do A if one chose to.) And who could deny that at most moments each of us is such that he would then be acting differently if he had chosen to act differently?

The case is otherwise with incompatibilism. To see why this is so, let us remind ourselves of why people become incompatibilists. They become incompatibilists because they are convinced by a certain sort of argument. My favorite version of it—which I reproduce from my book *An Essay on Free Will*[1]—turns on the notion of "having a choice about." Let us use the operator 'N' in this way: 'Np' stands for 'p and no one[2] has, or ever had, any choice about whether p'. The validity of the argument turns on the validity of two rules of deduction involving 'N':

Rule Alpha: From $\Box p$ deduce Np. ('$\Box$' represents "standard necessity": truth in all possible circumstances.)
Rule Beta: From Np and N($p \supset q$) deduce Nq.

Now let 'P' represent any true proposition whatever. Let 'L' represent the conjunction into a single proposition of all laws of nature. Let 'P$_0$' represent a proposition that gives a complete and correct description of the whole world at some instant in the remote past— before there were any human beings. If determinism is true, then $\Box$(P$_0$ & L. $\supset$ P). We argue from this consequence of determinism as follows.

1. $\Box$(P$_0$ & L. $\supset$ P)
2. $\Box$(P$_0$ $\supset$ (L $\supset$ P))   1; modal and sentential logic
3. N(P$_0$ $\supset$ (L $\supset$ P))   2; Rule Alpha
4. NP$_0$ Premise
5. N(L $\supset$ P)   3, 4; Rule Beta
6. NL   Premise
7. NP   5, 6; Rule Beta

If this argument is sound, then determinism entails that no one has or ever had any choice about anything. Since one part of "anything" is what any given person does, this amounts to saying that determinism entails that no one could ever have done otherwise. No one, I think, could dispute the two premises or Rule Alpha. The question of the soundness of the argument thus comes down to the question whether Rule Beta is valid. It is not my purpose in this paper to defend Beta. I reproduce this argument only to point out the central role that Beta (or something equivalent to it) plays in the incompatibilist's reasons for accepting his theory. I will go so far as to say that, in my view, one could have no reason for being an incompatibilist if one did not accept Beta. If one accepts Beta, one should be an incompatibilist, and if one is an incompatibilist, one should accept Beta.

What I propose to show in the sequel is this: Anyone who accepts Beta should concede that one has precious little free will, that rarely, if ever, is anyone able to do otherwise than he in fact does. I shall argue for this position as follows. I shall first show that if Rule Beta is valid, then no one is able to perform an act he considers morally reprehensible. I shall then extend this argument; by a similar sort of reasoning, I shall show that, given Rule Beta, no one is able to do anything if he wants very much *not* to do that thing and has no countervailing desire to do it. Finally, by more or less the same reasoning, I shall show that the validity of Rule Beta entails that if we regard an act as the one obvious thing or the only sensible thing to do, we cannot do anything but that thing.

In *Elbow Room*[3], Daniel Dennett has argued eloquently that he is simply *unable* to do anything he regards as morally reprehensible. Compatibilists may feel a bit uneasy about agreeing with Dennett about this. Really simple-minded and primitive compatibilists, those who hold that one can do something just in the case that one would do it if one chose to, *must* disagree with Dennett. Take Dennett's primary example, the torture of an innocent victim in return for a small sum. Dennett will concede, I am sure, that we can easily imagine situations in which he, being more or less as he is now, would succeed in carrying out such torture *if he chose to*. His point is that, being as he is, he would never choose to. *I* think that this is a perfectly good point, but, of course, it is a point that must be disallowed by the primitive compatibilist who identifies the ability to perform an act with the absence of environmental impediments to performing that act. Leaving aside the question of what more sophisticated compatibilists might say about such cases, let us turn to the incompatibilists. They, I maintain, must agree with Dennett. Dennett uses himself as an example. I will use myself. Let us consider some act I regard as reprehensible. I might, like Dennett, use torture as an example, but my acquaintance with torture is purely literary, and I should like to try to avoid that dreamlike sense of unreality that is so common in philosophical writing about morality. I will pick an example that touches my own experience. Recently, a member of my university, speaking on the floor of a College meeting, deliberately misrepresented the content of the scholarly work of a philosopher (who was not present), in an attempt to turn the audience against him. Suppose such a course of action were proposed to me. Suppose someone were to say to me, "Look, you don't want Smith to be appointed Chairman of the Tenure Committee, so tell everyone that he said in print that all sociologists are academic charlatans. (I've got a quotation you can use that seems to say that if you take it out of context.) Then the sociologists will block the appointment." Call the act that is proposed A. I regard lying about someone's scholarly work as reprehensible. And, while I should prefer not to see Smith appointed, I certainly wouldn't *think* of blocking his appointment by any such means. In short, I regard the proposed act A as being indefensible. (I mean in the actual circumstances: I might lie about the content of someone's scholarly work to prevent World War III, but the start of World War III is not *in fact* what hangs on my performing or not performing A.) I may even say that I regard doing A as being "indefensible, given the totality of information available to me." And, of course, I do not so regard *not* doing A: there's nothing much to be said against that. We may also suppose that I am unable (as things stand) to search out any further relevant information—the vote will come in a moment, and I must speak at once if my speaking is to affect it. Now consider the following conditional:

C If X regards A as an indefensible act, given the totality of relevant information available to him, and if he has no way of getting further relevant information, and if he lacks any positive desire to do A, and if he sees no objection to *not* doing A (again, given the totality of relevant information available to him),
then X is not going to do A.

What is the modal status of *C*? It seems to me to be something very like a necessary truth. What would be a conceivable circumstance in which its antecedent is true and its consequent false (i.e., X proceeds to do A)? If X changes his mind about the indefensibility of A (perhaps because of the intervention of some "outside" agent or force, or because of an access of new information, or because he suddenly sees some unanticipated implication of the information available to him)? If X just goes berserk? If so, build the non-occurrence of these things into the antecedent of *C*: he is not going to change his mind about the indefensibility of A and he is not going to go berserk.

It seems to me that there is no possible world in which C is false. What would it be *like* for *C* to be false? Imagine that X *does* do A. We ask him, "Why did you do A? I thought you said a moment ago that doing A would be reprehensible." He replies:

Yes. I did think that. I still think it. I thought that at every moment up to the time at which I performed A; I thought that while I was performing A; I thought it immediately afterward. I never wavered in my conviction that A was an irremediably reprehensible act. I never thought there was the least excuse for doing A. And don't misunderstand me: I am not reporting a conflict between duty and inclination. I didn't *want* to do A. I never had the least desire to do A. And don't understand me as saying that my limbs and vocal cords suddenly began to obey some will other than my own. It was *my* will that they obeyed. It is true without qualification that *I* did A, and it is true without qualification that I *did* A.

This strikes me as absolutely impossible. It's not, of course, impossible for someone to say these words—just as it's not impossible for someone to say, "I've just drawn a round square." But it is impossible for someone to say these words and thereby say something true.

Now consider the proposition that I consider the act A to be indefensible. I think it's pretty clear that I have—right now—no choice about how I feel about A. Like most of my beliefs and attitudes, it's something I just find myself with. (Which is not to say that I don't think that this attitude is well-grounded, appropriate to its object, and so on.) If you offered me a large sum of money, or if you promised—and I believed you could deliver—the abolition of war, if only I were to change my attitude toward A, I should not be able to take you up on this offer, however much I might want to. It is barely conceivable that I have the ability to change my attitude toward A over some considerable stretch of time, but we're not talking about some considerable stretch of time; we're talking about right now.

Let us now examine a certain Beta-like rule of inference, which I shall call Beta-prime:

From N x,p and N $x,(p \supset q)$ deduce N x,q.

Here 'N' is a two-place operator, and 'N x,p' abbreviates 'p and x now has no choice about whether p'. The one-place operator 'N' served my purposes in *An Essay on Free Will*, because there the premises of my argument concerned only propositions that were related in just the same way to all human beings, past, present, and future: laws of nature and propositions about the state of the world before there were any human beings. It is clear, I think, that whatever relation any given human being bears to such a proposition, any other given human being bears that relation, too. Since I was interested only in such propositions, I employed the impersonal and timeless one-place 'N'; it was simpler to do so. The arguments I wish to consider in the present paper, however, involve propositions about particular human beings and what they do at particular times, and their attitudes toward what they do at those times. For that reason, I need to use the person- and time-relative rule Beta-prime, and I must forego the convenience of Beta. And Beta-prime seems hardly less evident than Beta. The same intuitive considerations that support Beta seem to support Beta-prime, and it is hard to imagine a philosopher who accepts Beta but rejects Beta-prime.

Consider the following instance of Beta-prime:

N I, I regard A as indefensible
N I, (I regard A as indefensible ⊃ I am not going to do A)
hence, N I, I am not going to do A.

In this argument, 'I regard A as indefensible' is short for 'I regard A as an indefensible act, given the totality of relevant information available to me, and I have no way of getting further relevant information, and I lack any positive desire to do A, and I see no objection to *not* doing A, given the totality of relevant information available to me.' (Compare the antecedent of the conditional *C*, above.) The conclusion of this argument, written out in full, is 'I am not going to do A and I now have no choice about whether I am not going to do A'. Now the second conjunct of this sentence is a bit puzzling. But we may note that the sentences 'I have a [or *no*] choice about whether *p*' and 'I have a [or *no*] choice about whether not-*p*' would seem to be equivalent. Therefore, we may read the conclusion of the argument as 'I am not going to do A and I now have no choice about whether I am going to do A'. (The reason the original version of the conclusion seems puzzling is this: the mind looks for a function for that final 'not' to perform and finds none.)

The first premise of this argument is true, because, as we have seen, I (right now, at any rate) have no choice about whether I regard A as indefensible. The second premise is true because as we have seen, the conditional 'I regard A as indefensible ⊃ I am not going to do A' is a necessary truth, and no one has any choice about the truth-value of a necessary truth.

The general lesson is: if I regard a certain act as indefensible, then it follows not only that I *shall not* perform that act but that I *can't* perform it. (Presumably, 'I am not going to do A and I have no choice about whether I am going to do A' is equivalent to 'I can't do A'.)

This conclusion is not intuitively implausible. To say that you can do A (are able to do A, have it within your power to do A) is to say something like this: there is a sheaf of alternative futures spread out before you; in some of those futures you do A; and some at least of those futures in which you do A are "open" to you or "accessible" to you. Now if this picture makes sense (as a picture; it's only a picture), it would seem to make sense to ask what these futures are like. You say you can do A; well, what would it be like if you did? You say that a future in which you do A is "open" to you or "accessible" to you? Well, in what circumstances would you find yourself if you "got into" or "gained access to" such a future? If you can't give a coherent answer to this question, that, surely, would cast considerable doubt on your claim to be able to do A.

And suppose I do regard doing A as indefensible (for me, here, now). Then, I think, I cannot give a coherent description of a future (one coherently connected with the present) in which I proceed to do A. I have already considered what such an attempt would sound like ("Yes. I did think that...") and have rejected it—rightly—as incoherent.

We must conclude, therefore, that (given the validity of Beta-prime) I *cannot* perform an act I regard as indefensible, and that this is a perfectly intuitive thesis. Its connection with incompatibilism is displayed in the following argument.

(1) If the rule Beta-prime is valid, I cannot perform an act I regard as indefensible.

(2) If the rule Beta is valid, the rule Beta-prime is valid.

(3) Free will is incompatible with determinism only if Beta is valid.

hence,

(4) If free will is incompatible with determinism, then I cannot perform an act I regard as indefensible.

Throughout this little argument, 'I cannot perform an act I regard as indefensible' is to be understood in a *de re*, not a *de dicto* sense. It does not mean, 'Not possible: I perform an act I regard as indefensible'; it means, 'For any act *x*, if I regard *x* as indefensible, then I do not have it within my power to perform *x*'. (I don't mean to deny the *de dicto* statement; it is in fact true, but it doesn't figure in the argument.)

The defense of premise (1) of this argument has been the main task of the paragraphs preceding the argument.

Premise (2) seems undeniable because, as I have said, the intuitions that support Beta also support Beta-prime.

Premise (3) can be defended on this ground: the only reason known for accepting incompatibilism is that it follows from Beta. This, of course, does not *prove* that (3) is true. But it is unlikely that anyone would accept incompatibilism and reject Beta.

Let us now leave the topic of indefensibility and turn to desire—to cases of simple, personal desire having no moral dimension whatever.

Suppose that someone has an (occurrent) desire to perform some act. Suppose that this desire is very, very strong, and that he has no countervailing desire of any sort. (We have considered the case in which duty is unopposed by inclination. We now turn to the case in which inclination is unopposed by inclination.) Consider the case of poor Nightingale in C.P. Snow's novel *The Masters*. Nightingale wants to be a Fellow of the Royal Society—in the idiom of the 1980s, he wants this distinction so badly he can taste it. Every year, on the Royal Society's election day, Nightingale strides out to the porter's lodge of his Cambridge college and leaves *strictest* instructions that, if a telegram arrives for him, he is to be notified *immediately*. (He threatens the porter with summary dismissal if there is the slightest delay.) Now suppose that poor Nightingale, on the day of the election, is sitting in his rooms biting his nails and daydreaming about being able to call himself 'F.R.S.'. The telephone rings. He snatches it from its cradle and bawls, "Nightingale here," doubtless deafening his caller.

What I want to know is: *Could* he have refrained from answering the telephone? Was he able not to touch it? Did he have it within his power to let it ring till it fell silent? If what we have said above (in connection with indefensibility) is correct, he could have refrained from answering the telephone only if we can tell a coherent story (identical with the story we *have* told up to the point at which the telephone rings) in which he *does* refrain from answering the telephone. Can we? Well, we might tell a story in which, just as the telephone rings, Nightingale undergoes a sudden religious conversion, like Saul on the road to Damascus: All in a moment, his most fundamental values are transformed and he suddenly sees the Fellows of the Royal Society as cocks crowing on a dunghill. Or we might imagine that Nightingale's mind snaps at the moment the telephone rings and he begins to scream and break up furniture and eventually has to be put away. But, remember, neither of these things *did* happen. Let's suppose that they did not even come close to happening. Let's suppose that there was at the moment we are considering no disposition in the mind of God or in Nightingale's psyche (or wherever the impetus to religious conversion is lodged) toward a sudden change in Nightingale's most fundamental values. Let's suppose also that the moment at which the telephone rang was the only moment at which there was *no* possibility of Nightingale's mind snapping—it was a moment of sudden, intense hope, after all. Build these suppositions into our story of how it was with Nightingale up till the moment at which the telephone rang. Build into it also the proposition that no bullet or lightning bolt or heart attack is about to strike Nightingale. Call this story the Telephone Story. I am inclined to think that there is no possible world in which the Telephone Story is true and in which Nightingale does not proceed to answer the telephone. We have the following instance of the rule Beta-prime (imagine that the present moment is the moment at which the telephone rings):

N Nightingale, the Telephone Story is true.
N Nightingale, (the Telephone Story is true ⊃ Nightingale is going to answer the telephone)
hence,
N Nightingale, Nightingale is going to answer the telephone.

The conclusion may be paraphrased, 'Nightingale is going to answer the telephone, and he has no choice about whether to answer the telephone'. And the premises seem undeniably true.

The lesson would seem to be: If the rule Beta-prime is valid, then if a person has done A, and if he wanted very much to do A, and if he had no desires whatever that inclined him towards not doing A, then he was unable not to do A; not doing A was simply not within his power. An argument similar to the one given above shows that the incompatibilist ought to accept this consequence of Beta-prime.

Let us, finally, turn to a third kind of case. On many occasions in life, with little or no deliberation or reflection, we simply do things. We are not, on those occasions, in the grip of some powerful desire, like poor Nightingale. The things just seem—or would seem if we reflected on them at all—to be the obvious things to do in the circumstances. I suppose that on almost all occasions when I have answered the telephone, I have been in more or less this position. On most occasions on which I have answered the telephone, I have not been biting my nails in a passion of anxiety and impatience like Nightingale. On most such occasions, I have not been expecting the telephone to ring (not that its ringing *violates* any expectation of mine, either); with my mind still half on something else, I pick up the receiver and absently say, "Hello?" Obviously, mere habit has a lot to do with this action, but I do not propose to inquire into the nature of habit or into the extent of its involvement in such acts.

Now consider any such occasion on which I answered the telephone. I was sitting at my desk marking papers (say); the telephone rang. (I had not been expecting it to ring. I had no reason to suppose it would *not* ring.) I answered it. Without reflection or deliberation. I simply put down my pen and picked up the receiver.

Can we tell a coherent story in which (in just those circumstances) I simply ignore the telephone and go on marking papers till it stops ringing? Well, we might. Since the matter is a minor one, we need not postulate anything on the order of a religious conversion. We might simply assume that some good reason for not answering the telephone suddenly popped into my mind. (Didn't I have a letter recently from a man who claimed to be able to prove mind-body dualism from the fact that he had made several trips to Mercury by astral projection? Didn't he say that he would be calling me today to make an appointment to discuss the implications of his astral journey for the mind-body problem?) Or, again, we might imagine that I suddenly go berserk and begin to smash furniture. Or we might postulate a sudden Divine or meteorological or ballistic alteration of my circumstances. But we might also imagine that there exists no basis either in my psyche or my environment (at the moment the telephone rings) for any of these things. We may even, if you like, suppose that at the moment the telephone rings it is causally determined that no reason for not answering the phone will pop into my mind in the next few seconds, and that it is causally determined that I shall not go berserk or be struck dead.

This set of statements about me and my situation at the moment the telephone rang (and during the two or three minutes preceding its ringing) we may call the Second Telephone Story. It seems to me to be incoherent to suppose that the Second Telephone Story is true and that I, nevertheless, do not proceed to answer the telephone. And, of course, we have the following instance of Beta-prime:

N I, The Second Telephone Story is true.

N I, (The Second Telephone Story is true $\supset$ I am going to answer the telephone).

hence,

N I, I am going to answer the telephone.

The conclusion may be read: 'I am going to answer the telephone and I have no choice about whether to answer the telephone'. Its connection with incompatibilism can be established by an argument not essentially different from the one already given.

It seems clear that if the premises of this third instance of Rule Beta-prime are true, then we have precious little free will—at least assuming that Beta-prime is valid. For our normal, everyday situation is represented in the Second Telephone Story. It is perhaps not clear how many of the occasions of everyday life count as "making a choice." The light turns green, and the driver, his higher faculties wholly given over to thoughts of revenge or lunch or the Chinese Remainder Theorem puts his car into gear and proceeds with his journey. Did he do something called "making a choice between proceeding and not proceeding"? Presumably not: the whole thing was too automatic. The young public official, unexpectedly and for the first time, is offered a bribe, more money than he has ever thought of having, in return for an unambiguous betrayal of the public trust. After sweating for thirty seconds, he takes the money. Did he make a choice? Of course. Between these two extremes lie all sorts of cases, and it is probably not possible to draw a sharp line between making a choice and acting automatically. But I think it is evident that, wherever we draw the line, we are rarely in a situation in which the need to make a choice confronts us and in which it isn't absolutely clear what choice to make. And this is particularly evident if we count as cases of its being "absolutely clear what choice to make" cases on which it is absolutely clear *on reflection* what choice to make. A man may be seriously considering accepting a bribe until he realizes (after a moment's reflection on the purely factual aspects of his situation) that he couldn't possibly get away with it. Then his course is clear, because it has become clear to him that there is nothing whatever to be said for taking the bribe and a great deal to be said against it. He has not *decided* which of two incompatible objects of desire (riches and self-respect, say) to accept; rather he has *seen* that one of the two—riches—wasn't really there.

There are, therefore, few occasions in life on which—at least after a little reflection and perhaps some investigation into the facts—it isn't absolutely clear what to do. And if the above arguments are correct, then an incompatibilist should believe that on such occasions the agent cannot do anything other than the thing that seems to him to be clearly the only sensible thing.

Now there are *some* occasions on which an agent is confronted with alternatives and it is not clear to him what to do—not even when all the facts are in, as we might put it. What are these cases like? I think we may distinguish three cases.

First, there are what might be called "Buridan's Ass" cases. Someone wants each of two or more incompatible things and it isn't clear which one he should (try to) get, and the things are interchangeable; indeed their very interchangeability is the reason why it isn't clear to him which to try to get. (I include under this heading cases in which the alternatives are importantly different but look indistinguishable to the agent because he unavoidably lacks some relevant datum. Lady-and-tiger cases, we might call them.) Closely allied with Buridan's Ass cases, so closely that I shall not count them constituting a different kind of case, are cases in which the alternatives are not really interchangeable (as are two identical and equally accessible piles of hay) but in which the properties of the alternatives that constitute the whole of the difference between them are precisely the objects of the conflicting desires. We might call such cases "vanilla/chocolate cases." They are often signaled by the use of the rather odd phrase 'I'm trying to decide which one I want'—as opposed to '...which one to have'. I want chocolate and I want vanilla and I can't (or won't or don't want to) have both, and there is no material for deliberation, because my choice will have no consequences beyond my getting vanilla, or, as the case may be, chocolate. (Note, by the way, that someone who is trying to decide whether to have chocolate, to which he sometimes has an allergic reaction, or vanilla, which he likes rather less than chocolate, does not constitute what I am calling a "vanilla/ chocolate case.") Both vanilla/chocolate cases and "Buridan's Ass proper" cases are characterized by simple vacillation. Hobbes's theory of deliberation, whether or not it is satisfactory as a general theory, is pretty uncontroversially correct in these cases. One wavers between the alternatives until one inclination somehow gets the upper hand, and one ends up with a chocolate cone or the bale of hay on the left.

The second class of cases in which it is not obvious what to do (even when all the facts are in) are cases of duty versus inclination. Or, better, cases of general policy versus momentary desire. (For what is in conflict with the agent's momentary desire in such cases need have nothing to do with the agent's perception of his moral duty; it might have no higher object than his long-term self-interest.) I have made for myself a maxim of conduct, and no sooner have I done this than, in St. Paul's words, "...I see another law in my members, warring against the law of my mind." Our story of the young official and the proffered bribe is an example; further examples could be provided by any dieter. This class of cases is characterized by what is sometimes called moral struggle, although, as I have said, not all cases of it involve morality.

The third class of cases involves incommensurable values. (I owe this point to the work of Robert Kane.[4]) A life of rational self-interest (where self-interest is understood to comprise only such ends as food, health, safety, sex, power, money, military glory, and scientific knowledge, and not ends like honor, charity, and decency) versus a life of gift and sacrifice; caring for one's aged mother versus joining the Resistance; popularity with the public versus popularity with the critics. All these are cases of incommensurable values. Other cases would have to be described with more care to make sure that they fit into this class. The case of a young person wondering whether to become a lawyer or a concert pianist might belong to this class. But not if the question were, "In which profession should I make more money?", or "In which profession should I make the greater contribution to human happiness?" In those cases, values are not at issue, but only how maximize certain "given" values; the matter is one of (at best) calculation and (at worst) guesswork. The general form of the question that confronts the agent in true cases of the third type is, What sort of human being shall I be?, or What sort of life shall I live? And, of course, this does not mean, What sort of life is dictated for me by such-and-such values (which I already accept)? *That* question is one to be decided by calculation or guesswork. In cases of the third type, the agent's *present* system of values does not have anything to tell him. His values may tell him to become a professional rather than a laborer and an honest rather than a dishonest professional, but they do not tell him whether to become a lawyer or a pianist. (It may be that the values he could expect to have as a result of the choice would confirm that choice—see Kierkegaard on the moral versus the "aesthetic" life—but that's of no help to him *now*.) The choices in the third category are those that many philosophers call "existential," but I will not use this term, which derives from a truly hopeless metaphysic. As the cases in the first category are characterized by vacillation, and the cases in the second by "moral" struggle, so the cases in the third are characterized by *indecision*—often agonized indecision. The period of indecision, moreover, may be a long one: weeks, months, or even a really significant part of the agent's life.

I believe that these three cases exhaust the types of case in which it is not obvious to the agent, even on reflection, and when all the facts are in, how he ought to choose. Therefore, if our previous arguments are correct, the incompatibilist should believe that we are faced with a genuinely free choice only in such cases. (That is: in these cases, if in any. The incompatibilist may well believe that in some of *these* cases we have no choice about how to act, or, like d'Holbach and C.D. Broad, that even in these cases we have no choice about how to act.) It is not clear to *me* that in cases of the first type— "Buridan's Ass" cases—there is any conceivable basis for saying that we have a choice about what to do. Doubtless when we choose between identical objects symmetrically related to us, or when we choose between objects that differ only in those properties that are the objects of our competing desires, there occurs something like an internal coin-toss. (My guess, for what it's worth, is that we contain a "default" decision-maker, a mechanism that is always "trying" to make decisions—they would be wholly arbitrary decisions if it were allowed to make them—but which is normally overridden by the person; I speculate that when "vacillation" occurs, the person's control over the "default" decision maker is eventually suspended and it is allowed to have its arbitrary way.) I think that it's pretty clear that in such cases one has no choice about how one acts. If one tosses a coin, then one has no choice about whether it will land heads or tails. And, indeed, why should one want such a power—if the alternatives really are indifferent?

If this is correct, then there are at most *two* sorts of occasion on which the incompatibilist can admit that we exercise free will: cases of an actual struggle between perceived moral duty or long-term self-interest, on the one hand, and immediate desire, on the other; and cases of a conflict of incommensurable values.

Both of these sorts of occasion together must account for a fairly

small percentage of the things we do. And, I must repeat, my conclusion is that this is the *largest* class of actions with respect to which
the incompatibilist can say we are free. The argument I have given
shows that the incompatibilist ought to deny that we have free will
on any occasions other than these. It has no tendency to show that
the incompatibilist should say that we do act freely on these occasions. The argument purports to show that, given the principles from
which the incompatibilist derives his position, it is impossible for us
to act freely on occasions other than these. It has no tendency to
show that—given the incompatibilist's principles—it is possible for
us to act freely on any occasion whatever. It's like this: A biologist,
using as premises certain essential features of mammals and some
facts about Mars, proves that there could not be mammalian life on
Mars; such a proof, even if it is beyond criticism, has no tendency
to show that there *could* be any sort of life on Mars. That's as may
be. His proof just tells us nothing about non-mammalian life.

I will not discuss (further) the question of how much free will we
might have *within* these two categories. In the sequel, I wish to discuss
the implications of what I have argued for so far for questions of moral
blame.

I have argued that, if incompatibilism is true, free action is a less
common phenomenon than one might have thought. It does not,
however, follow that moral accountability is a less common
phenomenon than one might have thought. And this is the case even
on the traditional or "classical" understanding of the relationship between free will—that is, the power or ability to do otherwise than
one in fact does—and accountability. Nothing that has been said so
far need force the incompatibilist (the incompatibilist whose view
of the relation between free will and blame is that of the classical
tradition) to think that moral accountability is uncommon.

Let us see why. Would anyone want to say that the classical tradition is committed to the following thesis? "An agent can be held
accountable for a certain state of affairs only if either (a) that agent
intentionally brought that state of affairs about and could have refrained from bringing it about, or (b) that agent foresaw that that state
of affairs would obtain unless he prevented it, and he was able to
prevent it." I don't know whether anyone would want to say this.
My uncertainty is due mainly to the fact that philosophers discussing
problems in this general area usually talk not about accountability
for states of affairs— the *results* of our action and inaction—but ac-

countability (or "responsibility") for *acts*. This way of talking about these matters is confusing and tends to obscure what I regard as crucial points. However this may be, the classical tradition is not committed to this thesis, though it may be that some representatives of the tradition have endorsed it. This is fortunate for the tradition, because the thesis is obviously false. This is illustrated by "drunk driver" cases: I could not have swerved fast enough to avoid hitting the taxi, and yet no one doubts that I am to blame for the collision. How can that be? Simple: I was drunk and my reflexes were impaired. Although I was unable to swerve to avoid hitting the taxi, that inability (unlike, say, my inability to read minds) was one I could have avoided having. Or again: Suppose that when I am drunk it is not within my power to refrain from violently assaulting those who disagree with me about politics. I get drunk and overhear a remark about Cuban troops in Angola and, soon thereafter, Fred's nose is broken. I was, under the circumstances, unable to refrain from breaking Fred's nose. And yet no one doubts that I am to blame for his broken nose. How can that be? Simple: Although I was unable to avoid breaking his nose, that inability is one I could have avoided having. What these examples show is that the inability to prevent or to refrain from causing a state of affairs does not logically preclude being to blame for that state of affairs. Even the most orthodox partisan of a close connection between free will and blame will want to express this connection in a principle that is qualified in something like the following way:

> An agent cannot be blamed for a state of affairs unless there was a time at which he could so have arranged matters that that state of affairs not obtain.

And this principle is at least consistent with its being the case that, while we are hardly ever able to act otherwise than we do, we are nevertheless accountable for (some of) the consequences of *all* of our acts. (No one, I suppose, would seriously maintain that we can be blamed for *all* of the consequences of *any* of our acts. If I am dilatory about returning a book to the library and this has the consequence—apparent, I suppose, only to God—that a certain important medical discovery is never made, the thousands of deaths that would not have occurred if I had been a bit more conscientious are not my fault. And who can say what the unknown consequences of our most casual acts may be? Obviously, I can be blamed only for those consequences of my acts that are in some sense "foreseeable.") Consider this case.

A Mafia hit-man is dispatched to kill a peculating minor functionary of that organization. The victim pleads for his life in a most pathetic way, which so amuses the hit-man (who would no more think of failing to fulfill the terms of a contract than you or I would think of extorting money from our students by threats of failing them) that he shoots the victim in the stomach, rather than through the heart, in order to prolong the entertainment. Could he have refrained from killing the victim? Was it, just before he shot the victim, within his power to pocket his gun unfired and leave? If what has been said so far is true, probably not. Would it follow that he was not morally responsible for the victim's death? By no means. Given the kind of man he was, he was unable, in that situation, to have acted otherwise. But perhaps he could have avoided having that inability by avoiding being the kind of man he was. It is an old, and very plausible, philosophical idea that, by our acts, we make ourselves into the sorts of people we eventually become. Or, at least, it is plausible to suppose that our acts are *among* the factors that determine what we eventually become. If one is now unable to behave in certain ways—I am not talking about gross physical inabilities, like a double amputee's inability to play the piano—this may be because of a long history of choices one has made. Take the case of cold-blooded murder. The folk wisdom has it (I don't know if there is empirical evidence for this) that most of us have been born with a rather deep reluctance to kill helpless and submissive fellow human beings. But, if there is such a reluctance, it can obviously be overcome. And (so the folk wisdom has it) each time this reluctance is overcome it grows weaker, until it finally disappears. Suppose our Mafia hit-man *did* have a free choice the first time he killed a defenseless victim. He might have experienced on that occasion—though doubtless these terms were not in his vocabulary— something like a conflict between momentary inclination and long-term self-interest. Suppose he did kill his man, however, and that he continued to do this when it was required of him until he had finally completely extirpated his reluctance to kill the helpless and submissive. If he is now unable to pocket his gun unfired and walk away, this is, surely, partly because he has extirpated this reluctance. The absence of this normal reluctance to kill is an essential component of his present inability not to kill. If the folk wisdom is right, and let us suppose for the sake of the example that it is, then it is conceivable he could have avoided having his present inability. And, therefore, it may be, for all we have said, that he can properly be held to account for the victim's death. Given the causal and psychological theses contained in the folk wisdom, he may be accountable for the victim's death for the same reason that a drunk driver is accountable for an accident traceable to his impaired reflexes. (But, of course, I don't mean to suggest that the case of a man who has turned himself into a sociopath by a long series of free choices over many years is morally *very* much like the case of a man who has turned himself into a temporarily dangerous driver by one or two acts of free choice in the course of an evening.)

I have nothing more to say on the subject of moral blame. This is a difficult topic, and one that involves many other factors than the ability to act otherwise. (Coercion and ignorance, for example, are deeply involved in questions of accountability. And there is the dismally difficult question of what it is for a consequence of an act to be "foreseeable" in the relevant sense.) My only purpose in these last few paragraphs has been to give some support to the idea that the radically limited domain of the freedom of the will that the incompatibilist must accept does not obviously commit him to a similarly radically limited domain for moral blame. It may be that we are usually right when we judge that a given state of affairs is a given person's fault, even if people are almost never able to refrain from bringing about the states of affairs they intentionally bring about, and even if people are almost never able to act to prevent the states of affairs that they know perfectly well will obtain if they do not act to prevent them. For it may be that they could have avoided having these inabilities.[5]

Notes

1. See pp. 93-105.
2. That is, no human being. We shall not take into account the powers of God or angels or Martians.
3. See pp. 133ff.
4. See [2], Part II.
5. This paper was read at a conference on "Freedom and Mind" at McGill University in September, 1986, and as an invited paper at the 1987 meeting of the Central Division of the American Philosophical Association. On the latter occasion, the commentator was R. Kane. The paper was also read to the Philosophy Department at Virginia Polytechnic Institute and State University. The audiences on these occasions are

thanked for their useful comments, as are those who have been kind enough to correspond with me about the topics discussed herein. Special thanks are due to Daniel Dennett, Robert Kane, and Lawrence H. Davis.

References

1. Daniel C. Dennett, *Elbow Room: The Varieties of Free will Worth Wanting* (Cambridge, Mass. and London: Bradford Books, 1984).
2. R. Kane, *Free Will and Values* (Albany: State University of New York Press, 1985).
3. Peter van Inwagen, *An Essay on Free Will* (Oxford: The Clarendon Press, 1983).

Philosophical Perspectives, 3
Philosophy of Mind and Action Theory, 1989

PROXIMATE CAUSATION OF ACTION

Myles Brand
The Ohio State University

The Causal Theory of Action says, in essence, that an event involving a person is a human action just in case that event has the requisite causal antecedents. The event of a person's arm rising *is* the action of his raising his arm when, and only when, the arm's rising is caused by an appropriate event. This is a functional account of human action in that action is analyzed not by means of any 'intrinsic' properties, but in virtue of its causal roles. This theory was suggested by Donald Davidson in his classic paper "Actions, Reasons, and Causes" (1963), and has been advocated by many philosophers since that time (e. g., Goldman (1970)).

I, too, have defended the Causal Theory of Action, arguing that a person's immediately intending to do something, his intending to do it here and now, is in all cases the proximate cause of his doing it (Brand, 1984). Call this articulation of the theory the Thesis of Proximate Causal Intending, or (PCI).[1] Actions are always proximately caused by intendings. The key to explaining human action, according to (PCI), is to explain intending.

Some philosophers have recently objected to (PCI). They objected not on the grounds that it is a version of the Causal Theory of Action (though some of them, at least, do not embrace the Causal Theory), nor on the grounds that intending causes action, but rather on the basis of the more fundamental issue of whether there is any single type of event proximately causing actions (e. g., Thalberg, 1985; Hornsby, 1986; Davis, 1987). Some actions might be proximately caused by intendings, but others by the agent's desiring, or believing, or fearing, or hoping, or wishing, or some combination of these types of mental events or others—or indeed caused by some events that are not mental. If this objection can be sustained, then the role of intending in explaining action is not central and our net must be cast considerably wider to include a plethora of types of events, both mental and nonmental.

This debate is reminiscent of one between Davidson and Sellars. In Davidson's version of the Causal Theory, primary reasons are causes of actions, where, under a natural interpretation of the text, a primary reason is a combination of a pro-attitude toward actions of a certain kind and a belief that that kind of action can be performed. Pro-attitudes, in turn, include "desires, wantings, urges, promptings, and a great variety of moral views, aesthetic principles, economic prejudices, social conventions, and public and private goals and values" (1963, p. 68). Sellars, in rejecting Davidson's version of the Causal Theory, says:

> The main source of my discomfort is the expression 'pro-attitude.' Davidson is well aware that this is an omnibus term and lists, in the course of his discussion, some of the specific mental states in which this term applies. Yet he has little to say about this... [I]n his examples he tends to stress the onslaught of factual thoughts and leaves the relevant pro-attitudes to be relatively long term dispositions which constitute the mental background of the functioning of reasons (1973, p. 190).

Sellars here has two complaints about Davidson's view. First, Davidson has not focused on the proximate cause of action, but rather on the remote, background causes. Second, he has not identified a single, unique cause of action, but rather has listed a wide range of causes. Sellars' own version of the Causal Theory is that volitions proximately cause actions, where, on one reading, a volition closely resembles an intention to do something here and now.

On both counts, I contend, Sellars is correct. An adequate Causal Theory of Action should include both the claim that action is specified by its proximate cause and the claim that there is a unique proximate cause. Unfortunately, Sellars has not provided arguments for these claims. In this paper, I will provide a good reason for analyzing action by means of its proximate cause and a good reason for claiming that there is a unique type of proximate cause of action.

These reasons, by themselves, do not provide grounds for advocating any particular version of the Causal Theory, such as the one saying that immediate intendings are the proximate causes of action, that is, (PCI). Rather, the proceeding arguments undermine the skepticism about the need to specify a unique proximate cause of action. These reasons constitute a prolegomenon to any adequate Causal Theory of Action.

1. Proximate Causation

As a preliminary, some things need to be said about proximate causation. Let e, f, ..., range over individual events. I take events to be spatiotemporal particulars; that is, events have spatiotemporal boundaries and are not literally repeatable. I also take it that events are to be individuated finely, at least so that two or more events can co-occur in a single spatiotemporal region. However, details about the nature of events need not detain us (cf. Brand, 1984, Chap. 3). The relevant point is that I am taking events to be finely individuated spatiotemporal particulars. Further, let E, F, ..., range over types or kinds of events. Assuming universal closure, then, proximate causation between events is definable as follows:

(D1) e proximately causes f iff
    (i) e causes f and
    (ii) there are no events g_1, g_2, ..., g_n (where $n \geq 1$), distinct from e and f, such that e causes g_1 and g_1 causes g_2 and ... and g_n causes f.

If e causes f and e does not proximately cause f, then e *remotely causes* f. Observe that (D1) does not exclude the possibility that the effect f is overdetermined.

Sometimes we speak not of individual events proximately causing one another, but types of events standing in this relation, for instance, we say that punctures cause flat tires and that dropping a glass causes it to break. In these cases,

(D2) E proximately causes F iff every event e of type E that occurs is such that there is some event of type F that occurs and e proximately causes f, provided that nothing interferes.

So, every time a glass is dropped, it breaks. Note the clause "provided that nothing interferes" added to (D2). This clause excludes situations in which conditions are not normal. The glass will not break if it is made of specially reinforced material, or if the surface on which it lands is highly elastic, or so on. (It is notoriously difficult to specify precisely the content of this type of *ceteris paribus* clause, and I shall not attempt to do so here.)

Causation obtains between occurrent individual events. Thus, the relation of proximate causation between event types is parasitic on causal relations between individual events. Observe that here, too, overdetermination is not precluded.

One more definition is needed for our purposes: namely, again assuming closure,

(D3) E is the unique proximate cause of F *iff*
    (i) E proximately causes F, and
    (ii) there is no event type G distinct from E such that G proximately causes F.

The two crucial claims at issue can now be stated.

(PC) There are event types that proximately cause human action.

(UPC) There is an event type that is the unique proximate cause of human action.

In the context of the Causal Theory, (PC) points to a proximate causal relation between action and antecedent event types and (UPC) says that there is exactly one such antecedent type. An adequate Causal Theory of Action, I contend, depends on the truth of both (PC) and (UPC). To reinforce an earlier point, (PC) and (UPC) are necessary preliminaries to particular articulations of the Causal Theory.

2. Proximate Causation of Action

It is not enough that a Causal Theory list the background dispositions and attitudes leading to action. Rather, a—or *the*—proximate cause should be specified. For by specifying a proximate cause of action, *the problem of causal waywardness* is dissolved. This is the problem that has led Frankfurt to say "I believe that the causal approach is inherently implausible and that it cannot provide a satisfactory analysis of the nature of action" (1978, p. 157), a complaint echoed by more than one philosopher.

Consider the following example, derived from Frankfurt.[2]

> *Abel* is attending a party. He wants to spill his drink because he wants to signal to his accomplices to begin the robbery and he believes, in virtue of their prior agreement, that his spilling his drink will achieve that. But Abel is an inexperienced criminal and quite anxious. His anxiety makes his hand tremble, and so his drink spills. As a result, the robbery is committed.

Here the apparently appropriate antecedent mental events, a desire to signal to his accomplices and a belief that he can do so, caused the bodily event of spilling the drink; yet, Abel did *not* perform the action of spilling his drink. There was a wayward causal chain leading from the antecedent mental events to the bodily behavior. Spilling his drink was something that happened to Abel, in the way that a nervous twitch of one's shoulder or the blinking of an eye is. The existence of such wayward chains shows that causation by the apparently appropriate mental events is not sufficient for action, according to this objection.

First of all, this problem should be distinguished from another one with which it is often confused. Consider the following case, which derives from Chisholm (1966, pp. 29-30):

> *Carl* wants to kill his rich uncle because he wants to inherit the family fortune. He believes that his uncle is home and drives toward his house in order to perform the dastardly deed. His desire to kill his uncle combined with his belief that his uncle is home agitates Carl and he drives recklessly. On the way he hits and kills a pedestrian, who, as luck would have it, is his uncle.

In this situation, Carl performed several actions, for example, getting into his car and driving toward his uncle's house; these actions were caused by his desires and beliefs. But some of what happened did not go according to his plan, in particular, running down his uncle, which was fortuitous—for Carl, not his uncle. Carl killed his uncle, but unintentionally. The waywardness described in this story pertains to the intentionality of what Carl accomplished, not whether he performed any actions at all. We might label this kind of waywardness 'consequential waywardness,' to indicate that something is amiss about the consequences of the agent's actions. The problem about consequential waywardness is to be resolved by clarifying agents' plans for future action and the way in which the agent follows his or her plan.[3]

By contrast, the problem to which Frankfurt points in the story about Abel concerns the issue of whether a person performs any action at all. It challenges the very analysis of action. The Causal Theory says that something is an action of a person if and only if his bodily movements are caused by appropriate prior events. Davidson and others have claimed that a desire to do something and a belief that one can do it are the appropriate prior events. The possibility of causal deviance between these events and the resulting bodily behavior shows that being caused by these events is not sufficient for action. I label this 'the problem of antecedential waywardness.'

The resolution to the problem of antecedential waywardness for action should be obvious by now. Abel's desire and belief do not proximately cause his bodily behavior. His anxiety intervenes. An adequate Causal Theory should say that the requisite antecedent mental events *proximately* cause the action. There can be no causal space, as it were, for other events to interrupt the causal sequence.

Background attitudes can be easily interrupted before they cause behavior, and thus, are not good candidates for the characteristic causes of action. A complex event consisting of a desiring and believing appears to be a better candidate. But as Frankfurt's example shows, a desire and belief complex can also be interrupted. My own hypothesis is that intending—or more exactly, immediate, here and now, intending—is the superior candidate for the causal antecedent to action, in part because there is no opportunity for any event to intervene between it and the behavior. But whatever event type or event types are taken to be the requisite causal antecedents to action, they are to proximately cause the action.

It may be that the need for the proximity of the causal antecedents to action has been ignored by causal theorists because intervening events can sometimes be benign. Suppose again, but only for the sake of argument, that belief-desire complexes cause actions. Some events can intervene between this complex and the resultant behavior without altering the actional status of the behavior. It might happen that Abel's desire to begin the robbery plus his belief that he could do so causes him to imagine—to picture to himself—that he will spill his drink, and, in turn, his imagining that he will spill his drink causes him to spill it. Though his imagining intervened between his desire and belief and his behavior, we would grant that his spilling the drink was an action. The intervention of an imagining does not usually result in a wayward sequence.[4]

However, the Causal Theory of Action purports to identify all actions by means of their causal history. That there are some cases of benign intervention between the requisite causal antecedents and the behavior is otiose. If there are any cases that defeat the claim that the behavior is an action even though caused by the requisite antecedents, the Causal Theory is untenable. The original story of Abel is such a case. Or rather, it is such a case *if* the Causal Theory is formulated in a way that permits interruption in the causal sequence between the requisite antecedent events and the behavior. The possibility of interruption is eliminated when the requisite antecedent events proximately cause the behavior.

Proximate causation is consistent with overdetermination.[5] Suppose that an action were overdetermined by prior mental events. Say, Abel's desire to begin the robbery and his belief that he could do so proximately caused his spilling the drink *and simultaneously* his fear of focusing attention on himself made his grasp of the glass such that it also caused his behavior. On the supposition that a desire-belief pair is the requisite antecedent to action, Abel performed the action of spilling his drink, despite there being another event causally necessary and sufficient for that selfsame behavior. The Causal Theory of Action is threatened not by simultaneous overdetermining events, but by mental events intervening between the purported requisite causal antecedents to action and the resultant behavior.

At times, other solutions to the problem of antecedential waywardness have been proposed. One approach is to argue that the connection between the requisite antecedent mental events and the resultant behavior must be normal, and that determination of causal normalcy is a scientific matter. Goldman (1970, p. 62), for instance, has said that the desire and belief must cause the behavior "in a characteristic way." The specification of this characteristic or normal way, he adds, requires "extensive neurophysiological information, and I do not think it is fair to demand of a *philosophical* analysis that it provide this information." However, this approach to the problem misconstrues the function of scientific explanation. Neurophysiologists and other scientists studying human behavior record causal generalizations as they find them. These generalizations state information about the details of complex causal sequences in a proprietary vocabulary. But they do not yield a criterion for normalcy. At best, these sciences can tell us whether some type of causal sequence is statistically prevalent: that, however, is altogether different than providing a criterion for normalcy. There is nothing abnormal in the Abel story. Extreme anxiety sometimes does interfere with one's desires and beliefs. A scientific psychological account would specify the covering causal generalizations for this type of sequence; it would not relegate them to the 'abnormal.' Normalcy is a philosophic, not a scientific judgment, and as such should be built into the analysis of action, contrary to Goldman's claim.

To sum up, a main problem for the Causal Theory of Action is eliminating the possibility of waywardness between the causally requisite antecedent mental events and the resultant behavior. This problem is distinct from that of explaining waywardness in the execution of one's plan for a series of actions. The former type of waywardness focuses on the relationship between the mental antecedents to each action, and thus concerns the analysis of action; the latter type focuses on the consequences of what one does, and thus concerns the analysis of the intentionality of activity. The possibility of waywardness between the requisite mental antecedents and the behavior is eliminated if the requisite antecedents proximately cause the behavior. (To be cautious, we should say, strictly speaking, only that the requirement of proximate causation is sufficient to eliminate antecedential waywardness. It is not necessary if there is some other means to preclude antecedential waywardness.) In a word, then, a Causal Theory of Action resolves the problem of antecedential waywardness through a commitment to (PC).

3. Unique Proximate Causation of Action

If an event is caused, it is proximately caused. This result follows from the definition of 'proximate cause' on the conditions that individual events have duration and that a chain of causally related events is not dense. Since events are being viewed from the commonsense vantage point, these conditions are satisfied. If events were being treated as scientific constructs, and taken to be spatiotemporal points or time slices or some such, these conditions would not be justified. Here and throughout the discussion, the conceptual framework of commonsense is presupposed.

Every individual human action is an individual event. Clearly a physical action, such as my raising my arm this noon, is an event. Similarly, a mental action, such as my solving this chess puzzle in my head during lunch yesterday, is an event. There are special problems about the spatial location of mental actions; but these problems also pertain to nonactional mental events, such as my visually processing information presented by a distal array, and do not countervene the claim that mental actions are events. Now, since every action is an event, it follows that every action is proximately caused. Let us accept the Humean principle that if events are casually related, there is some causal generalization covering this relationship. Note that the acceptance of this principle does not require the acceptance of Hume's regularity analysis of singular causal statements. The defects of Hume's analysis of singular causal statements are well-known and need not be rehearsed here.[6] The Humean principle that causal generalizations cover individual causal relations is compatible with any adequate analysis of singular causal statements: it is even compatible with the view that there is a necessary connection in nature between cause and effect. The principle requires only that there be some covering generalization or other for every causal connection, however causation is to be finally understood.

Since the Humean principle pertains to all causal connections among events, it pertains to proximate causal connections. If one event proximately causes another, there is some causal generalization of this connection. It follows, then, that for every proximately caused action, there is some covering generalization.

Consider these generalizations somewhat more closely. A first suggestion for the general form of a causal generalization is:

(1) (e) $\{Ee \supset (\exists f) [Ff \& C(e, f)]\}$,

where e and f range over events, C is '...causes—,' and E and F are properties of events. For the generalization 'striking matches causes their igniting,' E is the property of being a striking of a match and F being an igniting of a match. Since types or kinds are properties, Ee says that e is of type E, or in this example, individual event e is of the type striking a match.

The general form (1) can be improved in several ways (cf. Davidson, 1967, esp. p. 699). For instance, a function specifying the temporal relations between cause and effect might be added. Hume held that causes precede their effects, and he has been widely followed on this point. But there might be genuine cases of simultaneous causation; for example, the downward movement of a lead ball from the time it comes into contact with a cushion to the time it comes to rest causing the cushion to be depressed. The temporal function would then have the force of saying that the effect did not precede the cause. That is,

$$(1') \ (e)(n) \ \{(Ee \ \& \ T(e) = n) \supset (\exists f) \ [Ff \ \& \ T(e) \geq n \ \& \ C(e,f)]\},$$

where n ranges over the rational numbers and '$T...$' assigns a number to an event to mark the time of its occurrence. Or, (1) might be modified to reflect the claim that causes are both necessary and sufficient for their effects. It is not only the case that if an individual cause were to occur, so would its effect given the circumstances, but also if the effect were to occur under the given circumstances, the cause would have also occurred. Thus,

$$(1'') (e)(n) \ \{(Ee \ \& \ T(e) = n) \supset (\exists f)[Ff \ \& \ T(f) \geq n \ \& \ C(e,f)\} \ \&$$
$$(e)(n)\{(Fe \ \& \ T(e) \geq n) \supset (\exists f) \ [Ef \ \& \ T(f) = n \ \& \ C(f,e)\}.$$

But these further modifications of (1) complicate the argument without substantially affecting it, and therefore will be suppressed.

Generalizations of the form (1) are indifferent as to whether effects are remotely or proximately caused. Since if an event is caused, it is proximately caused, and since there is, by Hume's principle, a causal generalization for every pair of causally related events, some generalizations of the form (1) will specify proximate causation. Let *PC* be the relation '...proximately causes—' Then a species of (1) is

$$(2) \ (e)\{Ee \supset (\exists f) \ [Ff \ \& \ PC(e,f)]\}.$$

Causal generalizations serve two related functions. They explain past events and predict future ones. If explanation and prediction are complete, the system is classically deterministic, or let us say *Laplacian*. That is, a Laplacian system is one such that there is a set of causal generalizations that gives the state of the system at any time given the state of the system at some time.

A closed system of billiard balls is Laplacian. Given the position and momentum of each ball at some time, we can by means of causal generalizations specify their positions and momenta at any other time. The system is closed in the sense that all forces acting on the balls are known. The dynamical laws for medium-sized macroscopic objects contain an implicit *ceteris paribus* clause pertaining to the closure of the system.

In much the same way, folk psychological systems are Laplacian. Suppose that Ronnie reports to Nancy that the house is aflame. Will Nancy attempt to escape? Maybe. We cannot predict her actions from this limited information. We need to know the content of Nancy's cognitive attitudes, as well as the sense and directions of her conative and affective attitudes. If we knew that Nancy was normal in every way, that she desired not to be harmed and that this was a desire on which she was prepared to act, and moreover that she believed that the house was indeed on fire, then, on the basis of folk psychological generalizations, we could predict that she would attempt to escape. Or if we knew that Nancy had these conative and affective attitudes but did not believe Ronnie, that she believed instead that Ronnie was providing misinformation, then we could predict by means of folk psychological generalizations that Nancy would not try to flee from the house.

The point is that once the psychological parameters are fixed, folk psychology enables us to predict action. Of course, in many situations the mental states of the actors cannot be fixed, and thus reliable predictions cannot be made. But once the set of mental states of the agent is specified, then, in principle, his or her action is predictable. Or alternatively, if the action is known and the background circumstances are also known, the mental state of the agent can be inferred. Both the criminal and civil law in establishing intent presuppose this feature of folk psychology. As in the case of physical systems, there is an implicit *ceteris paribus* claim saying that the system is closed, that is, there are no interfering external factors.

This point is worth stressing. It might appear that folk psychology is nonLaplacian. The reason is that we cannot always predict with confidence what persons will do. But this observation speaks to our lack of knowledge about the mental states of other persons and not to folk psychology being nonLaplacian. *If* we know the mental states of another person and *if* we know the relevant causal generalizations, we can predict with certainty what it is they will do. If we know someone's intention to act, the desires and beliefs that generated this intention, his long-term background attitudes, the relevant covering generalizations, and that there are no interfering conditions, then we can predict what he will do. We cannot predict from this information alone the consequences of his actions, since that requires knowledge of the physical state of the world; but we can predict the actions themselves. When predictions about future action cannot be made, it is because of epistemic deficiencies. Folk psychology, like all commonsense theories of the world, presupposes perfect predictability. Perfect predictability, however, is possible only in the presence of perfect information. To repeat, a complete specification of someone's mental states plus the set of folk psychological generalizations is sufficient to project his or her actions, *ceteris paribus*. And that is the same as saying that folk psychology is Laplacian.

Armed with this background account of causal generalization, let us return to (UPC), the thesis that there is a unique proximate cause of human action. The claim (UPC) is true if there is a causal generalization specifying an event type that is the unique proximate cause of action. Obviously, *either* (a) there is a causal generalization specifying an event type that is the unique proximate cause of action, *or* (b) there is no causal generalization specifying such an event type. I will argue for the first alternative (a), that there is a generalization specifying the unique proximate cause of action, by showing that the second alternative (b) is highly problematic. From this, (UPC) follows.

Suppose that there were no causal generalizations specifying an event type that is the unique proximate cause of action; that is, suppose that the second alternative (b) were the case. Since actions are proximately caused, there would be on this supposition causal generalizations of the forms

$$(3) \ (e)\{E_1e \supset (\exists f) \ [Af \ \& \ PC(e,f)]\},$$
$$(e)\{E_2e \supset (\exists f) \ [Af \ \& \ PC(e,f)]\},$$

$$\cdot$$
$$\cdot$$
$$\cdot$$

$$(e)\{E_ne \supset (\exists f) \ [Af \ \& \ PC(e,f)]\},$$

where A is the type human action and $E_1, E_2, ..., E_n$ are the types of events proximately causing actions. This statement entails:

$$(4) \ (e)\{E_1e \lor E_2e \lor ... \lor E_ne) \supset (\exists f)[Af \ \& \ PC(e,f)]\}.$$

However, a causal generalization of the form (4) is problematical. It seriously hinders the functions of explanation and prediction that causal generalizations are to serve. Suppose that we know that a person thrust his arm out the window of his car. On the basis of (4) we can only conclude that he did so because of either immediately prior desires or urges or aesthetic principles or economic prejudices or social conventions or what nots. Additional factual information *from an earlier time* than that at which he moved his arm is necessary to explain why he did so. This situation is importantly different from those involving other commonsense phenomenon. As noted in a case of moving billiard balls, it is required only that we know the state of the system at one time and the appropriate causal generalizations to explain its motion. But on this account, we would need to know the state of the system at two (or more) times for explanation of human action. An analogous argument can be made for the predictive function of causal generalizations.

The point can be restated by saying that, given our supposition of the second alternative (b) that there is no unique proximate cause of action, a system involving human actions is nonLaplacian; that is, it fails to be classically deterministic. This is a strong result. It harbors ill for a science of psychology. Psychology, on the one side, and physics and biology, on the other, would then be irreconcilably different. It is not merely that they are not unified and reducible one to another—something we have known for some time—but rather that the kinds of explanations and predictions they generate are radically different. Alternative (b) is contrary to the Laplacian nature of folk psychology.

Several objections might be made to this line of argument. First, it might be countered that physical systems are really nonLaplacian and, hence, do not diverge from psychological ones. Given a quantum mechanical framework, we can only assign a probability less than 1 to a prior cause on the basis of the current state of a physical system. In reply, it should be observed that we are dealing with the commonsense framework here, both for physical systems and psychological ones. On this perspective, quantum mechanical considerations are not relevant. In judging the flight of a baseball, we do not take into consideration the probability that it will suddenly alter its course or that its subatomic particles will suddenly break apart and disperse; the probability that either will occur is negligible and not of concern to baseball players. Moreover, if quantum mechanical considerations were considered relevant, they would affect physical systems and psychological ones equally. Arm thrustings and billiard ball movements are equally subject to the laws of quantum mechanics. But, if (4) covered human actions, there would be, in addition to any quantum mechanical uncertainty, uncertainty about the type of proximate causes. Quantum mechanical considerations, in short, do not eliminate the differences between physical and psychological explanations that a defense of (4) requires.

The second objection is that the claim that folk psychology is LaPlacian is really *contrary* to commonsense. Mental events can have multiple causes. Consider desires. We often talk about desires arising in diverse ways. For example, a desire to be sunning oneself on a warm beach might be said to arise from one's prior preferences; but it might also be said to be generated from a well-designed travel brochure. But if folk psychology is LaPlacian, then by the same logic that argued for a unique cause of action, there cannot be multiple causes of desire. Since there are multiple causes of desire, the objection concludes, folk psychology is not LaPlacian.

In response, consider more carefully the claim that there are multiple causes of mental events, such as desires. An occurrent desire is generated from background, dispositional preferences when, and only when, it is triggered by some event. A cause of an occurrent desire is complex: it involves both background states and a triggering mechanism. This total causal antecedent must be present if the effect, the occurrent desire, is to occur. This picture is fully in accord with the commonsense view of the mental, and does *not* speak to multiple, distinct causal antecedents to the selfsame desire.

One possible source of this objection is the conflation of multiple ways of describing the generation of desire with these being multiple causes of desire. One description might emphasize the background states, while another might focus on the triggering event (or, better, the perceptual belief of the triggering event's occurring). These descriptions purport to name *the* cause of the desire. But descriptions of 'the cause' are notoriously incomplete and context-dependent. To say that a desire to sun oneself on a warm beach arose from looking at a travel brochure is to name the cause of the desire, in the sense that it names that part of the total cause that is to be singled out in this context. This objection does not show that a mental event type can have more than one cause; at best, it succeeds only in showing that causes of mental events types can have myriad descriptions.

There is a further moral to be drawn from this objection. Folk psychological causal generalizations can be expected to be complex. Generalizations about desires is one case in point. The causal antecedent to desire is a complex event, one involving background dispositional states and triggering mechanisms. Another case in point is action. We should expect such generalizations to reflect that the cause of action is complex, consisting, I would argue, of the triggering of a motivational state within the context of an appropriate cognitive structure.

Folk psychological generalizations, as a result of their complexity, are difficult to state precisely. We should not assume that, since these generalizations occur within folk psychology, they will be simple or they will be known. Mostly, probably wholly, we operate with rough approximations to such causal generalizations. Folk psychology is committed to there being causal generalizations governing key sortal terms and that this set of generalizations constitutes a LaPlacian system, not that the generalizations are simple or known.

The third objection attacks the status of generalizations of the form (3) and (4). The level of abstraction of the sortal terms occurring in such generalizations is too high to yield a folk psychology that is predictive and explanatory about human action. For example, 'human action' would not occur as a sortal, but only something like 'behavior.' In the same way, 'desiring,' 'believing,' and 'intending' would not appear in these generalizations, but only some very general term such as 'pro-attitude.' At this level of abstraction, the objection continues, no predictions or explanations of human action are forthcoming.

Let us focus on the claim that 'behavior,' not 'human action,' will occur in these generalizations; the case for sortals referring to antecedent mental events is relevantly similar. We can admit that folk psychology is not precisely delineated. There is no codified theory that constitutes folk psychology. From this admission, however, it does not follow that there is nothing definite that can be said about folk psychology. Folk psychology is, basically, a reconstruction of commonsense thinking about the mind and about personhood. An adequate reconstruction is constrained by the conceptual framework of commonsense thought in this domain (cf. Brand, 1984, pp. 160-70).

In particular, commonsense dictates that there is a distinction between what persons do and what happens to them. As Wittgenstein noted some time ago, there is a critical difference between a person's raising his arm and his arm's merely going up. Folk psychology regiments this distinction by including causal generalizations containing 'human action' (or containing sortals for subclasses of actions). The general term 'behavior' includes both movements that are actions and those that are not actions. The sortal 'human action' represents the maximal level of abstraction permitted for folk psychology; folk psychology cannot contain only sortals that are more abstract than 'human action.' For if it contained only such sortals, if it contained, for instance, only 'behavior,' it would fail to reflect the crucial commonsense distinction between what we do and what happens to us. Whatever value Watson's, or Skinner's, behaviorism might have, it cannot substitute for folk psychology. In short, the premise of the objection that 'human action' is insufficiently abstract to be included in folk psychological generalizations is wholly without basis.

The final objection also attacks (3) and (4), but from the opposite direction. They are not causal generalizations at all, it might be said, since the type human action is not a natural kind and causal generalizations state relations between natural kinds. Human actions are varied and do not form a natural class. Thus, any difference between physical and psychological explanation based on (3) and (4) is apparent, not real.

In response, I would argue against the presumption of this objection that human actions do not form a natural kind. Mere diversity of instances does not preclude a kind from being natural. The list of mammals is highly diverse, ranging from squirrels that fly to dolphins that live in the sea; yet, they constitute a natural kind. Natural kinds are identified within the context of a theoretical perspective. Nature has many joints, and the ones on which we choose to focus depends on our background theoretical framework. The framework of folk or commonsense psychology recognizes action as a natural kind.

Admittedly folk psychology is somewhat amorphous; and this response might not fully persuade. If so, we should note that even if 'human action' is not a natural kind term, but rather a general term that includes natural kind terms referring to many types of actions, the same problem that arose for (4) will repeat itself. Consider some species of action, rather than the totality of action, say the species arm-thrustings. Presumably arm-thrustings constitute a natural kind. (If there is some hesitation about arm-thrustings, pick some other type; all that is needed for the response is that subclasses of human actions constitute natural kinds.) Now, by supposition, not all arm-thrustings have the same proximate cause, some being caused by desires, others by urges, others by fears, or so on. Thus, there is a causal generalization of the form (4) with *A* replaced by, say, *T* (for '... is an arm-thrusting'). This new causal generalization suffers from the same deficits of limited explanatory and predictive value as the original (4). To generate an argument with the force of the original one in which 'human action' appears as a kind term, these subarguments are to be repeated for each species of human action constituting a natural kind. Since there are presumably a finite number of such natural kinds, this tack would complicate matters but without any substantial change. The main point remains: a single type of event cannot have diverse proximate causes if the causal generalization is to have full explanatory and predictive power.

It may be that in the end psychological explanation is radically different from physical explanation, in that there is a kind of indeterminism for psychological phenomena that is absent in the case of physical phenomena. Certainly some philosophers have suggested indeterminism of the psychological. But that is a highly contentious position and the burden of proof lies with its advocates. The case must be made. It cannot rest merely on skepticism about there being a single event type that proximately causes action. That would make the job of the indeterminist too easy: it would, to paraphrase Russell, give by theft what should be earned by honest philosophical toil.

To sum up the argument, all events, including human actions, that are caused are proximately caused. The causal generalizations that cover individual cases of proximate causation of action either specify an event type that is the unique proximate of cause or they do not. If there is no causal generalization specifying a unique proximate cause of action, if the generalization has the form (3), there is a radical difference between commonsense psychological explanation and commonsense physical explanation, in that the former is indeterministic in a way that the latter is not. Since there is no apparent reason to believe that there is this radical difference, the claim that the causal generalizations covering human actions do not specify a unique proximate cause is untenable. Thus, these causal generalizations do specify a unique type of proximate cause of action. And, therefore, the thesis (UPC), which says that there is a unique type of proximate cause of human action, is justified.

4. Summary and Conclusion

A Causal Theory of Action specifies human action in terms of its causal role, in particular, in terms of its causal history. A theory of this type is threatened by the possibility of causal deviance or waywardness. The requisite antecedent events might occur in such a way that, despite causing the behavior, the claim that the behavior is actional is contradicted. If, say, a desire-belief complex were the requisite antecedent events, this complex event could cause the appropriate behavior by means of a causal sequence that involves severe nervousness or anxiety; in these cases, the behavior would be caused by the requisite antecedent events without achieving the status of action. Some constraints must be placed on the antecedent events. One natural constraint is that the requisite antecedent events proximately cause the action. In that case, there is no causal space, as it were, for intervening wayward events.

Moreover, the type of antecedent event that proximately causes action must uniquely do so. Otherwise, there would be a kind of causal indeterminism for human action that does not exist for physical events. Physical events, such as billiard ball collisions, when viewed from the macroscopic, commonsense vantage point, form a Laplacian system. The covering causal generalizations for these event pairs are such that the state of an object can be predicted from a single complete description of the system. But if there are multiple proximate causes of the same human action, it is not possible to predict what will happen in all cases on the basis of a single complete description of the system. Consequently, psychological explanation would be radically different from physical explanation. This result does not comport well with commonsense, folk psychology. While there are serious difficulties in *knowing* what antecedent mental events lead persons to act, it is not part of folk psychology that there are no such prior mental events. Certainly the claim that psychological phenomena are indeterministic needs extensive justification—even to make it plausible. Thus, the alternative, that there is a unique type of cause of human action, is justified.

Of course, the claim that there is a proximate cause of action and that that cause is unique does not say *which* type of event is the proximate cause. These claims only give shape or form to a Causal Theory of Action, not content. To do so would involve identifying a type of mental event that has the appropriate motivational and cognitive properties from which action can emanate. This type of mental event, it would seem, should be such that its occurrence moves the agent to act; moreover, it provides a representation about how the projected future action fits into the perceived environment and background of other planned actions, as well as providing a monitoring and guidance mechanism for the ongoing activity. My favorite candidate for this type of complex event is intending. But this is not the place to make that argument.[7]

Notes

1. Others have, of course, defended (PCI). See, for instance, Searle (1983).
2. Davidson (1973) presents similar examples. Though he thinks that these cases present a problem for the Causal Theory of Action, he does not, unlike Frankfurt, claim that it is a defeating objection.
3. See Brand (1986).
4. The defender of (PCI) would add that the imagining generated an immediate intending, which proximately led to the behavior, and *that* is the reason why the spilling is an action.
5. I assume here that there is genuine overdetermination, though I have reservations about this assumption (cf. Loeb, 1974).
6. See Brand (1979).
7. An earlier version was read at The Ohio State University, Bowling Green State University, and the University of Cincinnati. I profited from these discussions, and especially want to acknowledge the helpful comments of Michael Bradie. I also benefited from comments by Hugh McCann on that version.

References

Brand, Myles, "Causality" in *Current Research in Philosophy of Science*, Peter Asquith and Henry Kyburg, eds. (Philosophy of Science Association, 1979), pp. 252-281.

Brand, Myles, *Intending and Acting* (MIT Press, 1984).

Brand, Myles, "Intentional Actions and Plans" in *Midwest Studies in Philosophy X* (1986), pp. 213-230.

Chisholm, Roderick, "Freedom and Action" in *Freedom and Determinism*, Keith Lehrer, ed. (Random House, 1966), pp. 28-44.

Davis, Lawrence H., Review of *Intending and Acting, Philosophy and Phenomenological Research*, 47 (1987), 506-511.

Davidson, Donald, "Actions, Reasons, and Causes," *Journal of Philosophy* 60 (1963), 685-700. Reprinted in Donald Davidson, *Essays on Actions and Events* (Oxford, Clarendon Press, 1982), pp. 3-19.

Davidson, Donald, "Freedom to Act" in *Essays on Freedom of Action*, Ted Honerick, ed. (Routledge and Kegan Paul, 1973), pp. 137-156. Reprinted in Davidson, *Essays on Actions and Events*, pp. 63-87.

Davidson, Donald, "Causal Relations," *Journal of Philosophy* 64 (1967), 691-703. Reprinted in Davidson, *Essays on Actions and Events*, pp. 149-162.

Frankfurt, Harry, "The Problem of Action," *American Philosophical Quarterly* 15 (1978), 157-62.

Goldman, Alvin, *A Theory of Human Action* (Prentice-Hall, 1970).

Hornsby, Jennifer, Review of *Intending and Acting*, *Philosophical Review* 95 (1986), pp. 261-264.

Loeb, Louis E., "Causal Theories and Causal Overdetermination," *Journal of Philosophy* 71 (1974), 525-544.

Searle, John, *Intentionality* (Cambridge University Press, 1983).

Sellars, Wilfrid, "Action and Events," *Nous* 7 (1973), 179-202.

Thalberg, Irving, Review of *Intending and Acting*, *Canadian Philosophical Reviews* 5 (1985), pp. 145-147.

Philosophical Perspectives, 3
Philosophy of Mind and Action Theory, 1989

INTENTION AND PERSONAL POLICIES

Michael E. Bratman
Stanford University

1. Introduction

I am about to go running; I hear on the radio that the pollen count is high; I recall my general policy of not running when the pollen count is high; and so I decide not to run. Gregory asks me for help with his homework; I recall my general policy of helping him with his homework when he asks; so I decide to help him. While making my summer plans I note my general policy of always working on some foreign language; so I ensure that my summer plans include some language study. Getting into my car I am reminded of my general policy of buckling up my seat belt when I drive; and so I do.

In all these examples my practical reasoning and action are shaped by relevant general policies of mine. I will call these *personal policies* to indicate that I am confining my attention to the general policies of individual agents, rather than those of complex organizations like corporations or governments. Personal policies pervade our lives. A plausible model of the intelligent activity of beings like us should make room for and shed light upon the complex roles of such policies in our lives.

A common way of thinking about intelligent agency is in terms of a desire-belief psychology. On this approach, the agent's desires and beliefs give her various reasons for acting in various ways, and intelligent action is the output of psychological processes primarily involving such desires and beliefs. However, even before we begin to reflect on personal policies we can see, I think, that such a desire-belief psychology is too impoverished to do justice to central aspects of the kinds of rational agents we are. In particular, desire-belief models of intelligent action do not do justice to the role of future-directed intentions and partial plans in our ongoing planning and conduct. We need a model of intelligent agency in which intentions and partial plans are taken seriously as basic elements of the model, on all fours with ordinary desires and beliefs.

Or so, anyway, I have argued in recent publications, publications in which I have proposed a *planning theory* of intention.[1] According to this theory prior intentions are typically elements in larger partial plans for future action. And these partial plans shape further planning and action in characteristic ways, thereby helping us to coordinate our activities over time and with each other, and thereby helping us to extend the influence of present rational reflection to future action.

Once our model of agency takes such prior intentions seriously, we may seem to have a natural way of thinking about personal policies. In a typical case a future-directed intention concerns some particular occasion, an occasion that is more or less precisely specified by that intention. I may intend, for example, to go to Boston *tomorrow* or *some time next month*, or to finish this paper *today*. But we may also have intentions that are *general with respect to their occasions of execution*. We can have an intention to act in a certain way *whenever* a certain type of occasion is present, or an intention to act in a certain way on a *regular* basis. I can intend to help Gregory *whenever* he asks, or not to run *whenever* the pollen count is high; and I can intend to exercise (or to study a foreign language) *regularly*. This suggests that the planning theory of intention can be extended to include personal policies by seeing such policies as intentions that are general in this way: general with respect to their occasions of execution.

I believe that, in the end, this is a fertile way of approaching personal policies. But there is a complication. Intentions, I say, are typically elements of partial plans, plans that shape further planning and action. These plans typically concern particular, more or less specifically characterized occasions: I have my plans for next week, for when I see you, for spring quarter, and for today. Such plans can be thought of as kinds of *schedules*, schedules that help us promote coordination and extend the influence of deliberation over time. But personal policies will not normally be elements in such schedules, for these policies do not solely concern particular occasions, more or less specifically characterized. My policy of not running whenever the pollen count is high will not itself be part of my plan for today, though it may influence that plan. Indeed, even policies that are extremely close to our scheduling of activities will typically not themselves be elements in the resulting schedules. I have a friend whose policy is always to mail his tax return on April 15. This policy predictably leads each year to a policy-based intention to mail his return on that April 15. And this policy-based intention will be an element in his schedule-like plan for that day. But his general policy will not itself be an element of that plan.

I do not say that general policies will never be elements of such schedules. As Ron Nash pointed out to me, I might have a plan to finish my paper this quarter and adopt, as a means, the policy of starting work by 8 a.m. daily. This policy is in a way embedded in my schedule for completing my paper. Still, I think it is clear that because of their generality of application policies will not normally themselves be elements in plans that concern only particular occasions.

So my situation is this. The planning theory sees intentions as typically elements of coordinating plans, and tries to exploit this idea to provide a model of the role of intention in intelligent agency. I want to extend this model to include the central roles of personal policies in intelligent agency. I propose to do this in a way that exploits my earlier treatment of intention, by seeing such policies as certain kinds of general intentions. But I need to do this in a way that does not assume that policies are themselves elements in standard kinds of coordinating plans: schedule-like plans that solely concern particular occasions.

2. The planning theory: some basic ideas

The first step is to review some of the basic ideas of the planning theory about the role in intelligent agency of future-directed intentions concerning particular occasions.

Why bother with future-directed intentions anyway? Why not just cross our bridges when we come to them? I think there are two main answers. The first is that we are not frictionless deliberators. Deliberation is a process that takes time and uses other resources; because of this there are obvious limits to the extent of deliberation and reflection at the time of action. By settling on future-directed intentions we allow present deliberation and reflection to shape later conduct, thereby extending the influence of Reason on our lives. Second, we have pressing needs for coordination. To achieve complex goals I must coordinate my present and future activities. And I need also to coordinate my activities with yours. Future-directed intentions help facilitate both intra- and inter-personal coordination.

How? As I have already indicated, I believe that part of the answer comes from noting that future-directed intentions are typically elements of larger plans. My intention today to go to Boston next week helps coordinate my activities for the next several weeks, and my activities with yours, by entering into a larger plan of action—one that will eventually include specifications of how to get there and what to bring, and one that will be coordinated with, for example, my child-care plans and your plans for meeting me in Boston. And it will do this in ways compatible with my resource limitations and in a way that extends the influence of today's deliberation to next week's action.

Let me stop and clarify how I am using this notion of a plan. A first distinction that needs to be made is between plans as abstract structures and plans as mental states. When I speak here of plans I have in mind a certain kind of mental state, not merely an abstract structure of a sort that can be represented, say, by some game-theoretical notation. We can characterize important aspects of such mental states in terms of such abstract structures; but this should not lead us to loose sight of the distinction between the two. A more colloquial usage for what I intend in speaking of a plan might be 'having a plan'. But even after saying this there remains room for misunderstanding; for we need to distinguish two different senses of 'having a plan'. In one sense of 'having a plan' I can have a plan simply by having a kind of recipe—simply by knowing a procedure for achieving a certain end. In this sense I can have a plan for roasting lamb whether or not I actually plan to roast lamb. This contrasts with a second sense of 'having a plan'. In this second sense I have a plan to roast lamb only if I plan to roast it. It is this second kind of case that I intend when I speak of plans. Plans, as I shall understand them, are mental states involving an appropriate sort of commitment to action: I have a plan to A only if I plan to A.

The plans characteristic of a limited agent like me typically have two important features. First, my plans are typically *partial*. When I decide today to go to Boston next week I do not settle all at once on a complete plan for next week. Rather, I decide now to go to Boston, and leave till later deliberation about how to get there in ways consistent with my other plans. Second, my plans typically have a *hierarchical structure*. Plans concerning ends embed plans concerning means and preliminary steps; and relatively less specific intentions embed relatively more specific ones. As a result, I may deliberate about parts of my plan while holding other parts fixed. I may hold fixed certain intended ends, while deliberating about means or preliminary steps.[2]

The strategy of settling in advance on such partial, hierarchically structured plans, leaving lower-level decisions till later, has a pragmatic rationale. On the one hand, we need to coordinate our activities both within our own lives and socially, between lives. And we need to do this in ways compatible with our limited capacities to deliberate and process information. This argues for being planning creatures. On the other hand, the world changes in ways we are not in a position to anticipate; so highly detailed plans about the far future will often be of little use and not worth bothering with. Partial, hierarchically structured plans for the future provide our compromise solution.

With this partiality of plans go characteristic patterns of reasoning; for given the partiality of plans, we will frequently engage in reasoning in which our prior intentions play an important role as inputs. We will reason from a prior intention to further intentions concerning means or preliminary steps, or from a relatively less specific to a relatively more specific intention. In such reasoning we fill in partial plans in ways required for them successfully to guide our conduct.

Such reasoning is driven by demands that, other things equal, plans need to satisfy to serve well their roles in coordination and in extending the influence of deliberation. First, there are *consistency constraints*. Plans need to be both internally consistent and consistent with the agent's beliefs. Roughly, it should be possible for my plans taken together to be successfully executed in a world in which my beliefs are true. Second, though partial, my plans need to be filled in to a certain extent as time goes by. My plans should be filled in with sub-plans concerning means, preliminary steps, and relatively specific courses of action, sub-plans at least as extensive as I believe is now required to do what I plan. Otherwise they will suffer from *incoherence*.[3]

Associated with these two demands are two direct roles intentions and plans play as inputs in practical reasoning. First, given the demand for coherence, prior intentions frequently *pose problems* for further deliberation. Given my intention to go to Boston next week, I need soon to fill in my plan with a specification of some means to getting there. Second, given the need for consistency, prior intentions *constrain* further intentions. If I am already planning to conduct an evening seminar at Stanford the night before I go to Boston, I cannot consistently solve my problem of how to get to Boston by deciding to take the night flight.

Prior intentions, then, pose problems for deliberation, thereby establishing a major standard of *relevance* for options considered in deliberation. And they constrain solutions to these problems, providing a *filter of admissibility* for options. In these ways prior intentions and plans help make deliberation tractable for agents like us, agents with substantial resource limitations.

This gives us a natural model of the relation between two kinds of practical reasoning: the weighing of desire-belief reasons for and against conflicting options, and reasoning from a prior intention to derivative intentions concerning means and the like. Our model sees prior intentions as elements of plans, plans that are typically partial and that provide a *background framework* within which the weighing of desire-belief reasons is to occur. It is this framework that poses problems for such further reasoning and constrains solutions to these problems. So practical reasoning has two levels: prior, partial plans pose problems and provide a filter on options that are potential solutions to these problems; desire-belief reasons enter as considerations to be weighed in deliberating between relevant and admissible options.

All this requires that prior intentions and plans have a certain *stability*: prior intentions and plans resist being reconsidered or abandoned. If we were constantly to be reconsidering the merits of our prior plans they would be of little use in coordination and in helping us cope with our resource limitations. However, it would of course also be irrational to treat one's prior plans as irrevocable, for the unexpected does happen and our values do change. This suggests that rational agents like us need general strategies and habits that govern the reconsideration or abandonment of prior intentions and plans. Roughly speaking, their retention and non-reconsideration should be treated as the default, but a default that is overridable by certain special kinds of contingencies—as we might say, in the spirit of John Dewey, certain kinds of problematic situations.

I have emphasized that prior intentions and plans play a coordinating role. My prior intention to go to Boston next week, for example, helps support coordination within my own life and socially, between my life and the lives of others. We can now say more about how this works.

Concerning both social and intra-personal coordination we may distinguish three aspects. Begin with the intra-personal case. I achieve coordination within my own life, first, when I settle on needed means or preliminary steps. My prior intention supports such coordination in my life by driving relevant reasoning about means and the like, thereby leading me to needed additions to my plans. Second, coordination within my life requires me to constrain my other plans appropriately, given my intention to go to Boston next week. This is supported by the demand for intention-belief consistency. Satisfaction of this demand supports my efforts not to keep tripping over myself in the pursuit of complex goals.

Each of these two aspects of intra-personal coordination will have inter-personal analogues involving cases of group action. Abe, Barbara, and Claire intend together to paint the living room. So they need to settle on appropriate means. This will involve, in part, settling on who will do what. Who will buy the paint? sand the walls? and so on. Second, they need to ensure that the relevant intentions of each of them fit together consistently. If Abe plans to sand on Tuesday Claire cannot plan to paint on Tuesday, given their shared knowledge that these are incompatible activities. The group action of painting the room requires that they solve problems of means and constrain their activities in light of demands for consistency.

These first two aspects of coordination are linked to demands for coherence and consistency, demands I have already discussed. The third aspect of coordination—both intra-personal and inter-personal—introduces a further theme: the belief-supporting role of, for example, my intention to go to Boston. The crucial point is that both you and I make further plans on the assumption that I will go to Boston. You go on to plan to go to Boston so as to meet me there; and I go on to plan to visit my sister while I am in Boston. We both *plan on* my going to Boston. We can do this because my prior intention to go to Boston normally supports the expectation that I will in fact go there then. That is, my intention normally helps support your expectation that I will go there, thereby enabling you to plan on the assumption that I'll be there. And it normally helps support my expectation that I will go, thereby enabling me to plan on a similar assumption. But how is it that my intention can provide such support?

Part of the answer has already been suggested, and returns us to the first two aspects of coordination. My intention will normally lead me to reason about, and to fill in my plan with appropriate means and preliminary steps. And a concern with intention-belief consistency will tend to prevent conflicts that would stand in the way of my going to Boston. Further, my intention has a certain stability; so one can expect that it will not be easily changed. Still, there is a gap in the explanation as it has so far been presented. For all that we have said so far my intention might stay around, lead to reasoning about means and the like, and preclude conflicting intentions, and yet still not control my conduct when the time comes.

What we have not yet explicitly noted about intention, and what fills the gap in the explanation, is the common-sense observation that there is a tight connection between intending to act and endeavoring/aiming/trying so to act. If I have a present-directed intention to *A* and nothing prevents me I will normally proceed to act in a way that aims at *A*-ing—I will normally proceed at least to try to *A*, to endeavor to *A*. So an agent can normally be relied on at least to try to execute her intention when the time comes, if the intention is still around and if the agent then knows both that the time has come and what to do. It is because intentions are normally stable that they can normally be relied on to persist until the time of action. It is because intentions drive relevant means-end reasoning and the like that the agent can normally be relied on to put herself in a position to execute the intention and to know what to do when the time comes. And it is because of the demand for consistency that the agent can be relied on not to undermine her own efforts. Taken together these features of intention help explain how future-directed intentions normally help support coordination by supporting associated expectations of their successful execution.

In summary, then, the planning theory emphasizes the following aspects of future-directed intentions:

1. We bother with future-directed intentions primarily because of our needs to extend the influence of rational reflection over time and to promote coordination, both inter- and intra-personal.
2. Future-directed intentions support coordination in part by supporting associated beliefs in their successful execution.
3. Future-directed intentions are typically elements in larger coordinating plans. These plans are typically partial and hierarchical.
4. Future-directed intentions and partial plans have a characteristic stability.
5. Given the demand for coherence, prior partial plans pose problems for further planning.
6. Given relevant consistency constraints, prior partial plans provide a filter of admissibility on options.

Our job is to see how to extend these principles to the case of personal policies.

3. The extension to personal policies

My goal is to extend the planning theory to include personal policies. My plan for doing this is to see such policies as intentions that are general with respect to their occasions of execution. For this to work the central features of intentions that are highlighted by the planning theory need to be extendable to personal policies. It should be possible to characterize central features of the roles of policies in intelligent agency as natural extensions of the roles of intentions in schedule-like plans. How can we do this?

Turn to principles (1)-(6) of the planning theory. These describe basic aspects of the functioning of prior intention in limited, intelligent agency. What we need to do is to characterize basic aspects of the functioning of personal policies in terms of extensions of these principles. We have noted, however, that personal policies will not normally be parts of schedule-like plans of action. So principle (3) is not going to be very useful in characterizing the basic roles of personal policies. What we need to explore is the extent to which (1)-(2) and (4)-(6), properly interpreted and extended, can adequately serve this purpose. This is what I proceed to do, beginning with principles (1) and (2).

3.1. Why we bother with personal policies

Why do we bother with personal policies? Why don't we just buckle our seat belts when we come to them? At least part of the answer follows the lines of our account of intentions concerning a particular future occasion. First, the formation of general policies helps extend the influence of rational reflection: it is a partial solution to the problems posed by our limited resources for calculation and deliberation at the time of action. Second, general policies facilitate coordination, both intra-and inter-personal. Let me elaborate a bit on each of these points.

Concerning the extension of the influence of reflection, begin by recalling my intention to go to Boston next week. In arriving at this intention my present reasoning helps shape my action next week. As I have urged, this extension of the power of reason to shape later action is a primary rationale for the capacity and disposition to form future-directed intentions and plans. Similarly, when I form a general policy of buckling up, my present deliberation helps shape my conduct in various later circumstances. My capacity to plump for such a general policy thus helps extend the influence of my present reflection. As with the case of intentions concerned with a particular future occasion this is useful to me because it allows my later action to be grounded in earlier deliberation, rather than only in deliberation at the moment of action, when time may be quite limited. Indeed, this extension of the influence of my present deliberation is even more striking in the case of a general policy than in the case of an intention concerning a particular future occasion; for in settling now on a policy for many similar circumstances later I save myself from having to go through the same reflections on many different future occasions.

There may also be yet a further advantage to be gained by settling in advance on such general policies. Consider, for example, personal policies of buckling up and of not driving after drinking alcohol. The dangers of riding without seat belts, or of driving after drinking, may be difficult to appreciate on the particular occasions when such decisions present themselves. This may not be because of any pressure of time or lack of information, but rather because some may find it difficult to appreciate the risks of a single occasion of riding without seat beats or of drinking and driving.[4] Some may be more reliable at appreciating the relevant risks when they instead reflect on general ways of acting in recurrent situations. Such people might well find deliberation about general policies to be a more reliable guide to action than particular deliberations about particular cases at the time of action. For such people adopting a personal policy (of buckling up, for example) would be a way of compensating for a predictable unreliability in their reasoning concerning specific cases.[5]

Turn now to the coordinating role of personal policies. Like intentions concerned with a particular future occasion, personal policies will help support coordination within the agent's own life and socially, between lives. And this support for coordination will be in part by way of support for associated expectations of action, just as the extension of principle (2) predicts. A full explanation of this depends on the proposed extension of principles (4)-(6) to personal policies; for, as we have seen, the coordinating role of prior intentions is closely tied to their stability and their satisfaction of demands of coherence and consistency. While these extensions are the subject of my discussion below, we can still sketch some of the main ideas about coordination here.[6]

Personal policies will play coordinating roles—both intra-personal and social—at two different levels: at the level of the policies themselves, and at the level of the policy-based intentions concerning particular occasions in which these policies issue. And at each level there will be each of the three different aspects of coordination distinguished above. So we have, in effect, a 3x2x2 matrix resulting from the product of the three aspects of coordination, the distinction between intra-personal and social coordination, and the distinction between the policy level and the level of intentions concerning particular occasions.

Consider intra-personal coordination at the level of policies. My policy of preparing the next day's lecture the night before will support coordination with other policies of mine. First, it might lead me to further policies concerned with means to the successful execution of this policy—for example, a policy of leaving at home the main books for the course. Second, it will constrain other policies because of concerns with consistency: I will not also have a policy of going out to movies nightly. And it may even lead to policies aimed at ensuring such consistency, as when I settle on a policy of not scheduling evening appointments. Third, I will be able to construct further policies on the assumption that I will be preparing these lectures nightly. So I might, for example, settle on a policy of taking care of my children in the mornings prior to my lectures.

Now turn to the level of policy-based intentions concerning particular future occasions. My lecture-preparation policy will normally serve each day as the basis for an associated, policy-based intention to prepare my lecture that evening. And this policy-based intention will then help me plan the rest of my day in ways that help ensure that I bring home any other books that are necessary for preparing that particular lecture, do not make other, incompatible plans for that evening, and can make further plans for the evening on the assumption that I will prepare my lecture then. So at both these levels my personal policy helps support all three aspects of intrapersonal coordination.

My personal policies will also help support social coordination. Here let me focus on the third aspect of coordination: coordination as reliable, policy-based prediction. I have a policy of working in my office in the afternoons. This policy makes my whereabouts predictable to you, in ways that make it easier for us to pursue our collaborative research project. You can plan on discussing matters with me in my office in the afternoons, and I can plan on your knowing of my availability. By having various general policies I make my behavior increasingly reliable. I thereby enable others to plan on what I will do; and I thereby also make it easier for me to plan on the assumption that others know what I will be doing.[7]

So personal policies help both to extend the influence of rational reflection and to support various forms of coordination. To this we may add yet a further, distinctive reason for bothering with personal policies. Consider an example suggested to me by Mark Crimmins. A store owner may have a policy of asking for identification before accepting a personal check. One reason for this policy might be that on each particular occasion there really is a serious chance of a phony check, and acting on this policy reduces that risk on that occasion. But the owner may also have a different kind of reason for this policy. He knows that if he decides on a case by case basis whether to ask for identification, his customers will know that this is what he is doing, and so those who are asked for identification may well feel singled out and offended. By having a general policy of always requiring identification the store owner avoids this: no customer need feel singled out as particularly subject to suspicion. When the store owner acts on his policy his reasons for asking for identification essentially include the policy itself, and his general reasons for it; his reasons for action need not include any particular suspicion of the particular customer whose identification is being requested. By having his general policy he changes the reasons for which, in a particular case, he asks for identification; and this can have important social effects.

This case illustrates two points. The first echoes a theme from Rawls' discussion in "Two Concepts of Rules"[8]: I can have reasons for having a general policy which are not merely a summation of reasons I would have, even in the absence of the policy, for the particular acts mandated by the policy. Second, once I have a policy, it and my reasons for it infect my reasons for its execution in a particular case. Since the reaction of others to my conduct is to a large extent dependent on their understanding of my reasons for that conduct, this impact of my policy on my reasons for action may well have an important social impact.

So analogues of principles (1) and (2) will be true of personal policies; and there will also be further, distinctive grounds for bothering with such policies.[9] As I have noted, however, this extension to personal policies depends on their playing roles analogous to those described in principles (4)-(6). So we need to say what those analogues are. I will begin with principle (4), concerning stability.

3.2. Stability, defeasibility, and flexibility

Future-directed intentions and plans have a characteristic stability. They are held against a background of habits of reconsideration and abandonment such that their retention and nonreconsideration is the default. A similar point can be made about personal policies. They too will involve a resistance to being abandoned or reconsidered; otherwise it would be a waste of time to bother with them in the first place, and the stability of one's schedule-like plans would also be threatened. So there is a natural extension of principle (4).

There are, however, important complications. Some personal policies exhibit a characteristic kind of *defeasibility*; and some personal policies exhibit an important kind of *flexibility*. These properties of defeasibility and flexibility are both compatible with, and interact in important ways with the stability of policies, thereby complicating the route from policy to action.

Begin with defeasibility. When I intend to buckle up when I drive, or to change furnace filters every two months, I do not intend so to act *no matter what*. I am not committed to buckling up in certain emergency situations, or to changing filters in an earthquake. We might try building all these qualifications into the specification of what is intended, but the task seems hopeless as long as we avoid relatively uninformative specifications like "unless the circumstances make so acting inappropriate". Instead, we should just recognize that there is an inevitable defeasibility in many policies: there can be circumstances in which one will appropriately block the application of the policy to the particular case even though one will still retain that policy. In an emergency I do not give up my general policy of buckling up, but I might still block its application to my particular case and not bother with my seat belts.

This means that for many policies we need to make a distinction between *reconsidering* or *abandoning* the policy, on the one hand, and *blocking* its application to a particular case, on the other. Faced with new information about seat belts I might reconsider my policy concerning their use. But in an emergency situation I do not reconsider or abandon my policy, I only block its application to the particular case.

A similar distinction does not apply to the case of an intention concerning a particular, relatively specific future occasion. I intend to go to Boston next Tuesday. If next Tuesday I am unexpectedly ill and cannot execute my intention, I must simply abandon that intention. I do not have available to me the intermediate possibility of blocking its application to my present situation but retaining the intention nevertheless; for the intention is precisely about that very situation.

Matters are more complex with intentions that concern a single occasion but that specify the occasion rather broadly. Consider my intention to go to Boston sometime next week. For me to execute this intention, in a normal case, I need to settle on some specific day. Suppose I settle on next Tuesday, Tuesday arrives, and I am ill. I then abandon my intention to go to Boston on Tuesday; but I may still retain my intention to go to Boston sometime that week. So my treatment of my intention to go to Boston that week is in a way analogous to my treatment of my policy of buckling up in a case in which, due to an emergency, I block its application to a particular situation. But there is also an important difference. My policy of buckling up provides quite determinate guidance as to what to do on a particular occasion of getting in my car to drive: I am to buckle up. So when on that occasion I refrain from buckling up, I really must block the application of this policy. In contrast, my intention to go to Boston sometime during the week does *not* provide determinate guidance concerning what to do on Tuesday. So when I refrain from going to Boston on Tuesday I need not block the application of *this* intention to my present circumstances. What I need to do is *not* *execute* this intention in my present circumstance and *abandon* my more specific intention to go on Tuesday. When I refrain from going to Boston on Tuesday I do not exploit a *defeasibility* in my intention to go sometime that week. What I do exploit is a certain flexibility in its specification of the occasion for execution. I will return to this point below, where I will introduce the notion of *occasion flexibility*.

Defeasibility should be distinguished from instability. The stability of a policy is its resistance to reconsideration or abandonment. When a defeasible policy is blocked in application to a particular case that policy still remains in effect—it is neither abandoned nor reconsidered. Indeed, defeasibility and stability are in a way mutually supporting. One's dispositions of reconsideration and/or abandonment concerning a given policy, and one's dispositions to block the application of that policy in certain special cases should complement each other appropriately. For example, extreme stability will tend to bring with it a need for increased defeasibility—a need for an increased willingness to block the policy's application to a special case.

I remarked earlier that intelligent agents like us will need general strategies and habits of reconsideration of prior intentions and plans, and a similar point holds for habits of blocking general policies in application to special circumstances. In both cases one wants habits and strategies that exhibit a mean between the extreme of being too willing to reconsider a prior intention or block a policy, on the one hand, and of being too rigid in retaining or applying one's intention or policy, on the other. And in both cases there will be room for interesting varieties of common human failings like self-deception and weakness of the will.

Let me turn now to the property of flexibility. Begin by distinguishing two kinds of flexibility. First, both policies and intentions concerning a particular occasion normally leave open many details about their method of execution, details that need to be settled before execution can be successful. My policy of changing the oil in my car every 3000 miles does not specify, for example, what brand of oil to use. And my intention to go to a concert tomorrow does not yet specify which concert. My policy allows for flexibility when I get around to choosing brands; and my concert-going intention allows for flexibility in choosing a concert. Call this *method flexibility*. Second, intentions and policies can also provide for flexibility concerning their *occasions of execution*. For example, my intention to go to Boston sometime next week allows for flexibility in determining later just which day to go. Call this *occasion flexibility*.

Here I focus on occasion flexibility. The first step is to distinguish several different kinds. My intention to go to Boston sometime next week exhibits *one-time* flexibility. It leaves me flexibility concerning when next week to go; but it nevertheless concerns only a single future occasion. In contrast, policies may exhibit more complex forms of occasion flexibility. To say what these are, however, I need first to make a pair of distinctions between types of policies.

The first distinction is one I have already hinted at: a distinction between *situation-specific* and *situation-indefinite* policies. A situation-specific (*ss*) policy is a policy of acting in a certain way whenever one is in a certain type of situation. A ss-policy is a general intention to A whenever C, where the type of action and the type of situation may be specified at various degrees of generality. My general intentions to help Gregory when he asks, to change oil every 3000 miles, and to refrain from vigorous exercise when the pollen count is high are all ss-policies. In contrast, situation-indefinite (*si*) policies do not specify a recurrent kind of situation in which one is to act, but rather are policies to act in certain regular ways over an extended period of time. My policies of exercising regularly, of giving regularly to charity, of always studying some foreign language, and of always working on some new athletic skill are all si-policies.

Two caveats. First, as I am understanding this terminology, a policy concerning one's A-ing is not made situation-specific merely because it appeals to a condition necessary for one to be able to A. A policy, for example, of not smoking cigarettes might be expressed as a policy of not smoking in those circumstances in which cigarettes are present. But this latter condition of opportunity does not by itself make the policy situation-specific. The policy of not smoking cigarettes remains a si-policy; it contrasts, for example, with the policy of not smoking when in the company of non-smokers, which is an ss-policy. Second, we must be careful how we understand the progressive forms of the verbs used in the expression of these policies.[10] My policy of always working on some new athletic skill obviously does not require that I actually be working on that skill all the time, to the exclusion of other activities. I can be working on my backhand over the course of several weeks without constantly having a tennis racket in my hand! An si-policy need not be all-consuming.

Turn now to a second distinction: among si-policies we can draw a rough-and-ready line between policies that favor some positive course of action and those that are best seen merely as ruling out some specific way of acting. My policy of exercising regularly is an example of the former; my policy of not lying an example of the latter. Without stopping to explore the question of how exactly to draw this distinction, let us call the former *positive* si-policies, and the latter *negative* si-policies.

These distinctions in hand return to occasion flexibility. As I have noted, intentions concerning particular future occasions may exhibit one-time flexibility in their specification of that occasion. When I intend to go to Boston sometime next week my intention only specifies its occasion of execution in a fairly coarse-grained way. Now, many ss-policies will exhibit an analogous kind of occasion flexibility concerning repeated occasions. I might, for example, have a policy of going to a Giants game once each month. This policy repeatedly leaves me the kind of flexibility in specifying its occasion of execution that my intention to go to Boston sometime next week leaves me for a one-time occasion.[11] I will call the flexibility that my policy exhibits *repeated* occasion flexibility.

Now consider the positive si-policy of exercising regularly. This policy does not specify the situations in which one is to exercise. Concerning any particular opportunity for exercise it leaves it open whether to exercise then. It just requires that one somehow build exercise into one's life. I will call this kind of flexibility *general* occasion flexibility.

So ss-policies can exhibit repeated occasion flexibility; and positive si-policies can exhibit general occasion flexibility. The next point to make is that repeated and general occasion flexibility need, each of them, to be distinguished both from instability and from defeasibility.

To see this, begin by returning to my exercise policy and its general occasion flexibility. If I do not take advantage of a particular opportunity for exercise I need not thereby either be reconsidering or abandoning my policy of exercising regularly. I may refrain from exercising this time without in any way questioning my general policy: General occasion flexibility is not instability. Further, when I refrain from exercising I am not thereby rejecting a straightforward consequence of my policy for this particular case. My policy is not a policy of exercising *whenever* I have the opportunity. I may refrain from exercising without blocking the application of my policy to my case. So the fact that I may refrain from exercising without giving up my policy does not show that my policy is defeasible. General occasion flexibility is not defeasibility.

To highlight the difference between defeasibility and general occasion flexibility compare my si-policy of exercising regularly with your ss-policy of exercising on Tuesday nights. Suppose Tuesday night arrives and with it an earthquake. Neither you nor I engage in our exercise routines. But you needed to block the application of your policy to this particular case, thereby exhibiting your policy's defeasibility. In contrast, I needed only to exploit the general occasion flexibility of my policy. My si-policy will exhibit general occasion flexibility rather than defeasibility; your ss-policy exhibits defeasibility rather than occasion flexibility.

Analogous points can be made about repeated occasion flexibility. First, when I do not go to the Giant's game tonight I need not thereby reconsider or abandon my general policy of going to a Giant's game monthly. Repeated occasion flexibility is not instability. Second, my policy does not provide determinate guidance concerning my plans for tonight. So when I stay home tonight I need not block the application of this policy to my present situation. Repeated occasion flexibility is not defeasibility.

A complication is that, though repeated occasion flexibility is to be distinguished from defeasibility, one and the same ss-policy may exhibit the former on some occasions and the latter on others. I have a ss-policy of changing the oil in my car approximately every 3000 miles. In a serious oil shortage I might block its application to my particular case, thereby evidencing its defeasibility. But in a busy week I take advantage of its implicit occasion flexibility when I delay a bit before changing oil, waiting until the weekend when I have more time.

To sum up. Personal policies, like intentions concerning particular future occasions, will exhibit stability. But this stability is compatible both with defeasibility and with repeated or general occasion flexibility. These three features—stability, defeasibility, and flexibility—together make for a complex relation between the initial adoption of a personal policy and its later role in guiding practical reasoning and action.

This complexity will also infect, in corresponding ways, the kinds of expectancies of action that will be supported by personal policies. My policy of exercising regularly will support expectations of regular exercise, but by itself it will not allow someone to plan on the assumption that I will be at the gym tomorrow. So the extension of principle (2) to personal policies will need to be understood in an appropriately complex way.

3.3. The problems posed by personal policies

On the planning theory intentions guide further planning in two major ways: given the demand for coherence they pose problems for further planning to solve; and given demands for consistency they constrain admissible options. If our strategy of analysis is to succeed we need to show how personal policies play analogous roles in guiding and focusing further planning and practical reasoning.

Begin with the problem-posing role. There may seem to be a difficulty here, a difficulty tied to the recognition that personal policies are not themselves typically elements of schedule-like plans of action.

The difficulty is this: I have explained the problem-posing role of future-directed intentions in terms of the demand that plans of action be coherent. The notion of coherence at work here is one of coherence *within* a schedule-like plan. But if a personal policy is not itself an element of such a plan, how can it pose a problem of coherence within such a plan?

I think the point behind this question is well taken, but that it does not prevent us from seeing personal policies as playing a problem-posing role analogous to that played by intentions concerning particular future occasions. What is needed is an extension of the notion of coherence, an extension that proceeds in two directions. We need to introduce notions of coherence, or the lack of it, (a) *within policies* and (b) *between* one's plans and one's policies. I may know myself well enough to know that I will not be able successfully to execute my policy of writing my lectures nightly unless I also adopt a policy of leaving the relevant books at home in my study. So, given the former policy, I adopt the latter to avoid an incoherence *within* my policies. At home at night after dinner I see that I need to adopt an intention to work on my lecture now, for otherwise there will be an incoherence *between* my policy and my plans for the evening. Finally, having decided to work on my lecture now I need to figure out how. Otherwise I will be threatened with an incoherence *within my plans* for this evening.

So there are three kinds of coherence at stake: coherence within plans, between plans and policies, and within policies. This means there will be three kinds of partiality. The planning theory emphasizes that plans are themselves typically partial, leaving the specification of means, preliminary steps, and more specific courses of action to be filled in as time goes by. This is partiality within one's plans. But my plans may also be partial in the sense that they have yet to include elements needed to ensure coherence between them and relevant policies of mine. And my policies may themselves exhibit a kind of partiality, as mine do when I have the policy of writing my lectures in the evening but have yet to settle on an appropriate policy about where to keep the relevant books.

It follows that there will be three kinds of problems: problems of coherence within plans, of coherence between plans and policies, and of coherence within policies. It is the latter two sorts of problems that are central to the extension of principle (5) to personal policies. Here I focus on the demand for coherence *between* one's plans and one's policies.

Normally, the need for coherence between policies and plans results in a need to settle on a *specification* of a general policy. I ensure such coherence by adding to my plans a policy-based intention to carry out my policy on an appropriate occasion: for example, given my oil-changing policy and my recent use of my car I add an intention to change the oil in my car tomorrow. Notice that in adding this intention I do not settle on a *means* to changing my oil every 3000 miles. (Such a means might be, say, installing a light on my odometer set to go off every 3000 miles.) Rather, I settle on a *specific application* of my oil-changing policy. However, in doing this I then create within my plans a problem of means: in order to ensure coherence of my plans for tomorrow I need to settle on some means to changing the oil then.

Matters are a bit more complex for positive si-policies, given their characteristic flexibility; but a similar structure is nevertheless present. My policy of always studying some foreign language threatens me with incoherence between this policy and my summer plans, as long as these include no particular plans for language study. I solve this problem by settling on some plan or other for language study this summer, though I have a great deal of freedom in determining which language, under what circumstances, and so on. Again, consider my policy of exercising regularly. To avoid a threatened incoherence between this policy and my plans, my plans need to include some specification of this policy. I have great flexibility (concerning both method and occasion) in deciding on a particular specification of this policy; but nevertheless I solve the problem by adding to my plans some particular specification or other of my general policy. Once these specifications are added they will typically pose, within my plan, problems of means and the like. Having decided to work on my German this summer I need to figure out how; having decided to run today I need to figure out how to get to the track. Here again we need to distinguish between reasoning aimed at settling on a specific application of a general policy, and reasoning aimed at settling on a means to an intended end.

This difference, between settling on a specification of a general policy and settling on a means to an intended end, returns us to the distinction between instability and defeasibility. If I begin with the intended end of running today, but balk at some necessary means to so acting I will be rationally obliged to give up my intended end. As Kant observed: "Who wills the end, wills (so far as reason has decisive influence on his actions) also the means which are indispensably necessary and in his power."[12] This contrasts with a case in which one does not apply a policy to a particular case due to that policy's defeasibility; for in this latter case the fact that one does not settle on a specification of the policy in the particular case does not force one to give up the policy. In special circumstances I might block the application of my policy of buckling up to my emergency situation without abandoning that policy; for my policy is defeasible. Kant's point about the relation between intended ends and necessary means does not extend to the relation between policies and their specifications; and this highlights an important difference between these relations.

I have been discussing the demand for coherence between policies and plans, and a standard kind of problem generated by this demand. Policies pose problems of specification; and their specifications frequently pose, within their plans, problems of means and the like. But there is also another kind of problem that can be generated by the need for coherence between policies and plans. A policy can also *directly* pose a problem of means or preliminary steps, a problem that arises even before a particular specification of the policy enters into a plan of action for some particular occasion. For example, one's general ability to execute a policy may require that one take certain preliminary steps. I have a policy of buckling up when I drive: but I also have a car with broken seat belts. I need to fix the seat belts to be in a position successfully to act on my policy. So my policy of buckling up directly poses a problem for my planning, a problem of settling on appropriate preliminary steps. Until I settle on such preliminary steps there is a threatened incoherence between my policy and my plans. But this is a different sort of incoherence than that threatened in the case in which what is missing is a specification of the policy for a particular occasion. In the present case the policy directly poses a problem of preliminary steps for my plans: whereas in the earlier cases problems of means or preliminary steps were posed only indirectly, by way of particular specifications of policies.

In summary: Given the need for coherence between policies and plans, personal policies can pose problems of specification which then lead indirectly to problems of coherence within one's plans. And personal policies can also directly pose problems of means or preliminary steps for the agent's plans. Finally, personal policies can pose problems of coherence among the agent's policies themselves. In these ways one's personal policies drive further practical reasoning, practical reasoning aimed at developing one's policies and plans in ways that solve these problems.

3.4. The filtering role of policies

On principle (6) of the planning theory, future-directed intentions provide a filter on admissible options, given the demand for intention-belief consistency. In what ways will personal policies play an analogous role?

Begin by distinguishing several different kinds of policy-related consistency. First, there is consistency, or lack of it, *within* one's policies, given one's beliefs. Two policies of mine are inconsistent with each other, given my beliefs, if it is not possible for me to adhere to both of them given that my beliefs are true. So, for example, my policy of writing my lectures nightly will be inconsistent with yet another policy of playing basketball nightly, knowing, as I do, that I am unable to do both in the same evening. Notice that a pair of policies might potentially conflict in some possible but as yet unexpected situation without those policies being inconsistent in this sense. My policies of writing my lectures nightly and of helping Gregory with his homework if he asks, might come into conflict if Gregory waits until the evening to ask for help and I have a long lecture to write that evening. The mere possibility of such conflict might lead me to consider various conflict-resolving strategies; but it need not. As long as I do not expect this to happen my policies will be consistent in the sense specified.[13]

The second kind of consistency that is important here is consistency, given one's beliefs, *between* policies and intentions concerning particular future occasions. This kind of consistency can itself be usefully, if somewhat roughly, divided into two kinds. First, there may be a failure of consistency between a policy and an intention concerning a relatively narrow option. My policy of not running when the pollen count is high will, once I detect a high pollen count, be inconsistent with an intention to run. Second, a policy might be inconsistent not with an intention concerning a relatively narrow option, but only with a relatively extended plan of action. My policy of always studying some foreign language would not be inconsistent with many intentions concerning relatively narrow options, but would be inconsistent with a larger summer plan that did not leave room for language study.

I think it is clear that intelligent agency will require consistency of all three sorts, other things equal. Given these demands for consistency policies will play associated filtering roles. My policy of not running when the pollen count is high will, once I detect a high pollen count, filter out from my further consideration the option of running. My policy of preparing the next day's lecture the night before will not only filter out the option of going to a movie tonight; it will also filter out a policy of playing basketball nightly. And my si-policy of always studying a foreign language, while it will not filter out very many relatively narrow options that might come up in my planning for a day, will provide an important filter on more extensive plans, such as summer plans.

This last remark concerning the filtering role of positive si-policies needs some clarification. Consider again my si-policy of always studying some foreign language. If a potential summer plan is sufficiently complete so as to *preclude* (by my lights) language study then it will perforce be filtered out. But a summer plan, while making no specific provision for language study, might still be sufficiently incomplete so as not yet to preclude it. In such a case the plan need not yet be filtered out. However, if I were to plump for such a plan it would remain importantly partial and so threaten incoherence with my si-policy. I can coherently plump for the plan only on the assumption that I can later fill it in in a way that avoids this incoherence. So my si-policy will directly filter out some larger plans of action, and it will allow some plans through only on the assumption that in filling them in the threatened incoherence with that policy can later be defused. When larger but partial plans get through the filter on such an assumption they will need later to be filled in further. And at this point the filter imposed by the general policy will again come into effect.

So personal policies will impose a filter on other policies, on relatively narrow options, and on relatively extensive plans of action. Our theory provides for a useful extension of principle (6) to personal policies.

4. Conclusion: policies and plans

A plausible model of limited, intelligent agency should include intentions and partial plans. These attitudes are as integral to such agency as are desires and valuations, on the one hand, and beliefs on the other. I have tried to see how personal policies might be built into the planning theory's version of such a model. The main strategy is to see personal policies as intentions that are general in an appropriate way, while recognizing that these general intentions are not typically elements of schedule-like plans of action. We can fruitfully see personal policies in this way because five major aspects of the functioning of future-directed intentions—aspects expressed in principles (1)-(2) and (4)-(6) of the planning theory—can naturally be developed and extended in ways that shed light on the central roles of personal policies. We may call this the *extended planning theory*.

The extended planning theory provides us with a rich picture of the normal functioning of personal policies. Personal policies play an important role in helping us extend the influence of rational reflection on action, given our limits. They help support coordination, both intra-and inter-personal. Once formed they have a characteristic stability, though this is not, of course, to say that they are immune to revision in the face of problems. This stability is sometimes complemented by the properties of defeasibility or (repeated or general) occasion flexibility. Personal policies provide a filter on admissible options—both other policies, relatively limited options, and extended plans of action. Personal policies directly pose problems both of specification and of means and preliminary steps. Once specified a personal policy may lead indirectly to yet further problems of means, given the demand for coherence within one's plans. In posing such problems personal policies drive further practical reasoning. All this helps explain why personal policies frequently support associated expectations of action, expectations that can themselves support coordination, both intra-and inter-personal.

Return to the distinction between personal policies and those intentions concerning particular occasions that are characteristically elements of schedule-like plans. While this remains an important distinction, we now see that the relations among such policies and between policies and schedule-like plans are in certain ways plan-like: there are, we have seen, important demands of coherence and consistency both within one's various policies, and on their relations with one's plans concerning particular occasions. So, while personal policies will not typically be elements in schedule-like plans of action, the extended planning theory is in a good position to specify the central roles played by such policies in the reasoning and action of intelligent agents like us.[14]

Notes

1. See (Bratman, 1987) and other references and credits given there. For a brief overview of some of the ideas in this book see (Bratman, 1989). Portions of section 2, below, are taken from that essay, though I think my remarks here about coordination are less unsatisfactory than those to be found there. I discuss personal policies in (Bratman, 1986) and briefly in (Bratman, 1987), especially pages 87-92. In these earlier treatments my focus was on issues raised by policies for a general account of assessments of agent rationality, an account I detail in (Bratman, 1987). In this present essay I focus in a more detailed way on the ways in which personal policies shape intelligent planning and action.

468 / Michael E. Bratman

2. In describing plans as partial and hierarchical I exploit the fact that we can partially characterize the kind of mental state a plan is by appeal to abstract structures that can be partial and hierarchical. This is not, however, to identify plans with those structures, any more than I identify the mental state of believing a certain proposition with that proposition when I characterize that state in terms of properties of that proposition—e.g., its consistency with other propositions. (In these remarks I am attempting to respond to some comments of James Allen's in his useful discussion of an earlier paper of mine in (Allen, 1989).)

3. In (Bratman, 1987) I call this *means-end* incoherence, though I explain that I intend this notion to be understood broadly and to include incoherences induced by the absence of needed preliminary steps or specifications of relatively general intentions. Since I will be extending the notion of incoherence even further here (below in section 3) I have decided simply to use the term *incoherence*.

4. Perhaps because of a general difficulty many have in taking seriously certain kinds of low probabilities; or perhaps because of the particular temptations of, say, alcohol.

5. However, for some healthy skepticism about how widespread this phenomenon might be, see Paul Slovic's remarks as reported in (Allmann, 1985).

6. My sketch has been aided by comments from Mark Crimmins.

7. In the case just canvassed my policy helps coordinate our collaborative research project. But in making one a predictable actor in social contexts policies can support coordination at a considerably more abstract level. When the Department Chair has a well-known policy of being in her office in the mornings, a wide range of people, with a wide range of interests, can plan on seeing her then. This too is social coordination: the shared aim or intention is not some relatively specific project but rather something like the relatively abstract goal of participating in a well-functioning university.

8. (Rawls, 1955). Thanks to Carl Ginet for reminding me of the relevance of Rawls' essay.

9. I do not, of course, claim to have explored *all* such further grounds for bothering with policies.

10. As Dagfinn Follesdal once emphasized in conversation.

11. Of course, if it is June 30 and I have not yet gone to a Giants game I no longer have such flexibility. This is analogous to intending to go to Boston sometime during the week and finding oneself at the end of the week and still in Palo Alto.

12. (Kant, 1785), chapter II (Paton's translation).

13. See (Marcus, 1980) for a related discussion about consistency in ethics.

14. I was greatly aided by detailed comments from Sylvian Bromberger on an earlier draft of this paper. I also want to thank for their help Mark Crimmins, Dennis DesChene, Carl Ginet, David Israel, Ron Nash, and Martha Pollack. Work on this paper was supported in part by the Center for the Study of Language and Information, made possible in part through an award from the System Development Foundation.

References

Allen, James F. Two Views of Intention. In Philip R. Cohen, Jerry Morgan, and Martha E. Pollack (Eds.), *Intentions in Communication*, MIT Press, 1989.

Allman, W.F. Staying Alive in the 20th Century. *Science*, 85, October 1985, 31-37.

Bratman, Michael. Personal Policies. Working Paper #RR-7 (1986) in the Risk and Rationality Working Paper Series of the University of Maryland Center for Philosophy and Public Policy.

Bratman, Michael E. *Intention, Plans, and Practical Reason*. Cambridge: Harvard University Press, 1987.

Bratman, Michael E. What Is Intention? In Philip R. Cohen, Jerry Morgan, and Martha E. Pollack (Eds.), *Intentions in Communication*, MIT Press, 1989.

Kant, Immanuel. *Groundwork of the Metaphysic of Morals*, 1785, translated by H.J. Paton (Harper Torchbooks: New York, 1964).

Marcus, Ruth. Moral Dilemmas and Consistency. *The Journal of Philosophy*, 1980, 77, 121-136.

Rawls, John. Two Concepts of Rules. *The Philosophical Review*, 1955, 64, 3-32.

Philosophical Perspectives, 3
Philosophy of Mind and Action Theory, 1989

ACTIONS BY COLLECTIVES

Raimo Tuomela
University of Helsinki

I. Introducing Collective Actions

1. We commonly attribute actions to collectives. Thus, we use locutions like 'Firm F produced the goods G', 'Nation N_1 attacked nation N_2', 'The board dismissed Jones', 'The team scored', and so on. On the basis of examples like these it seems to be a worthwhile project to accept this commonsensical view at least in part and to think that true statements of the above kind can be made. I shall do so in this paper and investigate some central philosophically and conceptually interesting problems related to actions performed by collectives. I shall below be concerned especially with studying under what conditions attributions of actions to collectives can correctly be made.

The commonsensical view that actions can be and are commonly attributed to collective agents does not—under my construal of common sense at least—by itself entail that such attributions need be nonmetaphorical, nor does it entail the existence of collectives as supraindividual entities (see Section II below). And if collectives are construed as real entities, it must be admitted that they are entities clearly different from single human persons—to which action concepts and other mental concepts apply in the first place. Persons have (biological) bodies and perform bodily actions in contrast to collectives. Persons have a full-blown mental life while collectives do not. It can even be maintained that a collective is not a self-sufficient agent (e.g., in the sense of being capable of performing basic bodily actions).

Except for a few comments, I shall not below undertake a proper defence of the above semantical and metaphysical claims (which I am inclined to accept as correct). Irrespective of their correctness, it is possible to argue that the actions of collectives are "made up" or "constituted" by actions of persons. Indeed, this will be a central general thesis to be defended in this paper. Let me formulate the thesis in a preliminary manner as follows: If a collective (consisting presently of the agents $A_1,...,A_m$) does something X then at least some of its members, say $A_1,...,A_k$ (k equal to m or smaller) must, in the right circumstances, do something $X_1,...,X_k$, their parts; and in normal circumstances these parts serve to generate or "make up" X. (Strictly speaking, $X_1,...,X_k$ will be parts of a joint action of $A_1,...,A_k$ which need not be of the type X but which still can be taken to generate or bring about a token of X.) For instance, if one nation declares war against another nation, this may take place through appropriate actions by the members of its government, or its parliament or by its president. Or consider a hockey team's scoring. Some player or, perhaps players, did the scoring. Let us say that it was the "operative" members of the team (collective) who did it. The team's scoring was constituted by their actions. (Note that the statement about the team's scoring holds under different conceptions of how to define the membership of the team—cf. the players not presently on the ice.)

At this introductory stage I shall not go more deeply into the question whether all kinds of social collectives can be said to act. Here we will merely assume that at least typical social collectives such as groups and organizations can be taken to act; this will be substantiated, sharpened, and illustrated in our discussion to come.

2. While the main task of this paper is to clarify what is conceptually and philosophically interesting in actions performed by collectives, I shall start by introducing the notion of joint social action. A central claim of this paper is that actions by collectives are closely connected to relevant jointly performed individual actions; it is therefore appropriate to discuss joint actions at this stage.

In the way of a preliminary sketch, by a joint social action I mean an action performed by several agents who suitably relate their individual actions to each others' actions in pursuit of some joint goal or in adherence to some common rules, practices, or the like. Consider thus two or more agents' doing something X, say carrying a table or writing a book (linguistically, e.g., 'Tom and John wrote a book'). We are interested in the interpretation under which they *joint-ly* or *collectively* (rather than *distributively* and separately) did X. Or consider the still better example, 'All the king's men surrounded the castle'. Here the organized action of surrounding the castle is an irreducible joint action.

Joint social actions in our sense will include such diverse many-agent actions as carrying jointly a heavy table, playing tennis, get-ting married, greeting, asking questions and answering, conversing, and quarreling. Joint actions in this sense should be distinguished from actions performed by (single) collectives such as a group's solv-ing a problem, a bank staff's performing its daily routines, a com-munity's electing a leader, a nation's declaring war, and so on. But it is our central claim in this paper that actions by collectives are connected closely (and in a precise sense) to joint actions by the members of the collective.

To comment briefly on the classification of joint actions, let us distinguish between the logically presupposed *results* and other con-sequences and effects of actions. For instance, the window's open-ing is the result of the action of opening the window. Then we may ask whether, or to what extent, the full result event of a joint action comes about or is generated *causally* rather than *conventionally* or, as I shall below broadly say, "*conceptually*." For instance, two agents' carrying jointly a heavy table upstairs is causally brought about by their component actions of carrying the table. Technically speaking, the results, say r_1 and r_2, of the component actions causally generated the full result, say r, viz. the table's having been moved upstairs (by the agents' jointly carrying it). Although how "thinly" or "thickly" we conceive of the component actions affects the issue somewhat, it can be maintained that causal generation is all that mat-ters here. But consider next two agents' toasting by appropriately lifting their glasses. Here the full result of the social action, viz. a toasting getting performed (r), is conventionally generated by the individual glass liftings (r_1 and r_2), the results of the agents' compo-nent actions. Here we may assume that r is a mereological sum of r_1 and r_2 and that the conventional generation amounts to a redescription (according to the toasting-convention) of $r_1 + r_2$ as r. In many social actions (such as communicative actions, e.g. asking questions-answering) both causal and conventional (or "conceptual") generation play a role (see Tuomela, 1984, Chapters 5 and 6).

Another criterion of classification concerns whether the original agents themselves carry out the whole social action as members of the collective or whether at some point they employ some *represen-tatives* or "proxies" acting on its behalf. For instance, if properly authorized, a lawyer may buy a house for his client. He then represents his client relative to that action. When a nation declares a war or negotiates a treaty it is (or its members are) represented by, say, the Cabinet or perhaps the Prime Minister only; or when a worker's union negotiates a wage increase this takes place by means of its representatives.

II. What Are Collectives and Can All of Them Act?

1. In this section I will discuss actions by collectives more systematical-ly, starting with some linguistic and ontological considerations. The second subsection gives a brief classification of collectives capable of action on conceptual grounds.

Ware (1986) discusses the nature of collectives and actions by col-lectives. His approach is linguistic. He presents an analysis of several different kinds of sentences concerning collectives and their actions, and tries to reach ontological conclusions, as it were, from such linguistic considerations. As he has many interesting things to say about the topic and especially about various kinds of collective ac-tion, I shall start by considering his discussion.

To begin, consider the sentence "Marge and Liz lifted the piano." It can be given two interpretations, the *distributive* and the *collec-tive* (recall Section I). The distributive meaning relates the sentence to the conjunction of two statements to the effect that Marge lifted the piano and Liz lifted the piano. The collective interpretation says that they jointly (rather than separately) lifted it. Ware claims that the collective interpretation refers to an aggregate, a "sum in-dividual", which as a whole does things, without always involving all its parts.

There appear to be several logico-syntactic differences between the distributive and collective interpretations. For instance, distributive interpretation satisfies the so-called principle of contrac-tion while the collective interpretation does not satisfy it. Thus we cannot infer from "The boys carried the piano upstairs" (a collec-tively interpreted sentence) and "Bill is one of the boys" that Bill was involved. Analogously, the converse principle of expansion does not seem to apply either without recourse to sum individuals. Ware, following Massey (1976), claims that the collective interpretation somehow requires, in the way of ontology, that such holistic phrases as 'the boys' or 'the team', or what have you, refer to aggregate particulars, "sum individuals", in a mereological sense.

But it seems to me that one can do at least as well with a different individualistically acceptable ontological interpretation. The above kinds of linguistic considerations do not commit one to the sum individual— approach.[1] The alternative approach I have in mind is to have only single agents (and other needed nonaggregate particulars) in one's ontology and still accept that there are genuine collective (as well as distributive) interpretations of sentences purportedly about collectives. Consider thus the sentence "The group carried the piano upstairs." Let the group consist of Tom, Dick, and Harry, viz. these three persons plus some relevant social psychological relations between them (and towards the group or "us"). According to the present individualistic approach, the basic ontology required by that sentence is just these three persons, the relevant social relations (including their relevant attitudes towards each other and the "us") and their joint action of carrying the piano upstairs. (The ontology may also be taken to include the piano, upstairs, etc.) Here we have an individualistic ontology, one without social wholes.

In a deeper investigation we would presumably want to investigate the logical forms of sentences about collectives, although I am not sure what the logic would be—over and above standard first-order logic together with some suitable modal extension of it. Given that, we may consider a Tarskian semantics for this language. In such a semantics the elements in the domains would be merely persons, their actions, and other mentioned kinds of things; and we seem not to need here the mereological sum as a "truthmaker" or "satisfier". Anyway, linguistic arguments such as Massey's and Ware's cannot succeed in giving ontological conclusions, for there is, so to speak, no direct, unambiguous route from language to ontology. Any language can be connected to the world in a number of different ways in principle. (To assume that there is only one way would be to accept a rejectable form of the Myth of the Given.) But let me nevertheless say that it seems that one always has available the mereological sum in question in these cases without costly extra assumptions (the primitive overlap-relation, or alternatively the discreteness relation, needed for defining a sum can be regarded as readily available). In this sense the mereological approach becomes acceptable.

2. It is not necessary for the purposes of this paper to take a definite ontological stand concerning the nature of collectives. For linguistic reasons, we shall speak as if groups really existed (e.g. as suitable mereological sums of person-stages as Copp, 1984, suggests). Given the above discussion and our earlier examples we can now discuss what kind of social entities can act (and how).

First, we have social "face-to-face" collectives (more or less) structure. Thus crowds, defined with respect to a believed common interest or behavior-stimulus, are a case in point. Crowds, aggregates, assemblies, spontaneous gatherings of people, and related collectives can be said to act in virtue of the members' actions. Here the members do not, or at least need not always be, taken to represent or proxy or act *on behalf of* the collective (cf. Gruner, 1976, Londey, 1978). Thus in a riot the members of the collective typically perform their destructive actions *as members* of the collective without acting on its behalf. So we are here dealing with groups without much or any structure (and division of tasks and activities), and in such groups the members are (more or less) interchangeable or symmetrically related with respect to the goals and interests of the group.

On the other hand there are groups with structure. Often such structure is formally (e.g. legally) defined, in other cases it is determined informally (e.g. in terms of factually existing power relations).[2] For instance, organizations, institutions, and at least some teams belong here. Thus for example, a business corporation (an organization) is typically defined by a charter, by-laws, and by other related constitutive and regulative rules. This kind of formal collective acts via its organization, so to speak, and thus performs only "secondary" actions (in Copp's, 1979, terminology). The collective has positions to be filled by persons, and the positions are partly characterized by rules defining the roles of position-holders. The positions are not generally interchangeable (symmetric), and hence neither are position-holders with respect to their roles. That such formal collectives act via their organization then means in general that some position-holders (or possibly representatives of position-holders or representatives of such representatives, and so on) act on behalf of the collective.

As noted, a collective may be given structure in a number of different ways. A division of tasks and activities may be created by informal agreement (or by threat, force, or what have you), which does not make so much difference with respect to how the collective acts. We have distinguished between two modes of group action. We may then make a rough and ready distinction between three types of groups: 1) groups which can only act because some agents act on their behalf (cf. organizations); 2) groups which always or typically act in virtue of the members acting just as members of the group (cf. crowds); 3) groups which act in either the first or the second mode, depending on occasion (cf. a soccer team as i) playing versus as ii) receiving a prize bowl, with its captain representing it). In our earlier terminology, both kinds of active members can be called operative members, for it is in virtue of them that the collective performs its action. As to the capacity of a social collective to act, it does not seem to make much difference whether it is in some loose or strict sense face-to-face or whether its members (or positions) are interchangeable. The analysis of the actions by collectives to be given below is meant to apply to any social collective capable of action.

Social collectives in the sense meant in this paper are commonsensically taken to be capable of action; crowds, mobs, social groups, teams, organizations, institutions, and so on are simply understood as having goals and interests, which they are disposed to strive for by means of their actions. Classes of people such as red-haired women or something similar of course do not qualify as social collectives in this sense. (But if red-haired women organize themselves into a formal collective, then, as far as conceptual reasons are concerned, that collective will have the capacity to act.)

III. Two Theses on Actions by Collectives

1. Given the above discussion of the various ways actions can be performed by collectives I shall formulate a general thesis on the nature of actions by collectives. This thesis, which is surprisingly simple, is meant to apply to all kinds of social collectives in principle, although I will here substantiate and test it only in the case of informal groups and simple examples of organized collectives. The basic content of the thesis is that a group's intentional action requires (ultimately on conceptual grounds) that at least some of its members suitably act and that as a consequence the group will have acted. These acting members, as earlier, will be called operative members

and they include representatives which are strictly speaking non-members, a kind of substitutes and delegates of proper members of the group. Consider thus the following general analysis of a collective's doing something X intentionally relative to some relevant circumstances C, to be commented on later:

> (CA) A *collective*, G, *performed an action* X *intentionally* in circumstances C if and only if there were operative agents $A_1, ..., A_m$ of G such that $A_1, ..., A_m$ jointly performed X intentionally (in a relevant sense complying with the criterion (IA) to be presented below) in circumstances C.

This thesis analyzes *intentional* actions performed by collectives. Such actions are obviously as central in the case of collectives as they are in the case of single individuals. Thus, for instance, an intentional action by a collective is one for which it is legally and morally responsible. Our above analysis does not quite postulate group-minds (in analogy with the individual case) to account for intentionality, but it does implicitly postulate a kind of modern counterpart of group-minds, viz. we-intentions, to be shared at least by the operative members of the collective, as will be seen below.

The concept of joint action that the thesis (CA) relies on requires some further remarks. First, as an important special case we technically allow actions performed by one single individual, in order to have unified terminology (cf. the President representing his country). Furthermore, we accept the following liberal usage: in the context of (CA) we need not be able to say that the operative agents jointly do X (even in the above wide technical sense) but only that they jointly (in the indicated technical sense) do something which will bring about X. What they thus perform could be a joint action Y, nonidentical with X. To see the reason for this consider a case of a state's entering a treaty where the operative agents jointly ratified the treaty and did whatever was needed; but of course they did not jointly enter the pact even if they jointly brought about that the state entered the pact. However, given these qualifications, we shall below, for simplicity, typically speak of joint actions whenever the agents jointly bring about some result.

One further feature of (CA), worth noting here, is that because of the close connection (a non-accidental coextension based on conceptual grounds) it establishes between group action and joint action, some central properties attributable to joint action become rather straightforwardly attributable to group action. Social power is one such property: if, in the context of *(CA)*, the operative members have the social power to bring about X, then the group has the social power to do X. (Or so it can be argued at least, but we shall not here discuss the matter in detail.) Another feature, to be briefly commented on in Section III below, is that in the case of joint actions performable conjunctively as contrasted with those performable disjunctively the same distinction carries over to group action in virtue of *(CA)*.

The analysans of *(CA)* relies on the notion of (full-blown) *intentional* joint action. In order to characterize this notion we need (in my account, at least) to have an account of the intentionality of single-agent action. Put briefly, an action token u performed by an agent A was intentional if and only if there was a conduct plan of A such that A purposively brought about u because of this conduct plan (see Tuomela, 1977, pp. 320-325). In view of the above, I now propose for a joint action token u = <t,...,b,...,r> which may be assumed to exemplify a complex joint social action type (for a fuller discussion see Chapter 5 of Tuomela, 1984):

> *(IA)* A social action token u jointly performed by $A_1,...,A_m$ was (fully) *intentional* if and only if there were (complete) conduct plans K_i, one, respectively, for each A_i, i=1,...,m, such that $A_1,...,A_m$ purposively brought about u because of the social conduct plan $K = K_1\&...\&K_m$, where each conduct plan K_i makes essential reference to a we-intention (not necessarily one formed prior to action) that $A_1,...,A_m$ shared.

In this criterion for intentionally performed joint action the technical notion of conduct plan is used, which is my explication and expansion of the notion of a plan of action. The notion of we-intention appearing in *(IA)* can be given the following rough and ready explication sufficient for our present purposes (cf. Tuomela and Miller, 1988). We say that a member A_i of a collective G we-intends to perform a joint social action X if and only if i) he intends to do his part of X, ii) believes that the conceptual joint action opportunities for X obtain (e.g. that the other operative members are going to do their parts of X), and iii) believes that it is a mutual belief among the participating members of G that the conceptual joint action opportunities for X obtain. (See below for a formulation of *(CA)* employing the notion of the content of a we-intention.)

2. As earlier, we allow that the operative agents of G (viz. those ac-

tive agents in virtue of which G's action actually comes about) may include representatives for G who are not proper members of G (cf. lawyers in the case of a corporation, for example). The satisfaction of the right hand side of (CA) entails that $A_1,...,A_m$ performed some appropriate actions $X_1,...,X_m$ such that these actions generated or probably generated (and thus "made up") X, and this involves bringing about the result event of X. Here generation is understood in the sense of "purposive" (or "intention-preserving") generation as technically explicated by the relation $IG^*(u_1,...,u_m,u)$, to be read '$u_1,...,u_m$ purposively generated u', of Section II of Chapter 6 of Tuomela, 1984, such that the agents' conduct plans involved a relevant we-intention and where $u_1,...,u_m,u$ tokened $X_1,...,X_m,X$ respectively. As said, (CA) is meant technically to allow cases where only one agent acts as an operative member, even if then we do not have a proper joint action but only a single individual's action.

Note, furthermore, that (CA) could also have been formulated in more linguistic terms, taking as the analysandum something like "G performed X intentionally", but I have preferred the so-called "material" mode presentation, assuming that that mode is not quite so material as to determine the ontological commitments of the analysis.

Let us now consider in some more detail the distinction between the **operative** and the **non-operative** agents of G. We have said that the operative members are the actively acting ones (though possibly intentional omissions may be included in their relevant actions) in virtue of which the collective's action "really" comes about.

Thus both the representatives acting on behalf of a collective and its (active) members acting just as members are included among the operative agents. To reflect on our distinction a little more, consider a state's making a pact with another state. This takes place by, say, the Cabinet ministers' agreeing to the pact and the Prime Minister's signing it. Most citizens of the state do nothing relevant here, we may assume; the Cabinet represents them. But the state would not act fully intentionally unless the (non-operative) citizens were (at least to some degree or in some sense) aware that there are operative agents acting on their behalf, although they may not know who they are and in what roles they act nor exactly what relevant act they are performing. (Imagine a secret pact made in the name of the state by the Cabinet members without anybody else's faintest knowledge of it: the state did not act fully intentionally, I would say.) In some cases it may be appropriate to require the non-operative members to have a relevant conditional we-intention, where the condition might be that they are elected, or otherwise become, operative members, thus changing status from being non-operative ones (see Tuomela and Miller, 1988, on conditional we-intentions).

We may now in any case say that, in something like the above sense, the distinction operative/non-operative is an epistemic one: in the case of intentional actions performed by collectives also the non-operative agents so to speak "passively" participate in virtue of having some relevant awareness of what is going on in the collective. I shall not here try to spell out more clearly what the required passive participation must minimally be nor shall I try to give an analysis of how the operative representatives of collectives are selected, for I doubt that this can be done without performing empirical studies of the power and information structures of various collectives.

3. What are the circumstances C that (CA) relies on? It seems obvious that they must satisfy the right social and normative constraints. Thus the treaty proposal a Prime Minister signs does not qualify if it is unlawful. But he can intentionally do everything which he has the authority to do and which, accordingly, does not violate the role-rules defining the position of a prime minister. Similarly the members of the governing board of an institution obviously cannot nominate somebody for a post, say, if the board lacks the authority to do so, but they can do everything the rules of the organization permit. So, in general, we should demand that the circumstances C be such that the following at least "prototypically" holds: the ought-to-be rules (saying e.g. what the administration ought be like), ought-to-do rules (specifying e.g. what the position-holders ought to do in various circumstances), and may-do rules (specifying analogously which actions are permitted) characterizing an organization should not at least be intentionally violated by the position-holders.

If we concentrate on a single operative member A_i we may say this. Assume first that this agent is a position-holder in the collective. His actions as a position-holder are governed by some role-rules. A position may in fact be analyzed into a collection of roles, and roles may be characterized as conjunctions of role-rules—ought-to-do and may-do rules— related to possibly several joint or single actions. Accordingly, positions can, for our present purposes at least, be viewed as conjunctions of role-rules (cf. Tuomela, 1984, Chapter

8). Let us speak of "position-actions" in the case of actions satisfying (or "obeying") the position in question and of "role-actions" in the case of actions similarly satisfying a role related to the position. Given this simple schematic account, we can characterize the social-normative circumstances C as follows. Concentrating on one joint action type X, the suggestion is to regard C as the circumstances satisfying the role-rules pertaining to X (in a sense requiring the agents to act in the right roles, performing their role-related actions). The latter are understood to cover the role-rules for X_i, whenever A_i is performing X_i as his part in the context of our analysis (CA), in the case of all $i = 1,...,m$. It is also implicitly understood here that C also comprises all the (prior) satisfaction conditions (or the so-called "conceptual joint action opportunities") concerning the performance of X (hence e.g. the conditions related to the joint satisfiability of the X_i's). Put in simpler terms, when performing X_i in the context under discussion, A_i **is, at least in the prototypical cases, assumed to act in his X_i-related role**, viz. to obey the role-rules in question, and the obtaining of C will be assumed to account for that. (If some action is merely compatible with the role rules in question but not in a strict sense required or permitted by them, that action has not been performed in the right social and normative circumstances C.)

In the case of unorganized collectives we reason by analogy. In their case we may sometimes have a previously formed, but informal, division of tasks and activities, with accompanying expectations corresponding to the above kind of role-expectations in the case of organized collectives. Or there may be only an "on-the-spot" division of tasks and activities, and then the analogy with the organized collective may be only a dim one. But the circumstances C may in any case be defined analogously in the case of unorganized collectives, and when the division of activities and the conditions underlying it get dimmer (cf. crowds) so does C, but this obscurity lies more in the nature of the social phenomenon under discussion than in our conceptual analysis of it.

This characterization of C, even if tentative, serves to handle at least some, perhaps all problematic cases which relate to the social and normative content of the situation. Suppose for example that president Koivisto reproaches the government for something. Then he is not representing Finland, for he is not acting in his representative role, which concerns primarily matters related to foreign affairs. But acting in that representative role he may sign a pact and thus represent Finland. Note that acting in a role is not only a matter of performing appropriate kinds of actions but also acting in the right context. Consider now the president acting as himself in a movie or in a play, where he signs a pact giving away Finland to Sweden. This case is not real because he does not act in the right circumstances although he performs the right type of action.

I have meant my above analysis to apply at least to standard or prototypical cases. There are many kinds of borderline cases, which all fall more less short of satisfying the above conditions for C. And then the question arises whether they are close enough for satisfying the right social-normative conditions for the attribution of an action to the collective. Consider a case where a corporation supposedly buys a factory but where it was later found out that a legal mistake was involved. If the mistake was a minor one (e.g. a slip in a document) the case is close enough to the prototypic case to be rectified and to qualify as a sale, viz. an action by the corporation. But, to go to an alternative possibility, if the seller was later found out not to be the legal owner of the factory, after all, no change of ownership took place. Between these somewhat extreme cases (both of which, however, involve some kind of violation of C) the reader can invent all kinds of sophisticated examples.

My point here is that cases of collective action seem amenable to an analysis in terms of prototypes (which I take rather unproblematically to satisfy C) and similarity relations between them and cases violating C. "Sufficiently" similar cases qualify or may qualify as actions by collectives, the others do not. By this I mean that the problem is shifted to evaluating relevant similarities (related to rules and descriptive properties of actions) case by case. Think of a case where a country militarily invades another country, but that it is later found out that no proper authorization, required by the constitution of the country existed (e.g. the Government never made the appropriate decisions) although it was a common belief that it did. Largely on the basis of the descriptive features involved in the act of invasion we seem justified to say that the country (at least **de facto** if not **de jure**) invaded the other country. As another example consider Finland's President Ryti's signing the so-called Ryti-Ribbentrop Pact with Germany in 1944. However, Ryti acted in part as a private person and did not satisfy all the position rules concerning a president. He seemingly made a pact with Germany acting in a sense as an representative of Finland. While he seems to have made the pact with the approval of the Government this pact was (intentionally) never taken to the Parliament to be ratified by it, and so all the position rules were not satisfied. Now the Finns did not consider this to be a pact between the two countries while the Germans did, and here we have a real life example of the difficulties just discussed. And let me end by suggesting that when making *in casu* judgements of relevant similarity factual, a posteriori considerations may have to enter, and I conjecture that even the relevant criteria for making such judgements (nor all the required data) may not be available before a satisfactory empirical investigation of e.g. various types of collectives and occasions for acting.

I shall not in this paper try to clarify in more detail what the right normative and social circumstances amount to, and it may not perhaps be possible to do it without empirically investigating various types of collectives. Let me mention that Copp (1979) has discussed this problem, although in somewhat more general terms. Using his terms, we may agree that in the case of organized collectives, C must satisfy all the constraints entailed by the constitutional rules, laws and by-laws of organized collectives. Furthermore, in the case of unorganized collectives, C must satisfy relevant constraints concerning the composition and dynamics of, or patterns of interpersonal relations within, such collectives. These constraints form a kind of informal counterpart and analog of the constraining rules in the case of organized collectives.

4. I have here distinguished two different problems in accounting for the conceptual nature of actions by collectives. First, there is the discussed problem of giving the right normative and social circumstances C; secondly, a structural account of the relationships between the holistic, collective level and the individual level must also be given. I have concentrated on this second task. Accordingly, given the right C, I claim that (*CA*) is acceptable as an account of intentional actions by collectives. It also analyzes the sense in which individuals can bring about a collective's action and also the sense in which actions by collectives can be said to be constituted by actions of their members (and representatives). (See the analysis of the notion of constitution given in Tuomela, 1987).

Before discussing the truth of the thesis (*CA*), let me formulate yet another relevant thesis which does not distinguish between intentional and nonintentional actions and which seems not to be affected by the difficulties we encountered in the context of (*CA*). The thesis below connects a collective's actions, intentional or not, to its members' actions, intentional or not:

> (CA*) A *collective*, G, *performed an action* X in circumstances C if and only if there were operative agents $A_1,...,A_m$ of G such that $A_1,...,A_m$ jointly performed X in circumstances C.

I shall not here specifically discuss (CA*) except for noting that the concept of joint action we need in it will have to be the very broad one analyzed by formula (5.5) in Tuomela (1984). But, in any case, our discussion below will be seen to support this thesis.

IV. Are the Main Theses True?

1. Let us now begin our examination of the truth of (CA) and, in passing, also of (CA*). These analyses represent a kind of necessary coextension between macroconcepts and relevant microconcepts, we may say. But, apart from saying that the necessities can be argued to be ultimately based on conceptual considerations, I shall not here go deeper into that. Rather I shall regard these theses as philosophical analyses and take them to be necessary truths in the sense philosophical analyses in general can be so regarded.

The if-part of (CA) can be falsified by finding cases where a collective acts intentionally but where still no operative members are jointly intentionally doing anything relevant serving to bring about the collective's action (viz., in our earlier terminology, the result-event involved in the collective's action). The only if-part can be falsified by finding cases where, in the right circumstances, the operative members jointly perform something bringing about the result-event of the collective's action but where the collective cannot be taken to act intentionally under the relevant description. Our task below is to try to find out whether there are such counterexamples to (CA). And the tenability of (CA*) can be analogously handled. While we shall below proceed by examining example cases, let me mention another approach, which I have pursued in Tuomela (1987). It claims that the actions by collectives are *supervenient* on the relevant joint actions of the operative members. While I shall not in this paper use that approach, it is interesting to note that it gives an equivalent of (CA*) as its central result, thus showing that there are two routes to the same end.[3]

To return to (*CA*), when an informal collective does something intentionally the intentionality (purported aboutness, purpose) of its action, loosely speaking, derives directly from its members' relevant joint action. Thus if a dyad intentionally carries a heavy table upstairs the intentionality of this action resides in the dyad's members' actions making up an intentional joint action. And these component actions by the members were guided by the same we-intention, here typically the we-intention to carry the table upstairs. The presence of this we-intention in all the participants serves to make the total joint action and, as a consequence, also the collective's action intentional in the full-blown sense of the notion. Let us consider this in more detail.

The full-blown notion of intentionality is the admittedly idealized core notion from which all weaker notions of intentionality derive their significance. This full-blown notion is a core notion because of the analogy between the collective and the single agent, viz. we wish to view the collective as if it were a single agent. Consider a single agent's action X, e.g., his drinking a cup of coffee or reading an article. If X is intentional then it is purposively generated by his relevant willing-belief complex. This entails that the agent controls his action and is to some degree aware of it (or at least of the bodily actions involved in it). But to the degree that this kind of control over (and awareness of) the total action diminishes, the degree of intentionality also diminishes, *ceteris paribus*.

To clarify the analogy, consider the following collective action. Some people (perhaps unknown to each other) arrive at a public meeting at which a foreign guest with a hard-to-follow accent will speak. How do the listeners seat themselves? As it happens (we assume) they leave the first three rows completely vacant even if the talk would be easiest to follow from these rows. Instead they fill every seat from the fourth row on. Every auditor surely acted intentionally, whatever reason each one had for his choice of location. We can yet argue that the collective did not act intentionally because the control and awareness afforded by a relevant we-intention was lacking. But with such an effective we-intention (concerning rational seating) assumed to be shared by every auditor, and with the resulting joint action, the distribution of vacant and filled seats would certainly have been different. What I am trying to stress is that a we-intention, together with relevant beliefs, will make a collective an action-controlling unit comparable to a single agent but that such unity in the case of fully intentional social action cannot be arrived at without a relevant we-intention on the part of all acting agents. This idea naturally gives direct support to (CA) at least in the case of informal groups where all the members of the group are operative agents. My claim accordingly is that in such cases a group's action is (fully) intentional just in case all the members of the group act on the same relevant we-intention. Had some agents acted without the we-intention, the group's action, say X, would not have been fully controlled and unitary and hence not fully intentional (cf. (IA) above). The case of organized collectives is more problematic. Consider a formal collective like a corporation. The intentionality of the collective's action seems to derive in the first place from the public, constitutive and regulative rules of the corporation, and especially from its officially stated non-personal plans, programs, decisions, and what have you, which the representatives (the governing board, executives, etc.) are carrying out. The problem with respect to the truth of (CA) is to make sure that the joint action referred to by its right hand side is performed for the correct reason, viz. the collective's formal reason which makes the collective's action intentional. If the operative members had performed X jointly and intentionally but for a reason different from the collective's formal reason they might have brought about an action of the kind X by the collective, but the latter would not have been intentional under the correct description. So we must require the same source of intentionality both on the left hand side and on the right hand side of (CA). Thus the content of the operative agents' we-intention making their joint performance of X intentional must be essentially the same as the collective's reason making its action intentional. Speaking somewhat loosely, we can say that the intention making the collective's action intentional must coincide in its basic content with that of the we-intention in question. (How to clarify the notion of content technically and how, in doing so, to treat the minor differences stemming from the possible singular first person reference in the collective's intention and the reference to "we" in the case of the we-intention I shall not discuss here.) It is worth emphasizing that my requirement allows that the operative members have different motives and different views about what the group should do provided that they somehow arrive at the same relevant we-intention. Consider group decision making by a voting procedure where the majority rule is employed. Applying the rule will result in the specification of the relevant part of the we-intention.

In view of what we have above said about the close relationship between the intentionality of the collective's action and the intentionality of the operative member's relevant joint action, we can rewrite (*CA*), preserving its content, as follows:

(*CA*) A *collective*, G, *performed an action* X *intentionally* (for reason Rg) in circumstances C if and only if there were operative agents $A_1,...,A_m$ for G such that $A_1,...,A_m$ jointly performed X intentionally (for reason R_j) in circumstances C.

Here R_g of course means the group's reason and R_j the relevant joint action reason. R_j can be taken to refer to the content of the relevant we-intention in question (but see subsections 2 and 4 below for potential difficulties for this view). R_g and R_j are to be regarded as basically the same, as argued above. (Let me point out here that my analysis (*CA*) is compatible with weaker senses of intentional joint action than the one explicated by (*IA*), if need for the use of such a notion is demonstrated.)

Informal collectives can also act via their representatives. For instance, the members of a group may agree that a certain member will present the group's congratulation to a person celebrating his 60th birthday. Here the mechanism of group action is quite analogous to the case of formal collectives, the informal agreement and authorization replacing the rules of the formal organization such as the corporation discussed above. Accordingly, our theses are meant to apply here as well.

2. One can classify group action in terms of the tasks characteristic of the actions. I understand actions to be achievements which are responses to tasks, tasks involving the occurrence of the relevant result-events; cf. Section I. An important classification principle is accordingly the structural nature of tasks. Collective actions may be classified as *disjunctive* or *conjunctive* depending upon the kind of the tasks involved. Let us call an action by a collective purely disjunctive if it suffices that one of the participating agents brings about the result of the action. Group problem solving can be mentioned as an example: the group has solved the problem as soon as one of its members has. A purely conjunctive social action would be one requiring an active contribution from every participating agent (cf. two agents toasting each other). Naturally, many complex real-life social actions may involve as their parts both conjunctive and dis-

junctive tasks.[4]

Let us now consider some examples of the different ways in which actions by collectives can take place, keeping in mind also the above conjunctive-disjunctive dimension. (Most of the examples in this paragraph are from Ware, 1986). First, there are many things a group can do that its members cannot. A choir can encircle a piano, a team can cover a field, rallies can form, fill the mall, and disperse without any of the participants doing this, solo. From the point of view of the above classification these are indispensably conjunctive actions and also purely conjunctive with respect to the operative members (note that not all of the members of the collective need to participate). Next, there are many things that groups do that their individual members could but do not do (understanding 'could' here in a weak, conceptual sense). For instance, a team can win a game without all of the members taking part in all the matches. And groups can do what only one or two members of the group do, for example, the Chinese team reached the top of Mt. Everest even if only two members of the team went to the top. These are obviously examples of disjunctive actions. A still further kind of example to which the conjunctive-disjunctive classification also applies is group action by institutionally determined representation, cf. a nation's declaring war.

Consider now the truth of (*CA*) in relation to the above examples. First consider things a group can do but its members cannot. If a choir intentionally encircles a piano then its members surely must do their parts of the encircling, and those intentional component actions bring about the case that the members of the choir jointly encircle the piano: this is what the group's intentionally encircling the piano amounts to. How about things that groups do but that their individual members could do but do not do? A team with some of its members held in reserve can win a game. This being so, then of course the operative members jointly perform something, e.g. score a sufficient amount of goals, which in those circumstances amounts to the team's winning. In this sense the operative members brought about the team's winning. But note that a team cannot properly be said to win intentionally but only to try to win (intentionally), nor can its members intentionally bring about the team's winning although they can intentionally try to do it. Next consider cases where a group does (or can do) something when only one or very few of its members do it. Thus, for instance, a group may intentionally solve a problem when one of its members intentionally does it; and this accords with (*CA*).

Consider next cases where a collective acts via its institutionally determined representatives. For instance, suppose a nation (intentionally) declares war precisely in the case that the President does something appropriate which amounts to or brings about (in the sense of "purposive" of intention-preserving generation) the nation's declaring war. By taking the President to be the sole operative member, (CA) handles this fine. Note, too, that in more complicated cases of organized collectives the collective may contain subcollectives, whose actions will determine the collective's action. But even that presents no special problem to our analysis, it seems, for we can always go back to the subcollectives' joint actions and then combine them to get the whole collective's action via all the combined individual efforts. Of course we must then interpret the notion of joint action on the right hand side of (CA) broadly enough to cover this (cf. (5.5) of Tuomela, 1984, for a good candidate). But as far as I can see what was said earlier will suffice, although grinding out the same (or at least relevantly similar) intentional-making reason or purpose from all those (joint) actions of the separate subcollectives and other possible system-agents may not be so easy a task.

3. Ware (1986) compares single individuals and aggregate individuals, stressing their similarities. In that context he presents a (probably non-exhaustive) list of predicates applicable to both. In his analysis Ware presents five broad classes of predicates. His characterization of these is not entirely independent of his purported aggregate-ontology, but I shall try to ignore that, and consider here only how they apply to my above analysis of actions by collectives.

First we have 1) *cumulative predicates*, which are characterized as ones depending on the cumulative contribution of all the parts involved. The social whole is said to have the property in question because the parts make a common contribution through a related property. As an example consider "The group met at Hotel Helsinki". This can easily be analyzed in terms of the group members jointly coming there at the agreed upon time, and this is the case irrespective of whether the mentioned group sentence is taken to be made true by an aggregate or by single persons as sketched in section II.

Next we consider 2) *distributive predicates*. Ascriptions of these distribute across the parts uniformly. As an example sentence consider "The convoy advanced". This is to be analyzed in terms of the ships, viz. the members of the convoy, jointly advancing, and seems unproblematic for (CA) (and (CA^*)).

The third broad group is 3) *predicates of agency*. Among them 3)a) *predicates of whole agency* are used for ascriptions about what the whole does with all the parts being involved but without doing what the whole does. As an example consider "The assembly elected him". This example is analyzed in terms of the (operative) members jointly performing something which generated his being elected. Note that (*CA*) does allow that what the operative members jointly are *said* to do can be something "less" than X, but it has to bring about X in an intention-preserving way.

Next we consider 3)b) *predicates of contributed whole agency*. Ascriptions of these concern the whole's doing something because of the crucial involvement of some part and with the uninvolvement of many other parts. As an example we have "The hockey team used the power play". Here the operative members are those on the ice and playing, but the power play action can still be ascribed to the whole team, and this clearly fits (*CA*) (recall our earlier remarks on this kind of example).

As a third subgroup of predicates of agency we have 3)c) *predicates of variable agency*: what something does involves either the whole or some part doing it. As an example consider "Sonny and Cher sang ten songs". This sentence can be made true in a number of ways. Consider here only the interpretations where Sonny and Cher are regarded as a group, a dyad. This dyad's action or action-sequence can come about by Sonny and Cher singing together (in the strict sense) any number from one to ten songs and by their performing the rest separately. But also this entire action sequence counts as a joint action by them, for even when singing some songs separately they were taking part in an intentional joint activity generating or amounting to the dyad's performing ten songs intentionally.

As the final subgroup of agency predicates we consider 3)d) *predicates of necessarily partial agency* yielding ascriptions which are about what something does because necessarily a part does it. Consider "The crowd lynched the traitor". As a matter of factual necessity at most only a few members can be physically involved in the hanging of the traitor, we may suppose. They are the operative members who intentionally jointly hanged the traitor and they may also be said to have intentionally lynched him (or at any rate their hanging him in those circumstances generated the lynching). (*CA*) seems not to be in trouble in this case, either.

Ware's fourth broad group of predicates is called 4) *reciprocal predicates*. In this case there is reciprocity of parts in the sense illustrated by "The team conferred about their strategy". Here parts of the team are involved, and it is not necessary that these parts be individual members. If subgroups are involved, then (CA) must first be applied to them (cf. predicates of contributed whole agency), and then be used for the whole team. And here we take the operative members to be all the members of the team or, if parts are involved, only the operative members belonging to those parts.

The fifth broad group of predicates are the 5) *predicates of composition*. These predicates give the constitution or composition of something. Consider the sentence "The band marched in a heart-formation". Here the individuals in the band are assigned specific tasks involving their positions, but no problems for (CA) seem to be forthcoming.

4. Our theses (CA) and (CA *)) have so far gained support from this analysis of examples, and no counterexamples have been found. To end this paper, I shall present some potential criticisms of these theses. Let us first consider (CA). There are some putative problems that have to do with weaker senses of intentionality.

(CA) requires full-blown intentionality, viz. that all the operative agents intentionally perform their parts with the same we-intention. But there are examples in which intentional joint action can be said to take place without all the agents' having the relevant we-intention (and acting on it). For instance, there are various kinds of cases where some of the agents are to some degree misinformed about the situation at hand, or simply lack some pieces of information relevant for having the correct we-intention. Let us consider a spy ring's activities. The ring intentionally steals some information without all of the participants having knowledge of the total goal of the operation. Here it might be the case that an agent intends to do something, Z, and knows (or correctly believes) that Z is a subgoal of the group. This subgoal-relation might involve the agent's believing that there is an action, X, such that were he to intend to do X he would in those circumstances be justified in intending to do Z. The agent's so intending to do Z might accordingly strongly limit the class of actions that the group can perform, and thus the member in question might well be acting "in the right direction" without being exactly aware of the specific action X the group intends to perform. In the above cases the group's action is to at least some extent intentional. In response to this kind of case I really must insist on the distinction between full-blown intentional group action and to a lesser degree intentional group action. (*CA*) is concerned with the former. Its left hand side is concerned with full-blown intentional group action if and only if its right hand side is concerned with full-blown intentional joint action. Thus the kind of cases exhibiting weaker senses of intentionality do not directly affect (*CA*).

It needs to be emphasized once more that the notion of joint action in (*CA**) must be understood in a very broad sense which does involve the existence of a common goal but not necessarily the awareness of the operative agents concerning it (see the analysis (5.5) of Tuomela, 1984, for details). But even with this broad interpretation problems seem to arise. Let us consider one putative problem.

I shall discuss an example which Werhane (1985) discusses also. This example of collective action, which seemingly provides a counterexample to our (*CA**), is as follows: The American Telephone and Telegraph Company (AT&T) was recently accused of discrimination because it does not promote women and minorities to management positions. Whether or not this was a deliberate AT&T policy will perhaps never be fully decided, but let us assume here that it was not. Anyhow, looking at the pattern of company behavior, it is clear that women and minorities were not promoted. What really happened at AT&T I do not know, but the example at any rate helps us to see better the conceptual possibilities involved. At first glance, we seem to have here an action by a collective, viz. AT&T's discriminatory action (or a sequence of such actions), which we assume not to be an intentional group action (viz. the collective did not intentionally discriminate).

The corporative action of course takes place via some operative agents' actions, but nevertheless at least no intentional joint action by those operative agents seems to be involved (or so we assume, to make the case interesting). And could it be the case that not even unintentional joint action was involved? If so, isn't this a counterexample to the only if-part of (*CA**), for the corporation did act, didn't it? Now in order for there to be joint action in the broadest sense (see (5.5) of Tuomela, 1984) arguably a "we-attitude" in a wide behavioral sense must be involved. That is, the operative agents must then, loosely speaking, at least behave or be disposed to behave as if they were pursuing the common goal of not promoting minority people. If that indeed was the case, which seems unlikely, I propose we say that AT&T nonintentionally acted in a discriminative way.

(CA *) does stand in this case. But suppose not even such broad behavioral we-attitudes were involved. Then there was no joint action even in the broadest possible sense. I suggest we keep (CA *) and say here that the corporation did not really perform a discriminative action or pursue such a policy of action but rather that, discrimination was a consequence of something the operative members did while acting (promoting personnel) in their official capacity as position- or role-holders. The officials thus (unintentionally) performed discriminatory actions, but the corporation did not. It did not, because the operative members did not act jointly (even in the broadest possible sense of the notion). This is admittedly a borderline case, and I am suggesting we resolve it in a way satisfying (CA *). In this last case I am of course relying on (CA *) rather than testing it, but hasn't our principle already obtained much independent confirmation? When common sense intuitions are hazy we had better rely on theory.

Our above approach concentrated on an examination of whether commonsensical and linguistic examples of actions by collectives fit the schemas (CA) and (CA *). As mentioned earlier, there is also another route—examined in Tuomela (1987)—to the thesis (CA *). This other approach proceeds in a precise technical framework in terms of the notion of supervenience and argues that actions by collectives supervene on the actions of the operative members of the collective, and this yields an equivalent of (CA *). Together these two approaches to the same problem, by ending with the same general result, strongly indicate that that result indeed is tenable or at least worthy of more detailed investigation.

Notes

1. Actually the mereological approach cannot simply take collectives to be mereological sums of persons. First, the members of a collective may exist before the collective exists (or before they have joined it); thus their sum before that moment has no intimate relation to the collective. Secondly, mereological sums change with the change in persons involved in the sum, but collectives typically do not so change. One may try to repair this by taking collectives to be sums of "person-stages" over time such that the sum-stages at different time points are suitably structurally related or exhibit suitable unity. This idea has been explored and accepted in a lucid paper by Copp (1984).

2. We are dealing with two different dimensions here, viz. a) degree of organization and b) degree of formality. Collectives can be organized to different degrees and also their organization can be more or less formal (cf. Copp, 1984, on this).

3. In Tuomela (1987) it is shown that the notion of supervenience can also be used to elucidate the notions of constituting (viz. that a collective's action is constituted by its operative members' relevant actions) and representing or, which amounts to the same thing, acting on behalf of a collective.

4. Let us clarify the conceptual nature of disjunctive and conjunctive joint actions and actions by collectives. For this, we must explicitly speak of the *occurrence* of result events. Let thus $occ(r_j)$ stand for r_j's occurring. Then a purely or strictly disjunctive action by a dyad satisfies

(a) $occ(r) = occ(r_1) \lor occ(r_2)$,

while a purely conjunctive one satisfies

(b) $occ(r) = occ(r_1) \& occ(r_2)$.

(There are disjunctive and conjunctive actions in weaker senses where the individual and total results do not satisfy (a) or (b) but only e.g. a containment relation.) Here it is not necessary to distinguish between the result events of group actions and the corresponding result events of the joint actions of the operative members, given *(CA)* and *(CA*)*. Note especially that

$occ(r_1 + r_2) \neq occ(r_1) \lor occ(r_2)$,

viz. the occurrence of a sum $r_1 + r_2$ (as in the toasting example of section I) is different from either r_1's occurring or r_2's occurring. Completely analogously

$occ(r_1 \ r_2) \neq occ(r_1) \& occ(r_2)$.

Cases satisfying (b) are easy to come by while cases with $occ(r) = occ(r_1 \ r_2)$ are not. Analogously, we may discuss, for instance, cases of conditional dependence where

(c) $occ(r) = occ(r_1) > occ(r_2)$,

and cases where the occurrence of the individual results combine in more complex ways, truth-functional or not. (In the text we assumed that the conjunctive-disjunctive classification is the most central.)

References

Copp, D., 1979, 'Collective Actions and Secondary Actions', *American Philosophical Quarterly 16*, 177-186.

Copp, D., 1984, 'What Collectives Are: Agency, Individualism and Legal Theory', *Dialogue XXIII*, 249-269.

Gruner, R., 1976, 'On the Action of Social Groups', *Inquiry 19*, 443-454.

Londey, D., 1978, 'On the Action of Teams', *Inquiry 21*, 213-218.

Massey, G., 1976, 'Tom, Dick, Harry, and All the King's Men', *American Philosophical Quarterly 13*, 89-107.

Tuomela, R., 1977, *Human Action and Its Explanation*, Reidel, *Synthese Library*, Dordrecht and Boston.

Tuomela, R., 1984, *A Theory of Social Action*, Reidel, *Synthese Library*, Dordrecht, Boston, and Lancaster.

Tuomela, R., 1987, 'Collective Action, Supervenience, and Constitution", forthcoming in *Synthese*.

Tuomela, R. and Miller, K., 1988, 'We-Intentions', *Philosophical Studies 53*, 115-137.

Ware, R., 1986, 'Conjunction, Plurality, and Collective Particulars', manuscript.

Werhane, P., 1985, *Persons, Rights, and Corporations*, Prentice-Hall, Englewood Cliffs.

Philosophical Perspectives, 3
Philosophy of Mind and Action Theory, 1989

LINGUISTICS: WHAT'S WRONG WITH "THE RIGHT VIEW"

Michael Devitt
University of Maryland
Kim Sterelny
Australian National University

1. Introduction

What is linguistics about? A simple enough question, you might think, but one that has generated surprising controversy, much literature, and no very convincing answer.

The focus of the controversy has been on the transformational approach to syntactic theory, a central subdomain of linguistics. That will be our concern.

Jerry Fodor, who should know about such matters, says that "there are...really only two schools of thought on this question" (1981: 197). With careful neutrality he names these "the Right View" and "the Wrong View". The Right View is the standard view of Noam Chomsky and his followers, including Fodor. Fodor attributes the Wrong View (pp. 198-9) to Stephen Stich (1972) and Jerrold Katz (1977).[1]

The Wrong View is a sort of instrumentalism. The task of linguists is to construct a grammar that simply captures its data base, the linguistic intuitions of speakers; intuitions about grammaticality, ambiguity, passives, and so on. Provided the linguist gets things right at the level of the intuitive judgments, he has done all that is required. The theory is just an instrument for predicting some such judgments on the basis of others. According to the Wrong View, then, linguistics is not about anything beyond the concerns of those judgments; it is not about any deeper reality.

Related to our opening question is another: What does linguistics explain? The Wrong View holds that linguistics explains nothing: linguistic theory systematizes intuitive judgments but it does not explain them. The Wrong View is thus typical of instrumentalism.

Classical instrumentalism was motivated by a positivist epistemology and semantics. The Wrong View is not. Indeed, it has a perfectly respectable motivation. It arises from troubles with the Right View, together with an inability to see any other alternative to that view. We think that there is another alternative. If we are right, then the motivation for the Wrong View evaporates. So we shall not discuss that view any further.

The Right View is popular and familiar. Its main claim is that linguistics describes a grammar that has been internalized by each speaker; the grammar is, as they say, *psychologically real*. The speaker's linguistic competence consists in the internalization of this grammar (J. A. Fodor 1981: 199).[2] So, according to the Right View, linguistics is about linguistic competence. "Linguistics is simply that part of psychology that is concerned with one specific class of steady states, the cognitive structures that are employed in speaking and understanding" (Chomsky 1975b: 160).[3]

What does linguistics explain? According to the Right View, it is, like the rest of psychology, part of the explanation of behaviour. Most obviously, a grammar explains linguistic behaviour, but it is also relevant to the explanation of non-linguistic behaviour. To follow someone's instructions, for example, one must first *understand* them; that understanding utilizes the internalized grammar.

Chomsky insists on a distinction between competence and performance. The theory of performance is concerned with all the psychological factors that bear on the production and understanding of linguistic symbols. So it is concerned not only with the competence that is, according to Chomsky, the subject matter of linguistics, but also with such factors as memory, attention and interest. The theory of competence is the core of the theory of performance.

How can we tell what linguistics is about? Though we must take note of what linguists say it is about, we cannot rest content with that. Doing linguistics is one thing, reflecting on it, another. Linguists may have incorrectly abstracted the goal of their activity. We have to examine their activity for ourselves. The best reason that we can expect to find for thinking that linguistics is about *x* rather than *y* is that the considerations and evidence that have guided the construction of linguistic theory justify our thinking that the theory is *true* about x but not y. So we shall look to see which view of linguistics makes linguistic theory seem true.

Oversimplifying, our conclusions are as follows. The Right View is wrong; linguistics is not part of psychology. The right view is another one altogether, which we will call "Grandma's View". Our actual conclusions are much more complicated because of an important conflation. We will argue that the transformational linguists conflate two distinct theoretical tasks: one concerned with linguistic symbols and the other with linguistic competence.[4]

2. Two Versions of the Right View

The Right View holds that a grammar is an account of psychological reality. But what is it for a grammar to be internalized in the way this requires? There are two answers to this question.

A grammar is a set of rules generating all and only the sentences of a language. The set for any natural language is still largely undiscovered. Let us suppose, optimistically, that transformational linguists have discovered some members of the set for English. Call this fragment of a grammar, "G". Three ways we might describe a competent English speaker's relation to G are as follows:

1. She behaves as if she is governed by G
2. She is governed by G
3. She knows that G is part of the grammar for English and applies it.[5]

1 is not enough for the Right View because 1 can be true as the result of the speaker having internalized something other than G which yields the same behavioral output as G. The Right View requires either 2 or 3. Which? The most common expressions of the View suggest 3: the competence that linguistics describes is the speaker's tacit knowledge that the rules of the grammar are as they are; she has knowledge-that, or propositional knowledge, of G. We need a name for this version of the Right View. We shall call it "the Crazy Version". The Right View is sometimes presented in ways that seem to require only 2: there is no implication that the speaker knows about, or has any other propositional attitude toward, G. The only knowledge 2 might require is knowledge-how, a cognitive *skill*. We shall call this "the Sensible Version" of the Right View.

The differences between 1, 2 and 3 can be brought out by a simple analogy. Suppose that R is a rule for addition. So R is a mechanical procedure guaranteeing the right answer to problems of addition; it is an algorithm. Consider, now, a pocket calculator. We might describe it in any of the following ways:

1*. It behaves as if it is governed by R
2*. It is governed by R
3*. It knows that R is an algorithm for addition and applies it.

Clearly, 1* might be true without 2* or 3* being so. There are many ways to add and the calculator may be governed by a rule other than R; for example, R might be in the decimal notation and the governing rule in the binary notation. Next, 2* might be true without 3* being so. An object can be built so that it is governed by R, and thus have internalized R, and yet not explicitly *represent* R. And if it does not represent R it cannot have any propositional attitude toward R. Hence it cannot *know* about R. In the case of the calculator, we can be certain that it does not know about R, because it has been built in such a way that it could not know about anything.[6]

3. The Crazy Version of the Right View

Do transformational linguists believe the Crazy Version? The question has been aired at great length and yet, amazingly, no clear answer has emerged. They do not typically assert anything like 3, yet key figures believe that the speaker's relation to G is appropriately called knowledge (or something close).

Chomsky's favourite way of describing this knowledge is not helpful: he says that the speaker *tacitly knows the rules or principles* of her language. Unfortunately, the import of "knows the rules or principles" is not crystal clear. We are inclined to think it requires knowledge-that but there is room for doubt about this: perhaps mere knowledge-how is sufficient. The inclusion of 'tacitly' may seem to settle the question, for we ordinarily take a person's tacit knowledge to be propositions that he has not entertained but which he would acknowledge immediately in suitable circumstances. Thus, Ron tacitly knows that rabbits don't lay eggs; the thought has never crossed his mind, but he would deny that they laid eggs if the question were ever to arise. However, Chomsky knows better than anyone that the ordinary speaker would not acknowledge the rules of G. So this can't be what he means by 'tacitly'. Further, on occasions Chomsky explicitly denies that the speaker's knowledge is knowledge-that (1969a: 86-7; 1969b: 153-4).

The mystery deepens because the transformationalists so often write as if the speaker did have propositional knowledge of G and its consequences. Thus Chomsky describes the knowledge as a "system of beliefs" (1969a: 60-1; see also 1980: 225); as "a mental representation of a grammar" (1975a: 304). Learning a language is seen as learning a theory:

> It seems plain that language acquisition is based on the child's discovery of what from a formal point of view is a deep and abstract theory—a generative grammar of his language. (Chomsky 1965: 58)

Fodor describes Chomsky's view as propositional (1983: 4-10); it is the view that "your linguistic capacities...are...explained by reference to the *content of your beliefs*" (p.7). Finally, if the knowledge is not propositional, it must surely be knowledge-how. And, if we assume description 2, it is plausible to think that it is a particularly complicated piece of knowledge-how. However, Chomsky denies that it is knowledge-how (1969a: 87) or, at least, that it is knowledge-how without an "intellectual component" (1975a: 314-8).

Here and elsewhere (1975b: 162-4) Chomsky seems bent on undermining the distinction between knowledge-that and knowledge-how, between knowledge of facts and cognitive skills. Yet, as John Anderson says, this distinction "is fundamental to modern cognitive psychology" (1980: 223). Thus, long-term memory is taken to consist in the propositional (perhaps also imagistic representation of information (94-123). This is knowledge-that. On the other hand, cognitive skills like maze running, addition and chess playing, which may make use of representations of information, are not seen as consisting in such representations, but rather in, for example, "production systems" (222-92). These skills are knowledge-how.

We are left uncertain of the nature of the claim that the speaker has tacit knowledge of G.[7]

We set aside the exegetical issue for the substantive one. Is it reasonable to suppose that the ordinary speaker knows that G is part of the grammar for English and applies this knowledge in producing and understanding utterances? We think not. We think that 3, and hence the Crazy Version, are grossly implausible.

First, no one has produced a single good reason for the Crazy Version; the considerations adduced for the Right View are only ones for the Sensible Version; they are for 2 not 3.[8] In the face of twenty years of apparently overwhelming objections to the Crazy Version transformationalists have hardly conceded a point. When they do respond to the criticisms, they do so with obscurities. But mostly they continue on as if it is sheer pedantry to insist on the distinction between the two versions.[9]

Second, Gilbert Harman (1967) has raised the following problem for the Crazy Version. According to that Version, understanding a language requires representing its grammar. That representation must itself be in a language. What is it to understand that more basic language? If we suppose the more basic language is the same as the original language then we are caught in a vicious circle. If we suppose that it is some other language ("Mentalese" perhaps), then its grammar also has to be represented. This requires a still more basic language. And so on. The only way to avoid a vicious circle or an infinite regress is to allow that at least one language is understood directly, without representing its grammar. Why not then allow this of the original language, the one spoken?

Some linguists, particularly Fodor (1975; see also Chomsky 1969a: 87-8; 1969b: 155-6), have an answer to this question. They think that there are good reasons for supposing that in order to *learn* a language you have to understand another one already. However, we can understand that one directly, without representing its grammar, because it is not learned; it is *innate*. So, the answer to Harman requires a strong innateness thesis.

Third, Stich (1971, 1978) brings out the implausibility of the Crazy Version nicely by contrasting the speaker's relation to G with unproblematic cases of propositional knowledge. If a person knows that p, we expect him to be aware of p, or at least to be able to become aware of it when given a suitable prompt; and we expect him to understand expressions of p. The ordinary speaker quite clearly lacks this awareness and understanding for most of G. If a person knows that p, his knowledge should join up with other knowledge and beliefs to generate more beliefs. If a speaker has knowledge of G it is clearly not inferentially integrated in this way. Consider an example. Without tuition, a speaker is unlikely to have the conceptual recourses to understand even the relatively simple claim that 'NP --> Det + Adj + N' is a rule of English. If she tacitly knows that this is a rule, her knowledge is largely inferentially isolated from her other beliefs. Fourth, Stich's point is strengthened by an important aspect of the transformationalists' views. At its most explicit and extreme, this aspect sees the area of the mind that employs G, the sentence-parsing area, as *modular*. Fodor is the main exponent of modularity (1983), but Chomsky also speaks favourably of the idea (1980: 40-7).

In the functional organization of the mind, modular systems lie between transducers and the central processor. Transducers are the familiar sense organs which convert incoming stimuli into neural code. The central processor is the site of higher mental functions; what goes on there is what we would ordinarily think of as thinking. Modular systems analyze the raw data received from transducers and pass on some of the results to the central processor. These systems are "domain specific", specializing in a particular sort of stimulus; for example, sentences or faces. They are "innately specified" and "hardwired", "associated with specific, localized, and elaborately structured neural systems" (J.A. Fodor 1983: 36-7). They are "mandatory": there is no decision to operate; they are cognitive reflexes (pp. 52-3). Finally, and most importantly for Stich's point, they are "autonomous" (pp. 36-7). On the one hand, "there is only limited central access to the mental representations" that modular systems compute (p. 57). On the other hand, the systems have no access to information held elsewhere; they are "informationally encapsulated" (p. 64). Hence the inferential segregation that Stich points to.

The mere internalization of G in a module cannot involve the speaker in any propositional attitudes towards G, for the module is inaccessible to the central processor which is the site of her propositional attitudes. If the modularity thesis is right, the speaker no more knows G in virtue of being able to talk than she knows the principles of depth perception in virtue of being able to see. If the thesis is right, the only thing that could "know" G is the sentence-parsing module itself.

The modularity thesis is highly speculative and controversial. But even if it is false, Stich's point is still supported. If Chomsky is anywhere near right about the sentence-parser, it has many of the properties of a modular system. He thinks of it as a relatively encapsulated "mental organ" inaccessible to our general cognitive capacities. G is in a relatively autonomous system. The contrast between a speaker's propositional attitudes and her relation to G remains.

We conclude that description 3, and hence the Crazy Version of the Right View, are highly implausible, perhaps even crazy. It is time to consider the Sensible Version.

4. The Sensible Version of the Right View: Criticisms

The Sensible Version of the Right View does not require that the speaker represents G, a fragment of the grammar for English that linguists are on their way to discovering; she need have no propositional attitude to G. It accepts that knowledge of a language is a cognitive *skill*, and hence may be mere knowledge-how not knowledge-that. The Sensible Version does not require description 3, but it does require 2. If linguistic theory is to be true, G must be psychologically real in that it governs the behavior of each speaker and is descriptive of her competence. We doubt even this.[10]

The internalization of G requires the internalization of all the levels of analysis hypothesized by G: deep structure, intermediate structures, surface structure, and the rules.[11] This is what we doubt and what we shall be discussing in this section and the next. We do not doubt that *some* aspects of G are psychologically real, in particular those aspects that go into determining meaning. The nature and point of this qualification will become clearer in sections 6 to 8.

Why should we suppose that we are entitled to claim anything stronger than description 1? After all, grammars are like other algorithms. If there is one set of rules that generates a set of English sentences and assigns them appropriate meaning-relevant structures, there will be many; there will be a mathematical explosion of algorithms. Suppose G' is one of those alternative fragments of a grammar. Given that G' has the same output as G, why suppose that it is G rather than G' that is psychologically real? The evidence and considerations that have guided transformational grammarians provide insufficient reason for thinking that it *is* G.

(1) The early evidence for G was almost entirely about linguistic symbols: about which strings of words are grammatical; about the ambiguity of certain sentences; about the statement forms and question forms; about the synonymy of sentences that are superficially different; about the difference between sentences that are superficially similar; and so on. This evidence is linguistic, not psychological, and so does not seem to be the sort to throw immediate light on

what is in the head; on the precise nature of a speaker's competence, the mental state that plays the key role in her understanding and production of sentences. There is no basis in this evidence for thinking that the speaker has internalized G rather than the meaning-equivalent G'.

At this point, a protest is likely from old hands: "What you are referring to as linguistic evidence is really the evidence of the native speaker's intuitions. These intuitions reflect her underlying competence and are psychological. The role that they play as evidence shows that the grammar is indeed about competence." The protest raises difficult issues which we will take up later (section 9). We can set it aside now because it does not affect our claim that this evidence, even if the expression of intuitions, gives no reason for preferring G to G'.

(2) Transformationalists seek grammars that not only meet the linguistic evidence but are also simple and elegant.[12] So we can assume that G is simpler and more elegant than G'. But why is that a reason for thinking that G is psychologically real? Suppose that R is the simplest and most elegant algorithm for addition. On that basis alone we are not justified in ascribing R to any calculator. Perhaps the calculator is a child who adds by counting marbles. What is needed before ascribing R or G to an object is evidence about *its design*, about how it achieves its effect of producing additions or sentences. In the case of G, what is needed is psycholinguistic evidence.

These remarks against the bearing of the transformationalists' criteria of simplicity and elegance on psychological reality can be strengthened. First, the fact that G is more simple and elegant than its rivals is rather more evidence *against*, than evidence for, G being part of the grammar our brain is built to use. If innateness claims are right, our brains are specifically adapted to a certain class of grammars. Stephen Jay Gould (1980: 19-31) has used examples like the panda's thumb to show that adaptations are typically *not* maximally efficient engineering solutions to the problems they solve. For, adaptations are of pre-existing structures and this constrains the solutions possible. Second, as David Lewis has pointed out to us, the fact that G is maximally efficient and elegant from the grammarians' point of view does not entitle us to suppose it is optimal from the brain's point of view.[13]

(3) A dominant concern of transformational grammar has been language acquisition, which should provide psycholinguist

evidence.[14] However, until recently, attention to language acquisition has been more honorific than substantive:

> Many generativists assert that they aim to account for how children master their native languages, but the vast majority of their analyses do not contribute to that aim. (Hornstein and Lightfoot 1981b: 7)

Nevertheless, facts about language acquisition have more and more been playing a role in the construction of transformational grammars. We must see their bearing on the claim that G is psychologically real.

A language like English is a very complex system of rules. Yet, according to Chomsky and his followers, children learn this system quickly on the basis of meagre and misleading data. In particular, transformationalists emphasize the unavailability of negative data (that certain syntactic constructions do *not* occur), and the absence of systematic instruction about ambiguity.[15] There are certain sorts of errors that children do not make despite never having been warned against them. They end up making correct judgments about ambiguity despite the patchy and unsystematic evidence about ambiguity in their data. Given the lack of evidence available to the child, the transformationalists claim that it is highly implausible that language learning uses only the devices of empiricist learning theories. Rather, they claim, learning involves an innate language-acquisition device. This device constrains the grammar we can acquire. The system of constraints is called "universal grammar".

Recent versions of transformational grammar have presented a very rich picture of universal grammar: it is a set of principles that are incomplete schematizations of phrase-structure and transformational rules. They are completed, in learning, by fixing certain "parameters"; for example, fixing the ordering surface structure of basic constituents. The popular "government and binding" view exemplifies this approach.[16] So transformationalists claim that the only grammars that can be learnt are completions of the specified schematizations.

How might these considerations support G over G′ as an account of psychological reality? G might fit better than G′ into a theory of language acquisition: the decomposition of G into learned parameters and innately fixed principles might yield a more plausible account of language acquisition than the decomposition of G′. For learned parameters to be plausible, they should be simple, and robustly manifested in the child's linguistic experience. For innate principles to be plausible they must, at least, be ones that seem to play a role in the acquisition of other languages. We would also want to see evidence for the principles from the development of language in a child and from language processing.

We think that arguments along these lines do help to restrict the grammars that are candidates for psychological reality. In particular, we think that the transformationalists are on strong ground in their claims about the data available to children.[17] Nevertheless, we doubt that these arguments come close to establishing that G is psychologically real.

First, the evidence for the innate principles is not strong. Since these principles must play a role in the acquisition of all languages, we look to other languages for evidence of them. The trouble is that very few languages have been studied in sufficient depth to provide evidence. Worse, where in-depth studies seem to agree on an innate principle, there is a high risk that this agreement is imposed by the method of study rather than discovered in nature. Among the many alternatives to G equally compatible with the linguistic evidence, how many are tested for their ability to account for the acquisition of English? Very few: most are ruled out as candidates by the psychologically irrelevant consideration of simplicity; see (2) above. *And the same goes for all the other languages that have been studied in depth.* If the language-acquisition test for each language was applied to a much wider range of grammars, all with the same prima facie claim to being psychologically real, perhaps we would get agreement on different innate principles. More likely, we would get no agreement at all.

In sum, to the extent that the language-acquisition test depends on an appeal to independently motivated innate principles, it assumes that certain grammars for other languages are psychologically real. But their psychological reality is as much in question as that of G. What we need is a principled reason for ruling out the members of the mathematical explosion of grammars for each language. The theory of language acquisition does not supply this reason. The theory starts from—indeed, probably must start from—fairly detailed assumptions about the nature of the psychological states that are the end product of language acquisition.[18] And the nature of those states are precisely what is in question.

Interesting recent work on language development and processing provides some evidence for the innate principles, but cannot close the above evidential gap. Facts of language development have been shown to be consistent with the principles.[19] The worry is that the facts would be consistent with many other principles with equally good claims to being considered. The evidence from processing is not extensive and is controversial. It depends on substantial assumptions about the forms of rules and the nature of the processor.[20]

We have claimed that assumptions about innate principles do not deal with the mathematical explosion of alternative grammars in a principled way. Suppose that we were to set that aside, taking the apparent agreement between languages to be discovered not imposed. Our second doubt about the arguments from language acquisition is that we may still have a mathematical explosion to deal with. If there is one set of rules that can be plausibly decomposed into learned parameters and agreed innate principles, then there may be many.

Considerations of language learning certainly restrict the range of candidates to be part of the psychologically real grammar, but they do not establish that G is part of it. What is needed to establish this is much more direct psycholinguistic evidence.

(4) If G is psychologically real then it plays a role in performance, in the production and understanding of sentences. We can look to psycholinguistics for evidence that G and not G′ does indeed play this role. In principle, such evidence could settle the matter: evidence about reaction times,[21] the types of errors we make, the relative ease of understanding sentences, the order in which sentences are learned, and so on. Thus, suppose that according to G the active (e.g. 'Max bit Sam') is the basic form and the passive (e.g. 'Sam was bitten by Max') the derived form, but that according to G′ the reverse is the case. Now suppose that we discovered that actives are learned before passives; that they are easier to understand and remember; that fewer errors are made with them. Evidence of this kind would favour G over G′ as an account of psychological reality.

In practice, however, psycholinguistic evidence of this sort has not supported the view that G rather that G′ has been internalized by the speaker. We need to show that the deep structure, intermediate structures, surface structure, and the rules of G, have all been internalized. It is generally agreed that there is little evidence of this. There are problems even finding the transformationalist's levels and rules at all, let alone the particular details specified by G.[22] Even Robert Berwick and Amy Weinberg, who defend the psychological significance of transformational grammar, emphasize the great difficulty in getting performance data to bear on the psychological reality of grammars (1984: 35-45). The most that they hope to do is show the functional plausibility of the general principles of current transformational grammar.

We can sum up the discussion in this section as follows. To establish that G is psychologically real, hard psychological evidence is needed. Yet, as David Lightfoot points out, "the overwhelming mass of crucial evidence bearing on the correctness of grammar" has been linguistic (1982: 28).[23] This linguistic data cannot distinguish between many grammars generating the same sentences with the same meaning-relevant structures.

5. The Sensible Version of the Right View: Responses

What responses have been made to criticisms like ours? We shall start with one from David Marr.

Marr (1982) has used his well-known distinction between levels to defend Chomsky. Marr distinguishes three levels of understanding an information-processing device. The first is the *computational* level: it specifies *what* is computed and *why*. The second is the *algorithmic* level: it specifies *how* the computation is done. The third is the level of *implementation*: it specifies the way the computation is realized physically (pp. 22-5). Marr claims that the distinction between the computational and the algorithmic levels is "roughly [Chomsky's] distinction between competence and performance". He thinks that critics of Chomsky have overlooked the distinction between levels, and have criticized the grammar as if it were at the algorithmic level when it is actually at the computational level (p. 28).[24] The problem with this defense is that everything said at the computational level does still have to be true of the device. So all aspects of the grammar do have to be psychologically real; the speaker really must perform that computational task in all its detail. That is precisely what is in doubt. It is true, of course, that there may be many different ways of carrying out that task at the algorithmic level, differences which are not the concern of the grammar. But that is beside the point of our criticisms.

Nevertheless, we think that Marr's distinction helps to bring out what is right and wrong about the Right View. Briefly, we think that transformational grammar conflates Marr's computational and algorithmic levels. We shall discuss this in section 8.

Chomsky and his followers have a standard response to criticisms like ours.[25] They point out that their claim about grammatical rules is a typical scientific hypothesis based on *inference to the best explanation*. An account is needed of how we produce and understand English sentences. The best explanation of this is that we have built into us the very same rules that a variety of evidence suggests define English sentencehood. So we are entitled to infer that we do have those rules built in. The grammarians go on to draw attention to two aspects of this inference which it shares with *any* inference to the best explanation.

(i) It is irrelevant to argue that the conclusion of the inference may be wrong. *Of course* the evidence does not prove the hypothesis conclusively: it is *underdetermined* by the evidence like any other scientific hypothesis. Perhaps other hypotheses would provide better explanations. But again that is true of any hypothesis and is therefore beside the point. Until other hypotheses are produced we are entitled to accept this one.

(ii) When we accept a theoretical hypothesis we should interpret it *realistically*: it purports to describe an area of reality underlying our observations. The alternative view is instrumentalism: the view that an hypothesis is simply an instrument for predicting observations on the basis of past observations; it does not describe an underlying reality. Instrumentalism as a general doctrine is discredited and it would be unjustified discrimination to apply it to linguistics in particular.

In sum, the grammarians conclude that they are entitled to believe that their grammatical rules really do describe the reality underlying linguistic behaviour. That reality is psychological, the speaker's competence.

Chomsky offers a nice analogy (1980: 189-92). Suppose that physicists are unable to get any direct evidence about the inside of the sun. The best they can do is construct a theory of the inside that, if it were true, would explain the observed behaviour of the sun. Any such theory may be wrong of course, but they are entitled to believe the best one they can come up with.

We agree with these general observations. It is pointless to object that the conclusion of an inference to the best explanation might be wrong. And, certainly the conclusion should be construed realistically. (Sydney realism is the most virulent known strain.) However, we do not think that those general views yield the desired result in this particular case: they are insufficient to justify 2 and hence the Sensible Version.

The key question is whether the inference to the psychological reality of G is an *appropriate* one. Nobody knows how to codify inferences to the best explanation, but two conditions on appropriate ones are obvious enough. The proposed explanation must be both good and better than its rivals. It is no canon of science to accept a bad explanation because others are worse, nor to draw explanations out of a hat when we have a range of good ones.

Is G—say a Trace Theoretic version of transformational grammar—on the way to a good explanation of competence? Surely we must be agnostic here. So little is known of the computational mechanisms of the mind that we have no idea whether G is even a candidate for psychological explanation. Is G better than G'? Again, suspension of judgment is appropriate. What is the reason for preferring G to the many possible alternatives?

These remarks can be strengthened. Chomsky asks us to imagine that physicists have constructed a theory correctly predicting the sun's behaviour. If there was general agreement that this was a good theory and the best available, then its tentative endorsement would be appropriate. But transformational grammar is not yet in anything like that position. Our earlier supposition about G is indeed optimistic: there never has been a stable consensus about even the rough details of the form and structure of a grammar. We certainly wouldn't attribute solar reality to a theory that was supported largely by indirect evidence, was rejected by many experts, and which past experience suggested would be abandoned within five years.

In sum, inference to the best explanation does not warrant the conclusion that G is psychologically real. We are not justified in accepting description 2.

Where does our discussion leave the Sensible Version of the Right View? According to that version, linguistics is about competence—an internalized grammar—and is part of the explanation of behaviour. If that were the case, then the lack of justification for 2 would leave linguistic theory itself unjustified. This is a good reason for thinking that the Sensible Version is not right.[26] We think that it is indeed not right. But it is not entirely wrong either. A final verdict must wait on our discussion of the theory of symbols, and transformationalists' conflation of that theory with the theory of competence.

6. The Conflation of Symbol with Competence

Suppose we were to ask Grandma what linguistics is about. She would be likely to say: "language". If we pressed, we would hear about words and the way they fit together into sentences; about nouns and verbs, actives and passives, ambiguity, and so on. In brief, Grandma sees linguistics as being about the properties and relations of *linguistic symbols*. We doubt that we would hear a word from her about competence; not a glimmer of the Right View. This is a little embarrassing for Fodor, because he likes to think that Grandma, in her rough and ready way, is rather wise. We agree and only wish that he and Chomsky took more notice of her.

The problem is not that Chomsky and his followers deny what Grandma says. Rather, they conflate the idea that linguistics is about symbols with the idea that it is about competence. Further, they give priority to the latter.

In the opening pages of *Syntactic Structures*, the work that began transformational grammar, Chomsky describes linguistics as follows:

> The fundamental aim in the linguistic analysis of a language L is to separate the *grammatical* sequences which are sentences of L from the *ungrammatical* sequences which are not sentences of L and to study the structure of the grammatical sequences. (1957: 13)

The stated concern here is with linguistic symbols. Much discussion in transformational grammar gives the impression that this is indeed the concern. The discussion is about such matters as ambiguity, word order, and synonymy.

Nevertheless, as we have seen, the favoured way of describing the linguistic task is quite different. Thus, in another classical work, *Aspects of the Theory of Syntax*, almost in the same breath as some remarks like those quoted above, Chomsky says:

> The problem for the linguist...is to determine...the underlying system of rules that has been mastered by the speaker-hearer...Hence, in a technical sense, linguistic theory is

mentalistic, since it is concerned with discovering a mental reality underlying actual behavior. (1965: 4)

Here the concern is not with symbols, a human product, but with competence, a characteristic of the human mind. This is the Right View.[27]

Signs of the conflation are to be found in our recent discussion of the Sensible Version. We saw then that transformationalists use two different sorts of evidence in constructing a grammar. These bear directly on two quite different theories. The linguistic evidence bears directly on the theory of symbols and the psycholinguistic evidence bears directly on the theory of competence.

The properties of symbols that concern a grammar are *syntactic* properties. Full semantic properties—the properties that determine meaning—include reference. Reference involves word-world connections on which a grammar casts no light. Similarly, the competence that concerns a grammar is *syntactic* competence. Full semantic competence requires getting reference right. Reference is not fully determined by anything in the head. So, the conflation that we have been describing is that of the theory of the syntax of symbols with the theory of syntactic competence.[28]

These theories are very different. Linguistic competence is a mental state of a person that explains her linguistic behaviour; it plays a key role in *the production of* that behaviour. Linguistic symbols are the result of that behaviour; they are *the products of* that behaviour. They are datable placeable parts of the physical world: sounds in the air, marks on the page, and so on. They are not mental entities at all. A theory of a part of the production of linguistic symbols is not a theory of the products, the symbols themselves. Of course, given the causal relation between competence and symbol, we can expect a theory of the one to bear on a theory of the other. We consider that relation in section 8. But the relation does not make the two theories identical.

The theory of symbols is concerned with the properties of symbols that make them good for certain purposes. What is it about them that leads people to produce and respond to them as they do? The simple answer is that symbols have meaning. But then what is meaning? It has been discovered that syntactic properties are part of the answer.

Analogously, we might be interested in what makes a certain movement of a ball a good tennis shot. The answer would be in terms of such properties as speed, direction and height. Or we might be interested in what makes a certain chess move good. The answer would be in terms of the myriad possible game continuations; perhaps, in each of these the move gives white an advantage and no other move guarantees this. In all of these cases we are concerned with objects or events in the physical world "outside the head".

However, in each case we might have another concern which is very much with something "inside the head" (or, at least, "inside the body"). What is the explanation of the behaviour—certain movements of hand and arm, perhaps—producing good sentences, tennis shots or chess moves? To answer this, we need a psychological (perhaps, physiological) theory, a theory of competence; we need a theory that explains, for example, how white knew that that particular chess move was good. Such a theory is different from a theory of the objects produced by the behavioural output of a competence: different from a theory of linguistic symbols, tennis shots or chess moves.

The difference between the theory of symbols and the theory of competence can be made vivid by considering the many ways in which a person could be competent. According to the transformationalists, English competence consists in internalizing a grammar. They go further: all English speakers have internalized near enough the one grammar; competence has a uniform structure across the linguistic community. Even if this is so, it is not necessarily so. Many other grammars could agree on the meaning-relevant structures they assign to the sentences of English. Suppose that Martians became competent in English by internalizing one of these other grammars. The theory of Martian competence would have to be different from the theory of ours. Yet the theory of symbols would be the same, for it would still be English that they spoke. Returning to Earth, it would not matter a jot to the theory of symbols if competence among actual English speakers was entirely idiosyncratic.[29]

In sum, linguistic competence, together with various other aspects of the speaker's psychology, produces linguistic behaviour. That behaviour, together with the external environment, produces linguistic symbols. A theory of symbols is not a theory of competence.

The conflation of these two theories is bewildering. Why do transformationalists conflate them? We shall conclude this paper with a tentative diagnosis (section 10).

7. Grandma's View

Having distinguished symbols from competence, we urge Grandma's View of what linguistics is about: it is about symbols and explains the properties in virtue of which symbols have their roles in our lives; more cautiously, that is what it ought to be about and do. We shall argue for Grandma's View by saying more about the theory of syntax and, in the next section, more about its relation to the theory of competence. Some of these matters are discussed in more detail in our *Language and Reality* (1987: parts I-III).

(1) What are the purposes for which symbols are good? The purposes, as almost everyone has seen, are communicative ones. People use symbols to communicate information to each other about the human and nonhuman environment. People use them to greet, question, command, joke, offend, abuse, intimidate, and so on. These are social purposes. If our public language is also our main medium of thought, as we think it is, then linguistic symbols have another important, but not social, role in our lives.

(2) Symbols serve those purposes in virtue of their meaning. We mentioned above some properties that we think contribute to the explanation of the meaning. Those properties were syntactic, reflecting the concerns of this paper. In our view, syntax fits into the total explanation as follows. The core notion in the explanation of meaning is that of truth conditions; it is largely because a sentence has certain truth conditions that it has its role. The sentence's property of having those truth conditions is to be explained in terms of its syntactic structure and the reference of its parts. Reference is to be explained partly by a description theory but, ultimately, by a causal theory taking into account links to nonlinguistic reality. So syntax has its place in the explanation of truth conditions.

(3) The version of Grandma's View that we are urging takes linguistics to be about symbol *tokens*, datable, placeable, parts of the physical world. This version of the View should be distinguished from another which takes linguistics to be about symbol *types*. Talk of types is often just a convenient shorthand for talk of tokens of those types. If that were all that talk of linguistic types amounted to, the second version of Grandma's View would collapse into the first. However, at least one linguist, Katz (1977, 1981, 1984a), seems to take linguistics to be irreducibly about types. It is about Platonic objects just as mathematics is often thought to be. Fodor treats this as

if it has a fair chance of being the Worst View. His objection, which strikes us as sound, is that the Platonic view makes linguistics unempirical (1981: 205-6).

The view that linguistics is about tokens seems to have become discredited through its association with the anti-theoretical practices of pre-Chomskian structural linguistics. Clearly, this misguided past should not be allowed to count against the view.[30] Aside from that, there is a surprisingly popular objection to the view.[31] Crudely, linguistics can't be about tokens because there aren't enough of them. The grammar for English applies to a potentially infinite number of symbols. Yet there can be only a finite number of tokens. So, linguistics can't be about tokens.

One might as well object that a theory of tigers can't be about the beasts that stalk India and excite interest in zoos. Tiger theory is openended. It follows from the theory that if something led to the existence of a tiger token, then that token would be, say, carnivorous. Similarly, the grammar for English describes the characteristics of anything qualifying as a sentence of English. Its application is not limited to tokens actually produced. It follows from the theory that if something led to the existence of an English sentence token, then that token would be, say, tensed.

(4) In distinguishing the theory of symbols from the theory of competence, we may seem to have made it mysterious. We do think that linguistics, as the theory of symbols, has a certain autonomy from other theories, including psychology. However, we are physicalists and so must see this autonomy as only relative: in some sense, linguistics must ultimately be explained in physical terms. But this requirement does not remove the autonomy of linguistics any more than it removes that of, say, biology or economics.

Linguistics is a social science. Like all social sciences, it seems to be immediately dependent on psychological facts and facts about the natural environment. The nature of this sort of dependency is complex and hard to describe. Yet each social science proceeds largely undisturbed by the lack of a complete description. And so it should.

Consider some examples of this sort of dependency. What makes a physical object a pawn or a dollar? What makes a physical event a vote or unlawful? Nothing intrinsic to the objects and events in question; rather, it is the psychological states, within certain environments, of people involved with such objects and events. Exactly what states, what involvement, and what environment, is hard to say. Yet people quite properly feel free to theorize about chess, money, elections and the law. Similarly, we should feel free to theorize about linguistic objects and events.

It would be interesting to consider the way in which the syntactic properties that have concerned us in this paper are dependent on psychological fact. We must leave that to another place.[32]

8. Symbols and Competence

It is time for a verdict on the Right View. To give this we must first say a brief word on the relationship between the two theories that the transformationalists conflate: the theory of the syntax of a language and the theory of syntactic competence in the language.

The theory of syntax assigns to sentences structures that are relevant to the sentences' meanings. The theory of syntactic competence assigns to sentences structures that play a psychological role in the sentences' production and comprehension. The latter structures must include the former. For, the production and comprehension of sentences by the competent speaker requires the matching of those sentences with thoughts *having the same meaning-relevant structures*. To be competent is just to have the skill of matching sentences and thought that are, in this way, alike.

So, the meaning-relevant structure that the theory of syntax assigns to sentences must be the same as the meaning-relevant structure the theory of syntactic competence assigns to matching thoughts. But the theory of competence is interested in more than this structure: it is interested in *how* the speaker matches the meaning-relevant structures of sentences and thoughts. There are many different ways of matching involving many different structures. These differences are irrelevant to the theory of syntax but vital to the theory of competence because of its concern with the psychological processes that competence contributes to performance.

An earlier example helps to bring out the difference between the theory of syntax and the theory of competence. According to G the active (e.g. 'Max bit Sam') is the basic form and the passive (e.g. 'Sam was bitten by Max') the derived form, but according to G′ the reverse is the case. Since each sentence is assigned the same meaning-relevant structure by G and G′, this difference does not matter at all to the theory of syntax. Yet it is crucial to the theory of com-

petence. It is to settle precisely this sort of question that psycholinguistic evidence about acquisition, reaction times, and the like are
sought. This evidence has no immediate relevance to meaning.

Marr's earlier-mentioned distinction between the computational and
algorithmic levels (section 5) is helpful here. The computational
theory characterizes the nature of the task; "a mapping from one
kind of information to another" (1982: 24). In Marr's example of a
cash register, the mapping is from pairs of numbers into single
numbers; and, of course, that mapping has to get the addition right
(p. 22). So the characterization of the computational task that must
begin a theory of the register involves a piece of arithmetical theory.
In the case of a syntactically competent speaker, the mapping is between syntactic structures and sentences; and that mapping *has to
get the meaning right*. So the characterization of the computational
task that must begin a theory of competence involves a theory of
meaning-relevant structure. The problem with transformational grammar is that it goes beyond this linguistic task to questions of *how*
the speaker performs this task. It introduces analyses and psycholinguistic data that are irrelevant to the linguistic task. These analyses
and data bear on the algorithmic level. The conflation we have com-
plained of is roughly that of this algorithmic level with the computational level.

Marr claims that Chomsky's theory "is a true computational
theory": it "is concerned solely with specifying what the syntactic
decomposition of an English sentence should be, and not at all with
how that decomposition should be achieved" (1982: 28). But what
is involved in Chomsky's syntactic decomposition? It goes way
beyond the structure that is necessary to determine meaning. So it
goes way beyond the characterization of task required by a computational theory of the competent speaker. Though Chomsky is not
concerned with the algorithm for performance, his psychological approach to grammars seems clearly concerned with the algorithm for
competence. There are levels within the algorithmic level.

Consider now the verdict on the Right View. The View seemed
wrong because it made linguistic theory depend on a dubious inference to the best explanation: the psycholinguistic reality of G (section 5). (Perhaps this inference was made attractive to transformationalists by their conflation of theories; section 6.)

In contrast, Grandma's View makes linguistic theory seem probably
true. It makes the truth of the theory depend on an inference to the

best explanation that is not dubious: the linguistic evidence warrants acceptance of the linguistic reality of G. We have good reason to believe that symbols have the meaning-relevant properties that G assigns to them. The existence of alternative grammars like G' is no problem. G' is meaning-equivalent to G and so assigns the same meaning-relevant properties. It is therefore as linguistically real as G. The differences between G and G' are linguistically irrelevant. It would be nice to say simply that Grandma is right and Right is wrong. However, this would be far too simple.

First, we have seen that the meaning-relevant structure of thoughts that competence matches with symbols must be the same as that of the symbols. The theory of symbols supplies the characterization required for the computational level of the theory of competence. So, Grandma's View implies that there is some truth in the Right View.

Second, the psycholinguistic evidence that has gone into the construction of G is directly relevant to a theory of competence but not to a theory of symbols. This shows that linguistics, as currently practiced, is partly about competence not symbols. To this extent, the transformationalists' belief in the Right View has *made* it right and Grandma's View wrong.

These remarks are concerned with what *is* the case with linguistics. What *ought* to be the case? There are two tasks which, though related, ought to be kept distinct: one concerns symbols, the other competence. That is what we insist on. Both tasks are, of course, worthwhile and there is no point in arguing about which task we should *call* "linguistic". However, we suggest that it is natural to call the former, which is about language, "linguistic", and the latter, which is about a psychological state of people, "psycholinguistic". Adopting this usage, we conclude that linguistics ought to be about linguistic symbols. Grandma's View, which is largely right, ought to be entirely right.

Finally, our discussion has revealed a certain priority of linguistics over psycholinguistics. Just as a theory of competence at tennis or chess depends on a prior grasp of the nature of tennis or chess, so also does the psycholinguistic theory of competence at a language depend on a prior grasp of the nature of the language. This accords with the priority that Marr seems to imply (1982: 27-8) for the computational level over the algorithmic: understanding what is computed has some sort of precedence over understanding how it is computed.[33]

9. Linguistic Intuitions

We have mentioned (section 4) a likely protest against our argument: we have failed to take proper account of linguistic intuitions which play such a prominent role in the practice of transformationalists. These intuitions are speakers' linguistic beliefs: beliefs that a certain sequence of words is a sentence; that another is ambiguous; that two others are paraphrases, and so on. When we talk of the "linguistic evidence" for the theory of symbols, what we are really referring to are these intuitions. The evidence these intuitions provide is psychological (Fodor, Fodor, and Garrett 1975: 244). How then can the theory based on them not be psychological? So, how can it be so sharply distinguished from the theory of competence? Even though our intuitions do not support G over G' as an account of psychological reality, our rejection of the Right View seems too hasty.

We have said that, according to the Right View, linguistics is part of the explanation of behaviour. The important evidential role that transformationalists give to linguistic intuitions often leads them to claim that linguistics also, perhaps primarily, explains those intuitions.[34]

There are two quite different things that might be meant by a claim that intuitions are evidence. One is: *the fact that speakers have the intuitions* is evidence. The having of an intuition is a psychological phenomenon and so would be evidence for a psychological theory. In particular, to the extent that the speaker's competence is causally responsible for her having linguistic intuitions, they are indeed psychological evidence for the theory of competence. And to that extent, linguistics, if identified with the theory of competence, does explain the having of intuitions.

The having of an intuition can be evidence for a psychological theory even though the intuition is thought to be false. Thus, an atheist can take the having of religious intuitions to be evidence for or against a theory of, say, irrationality.

The alternative interpretation of the claim is importantly different in this respect. For the alternative is to suppose that the *content of the intuitions* is evidence. And that can be so if, but only if, the intuitions are likely to be true. The contents of true intuitions are evidence for a theory of the phenomena they are about. Indeed, strictly speaking, it is the phenomena, not our intuitions about them, that are the evidence. In this way, intuitions may be physical evidence, biological evidence, economic evidence, or whatever. They are psychological evidence only if they are about psychological phenomena.[35]

Insofar as the theory of symbols is supported by linguistic intuitions, it is supported by their contents. These intuitions are about linguistic symbols. So, to the extent that they are likely to be true, their contents are indeed evidence for a theory of symbols. They are not psychological evidence. Linguistics, if identified with the theory of symbols, explains what intuitions are about, not the having of those intuitions. Our distinction between tasks stands. The Right View should still be rejected.

There is a more subtle objection based on the role of intuitions.[36] The objection accepts that there are two tasks to be performed, but claims that their conflation is harmless, even appropriate, because the only way to throw light on symbols is by examining competence. For, our linguistic intuitions provide the only evidence for the theory of symbols; and it is plausible to see these intuitions as reflections of our underlying linguistic competence ("the voice of competence"). The Right View's failure to mention symbols is excusable because the theory of symbols is completely derivative from the theory of competence.

Something has already been conceded to this objection. We pointed out that the Right View is not entirely wrong because the same meaning-relevant structure is to be found in symbol and matching thought. So the theory of the structure of the one must also be a theory of the structure of the other.

Of course, the theory of competence is concerned with more than this structure of matching thoughts. It is concerned with other structures involved in matching. This concern is irrelevant to the theory of symbols. However, this does not undermine the objection. According to the objection, the theory of competence includes the theory of symbols but is wider than it.

It is the objection's claim of epistemic priority for the theory of competence that seems damaging to our position: the claim that the theory of symbols is derivative. This claim is based on assumptions about linguistic intuitions: (i) that they are the only evidence about symbols; (ii) that they are reflections of competence.

(i) must be an exaggeration. People produce and react to linguistic symbols. We can use information about such phenomena, and any other information we have about humans and their social life, in theorizing about symbols.

(ii) is more difficult to deal with. Suppose that description 3 were true of the speaker: her competence consists in tacit propositional knowledge of the grammar, as the Crazy Version requires. (ii) would then seem very plausible.

If the speaker has this knowledge of the grammar, it is plausible to see her intuitions as stemming from the knowledge in some way. Most simply, the intuitions might be seen as a straightforward inference from the knowledge, in which case her intuitions would be the very best evidence of the nature of her competence. However, linguists have generally preferred to see the intuitions as related less directly than this to the tacit knowledge: that knowledge, together with other factors, explain the having of intuitions (J. A. Fodor 1981: 200-1). Still, the intuitions would be largely reflections of the underlying competence, as (ii) claims. Since they largely reflect *knowledge*, they should be true, and hence good evidence of the nature of symbols.

However, the speaker's competence does not consist in tacit knowledge of the grammar. So (ii) must be reassessed.

We think it likely that a speaker's competence resides in a sentence-parsing module, or in something similarly inaccessible to the central processor (section 3). The central processor is the home of intuitions. Given the inaccessibility of the sentence-parser, it is an open question what role the module has in producing the intuitions. It is certainly unlikely that there would be anything close to the above straightforward inference. The module may not even "speak the same language" as the central processor.

What else but competence might have a role in producing linguistic intuitions? The central processor is the obvious candidate. Just as physical intuitions, biological intuitions, and economic intuitions can be produced by central-processor responses to the appropriate phenomena, so also can linguistic intuitions. These linguistic phenomena are not to be discovered by looking inward at our own competence but by looking outward at the social role that symbols play in our lives. When linguists do this now, they do not start from scratch. People have been thinking about these matters for millennia. The result of this central-processor activity is folk, or otherwise primitive, theory or opinion: the linguistic wisdom of the ages. The wisdom will be a good, albeit fallible and incomplete, guide to the nature of linguistic symbols.

Suppose that linguistic intuitions were entirely the result of central-processor activity, past and present. They would not then be reflections of competence and (ii) would be false. As a result, linguistics would not explain our having of the intuitions we have. Furthermore, the claim that the theory of competence is epistemically prior to that of symbols would be groundless.

Which of our two possible sources is mainly responsible for linguistic intuitions? The sentence-parser's main role is obviously to *do things with* language not to *provide us with thoughts about* language. Nevertheless, we think it likely that the sentence-parser does have a significant role with the most basic intuitions—for example, judgments of similarity and difference. Similarly, it is likely that the perception modules have a significant role with the most basic perceptual intuitions. However, it is unlikely that the perception modules are the sole source of those intuitions; recognition and classification depends partly on central memory. It is also unlikely that the sentence-parser is the sole source of basic linguistic intuitions. Many have argued that a person's linguistic intuitions are sensitive to her context.[37] If so they are sensitive to information represented in the central processor. Furthermore, to the extent that intuitions depend on the acquisition of theoretical concepts like *grammatical, ambiguous, passive*, and *noun phrase*, central processing will play a role.[38]

To sustain (ii), the central processor must have hardly any role in forming linguistic intuitions. It would have to be the case that our intuitions are largely uninfluenced by any thinking about linguistic phenomena, and by anything we learn about language at home and at school. Linguistic phenomena would have to differ from all other—physical, biological, economic, and so on—in failing to make us think.

In sum, we accept that there is a close relation between the theory of symbols and the theory of competence. However we do not accept that the role of linguistic intuitions shows that the conflation of the two theories is appropriate, nor that the former theory is epistemically prior to the latter. The intuitions are not simply the reflection of competence; we doubt that they are largely so. To the extent that they are not reflections, they are not, strictly speaking, evidence for the theory of symbols. The evidence is rather the linguistic phenomena that give rise to the intuitions. In any case, the intuitions are not the sole evidence for the theory. We see no reason to revise our verdict on the Right View.

10. Diagnosis of the Conflation

A major theme of this paper has been that linguists conflate the theory of the syntactic properties of symbols with the theory of syntactic competence. Why do they do this? We shall finish by hazarding a few guesses.

First, equivocation between taking 'knowledge' to refer to the *content* of knowledge and taking it to refer to the *state* of knowledge may lead to a slide from the theory of symbols to the theory of competence.[39] The initial conception of the task is to describe a language L. L is what L-speakers know; it is their knowledge. So the task is to describe L-speakers' knowledge. This follows, however, only if 'knowledge' refers to content. The slide comes if we move from this, and the fact that L-speakers' knowledge is their competence in L, to the conclusion that the task is to describe their competence. For this move holds only if 'knowledge' refers to the state.

Second, the fact that the grammarians tend to think of competence as propositional *knowledge* of syntax facilitates the conflation. For, a theory of competence would then be a theory of the syntactical rules known by the speaker. And if the speaker *knows* that a certain rule applies to a linguistic symbol then, of course, it does apply; knowledge implies truth. So, once the speaker's knowledge had been described, there would be nothing further to say about linguistic symbols.

Third, confusion over the nature and role of linguistic intuitions may be significant. We have seen (section 9) that if these intuitions are taken to be reflections of competence and also the only evidence for the theory of symbols, then it is plausible to see that theory as derivative from the theory of competence.

Fourth, the strange objection that linguistics can't be about symbol tokens because there aren't enough of them (section 7) has discredited the idea that linguistics can literally be about symbols at all. For that idea is then thought to be that linguistics is about types. If it were about such Platonic entities it could not be empirical. It may then be thought that linguistics can be made empirical, and able to accommodate the infinite number of sentences in a language, only by taking it to be about our *capacity* to produce and understand any of those sentences.

Fifth, the theory of symbols, like other social theories, is partly dependent on psychological facts. We think, though we have not argued, that this dependency is particularly striking in the case of the syntactic properties of the symbols. Perhaps this dependency prevents people from seeing the relative autonomy of the theory of symbols from psychology. These points are derived from our discussion. The next two are not. Sixth, it seems that it is hard to notice the difference between linguistic behaviour and linguistic symbols. Yet they obviously are different. The behaviour is a series of bodily movements, usually of vocal chords or hands. The symbol is an object in the world produced by the behaviour with the help of the environment, usually a sound or an inscription. The explanation of linguistic behaviour that is the concern of the theory of competence is a psychological description of its *cause*. The explanation of a linguistic symbol that is the concern of the theory of symbols is a semantic description of its *nature*. (In some sign languages the behaviour is the symbol, but that does not alter the point: we have a different explanatory interest in it *qua* symbol from *qua* behaviour.) Perhaps the failure to distinguish behaviour from symbol encourages the conflation of a theory that partly explains the former with a theory that explains the latter.

Seventh, we have found a place for syntax within a truth-conditional theory of meaning (section 7). Yet it is very difficult to see why we need such a theory. What does it explain?[40] We think that the distinction we have just made between linguistic behaviour and linguistic symbols is vital in answering this question (1987: sec. 9.4). The absence of a clear and agreed answer may lead people to miss the task of explaining symbols altogether.

In conclusion, the conflation of a theory of symbols with a theory of competence has caused confusion about the subject matter of linguistics. We think that the subject matter is largely, and ought to be entirely, symbols. Oversimplifying, Grandma is right, Right and Wrong are both wrong.[41]

Notes

1. The attribution to Katz is probably mistaken; see Katz 1984a.
2. Linguists of the Right persuasion thus use 'grammar' with a systematic ambiguity: both as the theorist's construction and as the possession of each native speaker (Chomsky 1965: 25).
3. Hornstein and Lightfoot claim that "a psychological interpretation for grammatical claims has often been adopted by modern writers and by some traditional grammarians" (1981c: 28n). Indeed, such an interpreta-

tion seems to have a long history; see Saussure 1916: 77,90.

4. After we had delivered an earlier version of this paper, our attention was drawn to an excellent paper, Soames 1984a. This takes a similar view to ours on the conflation and on what linguistics is about.

5. In an earlier work (1987: 134-42), we used the verb 'follow' instead of 'govern'. We have changed because 'following a rule' suggests to many that the rule is represented and so undermines the very distinction we are emphasizing.

6. Our three-way distinction between descriptions is analogous to Stabler's three-way distinction between levels of computational theory (1983: 391-2).

7. In recent years Chomsky has preferred the technical term 'cognize' to 'tacitly know' (1975b: 164-5; 1980: 69-70). However, the interpretative difficulty remains. Does cognizing G require standing in a "propositional attitude" to G or is it a mere skill?

8. Stabler's arguments (1983) are very persuasive to this effect, given his plausible interpretation of the Crazy Version using the computer analogy.

9. The most revealing exchange is that between Chomsky and Harman: Harman 1967; Chomsky 1969a; Harman 1969; Chomsky 1969b. See also Chomsky 1975a.

10. We are not the first doubters, of course; see, for example, Stich 1972, Pylyshyn 1972, and Katz 1977.

11. Berwick and Weinberg call this the view that the relationship between a grammar and the parser that embodies it is *transparent*. They seem, obscurely, to hold that the relationship could be less direct, yet the parser would still realize the grammar (1984: 75-82).

12. Baker puts the requirement, somewhat naively, as follows: "The rules should be as general as possible, so that they do not make the language appear to be more complicated than it actually is" (1978: 8).

13. The same point is made by Berwick and Weinberg 1984: 94-5.

14. We are indebted to a Maryland Mafia of Norbert Hornstein, David Lightfoot and Amy Weinberg for criticisms and suggestions that led to this discussion of language acquisition.

15. See particularly, Baker 1979; Hornstein and Lightfoot 1981c; Lightfoot 1981; 1982, especially: 15-21; in press.

16. Chomsky 1981a and 1982 are detailed expositions of this approach; Chomsky 1981b is an overview. See also Wexler 1982; Berwick and Weinberg 1984, chs 1 and 5; Van Reimsdijk and Williams 1986.

17. Even here some caution is appropriate: it is not always obvious what can be gleaned from data. For example, "the child may have intonational access to major phrase boundaries" (Gleitman and Wanner 1982: 37).

18. See, e.g., Gleitman and Wanner 1982: 27, 35.

19. See, e.g., Lightfoot in press.

20. Evidence for the innate principle of subjacency is provided by Berwick and Weinberg 1984: 153-71. J. D. Fodor 1985 is a detailed criticism, to which Berwick and Weinberg 1985 is a reply.

21. Pylyshyn has pointed out some problems in using reaction times as evidence in psychology (1980: 116-19).
22. For discussions based on the psycholinguistic evidence that go mostly against the case for the psychological reality of G, see Bresnan 1978: 1-3; Anderson 1980: 382-3; Lyons 1981: 259-60; Johnson-Laird 1983: 276-95.
23. An examination of actual arguments for a grammar confirms this. See, for example, Baker 1978: 3-27; Hornstein and Lightfoot 1981c: 17-24.
24. Support for this interpretation of Chomsky comes from his explicit rejection of the view that a grammar is a model for a speaker or hearer; see, e.g., 1965: 9, 139-40.
25. See, e.g., Chomsky 1980: 189-201.
26. "If linguistics is truly a branch of psychology ..., as is often unilaterally asserted by linguists, it is so far the branch with the greatest pretensions and the fewest reliable results" (Gazdar et al 1985: 5).
27. For some other examples of the conflation, see Chomsky 1966, and Katz 1971, ch. 4.
28. Philosophers typically make a similar mistake, conflating the theory of the full semantic properties of symbols—particularly of truth conditions—with the theory of full semantic competence. Dummett is the most explicit: "a theory of meaning is a theory of understanding" (1975: 99). Philosophers often compound this mistake by taking a propositional view of competence (cf. the Crazy Version). For references and criticisms, see Devitt 1981: 92-110; 1984: 205-11; Soames 1984b.
29. Katz makes a similar point; 1977: 266.
30. Katz remarks that the structuralist approach to grammars was "insufficiently abstract" (1984a: 18). But a theory of tokens *can be* as abstract as you like.
31. We have been confronted with this objection many times in conversation.
32. See Devitt in preparation.
33. Compare: "it is possible, and arguably proper, for a linguist (*qua* linguist) to ignore matters of psychology. But it is hardly possible for a psycholinguist to ignore language" (Gazdar et al 1985: 5).
34. See, for example, Lees 1957: 36; Chomsky 1969a: 81-2; Baker 1978: 4-5.
35. Katz makes a similar distinction between the "source" and "import" of intuitions; 1977: 258.
36. We are indebted to Jerry Fodor for an objection along these lines in response to an earlier version of this paper.
37. See, for example, Labov 1972: 192-201.
38. Cf Baker, who seems to regard all intuitive judgments as simply manifestations of competence (1978: 4-5).
39. For a passage suggestive of such a slide see Baker 1978: 3.
40. On this see Leeds 1978, Field 1978, Churchland 1979, and Stich 1983.
41. We are grateful for comments received when earlier versions of this paper were read in 1985 at the University of Sydney, La Trobe University and the University of New South Wales; and in 1986 at the University of Maryland. We are also indebted to Fiona Cowie and Stephen Stich.

References

Anderson, John R. 1980. *Cognitive Psychology and its Implications*. San Francisco: W. H. Freeman and Company.

Baker, C. L. 1978. *Introduction to Generative-Transformational Syntax*. Englewood Cliffs, NJ: Prentice-Hall, Inc.

Baker, C. L. 1979. "Syntactic Theory and the Projection Problem". *Linguistic Inquiry* 10: 533-81.

Baker, C.L., and J. J. McCarthy, eds. 1981. *The Logical Problem of Language Acquisition*. Cambridge, Mass.: MIT Press.

Berwick, R. C., and A. S. Weinberg. 1984. *The Grammatical Basis of Linguistic Performance: Language use and Acquisition*. Cambridge, Mass.: MIT Press.

Berwick, R. C., and A. S. Weinberg. 1985. "Deterministic Parsing and Linguistic Explanation". *Language and Cognitive Processes* 1: 109-34.

Bever, T. G., J. M. Carroll, and L. A. Miller, eds. 1984. *Talking Minds: The Study of Language in Cognitive Science*. Cambridge, Mass.: MIT Press.

Block, Ned, ed. 1981. *Readings in Philosophy of Psychology, Volume 2*. Cambridge, Mass.: Harvard University Press.

Bresnan, Joan. 1978. "A Realistic Transformational Grammar". In Halle, Bresnan, and Miller 1978: 1-59.

Chomsky, Noam. 1957. *Syntactic Structures*. The Hague: Mouton & Co.

Chomsky, Noam. 1965. *Aspects of the Theory of Syntax*. Cambridge, Mass.: MIT Press.

Chomsky, Noam. 1966. *Topics in the Theory of Generative Grammar*. The Hague: Mouton & Co.

Chomsky, Noam. 1969a. "Linguistics and Philosophy". In Hook 1969: 51-94.

Chomsky, Noam. 1969b. "Comments on Harman's Reply". In Hook 1969: 152-9.

Chomsky, Noam. 1975a. "Knowledge of Language". In Gunderson 1975: 299-320.

Chomsky, Noam. 1975b. *Reflections on Language*. New York: Pantheon Books.

Chomsky, Noam. 1980. *Rules and Representations*. New York: Columbia University Press.

Chomsky, Noam. 1981a. *Lectures on Government and Binding*. Dordrecht: Foris Press.

Chomsky, Noam. 1981b. "Principles and Parameters in Syntactic Theory". In Hornstein and Lightfoot 1981a: 32-75.

Chomsky, Noam. 1982. *Some Concepts and Consequences of the Theory of Government and Binding*. Cambridge, Mass: MIT Press.

Churchland, Paul M. *Scientific Realism and the Plasticity of Mind*. Cambridge: Cambridge University Press.

Devitt, Michael. 1981. *Designation*. New York: Columbia University Press.

Devitt, Michael. 1984. *Realism and Truth*. Oxford: Blackwell. (Princeton: Princeton University Press.)

Devitt, Michael. In preparation. "Meaning and Psychology".

Devitt, Michael and Kim Sterelny. 1987. *Language and Reality: An Introduction to the Philosophy of Language.* Oxford: Blackwell. (Cambridge, Mass.: MIT Press.)

Dummett, Michael. 1975. "What is a Theory of Meaning?" In Guttenplan 1975: 97-138.

Field, Hartry. 1978. "Mental Representation". *Erkenntnis* 13: 9-61. Reprinted with Postscript in Block 1981: 78-114.

Fodor, Janet Dean. 1985. "Deterministic Parsing and Subjacency." *Language and Cognitive Processes* 1: 3-42.

Fodor, Janet Dean, Jerry A. Fodor, and Merrill F. Garrett. 1975. "The Psychological Unreality of Semantic Representations". *Linguistic Inquiry* 6: 515-31. Reprinted in Block 1981: 238-52. (Page reference is to Block.)

Fodor, Jerry A. 1981. "Introduction: Some Notes on What Linguistics is Talking About". In Block 1981: 197-207.

Fodor, Jerry A. 1983. *The Modularity of Mind: An Essay on Faculty Psychology.* Cambridge, Mass.: MIT Press.

Gazdar, Gerald, Ewan Klein, Geoffrey Pullum, and Ivan Sag. 1985. *Generalized Phrase Structure Grammar.* Oxford: Basil Blackwell.

Gleitman, Lila R., and Eric Wanner. 1982. "Language Acquisition: The State of the State of the Art". In Wanner and Gleitman 1982: 3-48.

Gould, S. J. 1983. *The Panda's Thumb.* Harmondsworth: Penguin.

Gunderson, Keith, ed. 1975. *Minnesota Studies in the Philosophy of Science, Volume VII: Language, Mind, and Knowledge.* Minneapolis: University of Minnesota Press.

Guttenplan, S., ed. 1975. *Mind and Language.* Oxford: Clarendon Press.

Halle, Morris, Joan Bresnan, and George A. Miller, eds. 1978. *Linguistic Theory and Psychological Reality.* Cambridge, Mass.: MIT Press.

Harman, Gilbert. 1967. "Psychological Aspects of the Theory of Syntax". *Journal of Philosophy* 64: 75-87.

Harman, Gilbert. 1969. "Linguistic Competence and Empiricism". In Hook 1969: 143-51.

Hook, Sidney, ed. 1969. *Language and Philosophy: A Symposium.* New York: New York University Press.

Hornstein, Norbert, and David Lightfoot, eds. 1981a. *Explanation in Linguistics: The Logical Problem of Language Acquisition.* London: Longman.

Hornstein, Norbert, and David Lightfoot, eds. 1981b. "Preface". To Hornstein and Lightfoot 1981a: 7-8.

Hornstein, Norbert, and David Lightfoot, eds. 1981c. "Introduction". To Hornstein and Lightfoot 1981a: 9-31.

Johnson-Laird, Philip N. 1983. *Mental Models: Towards a Cognitive Science of Language, Inference, and Consciousness.* Cambridge, Mass.: Harvard University Press.

Katz, Jerrold J. 1971. *The Underlying Reality of Language and Its Philosophical Import.* New York: Harper & Row.

Katz, Jerrold J. 1977. "The Real Status of Semantic Representations". *Linguistic Inquiry* 8: 559-84. Reprinted in Block 1981: 253-75. (Page references are to Block.)

Katz, Jerrold J. 1981. *Language and Other Abstract Objects*. Totowa, N. J.: Rowman and Littlefield.

Katz, Jerrold J. 1984a. "An Outline of a Platonist Grammar". In Bever, Carroll, and Miller 1984: 17-48.

Katz, Jerrold J., ed. 1984b. *The Philosophy of Linguistics*. London: Oxford University Press.

Labov, W. 1972. *Sociolinguistic Patterns*. Philidelphia: University of Pennsylvania Press.

Leeds, Stephen. 1978. "Theories of Reference and Truth". *Erkenntnis* 13: 111-29.

Lees, Robert B. 1957. "Review of *Syntactic Structures*". *Language* 33: 375-407. Reprinted in Gilbert Harman (ed.), *On Noam Chomsky: Critical Essays*. Garden City, N. Y.: Anchor Press/Doubleday: 34-79. (Page reference is to Harman.)

Lightfoot, David. 1981. "The History of Noun Phrase Movement". In Baker and McCarthy 1981: 86-119.

Lightfoot, David. 1982. *The Language Lottery: Toward a Biology of Grammars*. Cambridge, Mass.: MIT Press.

Lightfoot, David. In press. "The Child's Trigger Experience: Degree-O Learnability". *Behavioral and Brain Sciences*.

Lyons, John. 1981. *Language and Linguistics: An Introduction*. Cambridge: Cambridge University Press.

Marr, David. 1982. *Vision: A Computational Investigation into the Human Representation and Processing of Visual Information*. San Francisco: W. H. Freeman and Company.

Pylyshyn, Zenon W. 1972. "Competence and Psychological Reality". *American Psychologist*: 546-52.

Pylyshyn, Zenon W. 1980. "Computation and Cognition: Issues in the Foundations of Cognitive Science". *Behavioral and Brian Sciences* 3: 111-32.

Saussure, Ferdinand de. 1916. *Course in General Linguistics*, eds, Charles Bally and Albert Sechehaye, trans., Wade Baskin, New York: McGraw-Hill Book Co, 1966. 1st. French ed., 1916.

Soames, Scott. 1984a. "Linguistics and Psychology". *Linguistics and Philosophy* 7: 155-79.

Soames, Scott. 1984b. "Semantics and Psychology". In Katz 1984b: 204-26.

Stabler, Edward P., Jr. 1983. "How are Grammars Represented?" *Behavioral and Brain Sciences* 6: 391-402.

Stich, Stephen P. 1971. "What Every Speaker Knows". *Philosophical Review* 80: 476-96.

Stich, Stephen P. 1972. "Grammar, Psychology, and Indeterminacy". *Journal of Philosophy* 69: 799-818. Reprinted in Block 1981: 208-22. (Page references are to Block.)

Stich, Stephen P. 1978. "Beliefs and Subdoxastic States". *Philosophy of Science* 45: 499-518.

Stich, Stephen P. 1983. *From Folk Psychology to Cognitive Science: The Case Against Belief*. Cambridge, Mass.: MIT Press.

Van Riemsdijk, H., and E. Williams. 1986. *Introduction to the Theory of Grammar*. Cambridge, Mass.: MIT Press.

Wanner, Eric, and Lila R. Gleitman, eds. 1982. *Language Acquisition: The State of the Art*. Cambridge: Cambridge University Press.

Wexler, Kenneth. 1982. "A Principle Theory for Language Acquisition". In Wanner and Gleitman 1982: 288-315.

Philosophical Perspectives, 3
Philosophy of Mind and Action Theory, 1989

BIOSEMANTICS AND THE NORMATIVE PROPERTIES OF THOUGHT

Graeme Forbes
Tulane University

1. Functions, norms and naturalism

That the semantic properties of words and sentences have normative aspects is a commonplace. According to some philosophers, particularly Dummett, these normative aspects individuate semantic properties. For example, in the case of a sentence, they individuate its meaning, or the proposition it expresses: the meaning is a rule that determines under what conditions the sentence is *properly* assertible or *justifiably* assertible (Dummett 1982). In Dummett's view, such normative criteria of meaning-individuation lead to non-truth-conditional semantics. Others have held that normative criteria can individuate meanings which determine full truth-conditions (Peacocke 1986). However that may be, the normativeness of the criteria which individuate meanings, or which determine which meaning is being expressed, has been seen by some, especially Kripke, as presenting an obstacle to a naturalistic explanation of meaning and related concepts. Thus, in his well-known discussion of the dispositional analysis of 'S means addition by "+",' Kripke writes: "Computational error, finiteness of my capacity, and other disturbing factors may lead me not to be *disposed* to respond as I *should*....The relation of meaning and intention to future action is *normative*, not *descriptive*" (Kripke 1982, p.37).

Naturalism about the semantic and the psychological is the view that a proper and complete understanding of these phenomena is formulable without countenancing forces of a sort not consonant with the forces currently recognized by physics,[1] or a kind of substance, or building block or property of material substance, of a radically different sort from those currently recognized by physics. The objection to naturalism Kripke is urging is that it involves a naturalistic fallacy, a doomed attempt to derive an *ought* from an *is* or a *would*, or at least from the wrong sort of *is* or *would*. For what facts gleanable from the natural world could explain why such-and-such is what *ought* to be said?

We need not be dumbstruck in the face of this question. Facts about design support ought-judgements. If the program I have just written fails to perform as I want it to, I may rewrite parts of the code and then say "It ought to work now". Here the goal of the program is derivative from the intentions of its creator, so this source of normativeness is not obviously one the naturalist can draw on, since intentional phenomena are part of the problem for naturalism. But design seems to be merely one way that the notion of how a thing ought to behave can have application. Normative concepts are applicable to anything with a function: if it is the function of a thing to φ then what it ought to do in appropriate circumstances is φ: φ-ing in those circumstances is what it is *supposed* to do or what it is *for*, and if it does not φ when it should, then it is *mal*functioning. And in evolutionary biology we seem to have a paradigm of how naturalistically *un*problematic facts about an object can determine that it or some feature of it has a function. Perhaps there is an analogous kind of explanation to be found of the normativeness of the semantic.

There are broadly speaking three philosophical approaches to the notion of function in evolutionary biology. First there is an eliminativist approach, according to which the appearance of goal-directedness in a system arises out of the way in which that system's subsystems are organized. On this view, the subsystems themselves do not have functions. So if there is a general organizational structure that is in common to systems exhibiting goal-directedness, an account of that structure would constitute an analysis of the teleological in non-teleological terms (see Nagel 1961 Ch. 12 and Rosenberg 1985 Ch. 3 for this approach).

It is not my intention here to try to evaluate this position. I simply note that it has some plausibility (see the clay-crystal example of the next section), and if correct would undermine the naturalist strategy of explaining the normative aspects of meaning by appeal to natural teleology. For it is hard to see how the meaning of a semantic primitive is to be explained as the product of the interaction of subsystems which themselves have none of the problematic normative features. Or rather, Kripke's challenge is essentially a query as to how that is to be done. If function and goal-directedness can be explained as suggested, then the appeal to biological function would just be an inessential detour on the way to a naturalistic theory. Perhaps such an approach could be said to *explain how* the normative features of the semantic arise. But the thrust of eliminativism in biology is that there is no significant unification to be made between the way that biosystems serve functions and the way that a deliberately designed artefact does, and as I already said, this has some *prima facie* plausibility. By contrast, one is not inclined to think that the normative aspects of meaning are just some kind of appearance: that is the strength of Kripke's point.

The attractiveness of the biosemantic turn appears to rest on the thought that evolutionary biology vindicates essentially ineliminable but naturalistically respectable concepts of function and goal. There are two accounts of teleological concepts as autonomous which render them naturalistically respectable, one *backward*-looking (the 'etiological' account) and the other *forward*-looking (the 'propensity' account). According to the etiological account, it is a function of a system to ϕ iff it is because of exercises of its capacity for ϕ-ing that the system (or more exactly, the genotype directing its construction) has continued to be reproduced despite the pressures of natural selection.[2] According to the propensity account, it is a function of a system to ϕ iff its capacity to ϕ confers on the system a propensity which enhances its prospects of reproducing in its natural environment. These two accounts seem to disagree only over extreme cases: if the world came into existence five minutes ago, no biosystem has a function etiologically construed, and if a system's capacity to ϕ no longer improves its survival chances because of environmental changes, ϕ-ing ceases to be its function on the propensity construal; see (Bigelow and Pargetter 1987) for a recent discussion.[3]

2. Thought-constituents as bearers of functions

The application of the etiological understanding of teleological notions to semantic concepts can be pursued in two different directions.

We might hold that the normative aspects of meanings arise from the intentions with which speakers express them, but that psychological states in general are to be explained naturalistically in teleological terms; this is the indirect approach I discuss in the next section. Alternatively, we might try applying naturalistic teleology directly in semantic analysis, pursuing the analogy with evolutionary biology. The main point of the analogy is that this approach, if successful, should enable us to avoid any appeal to intentions and purposeful design in explaining the workings of language, just as biology has no need of the hypothesis of an intentional designer of nature. This course has been pursued with ingenuity by Ruth Millikan (Millikan 1984). According to Millikan, words, and more generally conventional signs, have 'stabilizing proper functions'. That is, for each such sign, there is something it is supposed to do (hence 'proper function'), a something which 'tends at the same time to keep speakers using the device in standard ways and to keep hearers responding to it in standard ways' (op. cit. p. 32—hence 'stabilizing'). Millikan looks to the history of the use of a sign to derive the function which accounts for its proliferation, but the forward-looking, propensity account of function seems to fit her program equally well: neither requires an appeal to user intentions. A simple example to keep in mind is her proposal that the stabilizing proper function of a referring term is to 'precipitate acts of identification [on the part of the audience] of the variants in the world to which they correspond' (p.71). So we get normative constraints on the use and understanding of a referring term by speakers and hearers: if that is its function, certain things follow about how we should use it or respond to its uses.

Do such attributions of functions meet Kripke's objection to naturalism? I think they do not. The example just given highlights what from the naturalistic viewpoint must seem to be significant differences between the functions of conventional signs and the natural functions of biosystems. What a system does is something which can standardly be described in non-functional terms, that is, in the relatively unproblematic language of chemistry or physics. The activity in question turns out to be its function simply because of the way the environment happens to be. For instance, to choose an example far from the complexity of higher organisms, consider clay crystals.[4] We can imagine a certain type of clay crystal which because of its purely physical properties reshapes the structure of the beds of streams in which it is deposited so that more crystals of that sort are deposited until a small dam emerges. During the dry season the water in the resulting pools evaporates, exposing the underlying clay to the wind. The top layers are blown off as dust and some dust particles find their way into other streams. The dust particles have the physical property, some kind of structural defect, that causes damming, so the whole process starts again in these previously undammed streams. Hence this kind of clay spreads through the streams of the geographical region. On the etiological view, the structural defect of the clay crystals has a function, to build dams. And we can give a complete physico-chemical explanation of how it has the power to perform this function; in this case, the explanation would be from crystallography and the theory of flow dynamics.

By contrast, both the function of a name (to precipitate an act of identification on the part of an interpreter), and the basis of its ability to perform that function, are specifiable in the first instance only in naturalistically problematic terms: the etiological approach does not immediately legitimize the attribution of function to conventional signs (legitimize it from the naturalistic viewpoint) in the way it legitimizes attributions of function in biology from the viewpoint of contemporary science (which discounts vitalism, design etc.). The fact that the function of the sign is specified intentionally may not be a real difficulty to naturalism as such, for the point of attributing a function to the sign was simply to explain where the 'ought' in, say, 'the interpreter ought to think of x' comes from. Once we have accounted for the normativeness, perhaps we can add on a naturalistic theory of such notions as 'think of' (this is an element of the indirect approach to be discussed below). But the problem of explaining the basis of the sign's ability to perform its function seems more immediately serious for the direct approach.

The simplest way for something to have a function by convention is for its most influential prospective users to reach an agreement that that is how it is to be used; consider, for example, the Committee on Data for Science and Technology's 1986 standardization of the values of the fundamental physical constants, where it was *decided* to define the speed of light exactly and let the value of the meter be determined by empirical observation (Codata 1986). More general accounts, abstracting from explicit decision-making, are well known, (e.g. Lewis 1969). But we can put the conventional aspect to one side, since the main question is how it is possible for a sound or sequence of marks to precipitate an act of identification, to make a hearer think of a specific object. What is the analogue in this process of facts about flow dynamics?

The natural answer to the question about the basis of a conventional sign's power, still at the intentional level, is—to stay with the case of referring terms—that the sign is associated with a thought constituent and the thought-constituent is itself a way of thinking of a particular object. Here there are two things which need explanation: how is the association accomplished, and what is it for something to be a way of thinking of an object? And if the explanations should make use of notions which also have normative aspects, these again to be explained by attributing functions, we would like some guarantee that at some point there will be no further need for functional attribution, or else only for naturalistically unproblematic functional attributions.

Associated with referring terms are thought-constituents McDowell calls 'de re senses' (McDowell 1984). What is it that makes a sense a de one particular re x rather than another y? It is fairly widely accepted in contemporary philosophy of language that the $whole$ explanation cannot be given in terms of a's conceptual content (if it has any). Many writers would say that the crucial component is rather some special kind of causal relation that a stands in to x but not to y. Could the obtaining of such a relation be what underpins a's capacity to precipitate acts of identification of x, or more prosaically, to refer to x?

Take the case of demonstrative identification. No doubt one could not successfully demonstratively identify a man using tokens of the term 'that man' if one were causally isolated from the man in question. But merely that the use of the term is causally prompted by the man is far short of what is required to make the use a demonstrative identification: a scream might be causally prompted by the man but is not a demonstrative identification of him. What makes the sound the speaker produces a demonstrative identification has to do with the intentional background of the production, and the details here are controversial enough even in intentional terms: no one has come close to a realistic non-intentional account (see further note 7).

I said at the beginning of this discussion that normative aspects of semantic properties might be explained in terms of *designed* functions or in terms of *evolved* functions. Reflection on such a basic case as that of demonstrative identification strongly supports the commonsense view: that words are *designed* by us to perform certain functions, so that the normativeness in question derives from the intentions of speakers. Millikan has interesting arguments that Gricean intentions are not operative in the expression or grasping of thought (op. cit. pp. 60-70; see also Grice 1957). But the main source of the difficulties appears to be the complexity and sophistication of Gricean intentions. Much simpler intentional structures may underly language-use, as in Vlach's account of speaker-meaning in terms of commitment (Vlach 1981); and Kripke appeals to intentions that have explicit semantic content, such as the intention to use a name with the same reference as it has in the source from which the name was acquired (Kripke 1980, p.96). So it seems to me that at the point of the analogy with evolutionary biology where in the latter we see that there is no need to posit intelligent design to explain biological phenomena, the analogy in fact breaks down. A related point of breakdown, of course, is that with language it is not hard to point to candidates for the role of intelligent designers.

3. Teleology and psychological content

An indirect approach is one which handles semantic properties *via* an account of intentionality in general. This strategy must deal with all propositional attitudes—and on top of that the special case where the propositions themselves involve semantic concepts. A Gricean analysis of semantic concepts dissolves this extra layer of difficulty, but I will not take a stand on its feasibility, since my scepticism about the naturalistic project arises in connection with even the simplest propositional attitudes. The question is whether the indirect approach avoids the problem of giving a naturalistic account of such notions as 'refers to' or 'predicates of'. I shall argue that if we pursue the indirect approach we come to a point where we can go no further unless we have a naturalistic account of these notions.

It will be instructive of the problems to have before us a recent, sophisticated naturalistic proposal, that in (Stalnaker 1984). According to Stalnaker, beliefs and desires are states whose contents are determined by two aspects: what they *indicate*, and what *tendencies to bring about states of affairs* they bestow, where 'indicate' and 'tendency to bring about' are naturalistically explicable. The proposal may be summarized as follows:

> (A) The belief relation is the first component, and the desire relation the second component, of the unique pair $<B,D>$ such that B maps an agent's belief states into propositions and D maps the agent's desire states into propositions and the agent is disposed to act in ways that would tend to bring about the propositions in the range of D given the truth of the propositions in the range of B.[5]

(A) does not mention indication, which is only appealed to to select a *unique* $<B,D>$ from the range that may be consistent with the actual dispositions of an agent. This gives the following account of *believing that P*:

> (B) An organism G believes that P iff it has internal states of two kinds, b-states and d-states, such that (i) there is a unique pair of functions $<B,D>$ satisfying the conditions of (A) when G's b-states (d-states) are construed as belief states (desire states), (ii) the proposition P belongs to the range of B, and (iii) each b-state σ indicates the truth of the proposition $B(\sigma)$.

Stalnaker's account of indication is this (p. 13). A state of an object x indicates that its environment is in a state y iff there is a function f and an optimal or fidelity condition C such that if C obtains then the object is in state x iff the environment is in state $f(x) = y$.[6] Thus the shape of a shadow cast by a tree indicates the tree's shape when the sun is in a certain position, and its number of rings indicates its age.

Some rather serious objections arise to this naturalist strategy and its likely developments. First, it seems to me that the notion of indication is relevant at most to belief states whose contents are given by simple present-tense observation statements or past tense memory judgements or reports of one's own psychological states based on introspection. The indication criterion is supposed to settle the content of a state typically by looking at the state's causes. But consider all the belief-states whose contents are given by propositions which are classified as verification-transcendent in the literature on anti-realism (see e.g. Wright 1980, X-XII): in none of these will the environmental condition that verifies the belief-state (if it is true) be the cause of the belief-state—the cause will rather be, at best, traces of that condition. So by Stalnaker's lights, it is not a state which obtained in the distant past that is indicated by my belief that such-and-such was the case then: that belief-state at best indicates some present state whose causal antecedents trace to the past state (and there need not even be a present state of this sort). Indeed, the difficulty even arises over belief states which do not involve propositions usually classified as verification-transcendent, for example, a belief I may have about tomorrow's weather.[7]

Secondly, even in the case of present-tense perceptual judgements, the notion of indication may be problematic from the naturalistic point of view. For what are the fidelity conditions for a perceptual mechanism? 'Fidelity condition' is a normative notion, whose most obvious explanation employs the idea of the content of an experience somehow matching the perceived scene, which appears to import the intentional notions the naturalist is supposed to be eliminating: the question of whether there is matching is only settled once the content of the experience is settled. A likely move for the naturalist to make at this point is to turn again to teleology to account for the normativeness; perhaps the fidelity condition for a perceptual mechanism is just that condition whose obtaining allowed the mechanism to function in the way that gives it its survival value. However, this is too narrow, for we want to allow an organism perceptual beliefs if it is *somehow* managing to perceive its environment and forming beliefs on that basis, even if its natural apparatus has been substituted by some Heath-Robinson device of our making. What makes all the cases cases of perception has to do with the systematic dependence of the content of experience on features of the perceived scene. That is, what unifies the standard case with the strange variants philosophers might dream up is that the matching relation holds for a certain reason.[8]

There is also a broader obstacle to the use of indication to settle the content or meaning of a mental state. If indication comprises only what Grice (op. cit.) calls 'natural' meaning, then the concept is unproblematic from the naturalistic point of view but unhelpful to the project of explaining 'non-natural' meaning; for it seems little illumination about non-natural meaning can be gained by reflecting on 'natural' indication, in view of important features of non-natural meaning for which an account in terms of indication is difficult to

discern. One prominent problematic feature of non-natural indication is its potential for *falsely* indicating, a potential with no counterpart on the side of natural meaning. When fidelity conditions do not
obtain, the shadow may mislead an observer about the tree's shape.
But the unfaithful shadow does not *falsely mean* that the tree is such-
and-such a shape, since in fact it is not that shape. Yet the capacity
to mean that P, whether or *not* P is the case, is characteristic of a
system whose states have non-natural meaning.

The naturalist can once more appeal to teleological concepts.
Dretske and others have suggested that between natural and non-
natural meaning there lies something Dretske calls 'functional' meaning (Dretske 1986). For example, if a system is *designed* to produce
an effect E in circumstances S, then if E occurs, S is indicated (in
Dretske's sense) whether or not the system is functioning as intended: thus if the bell of a doorbell system sounds because of a short
circuit, it will still be correct to say that the bell's ringing indicates
or means (functional sense) that someone is at the door. So functional
meaning permits false indication, and there is therefore some prospect that it may afford an account of non-natural meaning.

But this proposal does not take us very far away from the 'effect
bearing traces of its cause' model of meaning whose inadequacy was
remarked upon in connection with verification-transcendent propositions: the teleological move merely substitutes final for efficient
causes. We are no closer to explaining the kind of meaning 'it's going to rain' has— regardless of what prompts the statement—in terms
either of the 'means' of 'those clouds mean rain' or of 'that behavior
means a predator is approaching' (where the behavior is the output
of a stimulus-response mechanism). It seems to me intuitively that
the difference between the natural and the functional 'means' is small
by comparison with the gulf between either of them and the non-
natural 'means'. Let me try to elaborate on this.

First, I should say that I doubt that 'functional meaning' is an intuitively accessible notion as Dretske intends it to behave. I do not
share Dretske's intuition that there is a sense of 'means' on which
a malfunctioning designed system or a product of evolution which
has been tricked 'mean' that the normal cause of their behavior is
present. If a philosopher surrounds an animal with paper-maché
predators and it responds as it would in a similar situation to real
predators, I can only hear the statement 'that behavior means ("tells
us") that there are predators nearby' as false, though I agree that

'that behavior *ought* to mean that there are predators nearby' is true.[9] It may be said that this is no matter: we can simply *define* a sense of 'means' or 'indicates' to play the required role. But in introducing a new primitive like this we undermine the idea that we already grasp some relatively less problematic concept which can be used to elucidate non-natural meaning. Indeed, it is somewhat presumptuous to use the word 'means' for this new notion. If we used some other term, say 'flags', insisting that 'E flags S' does not mean merely that E is behavior of a type whose function is to respond to states of the type of S, then there is a strong suggestion that we are importing elements of our understanding of non-natural meaning in conceiving of E flagging S though S does not obtain.

If the potential for false indication is a crucial property differentiating natural and non-natural meaning, we should ask what the source of this potential is. The naive view, with which I shall be content here, is that *expression* relations and *correspondence* relations play the main role. An assertion expresses a proposition, and a proposition P corresponds to a state of affairs; but the mere assertion-performance is no guarantee of the obtaining of the associated state of affairs. So far, this offers some support for the assimilation of non-natural to functional meaning, for the design of a doorbell mechanism may be said to set up a correspondence between the ringing of the bell and the presence of someone at the door; the evolutionary history of the squid's defence mechanism may be said to set up a correspondence between its squirting black inky substance into the surrounding water and its being under threat of attack. Consequently, when the mechanisms are triggered but not by the causes to which it is their functions to respond, we could say they falsely indicate someone's being at the door or the approach of a predator.

But this cannot be the whole story about the potential for false indication, since it does not explain why natural meaning does not allow for false indication. Why not say that if as a matter of natural necessity events of type E_1 are caused in 99 percent of the cases by events of type E_2, that sets up a correspondence between E_1-type events and E_2-type events, so that whenever an E_1-type event occurs in the remaining 1 percent of the cases, it falsely indicates the occurrence of an E_2-type event? Of course we could say this if we wanted to. It seems misleading, however, because the occurrence of an E_1-type event does not in any literal sense *make the claim* that an E_2-type event has occurred. We are really comparing events or occurrences here: the occurrence of the E_1-type event, the ringing of the bell, the squid's discharge, and the assertion of a proposition. Uncontroversially, in the first of these cases, no claim that such-and-such is the case is being made, while the last is the paradigm case of claim-making. But I think it is also clear that in the case of the squid's discharge, no claim about predators (or anything else) is being made, and if this is less clear in the case of the designed system, that is only because we have the intentions of the designer in mind (a resource the naturalist must abjure). The moral is that it is not enough to explain the possibility of false indication that we impute correspondence relations on the basis of natural facts, however salient those facts may be. The correspondence relations must be associated somehow with the practice of assertion or claim-making, a false proposition being the content of a false assertion. The practice of assertion is governed by the convention that in making an assertion one aims at the truth (Dummett 1973, Ch. 10). And no such aim can be attributed in the merely functional cases.

This point might be dismissed as irrelevant on the grounds that it is one thing for a state to be the bearer of non-natural meaning and another for that meaning to be asserted. Thus though the squid, in behaving as it does, is not making any claim about predators, its behavior bears a certain meaning nonetheless. But I doubt that there is any prospect of separating out the practice of assertion from the content of the acts of assertion. Non-natural meanings have to be the kinds of things apt for employment in acts aimed at expressing the truth. The type of state of affairs to which an assertion corresponds is determined by the proposition-constituents which the assertion-constituents express, the syntax of the assertion, and the state-constituents to which the proposition-constituents correspond. Here we are brought back to the problem of how to give a naturalistic account of why a word has the sense it does and why that sense has the reference it does, which I argued in the previous section to be matters which are determined at the first level of analysis by the intentions of language-users; I believe there is an ineliminable intentionality involved here which is the root reason why the indirect naturalistic strategy discussed in this section fails to find concepts in terms of which a plausible account of non-natural meaning can be formulated.

It would be an argument for naturalism if it could be shown that its failure would have intolerable consequences. In my view, Kripke's claim that there are no naturalistic facts which explain the normativeness of meaning still stands, and it might be claimed that this result justifies scepticism about the idea that there is a genuine fact about the content of a thought-constituent, thereby leaving the 'sceptical solution' Kripke attributes to Wittgenstein in possession of the field. But it may also be argued (as in McGinn 1984, p. 151) that the notion of genuine fact being appealed to here is too narrow. I think this reaction is likely to prove inconsistent with the naturalistic viewpoint, but that is a question-begging objection to it.[10]

Notes

1. A force intermediate between the weak and the strong force would be consonant with physics, while vital force or psi would not be.
2. Or whatever process it is which winnows alternatives, e.g. the process of being considered by God and found good or bad.
3. According to Bigelow and Pargetter, the etiological construal of 'function' renders functional explanation vacuous: one cannot explain why a system is there by saying that it has persisted because it serves the function of φ-ing, since by *definition* φ-ing is its function iff it is its capacity to φ which has explained its persistence to date (op. cit. p. 190). But there is no serious circularity problem here. A biologist can explain the persistence of a system by looking for something it has the capacity to do which, it is *a posteriori* reasonable to surmise, has given it an adaptive advantage. That something is its function, on the etiological analysis, but it is an empirical question what the system's capacities are and which might have given it an advantage (epistemic 'might'). Identifying a candidate completes an empirical explanation of why the system has persisted, and *calling* the candidate capacity the system's 'function' does not make the explanation any less empirical. Of course, one could equally well say that a biologist explains a system's persistence by finding something it does which *would* give it an adaptive advantage if circumstances were thus-and-so (the description to be derived from natural history). The smallness of this difference is why I think there is less to the etiology-propensity distinction than Bigelow and Pargetter make out.
4. This example is taken from (Dawkins 1986, pp. 153-8), which is itself based on the theories of the Glasgow chemist Graham Cairns-Smith. Dawkins' book is an extremely effective account of how evolutionary thinking undermines the otherwise near-irresistible support the facts of biology lend to the hypothesis of intelligent design underlying the natural world.
5. This summary is taken from (Field 1986, p.440). Field's counterfactual formulation has the failing that it is quite conceivable that if some actually false propositions in the range of the correct B function for S *were* true, this would bring with it circumstances in which S would not believe

546 / Graeme Forbes

those propositions. See (Forbes 1987) for further discussion of the details of Stalnaker's own formulations.
6. 'Environment' is being used in a wide sense here, to include states of the indicator.
7. In her paper "Biosemantics" (Chapel Hill Colloquium, October 1987) which she describes as "disinterring" her position on intentionality in *Language, Thought and Other Biological Categories*, Millikan suggested that what makes a representation a representation is that it is used as such by its consumers, and for a consumer to use something as a representation of x is for it 'to perform its tasks in accordance with a normal explanation for success only under the condition that [x is the case]' (pp.8-9). It seems that this criterion would never lead to ascription of verification-transcendent contents to representations. It is also not easy to believe that we can associate with each proposition 'tasks' (specified in naturalistically unproblematic terms) which are performed successfully in accordance with a normal explanation only if the proposition is true.
8. Teleological concepts may still have a role to play in a philosophical theory of perception. In (Davies 1983) it is argued that *what* is perceived may be determined teleologically: it is the function of perceptual apparatus to produce experiences that systematically depend on properties of the objects which are the first opaque objects in the line of sight, and not their function to produce experiences so depending on retinal images (pp. 419-20).
9. Similarly, if the doorbell rings as a result of a malfunction, 'that means someone is at the door' seems false to me on any natural interpretation. I intend the demonstratives in these examples to pick out the token events in question; there may be some 'type' interpretation on which the meaning ascriptions are correct, but then the phenomenon of false indication or misrepresentation has been missed.
10. I thank Radu Bogdan, Carolyn Morillo, Norton Nelkin and Christopher Peacocke for discussions which have improved this paper.

References

Bigelow, J. and Pargetter, R., 1987, "Functions", *The Journal of Philosophy* 84, 181-196.
Codata:1986, *Adjustment of the Fundamental Physical Constants*. London: Pergamon Press.
Dawkins, R., 1987, *The Blind Watchmaker*. Harlow: Longmans.
Davies, M. K., 1983, "Function in Perception", *Australasian Journal of Philosophy* 61, 409-26.
Dretske, F., 1986, "Misrepresentation", in Bogdan, R. (ed.), *Belief*, Oxford: Clarendon Press 1986.
Dummett, M., 1973, *Frege: Philosophy of Language*. London: Duckworth.
Dummett, M., 1982, "Realism", *Synthese* 52, 55-112.

Field, H., 1986, "Critical Notice: Robert Stalnaker, Inquiry", *Philosophy of Science* 53, 425-48.

Forbes, G., 1987, "Critical Review: Robert Stalnaker, Inquiry", forthcoming in *Synthese*.

Grice, H. P., 1957, "Meaning", *The Philosophical Review* 66, 377-88.

Kripke, S., 1980, *Naming and Necessity*. Cambridge: Harvard University Press.

Kripke, S., 1982, *Wittgenstein on Rules and Private Language*. London: Blackwell.

Lewis, D., 1969, *Convention*. New York: Blackwell.

McDowell, J., 1984, "De Re Senses", in Wright, C. (ed.): *Frege, Tradition and Influence*, 98-109. London: Blackwell.

McGinn, C., 1984, *Wittgenstein on Meaning*. New York: Blackwell.

Millikan, R., 1984, *Language, Thought and Other Biological Categories*. Cambridge: The MIT Press.

Nagel, E., 1961, *The Structure of Science*. London: Routledge and Kegan Paul.

Peacocke, C., 1986, *Thoughts: An Essay on Content*. London: Blackwell.

Rosenberg, A., 1985, *The Structure of Biological Science*. Cambridge: Cambridge University Press.

Vlach, F., 1981, "Speaker's Meaning", *Linguistics and Philosophy* 4, 359-91.

Wright, C., 1980, *Wittgenstein on the Foundations of Mathematics*. London: Duckworth.

Philosophical Perspectives, 3
Philosophy of Mind and Action Theory, 1989

SEMANTIC INNOCENCE AND PSYCHOLOGICAL UNDERSTANDING*

Jennifer Hornsby
Corpus Christi College, Oxford

1. Introduction

1.1 Semantics and Psychology

Philosophers' views about meaning and mind, about semantics and psychology and their relations, have proliferated in recent years: if one is looking for an account of these matters, then there are more and more in the philosophical literature to choose from. But reviewing that literature, one may be struck more by an idea that is common to a majority of the new accounts than by any of their subtle differences. The idea is roughly this. That if we are to give an account, of the sort that philosophers do, of intentional mental states, then we have two tasks. One is the task of dealing with the features of such states as beliefs and desire in virtue of which they play the role they do in causal explanation; the other is the task of saying how such states, and how the sentences of human language, relate to the world at large. Allow that semantics is a subject that makes mention of things in the world external to a subject, and let psychology be what we use to make sense of one another, then the idea is that psychology is one thing, semantics another. The present paper attempts to do something to dislodge this 'two-task idea'.

I take the two-task idea to be central in some of the work of at least Block, Field, Fodor, Harman, Loar, McGinn, Putnam and Schiffer (and one could name more).[1] There are too many variations on the theme for my descriptions of the two tasks to be acceptable as it

550 / Jennifer Hornsby

stands to all those whose views I have in mind.[2] And among those whom I take to share the two-task idea, there are differences of opinion as to quite how separate these two tasks can, or should, be kept, and as to how their connexion is to be conceived.

Something that unites all the philosophers I mentioned, and which is symptomatic of the two-task idea, is their confrontation of the question 'Why truth?'.[3] According to their idea, we can and should give an account of mental states which treats their attribution as having explanatory force and which includes the role of the states in linguistic productions and perceptions; but the account is separate from any which mentions connexions between those mental states and things in the world, or between bits of language and things in the world. Why then do genuinely semantic notions such as *truth* and *reference* loom so large when it comes to language and mind? Why, for instance do we think of names as referring, and of a person as related to the objects that we name in saying what she thinks? Why should truth-conditional accounts of meaning have been so pervasive in philosophy and linguistics? Semantics can't be made to go away, because we know that we are not in error when we say (speaking about our own language) such things as "'Everest' refers to Everest", or "An object satisfies 'is a mountain' iff it is a mountain". But if psychology is what we use to make sense of ourselves, and if the task of explicating psychology has no need of semantics, but uses only a notion of "conceptual role"[4], then why doesn't the subject of semantics simply lapse?

I find such a question strange. Or at least I find it strange that some philosophers seem to have become unwilling to contemplate the possibility that the reason why semantic notions persist in seeming ineliminable from accounts of the explanatory function of psychological and linguistic content is that they are ineliminable. I shall present a case for the view that accounts of content incorporating accounts of meaning given in the truth-conditional way constitute the foundational level of psychology. If that is right, it will seem that there is no *awkward* question 'Why truth?' to face up to.

The interpretational truth theories which I shall defend have often been claimed by their adherents to be or to serve as theories of meaning, and to help us to say or to show what knowledge of language consists in.[5] These claims are not at issue here. I want to place the emphasis slightly differently, however, and to suggest that interpretational truth-theories are illuminatingly seen in the context of providing an elucidation of the phenomenon of intentionality quite generally. In section 2 I present a unitary account of content, which is in competition with the two-task idea; and I do this in an attempt to make the two-task idea seem as superfluous as it seems to me to be strange. The point of the presentation is dialectical: I do not pretend to refute the two-task idea; but when I come to discuss it in section 3, I shall be in a position to suggest that its advocates have given a wrong impression of what the alternative to it might be.

1.2 Psychological Understanding and Semantic Innocence

People's having and gaining psychological understanding (as I shall speak of it) is a matter of their finding and coming to find one another intelligible. In particular cases, we find a person intelligible in knowing why she does what she does. And the concepts that we use when we manifest our possession of psychological understanding are the concepts that an account of mind and meaning are concerned with—such concepts as belief, desire and saying. They are concepts whose attribution in particular cases specifies a state of mind or a speech act using a 'that'-clause, a state of mind or a speech act with a content.[6]

An example shows that the notion of content relevant here may attach both to psychological states and to uses of language. Assume that (1) is correct. Then the content of a speaking of (2) is the same as a content of a belief of Bill's.

(1) Bill thinks that the sky is blue.
(2) The sky is blue.

If a person came out with both (1) and (2), then there would be something she had done twice, namely utter English words having the content that the sky is blue. Most likely there would also be things that she did only once—namely (a) state that the sky is blue (which she will have done in uttering (2) but not in uttering (1)), and (b) tell something of what Bill thinks (which she will have done in uttering (1) but not in uttering (2)). The content she states in uttering (2) is the content she states-that-Bill-thinks in uttering (1).

Davidson encouraged us to see this point as crucial to a correct account of the construction of speech reports when he insisted on what has been called the Principle of Semantic Innocence. This is the principle that the words which are used in saying what someone

has said (or, more generally, words in 'that'-clauses following propositional attitude terms) mean and refer to what they ordinarily
mean and refer to. Davidson himself used the principle to support
his paratactic account of indirect discourse.[7] But the present point,
encapsulated in the Principle of Semantic Innocence, may be less
controversial than any claim about the logical form of sentences containing 'that' clauses. It is simply that specifications of what people
think or want or hope or fear rely on the use of words as meaning
what they do when it is (e.g.) stated how things are. An account of
linguistic meaning has to be able to deal with utterances of both (1)
and (2) (along with all the other possible utterances); and an account
of psychological states presumably has to rely on a correct understanding of how utterances like (1) work.[8]

2. A Unitary Account of Content

2.1 Interpretational Truth Theories

Accepting the Principle of Semantic Innocence, one may hope that
an account of content will be suited to the treatment of the
use of language both to speak of the world at large and in making
psychological attributions. If there is a role which indicative sentences
play both as used by speakers assertorically, and as used in specifying the contents of people's states of mind, then seeing what it is
for them to play that role ought to illuminate our understanding of
both linguistic and non-linguistic action. An account of content, then,
should be fitted to the idea that a recurrent thing done with words,
a thing which is typically done whatever else is done, is: producing
sequences of sounds as having the content that they do.

Such an account recommends itself even if the use of words in
psychological attributions is not explicitly considered. Language users
have a stock of words whose relatively stable properties enable them
to convey their thoughts in a changing world. In the case of non
context-dependent words, the stable thing is what the words would
be uttered as contributing to content, and in the case of context-
dependent words the stable thing is something that contextually
determines what those words would be uttered as contributing to
content. Ineliminable from an account of the use of a particular
language, then, will be some theory on the basis of which one could

say, in the case of whatever sentence *s* any speaker of the language came out with:

At *t* she produced *s* as having the content that *p*.

And in any particular case, the (relatively) stable properties of individual words contained in *s*'s instance must be relied on in getting the correct thing to write in at the place of *p*.

Now the claim that a truth-conditional theory could serve as a theory of meaning for a language may be put by saying that it could be that a theory of truth, by virtue of its containing axioms stating properties of individual words, was such as to be targeted on theorems of this form: 'An utterance of *s* as uttered by *X* at *t* would be true iff *p*', *and* was such as to deliver such a theorem only where *X* would produce *s* at *t* as having the content that *p*. By 'interpretational truth-theory', I mean such a theory.

A distinction often made in discussion of theories of meaning is crucial here. On the one hand there are theories which treat particular languages, each of which can put one in a position to say what content any of the well-formed sentences of the particular language it deals with would be uttered as having. On the other hand there is an account (probably best not credited with the title of 'theory') which, as it is said, locates the concept of *meaning* in relation to other concepts, and which does so in part by seeing what a theory of meaning treating a particular language has to do, and how it might do that. In fact a further distinction might be made within this latter account between its statement of principles that would guide any actual empirical description of what speakers do, and a philosophical gloss which says how such principles would work together with a theory for a particular language. Here I shall think of the account as incorporating the principles about language use as well as the philosophical gloss on the whole. When thought of in this way, the account evidently goes beyond what anyone who started out looking for a philosophical analysis of linguistic meaning might have sought: it is an account of much besides meaning.

It is obvious that a theory of meaning (for a particular language, as opposed to the account requiring some settled conception of such a theory) does not describe the *use* even of the particular language productions of whose sounds by speakers it enables one to redescribe. For it is clearly not enough, if one is to say how a language is used, to be able to say 'She used sounds as having the content that ---'; one must be in a position to say also 'She said that ---', 'She asserted that ---', 'She warned that ---', 'She ordered that ---', 'She conveyed that ---'. These further things that are done when speakers produce sounds are things which aren't seen to be done until the theory of meaning is embedded within an account of force.

The division between a theory of meaning and a theory of force is a division within an account of language between what is specific to a particular language and what is not. What a speaker does with words depends on the content which those words have, and which, as a user of the language she utters those words as having. But once the content has been made determinate, there is nothing further which is specific to her language and which determines what she does.[9] The non-language specific character of the account in which a theory of meaning is seen to be embedded gives it its claim to serve as locating the concept of linguistic meaning quite generally. But to locate that concept generally is to see how it plays a role in conjunction with other concepts in making sense of people.

An interpretational truth-theory enables one to see speakers' productions of noises as contentful utterances by way of assisting in the task of seeing those productions as intelligible speech actions, having some purpose. But any hypothesis about the purpose of a person who used words on an occasion goes hand in hand not only with a hypothesis about the content of her utterance but also with a hypothesis about her mental states. Any such hypothesis is thus potentially confirmable or disconfirmable by reference at least to linguistic actions of that person and others who use the language on other occasions, and also to actions of any kind of that person on other occasions. We cannot understand people on the basis of what they do with words considered separately from all the other things they and others do. An account of the use of a language is just one part of a total account of the lives and minds of the people who speak it. If a theory of meaning is embedded in an account of force, an account of force is embedded in an account of mind, where an account of mind, if made explicit, would spell out (insofar as that is possible) everything that we effortlessly use in gaining psychological understanding. The principles I spoke of the account as incorporating must say everything that can be said to introduce our conception of a rational mind.

2.2 Saying

It is sometimes held that a theory of meaning should be targeted towards a theorem of the form *s* is true iff *p* just in case *s* can be used to *say* that *p*. But if one wants to keep it in mind that it is not only with *linguistic* actions that an interpretational theory is concerned, then formulations like this, using 'say', serve less well than the formulation using 'content',

And there is another reason to avoid the 'say' formulation: it is simply false that only a sentence having the content that *p* can be used to say that *p*.[10] Take the English sentence 'It seems to have been raining all summer'. If the notion of content is connected with recurrent properties of words, then the content that an interpretational theory of truth should show that sentence to be used as having is that it seems to have been raining all summer. But someone who utters that sentence might perfectly well be said to have said (say) that the weather hasn't been very good this summer. The former report, towards which an interpretational truth-theory is targeted, pays maximum respect to the fact of particular words having been used in a particular construction; but the latter report, which is typical enough of an everyday report of what someone did using words, does not pay particular attention to that fact. There is no definite answer to the question how far a non-quotational report of speech even by someone who uses the same language as the person reported, can deviate from the use of her words over again.[11] And as the present example can illustrate, this is a highly context dependent matter. Exactly which words can truly and fairly be used to say what was said by someone who came out with 'It seems to have been raining all summer' will depend, for instance, on what beliefs about the usual weather in the summer are shared by the original speaker, the reporter and the audience to the report. (That will depend in its turn, for instance, on where they live.) We usually accept far fewer substitutions in the slot in

s would be used by *X* at *t* as having the content that —

(which has been introduced for the purposes of theorizing) than we should accept in the slot in

X, if she used *s* at *t*, would have said that —

(which uses the everyday 'say').[12]

2.3 Content

Acceptable substitutions inside the slot in 'used as having the content that —' are guided (we have seen) by a conception of a theory of meaning as a theory that takes account of the recurrent features of individual words. The notion of content, then, is determined in part by the need to recognize syntactic structure in a language, and contents are accordingly finely discriminated. But exactly how finely they should be discriminated is only revealed in the broader framework where interpretational truth-theories have been located.

Frege held that it is a sufficient condition of the difference of two thoughts that it be possible for a person to have some attitude towards one and not the other. This is evidently the right criterion of difference for contents as conceived here. We cannot be indifferent whether we attribute (say) the belief that p or the belief that q to a person if we know that that person might believe that p and not believe that q; and we must use a notion of content which, like Frege's, precludes such indifference. Frege's principle is implicitly accepted in most discussions of opacity where it is acknowledged to be a sufficient condition of its being a non-sequitur to move from 'a believes that p' to 'a believes that q' that words that contribute differently to thoughts (in Frege's sense) be intersubstituted in the sentences that occur at the places of 'p' and 'q'.

Of course in practice we often feel justified in moving from ascriptions of a belief with one content to ascriptions of belief with what has to be counted another content. It may be in a strict sense a *non sequitur*, but nonetheless a safe bet, to move from 'Harriet believes that the present British Prime Minister is uncompromising' to 'Harriet believes that Margaret Thatcher is uncompromising'. Treating content in the Fregean way, it can often be taken for granted that if someone believes one thing she believes another. That this can be taken for granted is reflected in our reports of speech, as we have seen: We allow that someone's saying one thing is her (actually) saying what, according to the Fregean (modally defined) notion of content is another thing.[13]

When we appreciate how the Fregean psychological idea of a content has to work hand in hand with an account of linguistic content derived from facts about recurrent properties of words, we see that an interpretational truth-theory is sensitized to, and thus sensitive to, precisely the Fregean sense of words (or, in another idiom, to the conceptual repertoires of psychological subjects). For Frege, the sense of a word is what it contributes to a thought; and thoughts are the contents that the project of elucidating the propositional attitude concepts requires.

2.4 Indexicality

The presence in natural languages of indexicals has seemed to some people to stand in the way of the idea that one can simultaneously elucidate the role of *meaning* and the role of the concepts for intentional mental states generally. Evidently meaning and content cannot be equated if a single sentence (which "has some one meaning") can be used now with one content now with another. But there has been no equation of linguistic meaning and content here. Indexicals are words that contribute differently to the contents of utterances of sentences they occur in, though in contextually more or less predictable ways.

It needs to be acknowledged that not all thoughts are available to be entertained in all contexts. Suppose I overheard someone talking, and I tell you something of what she said. There are two ways in which my reports of her utterances will deviate from those that assign contents according to the Fregean notion. First, wanting to be understood as well as may be, I shall avoid expressing thoughts which aren't available to you, e.g. because you don't know the person spoken of. Second, in some cases I shall be literally unable to express the thoughts whose expression I wish to report. If, for instance, she was in a position to think about objects in ways which I now not in the presence of those objects can't think about them, I cannot say the contents of her utterances. Still, if I am trying to tell you what was said (in the ordinary sense), these constraints and limitations don't present insuperable problems: we have already remarked that someone can fairly and truly be said to have said that *p*, even though no utterance of hers had the content that *p* (according to the Fregean notion). Someone attempting to give a quite general theoretically motivated account of potential utterances of, say, 'He is hot' is, like me in the situation just envisaged, constrained by the need to be intelligible to whoever might learn from her account, and is limited by the unavailability to her of thoughts that others may have had in other times and places. Although the limitations are now in an obvious way more severe, they are of the same, not persistently problematic kind. The greater severity arises from the fact that 'having the content that —' is, as we have seen, a stricter notion than 'says that —'. And it arises also from the theoretically enforced need to generalize, to speak in abstraction about countless potential particular utterances. Obviously no one can know (say) whom 'he' as demonstrative pronoun would be used as referring to on all occasions. Forced to generalize, and wishing to say something intelligible in the abstract, the theorist says that utterances of (say) 'He was tired' would be used as saying, if anything, that some contextually demonstrated person was tired, noting that such utterances would have a certain sort of content, and elaborating perhaps on this 'certain sort'.

(Of course many indexicals present questions of their own; and there is much to be said under this head, and about modes of thought which can be discriminated more finely than any linguistic devices. But there is no reason to think that these questions would need to be ignored by someone who conceives of psychology in the way suggested here.[14])

2.5 Truth

In focusing here on the use to which an interpretational truth-theory can be put, may seem to have lost sight of the notion of truth. We should enquire now what role this notion plays—especially in view of my suggestion (section 1.1) that philosophers should avoid a position in which it requires some special accounting that *truth* and *reference* have ready application in connection with psychological understanding.

In the literature one finds two sorts of answers to the question how *truth* fits in with *interpretation* when interpretational truth-theories are at issue. According to the first answer, advocates of interpretational truth-theories are claiming that truth is a concept to which *meaning* can be reduced, or in terms of which it can be analyzed. According to the second, it is the purest accident that a theory of truth might do what a theory of linguistic meaning or a theory of content has to do. These answers are evidently at opposite extremes: the first sees the advocate of interpretational truth-theories as forging the closest of conceptual connexions between *truth* and *content*; the second sees the advocate as having no use at all for *truth per se*. Neither answer seems correct.

The first answer is obviously incorrect. It is presumably given by those who suppose that any account of content must be a philosophical analysis, so that if truth features in the account, content must be being analyzed in terms of truth. And it is small wonder that those who hold the view that the project which introduces interpretational truth-theories is an attempt at analysing 'content' or 'meaning', take the project to be misguided. They can be disabused of their view only by showing (as I have attempted to do) how and where truth enters into the project.

The second answer does not rest on any such evident misconception. I think that it is fuelled by the perfectly correct thought that what is relied on in interpretational theories for particular languages is the disquotational character of '*** is true iff —'. Now truth is a normative notion. So if one distinguishes truth's disquotationality from its normativity,[15] and tries to separate them, it looks as though only part of truth's character (and a relatively uninteresting part, it may be thought) does any work in truth-theories. It would indeed be an accident that truth was used if any property with one of truth's features (sc. disquotationality), even a property lacking one of truth's essential features (sc. normativity) might just as well have been used instead. But does truth really lose its normal, normative role in the context of interpretational truth-theories? Is disquotationality a genuinely separate feature? Admittedly truth's normative nature does not leap from the page if one is proving theorems inside such a theory. But that should not make one suppose that it somehow goes away. Attempts to separate disquotationality from normativity ignore the fact that it is virtue of possessing the disquotational feature that truth is the evaluative concept that it is. Consider that instead of 'Utterance u is true if and only if p', one could always say 'Utterance u is true if and only if it is indeed the case that p'.

What is certain is that it is only by conceiving potential utterances as *evaluable* for truth that one can have a conception of an interpretational truth-theory at all. To take a single example outside the realm of language use. It seems that to believe that p is (very roughly) to be disposed to acts in ways that would tend to satisfy one's desires in a world in which it were true that p. Such evidence as one has that someone believes something, then, if got from noticing ways in which she acts, relies on one's taking a view of how the world would be if what is believed were true, and of whether the world is indeed that way. How would the world be if it were true that p?

Well one has already said how it would be, if one has uttered a sentence with the content that p. What one says in saying how the world would be if a belief were evaluable as true is what one says in specifying the content of that belief, which one does in attributing the belief.

There is another way to see that truth plays its normal normative role here. Some people hold that truth is a property only of contents (or, as they may say, propositions), and they think that it follows that we ought not to predicate truth of sentences, as Tarski did. For their benefit, it is pointed out that predication of truth to a sentence as potentially uttered on an occasion could always be viewed as predication of truth to the content that the sentence is used to express.[16] In place of 'sentence s as used by X at t would be true iff —', then, we could put 'sentence s as used by X at t would express a content which is true iff —'. This way of putting it makes it clear that a theory of truth can be seen as matching contents which would be expressed by subjects with contents to be expressed by interpreters. Then we realize that coming to know an interpretational truth-theory is coming to be in a position to exploit the principle of semantic innocence in psychological understanding. Exploiting that principle is a matter of relying on the fact that we may use our words having their ordinary *semantic* properties in attributing beliefs to another. Everyday psychological understanding evidently makes no reference to a theory of truth. But it shares with the theorist's a reliance on the fact that utterances and states of mind are, like the utterances that report them, *truth*-evaluable, truth-*evaluable*.[17]

3. Two Task Accounts of Content

3.1 "Use" Theories of Meaning

Accounts of intentional phenomena that conform to what at the outset I christened the 'two task idea' have gained wide acceptance in the last few years. I have presented the unitary account of content in order that it may be seen as in competition with two-task accounts. It is not usually seen as a competitor, however. When it is introduced into discussion, wrong impressions are sometimes given of its status and pretensions. I hope to correct one such impression now, before turning to look at the genesis of the two-task idea.

Many philosophers who believe in a version of the two-task idea speak of a difference between 'truth-conditional theories of meaning' and 'use theories of meaning'.[18] They may make this contrast in order to suggest that one sort of theory is to be promoted as serving one, the other as serving the other, of their two putative tasks. But they can give the impression that an account centred on a truth-conditional theory is at most a partial one in anyone's view: they seem to rule out the possibility that truth-conditional theories should be promoted as playing a central role in an account designed to elucidate the nature of mental states quite generally—as of course they are by advocates of a unitary account.

Speaking of a difference between 'truth-conditional' and 'use' theories of meaning can be misleading in a further way. For suppose it is allowed that it is possible for a person to believe in something deserving the name of 'truth-conditions theory' but to reject the two-task idea. If truth-conditional theories and use theories are then contrasted, it looks as though such a person eschews something called a 'use theory'. But this is wrong. Certainly it is wrong if a "use theory" is associated with the name of Wittgenstein, or if it is associated with the slogan that meaning does not transcend use.

An interpretational truth-theory plays its role in an account of (*inter alia*) the *use* of language. And there is bound to be dispute between someone who supports a unitary account and someone who espouses some version of the two-task idea about how an account of language *use* is to be given. Such a dispute is part of a broader dispute about the nature of intentionality, and is reflected in a disagreement as to what the *use* of language should be thought to encompass. According to the conception already employed here, *use* includes all of the countlessly many things that people are heard as doing when a fellow speaker, or a theorist supplied with a theory of content and force, comes to understand them. This is a broad conception. According to another conception of *use*, which is invoked by two-task theorists from whose standpoint "use" and "truth-conditions" are in opposition, use includes only such facts about what people do with language as can be stated without yet allowing that speakers relate themselves to the world. This is a narrow conception. The two very different conceptions have presumably grown up in response to different theoretical demands.

What first made use conceptions of meaning attractive was the naturalistic idea that linguistic phenomena are, as it were, in the open:

an account of a language must allow (for example) that everything needed in its acquisition is accessible to those who in fact acquire it. This idea surely gives rise in the first instance to the broad conception of use: whatever might be counted as observable linguistic behaviour is a part of use. The narrow conception of use comes to be invoked (I think) when the focus is the individual language user, and her *dispositions* to linguistic behaviour are introduced. If dispositions themselves are thought of as states of individuals whose nature and correct individuation is independent of any conditions that obtain outside the individual, then the verbal behaviour towards which people can be thought of as disposed is inevitably restricted. I suggest that it is a particular individualistic conception of individuals' *dispositions* (characterized sometimes as their tacit knowledge), rather than anything in the idea of *use*, or of verbal behaviour itself, which has given rise to the newer and much narrower conception of *use*.[19]

If this is right, then it is at very best tendentious to suggest that a unitary account of content eschews a 'use' theory. On the one hand, a statement of the original, epistemological, motivation for speaking of 'use' appears to require the broad conception which is employed in the unitary account. On the other hand, it may be doubted whether the narrow conception of use corresponds to anything that anyone would ordinarily recognize as 'use': there is much one can say about language use, we ordinarily think, but it is hard to say anything about it if we are banned from using modes of speech report in which we make mention of objects beyond the language user. (For example, when I tell you that someone said that Quine wrote *Word and Object*, I seem to have told you something wholly about one of her uses of language; but this is not so according to the narrow conception.[20])

We should not allow a terminological manoeuvre to take us from the evident fact that accounts of intentional phenomena should be directed towards (*inter alia*) language use into automatic acceptance of the idea of a disposition which can be characterized both individualistically and as something which is recognizably a disposition to use language.[21] The advocate of a unitary account of content holds that a truth-conditional theory plays a crucial role within an account of the use of any language; and she denies that there is any workable conception of language use according to which an account of use could be separated from an account of the genuinely semantical aspects of a language.

Of course, though, it is not mere terminological manoeuvering which has been thought to recommend the two-task idea. The terminology may encourage us to forget that there was ever any other idea, but it has gained its hold because of arguments that are thought to demonstrate that semantical properties are a separable aspect of explanatory mental states. I turn now to look at some such arguments—to discuss the work of three authors selected to show something of how the two-task idea has gained ground in the last decade or so. (I shall not be concerned with the latest workings out of the idea.)

3.2 Putnam

Putnam's paper 'The Meaning of "Meaning"'[22] is seminal in the history of the two-task idea. Putnam there did not engage himself in the kind of rivalry that I am now trying to establish: when he criticized what he called Davidsonian semantics, he meant by 'Davidsonian semantics' a theory of meaning simply, and not the broader account (of section 2 here) which makes mention of such theories.

The difficulty that Putnam professed to find with Davidsonian semantics was that 'for many words, an extensionally correct truth-definition can be given which is in no sense a theory of the meaning of the word'.[23] Putnam's point was that either of the sentences '"Water" refers to water' and '"Water" refers to H_2O' might be used in a truth definition; we cannot distinguish between them in point of extensional correctness. But of course a theory of meaning ought not to be indifferent which of these sentences it made use of. Putnam's point can be put another way: two truth-theories can be equally good extensionally speaking, but not interpretationally speaking. But when we put the point in this way, we shall think of Putnam only as having recorded that a truth-theory needs to be constructed so as to be sensitive to all the psychological facts if it is to capture *meaning*. Of course this is how truth-theories have been envisaged here.

Putnam introduced Davidsonian semantics into a discussion of some natural assumptions about *meaning*. Above all, he wanted to draw attention to a difficulty he saw about combining two assumptions. (i) Knowing the meaning of a term is a matter of being in a certain psychological state. (ii) The meaning of a term determines its extension. In the context of the present discussion, we can think of

Putnam's criticism of Davidson as suggesting that Davidson paid attention to assumption (ii) at the expense of failing to acknowledge assumption (i): Davidson's account, according to Putnam, got the extension of terms right, but did so without caring about what is known by speakers of a language (speakers who, for instance, might, have no concept of H_2O, yet have a concept of water). In that case, we can see that the construal of Putnam's claim about extensional correctness, just given on behalf of Davidson, puts us in a position to meet Putnam's main point. For the requirement on a theory of psychological sensitivity, which we have seen comes down to the requirement that the theory be sensitive to Fregean sense, ensures that assumption (i) is met. Since the account incorporates that sensitivity in its mode of stating precisely the *extensions* of terms, assumption (ii) is also met.

The difficulty for Davidson that Putnam thought he saw was illustrated by way of his famous Twin Earth thought experiments. An ordinary, scientifically unsophisticated speaker of English knows what is meant by 'water'—a certain stuff, in fact H_2O. We are to imagine that Twin Earth is in nearly every way just like this earth, and that the Twin Earth counterpart of our English speaker inhabits an environment which contains a liquid which on the basis of the sort of observations that ordinary speakers ordinarily make cannot be distinguished from water; but the liquid on Twin Earth has a quite different chemical composition from water—it is XYZ. What would be meant by 'water' by the Twin Earth counterpart, then, will be something different from what we on Earth mean by 'water'. But, as Putnam says, what is in the head of our English speaker and what is in the head of his Twin Earth counterpart need not be relevantly different. So whatever state of a speaker constitutes knowledge of the meaning of a word, if it does indeed determine what is meant by the word, is not in the head. Many have thought that a case now been made for splitting knowledge of meaning and other psychological states into two parts—each part corresponding to one of Putnam's two assumptions, and each part imposing its own theoretical task. But the reply on Davidson's behalf has shown already that Putnam's (i) and (ii) can be combined. What the thought experiment suggests is that a problem would arise if one combined (ii) with the further assumption that psychological states are in the head (in whatever sense it is of 'in the head' that makes it seem evident that indeed there need be no relevant differences in the heads of the Earth speaker and the Twin Earth speaker). By themselves, Twin Earth thought experiments lend no support to the two-task idea. Notice that given the Principle of Semantic Innocence, Putnam's argument would affect psychological states generally, and not just states of knowing meanings: the state which I on Earth attribute by saying 'He believes that the lake fills with water each February', is, like the state which I attribute by saying 'He knows that "water" means water', a state of the Earth speaker, but not of the Twin Earth speaker with his indistinguishable head. And of course those who have taken some version of the two-task idea to be forced on us by Twin Earth examples have wished their idea to cover psychological states generally.

3.3 Fodor

Putnam gave the name of 'methodological solipsism' to the doctrine that mental states are literally in the head. And this was a doctrine that Fodor defended in his paper 'Methodological Solipsism as a Research Strategy in Psychology'.[24] The methodologically solipsist sort of psychology that Fodor hoped to promote he called Rational psychology. The sort of psychology which is used in psychological understanding, in which reference is made to things in the world beyond the subject when mental states are imputed, Fodor called Naturalistic psychology. And he said about Naturalistic psychology, 'It isn't a practical possibility and isn't likely to become one.'[25]

Now we know that what Fodor said about Naturalistic Psychology cannot be literally true, because naturalistic psychology is what we all actually use all the time. It seems that Fodor cannot really have been interested in everyday psychological understanding, and that he must only have meant that *if* we want psychology to meet certain standards—such as treating mental states as in the head—, then Naturalistic psychology must be deemed 'not a practical possibility and not likely to become one'. And yet it would be wrong to think that the Rational Psychology which Fodor favours for its practicability abjures psychological understanding. For the case Fodor makes for Rational Psychology relies on the principles that govern psychological understanding. It seems that Fodor thought, on the one hand, that the subject of the mind as we know it outside of laboratories isn't practicable, but on the other hand, that any practicable psychology would have to embody the principles that we work with in interpreting one another as·possessors of minds. Fodor's combination of hostility and friendliness towards Naturalistic Psychology can be explained. He thought that only one aspect of Naturalistic Psychology stood in the way of its being practically possible, and that that aspect could be peeled off, as it were, retaining everything that matters to psychological explanations as we know them. After the peeling off, there would be no obstacle to psychological explanation of the ordinary sort but conforming to his desired standards. For Fodor thought that only on one construal of psychological explanations are there problems of practicability, and on their problematic construal the explanations contain something extra, not really needed for explanatory purposes. As he put it: 'it's typically an opaque construal [of a propositional attitude context] that does the explanatory work'.[26]

Fodor's idea can be made clearer with one of his own examples. Suppose that some action of John's is explained by saying this

John believes that Cicero was a Roman orator.

Then there is an opaque construal of the sentence on which it would be invalid to substitute 'Tully' for Cicero, and a transparent construal on which the substitution would be valid. According to Fodor, one makes reference to Cicero himself, and thus to things in the world beyond John's head, only when one intends the transparent construal to be put on one's words. And the aspect of Naturalistic psychology to be peeled off is what is supposed to be distinctive of transparent construals—sc., roughly, reference.

Fodor's point about the connexion between opacity and explanatoriness has been registered here in the point that intersubstitutions of referring terms in the sentence which gives the content of a propositional attitude must for explanatory purposes show sensitivity to the *senses* of the words there. It is Fodor's other idea that must be questioned. This is the idea that *only* non-opaque construals make trouble for psychology—that it is only when we switch to a construal in which 'Cicero' can be replaced by 'Tully' that we have reference to Cicero, and thus in Fodor's view a threat to practicable psychology.

This other idea is in contravention of the Principle of Semantic Innocence. For according to Fodor's understanding of opacity, 'Cicero' is referred to in 'John believes of Cicero that he was a Roman orator' but not in 'John believes that Cicero was a Roman orator'. We must ask ourselves whether Fodor could really have had a reason to think that I refer to objects when I speak about them but not when I tell you what others think about them. Is it really that I refer to Cicero when I state that he was a Roman orator, but not when I state that John thinks that Cicero was a Roman orator?[27] If the answer is *No*, then it is wrong to suppose that when there is sensitivity to the sense of a term, it is not the role of that term to refer.

With the Principle of Semantic Innocence in place, the features of Naturalistic psychology which made Fodor find it a practical impossibility cannot be made to disappear. And we have been given no reason to think that there could be such a subject as Fodor's Rational psychology, which is supposed to embody sensitivity to sense but to make no references.[28]

3.4 McGinn

Unlike Fodor and others who adopt some version of the two task idea, McGinn engages in the sort of rivalry that I have tried to set up here. That is to say McGinn does not ignore the unitary account of content; in 'The Structure of Content' he criticizes it.[29] His criticisms take over at the point where Putnam's left off (section 3.2).

McGinn acknowledges the main point of section 3.2—that not any old truth theory, but only an interpretational one, is said by Davidson to serve as a theory of meaning. And McGinn is no opponent of the idea that truth-theories have a part to play in an account of meaning. But his view is that a theory of truth is 'constitutionally partial': the constraints on a theory of truth which ensure that it is interpretational are 'too strong if they are constraints on a definition of *truth*'.[30] McGinn means to suggest that insofar as a theory of content might be psychologically sensitive, that has nothing to do with its invocation of *truth*.

This suggestion was cast in doubt when it was argued that it is not an accident that *truth* plays the role it does in interpretational theories (section 2.5). Certainly it must be conceded that, as McGinn says, there could be a definition of truth that was in some sense correct but that was not 'strongly constrained'. It would be possible, for instance, to construct a theory whose canonical theorems were true and on the pattern of '*s* is true iff *p*', which was insensitive to differences of sense; and we might see fit to call such a theory 'a theory of truth-conditions'.[31] But it would be wrong to think that the constraints im-

posed on a theory of truth in section 2.1 that are meant to ensure
its interpretationality are *extra* constraints, additional to those imposed on some other imagined theory ('of truth-conditions'). For it
is not as if in the course of making sense of people, one could become
confident that one had a theory for their language which was extensionally correct, but have as yet no inkling of the senses of their terms.
As we saw in section 2, the idea of someone who supports the unitary
account of content is that *truth* is the very notion that will furnish
the theorist with materials to exploit the principle of Semantic
Innocence.

The question 'Why truth?' is thus easily answered in the context
of the unitary account (cp. section 1.1). To see exactly why that question is troublesome for McGinn will be to appreciate now the particular character of his own account. According to it, a theory of mind
and meaning not only has a part which specifies the truth-conditions
(in McGinn's sense) of utterances and states of mind, it contains also
another part which is needed to explicate the explanatory role of
such things—a theory of their intra-individual properties, said to
specify their cognitive role. 'We view beliefs as relations to propositions that can be assigned referential truth-conditions' and, as a
separate matter, 'we view beliefs as causally explanatory states of
the head whose semantic properties are, from that point of view,
as may be'.[32] The bearing of *truth*-evaluability on beliefs cannot
then be accounted for in terms of their explanatory properties. In
fact McGinn's own answer to the question 'Why truth?' is that truth
and reference may be located 'in the point of communication—in
the intention with which assertions (and other kinds of speech act)
are made. A hearer understands a speech act as an assertion just
if he interprets it as performed with a certain point or intention—
viz. to convey information about the world.'[33]

But there seems to be a problem about invoking specifically this
principle about *linguistic* understanding in explicating truth's salience
in our thinking about mind and meaning. The problem is that there
are principles which have an apparently similar status but which
govern interpretation more generally. Where McGinn wants to say
that *a* is taken to have asserted something only if she is taken to
purport to put forward something true, one could equally well say
that *a*'s wants are satisfied only when their contents come to be true,
or *a* succeeds in doing what she tries to to the extent that the beliefs
which explain her trying to do that are true[34]. But if we can

recognize a place for truth when we consider non-linguistic action and think about its explanation and its point, then it seems wrong to relegate truth to a place in which it works in the minds only of those engaged in communication, and to deny that the principles which embody people's rational explicability could contain essential mention of relations between the contents of beliefs and the things in the world that the contents concern.

It is when one appreciates the principle of Semantic Innocence at work in the area of giving psychological explanations that one seems bound to recognize the truth-evaluability of contents as indispensable from that area. Suppose I assert that Jane drove to Bedford, and then explain the action that I have asserted there was by saying that Jane believed that there was a zoo at Bedford. (It is common knowledge, let us suppose, that Jane might be hoping to visit a zoo.) Given that that which, in a simple assertion, is put forward as true is exactly that which, in an explanation of action, is put forward as a (true or false) content believed by the person whose action is to be explained (cp. section 1.2), it is hard to maintain a difference of attitude towards the relevance of truth-evaluability to my presentation of the content that Jane drove to Bedford and my presentation of the content that there was a zoo at Bedford. McGinn wants to sever our understanding of how utterances can transmit knowledge about the world (as they typically do in assertions) from our understanding of how utterances can feature in explanations of people's interactions with the world (as they often do when it is said what someone thinks).

But if the semantical properties of beliefs were really irrelevant to the explanatory status of beliefs, then it would seem that, in finding Jane intelligible, it would not be relevant that Bedford be seen as somewhere she drove to and somewhere she thought that there was a zoo. This does seem relevant.

McGinn's premise, which leads to the disconnexion of the semantical from the explanatory, is that 'beliefs play a role in the agent's psychology just in virtue of intrinsic properties of the implicated internal representations'. The premise (as McGinn allows[35]) amounts to the methodological solipsism which Putnam seemed to recommend and which Fodor attempted to find a painless way to endorse. The issue between those who give a unitary account and the two-task theorists then comes down to an issue about whether, as the two-task theorist maintains, it is not beliefs as we know them, having truth-evaluable contents, but only some part of beliefs, or (in McGinn's version) beliefs only under some partial aspect, that we rely on in psychological understanding.

There is of course a deeper motive than any we have seen for methodological solipsism and for the two-task theorists' claims about beliefs as they figure in explanations. (If there were no such deeper motive, the two-task idea would surely not be as prevalent as it is, nor its varieties as various.) The two-task theorists share a general view about the character of any respectable causal explanation, and this is a character lacked by psychological explanations as we know them. We have then to choose between holding that psychological explanations are in good order even though they lack this character and holding that we must revise our thinking about psychological explanatory states. The two-task theorists' revision would enable us to see them as participating in the character of explanations whose features they apparently lack.[36]

Nothing said in this paper could force a choice. But we do well to remember that the view that psychological explanation is special and *sui generis* was held by some philosophers long before the two-task idea was invented. And I hope here to have made it clear that we are not lost for an account of content if we do take psychological explanation to be relevantly special. Philosophical understanding of psychological understanding, as well as psychological understanding itself, can be governed by the Principle of Semantic Innocence.[37]

Notes

*Work towards this paper was undertaken while I was a Fellow at the Center for Advanced Study in the Behavioral Sciences, Stanford, California. I am grateful for financial support provided by the Andrew W. Mellon Foundation.
1. Ned Block (1986); Hartry Field (1977); Jerry Fodor (1980); Gilbert Harman (1982); Brian Loar (1981),(1982); Colin McGinn (1982); Hilary Putnam (1975); Stephen Schiffer (1980).

   I have not tried to keep track of all the variants. And I have not taken specific account of changes of views of these authors over the years. Putnam has come to side with Davidson on the subject of interpretation; but even in Putnam, 1983, he never draws conclusions incompatible with the two-task idea.
2. It can be hard to disentangle terminological from genuine differences among those who hold the idea. The word 'content' is used differently by different two-task theorists: *v.i.*, n.6.
3. There is a discussion of answers to this question, and an answer of his own, in section III of McGinn, 1982. I discuss McGinn's own answer in

section 3.4 below.

4. See, for what may be the first use of this notion, Hartry Field, 1977.
5. The claim that truth theories can do duty as theories of meaning pervades Donald Davidson's essays collected together in Davidson, 1984. My debt to these writings will be evident.
6. I assume, then, (i) that a state's having the content it does is what enables it to play the explanatory role that it does, and (ii) that a state's content is what is specified in a 'that'-clause when it is ascribed. Two-task theorists are prevented by their philosophical position from holding that (i) and (ii) are both true. And sometimes 'content' is used so that (i) is preserved, sometimes so that (ii) is.
7. See Davidson, 1968.
8. Davidson spoke of our 'pre-Fregean semantic innocence'; and Barwise and Perry (1983), who are responsible for naming the Principle, take their anti-Fregean stance to be all of a piece with their endorsement of the principle. It may then be questioned whether I have any right to help myself to a *Fregean* notion of content (below).

   Well, Davidson's point was that Frege's view that words in 'that'-clauses refer to their sense should not be allowed to supplant our naive view that they refer to what they ordinarily refer to. But once the Fregean notion of content is in place, the effect of Davidson's paratactic analysis is to ensure that matches as to content are what determine intersubstitutions in 'that' clauses. This of course is exactly the result achieved by Frege by having words there refer to their senses. (For a demonstration of how much in harmony Frege and Davidson may be, see John McDowell, 1980. And I should myself question whether Barwise and Perry have respected the Principle at the end of the day, although I cannot enter into this here.)
9. This would require qualification in a more precise account. There can be determinants of what is done with words which are not determinants of content but which are more or less accidentally language specific. (E.g. it might be that a particular tone of voice conventionally signalling that a question was to be taken as a polite request was used by all and only the speakers of some language.)
10. The notion of 'strict and literal saying' is sometimes introduced to escape the falsehood. But it is not the case that 'say' has any strict and literal sense of its own to be called on; so 'strict and literal saying', if invoked, requires stipulations such as I have introduced for 'content'.
11. See Quine, 1960, p. 218.
12. I think that the fact that there is so much more which determines what is said than which determines what content an utterance has is part of what has led to the anarchism that one finds in (for instance) Baker and Hacker, 1984. It is as if the vast discrepancy between what an account of the content of utterances yields (on the one hand) and what is required in an account of speech acts (on the other) leads these authors to think that there is nothing stable about our language stock which we rely on in being understood.

13. Thus we need not think, what Howard Wettstein claims (1986, p.205), that 'our practices of substituting one name for another are not nearly as restrictive...as Fregeans would lead us to believe'. Fregeans may distinguish between the restrictions imposed in one's accounts of natural language semantics and psychological understanding and the relaxations permitted by our practices.

14. And there is reason to think they need not be so ignored. See e.g. Evans, 1982.

15. See e.g. Soames, 1984.

16. See e.g. Davidson (in 1984).

17. I make no attempt here to accommodate utterances of non-indicative sentences or those propositional attitude states whose objects are not straightforwardly truth-evaluable. For some useful considerations about how the analogue of content for utterances in the imperative mood relates to the analogue of content for desires and intentions (considerations thus pertaining to the unification of semantics and psychology), see Hamblin 1987.

18. See some of the work in the issue of the *Notre Dame Journal of Philosophical Logic* in which Loar, 1982 is found.

19. For an example of this use of 'use', and attributions of it to others, see McGinn 1984, pp. 240-42.

20. 'Wholly' makes allowance for views according to which use is a part of what is reported in ordinary reports like this.

21. In 'Physicalist Thinking and Conceptions of Behaviour' (Hornsby, 1986), I drew attention to equivocations on 'behaviour'. If use is linguistic behaviour, so that use is what linguistic behavioral dispositions give rise to, then the two notions of use are parallel to the two conceptions of 'behaviour' that I distinguished there in criticizing modern physicalisms. (I tried there to put pressure on the two-task theorists' view of explanation which is discussed at the end of section 3.4.)

   Notice that talk of dispositions itself *need* not have altered anything: *of course* speakers of a common language are all *disposed* in some same ways by virtue of sharing a language.

22. Putnam (1975).

23. Ibid., p. 259.

24. Fodor (1980).

25. Ibid., p. 234.

26. Ibid., p. 234. Fodor's talk of opaque vs. transparent construals indicates that he thought that there is an ambiguity in e.g. 'John believes that Cicero was a Roman orator,' according as intersubstitution of 'Tully' for 'Cicero' is not or is permitted. (Disambiguation can then be achieved with 'John believes of Cicero that he was a Roman orator', in which intersubstitution is permitted.) But this is questionable. The appearance that there is a transparent reading may be fostered by the laxity in ordinary reports (see Section 1.4 above)—an inevitable and more considerable laxity when reporter and reported are differently situated (see section 1.6 above). It may then be that there are not two readings of sentences like 'John believes that Cicero...', but variations in how licit it

is to proceed as if one had the transparent style of report.

27. It might be held that this puts the point in a question-begging way: of course 'he' refers here, because that is the only way back-reference could be secured. But the onus is put on those who deny the Principle of Semantic Innocence: they owe us an account of how 'he' *could* secure such back reference.

Fodor comes close to acknowledging the Principle when he says that 'the intuitive opaque taxonomy is actually what you might call "semitransparent"' (p. 238). But what is at present at issue is whether an "entirely functional taxonomy" of the propositional attitude states is the same as any "pre-theoretic" one.

28. Fodor would now give a different account of these matters;see his 1987, Ch.2. I criticize his earlier one because I find that the phenomenon of opacity still leads people to suppose that reference can be pulled apart from sense. (I should want to bring the Principle of Semantic Innocence to bear in a discussion of Fodor's latest account.)

29. McGinn, 1982; already referred to—v.s. nn.3 and 19.

30. Ibid., p. 239.

31. If we did use the term 'truth-conditions' in this way, we should *eo ipso* be committed to McGinn's claim that 'it is no defect in a statement of truth-conditions that the expressions used differ merely in cognitive role (sense) from the expressions mentioned' (p. 239).

32. Ibid., p. 216.

33. Ibid., p. 226.

34. These are rough and readily stated principles, stated so as to connect with the thought that a belief that *p* disposes one to act in ways that will satisfy one's desires if it is true that *p* (cp. section 2.5).

35. Ibid., p. 208.

36. For more on this choice, see the editorial introduction to Pettit and McDowell, 1986.

37. For more on the costs of the two-task idea, see McDowell, 1986, sections 6-8.

References

Baker, G. P. and Hacker, P. M. S., 1984. *Language, Sense and Nonsense* (Blackwell, Oxford).

Barwise, J. and Perry, J., 1983. *Situations and Attitudes* (MIT Press, Cambridge, Mass.).

Block, N., 1986. 'Advertisement for a Semantics for Psychology'. In *Midwest Studies in Philosophy* (University of Minnesota Press).

Davidson, D., 1967. 'Truth and Meaning'. *Synthese* 17. Reprinted in Davidson, D., 1984, to which page references are given.

Davidson, D., 1968. 'On Saying That'. *Synthese* 19. Reprinted in Davidson, D., 1984, to which page references are given.

Davidson, D., 1984. *Inquiries into Truth and Interpretation* (Oxford University Press).

574 / Jennifer Hornsby

Evans, G., 1982. *The Varieties of Reference* (Oxford University Press).
Field, H., 1977. 'Logic, Meaning and Conceptual Role'. *Journal of Philosophy* LXXIV.
Fodor, J. A., 1980. 'Methodological Solipsism considered as a Research Strategy in Cognitive Psychology.' *The Behavioral and Brain Sciences* 3. Reprinted in Fodor 1981, to which page references are given.
Fodor, J. A., 1981. *Representations* (Harvester Press, Brighton, Sussex).
Hamblin, C.L., 1987. *Imperatives* (Blackwell, Oxford).
Harman, G., 1974. 'Meaning and Semantics'. In *Semantics and Philosophy*, eds. M. Munitz and P. Unger (New York University Press).
Harman, G., 1982. 'Conceptual Role Semantics', *Notre Dame Journal of Formal Logic* XXIII.
Hornsby, J., 1986. 'Physicalist Thinking and Conceptions of Behaviour'. In Pettit and McDowell (eds.), 1986.
Loar, B., 1981. *Mind and Meaning* (Cambridge University Press).
Loar, B., 1982. 'Conceptual Role and Truth-Conditions', *Notre Dame Journal of Formal Logic* XXIII.
McDowell, J., 1980. 'Quotation and Saying That'. In *Reference, Truth and Reality*, ed. Mark Platts (Routledge & Kegan Paul, London).
McDowell, J., 1986. 'Singular Thought and the Extent of Inner Space'. In Pettit and McDowell (eds.), 1986.
McGinn, C., 1982. 'The Structure of Content'. In Woodfield (ed.), 1982.
Pettit, P. and McDowell, J. (eds.), 1986. *Subject, Thought and Context* (Oxford University Press).
Putnam, H., 1975a. 'The Meaning of "Meaning"'. In *Language, Mind and Knowledge: Minnesota Studies in the Philosophy of Science*, Vol. VII, ed. Keith Gunderson (University of Minnesota Press, Minneapolis). Reprinted in Putnam, 1975b, to which page references are given.
Putnam, H., 1975b. *Philosophical Papers Vol. II: Mind, Language and Reality* (Cambridge University Press).
Putnam, H., 1982. 'Computational Psychology and Interpretation Theory', in Putnam, 1983.
Putnam, H., 1983. *Philosophical Papers Vol. III: Realism and Reason* (Cambridge University Press).
Quine, W. V. O., 1960. *Word and Object* (MIT Press, Cambridge, Mass.)
Soames, S., 1984. 'What is a Theory of Truth,', *Journal of Philosophy* LXXXI.
Schiffer, S., 1980. 'Truth and the Theory of Content'. In *Meaning and Understanding*, eds. H. Parret and J. Bouverese (Walter de Gruyter, Berlin, New York).
Wettstein, H., 1986. 'Has Semantics Rested on a Mistake?', *Journal of Philosophy* LXXXIII.
Woodfield, A. (ed.), 1982. *Thought and Object* (Oxford University Press).

Philosophical Perspectives, 3
Philosophy of Mind and Action Theory, 1989

SEMANTICS AND SEMANTIC COMPETENCE

Scott Soames
Princeton University

The central semantic fact about language is that it carries information about the world. The central psycho-semantic fact about speakers is that they understand the claims about the world made by sentences of their language. This parallel suggests an intimate connection between semantic theories and theories of semantic competence. A semantic theory should tell us what information is encoded by sentences relative to contexts. Since competent speakers seem to grasp this information, and since the ability to correctly pair sentences with their contents seems to be the essence of semantic competence, it might appear that a semantic theory is itself a theory of competence.

Such a view has, I think, been quite common. We are all familiar with syntacticians who tell us that their grammars are attempts to specify the grammatical knowledge in virtue of which speakers are syntactically competent. This knowledge is generally thought to include, though perhaps not be limited to, knowledge of which strings of words are genuine (or grammatical) sentences of the language. By extension, it would seem that a semantic theory ought to specify the semantic knowledge in virtue of which speakers are semantically competent. Presumably, this knowledge will include, though perhaps not be limited to, knowledge of the truth conditions of sentences.

The reason for focusing on truth conditions arises from the representational character of semantic information. A sentence that represents the world as being a certain way implicitly imposes conditions that must be satisfied if the world is to conform to the way it is represented to be. Thus, the semantic information encoded by a sentence determines the conditions under which it is true. There may be more to semantic information than truth conditions, but there is no information without them. Thus, if semantic competence consists in grasping the information semantically encoded by sentence, then it would seem that it must involve knowledge of truth conditions.

The view that linguistic theories of syntax and semantics may double as psychological theories of competence comes in two main forms. The more modest form requires theories of syntax and semantics to provide theorems knowledge of which explains competence; however, it does not require these theories to specify the cognitive states and processes causally responsible for this knowledge. In particular, it does not require the theoretical machinery used in linguistic theories to derive theorems about grammaticality or truth conditions to be internally represented components of any psychologically real system. It simply leaves open the question of how the knowledge characterized by correct linguistic theories is psychologically realized.

The more robust form of the view that linguistic theories may double as psychological theories of linguistic competence tries to answer this question. According to this view, syntactic and semantic theories are required not only to characterize the linguistically significant properties of sentences, but also to do so on the basis of whatever internally represented cognitive apparatus is responsible for speakers' recognition of these properties. In short, linguistic theories are required to specify both the knowledge needed for linguistic competence, and the mechanisms from which that knowledge arises.

Although the robust approach has been accepted by many syntacticians, it has also been highly controversial. I believe it should be rejected for syntax as well as semantics.[1] However, it is not my present target. What I would like to argue is that, at least in the case of semantics, the modest approach is also incorrect. Semantic theories do not state that which a speaker knows in virtue of which he or she is semantically competent. Semantic competence does not arise from knowledge of the semantic properties of expressions characterized by a correct semantic theory.

Knowledge of Truth Conditions

Let us begin with the basics. The job of semantics is to specify the principles by which sentences represent the world. It is impossible to represent the world as being a certain way without implicitly imposing conditions that must be satisfied if the world is to conform to the representation. Thus, whatever else a semantic theory must do, it must at least characterize truth conditions. For certain languages, there are two standard ways of doing this. One involves the construction of a Davidson-style theory of truth for the language. The other involves the construction of a theory, or definition, of a relativized notion of truth for the language, truth-with-respect-to a world w. Both theories can be thought of as entailing statements that give the truth conditions of sentences. In one case, these statements are instances of schema T; in the other they are instances of schema T_w. (Instances are formed by replacing 'P' with a paraphrase of the sentence replacing 'S'.)

Schema T: 'S' is true (in L) iff P

Schema T_w: 'S' is true (in L) w.r.t. w iff in w, P

Now it might be thought that knowledge of truth conditions is the key to semantic competence, and hence that competence is the result of knowing that which is stated by each instance of one or the other of these schemas. But this is false. Knowledge of truth conditions (in this sense) is neither necessary nor sufficient for understanding a language.

It is not sufficient since it is possible for even the logically omniscient to know that

1. 'Firenze é una bella città' is true in Italian (w.r.t. w) iff (in w) Florence is a beautiful city

while failing to believe that

2. 'Firenze é una bella città' means in Italian that Florence is a beautiful city

and believing instead that

3. 'Firenze é una bella città' means in Italian that Florence is a beautiful city and arithmetic is incomplete.

All that is necessary for this is for the agent to believe that (for any w) Florence is a beautiful city (in w) iff (in w) Florence is a beautiful city and arithmetic is incomplete. In short, true beliefs about truth conditions are compatible with false beliefs about meaning.

One sometimes sees it suggested that this problem can be avoided by requiring the agent's knowledge of truth conditions to encompass everything forthcoming from a finitely axiomatized theory of truth for the entire language. But this is not so. Given a first order language, one can always construct extensionally correct, finitely axiomatizable truth theories each of whose theorems resembles (4) in correctly giving the truth conditions of an object language sentence, while failing to provide a basis for paraphrase or interpretation.

4. 'Firenze é una bella cittá' is true in Italian (w.r.t. w) iff (in w) Florence is a beautiful city and arithmetic is incomplete.

Now imagine a person ignorant of the object language being given a finitely axiomatized theory of truth. Unless he is also given information about meaning, he will have no way of knowing whether it can be used to paraphrase and interpret object language sentences. In particular, he will have no way of knowing whether the result of substituting 'means that' for 'is true iff' in its theorems will produce truths, as in (2), or falsehoods, as in (3). Knowledge of truth conditions, even of this systematic sort, is simply not sufficient for knowledge of meaning, or semantic competence.[2]

It is also not necessary. Knowledge of truth conditions, as I have described it, presupposes possession of a metalinguistic concept of truth. Thus, the claim that such knowledge is necessary for understanding meaning entails that no one can learn or understand a language without first having such a concept. But this consequence seems false. Certainly, young children and unsophisticated adults can understand lots of sentences without understanding 'true', or any corresponding predicate.

Must they, nevertheless, possess a metalinguistic concept of truth, even though they have no word for it? I don't see why. Perhaps it will be suggested that a person who lacked such a concept couldn't be a language user, since to use language one must realize that assertive utterances aim at truth and seek to avoid falsity. But this suggestion is confused. The child will get along fine so long as he knows that 'Momma is working' is to be assertively uttered only if Momma is working; 'Daddy is asleep' is to be assertively uttered only if Daddy is asleep; and so on. The child doesn't have to say or think to himself, "There is a general (but defeasible) expectation that for all x, if x is a sentence, then one is to assertively utter x only if x is true." It is enough if he says or thinks to himself, "There is a general (but defeasible) expectation that one should assertively utter 'Mommy is working' only if Mommy is working; assertively utter 'Daddy is asleep' only if Daddy is asleep; and so on for every sentence." For this, no notion of truth is needed.[3]

The point here is not that this truthless substitute says exactly the same thing as its truth-containing counterpart. In general, meta-linguistic truth is not eliminable without loss of expressive power, and practical utility. The point is that it is not necessary to have such a concept in order to learn and understand a language. Thus, knowledge of that which is expressed by instances of schemas T and T_w is neither necessary nor sufficient for semantic competence.

Beyond Truth Conditions

The problem with such accounts of semantic competence can be expressed as follows: Even if the sentence replacing 'P' is a strict paraphrase of the sentence replacing 'S', the "connective"

5. '...' is true (in w) iff (in w) ...

used to relate them is too loose to provide the information needed for understanding, or knowing the meaning of, a sentence. Thus, knowledge of truth conditions (in this sense) cannot explain semantic competence.

How might knowledge of meaning be expressed? A natural suggestion is that what one knows when one knows the meaning of a sentence is something of the form

6. 'S' means that P

or

7. 'S' says that P.

However, two qualifications must be noted.

First, in general if x means or says that P&Q, then x means or says that P and x means or says that Q. For example, if Reagan meant or said that defense spending would increase and taxes would be cut, then he meant or said that defense spending would increase, and he meant or said that taxes would be cut. However, the sentence

'Defense spending will increase and taxes will be cut' does not mean in English that defense spending will increase; nor does it mean in English that taxes will be cut. When we say that a sentence means in English that so-and-so, we are, I think, saying that it expresses the proposition that so-and-so. An unambiguous conjunction expresses a single, conjunctive, proposition; it does not also express the propositions that its conjuncts do.

Second, when an object language sentence contains an indexical element, we don't want to identify its meaning with any of the different propositions it may be used to express. For example, I don't want to say that 'I live in New Jersey' means (says) that I (S.S.) live in New Jersey. The sentence doesn't mean something specifically about me, any more than it means something about anyone else. Rather, its meaning is what allows it to be used in different contexts to express different (but systematically related) propositions.

These qualifications can be accommodated by suggestion (8).

8a. The meaning of a sentence is a function from contexts of utterance to propositions expressed by the sentence in those contexts.

  b. Knowledge of meaning is knowledge of that which is expressed by instances of schema K. (Instances are obtained by replacing 'C' with a description of a context of utterance, and 'P' with a sentence that expresses the proposition that the sentence replacing 'S' expresses in the context described.) Schema K: 'S' expresses the proposition that P relative to the context C.

In formulating this schema, we take 'express' to be a three-place predicate relating sentences, contexts, and propositions. A semantic theory utilizing this predicate will assign propositions to sentences, relative to contexts, while deriving the truth conditions of a sentence from the proposition it expresses. The suggestion for relating semantics to semantic competence, then, is that a correct semantic theory will entail instances of schema K, knowledge of which explains semantic competence.

But what are propositions, and how are they assigned to sentences? One familiar suggestion is that propositions are sets of metaphysically possible worlds assigned to sentences by recursive characterizations of truth with respect to a world. Given such a truth characterization, one can define the proposition expressed by a sentence S to be the set of worlds w such that S is true in w.

However, this won't do. On this approach, necessarily equivalent propositions are identified—e.g. the proposition that Florence is a beautiful city is identified with the proposition that Florence is a beautiful city and arithmetic is incomplete. Thus, the approach predicts that anyone who believes the one believes the other, that any sentence which expresses the one expresses the other, and that anyone who knows that a sentence expresses the one knows that it expresses the other. These results are unacceptable.

It is important to note that the problem does not arise from the selection of metaphysically possible worlds as the truth-supporting circumstances in terms of which truth conditions are explicated, and propositions constructed. Given a background of relatively modest and plausible assumptions, one can reconstruct essentially the same problem for any fine-grained conception of truth-supporting circumstances that allows one to maintain the standard recursive clauses in a truth characterization for constructions like conjunction, quantification, and descriptions.[4] This means that no matter what one takes truth-supporting circumstances to be, one cannot identify the proposition expressed by a sentence with the set of circumstances in which it is true; nor can one identify a semantic theory with a characterization of truth with respect to a circumstance.

What is needed is a reversal of familiar semantic priorities. Instead of viewing propositions as artifacts of conceptually prior truth characterizations, we should construct semantic theories that directly assign propositions to sentences, and derive truth conditions of sentences from theories of truth for the propositions they express. In order for these propositions to serve as fine-grained objects of the attitudes they should encode both the structure of the sentences that express them and the semantic contents of subsentential constituents. In this way, sentences with significantly different structures may express different propositions even though they are true in the same truth-supporting circumstances.

I believe that these ideas can best be implemented by an essentially Russellian conception of semantics and semantic content.[5] This approach can be illustrated by considering an elementary first order language with lambda abstraction, a belief operator, and a stock of semantically simple singular terms, all of which are directly referential.[6] On the Russellian account, the semantic content of a variable relative to an assignment is just the object assigned as value of the variable; the semantic content of a closed (directly referential) term, relative to a context, is its referent relative to the context. The contents of n-place predicates are n-place properties and relations. The contents of '&' and '~' are functions, CONJ and NEG, from truth values to truth values.

Variable-binding operations, like lambda abstraction and existential quantification, can be handled by using propositional functions to play the role of complex properties corresponding to certain compound expressions.[7] On this approach, the semantic content of $\ulcorner[\lambda x\ Rx,x]\urcorner$ is the function g from individuals o to propositions that attribute the relation expressed by R to the pair $<o,o>$. $\ulcorner[\lambda x\ Rx,x]t\urcorner$ can then be thought of as attributing the property of bearing R to oneself to the referent of t; and $\ulcorner\exists x\ Rx,x\urcorner$ can be thought of as "saying" that g assigns a true proposition to at least one object.

The recursive assignment of propositions to sentences is given in (9).[8]

9a. The proposition expressed by an atomic formula $\ulcorner Pt_1,...,t_n\urcorner$ relative to a context C and assignment f is $<<o_1,...,o_n>, P^*>$, where P^* is the property expressed by P, and o_i is the content of t_i relative to C and f.

b. The proposition expressed by formula $\ulcorner[\lambda v\ S]t\urcorner$ relative to C and f is $<<o>,g>$, where o is the content of t relative to C and f, and g is the function from individuals o' to propositions expressed by S relative to C and an assignment f' that differs from f at most in assigning o' as the value of v.[9]

c. The propositions expressed by $\ulcorner\sim S\urcorner$ and $\ulcorner S\&R\urcorner$ relative to C and f are $<$NEG, Prop S$>$ and $<$CONJ, $<$Prop S, Prop R$>>$ respectively, where Prop S and Prop R are the propositions expressed by S and R relative to C and f, and NEG and CONJ are the truth functions for negation and conjunction.

d. The proposition expressed by $\ulcorner\exists v\ S\urcorner$ relative to C and f is $<$SOME, g$>$, where SOME is the property of being a non-empty set, and g is as in (b).

e. The proposition expressed by $\ulcorner t$ believes that $S\urcorner$ relative to C and f is $<<o,$ Prop S$>,$ B$>$, where B is the belief relation, o is the content of t relative to C and f, and Prop S is the proposition expressed by S relative to C and f.

f. The proposition expressed by a sentence (with no free variables) relative to a context C is the proposition it expresses relative to C and every assignment f.

On this approach, the meaning of an expression is a function from contexts to propositional constituents. The meaning of a sentence is a compositional function from contexts to structured propositions. Intensions (and extensions) of sentences and expressions relative to contexts (and circumstances) derive from intensions (and extensions) of propositions and propositional constituents. These, in turn, can be gotten from a recursive characterization of truth with respect to a circumstance, for propositions.

For this purpose, we let the intension of an n-place property be a function from circumstances to sets of n-tuples of individuals that instantiate the property in the circumstances; we let the intension of an individual be a constant function from circumstances to that individual; and we let the intension of a one-place propositional function g be a function from circumstances E to sets of individuals in E that g assigns propositions true in E. Extension is related to intension in the normal way, with the extension of a proposition relative to a circumstance being its truth value in the circumstance, and its intension being the set of circumstances in which it is true (or, equivalently, the characteristic function of that set). Truth relative to a circumstance is defined in (10).

10a. A proposition $<<o_1,...,o_n>, P^*>$ is true relative to a circumstance E iff the extension of P^* in E contains $<o_1,...,o_n>$.

b. A proposition $<<o>,g>$ is true relative to E (where g is a one-place propositional function) iff o is a member of the extension of g in E (i.e. iff g(o) is true relative to E).

c. A proposition $<NEG, Prop\ S>$ is true relative to E iff the value of NEG at the extension of Prop S in E is truth (i.e. iff Prop S is not true relative to E).
A proposition $<CONJ, <Prop\ S, Prop\ R>>$ is true relative to E iff the value of CONJ at the pair consisting of the extension of Prop S in E and the extension of Prop R in E is truth (i.e. iff Prop S and Prop R are true relative to E).

d. A proposition $<SOME, g>$ is true relative to E (where g is as in (b)) iff the extension of g in E is non-empty (i.e.

      iff g(o) is true relative to E for some o in E).

  e. A proposition $<<$o, Prop S$>$, B$>$ is true relative to E iff $<$o, Prop S$>$ is a member of the extension of B in E (i.e. iff o believes Prop S in E).

Earlier we considered the suggestion that a semantic theory issues in instances of schema K, and that knowledge of that which is expressed by these instances explains semantic competence. The key idea behind this suggestion is that it is knowledge of the propositions expressed by sentences, rather than knowledge of truth conditions, that is fundamental to understanding a language. We now have a conception of semantics that pairs object language sentences with propositions of the right sort. Does this mean that we have a semantic theory that entails instances of schema K?

No, it does not. Instead, the above theory, when supplemented with a theory of object language syntax and an interpretation of it's vocabulary, will issue in theorems of the kind shown in (11).

  11. '∃x Lx,n' expresses (with respect to every context) the proposition which is the ordered pair whose first coordinate is the property SOME, of being a non-empty set, and whose second coordinate is the function g which assigns to any object o the proposition which is the ordered pair whose second coordinate is the relation of loving and whose first coordinate is the ordered pair the first coordinate of which is o and the second coordinate of which is Nixon.

Let us suppose, for the sake of argument, that (11) is true, and hence that the description it gives of the proposition expressed by '∃x Lx,n' is accurate. Still, the theorem is not an instance of schema K. Moreover, knowledge of that which it expresses is neither necessary nor sufficient for knowing the meaning of the sentence, let alone for explaining speakers' understanding of it.

In essence the situation is this: We think of the instance (12) of schema K as containing a singular term t which denotes the proposition expressed by '∃x Lx,n'.

  12. '∃x Lx,n' expresses the proposition that something loves Nixon (with respect to every context C).

Corresponding to this, the semantic theory issues theorem (11), which contains a singular term t' that refers to the same proposition as t. However, t and t' are distinct, non-synonymous expressions; t is 'the proposition that something loves Nixon', whereas t' is the complicated definite description given in (11). As a result, (11) and (12) "say" different things. Thus, even if knowledge of meaning amounted to knowledge of that which is expressed by the latter, it would not amount to knowledge of that which is expressed by the former. Semantic competence is not the result of knowing these semantic theorems.

Suppose, however, that one were to make the assumptions in (13).

13a. The expression ⌈the proposition that P⌉ is a directly referential singular term that refers to the proposition expressed by P.

b. 'Dthat' is an operator which can be prefixed to any definite description D to form a directly referential singular term ⌈dthat D⌉ whose semantic content is the referent of D.[10]

c. A proper semantic theory can be formulated so as to entail theorems analogous to (11) in which 'dthat' is prefixed to the description of the proposition expressed.

d. If t and t' are directly referential singular terms that refer to the same thing, then substitution of one for the other in a sentence (outside of quotes) does not affect what proposition is expressed. Moreover, substitution of one for the other in propositional attitude constructions preserves truth-value; if ⌈x knows (believes) that ...t...⌉ is true, then so is ⌈x knows (believes) that ...t'...⌉.

From these assumptions it follows that knowledge of that which is expressed by (the newly formulated) semantic theorems just is knowledge of that which is expressed by instances of schema K.

In my opinion, these assumptions are more reasonable than commonly thought. Indeed, I am willing to accept them. However, even if they are accepted, they cannot be used to connect semantics with semantic competence. The reason they can't is that although they allow semantic theorems to be assimilated to instances of schema K, they make it possible to know that which is expressed by these instances without understanding object language sentences.

I take it that if propositions can be referents of directly referential singular terms, then they can be labeled using directly referential proper names. Suppose, then, that the proposition that mathematics is reducible to logic is labeled 'logicism'. Using the assumptions in (13), we can then conclude that (14) and (15) "say" the same thing, and that (16) and (17) have the same truth value.

14. Logicism is expressed by s.
15. The proposition that mathematics is reducible to logic is expressed by s.
16. x believes (knows) that logicism is expressed by s.
17. x believes (knows) that the proposition that mathematics is reducible to logic is expressed by s.

Thus, if it is possible to believe or know that logicism is expressed by a certain sentence without understanding that sentence, then it will be possible to believe or know the corresponding instance of schema K—namely (15)—without being semantically competent.

But this is possible. The case is analogous to one in which someone believes that a particular person authored certain axioms without knowing very much about the person. For example, someone being introduced to elementary number theory might be told that certain axioms were first formulated by Peano. On the basis of this, he may come to believe that Peano first formulated those axioms, even though he is not able to identify Peano, distinguish him from other mathematicians, or to accurately characterize him using any uniquely identifying description.

Now consider a student attending his first lecture in the philosophy of mathematics. He may be told that logicism is a proposition about the relationship between logic and mathematics, that formalism is a doctrine about the interpretation of mathematics, and so on. At this stage, the student may not be able to distinguish logicism from other propositions about the relationship between logic and mathematics; or to describe it in any informative way. Nevertheless, he may acquire beliefs about logicism. For example, he may be told, "Russell was a defender of logicism", and thereby come to believe that Russell defended logicism. He might even be told, "Logicism is expressed by sentence s", and thereby come to believe that logicism is expressed by sentence s. In order to acquire this belief, it is not necessary that he understand s. It might, for example, be written on the board and labeled 's', but contain unfamiliar terminology. In such a case, the student's knowledge that s expresses logicism does not make him a linguistically competent user of s.

When combined with the assumptions noted above, this observation leads to the conclusion that one can know that which is expressed by an instance

18. 'S' expresses the proposition that P (relative to C)

of schema K without understanding the object language sentence that replaces 'S'. It would seem, therefore, that knowledge of semantic theorems is not necessary and sufficient for semantic competence, even under the most favorable assumptions.

To recapitulate: If one doesn't adopt the assumptions in (13), then one's semantic theory will not provide instances of schema K; if one does adopt the assumptions in (13), then one can construct a semantic theory whose theorems express the propositions expressed by instances of schema K—however, under these assumptions knowledge of those propositions does not ensure understanding the object language. Either way, knowledge of semantic theorems is not necessary and sufficient for semantic competence.

Semantic Competence and "The Augustinian Picture"[11]

If this is right, then a familiar strategy for explaining semantic competence won't work. The strategy is based on the idea that competent speakers understand sentences in virtue of knowing precisely the information that a semantic theory provides—namely, the truth conditions of, and propositions expressed by, object language sentences. In attacking this idea I have argued that semantic knowledge and linguistic competence do not always coincide; the presence of one does not guarantee the presence of the other. Thus, semantic knowledge cannot, in general, explain linguistic competence.

There is, however, a more fundamental point to be made. Even in cases in which a linguistically competent speaker is semantically knowledgeable, his competence may not derive from his knowledge; rather, his knowledge may derive from his competence.

The examples in (19) provide a case in point.

19a. Pluto is a distant planet.
   b. 'Pluto' refers to Pluto.
   c. 'Pluto is a distant plant' is true (in English) iff Pluto is a

distant planet.
d. 'Pluto is a distant planet' expresses (in English) the
   proposition that Pluto is a distant planet.

I believe all of these things. The reason I believe them is not that I have seen or had direct contact with Pluto. On the contrary, my only contact with the planet has been an indirect one, mediated by representations of it. In my case, the most important of these has been the name 'Pluto'.

My beliefs about Pluto are similarly mediated. I believe that Pluto is a distant planet because I have read or been told that it is. I have read or been told "Pluto is a distant planet"; I have understood the sentence; and I have accepted it. It is important to note that this understanding did not consist in associating an identifying description with the name 'Pluto', and a descriptive proposition with the entire sentence. In acquiring the belief, I may or may not have associated a description with the name, and I may or may not have come to believe descriptive propositions as a result of accepting the sentence. Still, my belief that Pluto is a distant planet cannot be identified with any such descriptive belief. Even if the description I associate with the name is inaccurate and doesn't, in fact, pick out Pluto, my belief that Pluto is a distant planet is about Pluto (though the descriptive beliefs acquired at the same time may not be). Similarly, even if the descriptive beliefs turn out to be false, my belief that Pluto is a distant planet may remain true. Finally, the proposition I express by 'Pluto is a distant planet' is the same as the proposition that others express by the sentence, even if the descriptions we associate with the name are different.

In short, the explanation of my belief that Pluto is a distant planet involves the fact that, (i) I accept the sentence 'Pluto is a distant planet'; (ii) the sentence expresses the proposition that Pluto is a distant planet; and (iii) I am a competent speaker, and thereby understand the sentence. Moreover, my understanding the sentence is not a matter of my using it to express descriptive propositions that I might have come to believe on independent grounds.

Analogous points can be made regarding other attitudes I might have taken toward the proposition. If I had come to wonder whether Pluto was a distant planet, or to doubt that it was, my having that propositional attitude would have involved my having a certain attitude toward a sentence that expressed it. In short, the only epistemic connection I have with certain propositions is mediated through sentences that express them.

These considerations can be extended to the other examples (19b-d). For instance, I believe the propositions expressed by (c) and (d). However, these beliefs do not explain my understanding of (a). I don't understand the sentence because I have those beliefs. If anything, it is the other way around. My belief in the propositions expressed by (c) and (d) is (in large part) due to my understanding and accepting sentences (c) and (d), and to the fact that they mean what they do. Moreover, part of what it is for me to understand these sentences is for me to understand (a), which is a constituent of both. Thus, the direction of explanation in this case is not from beliefs to competence, but from competence to beliefs.

If this is right, then a natural and seductive picture of language acquisition and linguistic competence is fundamentally mistaken. According to this picture, we have the ability, prior to the acquisition of language, to form beliefs and entertain propositions. In setting up a language, we adopt certain conventions according to which sentences come to express these antecedently apprehended propositions. Learning the language amounts to learning for each sentence, which antecedently apprehended proposition it expresses.

The most fundamental thing wrong with this picture is that in the case of many sentences, we do not grasp the propositions they express prior to understanding the sentences themselves. As a result, coming to understand these sentences does not consist in searching through our stock of propositions to find the ones assigned to them. Rather, coming to understand the sentences is a matter of satisfying conventional standards regarding their use. Just what these standards are is not well understood. However, whatever they are, once they are satisfied, one is counted not only as understanding new sentences, but also as grasping new propositions. As a result, learning a language is not just a matter of acquiring a new tool for manipulating information one already possesses; it is also a means of expanding one's cognitive reach.[12]

This point is potentially more far-reaching than the examples I have used might indicate. Although my beliefs about Pluto are linguistically mediated, they need not have been. They could, presumably, have been acquired through direct, non-linguistic contact with the planet. Many of my beliefs about individuals are like this. For example, my beliefs about Plato are linguistically mediated; but they are also dependent on the fact that others have had direct contact with the man and have passed his name down to me.

In other cases, I have linguistically mediated beliefs about objects with which no one is, or could be, in direct epistemic contact—for example, beliefs about quarks, the addition function, and the cardinal aleph null. In my opinion, there are such objects; we do succeed in referring to them; and we acquire beliefs about them in virtue of understanding and accepting sentences about them. How this all comes about is a large and unanswered question. Somehow, using the word 'plus' in a certain way counts as referring to the addition function, despite the fact that our use is logically consistent with alternative hypotheses, as well as the fact that there is no direct apprehension of the function.[13] Certainly, we do not say to ourselves, "There is this particular arithmetical function that we have been thinking about which has so far remained nameless; let's call it 'plus'". The reason we don't is that our epistemic access to the function does not precede our ability to represent it linguistically; rather, the two are simultaneous.

These considerations dramatically undermine the "Augustinian" picture of language acquisition and linguistic competence given in (20).

20a. There are objects, properties, and propositions that we apprehend prior to understanding a language.

b. Linguistic expressions stand for these independently apprehended objects, properties, and propositions.

c. Understanding a language is the result of knowing which expressions stand for which objects—e.g. of knowing that 'Pluto' refers to Pluto, that '+' stands for the addition function, and that 'Quarks are subatomic particles' expresses the proposition that quarks are subatomic particles.

Clause (a) is true but incomplete, since there are objects we apprehend only through linguistic mediation. Clause (b) is false, if taken as a claim about linguistic expressions in general. However, the result of deleting the words "these independently apprehended" from it is true. Clause (c) is objectionable on two grounds. First, it has the dubious consequence that understanding an expression always coincides with knowing that the expression has certain semantic properties. Second, it wrongly suggests that semantic knowledge about what expressions stand for is conceptually prior to, and explains, semantic competence.

Semantics

Where does this leave semantics? I have suggested that a semantic theory must pair sentences with the propositions they express, and derive the truth conditions of sentences from those propositions. I have also noted that the knowledge provided by such a theory is not necessary and sufficient for semantic competence. However, I have argued that this is no defect, since the attempt to explain semantic competence as arising from semantic knowledge rests on an inadequate conception of the role of language in our cognitive lives— a conception that ignores the linguistic basis of many of our semantic and non-semantic beliefs. If this is correct, then one should not look to semantics for an account of semantic competence.

Instead, one should look to it for an explication of the representational character of language. The central semantic fact about language is that it is used to represent the world. Sentences do this by systematically encoding information that characterizes the world as being one way or another. Semantics is the study of this information, and the principles by which it is encoded.

A theory of this sort can be seen as accomplishing three main tasks. First, it tells us what sentences say relative to different contexts of utterance, and thereby provides the basis for interpreting what speakers say when they assertively utter sentences in various contexts, and what they believe when they believe that which is said by one or another assertive utterance. Second, the semantic account of truth conditions explicates a fundamental aspect of the relationship between language and the world. Third, the model-theoretic machinery in the theory provides a semantic account of meaning-determined logical properties and relations holding among sentences.

Theories of semantic competence are responsive to different concerns. Whereas semantic theories focus on the fact that sentences encode information that represents the world, theories of semantic competence focus on the fact that languages are things that people understand. This focus on understanding can be developed in two ways. On the one hand, one may ask for a conceptual analysis (in terms of social, behavioral, mental, or verificationist notions) of what it means to understand an expression, a sentence, or a language.

On the other hand, one may want an empirical theory that identifies the cognitive structures and processes that are causally responsible for the linguistic understanding of a particular person or group. Both types of concern with understanding are legitimate, and deserve to be developed. However, neither is essentially semantic, in the sense I have sketched.

This does not mean that there are no interesting connections between semantic theories of information encoding and psychological, or philosophical, theories of linguistic understanding. In fact, they complement one another. Semantic theories specify contents of expressions, but say nothing about the empirical factors that are causally responsible for their coming to have these contents. For certain words, it is plausible to suppose that they got their content from a causal-historical chain connecting tokens produced by different speakers to a real-world referent. This sort of foundational view has been an important supplement to recent semantic theories, even though particular causal-historical chains have no place in semantic theories themselves.

A similar point might be made about mental representations associated with sentences by speakers. A number of cognitive scientists believe that understanding a sentence involves the recovery, manipulation, and storage of abstract representational structures. This belief has led to the attempt to develop theories about how these representational structures are connected to sentences, and how they interact with other cognitive systems. Typically these theories posit rules that take syntactic structures as input and produce different linguistic objects as output, where these latter are thought of as playing some significant role in explaining speakers' understanding, their semantic judgements, or both. If they do play such a role, then they may also be important causal factors in explaining why the natural language sentences they are associated with encode the information that they do.

It must be remembered, however, that these mental representations are not themselves semantic contents. Rather, they are things that have content. Thus, a theory of the cognitive structures associated with sentences is no substitute for a semantics. Indeed, such theories tacitly presuppose a semantics; for to say of an abstract mental structure that it represents so-and-so is to say that it bears information that characterizes things as being a certain way, and thereby imposes truth conditions that must be satisfied if things are to conform to the representation. Making this explicit is the job of semantics.

Thus, there is a sense in which theories of mental representation are incomplete without an accompanying semantics. However, there may also be a sense in which semantics is dependent on theories of mental representation. It is not just that theories of mental representation may be needed to explain how expressions come to have the contents associated with them by a correct semantic theory. Such theories may also be needed to decide what semantic content a sentence has, and hence what semantic theory is correct. The crucial point involves the introduction of structure into semantic content. I have argued, both here and on other occasions, that the semantic content of a sentence cannot be analyzed solely in terms of truth conditions, but rather must be seen as a complex with a structure that parallels that of the sentence itself.[14] But this raises a question. What level, or levels, of sentence structure does semantic information incorporate?

In the case of the simple first order language used to illustrate my propositional semantics, the answer is obvious—surface structure, since that is all the structure there is. However, in the case of natural language the matter is more complicated. Perhaps speakers of natural languages associate sentences with psychologically real underlying representations. If they do, then perhaps the propositions expressed by these sentences encode not their surface syntax, but rather the syntax of their underlying psycho-semantic representations. I don't know whether these possibilities will be born out; but the idea behind them is not unreasonable. It may very well be that cognitive structures involved in understanding sentences are closely related to propositional structures involved in explicating attitudes like saying, asserting, and believing. If they are, then semantic theories of information and psychological theories of semantic competence may turn out to be theories which, though different, have a lot in common after all.

Notes

1. See my "Linguistics and Psychology," *Linguistics and Philosophy*, volume 7, number 2, 1984, pp. 155-179; and my "Semantics and Psychology," in *The Philosophy of Linguistics*, edited by J.J. Katz, Oxford University Press, 1985, pp. 204-226.

2. For a more extended discussion of this point, as it applies to Davidsonian truth theories, see J.A. Foster, "Meaning and Truth Theory," in *Truth and Meaning*, edited by Gareth Evans and John McDowell, Oxford University Press, 1976, pp. 1-32. Although Foster presses the point forcefully against Davidson, he exempts approaches based on theories of truth-with-respect-to a possible world from his criticism. This, in my opinion, is a mistake. In addition to extending to such theories, the basic argument can be made to apply to any attempt to found meaning, or knowledge of meaning, on theories of truth with respect to a circumstance— no matter how fine grained we make the circumstances (provided standard recursive clauses in the truth theory are maintained).

3. I am not here suggesting that the child really must repeat or represent the latter (truthless) instruction to himself. Thus, I am not claiming that the child must have the notion assertive utterance in order to learn a language. My point is a negative one. If there is anything to the suggestion that language learners must realize that assertive utterances aim at truth, that realization need not involve possession of a concept of truth. It may be that the child ultimately must come to realize something like the following: One is to say that Mommy is working only if Mommy is working, that Daddy is asleep only if Daddy is asleep; and so on. A truth predicate comes in handy in stating such rule, for it allows one to eliminate the 'and so on' in favor of quantification over assertions plus predications of truth. But handy or not, this logical technology is not necessary for learning.

4. See my "Lost Innocence," *Linguistics and Philosophy*, volume 8, number 1, 1985, pp. 59-71; my "Direct Reference and Propositional Attitudes," in *Themes from Kaplan*, edited by J. Almog, J. Perry, and H. Wettstein, Oxford University Press, 1988; and my "Direct Reference, Propositional Attitudes, and Semantic Content," *Philosophical Topics*, volume 15, number 1, 1987, pp. 47-87, reprinted in *Propositions and Attitudes*, edited by N. Salmon and S. Soames, Oxford University Press, 1988.

5. See the articles mentioned in the preceding note, plus N. Salmon, *Frege's Puzzle*, M.I.T. Press, 1986.

6. A directly referential singular term is one whose semantic content (relative to a context and assignment of values to variables) is its referent (relative to the context and assignment). It is this semantic content that such a term contributes to the information encoded (proposition expressed) by a sentence containing it.

7. Although this Russellian method is, I think, essentially on the right track, it does lead to certain technical problems in special cases. For example, as Nathan Salmon has pointed out to me, Russellian propositional functions must be defined on possible, as well as actual, individuals, in order to assign correct extensions to expressions in different possible worlds. This means that these functions cannot be thought of as set theoretic constructions involving only actually existing objects. Another problem involves non-well-foundedness. As Terence Parsons has observed, in order for the self-referential, but unparadoxical, (i) and (ii) to have their intended interpretations, the propositional functions corresponding to

the matrices in these examples must be defined on the propositions expressed by (i) and (ii).

  i. (x) (I assert x --> I believe x)
 ii. (x) (I assert x today --> x is expressible in English)

This is impossible, if the set theoretic conception of propositions and propositional functions is maintained.

These problems can, I believe, be avoided by taking the semantic contents of compound expressions to be complex attributes rather than propositional functions. For example, the content of $\ulcorner[\lambda v \ S]\urcorner$, w.r.t. a context C and assignment f, might be taken to be the property P of being an object o such that dthat [the proposition expressed by S w.r.t. C and an assignment f′ that differs from f at most in assigning o to v] is true. The extension of P at a world w will then be the set of objects o such that the relevant propositions containing them are true with respect to w (provided that a proposition has the one place property of being true, at a world w, iff the two place relation of being true-with-respect-to holds between it and w).

Other ways of assigning attributes to expressions (compound predicates) may also be found. For present purposes, I will leave the final resolution of this issue open, and continue in the text to use familiar Russellian propositional functions as contents of compound predicates.

8. This system is presented in my "Direct Reference, Propositional Attitudes, and Semantic Content", where it is explained more fully.

9. Nathan Salmon has suggested using this lambda construction to distinguish the propositions expressed by the complement clauses of (i-iii) from those expressed by the complements of (iv-v).

  i. Pierre says (believes) that London is both pretty and not pretty.
 ii. Pierre says (believes) that London is non-self-identical.
iii. Pierre says (believes) that London is not identical with itself.
 iv. Pierre says (believes) that London is pretty and London is not pretty.
  v. Pierre says (believes) that London is not identical with London.

This suggestion has the important virtue of allowing us to characterize (iv-v) as true while recognizing that (i-iii) are false. For more discussion, see N. Salmon, "Reflexivity," *Notre Dame Journal of Formal Logic*, volume 27, number 3, 1986, pp. 401-429, and my "Direct Reference, Propositional Attitudes, and Semantic Content"—both reprinted in *Propositions and Attitudes*.

10. See David Kaplan, "On The Logic of Demonstratives," *Journal of Philosophical Logic*, volume 8, 1979, pp. 81-98; reprinted in *Propositions and Attitudes*.

11. The allusion to Augustine refers to the passage quoted by Wittgenstein that opens *The Philosophical Investigations*.

"When they (my elders) named some object, and accordingly moved towards something, I saw this and I grasped that the thing was called by the sound they uttered when they meant to point it out. Their intention was shewn by their bodily movements, as it were the natural language of all peoples: the expression of the face, the play of the eyes, the movement of other parts of the body, and the tone of voice which expresses our state of mind in seeking, having, rejecting, or avoiding something. Thus, as I heard words repeatedly used in their proper places in various sentences, I gradually learnt to understand what objects they signified; and after I had trained my mouth to form these signs, I used them to express my own desires."

The "Augustinian Picture" criticized below may be seen as an unwarranted extension of these remarks about language acquisition to cover all aspects of language.

12. I am speaking here primarily about first language acquisition (though the point applies, with less force, to some cases of second language acquisition as well).

13. See S. Kripke, *Wittgenstein on Rules and Private Language*, Harvard University Press, 1982.

14. See note 4.

James E. Tomberlin is a Professor of Philosophy at California State University, Northridge, where he has taught since completing graduate study at Wayne State University in 1969. He has published more than fifty essays and reviews in action theory, deontic logic, metaphysics, philosophy of language, mind, religion, and the theory of knowledge. Besides editorship of the present series, he has edited *Agent, Language, and the Structure of the World* (Hackett, 1983), *Hector-Neri Castaneda, Profiles* (D. Reidel, 1986) and he co-edited *Alvin Plantinga, Profiles* (D. Reidel, 1985).